DIALOGUES OF CONFUCIUS

Dialogues of Confucius

THE COMPLETE TEXT OF THE *KONGZI JIA YU* 孔子家語

TRANSLATED WITH
A PHILOSOPHICAL INTRODUCTION,
BACKGROUND, AND COMMENTARY
BY BRIAN BRUYA AND WENWEN LI

PRINCETON UNIVERSITY PRESS
PRINCETON & OXFORD

Published by Princeton University Press
41 William Street, Princeton, New Jersey 08540
99 Banbury Road, Oxford OX2 6JX

press.princeton.edu

GPSR Authorized Representative: Easy Access System Europe—Mustamäe tee 50, 10621 Tallinn, Estonia, gpsr.requests@easproject.com

Title: Dialogues of Confucius: The Complete Text of the *Kongzi jia yu*, Translated with a Philosophical Introduction, Background, and Commentary

ISBN 9780691276465
ISBN (e-book) 9780691276472

Library of Congress Control Number: 2025942893

British Library Cataloging-in-Publication Data is available

Editorial: Rob Tempio and Chloe Coy
Production Editorial: Elizabeth Byrd and Theresa Liu
Jacket: Ben Higgins
Production: Erin Suydam
Publicity: William Pagdatoon

This book has been composed in Arno

Printed in the United States of America

10 9 8 7 6 5 4 3 2 1

To our teachers, Yang Chaoming 楊朝明 and Roger Ames,
and to their teachers, or as the Chinese say, our grandteachers,
Li Xueqin 李學勤, A. C. Graham, and D. C. Lau 刘殿爵.
We dedicate this book to their aspirations, and their
ancestral teachers' aspirations, to carry forward the *dao*.

CONTENTS

ACKNOWLEDGMENTS

WE BEGAN THIS PROJECT in 2018 and have incurred numerous debts of gratitude since then.

The project that initiated this collaboration was a fellowship for Brian at the Collaborative Innovation Center for Confucian Civilization at Shandong University. That was followed by a Fulbright for Brian at National Taiwan University. We are grateful to the faculty, staff, students, and administrators of both universities for their warm welcome and assistance, and to the Fulbright program for the opportunity to build new relationships and renew old ones.

We are grateful also to the University of Michigan's Lieberthal-Rogel Center for Chinese Studies for providing a subvention to cover the cost of indexing this book. We are also grateful to the university for providing Brian the status to access the Center's resources, as well as those of the university's vast library.

The library systems of Eastern Michigan University, Shandong University, and National Taiwan University have likewise been indispensable, as has the university interlibrary loan system. Liangyu Fu at the University of Michigan library deserves special thanks for always being ready to suggest resources and to help troubleshoot broken links and glitchy database connections.

The following databases were also indispensable: Chinese Text Project (ctext.org), 漢籍全文資料庫 (Academia Sinica; https://hanchi.ihp.sinica.edu.tw/ihp/hanji), Chinese Ancient Texts Database (Chinese Hong Kong University; www.cuhk.edu.hk/ics/rccat/en/database.html), 楚簡帛字典【清華篇】(cjbnet.org/qinghua), and CNKI (China Academic Journals Electronic Publishing House Co.; cnki.net).

For advice and encouragement, we thank Yang Chaoming 楊朝明, Roger Ames, Donald Munro, Robert Eno, Wim De Reu, Ben Hammer, Michael Ing, Alexus McLeod, Mark Csikszentmihalyi, C. C. Tsai, Zeng Zhenyu 曾振宇, Song Lilin 宋立林, Tang Ziheng 唐子恒, Wang Chenglüe 王承略, Jin Jingwen 金靜文, Duan Jiewen 段潔文, and many others whom we are surely forgetting.

Many thanks to the students in Brian's Comparative Philosophy courses in 2020 and in 2024, who bravely waded through our drafts and offered many useful comments.

Gratitude to our respective spouses, Yuling Bruya and Xing Zheng 邢政. We are infinitely grateful for their patience and encouragement when the project interfered with our regular lives.

In the final round of revisions before submitting the manuscript for proofing, we passed a small number of ideas about specific word choice through ChatGPT (OpenAI) and Gemini (gemini.google.com), which we used to make decisions about minor modifications.

Thanks, finally, to Oscar Zheng for generously sharing textual resources that would have otherwise been challenging to access, and to Cynthia Col for creating a comprehensive index that will be a great aid to the curious reader.

CHINESE RECENSION

WITH THE EXCEPTION of the two postfaces, which are from the *Si ku quan shu* edition (see below), the Chinese text of this book is based on the *Si bu cong kan* 四部叢刊 photolithographic edition of Huang Luzeng's 黄魯曾 Ming dynasty revision of a Song dynasty edition (hereafter referred to as the SBCK edition; 商務印書館), with reference to the following:

- Shanghai Guji Chubanshe 上海古籍出版社 photolithographic reproduction of the Wen Yuan Ge 文淵閣 edition of *Si ku quan shu* 四庫全書 (hereafter SKQS).
- Tongwen Shuju 同文書局 lithographic reproduction of a handwritten Song edition (hereafter Tongwen).
- The Liu family's Yuhai Tang 劉氏玉海堂 reproduction of a Song edition.

The following were also referenced. Our main reference was Yang Chaoming and Song Lilin (2013), which provides a comprehensive critical recension. In the text, we note only where our text (punctuation aside) deviates from both Yang and Song (2013) and SBCK. We enumerate the section divisions created by Yang and Song. To conserve space, Chinese text is not divided into paragraphs.

- *Zuo zhuan* 左傳, *Xunzi* 荀子, *Li ji* 禮記, *Da Dai li ji* 大戴禮記, *Xin xu* 新序, and *Shuo yuan* 説苑.
- Yang, Chaoming 杨朝明, and Lilin Song 宋立林. 2013. *Kongzi jia yu tong jie* 孔子家语通解. Ji'nan: 齐鲁书社.
- Wang, Guoxuan 王国轩, and Xiumei Wang 王秀梅. 2012. *Kongzi jia yu* 孔子家语. Beijing: 中华书局.
- Wang, Deming 王德明. 1998. *Kongzi jia yu yi zhu* 孔子家语译注. Guilin: 广西师范大学出版社.
- Chen, Shike 陳士珂, and Tao Cui 崔濤. 2017. *Kongzi jia yu shu zheng* 孔子家語疏證. Nanjing: 鳳凰出版社.
- Yang, Chunqiu 羊春秋, and Feng-Wu Chou 周鳳五. 2020. *Kongzi jia yu xin yi* 孔子家語新譯. Taipei: 三民書局.

But for a small number of instances where it seemed prudent to reserve original forms, variant characters were standardized following:

- Language and Information Management Division of the Ministry of Education of China 中国教育部语言文字信息管理司. 2016. *Handbook of Common Language and Character Standards* 常用语言文字规范手册. Beijing: 商务印书馆.

ABBREVIATIONS

BA *Bamboo Annals, Zhu shu ji nian* 竹書紀年 (Wang and Huang 1997)

CQZZ *Spring and Autumn and Zuo zhuan, Chunqiu Zuo zhuan* 春秋左傳 (Durrant, Li, and Schaberg 2016)

LNZ *Exemplary Women of Early China, Lie nü zhuan* 烈女傳 (Kinney 2014)

SBCK *Si bu cong kan* 四部叢刊 edition of the *Dialogues* (see under "Chinese Recension" above)

SJ *Shi ji* 史記 (Sima 1981)

SKQS *Si ku quan shu* 四庫全書 edition of the *Dialogues* (see under "Chinese Recension" above)

In poem references, refers to numbers in *Mao Shi* 毛詩 (Yuan and Tang 1983; Pei 1998)

Introduction

Modern scholars are justifiably excited whenever a bronze vessel bearing an inscription is unearthed. But earth is not the only thing that can bury authentic records.

—SHAUGHNESSY, *BEFORE CONFUCIUS*

The *Dialogues of Confucius*[1] is a rich source of the thoughts of Confucius (Kong Qiu 孔丘, 551–479 BCE), but it is also a mysterious book with a checkered past. For centuries it lay in obscurity, disdained as a forgery, and yet it was also appreciated enough by a significant number of people that it was passed down generation after generation while other less appreciated books were lost entirely. While some scholars publicly derided the book, other scholars privately esteemed it.

The mystery that lies at the heart of the *Dialogues*' textual history is how the manuscript suddenly burst onto the scene in the third century, conveniently

1. The title of this book in Chinese is *Kongzi jia yu* 孔子家語. The Chinese characters now pronounced *Kongzi* are how early Confucians generally referred to the person we know today as Confucius. *Jia* means home or family, and *yu* means conversation, dialogue, or discussion. Ever since the work of James Legge in the nineteenth century, *jia* in the title has been interpreted in English as school of thought, and *yu* has been understood to mean sayings. The first of these is correct but requires a bit of explanation. The second does not do justice to the Chinese. Legge says that the title should be translated, "Sayings of the Confucian Family" and explains, "Family is to be taken in the sense of sect or school" (Legge [1893] 2012, 132). The word *jia* (family or home) was a metaphor for a group of like-minded people bonded around a single philosophy. For this reason, the best rendering of *jia* is *school.* The word translated by Legge as "sayings" is *yu* 語. However, the word for *saying* in Classical Chinese, the language of the *Dialogues,* is more often *yan* 言 than *yu. Yu* typically involves one or more people in conversation. The term *yu* occurs as a word on its own thirty-three times in the *Dialogues,* and in only one of them (19.8) could it conceivably be interpreted as saying, in the sense of apothegm. Twenty-seven times it refers to two or more people in dialogue. The most clear-cut case is in 8.13: "Confucius encountered Chengzi. They pulled their carriages alongside each other and began to chat [*yu*]." Most

providing Confucius' own thoughts on hot-button philosophical concerns of the day. Where had it been prior to that? And if it really contained genuine thoughts of the sage from 700 years earlier, why had it remained hidden for so long?

It is impossible to know for certain the textual history of the *Dialogues*, but in what follows we lay out what we think is the most plausible scenario, a scenario that is supported by a growing body of evidence. We believe the *Dialogues* can provisionally be accepted as largely genuine and accurately portraying the activities and thoughts of Confucius. While some of it remains suspect, it can nevertheless be used as a resource for understanding Confucius, his interactions with his students, and his philosophy. After we describe the textual history of the *Dialogues*, we outline key philosophical ideas and terminology. There is much more philosophical work to be done on the *Dialogues* with respect to its placement in the intellectual sphere of the Warring States period and its relevance for philosophical theory today. We propose our outline as a useful starting point.

The Extant Account

The *Dialogues* has been handed down to us with three explanatory documents. They are translated at the end of this book as separate appendices, in purported chronological order. The first is self-identified as a postface, by Kong Anguo 孔安國 (late second century BCE; see figure 1).[2] Kong Anguo was a descendant of Confucius and a standout scholar of his day. According to this postface, there was originally a large set of manuscripts related to Confucius' interactions with his followers, rulers, and other dignitaries. From this set of manuscripts, the *Analects* was selected.[3] The remainder was preserved as the *Kongzi jia yu*, the dialogues of the school of

often in the *Dialogues*, *yu* acts as a verb, meaning to say to—one person speaking to someone else. Even a cursory reading of the book reveals that it belongs in the literary genre of the dialogue. (See further along in the introduction for a more nuanced discussion of *dialogue*.) Legge most often refers to the book not by its full title but as the *Narratives of the School*, apparently preferring a pithier, more descriptive translation. We follow Legge in this preference but substitute the more accurate *dialogues* for *narratives*. "Confucius" rather than "school" clarifies that the book is centered on the ideas and opinions of Confucius and not his students, and signals the book's synergy with—rather than its distance from—the *Analects* of Confucius.

2. The exact dates of Kong Anguo are unknown. Recent scholarship places his dates in a sixty-six-year range, his birth no earlier than 156 BCE and his death no later than 90 BCE (Sun 2007; Chen and Bai 2014; Huang 2017). Absent compelling reasons to the contrary, we accept that Kong Anguo is the author of this postface. See Kramers (1950) and Huang (2017) for arguments in favor of this position.

3. It came to be known in Chinese as *Lun yu* 論語, *Selected Dialogues*, which was translated by Legge ([1893] 2012) as *Analects*, a title that has largely stuck.

Five Chiefs, dates unknown
Xia Dynasty, ?–c. 1570 BCE
Shang Dynasty, c. 1570–1045 BCE
Zhou King Wen, r. 1099–1050 BCE
Zhou Dynasty, 1045–256 BCE
Western Zhou Dynasty, 1045–771 BCE
King Wu, r. 1049–1043 BCE
Duke of Zhou, r. 1042–1036 BCE
King Cheng, r. 1035–1006 BCE
Documents
Poems
Eastern Zhou Dynasty, 770–256 BCE
Spring and Autumn Period, 770–481 BCE
Confucius, 551–479 BCE
Warring States Period, 481–221 BCE
Early Warring States, 481–401 BCE
Zuo zhuan
Mozi, c. 468–c. 376 BCE
Middle Warring States, 400–301 BCE
The *Mozi*, c. 376 BCE
Shanghai Museum manuscripts, mid- to late 4th cent. BCE
Guodian manuscripts, mid- to late 4th cent. BCE
Mencius, c. 372–289 BCE
Zhuangzi, c. 369–c. 286 BCE
Late Warring States, 300–221 BCE
The *Mencius*, c. 289 BCE
The *Zhuangzi*, c. 286 BCE
Xunzi, c. 313–238 BCE
Zou Yan, fl. 250 BCE
Han Feizi, c. 280–233 BCE
The *Xunzi*, c. 238 BCE
The *Han Feizi*, c. 233 BCE
Qin Dynasty, 221–206 BCE
Han Dynasty, 202 BCE–220 CE
Former Han Dynasty, 202 BCE–8 CE
Kong Anguo, c. 156–c. 90 BCE
Sima Qian, c. 145–86 BCE
Liu Xiang, 79–8 BCE
Dai Sheng, fl. 1st cent. BCE
Xin Dynasty, 9–23 CE
Wang Mang, 45 BCE–23 CE
Liu Xin, 46 BCE–23 CE
[Han Dynasty]
Later Han Dynasty, 25–220 CE
Zheng Xuan, 127–200 CE
Wei-Jin Period, 220–420 CE
Wang Su, 195–256 CE
Kong Chao, 3rd cent. CE
Ma Zhao, fl. 240–249 CE
Sui Dynasty, 581–618 CE
Tang Dynasty, 618–906 CE
Yan Shigu, 581–645 CE
Song Dynasty, 960–1279 CE
Sima Guang, 1019–1086 CE
Su Zhe, 1039–1112 CE
Chao Gongwu, 1105–1180 CE
Hong Mai, 1123–1202 CE
Zhu Xi, 1130–1200 CE
Shi Shengzu, fl. c. 1241 CE
Ye Shi, 1150–1223 CE
Wang Bai, 1197–1274 CE
Yuan Dynasty, 1279–1368 CE
Ma Duanlin, 1254–1323 CE
Ming Dynasty, 1368–1644 CE
He Mengchun, 1474–1536 CE
Lu Zhi, 1496–1576 CE
Qing Dynasty, 1644–1911 CE
Fan Jiaxiang, d. 1768 CE
Qian Fu, fl. c. 1800 CE
Duan Yucai, 1735–1815 CE
Sun Zhizu, 1737–1801 CE
Chen Shike, fl. 1800 CE

FIGURE 1: Timeline of eras, persons, and texts in the introduction. Texts are arranged by estimated date of completion of earliest layer in public form, dates that are often speculative but still useful for comparing texts of possibly prior date. Key figures in the development and critique of the *Dialogues* are in bold. There is no standard periodization of the Warring States period into three phases. Ours divides it into roughly equal thirds around the century breaks.

Confucius. Some of the material of the *Dialogues*, Kong says, was of comparable quality to the contents of the *Analects*, while some was of lesser quality.

Kong says further that the *Dialogues* collection was passed down from teacher to student, and in the mid-third century BCE Xunzi 荀子 conveyed a collection to the king of Qin that contained 100 chapters (*pian* 篇) of the aforementioned material—the complete collection. After the empire was unified by Qin, Kong continues, the collection passed to the subsequent dynasty, the Han.

Sometime before 180 BCE, the new copy was absconded with by a member of the ruling elite. After he was chased out of power, the collection was dispersed into private collections. In 141 BCE, Kong continues, the collection was reacquired in pieces and stored in the imperial archives, where it was mixed in with other collections. Between 110 and 105 BCE, Kong says, he himself, in his official capacity, acquired the collection, organized it, and transcribed it from the ancient script into contemporary characters.

Kong Anguo's postface is followed by a second postface (appendix 2) by an anonymous author who must have lived some time contemporaneously with or just after Kong Yan 孔衍,[4] a grandson of Kong Anguo. It provides an extensive lineage and a brief biography of Kong Anguo, then says that after Kong Anguo finished his work on the *Dialogues*, turmoil among the ruling elite led him to set it aside, and that he passed away without ever officially submitting it to the crown. The statement mentions Han Emperor Cheng's 漢成帝 commissioning Liu Xiang 劉向 (in 26 BCE) to provide new editions of the classics and includes a petition to the throne written by Kong Yan justifying the need for recognition and study of the *Dialogues*. The petition, which is included, says that parts of the *Dialogues* had been poached by Dai Sheng (戴聖, fl. 1st cent. BCE) for use in his *Li ji* 禮記 compilation. Postface 2 concludes by saying that, although the petition was successful and the emperor ordered that the *Dialogues* be included in Liu's work, both the emperor and Liu passed away before it could be accomplished.

The third explanatory document (appendix 3) handed down to us with the *Dialogues* is designated as a preface, authored by Wang Su 王肅 (195–256 CE). In this preface, Wang Su says that he acquired the contents of the *Dialogues* from the Kong family home by way of one Kong Meng 孔猛, a descendant of Confucius. Finding it valuable and consistent with his own (at the time, controversial) interpretations of the classics, he presented it to the public along with his own explanatory notes. The preface concludes with two examples of how the *Dialogues* clears up opaque statements in the *Analects* and the *Chunqiu wai zhuan* 春秋外傳, respectively, the first involving the identification of an interlocutor of Confucius and the second pertaining to a statement describing the governing of the early ruler Yao.

4. This Kong Yan is distinct from the more well-known Kong Yan, who lived just after Wang Su.

The Controversy

When Wang Su brought the *Dialogues* to the public in the third century, it was broadly accepted as authentic. It was received as an important text, and its reputation was perpetuated through the Tang and into the Song dynasty. However, doubt was presumably first cast on it quite early, when Ma Zhao 馬昭 (fl. 240–249 CE), a younger contemporary of Wang Su and a defender of Zheng Xuan 鄭玄 (127–200 CE) against Wang Su, claimed that one poem in it had been fabricated.[5]

Zhu Xi 朱熹 (1130–1200), one of the most important and influential philosophers of the last millennium, refers to the *Dialogues* positively and even uses a passage of

5. The book where Ma Zhao's quote is purported to appear has been lost. The title of the lost book is *Sheng zheng lun* 聖證論. It is recorded as having been written by Wang Su, but only scattered quotations of it remain in other works. The surviving quote from Ma Zhao is found in Kong Yingda's 孔穎達 recension of the *Li ji* (Kong and Zheng 1866). Kong records Zheng Xuan's comment on a passage of the "Yue ji" chapter, along with Wang Su's opposing comment that adduces the *Dialogues*, and then Ma Zhao's accusation against Wang Su that his quotation from the *Dialogues* is an interpolation. The passage in the *Li ji* mentions a poem attributed to Shun, entitled "The Southern Wind" (*nan feng* 南風). Zheng Xuan's note says that the wording of the poem is "unknown" (*wei wen* 未聞). Kong then says:

> *Sheng zheng lun*, challenging Zheng, quotes from the *Shizi* 尸子 and the *Dialogues of Confucius*, as follows:
>
> In the past, Shun, playing the five-string zither, created a poem called "The Southern Wind." It goes:
>
> The soft blowing of the southern wind
> Can ease the tension of our people.
> The timeliness of the southern wind
> Can increase the prosperity of our people.
>
> Zheng had said that the words were unknown and that the meaning had been lost. Recently Ma Zhao says that they were added by Wang Su to the *Dialogues* and Zheng had not seen them. As for the *Shizi*, it belongs to miscellaneous theories and cannot be verified. This is why it was said that it was unknown.

The sequence of the debate is as follows: The *Li ji* mentions a poem; Zheng Xuan comments in his annotation of the *Li ji* that the poem is lost; Wang Su, in the *Sheng zheng lun*, says that the poem actually survives in two texts—the *Shizi and the Dialogues*; then Ma Zhao, also in the *Sheng zheng lun*, discounts both sources. The *Shizi* was a Warring States text that has not survived to the present but is mentioned in the *Bie lu* and is described briefly by Liu Xiang. There is evidence that it survived into Wang Su's time and then gradually disappeared over the course of the Tang and Song dynasties (Fang et al. 1994). No one is sure what exactly the contents of the *Sheng zheng lun* were, but with passages like that above, it clearly involved some kind of debate. According to Kramer's reconstruction of events, a debate was held during Wang Su's time between the followers of Zheng Xuan (one of whom was Ma Zhao) and Wang Su and his followers, and the *Sheng zheng lun* is a record of that debate. (Kong and Zheng 1866; Kramers 1950; Cheng 2013; Yang and Song 2013; Guo and Zhang 2019)

the *Dialogues* to emend a passage in the "Zhong yong 中庸."[6] However, it was in Zhu Xi's time, about 900 years after the *Dialogues* had come to light, that its authenticity was first doubted in a comprehensive way. And the *Dialogues* wasn't alone in this respect; it was a period when the core Confucian texts were being reevaluated on a large scale.[7]

Wang Bai 王柏 (1197–1274) was a leading scholar of *Li Xue* 理學 (Neo-Confucian) attempts to question the status of ancient texts. Of his forty-one works, his *Doubting the Poems* (*Yi shi* 疑詩) and *Doubting the Documents* (*Yi shu* 疑書) were the most widely circulated and commented on. These books have since been criticized for taking the doubting agenda too far; Wang Bai suspected, for example, that whole sections of the *Poems* classic were Han-dynasty interpolations. And yet Wang Bai's conclusion that Wang Su had forged the *Dialogues* proved to be influential.

Criticism of the *Dialogues* intensified during the Qing dynasty. Yao Jiheng 姚際恒 (b. 1647) included the *Dialogues* in a study of forged texts. Cui Shu 崔述 (1740–1816), a biographer of Confucius, denounced the *Dialogues* as a forgery. In 1767, Fan Jiaxiang 范家相 completed a monograph arguing against the authenticity of the *Dialogues* based in large part on two circumstantial claims: (1) that Wang Su leaned heavily on the *Dialogues* in his refutations of Zheng Xuan in the *Sheng zheng lun* and (2) that the *Dialogues* overlaps considerably with other texts. A few decades later, Sun Zhizu 孫志祖 (1737–1801) produced another lengthy critique of the *Dialogues*.

The three books by Wang Bai, Fan Jiaxiang, and Sun Zhizu largely settled the matter in China up until only recently, but there was never universal agreement. In addition to Zhu Xi, scholars such as Chao Gongwu 晁公武 (1105–1180), Ye Shi 葉適 (1150–1223), Shi Shengzu 史繩祖 (fl. c. 1241), Ma Duanlin 馬端臨 (c. 1254–1323), He Mengchun 何孟春 (1474–1536), Lu Zhi 陸治 (1496–1576), Qian Fu 錢馥 (fl. c. 1800), and Duan Yucai 段玉裁 (1735–1815) all averred that the *Dialogues*, in whole or in part, was genuine. Chen Shike 陳士珂 (fl. c. 1800) annotated the *Dialogues* and defended its authenticity.

The earliest extant mention of the *Dialogues* is in Liu Xiang's (79–8 BCE) *Bie lu* 別録, the first comprehensive bibliography of Chinese texts, which is preserved in *Han shu* 漢書, "Yi wen zhi" (c. 92 CE). This record is consistent with the supplementary material handed down in the *Dialogues* and suggests that the *Dialogues* existed some two centuries before Wang Su could have forged it (although the accusers say that Wang Su purloined the title for his forgery).

6. In addition to his positive comments and his use of the *Dialogues* in emending the "Zhong yong," Zhu Xi also said: "The *Dialogues* is merely a miscellaneous collection of old records put together by Wang Su. There are many problems with it. And yet, it is not a fabrication by Wang Su" (Huang 2017, 308). According to Huang Huaixin (2017), this ambiguity in Zhu Xi is what prompted his student Wang Bai's study of the *Dialogues* (see just below). Wang intended to set the record straight.

7. The summary of events in this paragraph and the subsequent two paragraphs draws from Kramers (1950), Yang and Song (2013), Huang (2017), and Li (2020).

A text with an intriguing history that parallels that of the *Dialogues* is the *Zhou li* 周禮, which appeared around 150 BCE. The *Zhou li* and the material that eventually made up the *Dialogues* are said to have passed through the hands of Xunzi (*Dialogues*) or one of his students (*Zhou li*). They then fell into the hands of collectors and were eventually donated to the imperial archives, where they languished until being rescued from obscurity when they were cited in a matter of contemporaneous importance. The *Zhou li* was raised from obscurity by Liu Xin 劉歆 (46 BCE–23 CE) in support of Wang Mang 王莽 (45 BCE–23 CE). Finding it suspicious that each of the texts came to prominence coincidentally to support a contemporaneous position, Song-dynasty Neo-Confucians—principally the scholars Sima Guang 司馬光 (1019–1086), Hong Mai 洪邁 (1123–1202), and Su Zhe 蘇轍 (1039–1112) in the case of the *Zhou li*, declared them forgeries.[8]

The *Zhou li* was reputed to have been authored by the Duke of Zhou (周公, r. 1042–1036 BCE), and in the Tang dynasty it was made an official Confucian Classic. For these reasons, it had many defenders, who pointed out that the text contained passages that predated Liu Xin and so could not have been an outright forgery by him. William Boltz says that "the conclusion that the [*Zhou li*] is a genuine pre-Han text remains convincing" (Loewe 1993, 29). Below, we shall see that a similar rationale can be applied to the *Dialogues*: passages predating Wang Su and even Kong Anguo, especially from excavated texts, add to a body of evidence justifying an earlier dating for the text.

Before getting to that, however, a complicating factor must be raised: namely, the ancient-script version of the *Documents* (*Shang shu* 尚書). The postface to the *Dialogues* was not the only such document attributed to Kong Anguo; the preface of the ancient-script *Documents* was as well. The *Documents*, as explained in the glossary, is an immensely important Confucian classic, the earliest strata of which date among the earliest of all Chinese transmitted expository texts. However, the version of the text that surfaced about the time of Wang Su had acquired many additional chapters. Although that version was heralded in subsequent centuries as authentic, later textual scholars surmised that the extra chapters had been forged. Although Wang Su never adduced those chapters, and although mention of them precedes their appearance in the Jin dynasty (after Wang Su's time), the certainty with which scholars have pronounced them to be forgeries has tarnished the *Dialogues* by association. Inevitably, whenever the possible forgery of one is raised, the possible forgery of the other is not far behind.[9]

8. See William Boltz's entry for the *Chou li* in Loewe (1993).

9. For overviews of the complicated controversy of the ancient-script *Documents*, see Nylan (2001), Edward Shaughnessy's entry on the *Shang Shu* in Loewe (1993), and Huang (2017). A similar guilt by association is found in discussions of the *Kong cong zi* 孔叢子, which is also often considered a forgery attributed to Wang Su, even though he never adduced it. See Ariel (1989) and Huang (2017) for lengthy discussions of the issues involved. Ariel concludes that the book is likely a forgery originating from circles related to Wang Su. Nevertheless, he says, "The ascription of the authorship of the [*Kong cong zi*]

The Most Plausible Scenario

The first scholar to make an extended argument in English justifying the genuineness of the *Dialogues* was Robert Paul Kramers (1950).[10] More recently, Chinese scholars have used new evidence from recently excavated texts that date back to the relevant time period to likewise argue for the genuineness of the *Dialogues*. Let us begin by discussing Kramers along with Yang Chaoming and Song Lilin (2013) as representatives of current Western and Chinese scholarship[11] on the matter before entertaining opposing viewpoints.

---

to Wang Su will remain a matter of conjecture, and one must always be prepared to be proved wrong when suggesting such a probability" (Ariel 1989, 62). In a review of Ariel's conclusion linking Wang Su to the *Kong cong zi*, Kramers says, "The case Ariel makes for the [*Kong cong zi*] to be a third century Confucian response to the new 'Neo-Taoistic' developments which replaced the orthodox Han synthesis seems to me to go too far. . . . It is a hypothetical exercise carried out with the greatest ingenuity, but to me it remains extremely unconvincing" (Kramers 1991, 156–57). Huang Huaixin agrees with Kramers that the *Kong cong zi* likely contains early matter, but with more additions and reworking by later contributors in the Kong family. Huang says, *Kong cong zi* "is definitely not the work of Wang Su. Although some of its contents are not genuine, unlike what others have said before, it is not entirely untrustworthy" (Huang 2017, 246). Huang's analysis goes so far as to attribute authorship and two layers of editorship to all twenty-three chapters of the *Kong cong zi*, with the earliest layer dating to the Qin dynasty.

10. Prior to Kramers, James Legge adduced the *Dialogues* many times in his prolegomena to the *Analects*, writing that it is "a very valuable fragment of antiquity, and it would be worthwhile to incorporate it with the *Analects*" (Legge [1893] 2012, 132). A. B. Hutchinson (1878, 1879, 1880) echoes this sentiment in the first partial English translation of the *Dialogues*.

11. Huang Mengshan (2014) summarizes a flurry of activity on the authenticity of the *Dialogues* up to 2014. Liu Jinyou (2019) provides an exhaustive literature review of contemporary work on the *Dialogues*. See also Ning Zhenjiang's (2017) introduction to his own collection of essays about the *Dialogues* for a literature overview. Two other book-length studies are worth mentioning. Liu Wei (2014) and Huang Huaixin (2017) both attempt comprehensive evaluations of claims in the history of the controversy involving the *Dialogues*. Liu divides arguments in the controversy into four "cases (*gongan* 公案)," evaluating their merits and influence. He finds that the arguments against the authenticity of the *Dialogues* stem, by and large, from misunderstandings, decontextualization, or their own motivations ancillary to the actual controversy. Huang's study is the most detailed and nuanced, beginning with an in-depth examination of the Kong family, first during the Former Han and then during the Later Han. He examines Kong Anguo and works attributed to him and his descendants, as well as works about the Kong family, such as *Kong cong zi*. He continues into the Wei-Jin period, examining the scholarship of the Kong family and then the advent of Wang Su and the *Dialogues*. These steps comprise most of the seven chapters of the book, from which Huang concludes that the contents of the Wang Su preface and the Kong Anguo postface relating to their relationship to the book are likely to be accurate. Huang goes on to examine the relationships between the *Dialogues* and other texts, including excavated texts, that have parallel passages, concluding that Kong Anguo's description in the postface

Kramers begins with the Kong family itself, prompted by Wang Su's preface. Wang Su says that he obtained the *Dialogues* material from his pupil Kong Meng, who is not attested elsewhere, and some have suspected that his existence was a fabrication by Wang Su. Kramers argues that this is highly improbable because (1) the Kong family was prominent at the time and would surely have objected to such an egregious fabrication, (2) the family actually sided with Wang Su at the time, and (3) Wang Su's foremost student was Kong Chao 孔晁, a leading member of the Kong family. The only way to make sense of these facts and still maintain that the *Dialogues* was forged by Wang Su is to assume the forgery represented a grand conspiracy involving the prestigious Kong family, which defies common sense.[12]

From here, Kramers moves on to the two postfaces (which he refers to as a single postface). He examines in detail each of the historical claims as well as the Kong family lineage. He tentatively concludes that the first postface is by the hand of the compiler of the *Dialogues* in the early Han dynasty (i.e., Kong Anguo) and that the second is of a later date, perhaps as late as Wang Su himself. However, Kramers insists that evidence in the preface and the postfaces should not count as evidence for or against the authenticity of the *Dialogues* itself.

Looking at evidence internal to the *Dialogues*, Kramers divides his examination into four parts. In the first part, Kramers examines numerous passages that are slightly different from parallel passages in other texts and that are so consistent with Wang Su's arguments in the *Sheng zheng lun* as to suggest intentional tampering on Wang Su's part. In the second part, Kramers examines suspicious consistencies between Wang Su's commentary in the *Dialogues* and the pseudo-Kong Anguo commentary in the ancient-script *Documents*. In the third part, Kramers examines "peculiarities" of the *Dialogues* that in some way suggest tampering by Wang Su. These three discussions are consistent with—and adduce many of the arguments from—historical critiques of the *Dialogues*.

In the fourth part, Kramers explains why one should refrain from drawing any kind of general conclusion from the first three. He says that there are other parts of the text that strongly suggest that Wang Su was working with an independent text. He points out that Wang Su's commentary corrects graphical errors in the text, which would not make sense if Wang Su had created the text himself. Nor would it make sense, unless Wang Su were utterly diabolical, that he forged the

still stands and that although the *Dialogues* is not an entirely pristine Warring States text, it is largely the edited form of a collection of Warring States material.

12. Paul Goldin pushes back against this objection: "We can say with some confidence, however, that in forging the [*Kong cong zi*] 孔叢子, Wang Su (or someone in his camp) displayed just the kind of cleverness that Kramers finds it impossible to attribute to him" (Goldin 1999, 135n53). Goldin himself cites Ariel (1989). See above our discussion of Ariel's work, and see below Goldin's five objections to Kramers.

text and then corrected apparent anachronisms in it (as Wang Su does, for example, in correcting Yan Hui's purported age).

The bulk of the fourth part is devoted to examining relationships between the *Dialogues* and other texts, including proto-texts and common source texts, that existed at the beginning of the Han dynasty: *Zuo zhuan* 左傳, *Guo yu* 國語, *Xunzi* 荀子, *Shuo yuan* 說苑, *Li ji*, and so on. Kramers says that the contents of the *Dialogues* are consistent with the description in Kong Anguo's postface, and that there is a large overlap with accounts of Confucius in extant historical records ("mixed up with events of the various states" [see appendix 1]). The *Dialogues* contains nearly all accounts of conversations between Confucius and his students that existed at that time ("words of the seventy-two students" [see appendix 1]), with the exception of stories in the *Zhuangzi* 莊子 that were considered apocryphal. There is very little overlap with the *Analects* or other focused collections such as the *Xiao jing* 孝經.

Kramers concludes that the *Dialogues* should be distinguished into two parts:

> a. A collection made up from the main early traditions about Confucius handed down by later followers of his school, with the purpose of providing a complement to the [*Analects*]. Excluded were, for the reason that they had their own transmission, the [*Xiao jing*], [*Kongzi san chao ji*], and [*Zengzi wen*]. All this constitutes the bulk of the collection.
> b. A series of texts, passages, and sentences, which are in agreement with theories propounded in the third century A.D. by Wang Su, of which he made use as evidence against the tenets of the influential school of [Zheng Xuan]; this is a minor portion of the collection. (Kramers 1950, 192)

What does Kramers make of the value of the *Dialogues* for the present day? He says:

> We may learn from it some more about Confucius as he was conceived in the early Han and also in pre-Han times; for [my] hypothesis would entail that part of the direct sources out of which the [*Dialogues*] was compiled have been lost themselves. . . . It does not make a great deal of difference whether the [*Dialogues*] was entirely compiled in the third century A.D. or partly also in the second or first century B.C.; to us it mainly represents the Confucian lore existing in the third century B.C., as Waley rightly has pointed out. (Kramers 1950, 198)

While Kramers refutes some of the claims of the accusers of Wang Su, he also accepts some. But many of these claims rest on certain questionable assumptions, such as that there was a distinct divide between Daoist and Confucian schools. For example, with reference to passages connecting Confucius to Laozi 老子, Kramers says, "trends provening from [Daoist] origins were placed within the Confucian frame-work" (168). Although a distinct line separating Daoism from Confucianism was popular in twentieth-century scholarship, recent archaeological evidence has thrown it into doubt. The affiliation between so-called Daoist and Confucian theory present in the *Dialogues* can now be seen as pointing in the direction of its authenticity rather than the opposite. This point will become clearer below.

Several archaeological discoveries over recent decades provide evidence that at least some parts of the *Dialogues* are of early origin (Liu 1981; He and Liu 1981). Yang and Song (2013) summarize these finds and their relevance to the *Dialogues*. In 1973, a set of bamboo manuscripts dating to the year 55 BCE were found in a tomb in Ding County, Hebei Province. Some of these bamboo slips constitute the *Analects*, and some overlap with portions of the *Dialogues*. Li Xueqin, a leading scholar in contemporary China, called these the "Bamboo [*Dialogues*]" (X. Li 1987, 61) since they were written on bamboo, the common writing medium of the period.

Yang and Song also cite an even earlier source. In 1977, a Han tomb dating to 165 BCE was excavated in Fuyang, Anhui Province (Wang and Han 1978). It contained another set of bamboo slips that overlaps with the *Dialogues*. The dating of 165 BCE puts it just before Kong Anguo's time.

These two finds contain passages that overlap passages scattered across the *Dialogues*. A more recent archaeological find includes a large portion of an entire brief essay (chapter 27) of the *Dialogues* and dates to an even earlier time. In 1994, the Shanghai Museum purchased a collection of ancient bamboo slips on the antiquities market. These have since been authenticated and found to date to the fourth century BCE (Ma 2001; Shaughnessy 2005).[13] This stunning discovery puts to rest any theory that the *Dialogues* is entirely a product of the Han dynasty or later.[14] But it does more than that. It also shows that terminology once associated only with Daoism also appeared in overtly Confucian texts. The text in question is called "Parent of the People" (*Min zhi fumu* 民之父母). Overlap between the Shanghai Museum text and *Dialogues* 27.2 is not complete, but there is a significant amount of identical wording, including passages about the "three absences." The Chinese for *absence* is *wu* 無, a term that, indeed, means an absence of something at a basic level. In Daoism, it gains a supererogatory meaning, which is also apparent in the essay in question. There is

13. Ma estimates a late-fourth-century date for the physical manuscripts, and Shaughnessy concurs. Because it is unlikely that an original manuscript would be buried, it is most likely that the essay had circulated for some time before it was copied and buried. That would likely position it toward the mid-fourth century at the latest.

14. Some might downplay this significance by saying that if, as some accusers have said, the *Dialogues* was merely copied from other texts, like the *Li ji*, then any such archaeological finds speak to the authenticity of the other texts, not to that of the *Dialogues*. As Kramers and others have shown, however, the most likely scenario is that it was not merely a matter of the *Dialogues* being a pastiche of other texts. It is more likely that the *Dialogues* and other related texts were instead based on an independent set of underlying texts. The excavated material supports the theory that there were independent lines of texts that formed the bases of the transmitted texts that we have today.

also mention in the passage of *qi* 氣, a term that, despite one anomalous passage in the *Mencius* (*Mengzi* 孟子), has been widely considered a notion adopted by Daoists and other metaphysicians but eschewed by the earliest Confucians. The adoption of these putatively Daoist ideas would have once marked the *Dialogues* as unequivocally late. The Shanghai manuscript version of this passage, along with other excavated texts (such as "Xing zi ming chu 性自命出"), turns that notion on its head.[15]

Xia Dekao (2012) quotes a common view of the development of literary styles in Warring States period China from a standard history of Chinese literature:

> The development of prose styles related to pre-Han thinkers can be divided into three stages. The first stage is composed of the *Analects* and the *Mozi*, the former being prose purely in the form of reported dialogues and the latter being a mix of reported dialogues and debates. The second stage is composed of the *Mencius* and the *Zhuangzi*, the former also based on the dialogue form but already developing into a dialogic form of essay; the latter has already developed from the dialogue form into a transitional form of thematic essays of focus arguments. With only a few exceptions, the *Zhuangzi* almost entirely transcends the dialogue form and has developed into the thematic essay. The third stage is composed of the *Xunzi* and *Han Feizi*, both of which represent the height of the pre-Qin thematic essay. (69)

According to Xia, this theory has been overturned by the several essays of the Shanghai Museum manuscripts, which predate the *Mencius* and *Zhuangzi* but already have the form of the thematic essay.

Do the preceding arguments and insights settle the matter of the authenticity of the *Dialogues* once and for all? Not entirely. Some scholars (e.g., Wu Kejing 2015) still believe that Wang Su, or someone of his time, created the *Dialogues* by pasting together passages from already existing texts and then altered them to suit their own philosophical position. Their main argument rests on comparing linguistic features of one passage to another. These scholars say that aspects of the language in the passages that overlap with other texts, including excavated texts, point to the *Dialogues* being a later text. But this kind of argument, relying as it does on tentative assumptions about (1) what kind

15. Scholars who have closely examined the relationship of the Shanghai Museum text with its parallels in the *Dialogues* and *Li ji* have differing opinions about ultimate provenance, but the predominant opinion appears to be that the Shanghai Museum manuscript predates the *Dialogues* and *Li ji* versions (Richter 2013; Ning 2017; Cook 2021). As Scott Cook reminds us, however, this does not devalue the transmitted texts. On the contrary, the existence of the manuscript version gives us reason to reevaluate the transmitted texts. Qi Dandan (2012) summarizes the already copious literature on just this topic and classifies newer scholarship into four categories: the relationship of Confucian ideas with Daoist ideas; the development of intellectual history and literary history; political philosophy; and *junzi* studies.

of linguistic features count as early and (2) when such features made their way into a text, amounts to little more than a series of ad hoc just-so stories.[16]

Although it would be an overstatement to say that Western scholars largely accept Kramers' conclusions, it is safe to say that few have challenged them in print. The most extensive example in English comes only in a long footnote to an excursus on the *Xunzi* from Paul Goldin. Goldin expresses confidence that the *Dialogues* is a forgery by "the infamous Wang Su" (Goldin 1999, 135n53). Goldin offers five brief arguments for his rejection of Kramers' work and his own refusal to believe "that anything in the [*Dialogues*], which purports to contain those sayings of Confucius not selected for incorporation into the *Analects*, can be taken without outside confirmation as an authentic document from the Warring States."

First, he appeals to the large overlap with other extant texts, offering a false dichotomy to account for the overlap: "[Either] Wang Su stole from everyone or . . . everyone took from a real [*Dialogues*]" (136n53). As we've seen above, there is a more

16. Wu Kejing cites as support for his theory a dissertation by Siu King Wai (2004) that purports to demonstrate, by so-called forensic linguistics, that the *Dialogues* is a heterogenous text, with parts dating from the late Warring States period to the late Han. While attempting to proceed from a comparative basis employing the entire set of early texts, the work provides no dating schema for texts and no statistical framework for linguistic analysis, and instead merely examines whether certain characters, or strings of characters, occur across certain texts, with single citations (if any) substantiating the dating for each text in his massive set. There are two further flaws with this approach. First, the number and length of texts of the Han dynasty (by traditional dating) far exceeds the number and length of texts of the pre-Qin period, and so it will be statistically more probable that any random string of characters will be present in the larger set of texts than the smaller set of texts. Without independent statistical analysis or other criteria for selecting strings of characters, finding them to be more common in the later and larger set of texts is not informative. There must first be a reason to select a character, or string of characters, for analysis (as we show in our own examples later in this introduction). Otherwise, one can be accused of cherry-picking examples. Second, if Kong Anguo did indeed edit the *Dialogues*, as we provisionally accept, he did it by transposing Warring States script into Han dynasty script (using manuscripts that were not entirely pristine), and anyone can see by looking at excavated bamboo strips that this was not a perfectly straightforward process. In cases of difficult-to-understand passages or illegibility, his reconstructed word choices could have occasionally reflected Han dynasty syntactic constructions. So, the mere presence of a small number of such constructions is not evidence that the text was originally a Han dynasty production. Something similar can be said for Wang Su's recension (though his edits would have been based on hermeneutics, not script). What's more, the *Dialogues* is a relatively large text, five times as large as the *Analects*. So, of course, there is more likely to be overlap of specific syntactic constructions with other texts. Siu doesn't say that there are 50 or 100 examples of such-and-such a construction in the *Dialogues*. He says there are 2, or 6, or even just 1, and from there makes sweeping generalizations. Such a small number of examples is likely statistically insignificant. But we can't know for sure without some sort of statistical framework or set of eligibility criteria, which, where available, are thinly justified in Siu's work.

nuanced position—namely, that there were multiple lines of transmission of the material now contained in the *Dialogues* and found elsewhere. The multiple-lines-of-transmission theory accounts for the many divergences in parallel passages across manuscripts; Goldin's theft theory does not.

Second, Goldin says that parallel passages in the *Dialogues* and the *Yanzi chunqiu* 晏子春秋 "seem" to originate in the latter rather than the former, "although this probably cannot be proved" (136n53).

Third, Goldin says that a single statement of more than one formulation—namely, *dao bu shi yi* 道不拾遺 (lost items were let lie), which is found twice in the *Xunzi* and in parallel passages in the *Dialogues* (1.1 and 1.3)—was a late Warring States cliché, implying that the *Dialogues* could not date from the early Warring States. This line of reasoning is similar to the vocabulary evidence adduced below with respect to the dating of *Zuo zhuan* and the *Art of War* (Sunzi *Bing fa* 孫子兵法). It is true that, outside of the *Dialogues*, the earliest extant use of this phrase was in the Warring States period. Does that demonstrate that the two uses of it in the *Dialogues* are evidence that the *Dialogues* was forged by Wang Su? Certainly not. At most, it shows that that one part of the two passages in question dates from the late Warring States period at the earliest (400 years before Wang Su's time). But even this conclusion is premature, for the argument rests on a fallacious appeal to ignorance. Just because there are no extant early Warring States texts that use the phrase in question does not mean that it was never used in that time period. (We have to remember that most of the texts of the period have been lost.) It could also, as a cliché, have been added later. We see in other evidence below that, based on periodization of vocabulary, the *Dialogues* is likely a product of the early or middle Warring States period, though later additions cannot be ruled out.

Fourth, Goldin says, "the language of the [*Dialogues*] is not like that of Confucius's day" (136n53). Goldin offers one piece of evidence for this sweeping claim—the use of the term *Ru* (see in the philosophical lexicon below), which occurs in one chapter of the *Analects* and in one chapter of the *Dialogues*, although in the *Dialogues* the entire chapter is devoted to the concept. Goldin says that such an interest in the term occurred "only after the development of rival schools—that is to say, long after the time when Confucius' disciples would have decided what to include in the [*Analects*] and what in the [*Dialogues*]." In fact, however, the description of the *Ru* in the *Dialogues* has no association with rivalry among schools and is instead a description of *Ru* as the very kind of *shi* 士 (see below) that Goldin says did occupy Confucius' thinking. If Kong Anguo's description of the contents of the *Analects* and *Dialogues* is correct, then the brief treatment in the *Analects* and the lengthier treatment in the *Dialogues* is what we should expect (see further discussion below).

In his final argument, Goldin says that Wang Su's justification for bringing the *Dialogues* to light was to supplement his own philosophical positions of the time. But, Goldin asks, given the overlap of the *Dialogues* with other texts, why could

Wang Su not simply appeal to those other texts? Wang Su implies, Goldin says, that material in the *Dialogues* is new, and yet most of it is not. Isn't this a contradiction?

Again, the situation is more complicated than Goldin makes it out to be. Wang Su himself, in his preface, points out two pieces of information in the *Dialogues* that are indeed new. But it is not the newness of the *Dialogues* that is important; what is important is the authority. Most of the ideas in the *Dialogues* can indeed be found in other texts, but their originating in the lineage of Confucius confers on them a degree of certainty—lacking from quotations in other texts—that they are in agreement with Confucius' own thinking. Further on in this introduction, we cite many examples of fresh perspectives offered by the *Dialogues*.

In fairness to Goldin, it is important to emphasize that his argument comes in but a single footnote, so extensive evidence and discussion should not be expected (although he repeats his accusation with equal certainty in Goldin [2020], citing his own note). Because it is the most extensive challenge to Kramers' conclusions that we have found in English, we feel that it deserves the foregoing lengthy discussion.

Before moving on, there are two further minor points worth mentioning. Consistent with Goldin's position, Wu Kejing (2015) points out that approximately 5 percent of the *Dialogues* is unique and does not overlap with any known text. An example is *Dialogues* 9.11, about hiding a piece of jade. Nothing about this passage points to Wang Su's anti–Zheng Xuan agenda, so Wu Kejing and other opponents of the authenticity thesis have to say either that it is a passage taken by Wang Su from a text that has since been lost or that the forger made it up to throw us off his scent. This latter claim is also employed when certain linguistic elements appear that would be anachronistic for a later text. For example, Wu Kejing notes that the word *ju* 居, which had gone out of style by Wang Su's time, still appears repeatedly in the *Dialogues*. His argument is that it must be the forger's intentional way of making the text look older than it really is. In our opinion, neither of these arguments is convincing. The more plausible account is Kramers'—that the compiler (most likely Kong Anguo) was working with a set of Warring States texts.

A final niggling point has to do with the whereabouts of the *Dialogues* after Kong Anguo purportedly created the text out of the pile of manuscripts that he found in the imperial archives. The story is that Kong Anguo kept a version of the manuscripts in the Kong family home, and Wang Su eventually brought them to light. But Kong Anguo wouldn't have taken a version home without also leaving a version, or at the very least the original manuscripts, in the archives. When Liu Xiang was later charged with producing texts out of the archival material and produced the *Shuo yuan*, which substantially crosses over with the *Dialogues*, why does he mention neither the *Dialogues* as a text he found in the archives (the one that Kong Anguo had put together) nor the manuscripts that Kong Anguo purportedly used?

Kramers provides an answer to this question. First, Liu Xiang *does* mention the *Dialogues*. It is listed right there in the *Bie lu* (preserved in *Han shu*, "Yi wen zhi"). It is true that the length listed is different from the current length (on one interpretation) and that the Tang-dynasty cataloger Yan Shigu 顏師古 (581–645 CE) said that the *Dialogues* mentioned in the *Bie lu* was not the same as the one circulating in his day. According to Kramers, a solution to this riddle can be found in the second postface to the *Dialogues*, which suggests that when Liu Xiang came across both the *Dialogues* and the *Da Dai li ji* 大戴禮記 and noticed the parallels, he mistakenly suspected that the former copied from the latter, and so he excised all the common passages from the *Dialogues*, shortening it substantially. If the second postface of the *Dialogues* is accurate, Liu Xiang passed away before completing work on his truncated version of the *Dialogues*, which Yan Shigu may have seen but which has since been lost.

The Authenticity of the Text

From the very beginning of classical studies in the Han right up to today, scholars have been sensitive to the possibility of the existence of forgeries among the classics. Whenever it was noticed that a text had suddenly been plucked from obscurity, suspicion would fall upon the plucker for the too-serendipitous discovery. But perhaps we can look at this process in a different way.

Hundreds, if not thousands, of texts were committed to writing during the Warring States period, and only a small fraction have come down to us today. Why were those few texts preserved? Because they were found to be relevant to the readers of their day. If that is the case, then it should not surprise us when one of those texts skidded along the precipice of the abyss like so many others, but unlike the others was saved by someone who found in it support for their theory of the day. It happened when the *Zhou li* was rescued "from the obscurity of the Han archives" (Boltz, in Loewe 1993, 27) by Liu Xin on behalf of Wang Mang, who wanted to legitimize his rule as a restoration of the Duke of Zhou's wise governance. It happened when Liu Xin rescued the *Zuo zhuan* and used it "for citing the text in arguments on omen interpretation, a form of discourse that was immensely influential in his era" (Durrant, Li, and Schaberg 2016, lviii).[17] And, we believe, it happened when Wang Su latched onto the *Dialogues* in his battle against the theories of Zheng Xuan.[18] All of these texts fell under suspicion as possible forgeries over the centuries, in part because their arrival happened just at the right time for those who deployed them

17. Michael Nylan (2001) adds that after Liu Xin, "the *Zuo* gained steadily in popularity within scholastic circles, no doubt because it was touted as promoting conservative values in this period of gradual reinfeudation" (262).

18. Hao Hong (2011) details aspects of the *Dialogues*' philosophy that are consistent with aspects of Wang Su's own thinking and would therefore have been a convenient supplement to his own position. In addition, Hao discusses aspects of the *Dialogues* that are inconsistent with Wang Su's ideas. These are conveniently ignored by Wang Su's accusers.

in philosophical disputes. But perhaps that convenience should be seen as a point in their favor rather than against them. That is, perhaps they survived simply because they were found relevant.

In his studies of the *Bamboo Annals* (*Zhu shu ji nian* 竹書紀年) and the "Shi fu" 世浮 chapter of the *Yi Zhou shu* 逸周書, Edward Shaughnessy (1997) has shown that sometimes authentic classics turn out to be hiding in plain sight. From the Qing dynasty forward, the new text version of the *Bamboo Annals* had widely been considered a forgery. Only in recent decades has it been accepted as genuine. By examining similarities between the new-text *Bamboo Annals* and bronze inscriptions, and by a close examination of the arrangement of the *Bamboo Annals*, Shaughnessy (following David Nivison) has shown that, in his words, "no serious student of early China will be able to disregard the testimony of the *Bamboo Annals*" (93). This same spirit and allied methods, we believe, should be applied to the *Dialogues of Confucius*.

We said above that we believe the *Dialogues* can "provisionally be accepted" to be authentic. What do we mean by that? When working with any premodern text of questionable origin, one has to do a kind of Bayesian calculus and determine one's own confidence threshold for putting it to use as representative of the thought of the particular historical figure in question. What is one's confidence level, for example, that the Gospels are representative of the thought of Jesus, or that the words of Plato's Socrates can really be attributed to Socrates? Similarly, how likely is it that Aristotle's works, discovered underground centuries after his death, are indeed his students' records of his lectures? These questions are impossible to answer definitively. If one seeks 100-percent confidence in attributing a text to an author before using the text as a representative of the author's thoughts, then a vast range of texts—even the plays attributed to Shakespeare (James and Rubinstein 2007)—would be off-limits.

None of Aristotle's own writings survive, and yet Aristotle is one of the most influential philosophers in the Western tradition. How can that be? Historical records tell us that Aristotle produced over 100 writings—letters, essays, dialogues, and poetry—but all of them have been lost (Anagnostopoulos 2013; Hatzimichali 2016). Instead, we have records of his talks recorded by his students that were mysteriously discovered hundreds of years after his death. The traditional story goes as follows:

> Strabo [c. 63 BCE–23 CE] informs us that after the death of Theophrastus all of his and Aristotle's books were bequeathed to [Aristotle's student] Neleus, who took them to his home town of Scepsis in the Troad, where his descendants kept them hidden from the book-thirsty Attalid kings. They made up their minds to sell the books eventually in the early first century [BCE], but to the rich bibliophile Apellicon of Teos, whose library was brought by Sulla [d. 78 BCE] to Rome and received some form of scholarly attention from the grammarian Tyrannio, who then passed them on to Andronicus of Rhodes. (Hatzimichali 2016, 81)

Andronicus made them public around the middle of the first century BCE. Some of Aristotle's other writings were still extant at the time, but the Andronicus corpus gradually eclipsed them until they were lost entirely.

But even the writings that are purported to be transcriptions of his lectures are suspect. According to Georgios Anagnostopoulos (2013), the texts that Andronicus received were unorganized, brief, fractured, and in generally poor condition. On top of this, he says, they were purported to be from Aristotle's library but not necessarily authored by Aristotle. That means, he continues, that they could have been written by members of his school or could instead have been merely outside works that Aristotle had collected.

Furthermore, Aristotle is not the only philosopher for whom determining authorship is a challenge. The fact is that the authorship of many texts of ancient origin is difficult to attribute with certainty. Philosophers, historians, and textual scholars contribute to the long process of reaching consensus in such cases, but the burden of decision-making falls most heavily on the scholar who wishes to position a thinker's ideas not only in the history of the tradition but also in the current conversation. Often, historians and textual scholars can plead ignorance and simply ignore any contemporary relevance a candidate text might have. They can put the decision off for another day, or provide a detailed analysis of various positions, without adopting any one of them. But a scholar hoping to put ancient ideas into conversation today would like to be able to attribute key ideas from the past not just to a particular school or text but to a particular person. How can that be done without full confidence of authorship attribution?

One of the most influential philosophical texts of the European medieval period is that of St. Dionysius the Areopagite. This text appeared in the sixth century, purporting to be the work of this direct disciple of St. Paul in the first century (Rorem 1993; Corrigan and Harrington 2019). The text became extremely influential in Christian philosophy when it was assumed to genuinely be by the first-century saint, and not until the fifteenth century was it determined that the text was a forgery and couldn't have been written until the fifth century at the earliest. Because the true author of the text was completely unknown, the later tradition has referred to the author as simply Pseudo-Dionysius, or False-Dennis.

Many texts from ancient times fall between the poles of confirmed authorship and confirmed forgery. What can we do about them? Some scholars would say that, where we lack absolute confidence, we should refrain from attributing authorship. The fact is, however, that authorship attribution rarely works this way. When scholars today attribute authorship of the *Nicomachean Ethics* or the *Politics* to Aristotle, they—we—are not claiming absolute knowledge of confirmed authorship. Rather, they—we—are claiming sufficient confidence for now. Perhaps later we will learn something new about the authorship. It is also a hermeneutic shorthand for grouping mutually consistent positions. Even if the historical Aristotle did not write the texts, they are sufficiently alike among themselves and sufficiently similar to what others said of Aristotle's thinking that grouping them under one author permits us certain insights into the texts as a body of work, allowing us to make inferences and fill gaps from one text to another.

Most scholars who work with reconstructions of ancient philosophy prioritize hermeneutic expedience over certainty of authorship, in a provisional rather than neglectful way. Some scholars focus on questions of authorship attribution—a worthwhile enterprise—and some make provisional attributions based on the best evidence available. In a book on the five Confucian classics, Michael Nylan (2001) makes direct, unambiguous attributions to the thoughts and actions of Confucius. For example:

- "Confucius had said little or nothing on questions [about human nature, etc.], possibly because he thought them unanswerable, more likely because in his lifetime such topics did not yet engross educated men" (26).
- "The down-to-earth conversations, relaxed jokes, and individualized question-and-answer sessions used by Confucius himself" (41).
- "Confucius himself was fully confident that the old Zhou culture he faithfully renewed would never die" (348).

Nylan justifies as follows:

> The source now commonly regarded as most reliable for the life and thought of Confucius is the *Analects* (*Lunyu* 論語), a work that purports to record conversations between Confucius and his disciples. But even the earliest passages in the *Analects* probably date to the fourth century BC, about a century or so after Confucius's death, and the *Analects* contains later traditions and outright interpolations. . . . Scholars cannot reasonably hope to discern precisely what the historical Master really thought or said. . . .
>
> I have tried to follow the formula whereby "Confucius" refers to the semifictional creation of the *Analects*' compilers, supplemented—where this is possible without doing real violence to the *Analects*' account of Confucius—by portraits of Confucius preserved in related canonical works of early date, including the [*Li ji*]. I follow this formula in the full knowledge that Confucius over time came to be "more than a man or a thinker, more even than a school of thought," a veritable "cultural phenomenon intertwined with the destiny of all of Chinese civilization." (364)

In his entry on Confucius in the *Stanford Encyclopedia of Philosophy*, Mark Csikszentmihalyi (2020) follows a similar formula, and, beyond the *Analects* and *Li ji*, names several other sources of the philosophy of Confucius:

> Expanding the corpus of Confucius quotations and dialogues beyond the *Analects*, then, requires attention to three additional types of sources. First, dialogues preserved in transmitted sources like the *Records of Ritual* [*Li ji*], the *Elder Dai's Records of Ritual* ([*Da Dai li ji*] 大戴禮記), and Han collections like the [*Dialogues*] *of Confucius* (*Kongzi jiayu* 孔子家語) contain a large number of diverse teachings. Second, quotations attached to the interpretation of passages in the classics preserved in works like the *Zuo Commentary* to the *Spring and Autumn Annals*, or *Han's Intertextual Commentary on the Odes* (*Han Shi waizhuan* 韓詩外傳) are particularly rich sources for readings of history and poetry. Finally, a number of recently archaeologically recovered texts from the Han period and before have also expanded the corpus.

The "Confucius" to which Nylan and Csikszentmihalyi refer is, by our reckoning, the same Confucius that appears in the *Dialogues*. A reference to one is a reference to the other. So, when we say that a certain idea or position can be attributed to Confucius, we are not saying that it is a fact that the historical Confucius definitely said it. Instead, we are provisionally claiming that, to our best understanding today, there is a coherent set of positions that we can attribute to the figure known as Confucius in a specific set of texts (primarily the *Analects* and the *Dialogues*), and that the position in question fits into that set.

There are quite a number of criteria used to determine where on the authenticity spectrum any particular text falls. When enough criteria are met to suggest that authorship can be ascribed, one criterion that stands out is coherence, both internal and external. Are the ideas in the text largely consistent throughout, and are the ideas in the text consistent with texts attributed to the same author? Though not all contradictions or inconsistencies have to be ruled out, a text should not come off as tracking back and forth across incompatible positions, as conveying ideas that clearly originate in a later tradition, or as being simply a collection of haphazard and unrelated ideas. There should, as with the purported teachings of Socrates, be some semblance of systematicity or development, or at the very least of persistent questioning or exploration of positions.

One of the tasks of a scholar working with an ancient text is to reconstruct it in a coherent way. That does not mean forcing coherence on it, by taking passages out of context or offering implausible interpretations. Rather, it means looking at passages that, on a surface reading, may seem unrelated or contradictory and showing how they are actually mutually informing. The more mutually informing passages there are in a text, absent contradictory passages, the more coherent it is.

The *Dialogues* is not a systematic text in the sense that it presents a single argument broken into parts. Its chapters, for example, do not build on each other and then culminate in a final conclusive statement. Nor do they work like premises of a single disordered argument. However, many chapters do contain cohesive thematic statements, and there are few obvious contradictions or serious anachronisms across chapters. The ideas presented are consistent with the ideas discussed in the *Analects* and with other early Confucian positions, such as those of Mencius (Mengzi 孟子) and Xunzi. It is, unquestionably, a Confucian text.

Where some discrepant ideas, such as presumably Daoist ideas, appear in the text, rather than presupposing that they are interpolations or markers of a later text, we can take them as evidence that during the Warring States period there was not a divide between two such schools, as is often assumed. This is one way that the *Dialogues* demonstrates its value.

Skeptics of the authenticity of the *Dialogues* begin with the assumption that it was forged in a time well after the era of Confucius and his students, and that it therefore reflects the language and concerns of the era of its forger. However, if the text is indeed a text of the Warring States period, as we provisionally accept that it is, then it must be looked at instead as a text that reflects the language and concerns of the Warring States period, or even of Confucius' own time, the late Spring and Autumn period. But where in this three-century span of time should we place it? Other Warring States texts pose a similar problem of precise dating, and it will help to look at how dating has been approached in two particular texts, the *Zuo zhuan* and the *Art of War*.

Yuri Pines (2002a, 2002b) takes a fairly conservative approach to dating in his study of the *Zuo zhuan*, a text that, like the *Dialogues*, could range in date from early to late Warring States period, but also possibly reflects ideas of the Spring and Autumn period. Of Pines' dating methods, two are applicable to the *Dialogues*. The first examines the occurrence of specific terminology, including *renyi* 仁義, *wanwu* 萬物 (all things/creatures), *li* 理 (order), *cheng* 誠 (sincerity), *zhi* 智 (wisdom), *wan sheng* 萬乘 (large—a reference to the size of a state), *buyi* 布衣 (commoner), *yin yang* 陰陽, and the words for crossbow (*nu* 弩) or crossbow trigger (*ji* 機, *shu* 樞). Following the Yuan-dynasty scholar Zhao Fang, Pines argues that, because of the rare incidence of these terms in the *Documents* and the *Poems* but their common incidence in middle and late Warring States texts, frequent occurrence of these terms in a text would preclude its dating to the early Warring States period.

Pines (2002b) also distinguishes between a received text and an Ur-text, the latter being a core original text that was modified over time into the received text that we have today. While many scholars despair at the prospect of dating received Warring States texts more precisely than a 300-year range, Pines suggests that it is possible to do so with Ur-texts. He tentatively establishes an early Warring States date for the *Zuo zhuan* text, which contains ideas from the Spring and Autumn period. Pines' overall method seems readily applicable to the *Dialogues*.

Tabulating the occurrence of the above terms in the *Dialogues*, a relatively early dating is suggested, as follows:

The *Dialogues* contains no references to the crossbow or its trigger.

The term *buyi* occurs just once (35.2) in the *Dialogues*.

The term *wan sheng* occurs just once (9.9) in the *Dialogues*.

The terms *ren* and *yi* (see the separate headings below) are pervasive across the text individually but occur in only eight passages as a pair. A similar proportion is seen in the Guodian 郭店 corpus (excavated texts dating to the middle Warring States period or earlier).

Pines highlights the term *li* 理 as a key marker of change in intellectual terminology during the Warring States period. He observes that it is absent in the *Analects*, occurs seven times in three passages of the *Mencius*, and appears "no less than 106 times in the *Xunzi*" (Pines 2002b, 699). The term *li* occurs in thirteen passages of the *Dialogues*, largely in the same sense of to order that it is used in the Guodian essays "Cheng zhi wen zhi 成之聞之" and "Xing zi ming chu 性自命出." Less commonly in the *Dialogues*, it is used as a noun, meaning something like norm or principle, similar to its apparent use in the Guodian essay "Zun de yi 尊德義." The Guodian "Yu cong 語叢" essays seem to use it in both of the above senses.

The term *cheng* occurs in twelve passages of the *Dialogues*, usually in the typical sense of describing a basic personality trait, which is how it is also used in the *Zuo zhuan* ("Wen" 18.7) and in "Cheng zhi wen zhi." *Dialogues* 8.6 and 29.2 could have a more profound sense of a cultivated virtue with cosmic overtones (a purported later usage). In both cases, however, they appear right at the end of the passage, with a clearly explanatory purpose, suggesting that they could be later additions.

The term *wanwu* occurs in 11 passages of the *Dialogues*, a much lower incidence than in the *Xunzi* (40), the *Zhuangzi* (55; 21 in the Inner Chapters), and even the *Laozi* 老子 (a.k.a. *Dao de jing* 道德經, 16). In the *Mozi* 墨子, it occurs in 6 passages. It occurs in 3 of the Guodian documents (*Laozi*, "Tai yi sheng shui 太一生水," and "Tang Yu zhi dao 唐虞之道"). Pines says there are two alternative forms for this cosmological concept: *qun wu* 群物 and *bai wu* 百物. The former appears in the Guodian texts "Xing zi ming chu 性自命出" and "Zhong xin zhi dao 忠信之道," and the latter occurs in the Guodian text "Yu cong." *Bai wu* occurs once (26.4) in the *Dialogues* but not in a cosmological sense. *Qun wu* does not occur in the *Dialogues*.

The term *zhi* 智 occurs in forty passages of the *Dialogues*, but this is the most questionable of Pines' criteria, for the term appears in the "Shao gao" chapter of the *Documents*, which is widely recognized as among the earliest chapters of our earliest Chinese expository text, and the term *zhi* 知 was commonly considered the graphic equivalent of *zhi* 智, making it virtually impossible to use *zhi* 智 as an independent criterion. For example, Stephen Durrant, Wai-yee Li, and David Schaberg (2016) repeatedly translate *zhi* 知 as "wisdom" in their translation of CQZZ (e.g., "Wen" 13.2; "Cheng" 17.6, 17.9; "Xiang" 21.5, 23.8). In addition, the term *zhi* 智 occurs repeatedly in the Shanghai Museum and Guodian manuscripts.

The term *yin yang* is also of questionable utility in dating texts. Pines himself acknowledges that the terminology occurs during the Spring and Autumn period, when it referred to "primary cosmic forces" (701). He adds, however, "it was not related to political thought or general philosophy; and this situation evidently remained intact until the late fourth century BC" (701). The term *yin yang* appears in five passages of the *Dialogues* (5.3, 26.1, 32.9, 32.10, 32.13). To what extent these instances represent an earlier or later usage and to what extent any later usage is representative of the *Dialogues* Ur-text are both open to interpretation.

A second dating criterion used by Pines (2002a) follows the scholar He Leshi 何樂士 (among others), who posits that the grammatical character *yu* 于 is more common in the Western Zhou and is substituted later for the equivalent *yu* 於, especially in conversation. The fact that *yu* 於 outnumbers *yu* 于 by a factor of eight in the *Dialogues* should be expected, since Confucius lived in the Eastern Zhou. The very presence of the character *yu* 于, by this criterion, may gesture toward an early dating; but then again, the term continues to occur throughout the Han dynasty.

A similar transition, Pines says, occurred with the character *qi* 其 being replaced with *qi* 豈 (岂) in rhetorical questions. *Qi* 其 is the older construction, he says. Pines examines the ratio of one to the other in the *Zuo zhuan*, the *Analects*, and the *Mencius*, finding that the ratio of *qi* 豈 to *qi* 其 in the *Zuo zhuan* (82:64, or 1.28) and the *Analects* (8:3, or 2.6667) closely matches, whereas the *Mencius* ratio (12.5) is much higher. The ratio in the *Dialogues* is 36:9, or 4.0. If this criterion is valid and our tabulations are accurate, it would suggest that the *Dialogues* lies closer in time to the *Zuo zhuan* than to the *Mencius*.

By Pines' two methods, the *Dialogues* Ur-text would seem to be of quite early dating: that is, from the early Warring States period, reflecting the thoughts and ideas of the time of Confucius in the late Spring and Autumn period. Some passages were likely added or embellished over time, as reflected in the few instances of late Warring States terminology.

The dating of Sunzi's *Art of War* ranges, in scholars' estimations, from the late Spring and Autumn (possibly Confucius' lifetime) to the late Warring States period. In tracing prior scholarship, Samuel B. Griffith (1971) discusses two avenues of dating. The first, like Pines' analysis, focuses on terminology in the text.[19]

The crossbow, as discussed above, is one such term; as noted, it does not appear in the *Dialogues*.

Another is the term *dai jia* 帶甲 (armored), which should not appear in a text of the Spring and Autumn period, Griffith says. This term does not appear in the *Dialogues*.[20]

19. Pines (2002b), without citing Griffith, also applies his lexical method to Sunzi's *Art of War* (which contains a term for crossbow trigger and the terms *li*, *yin yang*, and *renyi*), and concludes with a tentative date of mid-fourth century BCE.

20. It's unclear whether other references to *jia* (armor) would also be criteria for later dating. The term *jia* in reference to soldiers appears seven times in the *Dialogues* (1.3, 5.4, 22.5, 31.5, 35.3, 37.2, 41.17), but it also appears in the same sense countless times in CQZZ (e.g., "Yin" 1, "Huan" 6, "Min" 2, "Xi" 15, "Wen" 1, "Xuan" 2).

Jin 金, referring to counted money, as in *bai jin* 百金 or *qian jin* 千金, does not come into wide circulation, Griffith says, until the Warring States period. This usage is also absent from the *Dialogues*, despite many references to payments and to expensive or luxurious items. Five passages (5.1, 10.18, 16.2, 33.3, 41.17) refer specifically to payments or gifts in the form of *bi* 幣. Though the term later came to mean money, it earlier referred to goods used as payment, most commonly silk.

The division of generals into *shang* 上, *zhong* 中, and *xia* 下 did not occur until the Warring States period, Griffith says. These terms do not occur in the *Dialogues*, despite references to military campaigns.

The terms *ye zhe* 謁者 and *she ren* 舍人 (both of which indicate functionary roles), have meanings specific to the Warring States period, Griffith says. These terms do not appear in the *Dialogues*.

Griffith distinguishes between two senses of *wu xing* 五行, referring to changing phases and to elemental substances (the latter use being the earlier one, he says). However, he offers no textual support, and this is likely an outmoded theory (Major 1976).[21] The earliest known use of *wu xing* is either in the CQZZ ("Zhao" 25 and 32) or in the *Documents* ("Gan shi" and "Hong fan"). In both of these texts, correlative relations are established between the five phases and other "fives." We see a very similar correlative arrangement in the *Dialogues* (24.1–5, 32.9–10).

Following the Qing-dynasty scholar Yao Nai, Griffith says that the term *zhu* 主, while common across all early texts, comes to refer specifically to the sovereign only during the Warring States period, having previously referred, as a noun, to a minister (or other leadership role) but not to a head of state. The term *zhu* appears in the sense of sovereign in ten passages of the *Dialogues*. One wonders, however, how accurate this criterion is for dating texts, given that the same sense also appears in a Western Zhou layer of the *Documents* ("Duo fang") (Nylan 2001).

Finally, Griffith comments on the scale of warfare and how it steadily grew from a small, knightly affair during Confucius' time to massive battles of hundreds of thousands of soldiers, with siege machines, cavalry, and tax levies to fund it all, in the late Warring States period. In the *Dialogues*, we see a number of depictions of

21. A. C. Graham (1986) and John Major (1991), following Graham, distinguish between an early meaning of five processes and a later meaning of five phases. The former refers to materials put to use, and the latter to substances transforming into one another. Major says that the latter gets its textual expression in the *Huainanzi* 淮南子 (139 BCE). In addition to its similarity of usage with the *Zuo zhuan* and *Documents*, the use of *wu xing* in the *Dialogues* seems to also overlap with later uses, as in the *Huainanzi*, in that we see correlations of materials with rulers, colors, musical tones, and so forth, and we see clear references to phases passing one into the other, but without a sense of one overcoming (*sheng* 勝) another, as we see in the *Huainanzi* (derived from Zou Yan 鄒衍, fl. 250 BCE). We suggest that *Dialogues* chapters 24 and 32, where *wu xing* appears, represent an intermediate and distinctively Confucian stage that predates the *Huainanzi* (as well as Zou Yan's *wu de* 五德).

battle and preparation for battle (1.3, 22.9, 37.2, 41.2, 41.6, 42.9, 42.11, 42.16), none of which indicate a massive scale, instead describing fairly limited confrontations. For example, 41.2 and 42.16 depict different parts of the same battle. Section 41.2 begins, "Guo Shu, a high minister of Qi, attacked Lu. Ji Kangzi sent Ran Qiu [his household manager] as lead general to defend against the attack, with Fan Chi as second in command." This is obviously not a large-scale, well-planned battle of specialists with tactical and technical expertise. Similarly, 42.16 says: "A Qi army invaded Lu. Gongshu Wuren met a man entering the fortress leaning on his staff and out of breath. In tears, Wuren said, "We exhaust them with labor and burden them with taxes. It is impermissible for a *junzi* to not participate, for an official to not be willing to die. This being the case, dare I shrink from battle?" At that, he and his beloved servant boy Wang Yi rode forth on a chariot, rushed the enemy, and died in battle." Section 42.11 depicts a battle between Chu and Wu, which fielded comparatively large armies during Confucius' time. The scene we are shown is of ad hoc participation by members of the highest levels of the government. Shang Yang, the minister of labor, did his very minimum by shooting three Wu soldiers with his bow and arrow (covering his eyes as they fell) and then promptly left the battlefield. In the largest tactical preparation for battle that we see in the *Dialogues* (37.2), Yue pledges "the 3,000 soldiers within its borders" to Wu.

Taken together, the criteria that Pines and Griffith put forward to date the *Zuo zhuan* and Sunzi's *Art of War* and applied to the *Dialogues* reveal that the *Dialogues* can be considered of quite early date, closer to the beginning of the Warring States period than to its middle or end and describing events that could very well date to the time of Confucius.[22]

As raised above, one of the key intellectual historical questions relating to philosophy of the Warring States period is the dating of the rise of correlative cosmology founded on the metaphysical concepts of *qi* 氣, *yin yang* 陰陽, and the five phases (*wu xing* 五行). A. C. Graham (1986), in an influential study of this topic, summarizes his conclusions as follows:

22. Ruan Guoyi (2010) compared the *Dialogues* to Zhou- and Han-dynasty texts along two linguistic dimensions. He found that with regard to the percentage of disyllabic words, the *Dialogues* belongs in the middle Warring States period, and with regard to the proportion of compound words that are attributive as opposed to coordinate, the *Dialogues* resembles later Warring States texts. Tang Haipeng (2011) performed a linguistic analysis of the *Dialogues* along three dimensions. He found that the vocabulary of the *Dialogues* does not match the specific characteristics of the vocabulary of texts of Wang Su's time, that copulative constructions (*ye* 也 vs. *wei* 爲) are characteristic of Archaic Chinese (Zhou dynasty) rather than Middle Chinese (Wang Su's period), and that passive constructions (*yu* 于, *wei* 爲, *jian* 見) are characteristic of Archaic rather than Middle Chinese. He concludes that the *Dialogues* "is primarily a text of the archaic period, but not ruling out the possibility that Wang Su polished or rearranged portions, confined to a minority of chapters, namely chapters 5, 7, and 8" (95).

(1) Down to 300 BC philosophers had only a bare cosmological scheme, the Way, Heaven and Earth, the Four Seasons, the 10,000 things. But outside the philosophical schools, the court astronomers, physicians, musicmasters and diviners had a cosmology in which colours, sounds and tastes correlate with the Six [*Qi*] of Heaven (which included *yang* "sunshine" and *yin* "shade"), and the Five [*Xing*] (processes) of Earth give way to each other in the conquest cycle. There was a state cult of the Five Processes which may already have correlated them with the centre and Four Directions.

(2) After 300 BC the philosophical schools came to accept the Yin and Yang as the [*qi*] which are the assimilating and differentiating influences behind chains of pairs.

(3) Outside the philosophical schools, [Zou Yan] (c. 250 BC) explained the rise and fall of dynasties by the conquest cycle of the Powers ([*de*]) behind the Five Processes, and advised rulers who aspired to found the coming dynasty to correlate their ritual acts with the Power of Water. This required a shift of fours and fives from the Six [*Qi*] to the Five Powers, with the result that the placing of the Powers in the Four Directions implied motion in a generation cycle corresponding to the Four Seasons.

(4) During the third century BC cosmology enters philosophical literature in [*Guanzi*] and the [*Lü shi chunqiu*]. From the unification in 221 BC the First Emperor reigning by the Power of Water, the surviving schools took over the whole system of correspondences now indispensable to influence at court. The Five [*xing*] (now translatable as "Five Phases") took next place to Yin and Yang, as the [*qi*] which assimilate and differentiate chains of fours and fives, and move all of them through the generation and conquest cycles. (91–92)

All of this very good scholarship should come with one large caveat—namely, that the textual record is woefully incomplete. What Graham attempts to do here is akin to reconstructing the dating of a fifty-two-card deck of playing cards with just ten randomly appearing cards, only five of which are datable. Suppose the cards of the fifty-two-card deck had evolved and accumulated over several centuries, and suppose there were no face cards in the datable set of five but there was a jack in the other group of five. One might infer that the jack was a late invention. But if so, one would be committing the fallacy of argument from ignorance. As the old saw goes, absence of evidence does not equal evidence of absence. Just because we don't know there was a jack in the period represented by the datable set does not entail that there was never a jack at that time.[23]

23. This fallacy is pervasive in scholarship over the last century, and although the recent revelations of excavated texts have given many scholars pause, the pause has often been too brief. Dirk Meyer

The sinological case is more complex than this, but the same logical principles apply, and from the limited information we have, the same proportions appear to apply also. The "Yi wen zhi" section of the *Han shu* is the earliest catalog we have of extant literature, and it records some 13,000 scrolls during the Former Han dynasty. But many texts that have been excavated from the Warring States period are not recorded there, and only about 20 percent of those Former Han texts survive today. To reconstruct the intellectual history of the Warring States and Han periods with any kind of specificity regarding which concepts occurred when—relying almost entirely on textual evidence, as Graham does—is a fraught enterprise. And it risks misdating other texts that don't fit the incomplete scheme.[24]

The fact is that there is a lot we don't know about cosmological beliefs in the Warring States period. A case in point is the recent emergence of the importance of the concept of the Great Inchoate (*tai yi* 太一). This concept appears prominently in the *Huainanzi* and the *Lü shi chunqiu* 吕氏春秋, texts that date to the early Han dynasty, the Qin, or the very late Warring States period. Because of this, any other text of ambiguous dating where the term occurs, such as the *Dialogues,* would be, on this basis, dated no earlier than these two texts. However, in the excavated Guodian manuscripts, which date to about 300 BCE at the latest, and probably significantly earlier than that, contain an essay ("Tai yi sheng shui") dedicated entirely to the cosmological concept of the Great Inchoate. It turns out that the *Dialogues* discussion of the concept parallels the one in the excavated text, another hint suggesting the authenticity of the *Dialogues.*

---

provides an illustrative example. In a 2012 publication he writes, "To date, no single [excavated] manuscript has been found that contains [poems] alone. They exist only in quotations" (Meyer 2012, 248). This observation makes up part of an argument that the poems in Confucius' time and during the Warring States period were primarily oral, and so without firm graphic instantiations. Seven years after Meyer made this statement, an early- to mid-Warring-States-period manuscript containing only a collection of fifty-seven poems (also found in the transmitted *Poems*) came to light (Shaughnessy 2021; for a discussion of orality versus writing in the history of the *Poems,* see Shaughnessy 2015). We're not claiming that this manuscript entirely invalidates Meyer's conclusion, merely that the conclusion was based at least in part on an argument from ignorance (because we have no text, therefore . . .). Such an argument is fallacious, and any conclusions drawn from such an argument, absent more substantial arguments, must be viewed with skepticism.

24. Note the distinction we are making here between general terminology vs. philosophical terminology. Given a dearth of textual sources, it is safer to make dating generalizations with regard to common terminology (e.g., grammatical particles and terms from everyday language) and terms that can be tied to the historical or archaeological records. The size of armies are stated in texts, for example, and examples of crossbows have been found in tombs. Philosophical terminology, such as *wu xing,* because it is neither common nor datable historically or archaeologically, is much more difficult to pin down chronologically.

The "Tai yi sheng shui" essay also uses the terms *yin* and *yang* unequivocally as cosmogonic principles. Graham says this doesn't happen until after 300 BCE, by which he means that Zou Yan was the major progenitor of the idea. However, Graham offers a rare caveat, saying that although this is our first textual record of the idea, it probably was circulating earlier. The "Tai yi sheng shui" shows that he was correct in his caveat but that he didn't push the date far enough back. If the same principle—that an idea typically circulates before it is recorded—applies to the appearance of the *yin/yang* principle in the Guodian manuscripts, then it could go back at least to 400 BCE.

A concept Graham discusses elsewhere using the same logic is *qing* 情. Canvassing early literature, he concludes that, in pre-Han texts, *qing* never means emotions (his word is *passions*) as it comes to mean in the Han dynasty (Graham 1990b, 59). A corollary of this claim is that any text of ambiguous dating that contains the word *qing* with a connotation of emotions would have to date to no earlier than the Han. Here again we see the fallacy of appeal to ignorance. Just because we don't have a Warring States period text in which *qing* clearly has emotional connotations (Graham discounts its association with emotions in the *Xunzi* and ignores a relevant occurrence in the *Poems*) does not mean there never was one. It turns out that several of the Shanghai Museum and Guodian essays contain the word *qing*, with clear emotional connotations, likewise mirroring its use in the *Dialogues* (see, e.g., chapter 32).

Other concepts follow a similar pattern. Concepts once thought to be markers of late Warring States or post–Warring States arguments have turned up in the Shanghai Museum and Guodian manuscripts and may mirror usages in the *Dialogues*. These include, for example, an emphasis on affection, or closeness (*qin* 親), between the people and the leadership, a preference for education and *li* over legal punishments, and an emphasis on meritocratic succession.[25]

According to Shaughnessy (1997), "In attempting to determine the authenticity of a transmitted document three factors must be considered: the history of the text's transmission, its linguistic usage, and whether the content is consistent with the purported historical context" (37). Let us summarize our conclusions according to these three criteria.

First, the title of the *Dialogues* is found in the earliest Han bibliography of existing texts dating from the Warring States period received into the Han archives. It

25. Scott Cook (2012, 97–176) provides an overview of some of the main themes of the Guodian texts. The overlap in themes with the *Dialogues* is noteworthy and deserving of further exploration. Sarah Allan (2015) translates and analyzes four excavated texts, all having to do with early sages and meritocratic succession, revisiting her earlier work on the subject (1981), which looked only at transmitted texts (excluding the *Dialogues*). According to her, "This paradigm of abdication is the only alternative to the idea of dynastic cycle found in the Chinese tradition, and it did not survive the Qin and Han dynasties as an idea for an alternative form of succession" (2015, 11).

remained obscure until Wang Su, one of the "greatest scholars of the third century" (Shaughnessy 1997, 80), is made aware of a copy in the home of the descendants of Confucius. That copy includes two postfaces, one by the great scholar Kong Anguo, explaining its origins in the Warring States period and its subsequent journey up to its arrival in his hands, and relating how it was introduced to the Han emperor but, for political reasons, languished thereafter. Although there is more than one current version of the *Dialogues* text, the differences among them are minor, and so it is widely believed that our current *Dialogues* is essentially the one that Wang Su brought to light.

Second, the linguistic usage in the text has been shown above to be largely consistent with texts dating prior to the middle of the Warring States period, and, more importantly, largely different from texts dating after that period. As Shaughnessy demonstrated in his examination of the *Bamboo Annals,* and as Pines argues in reference to Warring States texts generally, minor textual anomalies do not delegitimize an entire text. We know with certainty that texts were commonly modified after their original recording. We also know with certainty that many characters were homographically interchangeable.[26] Therefore, some apparent anachronisms are to be expected.

Third, we also saw above that the contents of the *Dialogues* are largely consistent with what we know from textual and archaeological sources of the time of Confucius. (More detail is provided in specific footnotes to this translation.) Many criticisms of the *Dialogues* argue that it primarily reflects concerns of the Han-dynasty philosophical debates, but this is simply not the case. One method used by Shaughnessy that is implicit in his three criteria is the comparison of transmitted texts with archaeological finds. Such finds from the Warring States reveal substantial crossover of exact content, of language use, and of general subject matter between the *Dialogues* and manuscripts that date to the mid-Warring States period at the latest.[27]

26. Shaughnessy (2006) provides a thorough examination of what he calls the "instability" of texts during the Warring States period at the level of "the word, the pericope, and perhaps even the whole text" (60). See also Boltz (1997).

27. As we noted above, the archaeological finds themselves don't prove the authenticity of the *Dialogues,* but they raise the question of the ultimate value of the practice of doubting antiquity that began in the Song dynasty, gained steam during the Qing dynasty, and then accelerated in the twentieth century. Michael Loewe and Edward Shaughnessy offer a reasonable and sobering assessment:

> This archaeological verification of some received texts has given rise, especially in China, to a scholarly view which affirms the antiquity of most significant aspects of Chinese culture. This view is now referred to as that of the *Xingu pai* 信古派 (Believing in Antiquity School), in conscious distinction from the *Yigu pai* 疑古派 (Doubting Antiquity School). . . . In some of its expressions this belief in antiquity is doubtless exaggerated, owing as much to contemporary cultural chauvinism as to scholarly evidence; but such opinions are probably no more biased than

Whatever concerns Wang Su found in the text that supported his views are there not because he put them there but because his view was more consistent with an early Warring States view than was Zheng Xuan's, whose "propensity to exalt and mystify" (Nylan 2001, 41) Confucius was itself anachronistic. Because of Zheng Xuan's syncretism, "the classical traditions were impoverished, deficient in the play necessary to fire scholars' imaginations and prevent scholastic ossification" (Nylan 2001, 53). It was Wang Su who turned opinion away from Zheng Xuan and back to a more down-to-earth depiction of Confucius and his philosophy.

It is increasingly recognized that the *Analects* was not known as a completed text until the Han dynasty (Makeham 1996). A recent advocate for this recognition has been Michael Hunter (Hunter 2012, 2017; Hunter and Kern 2018). In contrast to the work of scholars who filter through passages attributable to a historical Confucius, Hunter works in the opposite direction, combing through the entire early corpus for all passages having to do with Confucius and working with them to see how Confucius was envisioned, not what Confucius thought. He argues "that the single-serving [Confuciuses] who emerge from [early] dialogues and anecdotes . . . are best read as literary projections of the values and virtues implicit in associated [Confucius said] material. In other words, [Confucius] was the figure he had to be in order to legitimate [Confucius said] discourse" (Hunter 2017, 97). Although Hunter agrees that the *Dialogues* contains "a large amount of material" from early sources (22), he maintains that "all [Confucius] texts are on an equal footing such that there is no a priori reason to read some sayings or stories before others" (19–20). This leads to his most controversial claim: that not enough evidence can be found "to justify continuing to read the [*Analects*] as the most authoritative [Confucius] text from the Warring States era and, thus, as a foundational work of pre-imperial Chinese thought" (11).

In this way, Hunter blows up our traditional model of viewing the *Analects* as an early—and thus more authoritative—Warring States Confucius-related text and all other Confucius-related texts as later and thus less authoritative. One need not go as far as Hunter and place the *Analects* as late as the Former Han. After all, as even Hunter admits, there are quotations from the *Analects* that predate the Han. As Edward Slingerland (2018) and Paul Goldin (2018) point out, there are other reasons to believe that the source material of the *Analects* is a product of the Warring States period.

The implications of the work of Hunter, Makeham, and others is that, conservatively speaking, the *Analects* should not be considered to be entirely a product of the

---

those of many Western attempts to negate this view, and each of its proposals needs consideration on its own merits. Despite all these reservations, it is hard to deny the conclusion that the archaeological discoveries of the past generation have tended to authenticate, rather than to overturn, the traditional literary record of ancient China. (Loewe and Shaughnessy 1999, 10)

early Warring States period, thereby losing its pride of place as the single authoritative source for the philosophy of Confucius. The consensus opinion among scholars today seems to be with Robert Eno (2018): that the *Analects* contains material that is both very early, reflecting actual dialogues of Confucius, and material that has been subsequently added or tampered with, reflecting later concerns. As we have seen above, the *Dialogues* also fits this model. As a result, on the whole (again, conservatively speaking), we are left with a radical reordering of authoritative Confucius-related source material.

As table 1 illustrates, recent scholarship overturns the prior model of the *Analects* as the only source for the philosophy of Confucius in two ways. First, it has knocked the *Analects* down a peg, demonstrating that it is not entirely a product of the early Warring States period.[28] Second, it has shown that other texts, and particularly the *Dialogues,* also have a claim to priority of both chronology and authority. With reference to the Ur-texts of the *Analects* and the *Dialogues,* we believe that table 1 depicts an important reevaluation of the sources of Confucius' thinking. Paul Goldin's statement in defense of the traditional dating of the *Analects* could just as well apply to the dating of the *Dialogues*: "A work that was *compiled* in a certain century does not necessarily consist of material *dating* from that same century" (2018, 92).

Table 1: Reevaluation of the chronological development of the *Analects* and the *Dialogues.*

Prior Scholarship		**Recent Scholarship**
c. 450–400 BCE	c. 230 CE	c. 450–350 BCE
Analects	*Dialogues*	*Analects, Dialogues*

Our aim here is not to show that the *Dialogues* should supplant the *Analects* as the single most authoritative source of the thought of Confucius. To an extent, we agree with scholars like Slingerland (2018), Goldin (2018), and Pines (2002b), who say that there are lexical or conceptual reasons for the priority of the *Analects.* This coheres with Kong Anguo's postface as well. Our argument is only that the *Dialogues* should rank a close second—that the *Dialogues* carries legitimate weight and in fact fills certain gaps in the philosophy of Confucius.

Examining the lexical and conceptual milieu of Confucius' time is essential for the dating of Confucian texts. But as Hunter (2018) has argued, there are limitations

28. See especially E. Bruce Brooks and A. Taeko Brooks (1998), who, working from earlier theories, hypothesize that *Analects* as we know it accreted steadily over the course of the Warring States period, from shortly after Confucius' death to the year 249 BCE, at a rate of 12.7 years per chapter.

to this approach—namely, that it rests on hard-to-verify presuppositions about which ideas were early and which were not.

One feature of the *Dialogues* that might tend to raise doubts in a contemporary reader is the inclusion of passages that appear clearly anti-philosophical by today's standards: for example, the mentions of mythological creatures, numerology, and fantastic occurrences (as in 25.3–4). However, the presence of a few such passages should not affect one's opinion of the overall philosophical quality of the text. First, it is to be expected. Kong Anguo himself says that some passages "belong to a lesser category—baseless, confused, and dispensable." But such passages are common for premodern texts generally. Throughout the Middle Ages, for example, Plato's most-read and most-influential dialogue was the *Timaeus,* a fanciful cosmology that postulates four basic elements appearing in fundamental geometric shapes, stating that things composed of them function according to their kind. Nevertheless, we don't devalue all of Plato on this basis. In Aristotle's *History of Animals,* he claims that some creatures come to life by spontaneous generation (546b.25), and that while human males can produce sperm at the age of fourteen, they cannot reproduce until the age of twenty-one (547b.20). But we don't devalue Aristotle's other theories on this basis. And although the social status of women remains low across the board, in China as in Europe, through these centuries, we don't devalue all works that reflect such views on that basis.

Another feature that might cast doubt on the authenticity of the text is the length of some of its passages. Could Confucius really deliver such fluent disquisitions on a number of subjects off the cuff, and could the transcription of them be accurate? Actually, such impromptu brilliance is not difficult to imagine. Educators regularly speak coherently and at length on complex topics in the classroom. And Aristotle's extant works are all written records of just such extemporaneous disquisitions, at much greater length.

We have seen that although there are characteristics of the *Dialogues* that suggest later alterations, there are also characteristics that point to the genuineness—that is, an early provenance—of the text. Eric Henry (2022) notes that a major flaw of the *Shuo yuan,* which overlaps significantly with the *Dialogues* in content, is its many anachronisms. Although there are some possible anachronisms in the *Dialogues* (e.g., 15.9, 15.16, 16.3, 31.3, 39.2, 43.24, 44.4), they are comparatively few, and there are many other passages that clearly point to historical consistencies. One of the more remarkable has to do with grave mounds, as explained in 42.26n24. The transition in Confucius' time and later from the use of authentic items to accompany the dead in burials to the use of cheap replicas is accurately reflected in section 43.25.

Consider also section 41.7, where Confucius says, "There is a record from ancient times that says, '*Ren* is overcoming oneself and returning to *li*.'" Whoever recorded this passage could not have both been familiar with the *Analects* as we have it today and considered it a paramount authority, because in the *Analects,* the saying is attributed directly to Confucius rather than being attributed by Confucius to an ancient text, which would rule out both Kong Anguo and Wang Su as authors of the passage. By general standards of textual analysis, common apothegms were attributed to Confucius more commonly as his stature increased over the centuries, suggesting that this passage in the *Dialogues* may even predate the similar passage in the *Analects.*

Similarly, there is a quotation from the *Documents* in 41.16, but the wording is different from the version of the *Documents* that we have today. The latter is unchanged in the relevant respect from Wang Su's time, so if he had forged this passage in the *Dialogues,* why would he have intentionally messed up the wording of one of the most important and familiar texts of Confucianism? It is highly unlikely that Wang Su, a towering scholar of his day, would get the quotation wrong. If we insist that he forged the *Dialogues,* the only explanation is that he did it intentionally to diabolically throw us off his scent. But that seems even less likely, just because he would have risked coming off as an amateur. The most plausible explanation is that the editor of the *Dialogues* was working from a distinct source that reflects a slightly different version of the *Documents,* a source which has since been lost.

Another inconsistency in the *Dialogues* with respect to the *Analects* occurs in *Dialogues* 25.1, where Min Ziqian is said to be the mayor of the city of Bi. This directly contradicts *Analects* 6.9, which says that Min Ziqian refused an offer to govern Bi. Historically, we can easily make sense of this by positing that he first refused, then later accepted (even though his initial refusal was so memorable that it was recollected in its own independent tradition). If the *Dialogues* was forged, it would be much more difficult to reconcile. How would such an accomplished scholar as Kong Anguo or Wang Su make such a trifling and embarrassing mistake?[29]

By the time of the Later Han dynasty, certain writings and deeds had been associated with Confucius' students (for example, that Zixia was responsible for transmitting several of the classics). But in the descriptions of Confucius' students in chapter 38, none of these common attributions are made, suggesting that the descriptions were written quite early. Further, by the Later Han, Confucius' student Yuan Xian and Confucius' grandson, who have the same *zi* (*zisi* 子思; see "Naming convention" in the glossary), had become conflated, as Mark Csikszentmihalyi (2004) has noted. In the *Dialogues* (including the postfaces), they are clearly

29. A similar contradiction occurs in the *Analects* itself, which is likewise resolved through a diachronic interpretation. In 6.8 Confucius praises Ran You's potential for governing, and in 11.17 Confucius condemns Ran You's actions in governing.

separate individuals. As early as Xunzi, Zisi (Confucius' grandson) was associated with the Wu Xing theory, and he gradually grew in reputation. He would have been in his thirties by the time Confucius passed away, and yet he is not mentioned at all in the main text of the *Dialogues* (Gao 1991). According to Gao Zhuancheng (1991), the mythical elevation of Zisi began as early as the *Mencius* and is evident in the *Li ji*, and yet is absent from the *Dialogues*. The fact that the *Dialogues* lacks these mentions does not prove that it is early, but a common accusation of the *Dialogues* is that it reflects beliefs and concerns prevalent during the Han dynasty. If that were true, these oversights would be difficult to explain.[30]

What gaps can the *Dialogues* fill? We have already mentioned that it can act as a bridge over the supposed divide separating Daoism and Confucianism. This divide was always fraught, and it was often denied by later cosmopolitan Confucians. Its tenuousness is evident in the mention of Shun governing by *wu wei* 無爲 in the *Analects*, in the emphasis on *xiao* (see below) in the *Laozi*, the positive description of *qi* in the *Mencius*, and the lengthy descriptions of *xin shu* 心術 in the *Guanzi* 管子 (which points to an early layer of Daoist-like thought but not from a canonical Daoist; Ricket 1998). The Shanghai Museum and Guodian manuscripts add to this uncertainty. All of these together give us license to reconceive the relationship between Confucius and Laozi. For some time in the Chinese tradition, and even among many Chinese scholars today, the default position was to view the story of Confucius visiting Laozi and studying from him (studying *li*, no less) as uncontroversial. But the common position among Western scholars today is just the opposite. Not only is the story controversial; it is dismissed as utter fiction by many scholars.[31]

We believe that there is no convincing reason to dismiss the connection out of hand. What we have is not only the story itself, often repeated, but also a set of conceptual relationships. If there is one thing that separates a Laozi/Zhuangzi/Daoist view from a Confucian view, it is that the former had less confidence than the Confucians in the ability of humans to make good on their intentions for transformational change around them. What we can't say, in our opinion, is that early Confucians never spoke of metaphysical matters like *qi*, the Great Inchoate, and correlative relationships. When, exactly, these ideas came on the scene and how quickly they spread are questions we simply cannot answer at present. What we can do instead is try to make sense of them in an expansive, Warring States Confucian philosophy that may represent the philosophy of Confucius himself. And we can say provisionally that some mid–Warring States Confucians, who were only a generation or two away from Confucius himself, believed that it did.

30. For a related bit of textual evidence, see 38.10n7.

31. A good example is Michael LaFargue (1992), who takes the *Dao de jing* 道德經 to be composed of circulating aphorisms recorded by a group of "Laoist" idealists alienated from mainstream society.

The *Dialogues* also adds context to some cryptic passages in the *Analects*. For example, *Analects* 9.18 and 15.13 both say, "I have yet to meet someone who is as enamored of *de* as he is of beauty." Because the word translated here as *beauty* is ambiguous, there has been debate about how to interpret it. *Dialogues* 38.29 provides the story in which Confucius purportedly made the comment. Depending on how one interprets the *Dialogues* passage, at minimum it provides context to the *Analects* passage, and at most it resolves the ambiguity.

According to *Analects* 5.6, "Confucius encouraged Qidiao Kai to take up a position as an official. [Qidiao Kai] replied, 'I am not sure that I am adequate to it.'" *Dialogues* 38.26 says, "Confucius said [to Qidiao Kai], 'You are old enough to work as an official now. Soon it will be too late.' [Qidiao Kai] replied in writing, "I am not sure that I am adequate to it.' Confucius was pleased at this response." This passage fills out the *Analects* story with a few details, but not in a way that seems intentional. For example, it seems to make little difference that Qidiao Kai replied in writing; rather, that detail suggests an alternative telling of the same story passed down by an independent voice.

In *Analects* 5.13, Zigong says, "You may hear our teacher's eloquence, but not the topics of inborn nature and the *dao* of *tian*." This statement happens to be an accurate depiction of the *Analects* but not of the *Dialogues*. What are we to make of that? First, it is a bare statement with no context. Because statements about metaphysical topics are indeed rare in the *Analects*, most scholars have understood the statement to be a general description about Confucius' lack of interest in such matters. However, it could just as well have been a statement to a specific person, or under some specific circumstance, or even a reference to the past as opposed to the present. If a main compiler of the *Analects* material was Zigong or his students, perhaps it was them, not Confucius, who found metaphysical topics uninteresting. Second, even in the *Dialogues* Confucius is reluctant to speak of arcane metaphysics. We think the best way to interpret Zigong's statement is as an overstatement—not because Confucius never spoke on such matters but because he did so infrequently and reluctantly.

We can see this reluctance in chapter 23 of the *Dialogues*. Zai Wo raises the question of legendary figures from the distant past, and Confucius seems reticent to engage. He does engage, though, and offers a long disquisition on the most plausible interpretation. At the end, however, he expresses his displeasure toward Zai Wo. In chapter 24, in a long disquisition on elemental metaphysics and past associations, Confucius attributes his knowledge to Laozi. In 25.3, a long numerological disquisition by Zixia receives a concurrence from Confucius, again adverting to Laozi. Chapter 25 ends with Zigong denying the importance of preceding metaphysical speculation and Confucius agreeing with him.

All of this taken together, we believe, suggests that there was a divide among Confucius' students and interlocutors with respect to the importance of metaphysical speculation, with Zixia, Zai Wo, and Duke Ai favoring it and Zigong and his students opposed. Confucius' own position was most likely somewhere in the middle—not convinced of the importance of such tangential speculation as numerology and the specifics of elemental metaphysics but perfectly willing to discuss the crucial relationship of humans to the cosmic *dao*. The *Dialogues* is valuable in offering us this insight.

Circling back for a moment to Zai Wo can lead us to another insight provided by the *Dialogues*. The entry on Zai Wo in SJ says the following:

> 宰我問五帝之德，子曰："予非其人也。"
>
> Zai Wo asked about the *de* of the Five Chiefs. Confucius said, "Yu is [or, I am] not one of them."

This line is often interpreted (even by Wang Su in his commentary on SJ) as Confucius' way of dismissing the topic and not engaging. In chapter 23 of *Dialogues*, however, Confucius does engage Zai Wo on this topic, and a version of the dismissive statement appears at the end of the chapter (which we translate, "Yu, you are not on the same level with those men"). Zai Wo's response is to acknowledge self-deprecatingly that he is not worthy of instruction. This situation, in which the beginning and ending of chapter 23 appear in SJ but with very different meanings, suggests that the story had circulated for some time before Sima Qian 司馬遷 (145–86 BCE, author of SJ) heard about it, and that by the time it got to him the participants had been reduced to caricatures of Confucius not engaging in arcane topics and Zai Wo being on the receiving end of Confucius' criticism.

The *Dialogues* also resolves another contradiction with SJ. Tantai Mieming is identified in SJ as ugly but in *Dialogues* 19.8 as handsome. The solution, also based on widely circulating caricatures, is explained in the entry "Tantai Mieming" in the glossary.

Analects 9.5 and 11.23 relate brief events having to do with Confucius encountering danger in the state of Song, but they do not provide the reason. *Dialogues* 22.5 provides a bit more background, stating that he was surrounded by armored soldiers led by one Jianzi of Kuang.[32]

As mentioned above, the circumstances of Confucius' departing Wei in *Analects* 15.1 and *Dialogues* 41.17 differ in the details. We believe that these are independent accounts of the same occurrence and that the *Dialogues* account is not only the more correct one but is more valuable in the details it provides.

In *Analects* 5.3, Confucius praises Fu Zijian as a *junzi* 君子 (see the philosophical lexicon below), but no context is given and there are no other mentions of him. The

32. The *Shuo yuan* adds that the reason was that Confucius, resembling Yang Hu, was mistaken for him.

Dialogues provides context for Confucius' praise in 14.7, 19.4, and 37.3 through concrete details about Fu's accomplishments in government, his positive attitude, and his skill at indirect communication (see also "Consultation" below).

In *Analects* 14.43, Confucius suddenly accosts a man named Yuan Rang. Because there is no additional context, Confucius comes off as officious and irascible. *Dialogues* 37.4 is a brief narrative about another interaction between Confucius and Yuan Rang, revealing Confucius to be a patient, loyal old friend of the ne'er-do-well Yuan Rang. The relationship depicted in the *Dialogues* episode suggests that the *Analects* passage is less about officiousness and irascibility than about friendly teasing.

In the *Analects*, the personal life and background of Confucius are merely hinted at. In the *Dialogues*, we are given numerous details, including that he is descended from Shang nobility. This illustrious past is often pointed to by skeptical scholars as an obvious fabrication, meant by later Confucians to burnish his image. However, actual circumstances in his day would support the lineage account. First, as explained below (see "*Shi*"), it was a common feature of *shi* during Confucius' time that they were descended in one way or another from nobility. It would be unusual, then, if Confucius were not also a descendant of nobility. Second, if people had sought to fabricate an illustrious beginning for Confucius, they would surely have made him a descendant of the Zhou royal household that he so revered, not a descendant of the rivals that the Zhou conquered. We believe that these details of Confucius' life should be taken seriously as genuine biographical sketches. Finally, the basic details of his ancestry are corroborated in CQZZ ("Zhao" 7.12).

Dialogues 38.12 fills in two gaps in the historical records, as explained in 38.12n11.

Dialogues 19.6 provides a rationale for Confucius' criticism of Xie Ye in CQZZ ("Xuan" 9.6).

Chapter 5 of the *Dialogues* gives us a much richer sense of the word *Ru*, which is frustratingly vague in early texts (see "*Ru*" below).

The *Dialogues* also gives us specific insight into the affective dimension of Confucius' ethics and political thought. See the individual entries "Affection," "*Li*," "Love," "*Ren*," "*Shu*," and "*Xiao*" below (see also Bruya 2024).

Chapter 32 of the *Dialogues* and the "Li yun" chapter of the *Li ji* are essentially the same essay but differ in important ways. Whereas some scholars have said that the "Li yun" chapter complicates the value of *li*, even blaming it for negative effects on society, the *Dialogues* version suggests no such ambiguity and remains consistent with the Confucian tradition of the clear value of *li* (see Bruya 2024). We believe that the *Dialogues* version, for its internal consistency, is the more authentic version of the essay.

Confucius' negative attitude in 41.15 and in CQZZ toward Fan Xuanzi's inscribing of law on a cauldron for all to see has long been a topic of debate among scholars (Ames 1983). The juxtaposition of the events in 41.14 and 41.15 provides a unique perspective. Taking the two passages together, we see that Confucius was not reacting to the inscribing of laws on a cauldron per se. In fact, the problem he sees is not about law at all but about leaders and their success or failure at effecting good government and acting as models for others. In 41.14, he praises a Jin leader who institutes real reform by depriving corrupt aristocrats of their economic base and installing capable and virtuous officials. In 41.15, a new Jin leader, with the problem of corruption among the elite still not entirely solved, goes in a different direction, creating a cauldron inscribed with laws that the elite already flaunt with impunity. Confucius' objection to this pageantry is that it is not a genuine attempt at reform and is instead mere window dressing.

It was with some surprise that scholars noted the presence of Confucian texts in the Guodian finds, because these occurred in the southern state of Chu, which had then been considered outside of the principal cultural sphere of Confucius. The Shanghai Museum manuscripts, by their writing style, likewise appear to be from Chu. Though finding Confucian texts in Chu may seem mysterious at first, there are some clues in the *Dialogues* that can help make sense of it. In 35.2, Confucius notes that the Zhou music traditions have been better preserved in the south, and he remarks, "The south is a place of vitality and nurturance." Confucius also notes in 16.4 that certain civil traditions have been lost, which is probably a reference to the devastating cultural losses from the razing of the Western Zhou capital in 771 BCE. These two clues, along with the archaeological finds, suggest that the south, particularly Chu, was a place of significant cultural refinement that had preserved some Zhou traditions better than Confucius' own region.[33]

In the biography of Confucius in SJ, Laozi warns Confucius about the dangers of officialdom, ending with the following:

> 爲人子者毋以有己，爲人臣者毋以有己。
>
> The best child is one who is not self-centered; the best minister is one who is not self-centered. (11.1)

Analogizing being a child to being a minister is consistent with Confucius' view of a dynamic patriarchal hierarchy (see "Hierarchy" below), but the statement has no

33. From an overview of archaeological finds in the Chu region, Lothar Von Falkenhausen concludes:

> Interpreting such findings in conjunction with the eloquent bronze inscriptions, we arrive at a picture of Chu during the Spring and Autumn period as a polity very much in the Zhou mold. . . . This would tend to negate the currently fashionable image of a "Chu civilization" that was radically different from that of the Zhou; such a distinction was certainly not operative at the ritual and the political level during the middle to late Spring and Autumn period. (Loewe and Shaughnessy 1999, 525)

apparent connection to the warning just preceding it, and in its redundancy it exhibits neither literary flair nor philosophical depth. The *Dialogues* narrates the same story and the same advice, but with slightly different wording:

> 無以有己爲人子者，無以惡己爲人臣者。
>
> The best child is one who is not self-centered; the best minister is one who does not engender spite in others.[34]

This ending makes much more sense. It connects with the preceding statement, exhibits literary flair, and offers advice that is consistent with Confucius' own views in many places in the text, such as 13.5 and 41.22. As such, it gives us some confidence that the rest of the story in chapter 11 may also track actual events.

What of the veracity of the text overall? From the preceding argument, it follows that the ideas presented in the *Dialogues* are a reliable representation of the ideas of Confucius. One must always keep in mind that they have been filtered through his students, or students of his students. This makes it difficult to say that Confucius himself used any particular wording. It may help to try to imagine the process in which these stories were set down. No doubt they were first passed down orally as first-person accounts. But first-person oral accounts eventually become third-person oral accounts, and on top of the possibility of natural flaws of memory, details can change when accounts go from one person to the next. In addition, stories are not necessarily passed on in a linear fashion. They expand through webs of communication and may circle back. Imagine a student who goes to his teacher with a tale about Confucius that he heard from someone else. The teacher may respond, "That's not how I remember it. I remember that Zixia was there, and when it was all over . . ." And so the same story gets passed on in different iterations, with different details. When it gets put down in writing, it achieves a level of authority. But what we are learning from excavated manuscripts is that written texts themselves did not follow a linear path of transmission. They can differ from each other in the same ways that oral transmissions can, and it can't be assumed that, once a text was set down in written form, that would be its final form.

The story in *Dialogues* 41.18 is just one of many examples that can be used to illustrate distinct transmission lines of a story. This story, relating a conversation between Confucius and Duke Ai of Lu about whether to launch an attack on Qi, also appears in both CQZZ ("Ai" 14.5) and *Analects* 14.21. All three versions recount the

34. The use of different negatives in the two sources is of little consequence. As Shaughnessy notes, "In conventional script, 毋 represents the prohibitive negative 'do not' or 'ought not.' However, in manuscripts, whether of the Warring States or even the Qin and Han periods, negatives are freely interchanged, such that 毋 often represents also the simple negative *wu* 'have not,' conventionally written 無 or 无." (Shaughnessy 2006, 39n77)

same occurrence, and there is some precise overlap in their wording, but there are also significant differences in wording, as well as differences in the details recounted. The *Analects* and the *Dialogues* versions refer to the Duke of Qi specifically and use the terminology for purificatory bathing, both of which differ from the CQZZ account. Only the *Dialogues* specifically says that the duke refused Confucius' suggestion and that Confucius initially acted after hearing about the murder. All three stories report a "three," but in different ways. CQZZ says that Confucius fasted for three days and that he "requested that the duke attack Qi *three*," which Durrant, Li, and Schaberg (2016) interpret as him requesting it three times. The *Dialogues* says that Confucius bathed over three days and specifies that Confucius made the suggestion to the duke three times. The *Analects* does not mention either of these threes and says that instead of the duke telling Confucius to tell it to the Ji family, he tells Confucius to tell it to the Three Families, which he did, and they refused.[35] One way of approaching these commonalities and divergences is to say that the author of the *Dialogues* had access to both CQZZ and the *Analects* versions and reconciled them, but it actually doesn't reconcile them, since it doesn't contain all of the information in both. It also doesn't take the *Analects* as an authority, since the *Dialogues* version disagrees with the *Analects* version about who the duke said to report it to, and it leaves out the *Analects* statement that Confucius reported it a second time. The best way to make sense of these three versions of the same story is that they started out as a single event that was transmitted orally, and as it was retold to (at least) three different people, who remembered some of it word-for-word but not all of it, and that those three versions were passed down orally until finally being recorded in writing.

Another example of a distinct parallel passage in the *Analects* is *Analects* 14.40, in comparison with *Dialogues* 41.19. Only two phrases—*san nian bu yan* 三年不言 (to not speak for three years) and 於冢宰三年 (to the prime minister for three years)—are identical in both, and it is not apparent that either passage is derived from the other. We can think of two ways to understand these differences. One is that the two accounts are sourced from two different lines of oral transmission. The other way takes us to Kong Anguo's postface, where he says of the entire corpus of Confucius

35. The passage in question is 之三子告不可, which comes on the heels of a statement by Confucius and is usually interpreted as part of a third-person narrative—he told the three families, and they refused. The *Dialogues* does not mention him going to three and instead only mentions that the duke told him to inform Ji, and so suggests another interpretation for the *Analects* passage—namely, that the line above could be part of the preceding statement from Confucius. Confucius replies to the duke that as for going to tell the three families, this is not to be done. This interpretation makes it clear that his conversation with the duke ended the matter as far as he was concerned and that his duty went only so far as informing the duke.

stories that were eventually separated into the *Analects* and the *Dialogues* that the passages put into the *Analects* are factual (*zheng shi* 正實) and of paramount importance (*qie shi* 切事). The rest, he says, were put into the *Dialogues*, suggesting that the *Dialogues* provides us with a wealth of details for the laconically stated facts of the *Analects*. The differences in these two versions of the story in *Dialogues* 41.19 and *Analects* 14.40 can serve to illustrate this principle. In the *Analects* version, Zizhang asks a question about a passage in the Documents regarding the Shang king Gaozong not speaking for three years, and Confucius provides a general statement about a three-year period of regency whenever a king passes away. In the *Dialogues* version, we see the same question and answer in different phrasings, with the addition of two examples from history to support the general statement. The *Analects* version provides the bare minimum of the story in succinct prose, and the *Dialogues* version offers more details.

Section 41.19 also provides a hint in a completely different direction. The exact dating of political events in the early Zhou has been the topic of much speculation and calculation, using a variety of means, one of which is calendrical mentions in bronzes dating to the time. One problem with using the bronzes is that there are occasionally internal contradictions, and one solution to resolving these contradictions is what Edward Shaughnessy calls the "dual first year" (Shaughnessy 1991, 151) or "double *yuan*" (Shaughnessy 2009, 19) theory. This theory states that the actual initial reign date of a Zhou king may differ from the reign date mentioned by a king in a bronze inscription, since the king considers his reign to begin after the mourning period for his father has ended. Section 41.19, in which Confucius says that a king did not participate in governing during the mourning period for the preceding king, is a powerful corroboration of this theory. And the theory corroborates the authenticity of the contents of the *Dialogues* while also validating the usefulness of the *Dialogues*.

Our advice, and our own practice, is to take the ideas in the *Dialogues* and *Analects* as generally accurate and representative of the philosophy of Confucius. The technical terminology is certainly reliable.[36] The coherence of ideas related to political theory, education, human nature, cosmology, and so on, can be said to represent the genuine theories of Confucius. The points of tension between or within texts are starting points for discussion and debate; places within or between texts where one passage or idea can supplement passages or ideas elsewhere provide a basis for further investigation. A reconstructed philosophy of Confucius from the resources of the *Analects* and the *Dialogues* is an immensely useful philosophical resource,

36. This is not to say that there are no unsolved problems around early philosophical terminology. The excavated texts have raised quite a number, but their vocabulary is also remarkably consistent with the vocabulary of the *Dialogues* and so suggests contemporaneity.

useful for study in its own right, for deploying in current theory, and for use in cross-cultural comparisons.

There may be scholars who have been indoctrinated into the belief that the *Dialogues* is a forgery and, having read the argument above, are still skeptical. Perhaps the experience of Pang Pu 龐朴, a leading Chinese scholar of recent times, might be instructive. In a 1963 article on methodology, Pang criticized the naivete of fellow scholars, writing, "Some comrades have used the *Dialogues of Confucius* to jump to conclusions without the least bit of analysis. The *Dialogues of Confucius* was forged by Wang Su of Wei during the Three Kingdoms Period—a conclusion established long ago by our predecessors. Although it might have some value as a reference for the scholarship and ideas of that time, what could ever come from studying it for the purpose of understanding the thoughts of Confucius?" (Pang 1963, 28).

By 2004, the excavated texts had changed Pang's view entirely: "Faced with the bamboo manuscripts, reconsidering chapter 27 of the *Dialogues* and [the parallel] chapter in the *Li ji*, one must admit that they certainly predate the *Mencius* and are definitely not counterfeits of a later date" (Pang 2004, 71). It is difficult to oppose his conclusion that "Confronting the fact of the bamboo texts, we are forced to . . . wipe away our prejudices and come to a fresh understanding" (72).

Translation Issues

An impressive glowing sign over a small restaurant in Ji'nan, China, advertised the English word "gruel." This translation of the Chinese word on the sign is perfectly correct, and exactly wrong. Lexically speaking, *gruel* is the most accurate translation of the Chinese *zhou* 粥. No doubt the designer of the sign had looked up *zhou* in a Chinese-English dictionary. In this sense, it is perfectly correct. However, the purpose of an advertisement is to attract people. In fast-food commercials, for example, we see a cosmetically perfect food specimen that attracts our attention and gets our mouths watering. The word *gruel* instead brings to mind malnourished orphans and insipid, watery porridge. That's why, as a translation on a restaurant sign, *gruel* is exactly wrong.

What are we to make of this situation in which the most accurate translation is actually not right for the situation? It shows us that the job of a translator is not to translate words per se, but to try to transfer the cognitive-affective associations in the mind of the original author as fully and succinctly as possible to the mind of the reader via a word or set of words that are semantically related. Because the meanings of words in any language branch out in countless lexical, cultural, and historical webs of association, fully transferring the set of associations from one language to another is never really possible, even in closely related languages such as French and Italian, or English and German. When a language is as distant from English as

Chinese, let alone Classical Chinese (the language of the *Dialogues*), the task is even more difficult.[37]

Take the word *hero* for example. Now think of any non-Western or premodern culture. Even if you don't know the language, you can imagine a word that is equivalent to the English word *hero*. Imagine what that foreign word conjures in the mind of a native speaker of that language. It certainly does not conjure a firefighter, an astronaut, Rosa Parks, or Daniel Boone, heroes that might come to mind for an American English-language speaker. Instead, it would conjure someone like Arjuna (India), Achilles (ancient Greece), or Guan Gong (premodern China). So even though we have essentially the same idea in different languages, the mental contents prompted

37. The challenges of translation, especially of culturally loaded concepts, has been discussed numerous times, trenchantly and at length. Derk Bodde (1955) stressed the compromises that translators must make and how a foreign-language text can open us up to revelations about our own culture. Walter Benjamin (1997) spoke to how the simple words for *bread* in German and French, while denoting exactly the same object, have quite different connotations in the respective languages. He suggested that a good translation barely touches the original and opens us up to a potential universal language, each language supplementing the others. Both Bodde and Benjamin stress the dangers of being too literal, "the slavish adherence to fixed rules" (Bodde 1955, 244) and how "word-for-word translation completely rejects the reproduction of meaning and threatens to lead directly to incomprehensibility" (Benjamin 1997, 161). In an influential article, Theo Hermans echoes this sentiment, saying, "in the cross-cultural study of translation we should drop the idea that what we are aiming for is a full and accurate representation of foreign concepts of translation" (Hermans 2003, 385). Hermans traces Kwame Anthony Appiah's notion of *thick translation* (Appiah 1993) back to Gilbert Ryle's notion of *thick description*, "patient engagement and interpretive, contextualizing negotiation" (Hermans 2003, 386). For Hermans, this means providing as fresh a rendering as possible, not relying on "standard vocabulary" and providing detailed scholarly apparatuses as required to bridge cultural divides, and "relish[ing] what Geertz calls 'the delicacy of . . . distinctions' more than 'the sweep of . . . abstractions'" (387). Of course, abstractions are the bread and butter of philosophy, but the distinctions among abstractions across cultures are too often ignored by translators of Chinese philosophy, as they rely on "standard" vocabulary, such as *righteousness* for *yi* 義 and *humanity/benevolence* for *ren* 仁. Martha P. Y. Cheung (2007) updates Hermans' view of thick translation specifically with respect to Chinese cross-cultural translation. In reference to her own translation volume, she explains:

> The manoeuvres of thick translation applied to the rendering of translation concepts in the Chinese tradition can be divided into two categories: local manoeuvres and structural manoeuvres. Local manoeuvres include translating according to context, and the use of bold type, transliteration and transcription. Structural manoeuvres include: the deployment of texts for historical contextualization, grounding and layering, and for the setting off of semantic reverberations; the use of headnotes to provide biographical information on the writers of the texts; the use of indexes and footnotes to provide explanatory and interpretive signposts for readers; and the writing of introductory and other essays on the architectural dimension of the project. (Cheung 2007, 31–32)

by the idea in individuals will be vastly different, even unrecognizable to a person using another language. The challenge for a translator is to make the gap between minds as small as possible and the associations and meanings as equivalent and rich as possible.

So what would be a good translation of *zhou* in the restaurant sign? *Zhou* is a kind of porridge usually made of rice or millet, but with a consistency that is often more like soup than oatmeal porridge. It is considered mild and nutritious, so much so that it is commonly fed to small children and elders who have trouble chewing but still need adequate nourishment. Anything can be added to *zhou* to provide flavor. Because it is often fed by a caregiver and can be fortified with nutritious, medicinal, or especially tasty tidbits, not to mention that its heat can warm you up on a cold winter day, the associations of *zhou* in contemporary, affluent Chinese society have to do with familial love, care, togetherness, safety, and deliciousness. Compare those to the associations we have in English with *gruel*, and it's easy to see why *gruel*, though accurate, would be wrong, even comically so, in an advertisement. Would *porridge* or *rice porridge* be better? Not as terrible, but associations of *porridge*

Thick translation, Cheung emphasizes, requires interpretive effort not just on the part of the translator but also on the part of the reader. We loosely follow Cheung's advice, but there is really nothing new in this approach, for Roger Ames and his collaborators have been taking this approach for decades. Ames emphasizes the need for fresh vocabulary in order to avoid imposing entrenched Western philosophical distinctions on the Chinese. Sometimes, when there is no adequate English equivalent of a term, the best course is to transliterate. At the risk of trying the reader's patience with another overlong quotation, we offer an instructive paragraph from Ames:

> By way of analogy, when we reflect on our best efforts in the discipline to read and teach classical Greek philosophy, many if not most of us do not have an expert knowledge of classical Greek and the original language texts. But in developing a sophisticated understanding of an extended cluster of the most important Greek philosophical terms—*logos, nomos, nous, phusis, kosmos, eidos, psyche, soma, arche, alethea,* and so on—we can with imagination, get beyond our own uncritical Cartesian assumptions and at least in degree, read these Greek texts on their own terms. In a similar way, by seeking to understand and to ultimately appropriate the key philosophic vocabulary around which the Chinese texts are structured, students will be better able to locate these canonical texts within their own Confucian intellectual and cultural assumptions. The only alternative to doing our best to take the tradition on its own terms is to participate in a further colonializing of Chinese philosophy and the truncating of its long history. We have to resist the unconscious and patently spurious assumption that this tradition's fairly recent encounter with the vocabulary of the Western academy has been its defining moment. Such an uncritical approach places the uniqueness, the heterogeneity, and the intrinsic worth of the Chinese philosophical tradition at real risk. (2021, xxi)

While we adopt Cheung and Ames' general thick translation method, our specific "maneuvers" are tailored to the requirements of our project.

in English come nowhere near to *zhou* in the comfort-food department. Though oatmeal can be made sweet and flavorful, it is still not nearly as rich in associations as *zhou*. *Chicken soup*, in English, has connotations of caregiving, safety, warmth, and nutrition; thus, in certain contexts, that could be the best translation. Though it wouldn't work for the restaurant sign, of course.[38]

This is the dilemma of a translator—conveying associations while maintaining fidelity to meanings. The webs of associations can never fully be conveyed across languages, so a translator must be creative and flexible, selecting the best word for the immediate context. That could mean that the very same Chinese word needs to be translated as different English words in the same text, and that the dictionary equivalent of a term is not necessarily its best translation. Sometimes it means that terms should not be translated at all.

Another example of a difficult-to-translate word is the Chinese *zaozi* 棗子. Its proper translation into English is *jujube*, but because most people don't know what a jujube is, and because in its common dried form a *zaozi* is red, date-shaped, and sweet, the word is often translated into English as *red date*, even though jujubes are not dates at all. If we were translating a novel in which a person recovering from an illness is fed *zhou* with a couple of *zaozi* in it, we might translate the terms as *rice porridge* with *red dates* and add an explanatory phrase or sentence about sweetness, warmth, love, and nutrition. If we were teaching someone to cook Chinese food, we probably wouldn't translate the terms at all and instead just retain *zhou* and *zaozi*, insisting that our interlocutor learn these important culinary terms. So prospective use also informs the translation.

We use both of these methods to translate terms in this book. Sometimes we add a few words to help convey the associations, and sometimes we keep the Chinese term itself when there is simply no good set of associations in English. As you can see, translation is especially tricky for culinary words. An example from the *Dialogues* has to do with several words for alcoholic beverages, the primary term of which is *jiu* 酒. In terms of manufacturing methods, *jiu* during the period in question is beer, but when you think of beer (even if you are a craft brewer), your default thoughts are probably of a beverage with a golden color in a glass that has a bubbly mouthfeel and a somewhat bitter flavor, and you likely associate it with watching sporting events or other warm-weather leisure activities. *Jiu*, however, wasn't golden (instead probably clear, whitish, or brownish-yellow), was probably sweet or aromatic (from

38. It's worth noting that in the culture of present-day China, English lettering on an advertisement is often just for aesthetic rather than informative purposes. From this perspective, any combination of letters is as good as any other. Also, the word *zhou* does appear in the *Dialogues*. We translate it as *thin soup* and *thin congee*. It doesn't necessarily have the same associations today as it did in ancient times, when it could connote wholesome simplicity or even privation.

various herbs), and was used in sacrificial ceremonies and formal banquets (Zhang and Xu 2020). From its appearance and use, *jiu* more closely resembles white wine, and since the term *wine* is reasonably broad, it is sometimes the best choice. However, section 32.14 of the *Dialogues* specifically mentions malt in the process of making *jiu*, so *wine* simply won't do as a translation in that passage.

A translator wants to be as transparent as possible and not make too many demands on the reader to seek information beyond the text, and therefore should prioritize the use of familiar terms and minimize jargon and archaisms. A key term in the *Dialogues* is *xian* 賢, which in early China referred to someone who, because of their virtue, wisdom, and capability, was either already a great leader/official or was seen as a great candidate to be employed as a leader/official. The term often used in English to translate *xian* is *worthy* (as in "So-and-so is a worthy"), which might have been the best translation 150 years ago, but in its noun form it's rarely a word that people use today to signify a competent or aspiring leader. We translate *xian* as *capable and virtuous* (or *a capable and virtuous person*) because, lacking a good equivalent in contemporary English, that combination of adjectives seems to provide the right balance of formality and familiarity.

Sometimes, however, a translator has a responsibility to challenge readers to venture beyond their comfortable vocabulary and even to challenge their own assumptions. Liberally translating *zhou* as "chicken soup" or *jiu* as "wine" when the context contravenes that meaning would be both misleading and irresponsible. In the *Dialogues,* which includes numerous technical terms that do not have good English equivalents, a translator has to decide when to challenge the reader and when to let the prose flow. If the English mirrored the Chinese lexically and grammatically, word for word, the translation would be more like a lexicon than a readable text.

We have tried to keep the technical details mostly in the background, and we have provided an extensive glossary at the end for the curious reader. There are nevertheless two situations where we typically allow the technical to intrude. The first involves terms that we feel have long been mistranslated or that we think are worth using to enrich the reader's vocabulary. For example, we occasionally translate *jiu* as beer, because even though by appearance and usage it most closely resembles wine, it really isn't wine, and we think readers of ancient Chinese texts should eventually get accustomed to calling it beer. It is a bit of cultural imperialism, after all, to take the medieval European law that defined beer as necessarily containing hops and to criticize its applicability to China on that basis as inappropriate or anachronistic. Similarly, the word *mount* is often misused by translators, especially in the case of so-called Mount Tai. In conventional geographical naming in English, the term *mount* is generally used for mountains that are named after a person (e.g., Mount Rainier, Mount Shasta, Mount Everest), whereas *mountain* is used for descriptive names (e.g., Bald Mountain, White Mountain, Table Mountain) (Geographical Names Board of Canada 2012). Since the Chinese *tai* 泰 is an adjective (meaning majestic or peaceful—see, for example, Peace Altar in 29.3) and not a person's name, it makes sense to refer to the famous mountain as Tai Mountain, not Mount Tai.[39]

The second situation in which we challenge the reader with our translation has to do with technical philosophical vocabulary. We see our translation as a *philosophical translation* in that, when we have to make the choice between technical accuracy and readability, we put our focus on the philosophical terminology. (Alternatively, we could have focused on political, ritual, religious, culinary, or artistic themes.[40]) This book's glossary explains many technical terms having to do with flora and fauna, personal and place names, the calendar, and so on, because we did not want to unnecessarily distract the reader's attention to such things in the translation itself. For philosophical terms, however, we often simply transliterate the term, forcing the reader to slow down and think about what the term on the page means and how it relates to other terms in the same semantic web (while also providing an extensive philosophical lexicon at the end of this introduction). We apply this method of flexible translation or transliteration liberally.

A good example of how we adjust our wording to make the English come off as naturally as possible is in our many translations of the Chinese term *ming* 命. A fuller explanation of the term is provided further below, but let us here explain our thinking behind some of our word choices.

One meaning of *ming* is to appoint to a position and, by extension, the position of employment. Consider the following translations:

- "Nodding in my first appointment [*ming*], bowing halfway in my second, bowing deeply in my third" (11.1).
- "If the sovereign is just, accept employment [*ming*]. If the sovereign is unjust, reject employment [*ming*]" (12.21).
- "Everyone did their jobs [*ming*]" (14.9).

39. Admittedly, this will be a hard lift, since even official documentation within China and by UNESCO uses the flawed translation. Further, we'd like to emphasize again that the mission in our translation is not to get every term as lexically and grammatically as accurate as possible, which would make the text uninteresting and unreadable. The practice of translation is the art of balancing readability and technical accuracy. Different translators make different decisions. Here, we are announcing our general method, with some specific examples.

40. If we had a different focus, we would make different translation decisions. For example, as explained in the glossary, we translate all the different terms for the head of the government bureaucracy as *prime minister*. If our focus were on political history, we would take pains to translate each distinct term individually and explain the differences in the different organizational structures. Here, however, translating them all as *prime minister* gets the general point across. Likewise, we elide "prognostication" with "divination," we translate a city *zai* 宰 as *mayor*, not *magistrate* or *city administrator*, and we do not distinguish the different terms referring to surnames, clan, or lineage names.

The first is a quotation from a historical figure in a serious setting and so requires formal language. The second is about a general principle that seems applicable even today, and so we use a more general term. The third describes a common office scenario and so uses the idiom common to such scenarios.

Another meaning of *ming* is to order, as in a superior ordering a subordinate to do something. Consider the following translations:

- "Confucius ordered [*ming*] Shenju Xu and Yue Qi to lead a group of soldiers in a counterattack" (1.3).
- "My father once proclaimed [*ming*] his wishes, saying . . ." (11.1).
- "The ruler of Wu sent an emissary to Lu to ask about the bone but said, "Don't tell him I asked [*ming*]" (16.2).

In the first, we see a military operation, where the term *order* fits the context in a straightforward way—a superior commands a subordinate to do something. In the second instance, a father is commanding a son to do something, but here the term *order* would seem to come off as too severe for the context, so we soften it to *proclaim his wishes,* which seems to be the more natural locution in English for the context.[41] In the third instance, we soften it to an outright euphemism that does double duty. The underlying meaning of the sentence is: Don't tell him I'm the one behind this situation (which involves an emissary asking a question on behalf of a ruler). This can be couched as: "Don't tell him I ordered you to do this." Changing *order* to *ask* covers both the ordering and the inquiring in a serendipitous way. *Ask* can be a euphemism for *order* in situations where one wants to avoid alienation, as when a teacher "asks" students to do an assignment.

Yet another meaning of *ming* is the ordering done by cosmic forces that are sometimes unavoidable. Consider the following translations:

- "The good and ill that happen to states and families are truly designated [*ming*] by *tian* and are not just in the hands of people" (7.6).
- "He adjusted his behavior in anticipation of determinations [*ming*] from *tian*" (12.21).
- "Majestic, regal, lofty heaven / Its ordinations [*ming*] never untoward" (15.4).

In the first and second translations, because it would come off as awkward in English to say that *tian*[42] *ordered* something, we soften the intentionality by using the terms *designate* and *determine.* The third is from a more archaic source that requires arch language to convey the meaning that fits the poetic context.

41. Compare to 9.9, however, where a more generalized father-son relationship seems to warrant the use of *to order.*

42. For a brief explanation of *tian* 天, see "Fate" below.

Sometimes the intentionality of *tian* in early texts is softened even further, to the point that it suggests a cosmic law rather than a command from on high. Consider the following translations:

- "Just as we are born [*ming*] with this one body, there is no substitute" (7.1).
- "There are three kinds of unnatural death [*ming*]" (7.7).
- "His lack of concern over his executed family shows his ability to evaluate unavoidable circumstances [*ming*]" (8.9).

In the first, *ming* is paired with the word *xing* 性, which means something inherent, and so although it is still coming from cosmic forces, those forces are naturalized appropriately in the English rendering. In the second, the meaning is that these same cosmic forces provide each of us with a general lifespan, but an individual can shorten that lifespan through choices made along the way. The most fluent way to refer to a lifespan that does not reach its natural allotment is *unnatural death*. In the third, a person's family has been killed, and the person, who is known for being more pragmatic than religious, can do nothing about it. The emphasis in the passage is on the resilience that allows him to move on. The gist of this is captured in the locution *unavoidable circumstances* (see "Fate" below).

Before discussing some of the technical philosophical terms that we highlight in this translation, let us discuss some of the political/government terms that we more or less gloss over. The structure of the government was of paramount importance to Confucius, and we'll describe it here in sufficient detail for the reader to grasp its importance.

The vocabulary we use to describe it and to translate related words relies heavily on terms drawn from the European feudal tradition. In a series of books and articles, Li Feng has made a convincing case that the so-called feudal system of the early Zhou dynasty did not resemble its European counterpart. He says, for example: "Similarities did exist between medieval Europe and the Western Zhou, such as a hierarchical power structure, a division of authority between the central court and the regional powers, and a limited central administration. But, medieval Europe and Western Zhou China were not the only societies with these features. The [European] feudo-vassalic institution was not about how to organize government or how to distribute power, but was a way to regulate personal relations among the ruling elite. It therefore differentiates medieval Europe from Western Zhou China" (F. Li 2003, 142).

Confucius lived during the Zhou dynasty (1045–256 BCE). Although referred to as a dynasty, the Zhou was not the kind of central authority that would dominate China from the Qin dynasty (221–206 BCE) onward. Instead, power was held by local rulers, who had an obligation to the Zhou king. It is this hierarchical structure with local autonomy that has led historians to compare the Zhou system with the European feudal system. As Li points out, the differences between the two systems, especially at the beginning of the Zhou dynasty (the Western Zhou) are stark, and the comparison often breaks down. However, during the Eastern Zhou dynasty (770–256 BCE), things had changed to more closely resemble the European system (notwithstanding points of distinction). Li says of the Eastern Zhou:

> The fall of the Zhou capital in 771 B.C. and the collapse of the Zhou central power resulted in a historical environment somewhat similar to that from which the feudo-vassalic institution arose in medieval Europe. Studies of political institutions in the Spring and Autumn and early Warring States period point to several major new inventions: written legal codes, . . . contracted political loyalty sealed with the oath of alliance as indicated by the covenant, . . . a new type of estate to which there was attached not the right of administration or justice but only right to derive revenue. All of these occurred at a time when many states were unable to organize themselves according to the traditional lineage bonds. (F. Li 2003, 144)

Thus, although there were dissimilarities between the political systems of medieval Europe and of China in the time of Confucius, there were also enough similarities that, for the purposes of this translation (which is to focus on the philosophical rather than the political/governmental), we adopt the European feudal vocabulary. States (or parts of states) are often referred to as fiefs or fiefdoms, we refer to vassals and lords (though we don't draw a distinction between the sovereign-subject vs. the lord-vassal relationship), and for the five noble ranks of the Eastern Zhou we use the terms *duke*, *marquis*, *earl*, *viscount*, and *baron*.[43]

That said, to the extent that the philosophy of Confucius is a political philosophy, the distinctive characteristics of the Zhou system cannot be glossed over in their entirety. Some of these crucial features must be understood in order to understand the philosophy of Confucius.

43. In their translation of the CQZZ, Durrant, Li, and Schaberg (2016) translate *guo* 國, instead of the common rendering of *state, as domain,* following a feudal theme (though they simultaneously distance themselves from that theme), pointing out that because boundaries between domains were vague and rulership was transferred by lineage, the term fits better than *state*. We adopt this convention occasionally to remind the reader of the similarities to feudalism while usually preferring the word *state* (or its more familiar synonym, *country*) because (1) in its most general sense, *state* refers to an autonomous political entity (which the *guo* effectively were), and (2), as Li (2003) shows, there was an important sense of borders as geographical boundaries between states (though nothing like in the modern nation-state). In other words, like Durrant, Li, and Schaberg, we are wary of the parallels between European feudalism and the Chinese system. But because of our respective subject matter (theirs being history, ours philosophy), we draw slightly different conclusions in translating key terms.

Philosophy in the *Dialogues*

It is not lost on us that the term *philosophy* has deep roots in the Greek tradition and had no Chinese equivalent up until the Chinese borrowed a Japanese neologism originally used to translate the word *philosophy* into Japanese. Nevertheless, to the extent that philosophy, as we understand it today, is the written record of an interrogation of nature and the human condition generally, with an intention of making sense of the world with minimal contradictions, China has had philosophy for some 3,000 years.

As stated, the glossary contains a whole host of terminology that will help the reader understand the text in as full a way as possible. It does not, however, contain philosophical vocabulary. For philosophical terms, we provide what follows. The terms are listed in alphabetical order for convenience, either in English or in Chinese transcription.

Before getting to the specific terminology, let us return to the notion of government mentioned above. Social organization was as important a topic for the Chinese as it was for the ancient Greeks. Although today Westerners trace the concept of democracy back to the Greeks, the greatest philosophers of that time were not fans of democracy per se. We should try, briefly, to understand why.

One idea, pervasive in ancient Greece and Rome and common throughout European history, has, for good reason, more recently fallen out of favor. That is the concept of the essentialism of human nature, particularly as it relates to value, birth, and, frankly, blood. There is a reason that slaveholding took root early in European civilization and that democracies were at first restricted to a certain subset of people, before going out of favor, even in that very limited form, for over a millennium. The reason was the common belief that some people are, by birth, better than others.[44] That is to say, some people are born leaders and others born followers—not in a metaphorical sense but in a sense of intrinsic value and capability. The political theory of human equality in Europe is of relatively recent origin, dating only to the Enlightenment (Rist 1982; Jorati 2023). For most of European history, there was instead a belief in a cosmic hierarchy on which each person's place was determined at birth. Marcus Aurelius, Stoic philosopher and emperor of Rome, for example, said, "It is clear that the inferior exist for the sake of the better and the better for the sake of each other" (Marcus Aurelius 1983, 5:16). Variations of this view persisted through monarchist positions in the eighteenth century, beliefs in phrenology in the late nineteenth century and Aryanism in the twentieth century. It is still with us today in varieties of racial supremacism.

44. Of course, the direction of causation may go the other way. The idea of essentialism was a post hoc justification for the social practice of the othering of humans beings, but the point still holds that the idea contributed to the perpetuation of the system.

Although there was an aristocracy in ancient China, even in some sense a divinely anointed aristocracy, there was also often an insistence that leaders must be capable, and that it was their capability and virtue, not their birth, that legitimized their authority. We see in the *Dialogues* that Confucius cared deeply about history and the lessons that it can teach us. One of the key lessons for him came in the form of very early rulers of Chinese legend: Yao, Shun, and Yǔ.

Yao is said in the *Dialogues* (15.8 and 23.4; also in other early texts) to have been an early and important leader of the Chinese. Instead of selecting his own sons to succeed him, he chose a simple fisherman and potter named Shun.[45] Shun, the narratives say, turned out to be an excellent choice, and he in turn eschewed his own sons in favor of Yǔ.[46] Yǔ also turned out to be an excellent choice, except that he selected his own son to succeed him, thus beginning the Xia dynasty, the first of the three most ancient Chinese dynasties. This was a turning point in Chinese political history, Confucius believed, but not in Chinese intellectual history. The belief that capability and virtue ultimately outweigh birth persisted, because there came to be a belief that, while the capacities of the monarch mattered, what also mattered were the capacities of the ministers who help the monarch create policy and who put those policies into effect. In *Dialogues* 14.7, Confucius says, "Yao and Shun were able to solicit help from the capable and virtuous. The capable and virtuous are the genesis of all good fortune, the captains of fate."

Cultivating and installing capable and virtuous leaders is one of the dominant themes of the *Dialogues*. Even when the subject is not explicit, it should be understood as implicit. You cultivate yourself in order to take your place in society, and anyone is capable of doing so. Once you take your place, you understand that you are there for the purpose of governing, not for your own benefit. More capability and virtue allow you to move up through the hierarchy. And if everyone thought and behaved in this way, the world would be a harmonious place in which everyone prospers. Confucius' teachings therefore focus on building capability

45. The *Dialogues* doesn't narrate the transmission of power from Yao to Shun but does imply it, saying that Yao selected Shun as his minister and that Shun succeeded Yao. The *Documents* ("Yao dian") makes the abdication explicit.

46. Tone marks are used in Chinese transcription in two places in this book. They are used throughout the glossary (except in its headwords). This is for the sake of disambiguation and clarity in the most technical part of the book. For the rest of the book, we favor readability over unnecessary precision. However, in cases where homophones would engender confusion, as in this case, where Yǔ might be confused with Yu (Zai Wo) or Yú (Youyu), we supply tone marks for the alternative names (see all three in the glossary). Some academics nowadays prefer to use tone marks throughout. In our opinion, this is unnecessary, and the appearance of precision gives the false impression that the pronunciation of early times was the same as today.

and virtue in the individual, and on creating space for the capable and virtuous in society.[47]

This sense of a dynamic hierarchy is crucial to understanding the philosophy of Confucius. When we think of hierarchy in contemporary times, our first sense may be one of stasis, authoritarianism, and coercion. And no doubt this kind of hierarchy existed in Chinese history. However, to make sense of Confucius' philosophy, we have to realize that an individual could indeed move up in the hierarchy. Though there was a sense in ancient China of a natural hierarchy, it was not the kind of natural hierarchy that is assumed in Marcus Aurelius or Plotinus. For Confucius the model natural hierarchy was the family. In this hierarchy, the parents or grandparents are on top and express the virtue of *ci* 慈 (caring kindness; see "Love" below) toward their children. The children, for their part, express *xiao* 孝 (filial love; see "*Xiao*" below) toward their parents (and grandparents), not just when they are children but into adulthood, for as long as their parents are alive, and even beyond.

However, for Confucius the natural hierarchy of the family is dynamic. The child grows up and becomes a parent, then a grandparent. While growing up and assuming one role after another (or different roles concurrently—sibling, uncle/aunt, spouse, etc.), one fulfills one's obligations of love and duty in each distinct relationship. These imply virtues that may be specific either to a familial role or to a level in the hierarchy. At the level of a child, one should master the virtue of *xiao*; at the level of a parent, one should master the virtue of *ci*. *Xiao* and *ci* are thus "directional" virtues, deployed in a certain direction within the hierarchy depending on one's place in that hierarchy.[48]

In Confucius' thinking, the natural hierarchy of the family stands as an analogy for the hierarchy of society more broadly, including the political hierarchy. Although he views the rulership explicitly as having a parental role, for the most part he does not carry over the familial directional virtues into the political arena but instead substitutes equivalents. When one first enters society, one is *zhong* (see below) rather than *xiao*. As one moves up, gains responsibilities, and takes a leadership role over subordinates, one expresses the virtue of *ren* (see below)—the equivalent of *ci*.

Zhong, then, is the virtue of playing one's role lower in the hierarchy: following instructions, learning, accepting orders, assiduously fulfilling tasks, offering

47. The tension in the political philosophy of the *Dialogues* between blood succession and meritocracy is worth exploring further. In 19.6, for example, Confucius distinguishes between two officials who are killed in the process of advising corrupt kings. The distinguishing feature seems to be their closeness to the king, which is in part mediated by blood relation. In 32.2, by contrast, he explicitly associated a decline in the *dao* with the monopoly of power by one family, and more generally with power being passed down through family lines.

48. See Ames (2011) for a robust theory of role ethics derived largely from the *Analects*, "Zhong yong," "Da xue 大學," and *Xiao jing* that is consistent with the view presented in the *Dialogues*.

opinions when relevant—the virtue of the functionary and the mentee. *Ren*, by contrast, is the virtue of the supervisor and the mentor: decisiveness, intelligence, wisdom, frugality, care, and kindness. In both of these roles, a kind of selflessness is felt and expressed. Not precisely a self-denying variety of selflessness—Confucius is fine with doing well while also doing good, as long as any wealth accumulated is not excessive—but a selflessness that puts the well-being of others, individually and as a group, ahead of one's own.

One way to understand the terms *ren, ci, xiao,* and *zhong* is to recall the classic three terms for love in Greek—*eros, philia, agape*—and apply a similar principle to the Chinese. We can think of all four Chinese terms as distinct kinds of love: love of parents toward children, love of children toward parents, love of leader toward followers, and love of follower toward leaders. The danger of melding the four concepts is of watering down distinctions, which is why we tend to maintain the distinct terms in the translation. But the benefit of doing so is the emphasis on the affective component, which is otherwise in danger of being lost. Confucius' teachings aren't just about fulfilling one's duty to someone on the hierarchy. Rather, each of these virtues is intended to be felt, and in this way bonds of affection will be created up and down the hierarchy (see "Affection" and "Love" below).[49]

In the philosophical lexicon that follows, we list twenty-eight umbrella concepts from the *Dialogues*, highlighting and explaining the key Chinese terminology, indexing all instances in the *Dialogues*, and providing a selection of illustrative examples from the *Dialogues*. The *Dialogues* is a rich resource of Confucian theory. Our explanations here are not intended to be complete and should be understood instead as starting points for understanding the philosophy of Confucius in the *Dialogues* and for a more expansive discussion of its details and nuances. More can be said about each of the items in this list, and about items not included, such as humility; humiliation/stooping to indignities; deference; the spreading of virtues, teachings, and emotions; harmony; caution; optimism; fame; responsiveness/flexibility; minorities/frontier peoples; innovation; moderation; moral psychology; managing the emotions of the people; relaxation; development; lenience/tolerance; aesthetic interpretation; sincerity; friendship; criminal justice; effort vs. effortlessness; philanthropy; the stewardship of, and attuning with, nature; and Confucius' view of rhetoric/eloquence.

The explanations of the following terms are derived, as far as possible, exclusively from their use in the *Dialogues*, with reference to other texts only as immediately relevant.

49. The hierarchical aspect of these terms, while important, should not be understood as inflexibly running in only one direction, for in some instances (e.g., 8.3 and 8.7) they run in the other direction, as well. As one rises through the hierarchy, one does not shed virtues cultivated at the lower levels but retains and expresses them appropriatley. Likewise, being lower on the hierarchy does not preclude one from expressing more expansive virtues.

Affection	Education	Love	*Shu* 恕
Congeniality	*Fa* 法	Meritocracy	*Xian* 賢
Consultation	Fate	*Minben* 民本	*Xiao* 孝
Dao 道	Hierarchy	*Ren* 仁	*Xin* 信
De 德	Independence	*Ru* 儒	*Yi* 義
Dialogue	*Junzi* 君子	Sage	*Zhong* 忠
Differentiation	*Li* 禮	*Shi* 士	*Zi* 自

Affection

There are several words in the *Dialogues* signifying relationships of affection. *Qin* 親 refers to one's parents and, by extension, to relatives, and to the feelings of close bonds with anyone. One of the insights of the *Dialogues* is its emphasis on building close relationships between the leadership and the people. (For a concrete example of affection between the populace and an official, see 42.10, in addition to the citations below of the use of specific terminology.) The Chinese word *qin* is one of the most commonly used technical terms in the *Dialogues*, appearing 179 times (in all uses), more often even than the names of the traditional Confucian virtues of *ren* and *yi*. In the *Analects*, by comparison, *qin* appears just nine times.[50] The term *mu* 睦 refers to strong, harmonious relationships of mutual consideration. The term *du* 篤 describes intensity of feeling or action, and this applies also to relationships, conveying the kindness and generosity that engenders affectionate relationships. See also "Love" below.

***Du* 篤** 3.2, 5.4, 6.2, 7.1, 12.7–8, 17.3, 19.4, 21.6, 22.3, 32.14, 37.3, 38.14

Thoroughly, to deepen[51]

50. Another contrast worth considering is its use in the *Mencius*, where Mencius says, "A *junzi* . . . is *ren* toward the people but not *qin*" (7A.45). Mencius does allow for building relations from top to bottom such that people feel *qin* for the leadership (1B.19, 3A.3), just not the other way around. He reserves the term mostly for affection toward parents and other relatives. However, in the essays "Zi yi 緇衣" (which occurs in the Shanghai Museum and Guodian manuscripts) and the "Wu xing 五行" (which appears in the Guodian manuscripts), both of which predate the *Mencius*, we see an echo of the *Dialogues*, in that *qin* in the upper level of governance is reciprocated in the form of *qin* from below.

51. Where possible, we include in this philosophical lexicon examples that provide a variety of dimensions in order to give a sense of how the idea is understood in context. The ordering of examples by use is unsystematic, and the number of examples under each is indicative of nothing. This lexicon is for interpretive and philosophical rather than lexicographic purposes. It may be helpful for understanding other Confucian texts of the early and middle Warring States period, such as the Shanghai and Guodian manuscripts, but it has been created solely with the *Dialogues* as the topic of study.

3.2 "If an enlightened king is able to thoroughly implement these three ultimates."
6.2 "For deepening relations between parents and children."

Devotion, devotedly

5.4 "Ruists . . . act devotedly without fatigue."
32.14 "Devotion between father and son."

Generous and kind

22.3 "A *junzi* is generous and kind at home."

Mu 睦 6.2, 14.8, 17.4, 32.1, 32.8, 32.13–14, 42.31

Close/strong relationship

14.8 "You'll never form close relationships with others by disparaging them in public instead of correcting them in private."
17.4 "If you establish love by beginning with your own parents, you can teach the people to have strong relationships."
32.8 "What is beneficial to people are trustworthiness and forging strong relations."

Consideration

32.14 "Common people protect each other through mutual consideration."

Qin 親 3.1–2, 4.1–2, 5.4–5, 6.1, 7.4–5, 8.2, 8.4–5, 8.10–14, 8.17, 9.1, 9.3, 9.7, 10.9, 10.11, 11.2, 12.3, 12.15–16, 12.21, 13.11, 14.8, 15.1, 15.17, 15.21, 16.3, 16.6–7, 17.1–5, 19.2, 19.4, 19.6, 19.10, 21.6–8, 22.1, 22.3, 23.5–6, 25.2, 26.4, 27.1, 28.2, 29.3, 32.1–2, 33.2, 34.1, 35.3, 36.3, 37.3–4, 38.1, 38.12, 39.2, 41.9, 41.14, 41.21, 41.25, 42.31, 42.32, 43.2, 43.3, 43.17, 43.25, 44.6

Parent, family member, relative

4.1 "Separate spheres for husband and wife, affection between parents and children, trustworthiness between ruler and ministers. Get these three right, and everything else will follow."
4.1 "The wife is the primary line of descent from the grandparents, and her child is their descendant. How could either of these not be held in high esteem? This is why a *junzi* is never without respect. And when it comes to respect, the most important thing is to respect one's person. The self, after all, is an offshoot of one's parents. How would one dare not hold it in high esteem? To disrespect one's person is to harm one's parents. Harming your

parents is harming the root. When the root is harmed, the branch is doomed."

5.5 "When recommending someone from an in-group, Ruists don't avoid family members."

6.1 "It came time to speak of the norms of funeral rites, the ordering of ancestors and gods inside temples, the grades of animals used in sacrifices, the display of sacrificial items, and the setting of dates of special occasions—all for the purpose of displaying respect during sacrificial ceremonies, differentiating the distance of living relatives."

8.10 "When I was younger, I loved to learn and so traveled all across the land. But when I returned home, I found that my parents had passed away in my absence. . . . A man wants to take care of his elderly parents, but his parents have already passed away. The things that go and never return are the years. Those you'll never see again are your parents."

8.12 "When I was taking care of my elderly parents, we often had to eat wild plants and weeds. I would walk twenty-five miles to carry a sack of grain home for my parents. After my parents passed away, I traveled south to Chu, where I was in charge of a large fief, I was paid ten thousand bushels of grain, I had plush seats in my carriage, and I ate food from ornate bronze cauldrons. I would rather, however, still be eating wild plants and weeds and carrying grain for my parents."

10.9 "*Xiao* children will put their all into the ceremony to honor their deceased parents."

17.1 "*Ren* has to do with people and relies on affection for one's parents and relatives as its first priority."

17.4 "If you establish love by beginning with your own parents, you can teach the people to have strong relationships. If you establish respect by beginning with your own elders, you can teach the people to live amiably. Teach them to be kind and to build strong relationships, and the people will prioritize their parents. Teach them with respect, and the people will prioritize their duty to the state. As soon as the people treat their parents with *xiao*, live amiably, and perform their duty to the state, and these policies can emanate outward to the whole land, anything is possible."

19.4 "I am able to give my salary to my parents and extended family, and so my relations with them have become closer."

19.6 "Xie Ye was a high official, not related by blood to the duke."

Proximity, to be close to, to approach

8.14 "Single-mindedness and faith are required for controlling oneself in close proximity to water."

23.6 "His *ren* was approachable."

To build/form/feel/maintain close bonds / bonds of affection / close ties / relations

3.2 "The people above will feel close bonds to the people below, and care for them as if caring for their own vital organs; and the people below will feel close bonds to the people above, like young children to their loving mother. When bonds like these are formed among those above and below, orders are subsequently followed, policies work, people embrace their virtue, the nearby happily pay allegiance, and the far away come to submit. They are the results of good government."

3.2 "Use compassion to make up for insufficiency; use *li* to curtail excess; stand by your word instead of putting on appearances. . . . Thus, there can be persuasion through awe without the need for armored soldiers, and there can be bonds of affection without bribing the people."

3.2 "It is said that the best *ren* in the world is that which can unite the whole world in bonds of ultimate affection."

8.5 "Jisun once gave me a thousand bushels of grain that I was able to distribute to others and from which I was able to build a base of good feelings."

8.11 "If you don't fit in, you won't be able to form close relationships. Without close relationships, conscientiousness toward others will be impossible."

9.3 "Pride will prevent the building of close relationships."

13.11 "I have heard that a country can be kept intact by forming close relations with neighboring countries."

14.8 "You'll never form close relationships with others by disparaging them in public instead of correcting them in private."

15.21 "Of those who are a model of conduct for others and work to improve their *li*, become as close as brothers to all those within hundreds of miles."

16.3 "In ancient times, the gift given by the king to someone of the same surname was precious jade, demonstrating closeness among relations."

19.2 "It is conscientiousness that allows you to build close ties in new relationships."

19.4 "Despite my work in the office, I still have time to visit the sick and attend funerals, so my relations with friends have deepened."

19.10 "Better to not be close to someone than to be close but not trust them."

21.6 "When society is flourishing, the people will feel a close bond with the leader."

21.7 "In this way, the upper and lower levels of society will maintain close ties and not become estranged."

21.8 "Therefore, if obedience must be forced, neither conscientiousness nor trustworthiness will ensue and the common people will not feel close to you."

To befriend, to cozy up to

3.1 "When the people above befriend capable and virtuous people, the people below also become more judicious in choosing friends."
5.4 "Ruists can be befriended but not bought."
16.7 "Yang Hu cozies up to wealth, not to *ren*."

Affection

4.1 "Separate spheres for husband and wife, affection between parents and children, trustworthiness between ruler and ministers. Get these three right, and everything else will follow."
4.1 "A leader expresses affection through respect. To neglect respect is to abandon affection. Without affection and respect, there is no esteem."
7.4 "If your court is conducted with *li* and upper and lower levels of society interact with mutual affection, then commoners across the land will see themselves as your people."
7.5 "If [a *junzi*] does not deeply love excellent behavior, then commoners will not feel profound affection for those above them."
10.11 "Excessive seriousness can lead to a loss of affection."
17.1 "*Ren* has to do with people and relies on affection for one's parents and relatives as its first priority."
43.3 "Being in the positions of son and minister allows him to show reverence for a sovereign and affection toward a parent."

To personally do something

4.1 "The culmination of the grand wedding occurred when a groom, wearing his *mian* crown, personally welcomed the bride."
12.3 "May I ask you to speak from your personal experience of having studied with them?"
12.16 "All that I've said just now about the behavior of these students of Confucius is based on my own personal experience."
27.1 "The *junzi* of old thus did not need to personally use words to express these."

Favorite

11.2 "The *dao* of *tian* has no favorites and prefers lying low."

Merit

16.6 "Dukes Huan and Xi were only distantly related to the Duke of Zhou, and they did not do anything in their lifetimes to accumulate merit sufficient to keep their temples intact."

Congeniality

The term *shun* 順 occurs in only two passages of the *Analects,* neither of which is of consequence. In the *Dialogues,* however, it acquires the status of a technical term. This can be seen especially in Chapter 32.[52]

At base, *shun* means to follow the flow of water. By extension, it came to refer to obedience, agreeableness, cooperativeness, congeniality, amiability, and so on.[53] Because of Confucius' insistence on independent thinking (see "Independence" below), we generally eschew the *obedience* interpretation in favor of other, more active interpretations of the term. *Shun* also refers to the effect of an action or circumstances, in the sense of its happening smoothly and in line with expectations, and to the mode of an action or affair as it occurs.

In chapter 32, we see a fascinating theorization of *shun,* in which the leadership accommodates the natural inclinations of the people, thereby causing the people to be receptive to the imperatives of the leadership. Mutual congeniality, resulting in needs being met at every level of the hierarchy, engenders a thriving, harmonious society.

52. Like the term *qin* 親, the term *shun* is an instance in which an emphasis in the *Dialogues* differs with the *Analects* but shares overlap with the Guodian and Shanghai Museum manuscripts and deserves further exploration. Ma Chengyuan (2001) notes the use of *shun* (and its opposite *ni* 逆) as a technical term in the essay "Xing qing lun 性情論" (a.k.a. "Xing zi ming chu," which appears in both the Shanghai Museum and Guodian manuscripts), drawing lexical parallels with other early texts, such as the *Documents,* an excavated bronze, the *Zhou li,* and the *Guanzi.*

53. It is interesting to compare *shun* (to flow with) to *liu* 流 (to flow). While the former has connotations of graceful control and fluency, the latter can have connotations of overwhelming force, a loss of control, or even negative consequences. See, for example, 5.3 (*liu yan* 流言, gossip), 7.1 (*cong wu ru liu* 從物如流, "drifts along with circumstances"), 8.14 (圜流九十里, "fierce rapids ran for dozens of miles downriver"), 23.4 (*liu si xiong* 流四凶, "exiled the four villains"), 25.1 (*min bi liu* 民必流, "the people will flee"), 28.2 (和樂而不流, "convivial without going overboard"), 35.2 (*de ru quan liu* 德如泉流, "*de* . . . gushed like spring water"), and 44.3 (*liu ti* 流涕, "broke into tears"). However, there is a sense of orderliness and positivity when *liu* refers to the transmission of something over time or distance, as in 8.11 (名 . . . 流聲後裔者, "fame that . . . extends even to one's descendants"), 9.5 (水 . . . 其流也, 則卑下, "in flowing, [water] remains low and bends"), 21.7 (道化流而不蘊, "the transformative powers of the *dao* will continue to flow without obstruction"), and 27.1 (*li zhou liu* 禮周流, "*li* . . . is circulating everywhere").

***Shun* 順** 1.3, 2.1, 3.1, 4.1, 5.3, 6.1, 8.6, 8.17, 9.1, 12.15, 12.21–22, 17.3–4, 18.4, 19.1, 20.1, 22.3, 23.1, 23.3, 25.1, 25.4, 26.2–3, 30.1, 31.4, 32.8, 32.13–15, 36.3, 41.6–8, 42.20. 43.17, 43.26

To follow, to obey

8.6 "Then the Duke of Zhou put himself out there in his efforts to transform the people, and the whole world followed him."
12.15 "In his unwillingness to kill emerging insects, you can see his following a humane way."
25.1 "People follow instructions without needing them repeated."
26.2 "Women follow the instructions from men."
26.3 "There are seven grounds for divorce . . . [including] disobeying in-laws."
41.8 "Realize *de* behavior / And other states will follow."

Congenial / congeniality, agreeably

1.3 "After Confucius took the reins of government. . . . Women were devoted and congenial.
3.1 "Have people practice *li* across every level of the hierarchy, establish it with *yi*, put it into effect agreeably, and then the people will reject bad behavior."
9.1 "There is a younger brother who cannot show respect to his older brother but expects his own younger brother to be congenial to him."
22.3 "Could it be that [the person not known as a *xiao* son] is not respectful in his person, or that his words are disagreeable?"
32.14 "*Ren* is the root of *yi* and the embodiment of congeniality."
32.14 "With congeniality, communication can be maintained across gulfs, space can be opened up in thick growth, connection can be made without friction, and there can be movement without collision. Only by clearly understanding congeniality can one safeguard against crisis."
32.14 "Devotion between father and son, consideration between siblings, and harmony between spouses. . . . Major officials following the law, minor officials minding their duties, official posts in good order, and sovereign and ministers improving each other. . . . When the king takes *de* as his chariot and ceremonial music as the driver, when lords across the land treat each other with *li*, when high ministers use the law to keep themselves in order, when low officials use trustworthiness to keep each other in line, and when common people protect each other through mutual consideration. . . . This is the Grand Congeniality. Congeniality is how one nurtures the living and sends off the dead, the standard for serving gods and spirits."
32.15 "People who lived in the mountains were not forced to move to the riverside. People who lived along shorelines were not forced to move to the

plains. Putting to use water, fire, metal, and wood for the sake of meals required proper timing. Unions between women and men were created in the winter, and noble ranks were conferred in the spring, each according to appropriate age and contributions. These are all examples of making things congenial. Congeniality is the only way to work with the people. This prevents natural disasters, such as floods, droughts, and insect pestilence. It also prevents human maladies, like plagues and famine. *Tian* did not stint its *dao*; the earth did not stint its treasures; and people did not stint their emotions. As a result, heaven gave sweet dew, the earth gushed forth spring water, mountains produced resources for tools and carriages, rivers produced the equine chart, *fenghuang* and *qilin* flourished in the countryside marshes, turtles and water dragons flourished in palace ponds, and the offspring of all of the other birds and beasts could be glimpsed just by looking down. There was no particular cause. It was just that the Ancient Kings were able to follow *li* and achieve *yi*, to embody trustworthiness and achieve congeniality. Such is the realization of congeniality."

To do just right, to sound just right

41.6 "That sounds about right."
41.7 "He did just right."

Smooth/smoothly, gracefully

5.3 "Ruists dress moderately and move gracefully."
6.1 "*Junzi* have taken [*li*] as a way to effect reverence and respect, exploiting its efficacy in instructing and ordering the common people. . . . Once this system was functioning smoothly, it came time to . . ."
26.3 "These are how the sages created smooth relationships between a man and a woman, stressing the beginning of a marriage."

To flow with, in tune with, in line with

23.1 "The Yellow Chief . . . governed the people in line with the cycles of nature."
23.3 "Gao Xin . . . was *ren* and dignified, wise and trustworthy, with *yi* that came from being in tune with heaven and earth."
25.4 "A king must . . . flow with the natural order when inactive."
32.13 "*Li* . . . is the broad way of attaining the *dao* of *tian* as well as flowing along with human emotions."

Consultation

There are a number of ways to conceptualize Confucius' ideal form of government. One useful way is as a *consultocracy*—rule by consultation. This term has been used by contemporary scholars (Ylönen and Kuusela 2019) to refer pejoratively to democracies that rely too heavily on consultants. The notion of consultation has also been used to refer to contemporary Chinese governing practices, in contrast to deliberative democracy (Li 2022). Both notions already in use overlap somewhat with Confucius' notion.

Confucius has been criticized for never opposing the authoritarian governments of his day, and he has been praised for emphasizing a government rooted in the concerns of the common people (Yong 2011), both of which are reasonable assessments. Confucius lived in a time of monarchical rule and did not question the existing power structure. However, he was instrumental in the transition from aristocratic rule to meritocratic rule (see "Meritocracy" below) beneath the level of the local potentate. He also saw the primary aim of government as providing for the security and prosperity of the people, which has led some scholars to label his political theory *minbenzhuyi* 民本主義—people as the root, or foundation (see "*Minben*" below).

The titular head of state in Confucius' time was the Zhou king, who was viewed as a father figure for the rulers of the various states of the land. This familial-federalist power structure meant that the ruler of each state had virtual independence but was constrained in practical terms by alliances among states (see "Superpower" in the glossary). There were several major states in Confucius' time. Lu, Confucius' native state, was originally enfeoffed to the Duke of Zhou, Confucius' cultural hero, and was viewed as inheriting the proper Zhou ritual. It was, however, fractious and weak, being ruled jointly by the three families Jisun, Mengsun, and Shusun. Just to the southwest was Song, Confucius' ancestral state and the home state of the remnants of the Shang people, whom the Zhou had displaced. To the northeast was Lu's main rival, Qi. To the northwest was the state of Wei, where Confucius spent approximately ten years in self-imposed exile. To the west of Song was Zheng, a small but influential state that was right on the border of Zhou, which was still further to the west. South of Zhou, Zheng, and Song was the vast state of Chu. To the east of Chu, along the coastline, were Wu in the north and Yue in the south. On the periphery were Yan in the northeast, Jin in the central north, and Qin in the far west. There were also scores of smaller states that during Confucius' time were steadily being absorbed by the larger states (see each state's individual entry in the glossary).

During his self-imposed exile, Confucius is said to have visited, in addition to Wei, Cao (sandwiched between Wei and Song), Zheng, Song, Chu, Chen, and Cai (the last two being tiny states along Chu's northern border). This traveling was in keeping with his theory of consultocracy, in that he went to these states to offer his services as adviser. Confucius had a collectivist view of governance which, like his view of hierarchy (see "Hierarchy" below), ranged from the state level through the family to the individual. Each person, according to one's relevant station and relationships, had a responsibility to both advise others and listen to the advice of others.

It seems fair to say that today, and for centuries back in Western history (at least to the Enlightenment, and perhaps even to the time of Plato and Aristotle), advice has been understood as a relevant data point in a rational calculus, which any rational individual could undertake in the same circumstance. Differing points of view fill gaps, but the rational calculus is intersubjectively available to anyone since, ideally, given the same unambiguous set of desiderata and facts, everyone will come to the same rational conclusion. By contrast, Confucius seems to see the decision-making process as collective. This is not to say that it is democratic or consensus-driven. Rather, though individuals make the decision, they are, in principle, incapable of thinking issues through entirely on their own. The two systems—individualist-rationalist vs. collectivist—are not necessarily mutually exclusive or non-overlapping, but the difference in emphasis seems significant and is worthy of further exploration.

Confucius believed that one of the keys to good governance was something like what Doris Kearns Goodwin (2005) would describe as the "team of rivals" that surrounded Lincoln. In 9.9 and 15.2, Confucius says that a ruler should have as advisers *zheng chen* 争臣, contending ministers, or ministers of different opinions. But he goes on to also say that a father should have sons of differing opinions and that individuals should have friends of differing opinions, so that rulers, fathers, and individuals can all receive good counsel and thereby reform their behavior as necessary. An individual alone is evidently insufficient; even the great rulers, he says, such as Tang and King Wu, had useful advisers and heeded their counsel.

In 14.2, Confucius says that there are five ways of advising a ruler, and he settles on the indirect method as his preference. The method of indirect advising, which has been discussed to some extent by scholars (Jullien 2000; Raphals 2016), is a strategy clearly evident in the *Dialogues* (e.g., in 14.4, 22.10, 37.3, and 41.7). This is not to say that direct advice is entirely eschewed; such advice is likewise evident in many passages (e.g., 1.2, 22.9, 37.2, and 42.4). The problem, Confucius says, is that it can sometimes be fruitless and even dangerous to give direct advice. Ministers like Xie Ye and Bigan, he says (19.6, 20.1), have been killed for it. Thus, any adviser needs to discern the aptitude of the ruler for accepting direct advice (19.6).

The following examples illustrate the concept of consultocracy:

8.1 "My ambition is to be a counselor to an enlightened sage-king."

9.9 "In the past, an enlightened king of a large state would have at least seven ministers of differing opinions to consult in order to avoid making serious errors in his conduct and actions. In a medium-size state, a ruler would have at least five ministers of differing opinions to consult, in order to avoid putting his state in danger. In a small state, a ruler would have at least three ministers of differing opinions to consult in order to avoid having his throne usurped. A father would have sons with differing opinions in order to avoid descending into impropriety. An aspiring young man would have friends of differing opinions in order to avoid immoral behavior."

10.2 "The king of Chu was a capable and virtuous leader! He ignored the might of being a superpower and focused on the trustworthiness of one adviser. If it weren't for Shenshu's trustworthiness, the king would never have been able to do the right thing. If it weren't for the king's wisdom and capability, he would never have been willing to listen to Shen's advice."

11.2 "People like me possessing the *dao* offer our services to rulers, but our advice goes unheeded. The *dao* is so difficult to put into practice these days."

14.2 "In regard to a conscientious minister advising a ruler, there are five ways that are broadly considered appropriate: deceptively, bluntly, authoritatively, directly, and indirectly. Indeed, when it comes to figuring out how to get a ruler to act, I prefer the method of indirect advice."

14.4 The king of Chu's minister Ziqi, offers direct advice, which the king refuses. The prime minister, Zixi, then offers indirect advice, which the king accepts.

14.7 "There are five men in this area who are more capable and virtuous than me and whom I have appointed as my advisers. They all guide me along the *dao*."

15.2 "There has never been a successful ruler who didn't have ministers of differing opinions to help him rectify his errors; likewise, for a father and his sons, an older brother and his younger brothers, and an up-and-comer and his friends. So, it is said that a ruler's errors are caught by his ministers; a father's errors are caught by his sons; an older brother's errors are caught by his younger brothers; one's own errors are caught by one's friends. When this occurs, countries remain whole, families remain harmonious, relations among father and sons and among brothers remain strong, and friendships remain solid."

15.19 "People who are not ready will not listen to good advice, just as a tree planted on unprepared ground will not thrive."

19.1 "Without advice from ministers, a leader of people will be unable to govern. Without guidance from friends, an up-and-comer will be unable to make good judgments."

19.6 "When Duke Ling of Chen engaged in dissolute behavior in court, Xie Ye advised against such behavior and was killed for it. This is similar to how Bigan died."

20.1 "If advisers were always listened to, Wu Zixu would not have been killed."
21.4 "If you are open to counsel from others, good advice will come daily."
22.10 Shi Yu's direct advice to King Ling of Wei went unheeded, and so upon his death, he instructed his son to leave his body outside his house instead of burying it according to proper *li*. When the king caught wind of this, he was so taken aback that he reflected on Shi Yu's previous advice and reformed his behavior. Confucius commented, "For the heroes of the past who were able to advise their sovereigns, they stopped at death. There has never been the like of Shi Yu, whose dead body continued giving advice."
25.1 "In ancient times, the king took his court advisers as his left and right hands."
29.3 "On the day of the prognostication, the king personally stands at the royal archery range, where he receives his mission, in order to show that he can listen to advice."
32.12 "With . . . advisers to his left and right, the king takes a position of non-action in the center."
37.3 When Fu Zijian was mayor of Shanfu, he was troubled by the duke's uninformed meddling. Fu Zijian requested the services of the duke's two beloved scribes, and while they were writing for him, he bumped one of them and then blamed him for poor writing. The scribe complained to the king, who then had an epiphany, vowing never to interfere in Fu's governing again.
41.7 The Chu high official Zige mentioned a poem to the king of Chu. The king asked Zige to recite it, after which the king was deeply troubled by it and subsequently reformed his behavior.

Dao 道

The term *dao* is the key distinguishing feature of pre-Qin Chinese philosophy and, as a technical term, is second only to *li* in its frequency in the *Dialogues*. Fundamentally, *dao* refers to how things should be, according to a cosmic standard that can be grasped by humans and applied through our ethical and political systems and behavior. The term can denote something as grand as a cosmic organizing force (4.2) and as minute as a method of swimming in roiling water (8.14). As in English, the concrete sense of way as a road or path was extended to refer to a way, or method, of doing something, but it retains an implicit normativity: *the* way is better than any alternative. This does not, however, imply a general sense of objective, one-size-fits-all natural law, for *dao* also retains a sense of particularity when it comes to any one person's individual path through life (e.g., 20.1, 26.1). Reconciling this tension between the general and the particular is one of the challenges of interpreting this multifaceted concept.

The term *dao* is often used by Confucius as a way of referring to social or political justice. The *dao* prevails (*you dao* 有道), or is followed, in a just society, and it goes into decline, or is not followed, in an unjust society. This is an identity relation, not a consequence relation. A just society is one in which the *dao* prevails, and vice versa. What is meant by *justice*? Fortunately, Confucius provides descriptions of what he means by societies that are just (7.4, 32.1) and those that are unjust (6.1, 25.1, 32.2).

1.1–3, 2.2, 3.1–2, 4.1–2, 5.3, 5.5, 6.1–2, 7.1, 7.4–6, 8.4–6, 8.9, 8.11, 8.14, 8.17, 9.3–5, 9.11, 10.1, 10.4, 10.10, 10.17, 11.1–2, 12.1, 12.15, 12.17, 12.21, 13.1, 13.3, 13.5, 13.7, 13.11, 14.3–4, 14.7, 15.1, 15.8–9, 15.14, 15.16, 15.21, 16.3, 16.6, 17.1–3, 18.8, 19.4, 19.7, 19.10, 20.1, 21.5, 21.7, 21.8, 22.1, 22.7, 23.1, 25.1–2, 25.4, 26.1–2, 28.1–3, 29.1, 30.1, 31.4, 32.1–4, 32.13, 32.15, 33.4, 35.3, 36.1, 37.3, 38.12, 38.17, 38.19, 39.3, 41.1, 41.15–16, 41.22, 41.25, 42.4, 42.6, 42.9, 42.12, 42.29, 42.31–32, 43.3, 43.6, 43.25–26, 44.2

Dao[54]

2.2 "It would go against all norms for superiors to lose sight of the *dao* and murder those below them."

3.1 "*Dao* is the way to illuminate *de*. And *de* is the way to venerate *dao*. *Dao* cannot be venerated without *de*, and *de* cannot be illuminated without *dao*. Take, for example, a great horse. If it is not treated according to its *dao*, it cannot be ridden across vast distances. Now consider a large country with multitudes of people. If they are not led according to *dao*, one cannot achieve the status of a superpower."

3.1 "This is what is called the *dao* of enlightened kings."

3.2 "States to which expeditions are sent will, of course, have already abandoned the *dao*."

4.1 "The most important thing in implementing human *dao* is good government."

4.2 "The *dao* of *tian* is like the unceasing movements of the sun and moon from east to west. The *dao* of *tian* is never obstructed and so is able to persist. The *dao* of *tian* is the spontaneity of processes that fulfills the nature of things. The *dao* of *tian* illuminates all things thus fulfilled."

6.1 "The elite defy the masses and attack people of *dao*."

7.1 "Look for those who live in the world of today while aspiring to maintain the *dao* of the ancients."

54. The ad hoc divisions in this section demonstrate the folly of trying to translate a word like *dao*, for even in English, the terms *way* and *path* are polysemic and ambiguous. However, making the divisions seems preferable to not making them.

7.1 "There are the levels of the commoner, the *shi,* the *junzi,* the *xian,* and the sage. Understanding these five is sufficient to be able to govern in accord with the *dao.*"

7.1 "Although he does not yet have the foundation to excel in the methods of the *dao.*"

7.1 "His *dao* is sufficient to transform the people."

7.1 "Through the dissemination of this great *dao,* selfhood is brought to full development."

8.4 "You are a natural-born *junzi* who just follows the *dao.*"

8.6 "When leaders achieve their *dao,* the people are orderly."

8.9 "Is this really the *dao* of a *ren* person?"

9.3 "What I'd like to ask you about is what to do if on one hand I try to properly practice the *dao* publicly but it is not accepted by society, or on the other hand I try to practice the *dao* privately but can't bear to do only that. If I don't wish to end up in trouble or to practice the *dao* in seclusion, is there a *dao* for me?"

9.3 "Don't contravene the *dao* when trying to display it."

9.4 "This is what is meant by the *dao* of reduction and further reduction."

9.5 "Confucius was observing a river flowing toward the east. . . . 'When it flows with an unstoppable force, it resembles the *dao.*'"

10.17 "Petty arguments harm *yi.* Petty words destroy *dao.*"

11.1 "He thoroughly understands the origins of *li* and music, and . . . he sees clearly the cycles of *dao* and *de.*"

11.1 "Confucius' *dao* was well respected and spread quickly."

11.2 "The *dao* of *tian* has no favorites."

11.2 "People like me possessing the *dao* offer our services to rulers, but our advice goes unheeded. The *dao* is so difficult to put into practice these days."

11.2 "Never forget the *dao.*"

13.5 "Merely obeying the leadership and following along with the times destroys the *dao.*"

13.11 "Sages can be attracted to immigrate by favoring *dao* and *de.*"

14.3 "Zhonghang Wenzi lost his country by violating the *dao* and abandoning *yi.*"

14.7 "There are five men in this area who are more capable and virtuous than me and whom I have appointed as my advisers. They all guide me along the *dao.*"

15.1 "A concern for posterity is the foundation of the *dao* of a stable society."

15.8 "As there is an increase (*yi* 益) in one's *dao,* there is a loss (*sun* 損) of one's self."

15.8 "Whenever the process of *tian dao* comes to maturity, it inevitably changes."

15.21 "I come to you with great enthusiasm to ask about the *dao* of serving a lord."

16.6 "Better than understanding him would be spreading his *dao* and enacting his transformative excellence."

17.1 "The *dao* of *tian* promotes life; the *dao* of people promotes governing; the *dao* of the earth promotes growth."

17.1 "There are five ways in this world of achieving *dao*. . . . The five ways are: lord-vassal, father-son, husband-wife, older brother-younger brother, and friend-friend."

17.2 "Cultivating yourself will allow the *dao* to be firmly established."

17.3 "Decide beforehand how to put the *dao* into action, and your success will be limitless."

17.3 "If those below do not feel supported by those above, the people will be impossible to govern. There is a *dao* for achieving support from those above—not being trusted by friends will result in not being supported by those above. There is a *dao* for being trusted by friends—not accommodating the wishes of one's parents will result in not being trusted by friends. There is a *dao* for accommodating the wishes of one's parents—not sincerely developing yourself upon introspection, you cannot accommodate the wishes of your parents. There is a *dao* for sincerely developing oneself—to not be clear about the good, one cannot sincerely develop oneself. Sincere development is the ultimate *dao* of *tian*. To sincerely develop something is the *dao* of people. To sincerely develop is to hit the mark without forcing it, to understand without overthinking, to effortlessly accord with the *dao*. It is how sages remain serene. Someone who acts on sincere development selects the good and stubbornly maintains it."

18.8 "Everyone understands the attractiveness of this *dao*, but none can set it in motion or put it into effect."

20.1 "Is there something wrong with my *dao* that it has come to this?"

21.7 "The transformative powers of the *dao* will continue to flow without obstruction."

22.1 "I am tired of studying and feel perplexed about the *dao*."

22.7 "I have begun putting myself below others but don't fully understand the *dao* of putting oneself below others."

25.1 "If the people have no self-discipline, they will be confused and lose their way. The high ancestors would certainly view this as disrupting the *dao* of *tian*. If the *dao* of *tian* is disrupted, the use of criminal punishments will soar, both upper and lower levels of society will resort to flattery, none will recognize the danger, and all will lack *dao*."

25.4 "A king must work with the *dao* when active and flow with the natural order when inactive."

26.1 "Differences in *dao* are called *fate*."
26.1 "One *yang*, one *yin*, the matching of odd and even—thereupon *dao* is unified and reproduction achieved."
26.2 "Following the *dao* of *tian*, men nurture the things in the world."
28.1 "If you have remained true to the *dao* to the age of eighty or above."
28.2 "How simple the *dao* of ruling really is."
28.3 "The *dao* of Wen and Wu is to be sometimes intense, sometimes relaxed."
29.1 "Sages illuminated the *dao* of *tian* through the Jiao sacrifice."
30.1 "To not slack in performing the sacrifices is the child's dao of attending to deceased parents."
30.1 "Achieving moderation through *li* is how to control the people's sensual desires, influence their tastes, and flow with the *dao* of *tian*."
31.4 "People were severely penalized for . . . throwing the government into turmoil by promoting heterodox *dao*."
32.1 "The Three Dynasties when the great *dao* flourished. . . . When the great *dao* flourished, impartiality reigned, capable and virtuous people were selected to lead, people were trustworthy, and strong relations were forged."
32.2 "These days, the great *dao* is obscured, and the entire land belongs to one family. People have feelings only for their own parents and look after only their own children. People hoard goods for themselves and put in effort to please others."
32.3 "*Li* is how the Ancient Kings inherited the *dao* of *tian*."
32.4 "When I look back at the *dao* of the Zhou."
32.13 "*Li* . . . is the broad way of attaining the *dao* of *tian* as well as flowing along with human emotions."
32.15 "*Tian* did not stint its *dao*; the earth did not stint its treasures; and people did not stint their emotions."
36.1 "To have the spirit of the landscape was to be earthy. To be stately and glorious was to be *de*. To be prized by all was to be *dao*."
38.17 "He was very knowledgeable and favored the ancient *dao*."
38.19 "He was poor and yet delighted in the *dao*."
39.3 "Confucius discussed the *dao* with him."
39.3 "It is a pity that you have not met an enlightened king who would allow you to spread your *dao* and *de* to all the people."
39.3 "Clarified the *dao* of the *Changes*."
39.3 "Now that the *dao* of Confucius has reached its ultimate expression, it will be spread without limit."
41.1 "Adhering to one's office is even better than adhering to the *dao*."
41.16 "King Zhao of Chu understood the general *dao*. It is fitting that he did not lose his state."

42.6 "The officials who came followed the *dao* of expressing gratitude for services rendered."
42.29 "Everyone practicing the *dao* has times when they can't bear something."
43.3 "The *dao* of father-son and sovereign-minister relationships."
43.6 "This seems to capture the *dao* of it."
43.25 "To use spirit items is to understand the *dao* of funerals."

Path, road, route, street

3.2 "In order for distant leaders to have their influence felt nearby, it is not that they must travel along roads but that their enlightened *de* be manifest."
5.3 "On roads, they don't jockey for the smoothest lane."
7.1 "He acts out of sincerity on the path of trustworthiness"
7.6 "Embark on a path of enlightened and nurturing rulership."
8.5 "And it was only after Nangong Jingshu got me a carriage that my path really began to open up. . . . Were it not for the gifts of these two, my own path was in danger of disappearing."
16.3 "Zhou King Wu . . . built roads throughout the land to all the frontier peoples."
37.3 "Qi invaded Lu, and their route passed through Shanfu."
41.25 "People with gray hair would not be left carrying burdens on the streets."

Way, method

1.2 "Lu uses the way of the *junzi* to guide their sovereign. You use the way of the barbarians to advise me."
4.1 "The grandfather of King Wen did this, paving the way for his kingdom and his family."
5.5 "They use the same methods as those constructing the Way."
6.2 "I once wanted to learn about the way of the Xia dynasty."
7.4 "What is the way to accomplish this?"
7.4 "If your court is conducted with *li* and upper and lower levels of society interact with mutual affection, then commoners across the land will see themselves as your people. Who will there be to invade? If you violate this way and the people naturally rebel, seeing themselves as your enemy, then who will be with you to protect the state?"
8.14 "You are very skillful. Do you have some certain method?"
12.15 "In his unwillingness to kill emerging insects, you can see his following a humane way."
15.9 "Would it be acceptable to set aside the ancient ways and simply follow one's own ideas?"

33.4 "The *weimao* hat is used in the way of the Zhou, the *zhangfu* hat is used in the way of the Shang, and the *wuzhui* hat is used in the way of the Xia."
35.3 "This is how the way of the Zhou reached the four directions."
38.12 "He was always mindful of the way of *xiao*."

Speech, things/behavior, custom, system, practice

7.1 "Without striving for excess eloquence, he pays close attention to his speech."
7.5 "They will both be willing to do detestable things to each other. . . . If a *junzi* does not deeply detest detestable behavior, he will also not deeply love excellent behavior. If he does not deeply love excellent behavior, then commoners will not feel profound affection for those above them. . . . This is how deeply the *Poems* loves excellent behavior."
42.12 "He conducted the proceedings according to Shang-dynasty custom."
42.32 "The system of ancestral lineage is always there."
43.26 "A double is part of the practice of the ancestral tablet."

Principle, natural principle, reason, standard

4.1 "There must have been some reason that the enlightened kings of the Three Dynasties were sure to respect their wives."
10.4 "It is a natural principle that, when you miss someone, you will cherish their special tree, and when you have a special reverence for someone, you will display deep respect for their place in the temple."
13.1 "There is also a high official by the name of Shi Qiu, who left Wei on principle."
20.1 "Having cultivated himself and established a moral foundation, a *junzi* does not alter his standards because of hard times."

Fairness (negated as corruption), just/justice, well, civic order

2.2 "Having displayed one's fairness and virtue for all to see, lead that way and the people will follow."
7.6 "Corruption was so rampant that the king's rule was about to be cut short."
8.6 "He attacked injustice."
8.17 "If horses are treated well, they will be tame livestock. If they are not treated well, then they will turn into enemies."
9.11 "When a government is thoroughly unjust, it is acceptable to go into seclusion. When a government is just, you need to don court vestments and reveal the jade."
12.17 "I've heard it said that in a just society capable and virtuous people are brought to prominence."

13.7 "Where is the just individual who is unable to humble himself before others?"
41.15 "The people were able to safeguard their livelihoods by respecting the civic order."
41.22 "Aspiring officials of the past worked conscientiously for the government when it was just but retired to avoid trouble when it was unjust."

To lead

12.1 "Confucius' method of instruction is to lead his students in with poetry and history."

De 德

The term *de* has been examined and explained by scholars in great detail (e.g., Graham 1989; Hall and Ames 1987; Nivison 1996b; Kline 2000). The wide range of connotations of *de* available in the *Dialogues* allows the reader to see the subtleties of the idea behind the term. In some important ways, the semantic web of *de* aligns with that of the English *virtue* as derived from the Latin *virtus*, which mirrors the Greek *arete*. All three terms refer fundamentally to a kind of efficacy within something. When that efficacy is positive, we refer to it as an excellence; and when that excellence has a moral quality, we refer to it as a virtue. But even the word *virtue* in English can retain the original sense of efficacy. For example, for 7.6 we translate, "By virtue of the sparrow, King Xin neglected to reform the government." *Virtue* in this passage is a translation of *de*. We often leave *de* untranslated because no English term (not even *virtue*) seems to adequately map its polysemy. Although it generally denotes virtue, it often goes beyond virtue toward a kind of moral charisma and a connection with the cosmic *dao*. Also, *de* often implies not merely a run-of-the-mill sense of virtue but a superlative sense, an internal natural excellence. We see in 10.1, for example, that under ideal conditions, even animals are able to express their *de*.

1.2, 2.2, 3.1, 3.2, 5.4–5, 7.1, 7.6, 8.1, 8.4, 8.8, 9.5, 10.1, 10.15, 10.18, 11.1–2, 12.1, 12.4, 12.9, 12.21, 13.11, 15.4, 16.3, 16.6, 16.9, 17.1, 17.3, 18.3, 18.8, 18.10, 18.12, 20.1, 21.3, 21.7, 23.3–4, 23.6, 24.2, 24.4–5, 25.1–4, 26.2, 27.1–2, 31.1, 32.9, 32.14–15, 34.1–2, 35.2, 36.1–2, 37.3, 38.1–4, 38.29, 39.3, 41.6–8, 41.12, 41.16, 41.24–25, 43.20

De

3.1 "*Dao* is the way to illuminate *de*. And *de* is the way to venerate *dao*. *Dao* cannot be venerated without *de*, and *de* cannot be illuminated without *dao*."
3.2 "Use compassion to make up for insufficiency; use *li* and self-restraint to curtail excess; stand by your word instead of putting on appearances. . . . In

order for distant leaders to have their influence felt nearby, it is not that they must travel along roads but that their enlightened *de* be manifest."

5.4 "Ruists . . . carry *ren* where they go and embrace *de* where they stay."

7.1 "Regarding the *xian*, his *de* never crosses the line, and his actions are right on target. His words are sufficient to serve as a model for all the world, without bringing harm to himself. His *dao* is sufficient to transform the people, without harming the root. . . . Regarding the sage, his *de* merges with heaven and earth; he changes and connects without premeditation; he sees all affairs through from beginning to end; he accords with the natural spontaneity of all things; and through the dissemination of this great *dao*, selfhood is brought to full development. His brightness rivals the sun and moon, and his transformations are spirit-like. The people below don't understand his *de*; even eyewitnesses can't make out its scope."

9.5 "In that [a river] ceaselessly spreads out to give life to all things, it doesn't do so actively; in this way, water resembles *de*. In flowing, it remains low and bends; this principle is worth cultivating in oneself; in this way, it resembles *yi*. When it flows with an unstoppable force, it resembles the *dao*."

10.1 "When Shun was sovereign, in his governing he valued life and detested killing. . . . His *de* matched the *de* of heaven and earth in his calm emptiness. . . . As a result, all within the four seas were affected by his powers, which flowed unimpeded to uncultured tribes. *Feng* soared and *lin* appeared, and the birds and beasts followed their *de*."

11.1 "If society fails to install the descendant of a sage, his *de* will still shine brightly across the era."

17.1 "The three ways of achieving *de* in this world are: wisdom, *ren*, and courage."

21.7 "The transformative powers of the *dao* will continue to flow without obstruction. Thus, governing begins in *de*."

25.1 "The reason nature looks on him with *de* and the people embrace him is that his governing is commendable and the masses esteem him."

25.3 "I have heard that in the *Changes* it says that each kind of living thing—people, birds, beasts, bugs—has its own even or odd number, which matches its original allotment of *qi*. Most people don't understand this. Only those who have achieved a high level of *de* are able to get to the root of it."

25.4 "Mountains represent accumulated *de*."

35.2 "Shun. . . . His *de*, which gushed like spring water, flows right down to today. . . . Shun started out as a commoner, and through accumulating *de* and possessing inner harmony, he ended as chief."

37.3 "Fuzi's *de* has had its effect. The people act in private as if the executioner were by their side."

Moral, virtue

1.2 "Such means are inauspicious, immoral, and improper. The sovereign would never do such a thing."

1.2 "A sumptuous banquet is for the purpose of bringing attention to the virtue of the sovereigns."

3.2 "Orders are subsequently followed, policies work, people embrace their virtue, the nearby happily pay allegiance, and the far away come to submit. They are the results of good government."

8.1 "'My ambition is to be a counselor to an enlightened sage-king, spreading the five transformative teachings, advising about ritual and music, making it so that the people don't have to build city ramparts or cross over moats. Instead, I would have swords and spears melted down and made into farming tools, and I would put oxen and horses out to pasture. No wife would have to worry about an absent husband, and the ravages of warfare and strife would disappear for a thousand years. . . .' Confucius said with gravity, 'Beautiful! This is virtue!'"

8.4 "A good official applies the law uniformly. With *ren* and compassion at the front of his mind, he engenders virtue. Severe or cruel intentions, on the other hand, engender resentment."

12.9 "*Xiao* is the genesis of *de*. *Ti* is its next step. Trustworthiness is the profound expression of virtue. Conscientiousness is its precise manifestation. Shen gets each of these four virtues just right."

18.8 "It is rare to see someone who favors strength over virtue and who comes to a good end."

20.1 "For a long time now, you have laid up virtue and borne *yi* in your breast."

20.1 "Having cultivated himself and established a moral foundation, a *junzi* does not alter his standards because of hard times."

31.1 "The highest form of governing uses virtue to teach the people and *li* to keep them well ordered."

Merit, favor

16.6 "In the good done by *li*, there is merit that accrues to one's ancestors, which does not allow for the temples to them to be destroyed. Dukes Huan and Xi were only distantly related to the Duke of Zhou, and they did not do anything in their lifetimes to accumulate merit sufficient to keep their temples intact."

18.10 "You have achieved *ren* when you never forget past favors and never dwell on past slights."

Power, contribution, virtue

7.6 "And so, by virtue of the sparrow, King Xin neglected to reform the government and instead piled cruelty on top of cruelty."

9.5 "The virtue of water is like this, and this is why a *junzi* never fails to stop and observe."

24.2 "Beginning with the power of wood to rule the land, kings follow in the same order."

24.4 "What was elevated was the power that was exploited for ruling. The sequence was as follows: The Xia people used metal for their ruling power; their color was black. . . . The Shang leaders used water for their ruling power; their color was white. . . . The Zhou leaders use wood for their ruling power; their color is red."

32.15 "Unions between women and men were created in the winter, and noble ranks were conferred in the spring, each according to appropriate age and contributions."

Dialogue

Dialogue is a literary form with a long tradition in the West that continues today. In Chinese literary history, there is also a long tradition, but it is rarely noted, which is odd because it goes all the way back to the *Analects*, the Chinese title of which—*Lun yu* 論語—was understood by the Chinese, James Legge tells us, as "Digested Conversations" (Legge [1893] 2012, 137). It is common to think of the *Analects* as a collection of sayings by Confucius, but Confucius was not spouting truisms; he was speaking to interlocutors, and his comments were targeted at the specific interlocutors. This is what makes them conversations, or dialogues, albeit brief ones.[55] In the *Mencius* and *Zhuangzi*, dialogues are embedded in larger essays. The Warring States text *Guo yu* is a collection of purportedly historical dialogues.[56] The Daoist "pure conversation" (*qing tan* 清談) of the Wei-Jin period culminated in the text *Shi shuo xin yu* 世說新語 (Old Tales and Fresh Conversations). In the Chan Buddhist tradition of the Song dynasty,

55. Mark Edward Lewis distinguishes two types of passages in the *Analects*: those that begin with an "enunciatory scene" (someone of authority says) and dialogues: "other passages [in the *Analects*] assume dialogue form in which a question is asked and answered, and sometimes a longer exchange takes place" (Lewis 1999, 57).

56. Chang I-jen, William Boltz, and Michael Loewe render the title into English as "dialogues or discourses of the state" (Loewe 1993, 263).

dialogues (called *wen da* 問答) are a common literary form. The dialogue tradition continued with neo-Confucians. So it shouldn't be controversial to say that China has a long tradition of the dialogue literary form,[57] and it should be even less controversial to consider this book an example of that form.

The dialogue, as a literary form, is distinct from the notion of dialectic, though the terms *dialogue* and *dialectic* are sometimes used interchangeably. Plato, for example, is known for his Socratic dialogues, but *dialogue* in this use is ambiguous. It refers to a literary form—the dialogue—that features the character Socrates, but what distinguishes a Socratic dialogue is the method of dialectic, which, according to Plato (*Republic, Phaedo*), is an ascent to the truth through a question-and-answer process of entertaining and then rejecting various positions. The opposing viewpoints and friendly antagonism in the dialectic method can also result in a conflation of the notions of *dialogue* and *debate*. Plato's dialogues often depict people debating, but the debating is not what makes them dialogues. For example, Plato's *Republic* and *Laws* adopt the literary form of the dialogue, but they are essentially disquisitions on the topic of political theory as it relates to philosophical anthropology, with little debating.

Was there a dialectic method in ancient China? There was certainly a tradition of debate or disputation (*bian* 辯). In fact, A. C. Graham's classic introduction to Chinese philosophy (Graham 1989) is based on this idea. He defines *bian* as "the distinguishing of the right alternative" (36)—in other words, getting at some version of the truth. Did early Confucians partake in *bian*? Absolutely, according to Ronnie Littlejohn and Qingjun Li (2022). This is evident in the *Mencius*, and it was common in the Jixia academy. Was the dialectic method of *bian* used by Confucius? Not exactly.

Confucius' use of the dialogue to get at a version of the truth requires a different route. According to Jeong-Gil Woo (2019), Confucius' use of dialogue, as depicted in the *Analects*, involves relationship-oriented communicativity, which rests on an assumption of responsivity; in education, one answers questions as a matter of course. In other words, there is a particularism in the philosophy of Confucius (Ames and Hall 2001; Van Norden 2007) that is not captured by a philosophical perspective that aims at general truths. This is the fundamental difference between a Socratic dialogue and a Confucian dialogue. For Plato, any two interlocutors can engage in dialogue to get at unchanging, impersonal truths. Platonic dialogue is truth-seeking. For Confucius, each dialogue is distinct because the interlocutors and

57. Donald Holzman (1956) traces this tradition from the *Analects* (which he calls the *Conversations*) right through to Wang Yangming 王陽明 (1472–1528). In an article on the role of dialogue in the *Analects*, Anthony Cua says, "The Confucian use of dialogues is a device to preserve the sense of the concrete—a testimony to the inherently dynamic spirit of Chinese philosophy" (1969, 33).

conditions are distinct, and thus the questions asked and the answers given will also be distinct (e.g., 14.1). Confucian dialogue is educative. That is not to deny the existence of universal truth for Confucians, but it also is not an affirmation of universal truth. Whether there are universal truths is not, we believe, a topic that would have interested Confucius.

The dialogues of Confucius, and the *Dialogues of Confucius*, are for the most part not dialectic in the sense of debate or in the sense of truth-seeking (though see 19.1 and 35.3), but they are dialogues in the sense of conversation and education. Education is a process of responding to particular needs of particular students (Dewey 1916) and is resistant to formulaic approaches. At the same time, because there are aspects of our society and our conceptions of philosophical anthropology that resemble Confucius' own (see, e.g., "Meritocracy," "Affection," and "Hierarchy"), the lessons conveyed in Confucius' dialogues are as relevant to our day as to his.

Differentiation

The term *bian* 辨/辯 straightforwardly means to distinguish, although *bian* 辯 can also refer to eloquence and disputation. It is easy to see how making distinctions and disputation are related, which also explains why the characters 辯 and 辨 are often used interchangeably. The term *bie* 別 means to separate, both physically and conceptually, and so it also refers to making distinctions. The idea of differentiation is central to Confucius' philosophy. Because of the emphasis on equality in contemporary Western philosophy, this emphasis on the making of distinctions may seem alien, but it really shouldn't. Contemporary notions of equality, or egalitarianism, generally rest on either ontological equality or on procedural equality of worth—no one person is fundamentally better than any other person, and so we all have the same basic obligations and rights. This contemporary notion of equality of worth does not preclude social differentiation. Parents and children, for example, have different rights and obligations vis-à-vis each other, as do employers and employees, government leaders and citizens, and so on. Although Confucius has no explicit theory of equal moral worth, his belief in meritocracy (see below) implies just such a tacit theory. What we see, then, is a theoretical inversion when comparing equality and distinctions between ancient China and the contemporary West. For early Confucians, social distinctions are explicit and equal worth is implicit. For us, social distinctions are implicit and equal worth explicit. We stress one and they stressed the other. However, one thing in the *Dialogues* that will grate on contemporary ears is the repeated use of *bie* to refer to distinctions between the sexes, with the conclusion from such distinctions that men and women belong in different spheres of activity.

Confucius stressed social differentiation because he believed that it is the foundation of *li*. We see this in many references—for example, in 6.1 and 28.2, both of which contain the terms *bie* and *bian*. Without distinctions there would be no *li*, and without *li* we would be at a loss about how to express directional virtues like *ren*, *ci*, *zhong*, and *xiao*. Consider the difference between the love (*ci*) that a parent shows a child and the love (*xiao*) that a child shows a parent. They both can involve the felt obligation of one to feed the other, but not at the same point in time. The parent will have a felt obligation to feed a small child, and an adult child will have a felt obligation to feed an elderly parent. Of course, it would be nearly impossible to fail to make such a distinction, but it is common for growing children to treat parents (among others) thoughtlessly. Repeatedly emphasizing the child's role in the household engenders due feelings of respect. Similar distinctions will apply outside the home, but these are not so straightforward, and they are dependent on those within the household. My feelings of respect for my grandfather will be much stronger than those I may feel for an elderly neighbor or an older stranger, but the explicit distinction of old/young inside the home is imperative in order to engender the feeling of respect for one's elders outside the home.

Confucius says that the virtue of *yi* allows for the making of distinctions (30.1). In this sense, *yi* seems to be a prerequisite of *li*.

Differentiation is as close to a theory of epistemology as we see in Confucius, and it is a necessary precondition of many facets of Confucius' ethical and political theory. Perhaps the easiest or most straightforward way to understand the importance of distinctions is in the contemporary political sphere, where we attempt to maintain the distinction between legislative and judicial prerogatives. Judges who are viewed as inappropriately making law are blamed for not clearly distinguishing their role from the role of legislators. By distinguishing roles, we also distinguish differential rights and obligations.

The term *ming* 明, which means bright or to make bright, also means clear by extension, and by further extension it can mean to clarify conceptually. We see this, for example, in 30.1.

Bian 辨/辯 6.1, 9.3, 27.1, 28.2, 36.3

6.1 "Without *li*, there would be no way to regulate and serve the gods of heaven and earth; to distinguish the positions of sovereign and minister, superior and subordinate, older and younger."

27.1 "Therefore, if you maintain *li* in your household, there will be clear divisions between elder and younger."

28.2 "The places of higher and lower status have thereby been distinguished."

36.3 "Because enlightened kings and sages of the past distinguished honor and age."

Bie 別 1.1, 1.3, 2.2, 4.1, 5.5, 6.1, 10.17, 13.1, 15.13, 17.5, 18.2, 24.3, 26.2, 27.1, 28.2, 29.2, 30.1–2, 31.2, 32.5, 32.9–10, 38.14, 39.2, 42.31

1.1 "Men and women maintained their distance in public."

1.1 "Confucius identified five different kinds of terrain."

4.1 "Separate spheres for husband and wife."

6.1 "Without *li*, there would be no way . . . to discriminate the proper interactions of men and women, parents and children, older and younger siblings, husband and wife, families and clans, or relatives and acquaintances."

6.1 "*Li* was used to regulate displays and clothing insignia in order to differentiate those of high honor and achievement from their counterparts . . . all for the purpose of . . . differentiating the distance of living relatives."

10.17 "In 'Chirp of the Osprey.' . . . A *junzi* appreciates the beauty of the poem and also learns about the natural distinctions of male and female."

13.1 "I've heard that Duke Ling doesn't display proper respect for differences in his own household."

17.5 "Setting standards in response to the nature of things, sages . . . built temples and altars so that sacrifices could be made at appropriate times of the year, thereby distinguishing close relatives from distant ones and teaching the people to remember the past and return to their beginnings."

18.2 "[The sound of someone's weeping] has something to do with parting in this life."

27.1 "Without *li* in the household, differences between elder and younger will be lost."

30.1 "Disrespect for higher-ups is caused by an absence of *yi*. *Yi* is how distinctions of status and worth are made and maintained. When distinctions of status and worth are made and maintained, the people will respect their superiors and revere their elders. The *li* of vassals meeting their lord is how *yi* is made clear. *Yi* must be made clear, and then the people will not transgress. And even though there may be statutes against disrespect, the people will not fall into the trap of criminal punishment by committing such a crime."

30.1 "Licentious sexual behavior occurs when the sexes are not differentiated into separate spheres, which leads to a loss of *yi* between husband and wife. Betrothal and wedding ceremonies are how the separate spheres of the sexes are maintained and how the *yi* of husband and wife is clarified. When the separate spheres of the sexes are maintained and the *yi* of husband and wife is clear, although there may be statutes against fornication, the people will not fall into the trap of criminal punishment by committing such a crime."

31.2 "In hearing criminal punishment cases. . . . Differentiations were made that involved discussing the gradient of severity and estimating the extent of the wrongdoing."

32.5 "If norms are disrupted, the differentiations upon which *li* is based will be lost. If such differentiations are lost, officials will no longer serve, and the people will no longer submit; such a country can be called defective."

42.31 "People are connected by their surname and thereby indivisible. If they need to help each other, they provide food without distinction."

Education

In the *Dialogues,* there is reference to three distinct forms of education: textual, characterological, and mimetic, all of which are vitally important to Confucius' overall philosophy. It is no accident that Confucius was known as an educator in his own time and is known today as China's First Teacher. The philosophy of Confucius is fundamentally a philosophy of education.

All three methods of instruction are evident in 12.1. Texts pertaining to poetry and speeches and events of earlier times "lead" the students. Specific virtues "guide" and "persuade" them, and modeling through *li* and music completes the process. These ideas are elaborated in 36.2, where the Six Classics are listed (see "Six Classics" in the glossary): the *Poems,* the *Documents,* the *Music,* the *Changes,* the *Li,* and the *Spring and Autumn,* which, respectively, make the people warm and sincere, knowledgeable and forward-thinking, pure with subtle and profound thinking, reverent and respectful, eloquent and historically aware, and broad-minded and kind. The overlap with contemporary liberal-arts education is readily apparent. The *Documents* and *Spring and Autumn* can be classed as history and politics, the *Poems* and *Music* would belong to the arts, the *Changes* qualifies as metaphysics, and the *Li* as ethics.

Section 36.2 is one of the few passages that discusses textual education for the masses. In the *Dialogues,* textual education most often appears in the back-and-forth between Confucius and his students, often with reference to direct quotations from the *Poems* or the *Documents.* One of the most revealing passages of the *Analects* in this regard is 17.9, which says that the *Poems* can help their reader in four ways: arouse, see, commune, and complain. First, they help arouse one's emotions; Confucius sees the human being as fundamentally emotional, and the poems stimulate emotions in positive ways. Second, they make us see more observantly by increasing our vocabulary and our awareness of the subtleties around us. Third, they help us live together harmoniously, exposing us to positive examples of others living together peacefully in the past. Fourth, they provide us with nuanced terminology and allusions to correct the behavior of others indirectly, thereby to complain without offending them (see "Consultation" above).

Emotions, for Confucius, are closely bound up with virtues and character. In fact, most virtues, for Confucius, have an affective component. Textual education is intellectual to the extent that it transmits knowledge and encourages reflection. In these respects, it also overlaps with contemporary liberal-arts education. The major ways that Confucius' idea of education differs from our modern ideal is in its emphasis on character-building and its emotional foundation. Texts can help in this process, and we see this largely through the many references to texts by Confucius to his students. In 22.1, for example, where Confucius repeatedly quotes the *Poems,* one of the quotations goes like this: "Be a model for your wife, / Extending to your brothers, / Thereby leading families and countries." For Confucius, this summarizes the mimetic aspect of education.

By *mimetic,* we don't mean intentional imitation, but rather the kind of emulation that young children engage in when they unconsciously absorb the behavior of those around them. Confucius sees mimetic education as common and pervasive, and this is why it is so important in his eyes for the leaders of society to act as models for others. We are constantly learning from those around us, and especially from those above us—all of whom thus have a special responsibility to act scrupulously and virtuously. There are often conversations in the *Dialogues* about the particular virtues (or lack of virtues) in specific people, past and present. Such conversations, rather than being gossip, are instead a method of learning and instruction.

There are key Chinese terms having to do with education in the *Dialogues. Jiao* 教 is the most common and most closely overlaps with the English *to teach* and *to educate,* but it also means to counsel. *Xun* 訓 means to train, instruct, or advise, and *hua* 化 means to transform or to reform. We see through the use of these terms that education is not just book learning for Confucius. It also includes skill-building and character transformation. We translate the "five *jiao*" (8.1, 25.2, 30.1) as the "five transformative teachings" because, as stated in 30.1, they are not just the transmission of knowledge but are intended to reform—or transform (*hua*)—the behavior of the people. Education, for Confucius, transforms the individual from an unformed, uncivilized, uncultured simple creature to a virtuous and learned member of a harmonious society. We see education used often in the *Dialogues* in the context of criminal punishment, with the suggestion that the best way to reduce unwanted behavior is through education, which includes reforming the behavior of the elite, who are educative models of proper behavior. *Xue,* to study or to learn, in Classical Chinese also means to imitate. See also "*Fa*" below.

Although Confucius was educating students who were often associated with the elite or aspired to enter the realm of the elite, his philosophy of education was not elitist. Sources of learning could come from anywhere, including children (14.6) and animals (10.17, 14.6, 18.2, 22.2). He also believed that education involved rationally scrutinizing existing ideas (see, e.g., 41.26) and that ideas for political reform could come straight from the people (41.10).

Three other relevant terms, not indexed here, are *wen* 聞, which means to hear and by extension to learn (e.g., 10.15); *wen* 問, which means to ask or to inquire; and *qu* 取, which means to choose and by extension can mean to choose to learn something (10.17).

Hua 化 2.2, 3.1, 4.1, 7.1, 8.6, 9.5, 10.1, 10.5, 10.18, 15.15, 16.6, 21.7, 23.3, 30.1, 31.1, 35.2, 37.3

To transform, to reform, to educate

2.2. "There may still be some wicked ones who refuse to be transformed."
3.1 "I'll tell you about true kings, who can transform the world without even stepping outside."
4.1 "From your person to their persons; from your children to their children; from your wife to their wives—a sovereign fosters these three, and as a result he has a transformative influence across the land."
7.1 "Regarding the *xian*. . . . His *dao* is sufficient to transform the people, without harming the root."
8.6 "The Duke of Zhou put himself out there in his efforts to transform the people, and the whole world followed him."
15.15 "Living with a good person is like entering a flower-scented room—after a while, you don't notice the fragrance, but you absorb it as your own [i.e., are transformed by]. Living with a bad person is like entering a fish stall—after a while, you don't notice the stink, but you absorb it as your own."
21.7 "If a commoner commits a serious offense, seek the reason, and use *ren* to help them reform."
30.1 "The Three Kings and the Five Chiefs transformed the people [by reforming *li*], even though criminal punishment was there for them to use."
31.1 "The transformational government of the sage requires the interplay of both criminal punishment and good governing. . . . Criminal punishment is used in cases where a person refuses to reform through instruction."
35.2 "By cultivating this music for the purpose of educating the people, [Shun's] rise was rapid. His *de*, which gushed like spring water, flows right down to today."
37.3 "Fuzi followed the duke's order and gained complete control of his government. Shanfu was subsequently well governed. He personally acted honest and sincere, he clarified the importance of being close to one's parents, he elevated kindness and respect, he spread *ren* far and wide, he spurred sincere integrity, and he acted with utmost conscientiousness and trustworthiness. The people were transformed by him."

Jiao 教 1.2, 2.2, 3.1, 6.1, 7.2, 7.6, 8.1, 8.8, 8.17–18, 9.2, 9.7, 10.5, 10.10, 11.1, 12.1, 12.21, 13.9, 14.7, 15.10, 15.18, 17.4–5, 19.1, 19.5, 21.1, 21.7, 23.1–3, 25.2, 26.2, 29.3, 30.1–2, 31.1, 32.5–6, 35.3, 36.2–3, 38.10, 38.23–24, 39.3, 41.24–26, 42.31, 43.3, 43.12

To educate, to instruct, to guide, transformative teaching, teaching, method of instruction, instruction, education

2.2 "If those in charge are not doing their jobs educating the people, it's not the fault of the people. . . . [E]ducation must come before punishment. . . . Teachings are in disarray, and punishments proliferate, confusing the people and luring them into traps."

6.1 "*Junzi* have taken [*li*] as a way to effect reverence and respect, exploiting its efficacy in instructing and ordering the common people so that they do not destroy the rhythms of their relationships."

8.1 "My ambition is to be a counselor to an enlightened sage-king, spreading the five transformative teachings."

8.17 "When a sage does something, he doesn't act simply on personal whims, because his actions may change the customs of the day and his teachings may spread widely among the people."

10.10 "People followed without being led and acted without being instructed."

12.1 "I've heard that Confucius' method of instruction is to lead his students in with poetry and history, to guide them with *xiao* and *ti*, to persuade them with *ren* and *yi*, and to model for them with *li* and music, culminating in cultured and virtuous individuals."

12.21 "Zhao Wenzi . . . was *xiao* toward his parents, reverential toward his brothers, and he selected the path of excellence without being taught to do so."

13.9 "To help [the people] live long, emphasize *li* and education and make harsh punishments few and far between."

14.7 "Your treating three people with the respect due to a father teaches by example the virtue of *xiao*. Your treating five people with the respect due to an elder brother teaches by example the virtue of *ti*."

14.7 "They all guide me along the *dao*."

15.10 "I offended you, and it took all your strength to teach me a lesson."

17.5 "A *junzi* remembers the past and returns to his beginnings, never forgetting that from which he sprang. In this way, he expresses respect and proper emotion, giving his all in his service, always pushing himself to the limit. This is called the great teaching."

23.2 "He instructed the masses in how to regulate their inner selves."

23.3 "Chief Ku . . . touched the people through his instruction, benefitting them greatly."

30.1 "Clarifying the *li* of mourning ceremonies is how to instruct people in *ren* and love, which in turn will cause people to don mourning attire and lament the deceased."

31.1 "The highest form of governing uses virtue to teach the people and *li* to keep them well ordered."

35.3 "These six were the major forms of education. . . . [T]he noble lords were taught how to act as proper younger siblings."

36.2 "You can tell a country's level of education as soon as you enter. If the behavior of the people is warm and sincere, they've been educated in the Poems. If they are knowledgeable and forward thinking, they've been educated in the Documents. If they are broad-minded and kind, they've been educated in the Music. If they are pure and their thinking subtle and profound, they've been educated in the Changes. If they are reverent and respectful, they've been educated in the Li. If they are eloquent and historically aware, they've been educated in the Spring and Autumn. However, if the Poems are studied superficially, people tend to be naive. If the Documents are studied superficially, people tend to scheme. If the Music is studied superficially, people tend to be extravagant. If the Changes is studied superficially, people tend to be dishonest. If the Li is studied superficially, people tend to be convoluted. If the Spring and Autumn is studied superficially, people tend to be rebellious."

36.2 "There are four seasons—spring, summer, fall, and winter—with wind, rain, frost, and dew; all are instructive. Weather patterns flow across the land—winds rise and thunder claps, affecting every creature on earth; all are instructive."

36.2 "The instructions of nature are intertwined with the sage."

36.3 "Zizhang asked about how sages teach. Confucius said, 'Shi, let me tell you about it. A sage merely clarifies *li* and music, brings them to public attention, then implements them.'"

41.25 "In the instruction of the sage kings, respect for elders inside and outside the family was promulgated starting from the palace to pedestrians on the street, to villages, to hunting parties, to the military. In this way, everyone felt it to be the *yi* thing to do, and no one would dare violate it their whole lives."

41.26 "Elders who refuse to teach and youth who refuse to learn are bad luck for society."

42.31 "It is up to our generation to instruct in the ways of harmony. It is an instruction from the Former Kings that cannot be altered."

43.12 "In ancient times, a son of nobility had a mentor outside the household and a motherly figure inside the household who were designated to teach the child."

Model behavior

3.1 "Safeguarding can occur once the seven kinds of model behavior are cultivated . . . cultivating the seven models of behavior internally conserves effort in leadership."

3.1 "'What are the seven kinds of model behavior, if I may ask?' Confucius replied, 'When the people above venerate the aged, it increases *xiao* among the people below. When the people above respect their elders, it increases respect for elder brothers among the people below. When the people above take joy in sharing wealth, it increases generosity among the people below. When the people above befriend capable and virtuous people, the people below also become more judicious in choosing friends. When the people above appreciate *de*, the people below are not secretive. When the people above shun corruption, contentiousness becomes shameful among the people below. When the people above are scrupulous and deferential, the people below become moderate. These are what are called the seven kinds of model behavior, and they are the root of governing the people. When models of behavior are set in the government, the people will be set right. The people above are examples for the people below. If the examples get it right, what will not be right?'"

To advise

1.2 "You use the way of the barbarians to advise me."

Xun 訓 7.1, 10.2, 14.8, 25.2, 39.3, 42.1

Training, instruction

25.2 "Crisis occurs when the soil is not cultivated, when finances are not ample, when the people are hungry and cold, when teachings and trainings are not circulated, when customs are perverted, or when the people emigrate."
42.1 "Having a vassal calling a king to him is not a good model for instruction."

Advice, to correct

10.2 "If it weren't for the king's wisdom and capability, he would never have been willing to listen to Shen's advice."
14.8 "You'll never form close relationships with others by disparaging them in public instead of correcting them in private."

Xue 學 1.1, 3.1, 5.2–5, 8.10–11, 9.2, 9.7, 10.15–16, 12.2, 12.7–9, 12.11, 12.13, 12.21, 13.7, 14.5, 15.8, 15.14, 16.4, 17.1, 18.5, 18.7, 19.1, 19.4, 20.1, 22.1, 28.1, 31.4, 32.8, 32.12, 32.14, 35.1, 35.3, 38.9–10, 38.24, 38.40, 41.2–3, 41.17, 41.26, 43.3

To study, to learn, learning, education

5.3 "Ruists . . . study night and day."

5.4 "Ruists study widely without limit."
8.10 "When I was younger, I loved to learn."
8.11 "Isn't it true that the effects of learning are the only thing that in the end will earn fame that reaches the four corners of the land and extend even to one's descendants? So a *junzi* must study."
9.2 "If you do not study when young, you will be incapable as an adult."
9.7 "Failing to industriously study when young and then as a result having nothing to teach when old—I consider this shameful."
10.15 "A *junzi* has three worries: to not have the opportunity to hear something worth hearing about; having heard about it, to not have the opportunity to study it; having studied it, to not have the opportunity to put it into practice."
12.7 "You can see his wisdom in his fondness for learning."
12.8 "If you want to learn the art of attending well to a guest, study with Chi."
12.13 "Wishing to hone his talent, he studies."
12.21 "He took ignorance as an opportunity to learn."
14.5 "That's why I take them both as elders to learn from and why I admire and respect them so much."
15.8 "As there is an increase in one's *dao*, there is a loss of one's self. One loses a sense of self-importance and uses the humility of emptiness to learn from others."
17.1 "Having a fondness for learning is akin to wisdom."
19.1 "I was asking what ability you have that could be brought to a higher level through study."
32.8 "What is meant by *human feelings*? Delight, anger, sorrow, fear, preference, aversion, and desire—these seven are unlearned abilities."
32.14 "Human emotions are the fertile ground of sages and kings, who . . . weed it by teaching. . . . Trying to enact *yi* without paying due attention to education is like sowing but not weeding. To pay attention to education but not match it with *ren* is like weeding but not harvesting."
35.1 "Confucius studied the zither with Shi Xiangzi."
38.40 "Beginning the process of education when still young is like creating inborn nature."
41.17 "I have studied how to conduct ceremonial sacrifices. I have not studied how to engage in armed conflict."
41.26 "Elders who refuse to teach and youth who refuse to learn are bad luck for society"
43.3 "When a crown prince learns well, the people of the country see it."

To imitate

10.16 "I take my inability and imitate Liuxia Hui's ability."

Knowledge

5.2 "I've heard it said that while a *junzi's* knowledge is far-reaching, his clothing stays closer to home."

School

32.12 "The three elders in schools."

Fa 法

The term *fa* means norm in the broadest sense. A law is a norm to be followed, as are a teacher, a rule, a way, a standard, an order, and a method. But each is followed in a different way, with different parameters of strictness. A key passage that helps put this ambiguity in perspective is 21.3: "When the normative model has been internalized, it is never far away, like a natural spring that never ceases flowing." The Chinese *fa xiang* 法象 (normative model) is explained in the glossary. Here, we are interested in the internalization of normative models. For Confucius, laws are not desirable as ways to control people's behavior because they offer only extrinsic motivation. Education (see above), on the other hand, is an intrinsic control of behavior because through the natural psychology of imitation, one internalizes external models of behavior. In 25.1, a norm (*fa*) is conceived as just such an internalized standard, which is contrasted with penal law. A norm has to be worth following, not just out of punishment. In this sense, norms inculcate self-discipline. Compare *Li* below.

1.1, 1.3, 2.2, 3.2, 5.4, 7.1, 7.3, 7.6, 8.4, 8.17, 9.5, 10.18, 13.3, 13.8, 14.8, 21.2–4, 22.5, 24.1, 25.1–2, 29.3, 30.1–2, 32.4–5, 32.12, 32.14, 38.14, 39.3, 41.2, 41.5, 41.15, 41.23, 42.8, 42.21, 43.3, 43.12

Method

1.1 "How about if we spread your methods throughout Lu?"
3.2 "Enlightened kings of the past employed methods that guaranteed boundaries."
7.3 "Please tell me about a method for selecting people."
10.18 "Where are there people who cannot be transformed by employing a leadership method such as this?"

Law, rule, penal system

1.1. "He created laws that only rarely needed to be applied."
1.3 "There was also a man named Shenkui, who lived a life of extravagance outside the law."

2.2 "We may think the penal system is effective, but can common people avoid falling afoul of it?"
5.4 "They always take harmony as the basis of *li* and adhere to rules even in leisure."
8.4 "A good official applies the law uniformly."
8.17 "The state of Lu had a law that funds required for ransoming back a citizen of Lu enslaved in another state could be sought from the Lu state treasury."
9.5 "In [water's] remaining level while at rest, it resembles the law."
14.8 "Someone who knows how to be an official benefits the people by respecting the law. Someone who is ignorant of how to be an official harms the people by perverting the law."
25.2 "Even if all leaders were the same in their officials and laws, some would achieve peace while others would end in turmoil. The difference would lie in how they handle their direction and speed."
30.1 "The cause of fraud, thievery, lawlessness, and recklessness is scarcity."
30.1 "If moderation through *li* has been put on full display and the five transformative teachings have been taught in their entirety and yet the people falter and fail to reform, you must clarify the laws, promulgate them, and enforce them."

To take after, model, exemplar, to model

7.1 "[The *xian*'s] words are sufficient to serve as a model."
13.3 "Jie . . . forgot the *dao* of the sages and ancestors, he destroyed their models of good behavior, and decimated the sacrificial rites passed down to him."
21.3 "When the normative model has been internalized, it is never far away, like a natural spring that never ceases flowing."
21.4 "When you model proper behavior in your own person, the people will follow."
22.5 "If I, having inherited the ways of the Ancient Kings and favoring the ancient exemplars, still incur disaster, that is not an error on my part but is due to circumstance."
24.1 "Ancient kings changed their dynastic periods following the model of the elemental phases."
29.3 "As prominent as the sun and moon, taking after heaven itself."
42.8 "When Zang Wenzhong managed the government of Lu, he left behind written models of excellent speech that are still with us."
42.21 "An excellent mourner. He can act as a model."
43.12 "If you go through with it, it would be in violation of the ancient *li* and upend the state's role as a model of behavior."

Norms

25.1 "Virtue and norms are tools for controlling the behavior of the people, like a bit and bridle for controlling the behavior of a horse."

25.1 "Someone who cannot guide the people abandons virtue and norms, using only criminal punishments."

25.2 "If virtue is abundant, that means norms are well honed. If virtue is not abundant, then reform the norms, by which you can bring all virtues to government without decline."

25.2 "An official who is capable of virtue and normative behavior is considered to have *de*. An official who is capable of acting according to virtues and norms is considered to have proper behavior. An official who is capable of bringing virtue and norms to full development is considered to have accomplishments. An official who is able to govern with virtue and norms is considered to have wisdom. Therefore, by evaluating the virtues, norms, and behavior of his officials, a leader ensures that things are put in order and accomplishments are made. It is essential that norms be reformed in the last month of the year and officials be evaluated in the first month of the year."

32.4 "When the nobility held agrarian and ancestral sacrifices, those at each level made offerings to their forebears, and the performer of the rite dared not alter the long-standing norms."

32.5 "If the position of the ruler is precarious, high ministers may turn on him, lower ministers steal, punishments turn grave, and customs be lost, disrupting norms. If norms are disrupted, the differentiations upon which *li* is based will be lost. If such differentiations are lost, officials will no longer serve, and the people will no longer submit; such a country can be called defective."

32.12 "With *li* performed in the five sacrificial ceremonies, norms are set right."

39.3 "Confucius . . . compiled the *Poems*, retold the *Documents*, set the form of the *Li*, organized the *Music*, wrote the *Spring and Autumn*, and clarified the *dao* of the *Changes*—all in order to preserve them for later generations as norms and models. His refinement and *de* are thus visible to all."

Strategy

41.2 "I only learned about the fighting strategy by happenstance."

Fate

There is an interesting parallel between the English word *order* and the Chinese word *ming*. *Order* comes from the Latin *ordiri*, meaning to initiate or maintain in an organized arrangement, especially with respect to persons or narrative events. *Order* thence becomes a verb for the transfer of intentions of arrangement and a noun for the arrangement itself. In Chinese, *ming* begins with the sense of a transfer of intention from a hierarchical position of power, and by extension comes to mean the organized circumstances resulting from that intention. Thus, in both English and Chinese, *order/ming* acts as both noun and verb to convey the intention of creating order and the ordered circumstances themselves.

In Chinese, there is an added complexity in the association of *ming* with *tian*. A key theme of the *Documents* is the justification by King Wen that the tyrannical behavior of Shang King Zhòu justified the transfer of *tian ming* from the Shang to the Zhou. *Tian* fundamentally means sky, and by extension an anthropomorphic power abiding in a celestial realm. Later, into the Spring and Autumn period, *tian* became increasingly paired with *di* (earth) to refer collectively to the anthropomorphic powers of the cosmos, and gradually to mean just the cosmos itself, or nature.[58] Thus, *tian*, depending on the context, can refer to an intentional spirit-like cosmic power or to the workings of nature, or to an ambiguous intermediate sense. *Ming*, by its association with *tian*, also transitioned from meaning circumstances ordered by a spirit-like cosmic power to meaning the accumulated circumstances of an ordered cosmos, with an emphasis on the circumstances as being unavoidable—hence the common translation as *fate* or *destiny*. Both senses of *ming*—the anthropomorphic cosmic sense and the naturalistic cosmic sense (and the ambiguity between them)—are evident in the *Dialogues*.

Confucius addresses the topic specifically in 26.1 and indirectly in 7.6, and these are where we see a key difference between the idea of fate in early China and the more familiar sense of fate from the Greek tradition. Whereas the Greeks emphasized the end-state of a cosmic plan (e.g., Oedipus would murder his father and marry his mother), the early Chinese (in addition to emphasizing a certain position after the accumulation of circumstances, as in 38.3) emphasized *ming* as a beginning. In other words, it may have been your fate to have been born a prince and mine a pauper, but that is only the starting point. What we do with that fate is up to us. Hence, *ming* can also mean life, as in a lifespan. We see a vivid example of the indeterminate perspective of *ming* in 7.7, where Confucius describes three ways in which one can unnaturally (*fei qi ming* 非其命) shorten one's life by making poor choices. A more determinate perspective can be seen in 8.9. In 7.7, things are not yet settled, and one's choices going forward can alter circumstances in a way that matters. In 8.9, nothing that one does can alter what has happened already.

58. Lothar von Falkenhausen (2006) observes from archaeological evidence a radical change in buried ritual bronzes in the late Western Zhou around 850 BCE, when there appears to be a de-emphasis of religious beliefs. Perhaps this was the beginning of the transition of *tian* from divine power to natural order.

***Ming* 命** 1.2–3, 3.2, 4.2, 5.3, 7.1, 7.6–7, 8.9, 9.9, 11.1, 12.4, 12.16, 12.18, 12.21, 13.5, 14.9, 15.4, 16.2, 16.4, 17.4–5, 20.1, 21.6, 22.2, 22.5, 22.9–10, 23.5, 26.1, 27.2, 28.1, 29.3, 30.2, 31.3, 31.5, 32.6, 32.13, 33.2, 35.3, 38.3, 38.12, 38.31, 39.1, 41.3, 41.6, 41.14, 41.16–17, 41.21, 41.27, 42.11, 42.26, 42.28, 43.1, 43.8, 43.12

To order/designate/proclaim/determine/ask/decide, ordination, edict, rules

1.2 "This cannot be something the Qi sovereign ordered other lords to do."
1.3 "Confucius ordered Shenju Xu and Yue Qi to lead a group of soldiers in a counterattack."
7.6 "The good and ill that happen to states and families are truly designated by *tian* and are not just in the hands of people."
9.9 "How can *xiao* mean for a son to merely follow the orders of his father? How can devotion mean for a minister to merely follow the orders of his sovereign?"
11.1 "My father once proclaimed his wishes, saying . . ."
12.21 "He adjusted his behavior in anticipation of determinations from *tian.*"
15.4 "Majestic, regal, lofty heaven / Its ordinations never untoward."
16.2 "The ruler of Wu sent an emissary to Lu to ask about the bone but said, 'Don't tell him I asked.'"
21.6 "When officials understand the inclinations of the people and work with their emotions, the people will be able to follow edicts."
31.3 "To demonstrate the seriousness with which he handled cases, the king would also take into account the three exculpatory factors in deciding a case and setting the punishment."
41.16 "According to the rules of sacrifice handed down by the founders of the Three Dynasties, one does not sacrifice beyond the purview of one's kingdom."

Royal

31.5 "The prohibited items were: royal or noble vestments and carriages . . ."

To name, to establish

16.4 "They named things after features of people's lives."
17.5 "Sages clearly established the terms *gui* and *shen* as guideposts for the people."

Appointment/employment/job, to hire

11.1 "Nodding in my first appointment, bowing halfway in my second, bowing deeply in my third."

12.21 "If the sovereign is just, accept employment. If the sovereign is unjust, reject employment."
14.9 "Everyone did their jobs."
41.14 "When he heard how Wei had hired Jia Xin, he considered it in line with conscientiousness."

Duty

17.4 "The people will prioritize their duty to the state."

To be born with, natural, unavoidable circumstance, fate/destiny

7.1 "Just as we are born with this one body, there is no substitute."
7.7 "There are three kinds of unnatural death."
8.9 "His lack of concern over his executed family shows his ability to evaluate unavoidable circumstances."
20.1 "One's behavior is a matter of one's own; one's life and death are a matter of circumstance."
22.2 "It is fate that I don't cross here."
22.9 "It must be destiny!"

Life

13.5 "They may even lose their lives for trying."

Hierarchy

The concept of hierarchy is closely related to the idea of differentiation (see above). Confucius believed that, from birth to death, we are constantly moving through hierarchies, and that we must learn to play the various roles at each stage of these dynamic processes. The key hierarchy is the family, and the key virtues are *xiao* in the children (including adult children) and *ci* in the parents. In society, especially in the government bureaucracy, the analogs are *zhong* in the lower strata and *ren* in the upper strata. We can think of it this way: *xiao* is to *ci* as *zhong* is to *ren* (*xiao*:*ci*::*zhong*:*ren*). Sections 6.1, 6.2, 26.4, and 43.17 are examples of passages that explicitly link the familial hierarchy with the government hierarchy. He also believes there are five stages as one moves up through society: commoner, *shi*, *junzi*, *xian*, and sage. Each of the stages and each of the directional virtues is philosophically significant in its own right, and so each has its own individual lexicon entry. (See "*ci*" under the entry for "Love.") Section 7.1 provides definitions of the five stages. Section 21.4 describes three tiers of the government hierarchy: sovereign, officials, and the people. The term for *family* is *jia* 家 (not indexed here, but see "*qin*" under

"Affection" above). Terms for government hierarchy (*official, sovereign,* etc.) are not indexed. See also "*Li*."

Deng 等 3.1, 6.1, 6.2, 17.1, 24.5

Hierarchy

3.1 "Have people practice *li* across every level of the hierarchy, establish it with *yi,* put it into effect agreeably, and then the people will reject bad behavior like hot water poured over snow."

6.1 Confucius said, "From what I've learned, *li* is the most important thing in the lives of the people. Without *li,* there would be no way to regulate and serve the gods of heaven and earth; to distinguish the positions of sovereign and minister, superior and subordinate, older and younger; or to discriminate the proper interactions of men and women, parents and children, older and younger siblings, husband and wife, families and clans, or relatives and acquaintances. For this reason, *junzi* have taken it as a way to effect reverence and respect, exploiting its efficacy in instructing and ordering the common people, so that they do not destroy the rhythms of their relationships. Once everyday affairs had been made productive in this way, *li* was used to regulate displays and clothing insignia in order to differentiate those of high honor and achievement from their counterparts, as well as those higher and lower in the hierarchy. Once this system was functioning smoothly, it came time to speak of the norms of funeral rites, the ordering of ancestors and gods inside temples, the grades of animals used in sacrifices, the display of sacrificial items, and the setting of dates of special occasions—all for the purpose of displaying respect during sacrificial ceremonies, differentiating the distance of living relatives, and ordering the placement of deceased relatives in the temples, and finally having the reunion feast for the whole clan. Each person could thus take heart in their social position, the bonds of beneficence and responsibility having been fastened. The leaders themselves were modest in their dwellings and frugal in their clothing and jewelry, refrained from commissioning elaborate carvings on their vehicles or ornate designs on their tableware, and didn't seek out rare delicacies or harbor hedonist aspirations. In this way, all the people reaped the same benefits. This is how the enlightened kings of the past put *li* into effect."

17.1 "*Li* arises out of the hierarchy of affection for one's parents and respecting capable and virtuous [*xian*] people."

Shangxia 上下 3.2, 4.1, 5.5, 6.1–2, 7.4, 13.5, 17.5, 21.7, 25.1–2, 27.2, 32.4–5, 34.1, 36.3, 42.18

Above and below

3.2 "The people below will feel close bonds to the people above, like young children to their loving mother."

6.2 "These rituals were for the purpose of calling down spirits in order to converse with the ancestors, for maintaining the relations between sovereign and minister, for deepening the relations between parents and children, for strengthening the relations between older and younger siblings, for ordering the relations between those above and below on the hierarchy, and for prescribing the proper roles for husband and wife." They called this "receiving the blessings of tian."

42.18 "This wife of Jisun truly understands *li*. Full of love and selflessness, she makes the perfect display up and down the hierarchy."

Independence

Although Confucius valued playing one's role conscientiously in our various hierarchies, one's loyalty to one's role was not viewed as unconditional. One should serve in government, for example, only when the government is sufficiently just and when one can make a significant contribution. And although valuing customary behavior (see "*Li*" below) may seem to imply valuing conformity, Confucius speaks against conformism.[59] In 41.10, we see an early instance of the public square and the importance of taking the voice of the people seriously in government policies. Key Chinese terminology include: *zi li* 自立, 5.3–4; *te li* 特立, 5.3; and *te li du xing* 特立獨行, 5.5.

The following examples are of the concept of independence, not just of specific terminology:

5.3 "Ruists . . . don't engage in corrupt behavior—so doesn't that make them hard to keep?"

5.3 "Ruists can be entrusted with goods and not desire them. They can be inundated with pleasures but not indulge in them. They can be menaced by mobs without flinching. They can be stopped by soldiers without cowering. They can face down personal advantage without compromising their *yi*. They can

59. William Theodore deBary saw in Confucius something resembling a liberal reformer:

The enduring value of humane experience was affirmed by Confucius in his efforts to conserve what was best in traditional culture. In this sense he could be called conservative. But Confucius was, at the same time, liberal in viewing past ideals and models as the basis for a critique of existing institutions and as a reminder of the greatness of which man was called by Heaven. . . . Confucian reformism was inspired by a positive commitment to human welfare and informed by a critical attitude toward established institutions which reflected an awareness of alternative possibilities for improvement. (1983, 7–8)

stand firm in the face of death. They neither regret the past nor worry over what is to come. Misspoken words are not repeated, and gossip is never pursued. They neither compromise their authority nor plot for more power. This is how they stand apart."

5.4 "Ruists take conscientiousness and trustworthiness as their armor, and take *li* and *yi* as their shield. They carry *ren* where they go and embrace *de* where they stay. In these they do not change, even under oppressive governments. This is their independence."

5.4 "Ruists study widely without limit, act devotedly without fatigue, don't slack even when alone, and don't get caught up when associating with elites."

5.5 "Ruists purify themselves by bathing in *de*. They speak their piece and then lie low. They quietly make matters right. If those above or below don't know what to do, Ruists hold their tongue and offer a helping hand, without expecting immediate results. . . . In times of good government, they don't take it for granted, and when things break down, they don't take part in the destruction. They neither gravitate toward those who agree with them nor repudiate those who disagree. This is how they stand apart and achieve independence."

5.5 "There are times when Ruists serve neither king nor lords. . . . Even if offered an entire state to themselves, they would consider it a mere trifle, refusing to be subject to anyone."

7.4 "If your court is conducted with *li*, and upper and lower levels of society interact with mutual affection, then commoners across the land will see themselves as your people. Who will there be to invade? If you violate this way and the people naturally rebel, seeing themselves as your enemy, then who will be with you to protect the state?"

9.9 "How can *xiao* mean for a son to merely follow the orders of his father? How can devotion mean for a minister to merely follow the orders of his sovereign? *Xiao* and devotion mean being able to thoroughly understand what one is following."

10.16 "To aim for the greatest good without conforming to others' behavior—this is wisdom."

11.2 "If others all rush over there, I alone stay over here. / If others all move to one place, I alone refuse to go."

12.21 "Not only does a sovereign select a minister to employ, but a minister also selects the sovereign to work for. If the sovereign is just, accept employment. If the sovereign is unjust, reject employment."

13.5 "Merely obeying the leadership and following along with the times destroys the *dao*. . . . When you try to do right in a world gone wrong, you are labeled deviant, if not downright monstrous."

20.1 "Having cultivated himself and established a moral foundation, a *junzi* does not alter his standards because of hard times. . . . [A] *junzi* who is especially skilled at cultivating the *dao,* with strong mainstays and supporting principles, need not be accepted by everyone. . . . Not being accepted is a sign of being a *junzi*."

20.3 "I have heard that those who receive gifts from others end up fearing them, and those who give them end up acting imperious. Even if the sovereign does not act imperious toward me for having given me the gift, how could I still not fear him?"

41.5 Confucius praises a historian who records an event that is unflattering to the prime minister.

41.17 "A bird selects the tree. Where is the tree that selects the bird?"

41.21 A mother admonishes her son rather than complying with his wishes (per the principle in 26.2).

41.22 "Aspiring officials of the past worked conscientiously for the government when it was just but retired to avoid trouble when it was unjust."

41.23 "There is relentless greed, so even if there were a new tax on fields, it would not be enough. If Jisun wants a method for taxation, the Zhou example is right there for him to follow. If he wants to go against it and act carelessly, why ask for my advice?"

Junzi 君子

In the ladder of moral achievement that Confucius lays out in 7.1, *junzi* is the middle of five rungs. The term in Chinese has a fortuitous overlap with the English *gentleman,* in that both originally referred to the nobility and came by extension to refer to someone who aspired through one's behavior to belong to the respectable upper class (see 4.2). For this reason, some also translate the term as *noble person,* playing on the dual meaning of *noble*. Roger Ames (2021) prefers *exemplary person* as a translation, emphasizing the modeling of virtuous behavior that Confucius says is intrinsic to this role. The level of the *junzi* is the most practical goal for Confucius' students, and what it is and how to achieve it are major topics of discussion. The level of *shi* is the starting point for one's journey to *junzi,* and the level of *xian,* just above the *junzi,* is a bit too elevated and laudatory to actually aspire to. The *junzi* is a leader who is continuously learning. The status of *junzi* is often associated with the virtue *ren*. The opposite of the *junzi* is the small-minded person.

Chapter 21 is a discussion on the topic of working in a government supervisory position, and in six out of the eight sections the path to success is couched in the language of the behavior of the *junzi*. Confucius concludes the chapter, "This is the ultimate way to govern the people, a primer for the person entering officialdom."

1.2, 2.1, 4.1–2, 5.2, 6.1, 7.1, 7.5, 8.3–4, 8.11, 8.13, 9.1–3, 9.5, 9.8, 9.10, 10.5, 10.8, 10.10–15, 10.17–18, 11.2, 12.2, 12.5, 12.12, 13.5, 13.7, 14.8, 15.1, 15.3, 15.5, 15.7, 15.14–15, 15.16, 15.18, 15.20–21, 17.1, 17.5, 18.1, 18.5, 18.9–11, 19.1, 19.4–5, 19.8–9, 20.1–2, 21.1–3, 21.5-.6, 21.8, 22.1–4, 23.1, 27.1, 29.3, 30.2, 31.1, 32.14, 35.1–2, 36.1, 37.1, 37.3, 38.13, 41.1, 41.3, 41.23, 42.5, 42.7, 42.12, 42.16, 43.5, 43.15, 43.18, 44.6

4.1 "A *junzi* is never without respect."

4.2 "Being a *junzi* means making a name for yourself. When you have made a name for yourself in the eyes of the common people, you are called a *junzi*. In this sense, you have made your parents into *jun* (nobility), and you are their *zi* (child)."

6.1 "*Junzi* have taken [*li*] as a way to effect reverence and respect, exploiting its efficacy in instructing and ordering the common people, so that they do not destroy the rhythms of their relationships."

7.1 "There are five levels of achievement. There are the levels of the commoner, the *shi*, the *junzi*, the *xian*, and the sage. . . . Regarding the *junzi*, his speech is always conscientious and trustworthy, harboring no resentment. He expresses *ren* and *yi* in his person without showing any sense of arrogance. His thoughts are penetrating and far-reaching, without getting caught up in any one thing. He acts out of sincerity on the path of trustworthiness, firm and confident without rest, as effortlessly as if others might be able to pass him but in the end cannot."

7.5 "A *junzi* behaves in ways that result in excellence for those around them."

9.8 "Yan Hui said, 'A wise person naturally understands. A *ren* person naturally cares.' Confucius said, 'This is the response of . . . a *junzi*.'"

10.5 "The *junzi* of the past took conscientiousness as their basic makeup and *ren* as their defense."

10.11 "A *junzi* is just familiar enough to bring about happy interactions and just serious enough for proper *li*."

10.13 "A *junzi* does his utmost in expressing respect for others."

11.2 "A *junzi*, understanding the impossibility of lording over others, keeps below them / Understanding the impossibility of leading others, keeps behind them."

15.5 "Minzi's sorrow was not yet forgotten, and yet he was able to use *li* to control it. Zixia's sorrow was completely worked through, and yet he was able to use *li* to extend it. Despite the differences, is it not right to label them both *junzi*?"

15.14 "There are four ways in which Hui conducts himself in the *dao* of the *junzi*: he is aggressive when it comes to putting *yi* into practice; he is docile when accepting admonishment; he is guarded when it comes to expecting an official salary; and he is cautious when it comes to governing his own person. There are three ways in which Shi Qiu conducts himself in the *dao* of the *junzi*: he respects his superiors even when not in office; he respects the spirits of his deceased ancestors even when not worshipping; he is strict with himself but lenient with others."

17.5 "A *junzi* remembers the past and returns to his beginnings, never forgetting that from which he sprang. In this way, he expresses respect and proper emotion, giving his all in his service, always pushing himself to the limit."

18.5 "Yan Hui asked about the *junzi*. Confucius said, 'Love is akin to *ren*, and moderation is akin to wisdom. A *junzi* understands this and is someone who neither takes himself too seriously nor takes others lightly.'"

18.9 "A *junzi* speaks with his actions."

18.10 "The way a *junzi* treats friends is that, when he knows in his heart that a friend has done something wrong, he cannot say, 'I didn't realize.' Such is a *ren* person."

18.11 "A *junzi* attacks his own faults, not the faults of others."

19.9 "A *junzi* admires people for abilities that exceed his own. . . . a *junzi* encourages the talents of others"

20.1 "A *junzi* never feels troubled. . . . Having cultivated himself and established a moral foundation, a *junzi* does not alter his standards because of hard times. . . . [A] *junzi* who is especially skilled at cultivating the *dao*, with strong mainstays and supporting principles, need not be accepted by everyone. . . . Not being accepted is a sign of being a *junzi*."

20.2 "A *junzi* cultivates himself, and before he encounters success he delights in the prospect of success. When he succeeds, he delights in the governing. In this way, a *junzi* is joyful his whole life, without a single day of anxiety."

27.1 "There is nothing in a *junzi*'s life for which there is not *li*."

35.2 "The music of a *junzi* is gentle and mild, possessing a sense of vitality and nurturance."

42.7 "A *junzi* should not make a superior feel threatened or a subordinate feel pressured."

43.5 "A *junzi* does not mourn to the point of illness or emaciation."

43.18 "A *junzi* does not accept support from people who engage in nefarious acts, does not participate in inciting disorder, does not profit from evil deeds, does not serve others for illicit purposes, does not cover up behavior that violates *yi*, and does not commit behavior that violates *li*."

Li 禮

Thomas Kuhn (1970) said that the most difficult thing about working with a paradigm of the past is understanding how otherwise intelligent people could attach importance to things we find relatively unimportant today. No one would deny that there is a certain social importance to etiquette and some ceremonies, but for most people they don't rise to the level of philosophical significance in contemporary society. What are the complexities, after all, of how an emcee toasts a guest, or how loudly one should wail at a funeral ceremony? For Confucius and early Confucians, such things were of profound importance and subtle complexity.

During the 2020 pandemic, when schools and offices closed and people were advised to curtail social interaction, we suddenly realized the profound significance of birthday parties, graduation ceremonies, weekly family dinners, and even the common handshake. Although none of these existed as such in early China, they are all examples of what Confucius would call *li*. *Li* are the norms, rules, and customs that guide social interactions. For Confucius, they are essential not just for harmonious social interactions but also for governing.

To see the significance of *li* for Confucius, we can draw a parallel between excess in our day and excess in Confucius' day. Excess in our day takes the form of hyperconsumerism and a concomitant disregard for such things as its environmental effects. Excess in Confucius' day took the form of the luxurious lifestyles of the ruling class (e.g., 41.7). Although these two kinds of excess are distinct, they are both rooted, Confucius would say, in natural human desires. An important function of *li* for Confucius is scaling back those desires. An important message from Confucius for our times is the role of the ruling class in this process. While excess in his day was not possible for the average person, he believed that the average person was still affected by the excess of the ruling class—in two ways. The most obvious way was that excess at the top leads to scarcity at the bottom. Another important way, and one that has implications for us today, is Confucius' belief that regular people take their behavioral cues from the most prominent people in society (see "Education" and "*Fa*" above). A disregard for moderation of desires in the ruling class becomes emulated by the people, leading to crass, dissolute behavior, as opposed to thoughtful, caring behavior.

Li, for Confucius, are all those time-tested customs that help us channel our natural emotions and desires in moderate, productive ways. We shake hands as a demonstration of good will. Holding a funeral ceremony allows for the expression of sorrow. Weddings are opportunities for expressing joy as well as avenues for the pairing of two people, which channel erotic desires while providing a basis for the loving interactions that are a family. See 42.18 and 42.21 for examples of Confucius' appreciation of the display of emotion through *li*.

We see a tension, however, between carrying out custom and expressing emotion. Confucius is confronted many times with the question of whether such-and-such a behavior is in accord with *li*. His fundamental criterion appears to be whether the behavior is an expression of sincere emotion. Lacking justification to contravene *li*, he seems to assume that one should follow established custom. But when there is evidence of sincere emotion, or when there is no established custom, sincere emotion trumps purported protocol. The function and purpose of *li* for Confucius, then, is to provide an outlet for desire and emotion while simultaneously moderating desire and emotion so that they are not disruptive or destructive. Notice in 42.16, for example, how he allows for a minor to be honored with the funeral ceremony of an adult under special circumstances. In 42.14 and 42.31, by contrast, he seems to stick inflexibly to ritual protocol. In both passages, the explanation may lie in the elevated position of the people in question, who should naturally act as examples for everyone else.

As stated above, Confucius is not a cultural elitist. He believes that any customary expression of sincere emotion appropriate to the situation is acceptable. In 43.11, for example, he mentions two Yi brothers, members of an ethnic minority, who presumably follow their own distinct customs and yet appropriately express sorrow for their deceased parents. And in 42.26, Confucius seeks to learn of the *li* of another distinct set of cultural customs from the state of Wu, expressing his approbation in the final sentence. In 35.2, he says that the south had preserved some ancient musical traditions better than his own region had.

With respect to exact protocol, there appears to be some tension in the text with regard to how exacting one should be. For example, in multiple passages (e.g., 1.3, 32.4, 42.8, 42.13, 42.14, 42.17, 42.31, and 43.22), Confucius comes off as an unforgiving stickler for detailed ritual protocol. Taken in isolation, such passages paint an unattractive picture of Confucius, rendering him largely irrelevant to philosophical conversations today. However, in the full context of the *Dialogues*, we see—also in multiple passages (e.g., 27.2, 42.12, 42.20, 42.25–28, 43.6, 43.11, 43.20, and 43.27)—that there is more to *li* than exacting protocol. Underpinning the protocol are feelings, which are expressed through the *li* in customary ways. Violations of custom are thus revelatory of a lack of genuine feeling. Because Confucius believes that bonds of affection are what hold society together, a lack of feeling is indicative of a breakdown in society. That said, Confucius can also be forgiving in certain circumstances. Not everyone has to be perfect all the time, but the onus is on those with more power in the hierarchy, because they are models for those below and have the power to affect people's lives. Notice in 43.15 that Confucius excuses a young up-and-comer, and in 42.25 he excuses anyone afflicted by poverty. In several passages (e.g., 42.24, 42.28, 43.15), Confucius' students object to violations of protocol and Confucius overrides their objections. In 30.2, he exempts common people who are too busy with their daily affairs from bothering with the petty details of ritual protocol. In 42.4, the protocols of *li* are modified during a famine. In 42.12, Ziyou chides Confucius for altering custom in a funeral ceremony (the most important of customs), and Confucius' retort is that it must be conducted "according to what is fundamental, and that's all there is to it." In 43.6, Confucius says, "*Ren* is what guides *li*. Thus, one must look inside oneself for *li*. For *li*, there is no guide to follow or deviate from, there is no absolute excess or deficiency. You simply follow *yi* and do what is appropriate."

For Confucius, there seems to be a dynamic relationship between emotion and *li*. While genuine feeling underpins, informs, and is expressed via *li*, *li* at the same time modulates, channels, and moderates the emotional expression. The goal for Confucius is to strike an exquisite balance in both emotional and ritual expression, one that also fits the practical and relational circumstances. Afflicted by poverty? Scale back. Distantly related? Scale back. Particularly affectionate bonds? Over-expression may be warranted, but not necessarily for those higher in the hierarchy who are models for those lower down, since those lower down may get the wrong impression and not understand the basis of the violation. You can see Confucius confronting the criterion of balance in the following passages: 10.11, 15.5, 26.4, 42.17, 42.25, 42.29, 43.6, 43.7, 43.9, 43.13, 43.20.

It's important to recognize that *li* is, in a sense, a one-size-fits-all solution, and yet every situation has its unique aspects. Confucius recognizes this and provides for allowances, although not necessarily appreciatively. See, for example in 42.23 and 42.24, his distinct responses to two individuals regarding the ending of the three-year mourning period for parents. In 42.24, a "man of Lu" begins singing on the very first day. In 42.23, Meng Xianzi has a ceremonial rack of bells and chimes all ready for playing and yet does not have them played. Both of these responses are acceptable for Confucius. The three-year mourning period is designed to allow people sufficient time to work through their bereavement, but Confucius recognizes that it will be sufficient for some and not for others. It was sufficient for the man of Lu but not for Meng Xianzi.

If that is true, then why does Confucius praise Meng Xianzi and backhandedly criticize the man of Lu? The potential differences across situations and individuals can be many and varied. Meng Xianzi may have a deeper level of self-cultivation than the man of Lu. Occupying a higher position, he may have a greater obligation as a model to those below him. He may have had a better relationship with his parents. And so on.

In 18.2, we see a family sell a grandson in order to pay for a grandfather's burial. In 42.25, Confucius offers a principle that would relieve the family of such a burden—namely, express *li* within one's economic means. And in 42.27, he contrasts the level of *li* appropriate to wealthy and poor families.

Li is far and away the most common technical term in the *Dialogues*, appearing 328 times, and whole chapters (i.e., 6, 27, 32, 33, 42, 43, and 44) are devoted to the topic of *li*. The terms *li* and *music* often occur as a pair, as if they had one and the same meaning. The way that music spreads emotion among those present helps us see how *li* does the same. The functions of music and *li* are, in this sense, equivalent.

The social basis of *li*, for Confucius, lies in the notion of differentiation, as is evident in 6.1. (See "Differentiation" above.)

1.1–2, 3.1–2, 4.1, 5.4–5, 6.1–2, 7.2, 7.4, 8.1, 8.11, 8.13, 9.9, 10.11, 11.1, 12.1, 12.4, 12.7–8, 12.15, 12.22, 13.9, 14.3, 15.1, 15.5–6, 15.9, 15.16, 15.21, 16.5–6, 17.1–3, 17.5, 18.1, 18.3, 18.12, 19.2, 19.5, 20.1, 21.1,

22.4–5, 22.10, 23.4, 25.2, 26.2, 26.4, 27.1–2, 28.1, 29.2–3, 30.1–2, 31.1, 32.1–8, 32.10–15, 33.1–3, 34.1, 35.3, 36.1–3, 37.2, 38.9, 38.23, 39.3, 40.1–2, 41.3, 41.7, 41.11, 41.17, 41.20, 41.23, 42.2–5, 42.8, 42.11–13, 42.15, 42.17–18, 42.22–23, 42.25–31, 43.2–3, 42.6–8, 43.11–12, 43.14–16, 43.18, 43.20, 43.22, 43.24, 44.1, 44.6, 44.7

3.2 "Use *li* and self-restraint to curtail excess. . . . Ultimate *li* is that by which the whole land is well governed without the need for deference."

4.1 "In the governments of ancient times, the most important thing was caring for others. The way to implement caring for others was through *li*."

5.4 "They always take harmony as the basis of *li* and adhere to rules even in leisure."

6.1 "From what I've learned, *li* is the most important thing in the lives of the people. Without *li*, there would be no way to regulate and serve the gods of heaven and earth; to distinguish the positions of sovereign and minister, superior and subordinate, older and younger; or to discriminate the proper interactions of men and women, parents and children, older and younger siblings, husband and wife, families and clans, or relatives and acquaintances."

12.8 "The three hundred rules of *li* can be learned with effort, but performing them three thousand times with due dignity and solemnity is truly difficult. . . . All of this can be accomplished through the simple act of attending well to a guest."

13.9 "To help [the people] live long, emphasize *li* and education and make harsh punishments few and far between."

15.1 "Grief is the foundation of the *li* in mourning customs."

15.6 "Respect is *li* without the ceremony."

17.1 "*Li* arises out of the hierarchy of affection for one's parents and respecting capable and virtuous people. *Li* is the root of good governing."

17.2 "Understanding the circumstances of lower officials will cause them to repay you with deeply felt *li*."

17.5 "Expressing feelings from top to bottom—that is the ultimate achievement of *li*."

27.1 "*Li* is the system for getting things just right . . . *li* is something that can prevent misbehavior and guarantee good behavior. . . . *Li* is the managing of affairs. . . . *Li* is where we find system and measure, where we find civility and good behavior, but actually putting *li* into effect is up to each individual."

30.1 "Achieving moderation through *li* is how to control the people's sensual desires, influence their tastes, and flow with the *dao* of *tian*."

30.2 "What is meant by saying that *li* is not expected of the common people is that the common people are so busy with their daily affairs that they are unable to be complete in their *li*. And so they were not expected to attend to every facet of *li*."

31.1 "The highest form of governing uses virtue to teach the people and *li* to keep them well ordered."

32.2 "*Li* flourishes in concert with nature. If someone is in power without proceeding from *li*, it will lead to calamity."

32.3 "*Li* is how the Ancient Kings inherited the *dao* of *tian*, how they governed people's emotions, how they maintained proper rankings of ancestors and gods, and how they performed proper funerals, village archery events, coming-of-age ceremonies, weddings, and audiences with the sovereign. Thus, when the *li* of sages is properly displayed, states and families throughout the world are able to achieve order through *li*."

32.7 "The common people govern themselves by virtue of modeling after the sovereign, achieve stability for themselves by supporting the sovereign, and bring themselves to prominence by serving the sovereign. This is how *li* is achieved and everyone's place decided."

32.8 "Other than through *li*, how can a sage govern such that the seven emotions are managed, the ten *yi* are cultivated, trustworthiness is promoted and strong relations are forged, deference is inculcated, and contentiousness is eliminated? He must be mindful of the primary desires for food, drink, and sex and of the primary aversions to death, poverty, and hardship. Desires and aversions are the two primary human motivations. They are concealed in people's hearts and unfathomable. With pleasure and aversion in people's hearts but not visible in their expressions, absent *li*, how can they best be channeled?"

32.13 "If one wishes to destroy a country, annihilate a family, or put an end to a person, first eliminate *li*."

32.14 "The sage refines the haft of *yi* and the ordering of *li* to govern human emotions. Human emotions are the fertile ground of sages and kings, who plow it by developing *li*. . . . *Li* harmonizes different *yi*."

32.15 "The differentiation inherent in *li* allowed for emotions to be supported and crises averted."

42.11 "There is *li* even in killing others."

42.18 "This wife of Jisun truly understands *li*. Full of love and selflessness, she makes the perfect display up and down the hierarchy."

42.22 "*Li* is such that things can be transmitted, they can be passed on."

42.25 "It is *li* enough to prepare the body for burial and expeditiously bury it according to one's means, absent an outer coffin. What is so harmful about poverty?"

42.27 "In a funeral, it is better to have an excess of sorrow and a lack of *li* than to have an excess of *li* and a lack of sorrow. In a sacrificial ceremony, it is better to have an excess of reverence and a lack of *li* than to have a lack of reverence and an excess of *li*."

42.29 "When the Ancient Kings established the system of *li*, those who exceeded the standards had to cut back, and those who couldn't achieve them had to try harder."

42.31 "We keep order with respect to the ancestors by paying due reverence to them according to their position in the family hierarchy. We keep order with respect to our descendants by building close ties with them. It is up to our generation to instruct in the ways of harmony. It is an instruction from the Former Kings that cannot be altered."

43.6 "*Ren* is what guides *li*. Thus, one must look inside oneself for *li*. For *li*, there is no guide to follow or deviate from, there is no absolute excess or deficiency. You simply follow *yi* and do what is appropriate."

43.7 "If a host does not lead with *li*, a guest will not wholeheartedly express *li*. If a host wholeheartedly expresses *li*, how could a guest dare not wholeheartedly express *li*?"

43.20 "Gongfu's mother was wise. After analyzing human behavior, she curtailed the over-expression of *li*."

Love

Three passages in the *Analects* speak to the topic of love generally:

- Confucius said, "To lead a large state, be respectful and trustworthy in your affairs, be frugal in expenditures, love others, and work the people at the right times" (1.5).
- Confucius said, "A student should be the good son at home and the good younger brother outside, should be cautious and trustworthy, should overflow with love for the people, and should befriend persons of *ren*" (1.6).
- Fan Chi asked about *ren*. Confucius said, "Love others" (12.22).

These passages are not at all ambiguous, and they clearly demonstrate the importance of the notion of love in Confucius' philosophy. And yet they are rarely discussed or highlighted. Perhaps this is because the idea occurs only a few more times in the *Analects* and is not amplified by Mencius or Xunzi. In the *Dialogues*, we do see an amplification, which suggests that these unambiguous passages in the *Analects* deserve more attention than they have received thus far.

The term *ai* has a wide range of connotations, from cherishing a loved one, to concern for distant relatives, to admiring a colleague, to caring for the populace, to undertaking an investigation with care and concern, to a culinary preference. As in English, where *love* is an intensification of *like*, *ai* in classical Chinese is an intensification of *hao* 好 (a preference for something). This is evident in lists of emotions across the early corpus, in which *ai* is interchangeable with *hao* (e.g., 32.8) and paired with its opposite *wu* 惡 (to dislike or detest). Because *love* in English can be a distant emotion without action, and *care* in English can imply action without emotion, and yet *ai* in classical Chinese sometimes connotes both emotion and action, we occasionally translate *ai* as *to love and care for* (e.g., 41.24) or *loving care* (15.17).

The term *en* 恩 is a less common term denoting love, but also with a fairly broad range—from fondness for one's parents, to the beneficence of a leader, to gratitude.

Ci 慈 and *xu* 恤 are more focused. *Ci* is a loving kindness or compassion from someone with more power or resources to someone with fewer. Most commonly, it refers to parental love, but it can also be used in the context of leadership. Generally, *ci* and *ren* are analogous, with *ci* used in the home and *ren* outside the home. *Ci* and *xiao* are love in opposite directions, *ci* from parents to children and *xiao* from children to parents.

Xu also means to love and care for, with a special emphasis on tenderness and empathy. It can be expressed from a parent to a child, but also—in a charitable sense—from a caring person with resources to a person without resources. (See also "Affection," "*Ren*," "*Zhong*," and "*Shu*.")

***Ai* 愛** 3.2, 4.1–2, 5.3, 8.18, 9.8, 10.4, 12.21, 13.1, 13.4, 13.10, 14.5, 15.17, 17.4–5, 18.5, 18.9, 21.2–3, 21.5, 23.5, 26.4, 30.1, 31.2, 32.7–8, 32.15, 34.2, 37.3, 38.15, 41.12, 41.24, 42.10, 42.18, 42.32

To love, to care for, to care, to cherish

3.2 "There is no greater *ren* than loving others."
4.1 "In the governments of ancient times, the most important thing was caring for others."
4.2 "You cannot fulfill yourself if you care about governing but don't care for the people."
9.8 "A wise person naturally understands. A *ren* person naturally cares."
10.4 "It is a natural principle that when you miss someone, you will cherish their special tree."
13.1 "Duke Ling's younger brother, Prince Qumou, has the wisdom to rule a large state and the trustworthiness to protect it. The duke employs and cherishes him."
13.10 "Someone who cherishes others is cherished by others. Someone who despises others is despised by others."
21.2 "Care for them without being too lenient in punishments."
21.5 "If you love and care for them, you will survive. If you detest them, you will perish."

26.4 "The resourcefulness that one brings to displaying love for one's father one should also bring to displaying love for one's mother."

34.2 "Look at the reverence of the Zhou people for the the Earl of Shao. They loved him and especially revered the tree under which he rested."

37.3 "Wuma Qi asked [a fisherman who was throwing back fish], 'People fish for the purpose of getting fish. Why are you letting them go?' The fisherman said, 'The big ones were *chou*, which our officials love.'"

41.24 "He used his own carriage to help people cross a river during the winter. This is love and care, not formal instruction."

42.10 "The people are pleased with those who love and care for them. Such a leader is invincible."

To stint

32.15 "*Tian* did not stint its *dao*; the earth did not stint its treasures; and people did not stint their emotions."

To admire

14.5 "That's why I take them both as elders to learn from and why I admire and respect them so much."

Loving attitude, loving concern, loving care, love, concern

8.18 "A loving attitude combined with compassionate treatment can help you embrace people in dire straits."

15.17 "If you are affluent and esteemed and yet can extend loving care to others, who will not draw close to you?"

17.4 "If you establish love by beginning with your own parents, you can teach the people to have strong relationships."

18.9 "A *junzi* may agitate people when advancing a cause of *yi* but otherwise treats them with loving concern."

30.1 "Clarifying the *li* of mourning ceremonies is how to instruct people in *ren* and love."

31.2 "All efforts were made to obtain eyewitness accounts and to maintain conscientiousness and concern."

42.18 "This wife of Jisun truly understands *li*. Full of love and selflessness, she makes the perfect display up and down the hierarchy."

42.32 "Although the sovereign is in an exalted position, he demonstrates his love and respect for his relatives by not disclaiming them even after a hundred generations."

Loved, beloved, favorite things

17.5 "These taught the people to foster the root, return to the beginning, and honor loved ones."
17.5 "The depth of his yearning was so profound that it was as if he could see his parents' favorite things."
37.3 "He sent his beloved scribes with a message for Fuzi."

Ci 慈 3.2, 6.2, 8.9, 12.21, 17.4, 21.3, 27.1, 32.8, 32.12, 43.12

(Parental) love, loving

3.2 "The people below will feel close bonds to the people above, like young children to their loving mother."
32.8 "What is meant by *human yi*? Love on the part of a father, *xiao* on the part of a son."

Compassion, love and compassion, kindness

6.2 "One to express *xiao* to the ancestors and one to show love and compassion to descendants."
12.21 "There was also Liuxia Hui. He was *xiao*, reverent, compassionate, and *ren*."
17.4 "Teach them to be kind and to build strong relationships."
27.1 "Flattery is the theft of compassion and *ren*."

Sympathy

8.9 "His own family was decimated in Qi, and he didn't seem at all concerned. This shows a lack of sympathy."

En 恩 6.1, 26.4, 38.12, 43.24

Beneficence, magnanimity

6.1 "Bonds of beneficence and responsibility having been fastened."
43.24 "The magnanimity he extends by doing so is incalculable."

Fondness

26.4 "A child with deep fondness for his parents displays it in mourning apparel, wearing simple, rough clothing for three years on their behalf. This custom stems from fondness. In the conduct of a household, fondness outweighs *yi*. Outside the home, *yi* outweighs fondness."

Gratitude

38.12 "Shen's stepmother responded to his assistance without gratitude."

Xu **恤** 3.2, 12.7, 14.7, 23.5

To give aid

3.2 "The poor and destitute were given aid."

To treat with tenderness, to take good care of

12.7 "He is respectful to the old and tender to the young."
14.7 "In regard to my governing, if a father takes good care of his children, his children will take good care of the disadvantaged and attend properly to funerals."

To empathize with

23.5 "He empathized with those far away and attended to those nearby."

Meritocracy

In 7.1 we see the five stages of accomplishment (see "Hierarchy" above), and in chapter 5 we see the disciplined, virtuous, and hopeful *Ru* prepared for taking on a post in the government (see "*Ru*" below). Both are indicative of the belief in Confucius' time that any man could enter the government and serve at the highest levels. Confucius was viewed as a teacher (see "Education" above), who could help ambitious young men improve their prospects.

Although the term *meritocracy* is of relatively recent origin in English, we see in the *Dialogues* that the Chinese had a term for it quite early. The term is *xianzheng* 賢政 (3.2)—government by the capable and virtuous.[60] The implication is that one's socioeconomic background and status in the hierarchy are unimportant when being considered for an administrative position. What matters is one's competence and virtue.

According to Confucius, meritocracy is the ideal form of government and can be traced back to the earliest Chinese rulers. In chapter 23, the Five Chiefs are discussed.

60. Though the term itself is extremely rare in early texts and is not recognized as a word in Chinese dictionaries, it is not uncommon in secondary literature on early Chinese philosophy. The Qing-dynasty translator Yan Fu 嚴復 used the term *xianzheng* as a translation of Aristotle's *aristocracy*, emphasizing the cultural sophistication of the rulers as opposed to their social status.

They are legendary heroes commonly extolled across the early Chinese corpus. In Confucius' description, one follows another as the paramount ruler of China, but in none of the cases is the rulership post passed from father to son. Each of these heroes is described as a man of great ability, innovation, wisdom, and virtue. Shun, the one who appears most commonly throughout the *Dialogues* as Confucius' particular favorite, was also apparently born a commoner; Confucius says he was a fisherman and a potter.

Coming chronologically after the Five Chiefs, Confucius' model rulers are the Three Kings, the founders of the Xia, Shang, and Zhou dynasties. Yǔ succeeded Shun and began the Xia dynasty. Eventually, the Xia went into decline, and the corrupt last ruler was conquered by Tang, the founder of the Shang dynasty. The cycle repeated, and Zhou King Wu conquered the Shang. Though Confucius never directly repudiates the monarchical system, he says repeatedly that a sovereign should have all the virtues of a great leader, and he seems perfectly comfortable envisioning a corrupt ruler being toppled by a capable and virtuous replacement of a different bloodline.

Confucius' emphasis on meritocratic government comes at the level between that of the commoner and that of noble inheritance. During his time, there was a large pool of ambitious young men (*shi* 士; see below) hungry for education and opportunities who viewed themselves as being, or rising, above the status of farmers and tradesmen. It's not clear how gradually or suddenly young commoners began to be allowed into the government, but credit is often given to Duke Huan of Qi, who hired the commoner Guan Zhong (see the glossary), whose radical reforms resulted in Qi becoming the first superpower of the Spring and Autumn period. Later, Jin followed suit, and then Qin. By Confucius' time, it was widely recognized that hiring capable men was the path to dominance. However, since power and privilege are rarely surrendered voluntarily, whatever meritocratic ideals had begun circulating were never fully realized.[61]

Meritocratic standards, in Confucius' eyes, applied even to one's status after death (34.1).

Various ideals associated with meritocracy in the *Dialogues* include education (see above), *shi* (see below), fostering the talents of others, recognizing the talents

61. Drawing from the archaeological record, Falkenhausen (2006) says, "at least in ritual contexts, the previous all-important distinctions between ranked-élite and unranked-commoner segments of lineages became blurred after the middle of the Eastern Zhou" (394)—that is, right about the time of Confucius. Falkenhausen describes a consistency between Confucius' meritocratic leanings and archaeological evidence but cautions against drawing a causal connection. See Allan (2016) for a treatment of legends in early transmitted texts that express the tension between hereditary and meritocratic succession in early political theory, and see Allan (2015) for a treatment of excavated texts on the same theme.

of others, elevating the talents of others (*xian*; see below), and *junzi* (see above). Individuals commonly associated with meritocracy and the resulting good government include Yao, Shun, Guan Zhong, and Zichan (see their separate entries in the glossary).

The following examples illustrate the concept of meritocracy:

1.1 Confucius, who was not an aristocrat, was hired as mayor of the town of Zhongdu and subsequently promoted to minister of justice for the state of Lu.

1.3 Confucius, the non-aristocrat, advises the duke of Lu to demolish the city walls of the three most powerful aristocratic families in Lu, thus both symbolically and in reality reducing the aristocratic hold over the Lu government. In the same section, we see that Zhong You (Zilu) is Jisun's household manager. This was a comparatively powerful position. Working in an administrative position in an aristocratic household was a common stepping stone for a *shi*.

3.2 "The capable and virtuous were hired and promoted, while worthless pretenders were demoted and fired."

3.2 "The greatest enlightenment in the world is that which can raise up the most capable and virtuous. . . . [T]here is . . . no greater meritocracy than having capable and virtuous people in office."

5.1 "Ruists sit like jewels on cushions, ready to be hired; they study night and day, ready to answer queries; they fill their breasts with conscientiousness and trustworthiness, ready to be promoted; and they act confidently, ready to be selected. These are ways in which they establish themselves."

5.4 "If a sovereign appreciates their ideas and hires them, they work with dedication."

5.5 "Ruists don't avoid family members, and when recommending from an out-group, they don't neglect those they have reason to resent. In their successes, they don't seek a large salary. They recommend other capable and virtuous people, without expectation of reward. Sovereigns achieve their goals, and the people depend on the Ruist's *de*."

8.12 We see Zilu's poverty before he entered government and his relatively comfortable circumstances afterward.

10.1 "Shun . . . recruited men who were capable and virtuous and replaced the ones who weren't."

12.17 "I've heard it said that in a just society capable and virtuous people are brought to prominence. They are employed as leaders, and the people follow them."

13.1 "There is also an official named Lin Guo. Whenever he comes across someone capable and virtuous, he always recommends him to the duke.

If that person is fired for cause, Lin surrenders his own salary to make up for the loss. As a result, Duke Ling has no worthless officials on the payroll because he recognized Lin as capable and virtuous and showed esteem for him."

13.2 "Zigong asked Confucius, 'Of the ministers working today, which is the most capable and virtuous?' Confucius replied, 'I don't know of any. . . . You have heard of people who are capable and virtuous by virtue of their own efforts, but have you heard of those who are capable and virtuous by virtue of recommending others who are capable and virtuous?' Zigong replied, 'Yes, those who recommend the capable and virtuous are themselves capable and virtuous.'"

13.6 "What is the first priority for a capable and virtuous leader ruling a country?"

13.7 "When the Duke of Zhou held the esteemed position of prime minister and was controlling the reins of the government, he still humbled himself before ordinary people by meeting with 170 of them each day. . . . This is how he was able to hire the best people."

14.7 "There are five men in this area who are more capable and virtuous than me, and whom I have appointed as my advisers."

14.7 "Yao and Shun were sure to solicit help from the capable and virtuous. The capable and virtuous are the genesis of all good fortune, the captains of fate."

14.8 "To fire one capable and virtuous person just to hire another is akin to expropriation. To fire a capable and virtuous person in order to hire an unwise and incapable person is akin to assault."

17.1 "*Yi* has to do with appropriateness and relies on respecting capable and virtuous people as its first priority. *Li* arises out of the hierarchy of affection for one's parents and respecting capable and virtuous people."

17.2 "There are nine requirements to become a state renowned throughout the land. They are . . . (2) show reverence for capable and virtuous people."

17.3 "The way to show reverence for the capable and virtuous is to eschew slander, distance yourself from debauchery, disesteem wealth, and esteem virtue."

19.9 "A *junzi* encourages the talents of others, while a small-minded person seeks to get the best of others by suppressing their talents."

20.1 "King Zhao of Chu hired Confucius."

20.3 Zengzi is depicted working in the fields in tattered clothes. When he is offered a fief by the duke of Lu for nothing, he refuses on principle.

21.5 "If you labor over selecting people, you can relax in doing your work."

25.2 "Disquiet occurs when the capable and virtuous lose their positions of leadership."

27.1 "Even if someone who works in the fields were to implement them, he would be revered as a sage."
32.1 "When the great *dao* flourished, impartiality reigned, capable and virtuous people were selected to lead."
33.1 "For all born in this world, none is superior by birth."

Minben 民本

There are passages in the *Dialogues* about the need to control the people and keep them calm, to pacify them, to win them over, and to transform them. Read uncritically, these passages might suggest an autocratic or monarchical political theory according to which the people exist for the sake of the ruler—to be bent according to his will—or a natural-law theory according to which the ruler properly belongs in his place and the people in theirs. The latter is closer to the political theory we see in the *Dialogues*, but the proper role of the ruler obtains only through governing for the sake of the people. It is very much a government *for* the people, though not *of* or *by* the people (but see "*Zi*" below).

A popular view of Confucian political theory that is democracy-adjacent is called *minben* 民本 ("people as the root"), a figure of speech that appears as early as the *Documents* ("*min wei bang ben* 民惟邦本 people are the root of the state," in the chapter "Wu zi zhi ge"). Following and responding to such thinkers as Liang Qichao and Jin Yaoji, Yong Xia (2011) explains, "The core subject of *minben* is not the sovereign, nor does it mean that the sovereign takes the people as his root, but that the people are the principal actors, the people are the root, the sovereign is an offshoot of them" (28). A pithy, Greek-derived neologism for *minben* might be *demorhiza* (*demo* = people; *rhiza* = root), as in "Confucius favored a demorhizic form of government."

Dialogues 32.7 offers an exceptionally nuanced passage that could easily be read as something right out of Han Feizi 韓非子, with the ruler justifiably manipulating the people toward his own ends. A demorhizic reading, however, derived from consideration of the *Dialogues* as a whole, reveals an interdependent relationship between the people and the ruler, with the ruler as a model of good behavior and the people emulating the ruler. What it means when one person emulates the behavior of another is where the nuance comes in. The only way to make sense of this passage in the context of the *Dialogues* is to see the ruler and the people as fundamentally interdependent (see "Affection" and "*Fa*" above).[62]

62. Erica Brindley (2010) posits a similar kind of interdependence in her notion of "holistic individualism" (xi), which is the best way, she says, to conceive of the individual in early Confucianism. Roger Ames (1983) traces a Confucian-Legalist political theory of *li min* 利民 in the *Huainanzi* that is a close parallel to what we are calling *minben* in the *Dialogues*. Differences between them, such as the

In 41.10 (the public square) and 41.12 (a protest poem), we see depictions of the relevance of the voices of the people.

The following examples illustrate the concept of *minben*:

3.2 "The purpose of hunting and fishing is not to fill up the mansions and palaces. The purpose of levying taxes on the people is not to fill up the state's treasury."

7.4 "If your court is conducted with *li* and upper and lower levels of society interact with mutual affection, then commoners across the land will see themselves as your people. Who will there be to invade? If you violate this way and the people naturally rebel, seeing themselves as your enemy, then who will be with you to protect the state?"

10.1 "When Shun was sovereign, in his governing he valued life and detested killing. In his hiring, he recruited men who were capable and virtuous and replaced the ones who weren't. His *de* matched the *de* of heaven and earth in his calm emptiness. His transformative powers matched the four seasons in his ability to usher in change. As a result, all within the four seas were affected by his powers, which flowed unimpeded to uncultured tribes. *Feng* soared and *lin* appeared, and the birds and beasts followed their *de*. The one and only reason for all of this was his valuing of life."

13.9 "As for the crucial aspects of good government, nothing is more important than helping the people live long and prosper."

14.8 "Someone who knows how to be an official benefits the people by respecting the law. Someone who is ignorant of how to be an official harms the people by perverting the law. Such is the genesis of resentment."

15.20 "Without water, a boat can't go, but if water gets in, it will sink. Without the people, a leader can't govern, but if the people rise up, he will be toppled."

21.2 "Oversee the people without the defect of being inflexible toward them. Win them over without offending them through frank speech. Take their measure without deceiving them through rhetoric. Nurture them without disturbing their regular calendar. Care for them without being too lenient in punishments. By doing these things, your position will be stable, your reputation will be made, and you will have earned the allegiance of the people."

21.3 "An intelligent ruler is always tolerant in dealing with the people. Through love and tenderness toward them, the people will be able to achieve their own ends."

Dialogues' emphasis on affection and the ultimate expendability of any particular ruler, deserve further exploration.

23.1 "The Yellow Chief . . . studied astronomy and developed the use of water, fire, and other natural resources, devoting all of his energy to fostering a flourishing populace."

23.4 "Chief Yao . . . put the needs of the people first."

32.15 "People who lived in the mountains were not forced to move to the riverside. People who lived along shorelines were not forced to move to the plains. Putting to use water, fire, metal, and wood for the sake of meals required proper timing. Unions between women and men were created in the winter, and noble ranks were conferred in the spring, each according to appropriate age and contributions."

41.10 "People retreat to the school as a diversion and spend time talking about what's right and what's wrong in the government. What they approve of, we try to put into practice. What they disapprove of, we try to reform."

42.4 "During a bad year, ride a nag; halt all corvée labor; do not repair roads; in supplication ceremonies, use silk and jade for offerings; do not use bells and chimes during sacrificial ceremonies; and when animals are offered in sacrifice, use second-rate animals. This is the *li* of how a capable and virtuous ruler humbles himself in order to save the people."

Ren 仁

Ren is the primary cultivated virtue for Confucius, and it was often incompletely understood by his students, as depicted in the *Analects*. The *Dialogues* provides us with a much clearer picture. *Ren* is most often used as a directional virtue of care and mentorship from someone of an elevated position on the social hierarchy to someone of a lower position, analogous to the love and care of a parent for a child. But it is not exclusively used in this way. *Ren* can also be applied to friendships, as when helping a friend improve (18.10), to self-sacrifice in the aid of one's country (19.6), to creatures of the environment (23.1), and to those of elevated positions in the spiritual hierarchy (27.1). These extensions suggest that *ren* is an expression of care to those in one's charge or to those one has the power to help. This power can come from one's position in the hierarchy or from personal capacities, the latter of which justifies the former in a just society.[63] As one moves up through a hierarchy and expresses virtues appropriate to one's position, the expression of those virtues can foster the expression of virtues in people below. *Ren* is involved in this virtuous

63. For a concept related to the directionality of virtue, see the concept of agent-relative obligation in Van Norden (2007). For a description of the directionality of *zhong* 忠 and *shu* 恕, see Nivison (1996a). For a concrete example of directional virtues attached to specific roles, see 32.8: "Love on the part of a father . . ."

cycle to the extent that the expression of *ren* in society fosters the expression of *xiao* (see below) in households (30.1). Like the notion of love in Western culture, *ren* is an emotive virtue, not purely an intellectual virtue—it is a feeling (43.6). It is important to also understand that although Confucius sees *ren* as a virtue that is cultivated, like culture more broadly, he also sees it as arising spontaneously from the grassroots. In 8.3, for example, a gift from a commoner is an expression of *ren*.

3.1–2, 4.2, 5.3–5, 7.1, 7.7, 8.3–4, 8.8–9, 9.8, 9.10, 10.5, 10.10, 10.12, 10.16, 10.18, 11.1, 12.1, 12.10, 12.14–15, 12.21, 15.6, 15.21, 16.7, 17.1, 18.3–6, 18.10, 19.1, 19.6, 20.1, 20.4, 21.7, 22.5, 23.1, 23.3–4, 23.6, 25.2, 25.4, 27.1, 30.1, 32.5–8, 32.12, 32.14, 36.1, 37.2–3, 38.1, 38.11, 38.15, 41.7, 41.10, 43.6, 43.25, 44.4

3.1 "If sovereigns first cultivate *ren* in themselves, then the high ministers will be conscientious and the lower ministers will be trustworthy."

3.2 "The best *ren* in the world is that which can unite the whole world in bonds of ultimate affection."

3.2 "There is no greater *ren* than loving others."

5.5 "Gentle kindness is the root of *ren*. Cautious reverence is the ground of *ren*. Open tolerance is the operation of *ren*. Easy association is the aptitude of *ren*. *Li* and self-restraint are the face of *ren*. Conversation is the culture of *ren*. Music is the harmony of *ren*. Generosity is the spreading of *ren*. All Ruists possess these aspects of *ren*, and yet none dare to call it *ren* in themselves."

8.3 "I have heard that in the past people didn't like food to go to waste and would prefer to give it to others than to let it spoil. These are people of *ren*."

9.8 "A *ren* person naturally cares."

12.10 "His transparency toward the common people amounts to *ren*."

12.15 "In his unwillingness to cut tall grasses, you can see his *shu* and *ren*."

18.5 "Love is akin to *ren*."

18.10 "You have achieved *ren* when you never forget past favors and never dwell on past slights."

19.6 "He used his death as a way of exhortation, hoping that, after he was gone, the king would come to regret his error and reform. His intentions were fundamentally *ren*."

20.4 "A person of *ren* is incorruptible."

23.1 "He extended his *ren* and care to the birds, the beasts, and the bugs."

23.4 "Chief Yao . . . was as *ren* as the heavens"

27.1 "The *li* of the Jiao and She sacrifices are how *ren* is expressed to the recently deceased. The *li* of the Di and Chang sacrifices are how *ren* is expressed to the ancestral line. The *li* of laying out food offerings are how *ren* is expressed at a funeral. The *li* of *xiang* archery banquets are how *ren* is expressed to one's neighbors around town and extended family. The *li* of informal banquets are how *ren* is expressed to one's guests at home."

30.1 "An absence of *xiao* behavior is caused by an absence of *ren* behavior, which in turn is caused by impropriety in mourning ceremonies. Clarifying the *li* of mourning ceremonies is how to instruct people in *ren* and love."

32.8 "*Ren* on the part of a sovereign, conscientiousness on the part of a minister."

32.14 "*Ren* is the root of *yi* and the embodiment of congeniality. . . . To pay attention to education but not match it with *ren* is like weeding but not harvesting. To match education with *ren* but not create a comfortable atmosphere through ceremonial music is like harvesting but not eating."

41.7 "*Ren* is overcoming oneself and returning to *li*."

43.6 "*Ren* is what guides *li*."

Ru 儒

The word *Confucianism* refers to the Chinese *Ru* school of thought. It is not like Marxism or Aristotelianism, however, in which the school of thought grew up around the work of a person and was named after that person. The word *Ru* 儒 appears to predate Confucius, though not by much,[64] and there were *Ru* in his time that were not necessarily associated with him. He associated himself with the category *Ru*, and after his lifetime the category became exclusively associated with him.

Because of its lack of textual adumbration in very early texts, scholars have struggled to fill out its definition, variously interpreting it as scholar, classicist, and ritual specialist. Even in the *Dialogues*, it appears in only one chapter in the relevant sense. Fortunately, the chapter is dedicated to the idea.

The *Ru* of Confucius' time appear to have been relied on for their special understanding and knowledge of *li* (see above), which was acquired at least in part through textual study. This explains the different interpretations of the term. We don't know exactly what, if anything, Confucius added to the notion. From chapter 5 (among other sources[65]), we can glean that the *Ru* were sometimes popularly viewed as something akin to the Pharisees in the New Testament—sticklers for ritual protocol with a tendency to be unforgiving, officious, and even hypocritical. But chapter 5 is also an eloquent defense of the *Ru* by Confucius and can give us a sense of how the term *Ru* was elevated from a pejorative of officiousness to an esteemed school of

64. The term *Ru* doesn't appear at all in the *Documents*, the *Poems*, or BA, and does not appear in the CQZZ (in the relevant sense) until the time of Confucius.

65. Mark Csikszentmihalyi (2004) provides a thorough background of Warring States depictions of *Ru*, both pro and con.

thought. There is an emphasis in chapter 5 on the independence of the *Ru* (see "Independence" above).

5.2–6
5.2 "Your clothing—is that Ruist clothing?"
5.3 "Ruists sit like jewels on cushions, ready to be hired; they study night and day, ready to answer queries; they fill their breasts with conscientiousness and trustworthiness, ready to be promoted; and they act confidently, ready to be selected."
5.3 "The Ruist way of life can appear austere and difficult. Whether standing or sitting, they are respectful and reverent. In speech, they are always sincere and trustworthy. In their behavior, they are always conscientious and upright."
5.3 "Ruists can be entrusted with goods and not desire them. They can be inundated with pleasures but not indulge in them."
5.4 "Ruists study widely without limit, act devotedly without fatigue, don't slack even when alone, and don't get caught up when associating with elites. They always take harmony as the basis of *li* and adhere to rules even in leisure. They admire the capable and virtuous, and they are accepting of the masses, seeking to patch up any minor falling-out. This is how they are open and tolerant."

Sage

At the top of Confucius' ladder of achievement (see 7.1), the sage is the ultimate expression of human potential. Confucius never identifies any contemporary as a sage, reserving the term for ancient kings of the past. In the *Dialogues*, Confucius is the only contemporary identified as a sage. According to the many descriptions of past sages, a sage has some specific characteristics. A sage restores unity between human nature and nature broadly, working with, not against, the spontaneous forces of nature. The sage is also an innovator, suggesting, contrary to many descriptions of Confucianism, that the highest achievement in Confucianism is creative contributions to humanity, not merely perpetuating established custom. Further, a sage works with, not against, human nature to govern, which, from outside appearances, comes off effortlessly.

Sheng (ren) **聖（人）** 4.1, 5.1, 6.2, 7.1, 8.1, 8.17, 11.1, 13.3, 13.11, 14.3, 14.6, 15.4, 16.6, 17.3, 17.5, 18.4, 19.1, 19.3, 20.1, 21.7, 25.2, 25.4, 26.2–4, 27.1–2, 29.1, 30.1, 31.1, 32.3, 32.6–8, 32.10, 32.13–14, 35.1, 36.2–3, 37.2, 38.10, 39.2–3, 40.2, 41.2, 41.21, 41.25–26

6.2 "Later, sages appeared and made their contributions. They fashioned uses for fire, such as for casting bronze and firing clay. They discovered methods for making houses and buildings, windows and doors."

7.1 "Regarding the sage, his *de* merges with heaven and earth; he changes and connects without premeditation; he sees all affairs through from beginning to end; he accords with the natural spontaneity of all things; and through the dissemination of this great *dao*, selfhood is brought to full development. His brightness rivals the sun and moon, and his transformations are spirit-like. The people below don't understand his *de*; even eyewitnesses can't make out its scope."

8.17 "When a sage does something, he doesn't act simply on personal whims, because his actions may change the customs of the day and his teachings may spread widely among the people."

11.1 "Confucius is the descendent of a sage."

17.3 "To sincerely develop is to hit the mark without forcing it, to understand without overthinking, to effortlessly accord with the *dao*. It is how sages remain serene."

26.4 "The sages created the customs of mourning according to this pattern of abatement of sorrow."

31.1 "The transformational government of the sage requires the interplay of both criminal punishment and good governing."

32.7 "Whenever a sage is able to form the whole world into one family, to form the whole country into one person, it doesn't occur just by thinking about it. One must understand people's feelings, proceed from *yi* accordingly, be clear about both the benefits and harms to them, and only then take action."

32.8 "Other than through *li*, how can a sage govern such that the seven emotions are managed, the ten *yi* are cultivated, trustworthiness is promoted and strong relations are forged, deference is inculcated, and contentiousness is eliminated? He must be mindful of the primary desires for food, drink, and sex and of the primary aversions to death, poverty, and hardship. Desires and aversions are the two primary human motivations. They are concealed in people's hearts and unfathomable. With pleasure and aversion in people's hearts but not visible in their expressions, absent *li*, how can they best be channeled?"

32.10 "In creating guides for behavior, the sage necessarily takes heaven and earth as the root, *yin* and *yang* as the sprout, the four seasons as the handle, the sun and stars as the mainstays, the moon as the measure, deceased ancestors as companions, the five elemental phases as constituents, *li* and *yi* as implements, human feelings as fertile ground, and the four auspicious creatures as domestic animals."

32.13 "Only sages fully understand that *li* must not be dispensed with."

32.14 "Human emotions are the fertile ground of sages and kings, who plow it by developing *li*, plant in it by displaying *yi*, weed it by teaching, bring a feeling of community through creating a foundation of *ren*, and create an atmosphere of stability through playing ceremonial music."

39.3 "Confucius is heir to the former sages."

41.2 "Ran You said, 'Indeed, I learned it under Confucius, who is a great sage.'"

41.25 "In the instruction of the sage kings, respect for elders inside and outside the family was promulgated starting from the palace to pedestrians on the street, to villages, to hunting parties, to the military. In this way, everyone felt it to be the *yi* thing to do, and no one would dare violate it their whole lives."

Shi 士

In 7.1, Confucius lists five levels in a hierarchy of moral achievement: commoner, *shi*, *junzi*, *xian*, and sage. The *shi* is the entry-level position, the low official. *Shi* also denotes an ambitious young person. One key to understanding Confucius' overall philosophy is to understand his fundamental belief in meritocracy (see above)—that through hard work, ability, and moral cultivation, one may start out at a low social level and rise to the highest ranks in the land.

The original meaning of *shi* is not well understood,[66] but there seems to be some consensus that, in the Western Zhou, *shi* referred to the lowest rung of the aristocracy. An important element of the idea of *shi* is that, although major noble titles were handed down to the firstborn son of the wife (see "Wife" in the glossary), other sons did not drop out of the aristocracy altogether. Instead, they became known as *shi*. This status put them a step above the commoner (farmers, tradesmen, etc.) and gave them access to education, low positions in the government, and administrative positions in the households of the higher nobility. They were also the soldiers that fought on behalf of their lords. This is why the term is sometimes translated *knight*. As the decades and centuries passed during the Zhou, in which polygynous noble families proliferated, there grew a vast labor pool of *shi*—educated young men with ambition and motivation.

By the time of Confucius, as we see in the *Dialogues*, the term had largely lost its meaning of low-status aristocracy and had come to refer to low-level government functionaries and ambitious young men.

1.2–3, 3.1–2, 5.4, 7.1, 7.3, 7.7, 8.4, 8.10, 8.13, 8.18, 9.1, 9.8–9, 10.10, 11.1, 12.14, 13.1, 13.3, 13.7, 13.11, 15.2, 15.11, 15.13, 16.10, 17.2–3, 19.1–2, 19.8, 20.4, 22.3–6, 25.2, 28.1, 31.2–3, 32.5, 32.14, 33.1, 33.3, 34.1, 35.3, 37.2, 39.1–2, 41.1, 41.10, 41.21–22, 42.6, 42.16, 43.15, 43.20, 43.23, 44.1

66. In an examination of the term, Zhou Xiaomin and Xie Yangju (2021) describe eight competing theories in the scholarly literature to explain *shi*. See Yu (2003) for a book-length treatment.

Shi

7.1 "There are five levels of achievement. There are the levels of the commoner, the *shi,* the *junzi,* the *xian,* and the sage. Understanding these five is sufficient to be able to govern in accord with *dao.*"

7.1 "The *shi* is someone who has direction and who latches onto certain plans. Although he does not yet have the foundation to excel in the methods of the *dao,* he has set his mind on following the *dao.* Although he has not yet mastered the many excellences required, he is in the process of mastering them. Thus, without striving for excess knowledge, he pays close attention to his current pursuit of knowledge. Without striving for excess eloquence, he pays close attention to his speech."

Official (often with an emphasis on being at a lower level and aspiring to rise), potential up-and-coming official, aspiring official, young official, low official

3.2 "Ultimate music is that by which the people are harmonized without making a sound. If an enlightened king is able to thoroughly implement these three ultimates, the nobility will recognize the legitimacy of the king, officials will loyally serve, and the people will willingly exert themselves."

3.2 "An enlightened king of the past was sure to have a thorough knowledge of the names of all potential up-and-coming officials, and not just their names but also their qualities, their skills, and where they resided, and then he would honor them with official rank across the land."

5.4 "If a sovereign appreciates their ideas and hires them, they work with dedication, and if a sovereign does not appreciate their ideas, they do not attempt to ingratiate themselves in order to be hired. This is their situation as aspiring officials."

7.3 "With young officials, they must first be scrupulous, and from those one selects for intelligence and ability."

33.3 "The king acts as host himself, and the *li* of this is unchanged right down to low officials."

Person/people (often with an emphasis on being a youth with aspirations), aspiring men, someone who is on his way, aspiring young man, people working their way up the ladder, prospect, up-and-comer

7.1 "Duke Ai asked Confucius, 'I'm interested in selecting aspiring men to work in the government and would like to ask you how to go about doing that.'"

7.7 "Wise and *ren* people live well-regulated lives."

9.8 "Confucius said, 'This is the response of someone who is on his way.' . . . Confucius said, 'This is the response of someone who is on his way and who is a *junzi.*'"

9.9 "An aspiring young man would have friends of differing opinions in order to avoid immoral behavior."
11.1 "Many people working their way up the ladder today have brilliant, perceptive, analytical minds, but because they enjoy criticizing others, they bring themselves perilously close to death."
12.14 "Confucius had such confidence in his ability to effect *ren* that he considered him a unique prospect."
19.1 "Without guidance from friends, an up-and-comer will be unable to make good judgments."
33.1 "Whether for the crown prince or an average up-and-comer, the *li* does not change."

Soldier

1.2 "Soldiers, grab your weapons!"

Shu 恕

The term *shu* appears in just two brief passages of the *Analects* and yet is commonly vaunted as one of Confucius' most important concepts. This is because in one of those passages, when asked, "Is there a single word that can inform my behavior for the rest of my life?" Confucius responds, "That would be *shu*—do not spread to others what you do not wish for yourself." This passage is commonly misunderstood in two respects. First, *spread* (*shi* 施) is usually translated *do*, but this is misleading. There is a temporal aspect to *shu* such that it is not a one-off interaction. Second, *shu* is often incorrectly translated as *reciprocity*. This is understandable because there is certainly a sense of reciprocity in it (see 9.1, for example), but other usages, including those in the *Dialogues*, show that *shu* is fundamentally a variety of love in the form of compassion that involves a mindfulness of not wanting to be on the receiving end of uncompassionate treatment from others. Here, we generally render it *compassion* when we don't leave it in transliterated form. The three emotions not reciprocated in *Dialogues* 9.1 are varieties of love—*zhong*, *xiao*, and *ti* (love from a younger sibling to an older sibling). The point of the *Analects* passage in question is: you don't want others to treat you uncompassionately, so you should be compassionate to others. This distinction becomes apparent in the seven passages in which *shu* is used in the *Dialogues*, especially 9.1.[67] In four of the

67. The way 9.1 posits imagining what one would want from someone in the same role as oneself as a definition of *shu* perfectly aligns with Paul Goldin's (2011) interpretation of the term. Drawing from "Zhong yong" 13, and following David Nivison (1996a), Goldin says, "*Shu* is a relation not between two individuated people, but between two social roles. How does one treat one's father? In the same way that one would want to be treated by one's son *if one were a father oneself*" (16).

passages, *shu* is closely associated with *ai* 愛 or *ren* 仁. See also "Love" above and 12.15n17.

8.4, 8.18, 9.1, 12.15, 18.4, 18.6, 27.2

Shu

9.1 "A *junzi* understands three lessons of *shu*. (1) There is a minister who cannot serve his sovereign but expects his subordinates to assist him—this is not a case of *shu*. (2) There is a child who cannot be *xiao* to his parents but expects his children to requite him—this is not a case of *shu*. (3) There is a younger brother who cannot show respect to his older brother but expects his own younger brother to be congenial to him—this is not a case of *shu*. When people with aspirations for office can understand the basis of *shu*, that is when they can be said to have set themselves right."

12.15 "In Chai's . . . unwillingness to cut tall grasses, you can see his *shu* and *ren*. The great reverence of Tang the Accomplished was made possible through his *shu*."

18.6 "For *ren*, you can't do better than *shu*. When you know what not to do, then you know exactly what to do."

Compassion, compassionate treatment (associated with mindfulness of one's own dislike for uncompassionate treatment)

8.4 "A good official applies the law uniformly. With *ren* and compassion at the front of his mind, he engenders virtue. Severe or cruel intentions, on the other hand, engender resentment."

8.18 "A loving attitude combined with compassionate treatment can help you embrace people in dire straits."

18.4 "Despite [Zang Wenzhong's] wisdom, there are reasons he was not accepted in Lu. He was not congenial in his work, nor was he sufficiently compassionate. The Xia shu says, 'Stay mindful here and now. Be congenial and spread compassion.'"

27.2 "In costume-less mourning, the heart opens in compassion."

Xian 賢

In 7.1, Confucius describes a ladder of achievement, from commoner to *shi*, to *junzi*, to *xian*, to sage (see the separate entries above). The sage is such an exalted category that no such contemporary is identified by Confucius, but whether to apply the term *xian* to people is a matter of common speculation for Confucius and his circle. The term *xian* applies only to outstanding leaders or advisers and to those who are fit to lead or advise. And they can be from any walk of life. This category of person, according to Confucius, is highly capable of governing and possesses virtue that extends to the entire populace. However, we see in the examples of Guan Zhong, Yan Pingzi (two prime ministers of Qi at different times; 42.7), and the king of Chu (10.2), that even a *xian* is not infallible and can sometimes be shortsighted. The term is most commonly used in the context of recognizing and elevating (or failing to do so) those who are fit to lead or advise. Someone who recognizes and elevates a *xian* is also *xian*. In 18.4, we see that a potential *xian* may be wise, but if they are not *ren*, they do not qualify as *xian*.

2.2, 3.1–2, 5.4–5, 7.1–2, 8.13, 9.7, 10.1–2, 10.8, 12.1–3, 12.16–17, 13.1–2, 13.5–6, 14.3, 14.7–8, 15.8, 15.12, 15.15–16, 15.19, 17.1–3, 18.4, 20.1, 21.5, 22.2–3, 22.9–10, 25.2, 28.1, 32.1, 33.2, 38.27, 39.1, 41.14, 41.26, 42.4, 42.7

Xian

7.1 "Regarding the *xian*, his *de* never crosses the line, and his actions are right on target. His words are sufficient to serve as a model for all the world, without bringing harm to himself. His *dao* is sufficient to transform the people, without harming the root. He brings prosperity to society so that people needn't accumulate wealth, and he spreads it widely so that people needn't worry about poverty."

Capable and virtuous

12.17 "I've heard it said that in a just society capable and virtuous people are brought to prominence. They are employed as leaders, and the people follow them."

13.2 "Those who recommend the capable and virtuous are themselves capable and virtuous."

14.7 "Fu said, 'There are five men in this area who are more capable and virtuous than me, and whom I have appointed as my advisers. They all guide me along the *dao*.' Confucius breathed a sigh of relief and said, 'The capable and virtuous are the genesis of all good fortune, the captains of fate.'"

14.8 "To fire one capable and virtuous person just to hire another is akin to expropriation. To fire a capable and virtuous person in order to hire an unwise and incapable person is akin to assault. . . . To conceal someone else's excellence is called stifling the capable and virtuous."

17.1 "*Yi* has to do with appropriateness and relies on respecting capable and virtuous people as its first priority. *Li* arises out of the hierarchy of affection for one's parents and respecting capable and virtuous people."

Xiao 孝

The mystery of the importance of *li* in early China also goes for the importance of *xiao*, which refers to the kindness, love, and respect due to a parent from a child (including, and especially, adult children). Confucius says in the *Analects* (1.2) that *xiao* is the root of *ren*. If *ren* is Confucius' most exalted virtue, then *xiao* must be his most fundamental. But why? The *Dialogues* gives us some clarity. In the *Dialogues* the importance of *xiao* applies also to its being the foundation of the virtues *yi* (acting appropriately, morally, justly; see below) and *li* (acting in accord with ritual propriety; see above). It is a feeling of love toward one's parents, even when they have passed on. Imagine a person who was unable to love even their parents. If you can't love even your parents, who can you love? How could such a person possibly take a position in society and treat others with love and kindness? Love of one's parents is the easy case, on which we build and from which we extend. But without that foundation, there is nothing on which to build.

The "easy" part of *xiao* deserves further exploration. A paradigm case in Confucius' eyes is that of Shun, whose parents were not only abusive toward him but murderously so (15.10). For Shun, loving his father could not have been easy. And yet he was still *xiao*, and on account of this he was seen by Yao as a potential leader of others. *Xiao* is a complex combination of love, duty, kindness, and respect. It's easy to love loving parents, and for those parents who are not so easy to love, we must remember the sacrifices they have made for us and how they cared for us from infancy. We take this complex combination of love, duty, kindness, and respect for those closest to us in our lives, enter society, and extend that complex combination to those above us on the hierarchy, in an attempt to perform our duties and forge bonds of intimacy—bonds that, in a sense, replicate the parent-child relationship.

The Shanghai Museum essay "Nei li 内禮" (Hou 2018) provides a useful description of *xiao*. First, it says, "In a *junzi*'s establishing *xiao*, love is what's used and *li* is what's prized" (218). Then, it says, "When a *junzi* serves his parents, there should be no private joys or worries. What your parents find joyful, you should find joyful. What your parents worry about, you should worry about" (218).

Xiao can also refer to veneration for ancestors (6.2), as well as care and respect for elders generally.

The term *ti* 悌 refers to the same kind of love and respect as *xiao* but directed to an elder brother. It is occasionally paired with *xiao* (3.2, 12.1, 28.1, 41.25); it can also stand alone in the same sense of respect for elders generally (41.25).

Xiao 孝 2.2, 3.1–2, 4.2, 6.2, 8.17, 9.1, 9.9, 10.9, 12.1, 12.4, 12.9, 12.21, 14.7, 15.1, 15.10, 17.4–5, 22.1, 22.3, 23.5, 28.1, 30.1, 32.8, 32.12, 35.3, 38.2, 38.12, 38.14, 41.25, 42.25, 43.17, 43.26

Xiao

2.2 "A country must make *xiao* a priority."

3.1 "When the people above venerate the aged, it increases *xiao* among the people below."

6.2 "They took the carcasses, whether dog, pig, cow, or goat, along with the contents of the ritual vessels—grains, vegetables, congee, etc.—and boiled it all together, then used it to pronounce declarations, one to express *xiao* to the ancestors and one to show love and compassion to descendants."

8.17 "I would like to say that people are conscious after they die, but I fear that doing so would encourage very *xiao* people to go overboard and endanger their own lives during the mourning process. I would also like to say that people are not conscious after death, but I fear that doing so would encourage less *xiao* people to abandon their deceased parents without burying them."

9.9 "How can *xiao* mean for a son to merely follow the orders of his father? . . . *Xiao* and devotion mean being able to thoroughly understand what one is following."

10.9 "*Xiao* children will put their all into the ceremony to honor their deceased parents."

12.1 "I've heard that Confucius' method of instruction is to lead his students in with poetry and history, to guide them with *xiao* and *ti*, to persuade them with *ren* and *yi*, and to model for them with *li* and music, culminating in cultured and virtuous individuals."

12.9 "*Xiao* is the genesis of *de*."

14.7 "Your treating three people with the respect due to a father teaches by example the virtue of *xiao*."

15.1 "*Xiao* is the foundation of the *yi* in establishing oneself."

17.4 "As soon as the people treat their parents with *xiao*, live amiably, and perform their duty to the state, and these policies can emanate outward to the whole land, anything is possible."

17.5 "On the day after the sacrifice, he couldn't sleep as the sun rose, having his parents on his mind. He reached out to them with respect, and his remembrance continued long afterward. On the day of the sacrifice, there is always a mixture of joy and sorrow. At the banquet there is always joy, and when it ends there is always sorrow. These are the sentiments of a *xiao* child."

30.1 "When the *li* of mourning ceremonies is clear, the people will be *xiao*."

32.8 "What is meant by *human yi*? Love on the part of a father, *xiao* on the part of a son, helpfulness on the part of an older brother, solicitude on the part of a younger brother, *yi* on the part of a husband, coordination on the part of a wife, mentoring on the part of an elder, congeniality on the part of a younger person, *ren* on the part of a sovereign, conscientiousness on the part of a minister."

35.3 "Through the king's communicating with ancestors in court ceremonies, the people learned to be *xiao*."
42.25 "Zilu inquired of Confucius, 'Poverty is so harmful. One is unable to care for one's parents while they are alive and unable to afford a proper ceremony when they pass on.' Confucius said, 'It is *xiao* enough to make one's parents happy by serving them beans to eat and water to drink. It is *li* enough to prepare the body for burial and expeditiously bury it according to one's means, absent an outer coffin. What is so harmful about poverty?'"
43.26 "This is something that a person who feels *xiao* does naturally after a person passes away."

To be good to elders

3.2. "Guidance was given to youth who were good to their elders."
28.1 "Youths who are good to their elders."

Ti **悌** 3.1, 3.2, 12.1, 12.9, 14.7, 28.1, 32.8, 41.25

Ti

12.1 "I've heard that Confucius' method of instruction is to lead his students in with poetry and history, to guide them with *xiao* and *ti*, to persuade them with *ren* and *yi*, and to model for them with *li* and music, culminating in cultured and virtuous individuals."
12.9 "*Xiao* is the genesis of *de*. *Ti* is its next step."
14.7 "Your treating five people with the respect due to an elder brother teaches by example the virtue of *ti*."

Respect for elder brothers

3.1 "When the people above respect their elders, it increases respect for elder brothers among the people below."

To be good to elders, respect for elders

3.2. "Guidance was given to youth who were good to their elders."
28.1 "Youths who are good to their elders."
41.25 "In the instruction of the sage kings, respect for elders inside and outside the family was promulgated starting from the palace to pedestrians on the street, to villages, to hunting parties, to the military. In this way, everyone felt it to be the *yi* thing to do, and no one would dare violate it their whole lives."

Solicitude on the part of a younger brother

32.8 “What is meant by *human yi*? Love on the part of a father, *xiao* on the part of a son, helpfulness on the part of an older brother, solicitude on the part of a younger brother, *yi* on the part of a husband, coordination on the part of a wife, mentoring on the part of an elder, congeniality on the part of a younger person, *ren* on the part of a sovereign, conscientiousness on the part of a minister.”

Xin 信

Xin, which we typically translate as *trustworthiness,* is often paired with *zhong* (see below), and like *zhong* it is often a reference to a virtue of someone lower on the hierarchy. Also, like *zhong, xin* is a matter of building close relationships based on a feeling of trust. Yet, more often than with *zhong, xin* is also recommended for those in elevated positions.

There is a subtle difference between honesty and trustworthiness. The former is a matter of truth-telling and not deceiving. The latter is a matter of backing up one's speech with actions. In the practical sphere of Confucius' philosophy, it is standing by one's word that builds trusting and affectionate relationships between upper and lower echelons of society.

1.3, 3.1–2, 4.1, 5.3–6, 7.1, 7.6, 8.7, 8.14, 9.3, 10.2, 11.2, 12.9, 12.14, 12.21–22, 13.1, 13.4, 14.6, 14.8–9, 15.6, 15.12, 16.4, 16.7, 17.3, 19.2, 19.9–10. 20.1, 20.4, 21.2, 21.8, 23.1, 23.3, 23.6, 30.1, 31.1, 32.1, 32.8, 32.13–15, 36.1, 37.2–3, 38.26, 41.2, 41.7, 41.10, 41.17, 41.20, 41.26

To stand by one's word

3.2 “The purpose of hunting and fishing is not to fill up the mansions and palaces. The purpose of levying taxes on the people is not to fill up the state's treasury. Use compassion to make up for insufficiency; use *li* to curtail excess; stand by your word instead of putting on appearances. . . . The people will have faith in such leaders as surely as the extreme temperatures of winter and summer put everyone to the test.”

Trustworthiness, trustworthy

5.3 “Ruists don't prize gold or jade and instead take conscientiousness and trustworthiness as their treasures.”

5.4 “Ruists take conscientiousness and trustworthiness as their armor, and take *li* and *yi* as their shield.”

5.6 "Duke Ai's words soon became more trustworthy."
7.1 "Regarding the *junzi*, his speech is always conscientious and trustworthy, harboring no resentment."
10.2 "He ignored the might of being a superpower and focused on the trustworthiness of one adviser. If it weren't for Shenshu's trustworthiness, the king would never have been able to do the right thing."
12.9 "Zeng Shen. . . . What he pledges to others is unfailingly trustworthy."
12.9 "Trustworthiness is the profound expression of virtue."
12.21 "Zhao Wenzi . . . served with *yi* and was trustworthy in his actions."
12.22 "In his position as labor minister, he was trustworthy and seemed to enjoy taking his responsibilities head-on."
13.1 "Prince Qumou has the wisdom to rule a large state and the trustworthiness to protect it."
13.4 "Conscientiousness helps you get along with others. Employers appreciate people who are trustworthy."
14.6 "The words of a sage are trustworthy and can be substantiated."
14.9 "This shows that the people are working hard in response to Yóu using reverence and respect as a sign of his trustworthiness. On entering the city, the exteriors of the walls and houses are in good condition, and the trees and plants are flourishing. These demonstrate that, in response to Yóu using conscientiousness and trustworthiness as a sign of his broad-mindedness, the people are not negligent."
17.3 "The way to encourage lower officials is to reward conscientiousness and trustworthiness with substantial salaries. . . . [N]ot being trusted by friends will result in not being supported by those above."
19.2 "It is trustworthiness that allows you to carry through on your words, though speaking little."
21.8 "If as a *junzi* you wish your speech to be treated as trustworthy, nothing is better than hollowing yourself out. . . . Therefore, if obedience must be forced, neither conscientiousness nor trustworthiness will ensue, and the common people will not feel close to you. If interior and exterior do not resonate, the common people will not trust you."
37.2 "Eloquent words can undermine trustworthiness."

Faith

8.14 "When I go underwater, I rely on single-mindedness and faith. And when I come out, I also rely on single-mindedness and faith. Single-mindedness and faith are what I entrust my body with in the waves. I can't rely on just the work of self-preservation."

Yi 義

One meaning of *yi* is to mean, in a semantic sense. Beginning with meaning is a good way to understand *yi*. If I don't understand the meaning of a term, I am less likely to act according to that meaning. For example, if I am instructed to walk gingerly but I don't know what *gingerly* means, I will be unable to follow the instructions. Likewise, if I aim to be courageous but mistake brazenness for courage, I will fall short of my own ambitions. Grasping semantic meaning is thus a necessary precondition of the ability to act appropriate to that meaning. (*Meaning* can have additional connotations of intention, as in "What do you mean by that?" and import, both of which are also found in the *Dialogues*.)

To act appropriately, for Confucius, means to act appropriate to the meanings of the many differentiated terms in social relationships (see "Differentiation" above, and especially 28.2, 30.1, 32.8, and 36.3). For Confucius, the differentiated terms of social relationships are especially important in government posts, with many competing concerns, not the least of which is one's own potential benefit. From its many occurrences in the dialogues, *yi*, in short, refers to moral courage based in humility and a sense of responsibility and justice. It is sometimes paired in the second position with *ren* or *li*. Many Confucian virtues (e.g., *ren* and *li*) have their origins in normal human emotions. A distinguishing feature of *yi* is that it stems more from a sense of the fit of an action to external circumstances than from an inner feeling. (See, for example, 26.4, 36.3, and 41.9.) However, in 32.8, after human *qing* 情 is identified with emotions, human *yi* is identified with familiar relational virtues, such as *ci* and *ren*, all of which are underpinned by love. Similarly, in 15.1, it is said that "*Xiao* is the foundation of the *yi* in establishing oneself." *Yi* is also viewed as flexible, not rigid (see 9.5).

1.2, 2.2, 3.1, 3.2, 5.3–5, 6.1, 7.1, 7.6, 7.7, 8.9, 9.5, 9.9, 10.2, 10.14, 10.17, 12.1, 12.14, 12.21, 14.2–3, 15.1, 15.9, 15.10, 15.14, 16.4, 17.1, 18.1, 18.3, 18.9, 19.5, 20.1, 22.2, 22.5, 22.9, 23.2–3, 24.1, 25.2, 26.2, 26.4, 27.1–2, 28.1–2, 29.3, 30.1, 31.1–2, 32.5–8, 32.10, 32.12, 32.14–15, 36.1, 36.3, 37.1–2, 38.10–11, 38.33, 39.3, 41.2, 41.4, 41.9, 41.14, 41.19–20, 41.25, 41.27, 42.31, 43.3, 43.6, 43.16, 43.18

Yi

2.2 "The Documents say, 'Punishments and executions must be handled according to *yi*, not by one's whims.'"

5.3 "Ruists . . . don't pray for land and instead take *ren* and *yi* as their property."

7.6 "After three years, people from far away so admired his *yi* that sixteen states came to express their esteem."

10.14 "Confucius said to Zilu, 'A *junzi* uses the heart to lead the senses, establishing *yi* through courage. The small-minded person uses the senses to lead the heart, mistaking impertinence for courage.'"

15.1 "*Xiao* is the foundation of the *yi* in establishing oneself."

15.14 "He is aggressive when it comes to putting *yi* into practice; he is docile when accepting admonishment."

17.1 "*Yi* has to do with appropriateness and relies on respecting capable and virtuous people as its first priority."

18.3 "The addition of *ren, yi, li,* and music make for the conduct of the developed person."

18.9 "And so a *junzi* may agitate people when advancing a cause of *yi* but otherwise treats them with loving concern."

22.9 "Coercing me to agree violated *yi.*"

23.3 "He was *ren* and dignified, wise and trustworthy, with *yi* that came from being in tune with heaven and earth."

26.4 "The manifestations of *li* take after the five elemental phases, and its *yi* lies in the four seasons. We can take the *li* of mourning as an example. Involved are: fondness, *yi*, austerity, and contingency. . . . Outside the home, *yi* outweighs fondness. The resourcefulness that one brings to respecting one's father one should also bring to respecting one's sovereign. Respecting those who deserve respect and esteeming those who deserve to be esteemed are the best way to be *yi*. And so one wears simple, uncomfortable clothes for three years in mourning one's sovereign. This custom stems from *yi*."

30.1 "Disrespect for higher-ups is caused by an absence of *yi*. *Yi* is how distinctions of status and worth are made and maintained. When distinctions of status and worth are made and maintained, the people will respect their superiors and revere their elders. The *li* of vassals meeting their lord is how *yi* is made clear. *Yi* must be made clear, and then the people will not transgress. And even though there may be statutes against disrespect, the people will not fall into the trap of criminal punishment by committing such a crime. . . . Licentious sexual behavior occurs when the sexes are not differentiated into separate spheres, which leads to a loss of *yi* between husband and wife. Betrothal and wedding ceremonies are how the separate spheres of the sexes are maintained and how the *yi* of husband and wife is clarified."

32.5 "*Li* is the lever by which the ruler . . . asserts *ren* and *yi.*"

32.6 "Decrees . . . applied to ancestral temples have to do with *ren* and *yi*."

32.7 "When calamity is imminent, a sovereign willingly dies on behalf of his country in accord with *yi*."

32.7 "One must understand people's feelings, proceed from *yi* accordingly, be clear about both the benefits and harms to them, and only then take action."

32.8 "What is meant by *human yi*? Love on the part of a father, *xiao* on the part of a son, helpfulness on the part of an older brother, solicitude on the part of a younger brother, *yi* on the part of a husband, coordination on the part of a wife, mentoring on the part of an elder, congeniality on the part of a younger person, *ren* on the part of a sovereign, conscientiousness on the part of a minister—these ten refer to human *yi*."

32.14 "*Li* is the realization of *yi*. *Li* harmonizes different *yi*."

32.14 "*Yi* is the differentiation of norms and the regulation of *ren*. With it, there can be harmony among the norms and attention paid to *ren*. Strength comes with its achievement and demise with its loss. *Ren* is the root of *yi* and the embodiment of congeniality."

36.3 "In a well-designed house, there are inner quarters for family life and an eastern staircase for welcoming guests. A mat allows for positioning superior and subordinate. A carriage allows for positioning left and right. In walking with others, there is room for walking side by side or single file. In standing with others, there is an order to it. These are all the *yi* of the ancients."

37.1 "A person . . . can achieve his ambitions without offending against *yi*."

41.2 "Ran Qiu did what Fan Chi suggested, and the troops followed him. When the troops entered battle with the Qi army, the Qi army turned and fled. Ran You was able to attack at will with his dagger-axe. Confucius heard about this and said, 'This is *yi*.'"

41.14 "Weizi's way of promoting people, neither losing those close to him nor losing the opportunity to elevate those who were strangers to him, can be considered *yi*."

41.20 "Ceremonial implements symbolize *li*. *Li* brings about *yi*. *Yi* produces benefits. Benefits devolve to the common people. Such are the workings of the government."

43.3 "By making clear the succession of his own state of Lu to his son Bo Qin, he helped King Cheng understand the *yi* of the relationships of father-son, sovereign-minister, and elder-youth."

To mean, meaning, content

3.2 "May I ask what you mean by these?"

18.1 "Your words ring true, and they have a deeper meaning. I'd like to hear you say a little more."

38.10 "He was well-versed in the *Poems*, fully understanding their meanings."

39.3 "He selected the transmitted records of the great thinkers, checking and analyzing their content."

Important

41.21 "Why is it so important?"

Opinion

29.3 "I have heard that the king . . . does a *gui* prognostication at his father's temple to get the opinion of his revered ancestors and his loving father."

To do the right thing

5.5 "When there is agreement about the right thing to do, they charge forward."
10.2 "If it weren't for Shenshu's trustworthiness, the king would never have been able to do the right thing."

Moral behavior, proper behavior

9.9 "An aspiring young man would have friends of differing opinions in order to avoid immoral behavior."
15.10 "He would have been letting his father sink into iniquity."
22.2 "If even birds and beasts know enough to avoid those whose behavior is improper, how much more so should people?"

Responsibility, duty, concern

6.1 "Each person could thus take heart in their social position, the bonds of beneficence and responsibility having been fastened."
8.9 "But Guan Zhong's sense of his own potential for achievement overrode his narrow sense of duty."
26.2 "Instead of narrow concerns of their own, there are three compliances."

Justice

25.2 "Injustice occurs when criminal punishments surge and when misbehavior in society cannot be checked."

Zhong 忠

Zhong is a key virtue of someone in the capacity of an official, or anyone lower on the social/power hierarchy. It is equivalent to the virtue of *xiao* (see above), which applies in the context of the family. As a child is *xiao* to a parent, so an official is *zhong* to a superior (to the office, not to the person). *Zhong* is often paired with *xin* (trustworthiness; see above), and it is viewed as being fostered in lower ranks through the *ren* behavior of a superior. The *zhong* of an official works both up and down the hierarchy, building bonds of intimacy and trust in all directions. Sometimes *zhong* ends in the ultimate sacrifice, but for Confucius, even *zhong* has its limits. One should never engage in unscrupulous behavior in the name of loyalty, and if a government is rotten to the core, one should resign until moral order has been restored.[68] (See also "Independence.")

1.3, 3.1, 5.3–4, 7.1, 8.7, 8.9, 8.11, 8.14, 10.5, 10.18, 12.9, 12.21, 13.3–4, 13.11, 14.2, 14.4–5, 14.9, 15.2, 15.21, 17.3, 17.5, 19.2, 19.6, 20.1, 21.2, 21.8, 22.10, 30.2, 31.2, 32.8, 36.1, 37.3, 41.10, 41.14, 41.22, 43.17

Conscientious, conscientiousness

3.1 "If sovereigns first cultivate *ren* in themselves, then the high ministers will be conscientious and the lower ministers will be trustworthy."
5.3 "Ruists . . . fill their breasts with conscientiousness and trustworthiness, ready to be promoted. . . . Ruists don't prize gold or jade and instead take conscientiousness and trustworthiness as their treasures."
8.11 "Without close relationships, conscientiousness toward others will be impossible. To act unconscientiously is contrary to *li*."
10.5 "The *junzi* of the past took conscientiousness as their basic makeup and *ren* as their defense. Without leaving their humble cottages, they were known for hundreds of miles around. If there was some uncivil behavior, they would transform it with their conscientiousness."
12.9 "Trustworthiness is the profound expression of virtue. Conscientiousness is its precise manifestation."
15.2 "Conscientiously spoken words are hard to hear but beneficial to one's conduct."
17.5 "In the past, when King Wen performed sacrifices, he served the dead just as if he were serving the living, he yearned for the dead as if he had no wish to go on living, he would inevitably be struck with grief on the anniversary of his parents' death, and when they were brought up in conversation it was

68. Goldin (2008) makes a persuasive case that *zhong* 忠 in its earliest usage is closely related to *zhong* 中, impartiality, and does not mean loyalty, which only comes later. His preferred translation of the term is "being honest with oneself in dealing with others" (170), with an emphasis on *dealing with others*. Goldin feels that the translation *conscientious* does not adequately express the interpersonal aspect of the term. We prefer the *conscientious* translation and let the context demonstrate the interpersonal nature of the interactions. Overall, we largely concur with Goldin. However, Goldin draws a bright line around the *Analects* and says that *zhong* in CQZZ carries meanings of both impartiality and loyalty (Goldin 2018), glossing over the fact that the ideas in the *Analects* and CQZZ are likely coterminous (Pines 2002a), which undermines his claim that the loyalty interpretation comes only after the *Analects*. By Goldin's standard, the comparatively rare use of *zhong* as *loyalty* in the *Dialogues* is another hint to the early date of the *Dialogues*. For a detailed discussion of *zhong* in CQZZ, see Pines (2002a).

as if they were right in front of him. This is an example of conscientious lineal sacrifice."

19.2 "It is conscientiousness that allows you to build close ties in new relationships."

21.8 "If obedience must be forced, neither conscientiousness nor trustworthiness will ensue, and the common people will not feel close to you."

43.17 "A *xiao* son does not follow his emotions if it means harming his parents, just as a conscientious minister does not engage in unseemly acts that would harm his sovereign."

Loyalty, faithfulness

8.9 "Then Shao Hu took his own life, but Guan Zhong didn't. This shows a lack of loyalty."

22.10 "His faithfulness moved his sovereign."

Single-mindedness

8.14 "When I go underwater, I rely on single-mindedness and faith. And when I come out, I also rely on single-mindedness and faith. Single-mindedness and faith are what I entrust my body with in the waves."

Zi 自

Often the term *zi*, which can indicate a strong sense of agency, of taking the initiative, can be left untranslated in English because English connotations of human action already convey a robust sense of agency. For example, in 21.5 *zi* appears three times, emphasizing that the selection process is agentive: "A woman must select just the right fabric, an artisan must select just the right material to work with, and a capable and virtuous leader must select just the right people to surround himself with." We could add *himself* or *herself* after each of the sentence subjects, but the English is sufficiently agentive already.

Zi can connote a sense of agency that is agentive in that there are no external contributions, ranging from aid (an infant that can say its own name; 23.3) to coercion (a criminal who freely comes forward; 30.2). It is most often a freedom from constraint, which can have a positive sense, as in 23.3 and 30.2, but it can also have a negative sense (as in the farmers who, in urgent circumstances, want to harvest grain growing in others' fields; 37.3).

In traditional Western action theory, nature itself is viewed as a constraint on human action, for which the notion of free will has been the preferred solution. In early China, nature is viewed as a source of unconstrained action that should be emulated rather than transcended or overcome (Bruya 2010). In 7.1, the sage accords with *ziran* 自然, the natural spontaneity of all things. In 38.40, habits are described as *ziran,* the unfolding of nature itself. But even in contemporary English, "nature" can also refer to a normal, positive, unhindered course of events. For example, in 22.3 a suitable translation of a description of a normal course of events goes like this: if you cultivate yourself, your name will naturally be established (*zi li* 自立).

Another use of *zi li* brings us back to freedom from constraint, this time in the form of corrupt influence. In 5.4, Ruists are able to *zi li*—stand on their own, be independent—despite the corrosive influences around them. This conveys a general sense of autonomy that is distinct from specific cases of taking the initiative, and it also has implications for political theory that may not be immediately apparent. In 21.3, for example, it says that if a *junzi* leads in a certain way, the people will be self-governed (*zi zhi* 自治)[69]—that they will generally manage themselves without being managed by someone else. We also see a leader engendering this sense of general autonomy in 21.7:

> When crooked people must be set straight, make it so they achieve it of their own accord [*zi de* 自得]. When the worried require comfort, make it so they seek it of their own accord [*zi qiu* 自求]. When the immoderate require moderation, make it so they find it of their own accord [*zi suo* 自索].

Here, we see the interdependence between the people and the ruler that signals a unique sense of self-governance. See 41.10 for a specific instance of this kind of affective solidarity. (See also "*Minben*" and "Independence" above.)

***Zi* 自** (in the sense described above; other senses [*proceeding from* and *action to/for oneself,* with the self as object] are not indexed) 5.4, 7.1, 7.7, 8.9–10, 8.17, 9.3, 9.8, 10.3, 13.11, 14.8, 15.10, 15.14, 15.21, 16.9, 19.1, 19.6, 20.3, 21.3, 21.5, 21.7–8, 22.3, 23.3, 26.2, 26.4, 28.2, 29.2, 30.2, 32.7, 33.2–3, 37.2–3, 38.11, 38.32, 38.40, 41.5, 41.9, 41.14, 41.17, 41.26, 42.2, 42.4, 42.6, 44.5

5.4 *Zili* 自立 "This is their independence."
7.1 *Ziqiang* 自强 "A *junzi* . . . acts out of sincerity on the path of trustworthiness, firm and confident without rest."
7.1 *Ziran* 自然 "The sage . . . accords with the natural spontaneity of all things."
7.7 *Zi qu* 自取 "Brought on by one's own actions."
8.9 *Zi caishen* 自裁審 "His lack of embarrassment when shackled just shows his ability to see and judge events clearly for himself."

69. Rather than referring to each individual managing himself here, this passage could just as well refer to people working as a collective to manage themselves. The end of the passage suggests the second interpretation: "Through love and tenderness toward them, the people will be able to achieve their own ends." In other words, each striving toward his own ends will eventuate in a well-ordered society—a very contemporary-sounding notion of self-governance. See 8.6 and 10.10 for examples of the self-ordering of the people.

8.10 *Zi jue* 自覺 "I have suffered three losses and am realizing them only late in life."
8.17 *Zi zhi* 自知 "You will find out for yourself someday in the future."
9.3 *Zi yi wei* 自以爲 "I . . . don't consider myself to be incapable."
9.8 *Zi zhi . . . zi ai* 自知 . . . 自愛 "A wise person naturally understands. A *ren* person naturally cares."
10.3 *Zi shi* 自筮 "Confucius once did a divination with yarrow stalks."
13.11 *Zi lai* 自來 "I want sages to choose to immigrate here."
14.8 *Zi yu* 自與 "To take credit for the good deeds of others is robbery."
15.10 *Zi yi wei* 自以爲 "Believing he had done nothing wrong."
15.14 *Zi zhi* 自知 "I realize."
19.1 *Zi zhi* 自直 "Straight without being shaped."
20.3 *Zi zhi* 自致 "The sovereign offered the gift of his own initiative."
21.3 *Zi zhi* 自治 "The people will be self-governed."
21.3 *Zi de* 自得 "The people will be able to achieve their own ends."
21.5 *Zi ze* 自擇 "A woman must select just the right fabric, an artisan must select just the right material to work with, and a capable and virtuous leader must select just the right people to surround himself with."
21.7 *Zi de* 自得 "When crooked people must be set straight, make it so they achieve it of their own accord."
21.7 *Zi qiu* 自求 "When the worried require comfort, make it so they seek it of their own accord."
21.7 *Zi suo* 自索 "When the immoderate require moderation, make it so they find it of their own accord."
22.3 *Zi li* 自立 "Your name will naturally be established."
23.3 *Zi yan* 自言 "Being able to say his name."
26.2 *Zi hun* 自婚 "Marry as they may."
26.4 *Shen zi zhi shi* 身自執事 "Everything is prepared by the family themselves."
28.2 *Zi ru* 自入 "The other guests enter on their own."
29.2 *Ziran* 自然 "Natural bodies."
30.2 *Zi ding* 自定 "The high ministers themselves created terms."
30.2 *Zi qu* 自取 "You have chosen to come here of your own accord."
32.7 *Zi zhi* 自治 "Common people govern themselves."
32.7 *Zi an* 自安 "Achieve stability for themselves."
33.2 *Zi lai* 自來 "Has continued on its own."
33.3 *Zi wei zhu* 自爲主 "The duke himself acts as the host."
37.2 自爲子貢御 "The king of Yue welcomed Zigong on the outskirts of the capital and personally acted as his driver."
37.2 *Zi fa* 自發 "He launched an attack on his own against Qi."
37.3 *Zi shou* 自收 "There is no time for everyone to go out and harvest as they normally would."
37.3 *Zi qu* 自取 "If I make the people feel that they can take things at will."

38.11 *Zi wu* 自務 "Marched to his own drummer."
38.32 *Zi wan sheng er* 自晚生耳 "I suspect that you are just someone who naturally has children late and that it is no fault of your wife."
38.40 *Ziran* 自然 "Habits are like the unfolding of nature itself."
41.9 *Zi zhi* 自知 "Yongzi knew that he had committed a crime."
41.14 *Zi qiu* 自求 "Fortune will come."
41.17 *Zi zhi zhi* 自止之 "Kong Wenzi stopped him."
41.26 *Zi yi* 自益 "Harming someone else for personal gain."
42.2 *Zi wei shi guo* 自爲石椁 "Huan Tui was having a stone coffin made for himself."
42.2 *Zi wei zhi* 自爲之 "All of these are done by one's auxiliaries and children and cannot be predicted ahead of time, let alone performed by oneself."
42.6 *Zi wei* 自爲 "Some local officials came of their own initiative on behalf of those putting out the fire."
44.5 *Zi chu* 自出 "Confucius went to the gate personally to receive it."

Confucius' Students

As stated above, Confucius' students largely identified as *shi* (dispossessed descendants of aristocracy or royalty) and aspired to be *junzi*, or even better. In other words, they generally came from humble backgrounds and aspired to climb the ladder of officialdom. Theirs were simultaneously goals of prestige, material aspiration, and political as well as moral idealism. Students wanted to do good for society and, if circumstances permitted, they could also do well for themselves. The content of Confucius' dialogues with his students range from moral self-cultivation that would make one a virtuous leader, to the metaphysics underpinning a malleable human nature, to the psychology of human nature and political motivation, to sociopolitical organization for the welfare of the people, to effective leadership, to educational theory, to historical events and their contemporary relevance, to judging character, and so on.

The educational categories identified in the *Analects* (11.3) specifically are: virtuous conduct, speech, governing, and cultural learning. Under those four categories, ten students are identified by name, suggesting that each student especially excelled at one of them. For example, the four identified as excelling at virtuous conduct are Yan Hui, Min Ziqian, Ran Geng, and Zhonggong. It is probably not a coincidence that they are also the first four listed, in the same order, in the *Dialogues*' list of students (chapter 38) and in another list in SJ. In fact, the ten students listed in the *Analects* passage are also the first ten who appear in both the *Dialogues* list and the SJ list. The only difference is that the SJ list observes exactly the same order as in the *Analects*, while in the *Dialogues* the two listed under "speech" appear ahead of the two listed under "governing."

Although the above fact connects the lists in the three texts together, there are good reasons to believe that the *Dialogues* list and the SJ list, while perhaps having the same ultimate origin, diverged at some point well before SJ was recorded, making the *Dialogues* version the earliest one we currently possess.[70]

The differences in the two lists are numerous and minor, but not insignificant. Of the "seventy-two" students, the *Dialogues* lists seventy-six and SJ seventy-seven.[71] Not all of the names fully match, however, and sometimes matching them becomes a phonological and graphical guessing game; but of the plausible attempts, four names on the *Dialogues* list and five on the SJ list lack respective matches.[72] These mismatches support the notion that the *Dialogues* list is both earlier and independent of the SJ list. First, SJ includes all of the students mentioned in the *Analects* (except the mysterious Lao 牢 [9.7]), whereas the *Dialogues* lacks Gongbo Liao 公伯寮(繚). Second, the puzzle of the identity of Lao in the *Analects* is actually solved in the *Dialogues*. According to 38.33, Lao is the given name of Qin Lao, also known as Qin Zhang, a story about whom appears in *Dialogues* 43.18 and CQZZ ("Zhao" 20.4). Wang Su mentions this in his preface (appendix 3).

In chapter 12 of the *Dialogues*, Wenzi of Wei wheedles evaluations out of Zigong for twelve of Confucius' students. This list, in addition to *Analects* 11.3, the SJ list, and the list in *Dialogues* chapter 38, is a valuable source of information about Confucius' students and deserves further study. For now, we'll make two brief observations.

Wenzi wants to know which of Confucius' students, other than Zigong himself, are most *xian*—capable and virtuous; in other words, which are most qualified to be leaders in their own right. Of the ten students in *Analects* 11.3, three are not included: Min Ziqian, Ran Geng, and Zai Wo. For Zai Wo, it goes without saying that his noted eloquence in the *Analects* was no qualification for office, given his other defects. The exclusion of Min Ziqian and Ran Geng is consistent with their smaller role in the *Dialogues* compared to the *Analects*. Also excluded are Sima Ligeng and Fan Chi, two students that D. C. Lau (1979) identifies as prominent students of Confucius in the *Analects*.

One inclusion in Zigong's list is even more revealing—that of Tantai Mieming. Because Tantai Mieming occurs only once in the *Analects*, in a passage in which he is vaguely praised by Ziyou, Lau (1979) reasonably excludes him from among

70. Brooks and Brooks (1998) provide an extensive comparison between the list of students in the *Dialogues* and the one in SJ, agreeing that the *Dialogues* list predates the SJ list, but they go further and posit an even earlier list from which both are derived.

71. Brooks and Brooks (1998) say that the *Dialogues* list also contains seventy-seven names, adding Yan He 顏何 (SJ #72) between Shuzhong Hui and Qin Zu (*Dialogues* 38.40, 38.41). Their basis for the addition is not made explicit.

72. Brooks and Brooks (1998) attempt to reconcile the two lists, reducing them to one "original" list of seventy students. Li Qiqian (1987), going in the opposite direction, scours the early corpus and later scholarship, compiling a list of ninety-seven names of legitimate candidates of historical students of Confucius.

Confucius' genuine students. And yet here Zigong identifies him as one of Confucius' most accomplished students.

There has been much speculation among scholars about the transmission of Confucius' teachings after his death and about the possible development of factions among his students and their successors. The *Dialogues* does not reveal much on this subject, as would be expected in a genuinely early text, prior to the development of any such factions. The most the *Dialogues* reveals lies in the names included in Zigong's list and the length and quality of descriptions in chapter 38. The only potential major transmitter of Confucius' teaching not on Zigong's list is You Ruo, who plays a larger role in the *Analects* than in the *Dialogues,* and whom SJ identifies as Confucius' first immediate, but failed, successor.

The two students with the longest descriptions in *Dialogues* 38 are Zixia and Zengzi, suggesting that they were especially esteemed by, or close to, those compiling the list. This is consistent with Lau's observation that "the Confucian tradition was shaped by" them (219). In chapter 38, only Zixia is identified as a teacher. From the description, he accepted students publicly, like Confucius, and was also teacher and adviser to Marquis Wen of Wei. This is consistent with the SJ account.

Conclusion

There are good reasons to now believe that the *Dialogues of Confucius* is a genuine text from the early to middle Warring States period that, by and large, faithfully represents the words and deeds of Confucius and his students. More work needs to be done on the excavated manuscripts in the Shanghai Museum manuscripts collection, the Guodian collection, the Tsinghua University collection, and the Anhui University collection, all of which appear contemporaneous and contain numerous parallel and related texts. Similarly, there is much work to be done demonstrating the relationships between the *Dialogues* and other earlier texts, most notably the *Documents, Poems,* and CQZZ. The most extensive and reliable arguments in favor of the authenticity of the *Dialogues* can be found in Kramers (1950) and Huang (2017). Arguments against its authenticity (Goldin 1999; K. Wu 2015) are largely out of date, vague, unreliable, or highly speculative (Liu 2014; Huang 2017).

If one is to take the *Dialogues* as genuine, what is to be gained? Because it can be viewed as a companion volume to the *Analects,* the *Dialogues* supplements the philosophical positions of the *Analects* by providing context, more expansive discussions of familiar topics, and explorations that extend the philosophical reach of the *Analects.* One of the long-standing drawbacks of the *Analects* is its brevity and narrow scope, and so Confucians have commonly turned toward other texts to fill out its theory—texts like the "Da xue" and the "Zhong yong," two chapters of the *Li ji.* These texts expand Confucian theory into moral psychology, sociopolitical philosophy, and cosmology, but there has also been a nagging doubt as to the legitimacy of this expansion. The inclusion of the *Dialogues* and excavated texts in this discussion not only affirms the legitimacy of this expansion but also provides further nuances and details. As the textual record expands, so does our understanding of a comprehensive philosophy of Confucius.

We invite the reader to begin their own exploration of this more expansive theory. We hope that readers and scholars will use it to both enrich their own lives and to demonstrate its usefulness and relevance in the broader philosophical conversation today. We believe that this rich resource has much to offer and have provided an outline of a philosophical lexicon here and numerous footnotes throughout the text to begin the conversation.[73]

73. With such a large undertaking we are bound to have committed many errors and oversights. We welcome corrections. Much work remains to be done. For example, just before going to press we noticed a line in the "Bao xun 保訓" essay of the Tsinghua University collection of excavated manuscripts that bears an interesting resemblance to a curious line in the *Dialogues*. In note 16 on page 13 above, we remark on how Kong Anguo, working from an ancient, defunct script, would have had to make choices when rendering the text into the script of his day, a process that could account for Han dynasty word choices making their way into an early Warring States period text. The curious line in the *Dialogues* is: *Shun qi buyi* 舜起布衣, Shun started out as a commoner. The line is curious because *buyi* was an idiomatic term for commoner in Kong Anguo's day but not during the time of Confucius. The "Bao xun" essay, which dates much closer to the time of Confucius, has the following line: *Shun jiu zuo xiaoren* 舜舊作尖, Early on, Shun was a commoner. The term for *commoner* here is an archaic term in two senses. First, the character itself was not in circulation in the script that Kong Anguo used. So, he would have had to select an equivalent. Because 尖 is a rare variant compound of the two characters *xiao* 小 and *ren* 人, the most straightforward thing to do would be to disassemble it into its component parts as *xiaoren* 小人. However, the second way in which it is archaic is that in Confucius' time, *xiaoren* had two overlapping meanings: (1) commoner (its archaic meaning) and (2) small-minded person (the opposite of *junzi*, of a much more recent vintage). Confronted with an example in which Shun is described as a *xiaoren*, Kong Anguo would have eliminated small-minded person as a possible interpretation, and yet that was the predominant interpretation of *xiaoren* in the relevant time period (as is evident in its use elsewhere in the *Dialogues*). The best solution to this problem would be to use a term that did not carry the same ambiguity, and the word *buyi* accomplished that, meaning only commoner. This explains how a term not used in Confucius' time could have found its way into the mouth of Confucius. Of course, this is just speculation, but it is justifiable.

1

Minister of Lu

In this chapter, the groundwork is laid for Confucius' role as statesman. He is depicted as an effective—if severe—leader who can hold his own at the highest levels of officialdom and diplomacy. We learn that *li* is his desired modus operandi. His apparent severity is tempered with a concern for those at all levels of society, such that the needs of all are met, which is accomplished through a stable, peaceful social order based in *li*.

1.1

孔子初仕，爲中都宰，制爲養生送死之節：長幼異食，强弱異任，男女別塗，路無拾遺，器不雕僞。爲四寸之棺、五寸之椁，因丘陵爲墳，不封不樹。行之一年，而西方之諸侯則焉。定公謂孔子曰："學子此法以治魯國，何如？"孔子對曰："雖天下可乎，何但魯國而已哉！"於是二年，定公以爲司空。乃別五土之性，而物各得其所生之宜，咸得厥所。先時，季氏葬昭公于墓道之南。孔子溝而合諸墓焉，謂季桓子曰："貶君以彰己罪，非禮也。今合之，所以揜夫子之不臣。"由司空爲魯大司寇，設法而不用，無奸民。

In Confucius' first official position he was mayor of the town of Zhongdu. In this position he effectively regulated important aspects of life: elders and children were fed according to their distinct needs; the strong and the weak were accorded labor appropriate to their abilities; men and women maintained their distance in public;[1]

1. *Men and women maintained their distance in public, nan nü bie tu* 男女別塗: The exact meaning of this clause is vague, and commentators disagree about the best interpretation. The basic idea is that there was some kind of separation or distinction (*bie* 別) between men and women in the streets. Actual custom of the time has not been preserved. The context of Confucius' good leadership suggests that the custom contributed to the safety, good order, and respectful feelings that resulted from such leadership. Section 4.1 provides important context. There, the term *bie* is used in reference to husbands and wives and interpreted as separating them into different spheres of activity. Toward the end of that section, wives are identified as the primary line of descent, who must be accorded a high level of respect

lost items were let lie; handicrafts were simply adorned; and the dead were accorded dignified burial, with inner caskets four inches thick, outer caskets five inches, interred against hillsides as burial mounds, but without mounds of their own nor marked with a sapling.[2] After one year, even nobles from western states[3] were following his lead.

Duke Ding of Lu said to Confucius, "How about if we spread your methods throughout Lu?"

Confucius replied, "It could be the whole land. Why restrict ourselves to Lu?"

And so, the following year, the duke named Confucius minister of public works. Confucius identified five different kinds of terrain, thus allowing different kinds of agricultural products to be cultivated according to their distinct requirements, and all flourished.

Previously, Ji Pingzi had had Duke Zhao buried to the south of the ducal burial ground. Confucius had the duke's body exhumed and buried alongside the other ducal tombs. He said to Ji Huanzi, "To belittle a sovereign like that, thereby exposing one's own culpability, is a violation of *li*. Having now discreetly returned him, we have concealed your father's disloyalty."

Confucius was subsequently promoted to minister of justice, in which position he created laws that only rarely needed to be applied and so did not interfere in the common people's lives.

1.2

定公與齊侯會于夾谷，孔子攝相事，曰："臣聞有文事者，必有武備；有武事者，必有文備。古者諸侯並出疆，必具官以從，請具左右司馬。"定公從之。至會所，爲壇位，土階三等，以遇禮相見，揖讓而登，獻酢既畢，齊使萊人以兵鼓譟，劫定公。孔子歷階而進，以公退，曰："士以兵之！吾兩君爲好，裔夷之俘，敢以兵亂之，非齊君所以命諸侯也。裔不謀夏，夷不亂華，俘不干盟，兵不偪好，於神爲不祥，於德爲愆義，於人爲

---

by their husband. The section explains the relationship between affection and respect among different levels of a hierarchy. In section 30.1, separating the sexes into different spheres is said to prevent licentious behavior.

2. There is a long history in the China Central Plains, which continues to this day, of marking a grave with a mound of dirt and perhaps a sapling of an evergreen tree. In the countryside in Henan, for example, farmers' fields are dotted with such mounds. The conventional thinking in the time of Confucius and later (see, e.g., chapter 44, which is consistent with the archaeological record), however, was that this tradition did not go back to the early Zhou and so was not necessarily a best practice in terms of *li*. The reference here suggests, then, that Confucius was creating a reform that harked back to an earlier, better period. Notice, however, his own personal actions in chapter 44. (Wu 1998)

3. The state of Lu was situated toward the eastern edge of the Zhou empire and was relatively small and weak. Therefore, *western states* refers to the other Zhou states in a general sense.

失禮，君必不然。"齊侯心怍，麾而避之。有頃，齊奏宮中之樂，俳優侏儒戲於前。孔子趨進，歷階而上，不盡一等，曰："匹夫熒侮諸侯者，罪應誅，請右司馬速刑焉。"於是斬侏儒，手足異處。齊侯懼，有慚色。將盟，齊人加載書曰："齊師出境，而不以兵車三百乘從我者，有如此盟。"孔子使兹無還對曰："而不返我汶陽之田，吾以供命者，亦如之。"齊侯將設享禮，孔子謂梁丘據曰："齊魯之故，吾子何不聞焉？事既成矣，而又享之，是勤執事。且犧象不出門，嘉樂不野合。享而既具，是棄禮。若其不具，是用秕稗。用秕稗君辱，棄禮名惡，子盍圖之！夫享，所以昭德也。不昭，不如其已。"乃不果享。齊侯歸，責其群臣曰："魯以君子道輔其君，而子獨以夷狄道教寡人，使得罪。"於是，乃歸所侵魯之四邑及汶陽之田。

Duke Ding and the Qi sovereign[4] held a summit at Jiagu.[5] Confucius, managing the summit, remarked: "I have heard that in diplomatic affairs one must have military readiness, just as in military affairs one must have diplomatic readiness. Whenever nobles of old ventured across the border, they were sure to take a contingent of officers. I suggest that you prepare your war cabinet." Duke Ding followed Confucius' advice.

At the summit, an earthen terrace[6] with three steps above level ground had been prepared. The sovereigns exchanged formal greetings and then ascended the terrace. They offered toasts, after which Qi brought up performers from Lai playing drums and brandishing weapons that appeared to threaten Duke Ding. Confucius leapt up the stairs, backed the duke away from the performers, and said, "Soldiers, grab your weapons! These two sovereigns are attempting to make peace, and the frontier people captured by Qi dare to bring weapons to destroy the process. This cannot be something the Qi sovereign ordered other lords[7] to do. Frontier peoples should not plot to sow discord in the central states. Captured prisoners should not interfere in treaties. Weapons should not be used to threaten friends. Such means are inauspicious, immoral, and improper. The sovereign would never do such a thing."

Embarrassed, the Qi sovereign waved off the performers. After a time, Qi sent out the palace music troupe, which included dwarfs dancing and jesting in front of the sovereigns. Confucius rushed forward, again leapt up the stairs, and said emphatically, "Commoners confounding lords is a crime that deserves punishment. May the minister of war carry it out immediately."

The dwarfs were cut in two at the waist, torso and legs falling to the ground separately. The Qi sovereign expressed fear and shame.

4. Duke Jing.

5. According to CQZZ ("Ding" 10.2), this event occured in the year 500 BCE.

6. See "*Tai*" in the glossary.

7. Other lords, *zhu hou* 諸侯: the nobility of Qi, presumably (see, for example, the banquet preparations just below).

When it was time to finalize the treaty, the Qi side added a clause: "If Qi sends troops across its border, Lu must send three hundred war chariots to assist." Confucius instructed Zi Wuhuan to add the clause: "Qi shall return occupied land north of the Wen River."

When Confucius realized that a Qi nobleman was preparing a sumptuous banquet to celebrate, Confucius said to Liangqiu Ju, "Surely, you must be familiar with the ancient traditions of Qi and Lu. Celebrating an accomplishment with a sumptuous banquet is needlessly overworking the staff, not to mention that certain sacrificial vessels are not meant to leave the palace at all, nor should orchestral music[8] be performed out in the wilds like this. To go through with the celebration with all of the necessary paraphernalia would be to go against *li*. To try to do it without the necessary vessels and utensils, you would have to use inferior items. Is it your plan to insult the sovereigns with inferior items and ruin your reputation by violating *li*? I suggest you think hard about it first! A sumptuous banquet is for the purpose of bringing attention to the virtue of the sovereigns. When it can't accomplish that, it's best to not do it at all."

In the end, the banquet was not held.

As the Qi sovereign was returning home, he rebuked his ministers, saying, "Lu uses the way of the *junzi* to guide their sovereign. You use the way of the barbarians to advise me, and you wronged Lu in the process!"

Subsequently, he returned four cities to Lu, including their surrounding farmland north of the Wen River.[9]

1.3

孔子言於定公曰："家不藏甲，邑無百雉之城，古之制也。今三家過制，請皆損之。"乃使季氏宰仲由隳三都。叔孫不得意於季氏，因費宰公山弗擾率費人以襲魯。孔子以公與季孫、叔孫、孟孫入于季氏之宮，登武子之臺。費人攻之，及臺側，孔子命申句須、樂頎勒士衆下伐之，費人北，遂隳三都之城。强公室，弱私家，尊君卑臣，政化大行。初，魯之販羊有沈猶氏者，常朝飲其羊以詐市人；有公慎氏者，妻淫不制；有慎潰氏，奢侈逾法；魯之鬻六畜者，飾之以儲價。及孔子之爲政也，則沈猶氏不敢朝飲其羊，公慎

8. *Orchestral music, jia yue* 嘉樂: excellent music. Given the context, this seems to refer to musical instruments generally reserved for august occasions. Du Yu 杜預 says that it refers to music played on bells and chimes (i.e., orchestral music). (Luo 1994)

9. CQZZ ("Ding" 10) relates a version of this story and identifies the cities as Yun 鄆, Huan 讙, and Guiyin 龜陰. Two further points can be made. First, about the size of the concession: The swath of land from Yun in the West through Huan to Guiyin in the north ran the length of more than half of Lu's northern border at the time. That is a significant amount of territory. Second, about the text: The *Dialogues* says four cities, while CQZZ names three specific cities. Since one of the cities CQZZ names has two characters, it suggests (there being no serial comma in early texts) that a misunderstanding arose sometime in the transmission of this section. (Tan 1996)

氏出其妻，慎潰氏越境而徙，三月，則鬻牛馬者不儲價，賣羊豚者不加飾。男女行者別其塗，道不拾遺，男尚忠信，女尚貞順。四方客至於邑，不求有司，皆如歸焉。

Confucius said to Duke Ding, "In the political structure of ancient times, high officials did not quarter armed soldiers, nor did cities other than the capital have their own walled defenses. The Three Families[10] violate this system. I recommend that you have their city walls demolished."

And so, Zhong You, Jisun's household manager, was appointed to demolish the three walls. Shusun,[11] unhappy with Jisun, teamed up with Gongshan Furao, mayor of Bi (Jisun's city), who led the people of Bi in an attack on the Lu capital. Confucius led the duke, along with the leaders of the Jisun, Shusun, and Mengsun clans, to take refuge atop the Tower of Wuzi in Jisun's palace in the Lu capital. The Bi people invaded, and as they approached the tower, Confucius ordered Shenju Xu and Yue Qi to lead a group of soldiers in a counterattack. The Bi people were defeated and fled. Subsequently, the three walls were demolished.[12] This strengthened the central government and weakened the Three Families. With the sovereign in the position of honor and the ministers in the position of service, government reforms were carried out on a large scale.

Originally in Lu, there was a seller of goats by the name of Shenyou. He would often gorge his goats with water in the morning as a way of cheating his customers. There was also one Gongshen, whose wife was promiscuous and uncontrollable. There was also a man named Shenkui, who lived a life of extravagance outside the law. And in general, the sellers of meat and livestock of all kinds[13] in Lu enhanced the appearance of their products[14] in order to get better prices. After Confucius took the reins of government, though, Shenyou didn't dare gorge his goats anymore, Gongshen divorced his wife, Shenkui emigrated, and after three months, sellers of meat and livestock no longer enhanced the appearance of their products. Men and women maintained their distance in public. Lost items were let lie. Men were conscientious and trustworthy. Women were devoted and congenial. Visitors from all directions came to the capital and felt right at home, with no need to seek redress from local authorities.

10. *Three Families*: see under "Ji Huanzi" in the glossary.

11. *Shusun*: Shusun Zhe. See the glossary.

12. A version of this story appears in the CQZZ ("Ding" 12.2) but differs in some details. For one, Confucius' role is much diminished. For another, the CQZZ version states that, after two walls were destroyed and it came time to destroy the Mengsun wall, Mengsun balked and his wall remained standing. SJ ("Kongzi shi jia") follows the CQZZ version almost verbatim.

13. *Sellers of meat and livestock of all kinds, yu liu chu zhe* 鬻六畜者: sellers of the six domestic animals (horses, cattle, goats, chickens, dogs, swine).

14. *Enhanced the appearance of their products, shi zhi* 飾之: decorated them. It's not clear whether these were sellers of the live animals or sellers of the meat.

2

Beginning with Denouncement

The theme of Confucius as a high-placed and severe leader continues. He is particularly severe with those who would disrupt the functions of government intended for the welfare of the people and who would direct such functions, through deceit and misinformation, to their own personal benefit.

Confucius' apparent severity is tempered further in this chapter through the description of his view of education vis-à-vis the law. Notwithstanding the unfortunate dwarfs in chapter 1, severe punishments should be reserved for those in high positions, who (1) should know better and (2) have the power to spread corruption broadly. Order among the people, Confucius believes, should be achieved through education, not severe punishment.

We are introduced also to Confucius' students Zhong You (Zilu), who dares admonish Confucius, and Ran You, a competent leader in his own right, who was one of several of Confucius' students who worked for the powerful Ji family.

2.1

孔子爲魯司寇，攝行相事，有喜色。仲由問曰："由聞君子禍至不懼，福至不喜。今夫子得位而喜，何也？"孔子曰："然，有是言也。不曰'樂以貴下人'乎？"於是朝政七日而誅亂政大夫少正卯，戮之于兩觀之下，尸於朝三日。子貢進曰："夫少正卯，魯之聞人也，今夫子爲政而始誅之，或者爲失乎？"孔子曰："居，吾語汝以其故。天下有大惡者五，而竊盗不與焉。一曰心逆而險，二曰行僻而堅，三曰言僞而辯，四曰記醜而博，五曰順非而澤。此五者，有一於人，則不免君子之誅。而少正卯皆兼有之：其居處足以撮徒成黨，其談說足以飾邪滎衆，其强禦足以反是獨立。此乃人之奸雄者也，不可以不除。夫殷湯誅尹諧、文王誅潘正、周公誅管蔡、太公誅華士、管仲誅付乙、子産誅史何，是此七子皆異世而同誅者，以七子異世而同惡，故不可赦也。《詩》云：'憂心悄悄，愠於群小'，小人成群，斯足憂矣。"

Confucius was at one time both minister of justice and prime minister of Lu.[1] Zhong You, noticing a delighted expression on Confucius' face, asked, "I've heard that a *junzi* neither panics in adversity nor delights in good fortune. You seem delighted in your new position. Why is that?"

Confucius responded, "Yes, there is such a saying. Isn't it also said, 'Take pleasure in a position of humble leadership'?"

After being in a leadership role at the court for seven days, Confucius denounced Deputy Mao, a high official, for corrupting the governing processes. Mao was humiliated beneath the two towers outside the palace and then brought inside the court, where for three days he played the role of a corpse.[2] Zigong approached Confucius

1. The CQZZ ("Ding" 1.4) mentions in the year 509 BCE that Confucius was minister of justice for Lu. The *Xunzi* version of this story (28.2) has Confucius acting as prime minister. The *Dialogues* version has him in both positions simultaneously.

2. *Zhu* 誅, translated here as "denounced," can also mean executed, and *shi* 尸, translated here as "played the role of a corpse," can also be translated simply as "corpse." Although this line is often interpreted to mean that Confucius had Deputy Mao executed, there are two reasons to reevaluate. First, in the subsequent examples of Guanshu and Caishu also being subjected to *zhu*, our main sources—the *Documents* ("Zhou shu") and SJ ("Zhou ben ji," "Guan Cai shi jia")—show that Caishu was not executed. The case of Guanshu is also informative because in the SJ ("Guan Cai shi jia"), he and his co-conspirator, Wugeng, are described as receiving different punishments—one being *zhu* 誅 and the other being *sha* 殺, the latter of which generally means to kill (though it can also mean to exile). (The other five criminals listed are not historically attested.) The ambiguity of *zhu* here and in SJ seems to stem from the ambiguity of an archaic synonym in the *Documents*. According to the *Documents* ("Zhou shu"), Guan was subjected to *bi* 辟 and Cai was imprisoned. *Bi* 辟 can mean either to repudiate or to punish (but not necessarily execute); in fact, in its other instances in the *Documents*, it never seems to mean to execute and it is even set off against the punishment of execution, except in one passage where, after several kinds of *bi* punishments have been listed, the guilty one is subjected to *da bi* (the great punishment). Taken together, these points suggest that it would not make sense to interpret *zhu* as to execute. Second, in the very next section of this *Dialogues* chapter, Confucius laments the standard practice of summary execution. It is straightforward to translate the word *zhu* as to denounce; thus, following the reasoning above, we see it as the most fitting translation in this context. The word *shi* is more challenging to make sense of if *zhu* is interpreted as to denounce. *Shi* means corpse, and by extension it was used to denote the common practice of one person being designated the surrogate of a dead ancestor at a funeral ceremony, partaking of ritual offerings and conferring blessings on the family (see, for example, 32.5). We see *shi* used in a related metaphorical way in 10.24 (alternatively 10.16) of the *Analects*: "[Confucius] didn't sleep [like] a corpse." In this case, it probably refers not to a corpse per se but merely to a formal and solemn appearance. Confucius' point in *Analects* 10.24 seems to be that, when one goes to bed, it is a time to be relaxed and not caught up in the formalities of ritual. This meaning can be extended to the episode in question. Mao's attitude when punished must reflect the seriousness of the matter. He was forced to take his punishment, perhaps being criticized repeatedly over three days, while maintaining a bearing of formality and solemnity. Further passages in the *Dialogues* that support the interpretation here include 2.2, 3.2, 6.1, 14.4, 14.8, 15.8, 22.2, and 37.2. Passages that support

about this, asking, "Deputy Mao is an eminent person in Lu. As soon as you get control of the government, the first thing you do is denounce him. Isn't that a mistake?"

Confucius said, "Stay a minute, and I'll explain my reasons. There are five kinds of abominations in this world, and I'm not speaking of something like common thievery. The first is sinister contrariness; the second, strident distortion; the third, defending falsehoods; the fourth, being broadly misinformed; and the fifth, doing wrong and obscuring or validating it through generosity to others. Someone caught engaging in any one of these wouldn't be able to avoid being denounced by the sovereign, and Deputy Mao was guilty of all of them. He cultivated a faction of loyal followers at his place of residence; in his discourse, he covered up his own corruption while flattering whole groups of people; and he built up a line of defense that was sufficient for him to rebel and hold power independently. This kind of vile usurper must be removed. Consider that Tang of the Shang dynasty denounced Yin Xie, King Wen denounced Pan Zheng, the Duke of Zhou denounced Guan and Cai, the Grand Duke denounced Hua Shi, Guan Zhong denounced Fu Yi, and Zichan denounced Shi He—seven eminent people from different times, and all were denounced, seven eminent people from different times guilty of unpardonable abominations. The Poems say, 'Silent in worry, / Resented by small-minded cliques.'[3] When small-minded men form cliques, that is the time to worry."

2.2

孔子爲魯大司寇，有父子訟者，夫子同狴執之，三月不別。其父請止，夫子赦之焉。季孫聞之，不悦，曰："司寇欺余，曩告余曰：'國家必先以孝。'余今戮一不孝以教民孝，不亦可乎？而又赦，何哉？"冉有以告孔子。子喟然嘆曰："嗚呼！上失其道而殺其下，非理也。不教以孝而聽其獄，是殺不辜。三軍大敗，不可斬也；獄犴不治，不可刑也。何者？上教之不行，罪不在民故也。夫慢令謹誅，賊也；徵斂無時，暴也；不試責成，虐

interpreting *zhu* as to execute are 1.2 and 13.3. The term *zhu* appears once in the *Analects* (5.10), where it cannot possibly mean to execute and clearly means something like to criticize instead. Kramers (1950) translates all instances of *zhu* as *to punish* (and translates *lu* 戮 [to massacre, to humiliate] as to execute). John Knoblock (1994), in his translation of the *Xunzi*, translates the first instance of *zhu* in this passage as *to execute* and subsequent instances in the same passage as *to punish*. Eric Hutton (2014), in his translation of the *Xunzi*, uniformly translates the term in this passage as *to execute*. This story also appears in *Shuo yuan* 15.27, where Henry (2022) translates the term as *execute*, for the obvious reason that *Shuo yuan* 15.25 adds that Confucius had Mao beheaded.

3. These lines appear in the poem "The Cypress Boat" (#26) and can be found today in the "Bei feng" section of the *Poems*. On the surface, the poem appears to be a girl's lament on being mistreated by someone in her large household, with no help from those around her. Many commentators have also interpreted it as an allegory for a neglected aspiring official. This latter interpretation is consistent with its usage here.

也。政無此三者，然後刑可即也。《書》云：'義刑義殺，勿庸以即汝心，惟曰未有慎事。'言必教而後刑也。既陳道德，以先服之；而猶不可，尚賢以勸之；又不可，即廢之；又不可，而後以威憚之。若是三年，而百姓正矣。其有邪民不從化者，然後待之以刑，則民咸知罪矣。《詩》云：'天子是毗，俾民不迷。'是以威厲而不試，刑錯而不用。今世則不然，亂其教，繁其刑，使民迷惑而陷焉，又從而制之，故刑彌繁，而盜不勝也。夫三尺之限，空車不能登者，何哉？峻故也。百仞之山，重載陟焉，何哉？陵遲故也。今世俗之陵遲久矣，雖有刑法，民能勿逾乎？"

When Confucius was minister of justice, a father and son came to him with a legal dispute. Confucius jailed them both, keeping them in the same cell for three months. When the father pleaded for it to end, Confucius pardoned them. Jisun heard about this and was displeased. He said to Confucius' student Ran You, "I feel deceived by the minister of justice. He once told me, 'A country must make *xiao* a priority.' In order to teach the people this, I had someone executed for being un-*xiao*. Isn't that the right thing to do? Then Confucius goes and pardons the same type of behavior. Why is that?"

Ran You reported this remark to Confucius. Confucius sighed deeply and said, "Oh my! It would go against all norms for superiors to lose sight of the *dao* and murder those below them. To try cases of un-*xiao* behavior without first teaching *xiao* is to murder the innocent. You don't execute soldiers for losing a battle. And you don't apply corporal punishment if the justice system is already unfair. Why? If those in charge are not doing their jobs educating the people, it's not the fault of the people. It is criminal to be lax in decrees but strict in punishment, tyranny to institute a draft at an inopportune time, and cruelty to expect perfection without a period of trial and error. It is only when a government is free of these three kinds of error that one can institute strict punishments.

"The Documents say, 'Punishments and executions must be handled according to *yi*, not by one's whims. One can only say that these have never been handled with care.'[4] This is to say that education must come before punishment. Having

4. This passage resembles a passage from the "Kang gao" chapter of the "Zhou shu" section of the *Documents*. The Duke of Zhou, on behalf of the young King Cheng, is enfeoffing the duke's younger brother, Kang, at Wei, the old Shang capital, and instructing him to follow the legal ways of the Shang (from its glory days). The passage in its current form says: "Follow Shang laws to ensure that punishments and executions be handled according to *yi*, not by your whims. If you are able to fully follow the Shang ways, it will be called orderly. Otherwise, it will be labeled as never having gone smoothly. 用其義刑義殺，勿庸以次汝封。乃汝盡遜曰時敘，惟曰未有遜事。" In the *Dialogues* version, the conditional sentence "If you . . . called orderly" does not appear, and instead of *xun* 遜 (smoothly) in the next sentence of the *Documents* version, there is *shen* 慎 (to handle with care) in the *Dialogues* version. The "Kang gao" chapter is one of the mostly commonly quoted chapters of the *Documents* during the Warring States period and is from a very early historical layer of the *Documents*.

displayed one's fairness and virtue for all to see, lead that way and the people will follow. For those who remain unreformed, exhort them to emulate the capable and virtuous leaders of the past. For the still recalcitrant, threaten them with removal. For those remaining, they should be awed into submission by one's authority. Over three years of this, the people will reform. There may still be some wicked ones who refuse to be transformed. They are the ones you may punish, and the people will all recognize them as guilty.

"A poem says:

Support the king in this way,
Keep the people from going astray.[5]

"Therefore, do not threaten coercion and do not use harsh punishments. But rulers think differently today. Teachings are in disarray, and punishments proliferate, confusing the people and luring them into traps. If one responds with more severity, punishments will continue to proliferate, and one will never triumph over crime.

"When is an empty wagon unable to climb a three-foot ramp? When the ramp is too steep. When is a full wagon able to climb a thousand-foot hill? When the slope is a faint incline. It has been too long now that the justice system has been a faint incline for the people. We may think the penal system is effective, but can common people avoid falling afoul of it?"

5. This poem, entitled "Lofty Nan Mountain" (#191), under one plausible interpretation, is a lament about the disastrous governance of the prime minister Yin under Zhou King You. It can be found in the "Xiao ya" section of the *Poems*.

3

A King's Speech

Chapter 3 is the first chapter in the book that is an extended dialogue with one student on a single theme. The student is Zengzi, one of Confucius' most accomplished students, and the topic is meritocratic government, resonating with chapters 21 and 32. In Confucius' ideal form of government, compassionate rule from above creates bonds of trust and good feeling with the people below, who are allowed to live lives unburdened by the government, and who naturally emulate the frugal, virtuous behavior of their leaders. We are introduced to the key terms *dao, de, xiao,* and *ren,* all of which are reinforced by *li.*

3.1

孔子閑居，曾參侍。孔子曰："參乎！今之君子，唯士與大夫之言可聞也。至於君子之言者，希也。於乎！吾以王言之，其不出户牖而化天下。"曾子起，下席而對曰："敢問何謂王之言？"孔子不應，曾子曰："侍夫子之閑也，難對，是以敢問。"孔子又不應。曾子肅然而懼，摳衣而退，負席而立。有頃，孔子嘆息，顧謂曾子曰："參，汝可語明王之道與？"曾子曰："非敢以爲足也，請因所聞而學焉。"子曰："居，吾語汝。夫道者，所以明德也；德者，所以尊道也。是以非德道不尊，非道德不明。雖有國之良馬，不以其道服乘之，不可以道里。雖有博地衆民，不以其道治之，不可以致霸王。是故昔者明王内修七教，外行三至。七教修然後可以守，三至行然後可以征。明王之道，其守也，則必折衝千里之外；其征也，則必還師衽席之上。故曰内修七教而上不勞，外行三至而財不費。此之謂明王之道也。"曾子曰："不勞不費之謂明王，可得聞乎？"孔子曰："昔者帝舜，左禹而右皋陶，不下席而天下治。夫如此，何上之勞乎？政之不平，君之患也；令之不行，臣之罪也。若乃十一而税，用民之力，歲不過三日，入山澤以其時而無征，關譏市廓皆不收賦，此則生財之路，而明王節之，何財之費乎？"曾子曰："敢問何謂七教？"孔子曰："上敬老則下益孝，上尊齒則下益悌，上樂施則下益寬，上親賢則下擇友，上好德則下不隱，上惡貪[1]則下耻争，上廉讓則下耻節，此之謂七教。七教者，治民之本也。政教定，則本正也。凡上者，民之表也，表正則何物不正？是故人君先立

1. Corrected *pin* 貧 to *tan* 貪, following SKQS and Tongwen editions.

仁於己，然後大夫忠而士信，民敦俗璞，男慤而女貞，六者，教之致也！布諸天下四方而不窕，納諸尋常之室而不塞，等之以禮，立之以義，行之以順，則民之棄惡，如湯之灌雪焉。"

One day, Confucius was relaxing and Zeng Shen was attending to him.

Confucius said, "Shen, nowadays with respect to sovereigns, all we hear are the voices of low and high officials. Rarely do we hear the words of a sovereign. It's too bad! I'll tell you about true kings,[2] who can transform the world without even stepping outside."

Zengzi stood up, stepped off the mat, and said, "What is meant by 'speech of a true king?'"

Confucius didn't respond.

Zengzi said, "I'm just here to see if you need anything while relaxing. It's a difficult topic, and that's why I asked."

Again, Confucius did not respond.

Zengzi stood there, timidly respectful. He politely shifted his skirts as if to leave, standing with his back to the mat.

After a time, Confucius sighed again, looked over at Zengzi and said, "Shen, can you speak to the topic of the way of an enlightened king?"

Zengzi said, "I wouldn't presume to be competent to do that. Please do me the favor of allowing me to learn what you know about it."

Confucius said, "Sit down, and I'll tell you. *Dao* is the way to illuminate *de*. And *de* is the way to venerate *dao*. *Dao* cannot be venerated without *de*, and *de* cannot be illuminated without *dao*. Take, for example, a great horse. If it is not treated according to its *dao*, it cannot be ridden across vast distances. Now, consider a large country with multitudes of people. If they are not led according to *dao*, one cannot achieve the status of a superpower. This is why enlightened kings of the past cultivated the seven kinds of model behavior internally and achieved the three ultimates externally. Safeguarding can occur once the seven kinds of model behavior are cultivated. And military expeditions can occur once the three ultimates are achieved. By following the *dao* of enlightened kings, safeguarding guarantees a reach of a thousand miles, and expeditions will no doubt return safely. That's why it is said that cultivating the seven models of behavior internally conserves effort in leadership, and achieving the three ultimates externally conserves finances. This is what is called the *dao* of enlightened kings."

Zengzi asked, "May I learn more about the enlightened king who wastes neither effort nor finances?"

2. True king, *wang* 王: an idealized king, the kind of leader that Confucius wished could rule.

Confucius responded, "Consider Chief Shun of former times. He was aided by Yǔ and Gao Yao. He never left his mat, and yet the whole land was well governed. Where is his effort in leadership? If a government is unfair, it is the fault of the sovereign. If fair decrees are not followed, it is the fault of the vassals. Take ten percent in taxes. Don't conscript the people to work more than three days in a year. Let the people hunt in the mountains and marshes at appropriate times of the year without obligation. Arrange for inspections of market stalls, but don't take a levy. This is the path to building wealth, and the enlightened king does it through thrift. Where is the waste in finances?"

Zengzi asked, "What are the seven kinds of model behavior, if I may ask?"

Confucius replied, "When the people above venerate the aged, it increases *xiao* among the people below. When the people above respect their elders, it increases respect for elder brothers among the people below. When the people above take joy in sharing wealth, it increases generosity among the people below. When the people above befriend capable and virtuous people, the people below also become more judicious in choosing friends. When the people above appreciate *de*, the people below are not secretive. When the people above shun corruption, contentiousness becomes shameful among the people below. When the people above are scrupulous and deferential, the people below become moderate. These are what are called the seven kinds of model behavior, and they are the root of governing the people. When models of behavior are set in the government, the people will be set right. The people above are examples for the people below. If the examples get it right, what will not be right?

"Therefore, if sovereigns first cultivate *ren* in themselves, then the high ministers will be conscientious and the lower ministers trustworthy, the people will be honest and customs down-to-earth, men will be dutiful and women devoted. These six are the results of modeling behavior. Have them spread to the four corners of the land and they won't be spread too thin; have them fill the smallest household and they won't be too much. Have people practice *li* across every level of the hierarchy, establish it with *yi*, put it into effect agreeably, and then the people will reject bad behavior like hot water poured over snow."

3.2

曾子曰:"道則至矣,弟子不足以明之。"孔子曰:"參以爲姑止乎?又有焉。昔者明王之治民也,法必裂地以封之,分屬以理之,然後賢民無所隱,暴民無所伏。使有司日省而時考之,進用賢良,退貶不肖,然則賢者悅而不肖者懼。哀鰥寡,養孤獨,恤貧窮,誘孝悌,選才能。此七者修,則四海之內無刑民矣。上之親下也,如手足之於腹心;下之親上也,如幼子之於慈母矣。上下相親如此,故令則從,施則行,民懷其德,近者悅服,遠者來附,政之致也。夫布指知寸,布手知尺,舒肘知尋,斯不遠之則也。周制三百步爲里,千步爲井,三井而埒,埒三而矩,五十里而都,封百里而有國,乃爲稿積資聚焉, 恤行者之有亡。是以蠻夷諸夏, 雖衣冠不同, 言語不合, 莫不來賓。故曰'無市而民不乏, 無刑而民不亂'。田獵罩弋, 非以盈宮室也; 徵斂百姓, 非以盈府庫也。慘怛以補不足, 禮節以損有餘, 多信而寡貌, 其禮可守, 其言可覆, 其跡可履。如飢而食, 如渴而飲, 民之信之, 如寒暑之必驗。故視遠若邇, 非道邇也, 見明德也。是故兵革不動而威, 用利不施而親, 萬民懷其惠。此之謂明王之守, 折衝千里之外者也。"曾子曰: "敢問何謂三至?"孔子曰: "至禮不讓而天下治, 至賞不費而天下士悅, 至樂無聲而天下民和。明王篤行三至, 故天下之君可得而知, 天下之士可得而臣, 天下之民可得而用。"曾子曰: "敢問此義何謂?"孔子曰: "古者明王必盡知天下良士之名, 既知其名, 又知其實, 又知其數及其所在焉。然後因天下之爵以尊之, 此之謂至禮不讓而天下治。因天下之祿以富天下之士, 此之謂至賞不費而天下之士悅。如此則天下之名譽興焉, 此之謂至樂無聲而天下之民和。故曰: '所謂天下之至仁者, 能合天下之至親也; 所謂天下之至明者, 能舉天下之至賢者也。'此三者咸通, 然後可以征。是故仁者莫大乎愛人, 智者莫大乎知賢, 賢政者莫大乎官能。有土之君修此三者, 則四海之內供命而已矣。夫明王之所征, 必道之所廢者也。是故誅其君而改其政, 弔其民而不奪其財。故明王之政, 猶時雨之降, 降至則民悅矣。是故行施彌博, 得親彌衆。此之謂還師衽席之上。"

Zengzi said, "I don't quite understand what is meant by 'the culmination of *dao*.'"

Confucius replied, "Shen, do you think that's the end of it? There is more to it. In governing the people, enlightened kings of the past employed methods that guaranteed boundaries by dividing up the land and guaranteed order by creating levels of subordination. Subsequently, capable and virtuous people had no space for seclusion, and rebellious people had no place to hide. Officers were sent out on daily inspections and regular investigations. The capable and virtuous were hired and promoted, while worthless pretenders were demoted and fired. As a result, the virtuous and capable were happy, and the worthless pretenders afraid. Widows and widowers were met with compassion, the orphaned and childless were taken care of, the poor and destitute were given aid, guidance was given to youth who were good to their elders, and those of talent and potential were selected for advancement. When these seven are cultivated, there will be no need to punish people anywhere within the four seas. The people above will feel close bonds to the people below, and care for them as if caring for their own vital organs; and the people below will feel close bonds to the people above, like young children to their loving mother. When bonds like these are formed among those above and below, orders are subsequently followed, policies work, people embrace their virtue, the nearby happily pay allegiance, and the far away come to submit. They are the results of good government.

"To know the length of a *cun*,[3] extend a finger. To know the length of a *chi*, open your hand. To know the length of a *xun*, spread your arms. These measurements are

3. *Cun*: See the "Weights and Measures" section at the beginning of the glossary.

always nearby. According to the Zhou system of measurements, a *li* is 300 *bu* [strides], a *jing* is a thousand square *bu*, a *lie* is three *jing*, and three *lie* make a *ju*. A walled capital is about fifty square *li*.[4] Grant a fief of a hundred square *li*, and you have a state sufficient to accumulate monetary and material wealth and to assist travelers in need. And so, even though their customs vary and they don't speak the same language, all of the Xia kingdoms and non-Xia peoples will come to pay allegiance. This is why it is said: Even without markets, the people won't feel want; even without punishments, the people won't be disorderly.

"The purpose of hunting and fishing is not to fill up mansions and palaces. The purpose of levying taxes on the people is not to fill up the state's treasury. Use compassion to make up for insufficiency; use *li* and self-restraint to curtail excess; stand by your word instead of putting on appearances. Such *li* can be safeguarded; such words can be repeated; such tracks can be followed, as surely as eating follows hunger and drinking follows thirst. The people will have faith in such leaders as surely as the extreme temperatures of winter and summer put everyone to the test. In order for distant leaders to have their influence felt nearby, it is not that they must travel along roads but that their enlightened *de* be manifest. Thus, there can be persuasion through awe without the need for armored soldiers, and there can be bonds of affection without bribing the people. The people will appreciate such attention. This is what is called safeguarding by an enlightened king, which can be extended thousands of *li* away."

Zengzi said, "May I ask about the three ultimates?"

Confucius responded, "Ultimate *li* is that by which the whole land is well governed without the need for deference. Ultimate compensation is that by which officials are pleased without any waste. Ultimate music is that by which the people are harmonized without making a sound. If an enlightened king is able to thoroughly implement these three ultimates, the nobility will recognize the legitimacy of the king, officials will loyally serve, and the people will willingly exert themselves."

Zengzi said, "May I ask what you mean by these?"

Confucius responded, "An enlightened king of the past was sure to have a thorough knowledge of the names of all potential up-and-coming officials, and not just their names but also their qualities, their skills, and where they resided, and then he would honor them with official rank across the land. This is what I mean by the whole land being well governed without the need for deference. He used salaried positions across the land to pay rising officials across the land. This is what I mean by officials being pleased without any waste. As a result, the fame of the enlightened king spread across the land. This is what I mean by the people being harmonized with soundless music. And so it is said that the best *ren* in the world is that which

4. *Li*: In addition to the glossary entry, see 41.6n16.

can unite the whole world in bonds of ultimate affection; the greatest enlightenment in the world is that which can raise up the most capable and virtuous. Only when the three ulimtates are all mastered can military expeditions be sent forth. Thus, there is no greater *ren* than loving others, no greater wisdom than recognizing the worth of others, and no greater meritocracy than having capable and virtuous people in office. Therefore, if any local sovereign can cultivate these three, everyone within the four seas will simply submit.

"States to which expeditions are sent will, of course, have already abandoned the *dao*. For this reason, the conquered sovereign is to be punished and the government reformed. The people are to be met with sympathy, and no wealth is to be confiscated. In this way, the government of the enlightened king is like a timely rain—when it comes, the people rejoice. And so the more widespread such policies are, the more hearts of people everywhere will be won. This is what I meant when I referred to the expeditions returning safely."

4

The Grand Wedding

In an extended conversation with the young Duke Ai, Confucius places human actions in a cosmic context of connection, from the vastness of the *dao* of *tian* to daily acts of looking after one's parents. Tied together are the leadership's love and concern for the people, family bonds of the immediate household, and family bonds across generations. The major virtues depicted are *xiao*, trustworthiness, and *ren*, mediated and carried out, again, via *li*. Modeling good behavior has a transformative influence on others.

4.1

孔子侍坐於哀公。公問曰:“敢問人道孰爲大?”孔子愀然作色而對曰:“君及此言也,百姓之惠也,固臣敢無辭而對。人道政爲大。夫政者,正也。君爲正,則百姓從而正矣。君之所爲,百姓之所從。君不爲正,百姓何所從乎?”公曰:“敢問爲政如之何?”孔子對曰:“夫婦别,男女親,君臣信。三者正,則庶物從之。”公曰:“寡人雖無能也,願知所以行三者之道。可得聞乎?”孔子對曰:“古之政,愛人爲大。所以治愛人,禮爲大。所以治禮,敬爲大。敬之至矣,大婚爲大。大婚至矣,冕而親迎。親迎者,敬之也。是故君子興敬爲親,捨敬則是遺親也。弗親弗敬,弗尊也。愛與敬,其政之本與!”公曰:“寡人願有言也,然冕而親迎,不已重乎?”孔子愀然作色而對曰:“合二姓之好,以繼先聖之後,以爲天下宗廟社稷之主。君何謂已重焉?”公曰:“寡人實固,不固安得聞此言乎!寡人欲問,不能爲辭,請少進。”孔子曰:“天地不合,萬物不生。大婚,萬世之嗣也。君何謂已重焉?”孔子遂言曰:“内以治宗廟之禮,足以配天地之神;出以治直言之禮,以立上下之敬。物耻則足以振之,國耻足以興之。故爲政先乎禮。禮,其政之本與!”孔子遂言曰:“昔三代明王,必敬妻子也,蓋有道焉。妻也者,親之主也;子也者,親之後也,敢不敬與?是故君子無不敬。敬也者,敬身爲大。身也者,親之支也,敢不敬與?不敬其身,是傷其親;傷其親,是傷本也;傷其本,則支從之而亡。三者,百姓之象也。身以及身,子以及子,妃以及妃。君以修此三者,則大化愾乎天下矣。昔太王之道也如此,國家順矣。”

Confucius sat in attendance on Duke Ai. The duke asked, “May I ask what is most important in implementing human *dao*?”

Confucius suddenly took on a serious expression and responded, "It is to the people's great benefit that you ask this question, your majesty. How could I refuse to respond?

"The most important thing in implementing human *dao* is good government. The key to good government is integrity. When the sovereign leads with integrity, the people follow along and also live with integrity. Whatever the sovereign does, the people follow along. If the sovereign does not lead with integrity, how could the people be expected to live with integrity?"

The duke said, "May I ask about how to achieve good government?"

Confucius responded, "Separate spheres for husband and wife, affection between parents and children,[1] trustworthiness between ruler and ministers. Get these three right, and everything else will follow."

The duke said, "Although I am incapable, I would like to hear more about how to bring about the *dao* of these three."

Confucius replied, "In the governments of ancient times, the most important thing was caring for others. The way to implement caring for others was through *li*. The way to implement *li* was through respect. The culmination of respect was in the grand wedding.[2] The culmination of the grand wedding occurred when a groom, wearing his *mian* crown, personally welcomed the bride. To personally welcome the bride is to show respect for her. Thus, a leader expresses affection through respect. To neglect respect is to abandon affection. Without affection and respect, there is no esteem. Care and respect—these are the root of good government."

The duke asked, "I would just like to say that wouldn't it be going overboard to personally welcome my bride while wearing the *mian* crown?"

Confucius turned serious again and replied, "How can you say that the goodness of uniting two families, which continues the line of the former sages, with these descendants being masters of ceremony in the most important rituals across the land, is going overboard?"[3]

1. *Parents and children, nan nü* 男女 (male and female): A parallel passage in the *Li ji* has *fu zi* 父子 (father and child). Because *nan nü* can mean children, the most inclusive translation here is "parents and children."

2. *Grand wedding, da hun* 大婚: This is an uncommon locution. Commentators generally agree that it refers to the wedding of royalty or nobility.

3. The duke objects that a wedding's level of significance does not warrant the *mian* crown, which was apparently reserved for the most august occasions. Confucius demonstrates the unparalleled stature of the sovereign's wedding by putting it in terms of reverencing the lineages of the former sages. The general principle is that a ruler of a state, being in the ancestral line of a former sage, acts as master of ceremonies for the most important rituals (*zong miao she ji* 宗廟社稷) in the land, and a ceremony crucial to that process is itself of the highest stature.

The duke said, "I'm very thick. If I weren't, why would I be in need of hearing these things? I'd like to ask more, but I'm really not sure what to say. Perhaps you could explain it to me slowly."

Confucius said, "Without the unity of heaven and earth, the cycle of life would not continue. The great marriage is the continuation of the human lineage. How can concern for it be going overboard?"

Confucius then said, "At home, taking care of the *li* of the ancestral temple is sufficient to accommodate the spirits of heaven and earth. Externally, taking care of the *li* of straightforward speech allows for the establishment of respect among upper and lower levels of society. A faux pas at home is enough to jolt you into awareness; a national embarrassment is enough to really wake you up.[4] Thus, a good government prioritizes *li*. *Li* is the root of just such a government."

Confucius continued, "There must have been some reason that the enlightened kings of the Three Dynasties were sure to respect their wives. The wife is the primary line of descent from the grandparents, and her child is their descendant. How could either of these not be held in high esteem? This is why a *junzi* is never without respect. And when it comes to respect, the most important thing is to respect one's person. The self, after all, is an offshoot of one's parents. How would one dare not hold it in high esteem? To disrespect one's person is to harm one's parents. Harming your parents is harming the root. When the root is harmed, the branch is doomed. These three are symbolic of the common people. From your person to their persons; from your children to their children; from your wife to their wives—a sovereign fosters these three, and as a result, he has a transformative influence across the land. Long ago, the grandfather[5] of King Wen did this, paving the way for his kingdom and his family."

4.2

公曰:"敢問何謂敬身?"孔子對曰:"君子過言則民作辭,過行則民作則。言不過辭,動不過則,百姓恭敬以從命。若是則可謂能敬其身,敬其身則能成其親矣。"公曰:"何謂成其親?"孔子對曰:"君子者也,人之成名也。百姓與名,謂之君子,則是成其親爲君而爲其子也。"孔子遂言曰:"愛政而不能愛人,則不能成其身;不能成其身,則不能安其土;不能安其土,則不能樂天。"公曰:"敢問何能成身?"孔子對曰:"夫其行己不過乎物,謂之成身。不過乎,合天道也。"公曰:"君子何貴乎天道也?"孔子曰:"貴其不已也。如日月東西相從而不已也,是天道也;不閉而能久,是天道也;無爲而物成,是天道也;已成而明之,是天道也。"公曰:"寡人且愚冥,幸煩子之於心。"孔子蹴然避席而對曰:"仁人不過乎物,孝子不過乎親。是故仁人之事親也如事天,事天如事親,此謂孝

4. *Wake you up*: to become more aware of the importance of *li*.

5. The ambitions and virtuous governing of the Zhou lineage were said to have begun with King Wen's grandfather, Dan Fu.

子成身。"公曰："寡人既聞如此言，無如後罪何？"孔子對曰："君之及此言，是臣之福也。"

The duke said, "I'd like to ask what you mean by 'respect one's person.'"

Confucius responded, "Offensive[6] speech by a leader will be normalized by the people. Offensive actions by a leader will be codified by the people. What about non-offensive speech and actions that are normalized and codified? The common people will obey these with reverence and respect. This is what I mean by respecting one's person. Respecting your person will enable you to fulfill[7] your parents."

The duke asked, "What do you mean by 'fulfill your parents'?"

Confucius responded, "Being a *junzi* means making a name for yourself. When you have made a name for yourself in the eyes of the common people, you are called a *junzi*. In this sense, you have made your parents into *jun* [nobility], and you are their *zi* [child]."

Confucius continued, "You cannot fulfill yourself if you care about governing but don't care for the people. If you don't fulfill yourself, you won't be comfortable where you live, and if you are not comfortable where you live, you won't be able to rejoice in *tian*."

The duke said, "I'd like to ask what you mean by 'fulfill yourself.'"

Confucius replied, "'To fulfill yourself' means to behave as yourself without going beyond what you are. To not go beyond is to be in unity with the *dao* of *tian*."

The duke asked, "How does a *junzi* prize the *dao* of *tian*?"

Confucius said, "You prize it for never ceasing. The *dao* of *tian* is like the unceasing movements of the sun and moon from east to west. The *dao* of *tian* is never obstructed and so is able to persist. The *dao* of *tian* is the spontaneity of processes that fulfills the nature of things. The *dao* of *tian* illuminates all things thus fulfilled."

The duke said, "Although I am simple and dim, I wonder if I could trouble you to go a bit deeper into the matter."

Confucius, surprised by the duke's interest, rose from his mat, and responded, "Achieving *ren* doesn't go beyond the nature of things. Achieving *xiao* doesn't go beyond attending to one's parents. And so, for a person of *ren* to be in service to one's parents is like being in service to *tian*. Being in service to *tian* as one is in service to one's parents—this is what it means for a *xiao* child to fulfill oneself."

The duke said, "Now that I've listened to what you've said, what if I slip up in the future?"

Confucius replied, "I feel fortunate just to have you listen to what I've said."

6. *Offensive, guo* 過: There are many ways to interpret *guo*. It means fundamentally to cross a boundary, i.e., transgress, and so it can be rendered as *mistaken, extreme, aggressive, distasteful, provocative, abusive,* and so on. The point here is that whatever transgressions are made by the leader, they are taken as models for speech and behavior by the people.

7. *Fulfill, cheng* 成: As in 17.1n12 below, *cheng* means to bring to fruition or full development.

5

Ruist Behavior

This chapter opens with Confucius' student Ran Qiu in conversation with Ran Qiu's employer, Jisun. In an exchange that will be echoed in 41.17, Ran Qiu recommends that Jisun entice Confucius to return home. Between the events of chapters 1–2 and chapter 5, Confucius, frustrated with corrupt, ineffective rulership of Lu, went into self-exile, spending a decade or more traveling from state to state offering his services, with the state of Wei as his home base. As in chapter 4, the main dialogue takes place between Confucius and the young Duke Ai, who seems genuinely receptive.

In what may be the most eloquent chapter of the *Dialogues*, we get a rare description of the *Ru*, a social category with which Confucius himself identifies, but which we see at the end of the passage is commonly disparaged. The ideal *Ru*, Confucius says, is constantly in a mode of preparation and readiness, is fair and objective, aloof from social vicissitudes, simple and frugal in lifestyle, accustomed to poverty and other hardships, open and tolerant, mindful of the people, industrious, and independent. The *Ru* lives a life of service but refuses to be "subject to anyone."

5.1

孔子在衛, 冉求言於季孫曰: "國有聖人而不能用, 欲以求治, 是猶却步而欲求及前人, 不可得已。今孔子在衛, 衛將用之。己有才而以資鄰國, 難以言智也。請以重幣迎之。"季孫以告哀公, 公從之。

When Confucius was in the state of Wei, his student Ran Qiu remained in Lu and one day said to the nobleman Jisun, "When a state wishes to implement good government and has a sage who can help do that and yet doesn't employ him, it is like trying to catch up with someone by going backward—you will never be able to do it. Confucius is in Wei now, and they will employ him. Giving one's own talent away to a neighboring state—it's hard to call that wisdom. I suggest that you offer him a hefty sum and welcome him back."

Jisun relayed the suggestion to Duke Ai, who went along with it.[1]

5.2

孔子既至舍，哀公館焉。公自阼階，孔子賓階，升堂立侍。公曰："夫子之服，其儒服與？"孔子對曰："丘少居魯，衣逢掖之衣。長居宋，冠章甫之冠。丘聞之，君子之學也博，其服以鄉，丘未知其爲儒服也。"公曰："敢問儒行？"孔子曰："略言之，則不能終其物；悉數之，則留更僕未可以對。"

Confucius arrived at his lodgings, and Duke Ai visited him there. The duke ascended by the east staircase and Confucius by the guest staircase,[2] then Confucius stood in attendance on the duke. The duke said, "Your clothing—is that Ruist clothing?"

Confucius responded, "I grew up here in Lu, and we wore this kind of robe with the sleeves wide under the arms. Then I lived for a time in Song,[3] where it was the custom to wear this kind of hat made of black fabric. I've heard it said that while a *junzi's* knowledge is far-reaching, his clothing stays closer to home. I don't know if this counts as Ruist clothing."

The duke said, "Dare I ask about Ruist behavior?"

Confucius said, "I'll give you a brief account, but we won't cover everything. If I were to give you a detailed account, we would be here until your servants change shifts."

5.3

哀公命席。孔子侍坐，曰："儒有席上之珍以待聘，夙夜强學以待問，懷忠信以待舉，力行以待取。其自立有如此者。儒有衣冠中，動作順，其大讓如慢，小讓如僞。大則如威，小則如愧，難進而易退，粥粥若無能也。其容貌有如此者。儒有居處齊難，其起坐恭敬，言必誠信，行必忠正，道塗不争險易之利，冬夏不争陰陽之和，愛其死以有待也，養其身以有爲也。其備預有如此者。儒有不寶金玉，而忠信以爲寶；不祈土地，而仁義以爲土地；不求多積，多文以爲富。難得而易禄也，易禄而難畜也。非時不見，不亦難得乎？非義不合，不亦難畜乎？先勞而後禄，不亦易禄乎？其近人情有如此者。儒有委之以財貨而不貪，淹之以樂好而不淫，劫之以衆而不懼，阻之以兵而不懾。見利不虧其義，見死不更其守。往者不悔，來者不豫，過言不再，流言不極，不斷其威，不習其謀。其特立有如此者。

1. According to CQZZ ("Ai" 11.6), this episode occurred in the year 484 BCE.

2. In a traditional formal hall, the hall faces south, and there is a dais in the center, with staircases on the east and west sides. The east side staircase is designated for the host and the west staircase is designated for the guest.

3. *Song*: Confucius' ancestral state.

The duke ordered a mat prepared, and Confucius sat down in attendance, saying, "Ruists sit like jewels on cushions, ready to be hired; they study night and day, ready to answer queries; they fill their breasts with conscientiousness and trustworthiness, ready to be promoted; and they act confidently, ready to be selected. These are ways in which they establish themselves.

"Ruists dress moderately and move gracefully. In great matters their deference appears arrogant, while in small matters artificial. They can, therefore, come off as intimidating in the former and as embarrassed in the latter. This makes progress difficult and backsliding easy, as their unpretentiousness makes them seem incapable. This is how they present themselves to others.

"The Ruist way of life can appear austere and difficult. Whether standing or sitting, they are respectful and reverent. In speech, they are always sincere and trustworthy. In their behavior, they are always conscientious and upright. On roads, they don't jockey for the smoothest lane. In extreme weather, they don't compete for the cooler or warmer places. They cherish their life in order to have an opportunity to serve. They take care of themselves in order to perform beneficial acts. This is how they prepare themselves.

"Ruists don't prize gold or jade and instead take conscientiousness and trustworthiness as their treasures. They don't pray for land and instead take *ren* and *yi* as their property. Instead of seeking to accumulate things, they take culture as their wealth. They are hard to find but easy to reward. They are easy to reward but hard to keep. They appear only when needed—so doesn't that make them hard to find? They don't engage in corrupt behavior—so doesn't that make them hard to keep? They expect their compensation only after putting in their work—so doesn't that make them easy to reward? This is how they associate with others.

"Ruists can be entrusted with goods and not desire them. They can be inundated with pleasures but not indulge in them. They can be menaced by mobs without flinching. They can be stopped by soldiers without cowering. They can face down personal advantage without compromising their *yi*. They can stand firm in the face of death. They neither regret the past nor worry over what is to come. Misspoken words are not repeated, and gossip is never pursued. They neither compromise their authority nor plot for more power. This is how they stand apart."

5·4

"儒有可親而不可劫，可近而不可迫，可殺而不可辱。其居處不過，其飲食不溽。其過失可微辯而不可面數也。其剛毅有如此者。儒有忠信以爲甲冑，禮義以爲干櫓，戴仁而行，抱德而處。雖有暴政，不更其所。其自立有如此者。儒有一畝之宮，環堵之室，蓽門圭窬，蓬户甕牖，易衣而出，并日而食。上答之，不敢以疑；上不答之，不敢以諂。其爲士有如此者。儒有今人以居，古人以稽。今世行之，後世以爲楷。若不逢世，上所不受，下所不推，詭諂之民有比黨而危之，身可危也，其志不可奪也。雖危起居，猶竟信其志, 乃不忘百姓之病也。其憂思有如此者。儒有博學而不窮, 篤行而不倦, 幽居而不淫, 上通而不困。禮必以和, 優游以法, 慕賢而容衆, 毀方而瓦合。其寬裕有如此者。

"Ruists can be befriended but not bought, approached but not forced, killed but not disgraced. They neither live in opulence nor feast on delicacies. Their errors may be cause for slight remonstrance but never open rebuke. This is how they are steadfast.

"Ruists take conscientiousness and trustworthiness as their armor, and take *li* and *yi* as their shield. They carry *ren* where they go and embrace *de* where they stay. In these they do not change, even under oppressive governments. This is their independence.

"Ruists live in small houses or humble cottages, with wicker doors and narrow windows. Their homes may be crumbling and in disrepair. They may have to trade clothes with other family members before going out or ration their food to one meal per day. If a sovereign appreciates their ideas and hires them, they work with dedication, and if a sovereign does not appreciate their ideas, they do not attempt to ingratiate themselves in order to be hired. This is their situation as aspiring officials.

"Although Ruists are of today, they prefer prior ages; although they live in this age, it is the people of the future who will emulate them. If their own time cannot accommodate them, if no one above is willing to hire them and no one below to endorse them, if devious people conspire to harm them, and even if their persons are in danger, their resolve cannot be shaken. Even if encountering hardship in their daily life, they will persist in their resolve, never forgetting the plight of the people. These are things they dwell on.

"Ruists study widely without limit, act devotedly without fatigue, don't slack even when alone, and don't get caught up when associating with elites. They always take harmony as the basis of *li* and adhere to rules even in leisure. They admire the capable and virtuous, and they are accepting of the masses, seeking to patch up any minor falling out. This is how they are open and tolerant."

5·5

"儒有内稱不避親, 外舉不避怨。程功積事, 不求厚祿。推賢達能, 不望其報。君得其志, 民賴其德。苟利國家, 不求富貴。其舉賢援能有如此者。儒有澡身浴德, 陳言而伏, 靜言而正之, 而上下不知也, 默而翹之, 又不急爲也。不臨深而爲高, 不加少而爲多。世治不輕, 世亂不沮。同己不與, 異己不非。其特立獨行有如此者。儒有上不臣天子, 下不事諸侯, 慎靜尚寬, 底厲廉隅, 强毅以與人, 博學以知服。雖以分國, 視之如錙銖, 弗肯臣仕。其規爲有如此者。儒有合志同方, 營道同術, 並立則樂, 相下不厭, 久别則聞流言不信, 義同而進, 不同而退。其交有如此者。夫温良者, 仁之本也; 慎敬者, 仁之地也; 寬裕者, 仁之作也; 遜接者, 仁之能也; 禮節者, 仁之貌也; 言談者, 仁之文也; 歌樂者, 仁之和也; 分散者, 仁之施也。儒皆兼此而有之, 猶且不敢言仁也。其尊讓有如此者。

"When recommending someone from an in-group, Ruists don't avoid family members, and when recommending from an out-group, they don't neglect those they have reason to resent. In their successes, they don't seek a large salary. They recommend other capable and virtuous people, without expectation of reward. Sovereigns achieve their goals, and the people depend on the Ruist's *de*. In focusing on benefiting the state and its families, Ruists seek neither wealth nor honor. This is how they elevate and assist the capable and virtuous.

"Ruists purify themselves by bathing in *de*. They speak their piece and then lie low. They quietly make matters right. If those above or below don't know what to do, Ruists hold their tongue and offer a helping hand, without expecting immediate results. They don't stand on a precipice to appear taller or add a little to seem like a lot. In times of good government, they don't take it for granted, and when things break down, they don't take part in the destruction. They neither gravitate toward those who agree with them nor repudiate those who disagree. This is how they stand apart and achieve independence.

"There are times when Ruists serve neither king nor lords. They remain cautiously quiet and keenly open. They hone and polish[4] themselves in every respect, becoming steadfast as a way to preserve friendships and studying broadly as a way to understand what to undertake next. Even if offered an entire state to themselves, they would consider it a mere trifle, refusing to be subject to anyone. This is how they meticulously make their way.

"Ruists take the same route as those of similar ambitions. They use the same methods as those constructing the Way. They rejoice in standing together, and there is no resentment when there are changes in status. They don't believe rumors about those who've gone away. When there is agreement about the right thing to do, they charge forward; when there is disagreement, they back away. This is how they interact with others.

"Gentle kindness is the root of *ren*. Cautious reverence is the ground of *ren*. Open tolerance is the operation of *ren*. Easy association is the aptitude of *ren*. *Li* and self-restraint are the face of *ren*. Conversation is the culture of *ren*. Music is the harmony of *ren*. Generosity is the spreading of *ren*. All Ruists possess these aspects of *ren*, and yet none dare to call it *ren* in themselves. This is how they are respectfully modest."

5.6

"儒有不隕穫於貧賤，不充詘於富貴，不溷君王，不累長上，不閔有司，故曰儒。今人之名儒也妄，常以儒相詬疾。"哀公既得聞此言也，言加信，行加敬，曰："終歿吾世，弗敢復以儒爲戲矣。"

4. We interpret *di li* 底厲 as *di li* 砥礪, following Yang and Song (2013).

"Ruists don't lose hope due to poverty or low station, nor do they feel elated in times of wealth and recognition. They do not allow themselves to be sullied by a ruler, implicated with superiors, nor brought to grief by colleagues. Thus, I call them *Ru*. But nowadays people misapply the label *Ru*, using it as a pejorative."

After hearing this discourse, Duke Ai's words soon became more trustworthy and his behavior more reverent. He said, "I will never again in my life make fun of Ruists."

6

Questions concerning *Li*

This chapter presents Confucius' discussion of *li* in two parts, first with the young Duke Ai and then with Confucius' student Yan Yan. It builds on the role of *li* in governing but takes us back to *li*'s humble origins. The paramount importance of making distinctions is emphasized, not just as a preliminary condition of *li* but also as a function of *li*. Also emphasized is the need for frugality among the leadership, and the benefit it accords the people.

6.1

哀公問於孔子曰: "大禮何如? 子之言禮, 何其尊也!"孔子對曰: "丘也鄙人, 不足以知大禮也。" 公曰: "吾子言焉!"孔子曰: "丘聞之, 民之所以生者, 禮爲大。非禮則無以節事天地之神焉; 非禮則無以辯君臣、上下、長幼之位焉; 非禮則無以别男女、父子、兄弟、婚姻、親族、疏數之交焉。是故君子此之爲尊敬, 然後以其所能教順百姓, 不廢其會節。既有成事, 而後治其文章、黼黻, 以别尊卑、上下之等。其順之也, 而後言其喪祭之紀、宗廟之序, 品其犧牲, 設其豕腊, 修其歲時, 以敬其祭祀, 别其親疏, 序其昭穆, 而後宗族會醼。即安其居, 以綴恩義, 卑其宫室, 節其服御, 車不雕璣, 器不彫鏤, 食不二味, 心不淫志, 以與萬民同利。古之明王, 行禮也如此。"公曰: "今之君子, 胡莫之行也?" 孔子對曰: "今之君子, 好利無厭, 淫行不倦, 荒怠慢遊, 固民是盡, 以遂其心, 以怨其政。忤其衆, 以伐有道。求得當欲, 不以其所; 虐殺刑誅, 不以其治。夫昔之用民者由前, 今之用民者由後。是即今之君子莫能爲禮也。"

Duke Ai asked Confucius, "Why is *li* so important? When you speak of it, why do you treat it with such reverence?"

Confucius responded, "As an ignorant person myself, I am unfit to understand the great importance of *li*."

The duke said, "Please, sir, speak of it."

Confucius said, "From what I've learned, *li* is the most important thing in the lives of the people. Without *li*, there would be no way to regulate and serve the gods of heaven and earth; to distinguish the positions of sovereign and minister, superior and subordinate, older and younger; or to discriminate the proper interactions of men and women, parents and children, older and younger siblings, husband and wife, families and clans, or relatives and acquaintances. For this reason, *junzi* have taken it as a way to effect reverence and respect, exploiting its efficacy in instructing and ordering the common people so that they do not destroy the rhythms of their relationships.[1]

"Once everyday affairs had been made productive in this way, *li* was used to regulate displays and clothing insignia in order to differentiate those of high honor and achievement from their counterparts, as well as those higher and lower in the hierarchy. Once this system was functioning smoothly, it came time to speak of the norms of funeral rites, the ordering of ancestors and gods inside temples, the grades of animals used in sacrifices, the display of sacrificial items, and the setting of dates of special occasions—all for the purpose of displaying respect during sacrificial ceremonies, differentiating the distance of living relatives, ordering the placement of deceased relatives in the temples, and finally having the reunion feast for the whole clan. Each person could thus take heart in their social position, the bonds of beneficence and responsibility having been fastened. The leaders themselves were modest in their dwellings and frugal in their clothing and jewelry, refrained from commissioning elaborate carvings on their vehicles or ornate designs on their tableware, and didn't seek out rare delicacies or harbor hedonist aspirations. In this way, all the people reaped the same benefits. This is how the enlightened kings of the past put *li* into effect."

The duke asked, "So why don't the political elite do this today?"

Confucius responded, "Nowadays, elite figures never tire of pursuing personal benefit, never weary of indulging in hedonist desires, and prefer to engage in indolent amusements. No doubt, this dissolute abandon will drive the people to their limit and result in their resentment of the government. The elite defy the masses and attack people of *dao*. In pursuing their immediate desires, they fail to live up to their positions. With ruthless murders and harsh punishments, they fail to effect good government. In the past, leaders of the people proceeded from the former, and today they proceed from the latter. This is why society's elite are unable to put *li* into effect today."

6.2

言偃問曰:"夫子之極言禮也, 可得而聞乎?"孔子言:"我欲觀夏道, 是故之杞, 而不足徵也, 吾得《夏時》焉。我欲觀殷道, 是故之宋, 而不足徵也, 吾得《乾坤》焉。《乾坤》之義, 《夏時》之等, 吾以此觀之。夫禮初也, 始於飲食。太古之時, 燔黍擘豚, 污樽抔

1. This sentence seems to mark a shift from the subjunctive mood in the preceding sentence to a description of historical developments in the subsequent paragraph.

飲，蕢桴土鼓，猶可以致敬鬼神。及其死也，升屋而號，告曰：'高！某復！'然後飲腥苴熟。形體則降，魂氣則上，是謂天望而地藏也。故生者南嚮，死者北首，皆從其初也。昔之王者，未有宮室，冬則居營窟，夏則居橧巢。未有火化，食草木之實、鳥獸之肉，飲其血，茹其毛。未有絲麻，衣其羽皮。後聖有作，然後修火之利，範金合土，以爲宮室、户牖。以炮以燔，以亨以炙，以爲醴酪。治其絲麻，以爲布帛。以養生送死，以事鬼神。故玄酒在室，醴醆在户，粢醍在堂，澄酒在下。陳其犧牲，備其鼎俎，列其琴、瑟、管、磬、鐘、鼓，以降上神與其先祖，以正君臣，以篤父子，以睦兄弟，以齊上下，夫婦有所。是謂承天之祜。作其祝號，玄酒以祭，薦其血毛，腥其俎，熟其殽。越席以坐，疏布以冪。衣其浣帛，醴醆以獻，薦其燔炙。君與夫人交獻，以嘉魂魄。然後退而合亨，體其犬豕牛羊，實其簠簋籩豆鉶羹，祝以孝告，嘏以慈告，是爲大祥。此禮之大成也。"

Yan Yan asked, "May I hear a straightforward account of *li*?"

Confucius said, "I once wanted to learn about the way of the Xia dynasty, so I went to Qǐ, but there wasn't enough evidence there. I did get a Xia almanac, though. I once wanted to learn about the way of the Shang, so I went to Song,[2] but there wasn't enough evidence there, either. I did learn their theory of *qian* and *kun*, though.[3] So let's look at *li* from the perspective of the changes of *qian* and *kun* and the hierarchy in the Xia almanac.

"The first step in *li* began in the culinary. In the earliest times, they roasted[4] millet and tore apart boar meat with their hands. A hole in the ground served as pitcher, and they drank from it with cupped hands. For music, they used amaranth stalks to beat on earthenware drums. This is how they were able to express

2. Prior to the imperial period of Chinese history, which began with the Qin dynasty in 221 BCE, there was a long period known as the Three Dynasties, which were the Xia, Shang, and Zhou. Confucius lived during the second half of the Zhou dynasty. The Zhou conquered the Shang in the century prior to the year 1000 BCE. The vestiges of the royal house of Shang were enfeoffed with the Song state (which is where Confucius' ancestors are said to be from, though Confucius himself was born and raised in Lu). It is said that the Shang conquered the Xia and enfeoffed the vestiges of the Xia royal house with the state of Qǐ 杞. The point of these lines of text seems to be that Confucius reached back to the earliest days of Chinese civilization to recover the cultural traditions of *li*, and did so by traveling to the two states where the oldest traditions were likely to have been preserved. His own home state of Lu was enfeoffed to the son of the Duke of Zhou, who was attributed with creating the primary *li* of the Zhou dynasty. Although Confucius adored the Zhou *li* and was considered a master of that system, he apparently felt it necessary to go back even further, to its earliest roots. *Analects* 3.9 also mentions Confucius' view that relevant information in Qǐ and Song was scant.

3. *Qian* and *kun* are the two primary hexagrams of the *Changes* (see the glossary) and are polar opposites in meaning. They are often equated with *yang* and *yin*, respectively. This may be a reference to Confucius' acquisition of some early source of the sixty-four hexagrams.

4. That is, instead of boiling it.

reverence for the spirits and gods. When it came to death, they climbed up on rooftops, yelling, "Oh, So-and-so, come back!" Then they would deposit something uncooked in the mouth of the deceased and wrap something cooked to bury. Then the body would go down and the spirit would go up. This is called turning to the sky while interning in the earth. The living were aligned with the south, and the head of the deceased was aligned with the north. These were the beginnings of our system of *li*.

"Before kings had any kind of palace or building of their own, they camped in caves during the winter and nested in trees during the summer. Before fire was used for cooking, they subsisted on fruits and nuts and on the flesh of birds and beasts, drinking their blood and ingesting their fur. Before there was silk and burlap, clothing was made of feathers and hides.

"Later, sages appeared and made their contributions. They fashioned uses for fire, such as for casting bronze and firing clay. They discovered methods for making houses and buildings, windows and doors. They devised different ways of cooking meat, such as roasting, baking, boiling, and broiling, along with methods for making alcohol,[5] both sweet and sour. They turned silk and hemp into fabric. These were all used to nurture the living, send off the dead, and serve the ancestors and gods.

"Complex rituals were created that involved placing alcoholic drinks of different colors and viscosities in specialized vessels positioned at certain places indoors. Sacrificial meats were also prepared and displayed in distinct kinds of vessels, in addition to orchestras arranged according to instrument. These rituals were for the purpose of calling down spirits in order to converse with the ancestors, for maintaining relations between sovereign and minister, for deepening relations between parents and children, for strengthening relations between older and younger siblings, for ordering the relations between those above and below in the hierarchy, and for prescribing the proper roles for husband and wife. They called this 'receiving the blessings of *tian*.'

"They devised names for the gods that were to be worshipped, and then sacrificed to them using dark liquor[6] and the blood and pelts of animals, along with both raw and partially cooked meat. They used reed mats for sitting, covering them with coarse cloth. They dressed in fresh clothing, making offerings of beer brewed both sweet and sour, along with baked and broiled meats. The male and female head of the household

5. See "Alcohol" in the glossary for more detail.

6. Dark liquor, *xuan jiu* 玄酒: Wang Su, incorrectly claiming that there was no alcohol in the earliest times, takes the combination of *xuan* (dark) and *jiu* (alcohol) to mean pure water. We take the words at face value. We assume that Confucius was attempting to provide an accurate representation of early *li*, and there is evidence of alcohol at the earliest stages of civilization. Besides, other kinds of alcohol are also mentioned in the same section, referring to the same period of time.

took turns making offerings, praising the spirits. When it was over, they took the carcasses, whether dog, pig, cow, or goat, along with the contents of the ritual vessels—grains, vegetables, congee, etc.—and boiled it all together, then used it to pronounce declarations, one to express *xiao* to the ancestors and one to show love and compassion to descendants. This was all highly auspicious. It is the great accomplishment of *li*."

7

Five Levels of Achievement

As the title says, chapter 7 introduces us to the crucial idea of the five levels of achievement, a bedrock notion of Confucius' meritocratic vision. Duke Ai, raised in the pampered seclusion of the palace, worries that he does not have the requisite personal experience to recognize qualified individuals. After reassuring him, Confucius discusses the importance of building affectionate bonds at all levels of society. The final two episodes touch on the historical transition in China from superstition to a more naturalistic perspective.

7.1

哀公問於孔子曰："寡人欲論魯國之士，與之爲治，敢問如何取之？"孔子對曰："生今之世，志古之道；居今之俗，服古之服。舍此而爲非者，不亦鮮乎？"曰："然則章甫絇履，紳帶縉笏者，皆賢人也。"孔子曰："不必然也。丘之所言，非此之謂也。夫端衣玄裳，冕而乘軒者，則志不在於食焄；斬衰菅菲，杖而歠粥者，則志不在於酒肉。'生今之世，志古之道；居今之俗，服古之服'，謂此類也。"公曰："善哉！盡此而已乎？"孔子曰："人有五儀：有庸人，有士人，有君子，有賢人，有聖人。審此五者，則治道畢矣。"公曰："敢問何如斯可謂之庸人？"孔子曰："所謂庸人者，心不存慎終之規，口不吐訓格之言，不擇賢以托其身，不力行以自定。見小闇大，而不知所務；從物如流，不知其所執。此則庸人也。"公曰："何謂士人？"孔子曰："所謂士人者，心有所定，計有所守。雖不能盡道術之本，必有率也；雖不能備百善之美，必有處也。是故知不務多，必審其所知；言不務多，必審其所謂；行不務多，必審其所由。智既知之，言既道之，行既由之，則若性命之形骸之不可易也。富貴不足以益，貧賤不足以損。此則士人也。"公曰："何謂君子？"孔子曰："所謂君子者，言必忠信而心不怨，仁義在身而色無伐，思慮通明而辭不專。篤行信道，自強不息，油然若將可越而終不可及者。此則君子也。"公曰："何謂賢人？"孔子曰："所謂賢人者，德不逾閑，行中規繩，言足以法於天下而不傷於身，道足以化於百姓而不傷於本。富則天下無宛財，施則天下不病貧。此則賢者也。"公曰："何謂聖人？"孔子曰："所謂聖者，德合於天地，變通無方，窮萬事之終始，協庶品之自然，敷其大道而遂成情性。明並日月，化行若神。下民不知其德，睹者不識其鄰。此謂聖人也。"

Duke Ai asked Confucius, "I'm interested in selecting aspiring men to work in the government and would like to ask you how to go about doing that."

Confucius responded, "Look for those who live in the world of today while aspiring to maintain the *dao* of the ancients. Look for those who abide in the customs of today while wearing the clothes of the ancients. Isn't it rare to find men who maintain this way of life and yet are not the kind of men you are looking for?"

The duke said, "So, all of the men with old-fashioned hats, with tassels on their shoes, and with a bamboo tablet tucked in a wide belt are capable and virtuous?"

Confucius said, "Not necessarily. That's not what I meant. People who are somberly dressed in ceremonial robes and caps and ride in proper coaches do not aspire to eat spicy food.[1] People who are deep in mourning and moved to wear burlap clothes and reed sandals and able to subsist on thin congee will not be preoccupied with liquor and rich food. That is what I meant in saying, 'Look for those who live in the world of today while aspiring to maintain the *dao* of the ancients. Look for those who abide in the customs of today while wearing the clothes of the ancients.'"[2]

The duke replied, "Well said! And that's all there is to it?"

Confucius said, "There are five levels of achievement. There are the levels of the commoner, the *shi*, the *junzi*, the *xian*, and the sage. Understanding these five is sufficient to be able to govern in accord with the *dao*."

The duke said, "May I ask what is meant by the level of the commoner?"[3]

Confucius said, "A commoner forgets the rule to be cautious to the end and never utters words of wisdom. He doesn't care to turn himself into a virtuous and capable person worthy of being selected, nor does he make an effort to control himself. He sees narrow concerns but not broad ones, and he has no sense of what to strive for. He drifts along with circumstances, unsure of what to grab onto. This is the level of the commoner.

The duke asked, "What about the *shi*?"

1. People who wear the simple, somber attire of the *Ru* do not aspire to live in luxury.

2. See 10.12 for a similar sentiment.

3. *Commoner, yong ren* 庸人: mediocre person. We use the word *commoner* in two distinct senses in this translation. In one sense, it is opposed to aristocrat, or noble. It refers to someone without rank. (Other terms in the text translated as *commoner* in this sense include *pifu* 匹夫, *baixing* 百姓, *min* 民, *shu ren* 庶人, and *buyi* 布衣.) In the second sense, as in the passage in question, it is used to refer to those who are ordinary in the sense of mediocre—those who do not strive to excel or better themselves. Because the word *shi* 士 has an original sense of dispossessed nobility and an extended sense of one striving to improve, the term *commoner* is opposed to *shi* in both senses. What is important to keep in mind with regard to Confucius' meritocratic philosophy is that finding oneself in the position of being a commoner is a starting point, not an innate characteristic or an ineluctable fate.

Confucius replied, "The *shi* is someone who has direction and who latches onto certain plans. Although he does not yet have the foundation to excel in the methods of the *dao*, he has set his mind on following the *dao*. Although he has not yet mastered the many excellences required, he is in the process of mastering them. Thus, without striving for excess knowledge, he pays close attention to his current pursuit of knowledge. Without striving for excess eloquence, he pays close attention to his speech. Without striving to do too much, he pays close attention to his motivations. Knowledge lies in the knowing; speech lies in the speaking; action lies in the motivation. Just as we are born with this one body, there is no substitute.[4] Wealth does not improve one's life, nor does poverty harm it. This is the level of the *shi*."

The duke asked, "What about the *junzi*?"

Confucius replied, "Regarding the *junzi*, his speech is always conscientious and trustworthy, harboring no resentment. He expresses *ren* and *yi* in his person without showing any sense of arrogance. His thoughts are penetrating and far-reaching, without getting caught up in any one thing. He acts out of sincerity on the path of trustworthiness, firm and confident without rest, as effortlessly as if others might be able to pass him but in the end cannot. This is the level of the *junzi*."

The duke asked, "How about the *xian*?"

Confucius replied, "Regarding the *xian*,[5] his *de* never crosses the line, and his actions are right on target. His words are sufficient to serve as a model for all the world, without bringing harm to himself. His *dao* is sufficient to transform the people, without harming the root.[6] He brings prosperity to society so that people needn't accumulate wealth,[7] and he spreads it widely so that people needn't worry about poverty. This is the level of the *xian*."

4. *Knowledge lies . . . no substitute*: The meaning here is elusive. Kramers (1950) translates: "Thus, when he knows what he ought to know, says what he ought to say, and has [a course] along which to act, then it will be as unchangeable [for him] as [his holding sacred] life and limbs" (brackets are Kramers').

5. *Xian* 賢: This term is usually translated elsewhere in this text as "capable and virtuous." It specifically refers to people who are fit for a position in government leadership because of their ability and virtue. We leave it untranslated here to convey its use as a technical term.

6. *Harm to himself . . . harming the root:* The potential harm in these two sentences is twofold. First, there is the problem of becoming prominent. In order to do good on a large scale, one must become prominent, but prominence always brings the risk of unintentionally offending others, inciting envy in others, or appearing to be a threat to others in power, any one of which could bring harm down on oneself. Second, there is the problem of potentially straying from ethical principles, believing that the ends justify the means. The *xian* manages to effect good in the world while avoiding these two potential harms.

7. *Prosperity . . . wealth* 富則天下無宛財: A straightforward reading of the Chinese is: *Wealth that doesn't incite envy anywhere in the world*, seemingly referring to the *xian*'s wealth. In other words, their success in ordering society may, as a result, bring them wealth, but the wealth will not bring them harm. A parallel passage in the *Xunzi*, with a slightly different wording (富有天下而無怨財: prosperous to the

The duke asked, "What of the sage?"

Confucius replied, "Regarding the sage, his *de* merges with heaven and earth; he changes and connects without premeditation; he sees all affairs through from beginning to end; he accords with the natural spontaneity of all things; and through the dissemination of this great *dao*, selfhood is brought to full development.[8] His brightness rivals the sun and moon, and his transformations are spirit-like. The people below don't understand his *de*; even eyewitnesses can't make out its scope. This is the sage."

7.2

公曰:"善哉!非子之賢,則寡人不得聞此言也。雖然,寡人生於深宮之内,長於婦人之手,未嘗知哀,未嘗知憂,未嘗知勞,未嘗知懼,未嘗知危,恐不足以行五儀之教,若何?"孔子對曰:"如君之言,已知之矣。則丘亦無所聞焉。"公曰:"非吾子,寡人無以啓其心,吾子言也。"孔子曰:"君入廟,如右,登自阼階,仰視榱桷,俯察機筵,其器皆存,而不睹其人。君以此思哀,則哀可知矣。昧爽夙興,正其衣冠,平旦視朝,慮其危難,一物失理,亂亡之端。君以此思憂,則憂可知矣。日出聽政,至於中冥,諸侯子孫,往來爲賓,行禮揖讓,慎其威儀。君以此思勞,則勞亦可知矣。緬然長思,出於四門,周章遠望,睹亡國之墟,必將有數焉。君以此思懼,則懼可知矣。夫君者,舟也;庶人者,水也。水所以載舟,亦所以覆舟。君以此思危,則危可知矣。君既明此五者,又少留意於五儀之事,則於政治何有失矣?"

The duke said, "Excellent! If not for the *xian* in you, I wouldn't be able to learn about these ideas. I'm afraid that because I was born deep in the palace, raised by palace women, and have never known grief, worry, toil, fear, or danger, it will be impossible for me to put into practice the teachings of the five levels. What can I do?"

Confucius replied, "From what you just said, you already know what to do. And so there is nothing more for me to add."

The duke said, "If it weren't for you, I wouldn't have opened my mind this far. Please, sir, tell me."

---

point of possessing the whole world but without inciting resentment), reinforces this interpretation. We follow commentators, however, who interpret *yuan* 怨 (via cognates *yuan* 苑 and *yun* 蘊) as to accumulate. In the first interpretation, the emphasis is on the perspective of the *xian* and what happens to him, and in the second, it is on the perspective of the people and what the *xian* accomplishes for them.

8. *Selfhood is brought to full development, cheng qing xing* 成情性: *Qing* and *xing* both carry a fundamental sense of inherence and connote a resultant behavioral tendency. The emotive aspect is often more apparent in *qing*, and the inherence is often more apparent in *xing*. Both are understood as malleable and dynamic. *Xing* is translated variously here as *(inner) self* (7.1, 7.7, 23.2, 26.4), *(inner) nature* (10.12, 15.16, 18.3, 26.1, 29.2, 38.40), *natural inclination/tendency* (21.6, 25.4), and *character/personality* (38.10, 38.30, 39.2). *Qing* occurs even more often, with an even wider variety of translations (*emotion, sentiment, feeling, favor, behavior, relationship, sensitive and responsive to, urge, tendency, one's all, truthful,* and *nature*). It commonly connotes emotional expression.

Confucius responded, "You enter the temple, and to the right you ascend the main staircase.[9] Above you see only beams and rafters, and all around you see only the mats for paying respect to your deceased family. The ritual vessels are all there, but the people themselves have passed. You can come to understand grief by reflecting on this experience.

"You wake before dawn and dress, then you hold court as the sun begins to rise. You are faced with one crisis after another, and one error in judgment can be the seed of chaos down the road. You can come to understand worry by reflecting on this experience.

"You hold court from dawn straight through until dark, meeting with lords of all ranks from across the land. With each, you must exchange formal greetings and remain vigilantly dignified and serious at all times. You can come to understand toil by reflecting on this experience.

"Pensive and brooding, you exit a city gate. You look around and then off into the distance. Your eyes glimpse numerous ruins of kingdoms long fallen. You can come to understand fear by reflecting on this experience.

"A sovereign is a boat, and the people are water. Water not only supports a boat, but it can also capsize it. You can come to understand danger by reflecting on this.

"When you are able to understand these five things and are able to give some thought to the five levels, what errors will there be in governing?"

7·3

哀公問於孔子曰: "請問取人之法。"孔子對曰: "事任於官, 無取捷捷, 無取鉗鉗, 無取啍啍。捷捷, 貪也; 鉗鉗, 亂也; 啍啍, 誕也。故弓調而後求勁焉, 馬服而後求良焉, 士必慤而後求智能者焉。不慤而多能, 譬之豺狼不可邇。"

Duke Ai asked Confucius, "Please tell me about a method for selecting people."

Confucius replied, "For people who would take up a position as an official, do not select those who are too driven, those who are pinched,[10] or those who are talkative. The driven may end up greedy; the pinched may end up disloyal; and the talkative may blather nonsense.

"With bows, they must first be well-strung, and from those one selects for power. With horses, they must first be tame, and from those one selects for excellence. With

9. See 5.2n2. Right corresponds to east.

10. *Driven . . . pinched, jiejie . . . qianqian* 捷捷 . . . 鉗鉗: The meanings of these terms are difficult to pin down in this context but appear to be metaphorical, the first having to do with being energetic and the second with something being squeezed tight. A parallel passage in the *Xunzi* has the terms in unreduplicated form, where Knoblock (1994) translates them as *clever . . . glib,* and Hutton (2014) as *self-important . . . domineering.* Kramers (1950) renders them *quick-witted . . .* and *glib-tongued.* We stay as close as possible to straightforward interpretations that comport with the context.

young officials, they must first be scrupulous, and from those one selects for intelligence and ability. If a young official is capable but has no scruples, you would want to be as close to him as to a vicious wolf."

7.4

哀公問於孔子曰："寡人欲吾國小而能守，大則攻，其道如何？"孔子對曰："使君朝廷有禮，上下相親，天下百姓皆君之民，將誰攻之？苟違此道，民畔如歸，皆君之讎也，將與誰守？"公曰："善哉！"於是廢山澤之禁，弛關市之稅，以惠百姓。

Duke Ai asked Confucius, "I wish to be able to protect our state when it is small and weak and to be in a position to invade others when it is large and powerful. What is the way to accomplish this?"

Confucius replied, "If your court is conducted with *li,* and upper and lower levels of society interact with mutual affection, then commoners across the land will see themselves as your people. Who will there be to invade? If you violate this way and the people naturally rebel, seeing themselves as your enemy, then who will be with you to protect the state?"

The duke said, "Excellent!" He immediately attempted to relieve the burden on commoners by ending the prohibition against entering restricted terrain[11] and by eliminating the market tax.

7.5

哀公問於孔子曰："吾聞君子不博，有之乎？"孔子曰："有之。"公曰："何爲？"對曰："爲其有二乘。"公曰："有二乘，則何爲不博？"子曰："爲其兼行惡道也。"哀公懼焉。有間，復問曰："若是乎？君之惡惡道至甚也。"孔子曰："君子之惡惡道不甚，則好善道亦不甚，好善道不甚，則百姓之親上亦不甚。《詩》云：'未見君子，憂心惙惙。亦既見止，亦既覯止，我心則悅。'《詩》之好善道甚也如此。"公曰："美哉！夫君子成人之善，不成人之惡。微吾子言焉，吾弗之聞也。"

Duke Ai asked Confucius, "I've heard that you don't play board games.[12] Is that true?"

Confucius replied, "Yes, it is."

The duke said, "Why is that?"

11. *Terrain, shan ze* 山澤: probably refers to land designated as the duke's private hunting grounds.

12. *Board games, bo* 博: This may refer to a specific game popular at the time but now lost. Kramers (1950) provides a detailed description based on commentaries. Since the word *bo* evolved to refer solely to gambling, this game may have involved gambling, and so that may be part of the context of Confucius' objection.

Confucius responded, “In doing so, two people seek to get the better of each other.”

“And why would that stop you from playing?”

“Then they will both be willing to do detestable things[13] to each other.”

The duke was taken aback by this.

After a time, the duke asked, “Is that so? Then you must deeply detest those who do detestable things.”

Confucius replied, “If a *junzi* does not deeply detest detestable behavior, he will also not deeply love excellent behavior. If he does not deeply love excellent behavior, then commoners will not feel profound affection for those above them. The Poems say:

Not having seen my *junzi*,[14]
I am wracked with worry and sorrow.
If I can only see him,
If I can only lay eyes on him,
My heart will swell with joy.

This is how deeply the Poems loves excellent behavior.”

The duke said, “Wonderful! A *junzi* behaves in ways that result in excellence for those around them, not in detestable ways. If you hadn’t told me this, I wouldn’t have heard it from anyone else.”

7.6

哀公問於孔子曰: “夫國家之存亡禍福, 信有天命, 非唯人也。”孔子對曰: “存亡禍福皆己而已, 天災地妖不能加也。”公曰: “善! 吾子之言, 豈有其事乎?”孔子曰: “昔者殷王帝辛之世, 有雀生大鳥於城隅焉, 占之, 曰: ‘凡以小生大, 則國家必王而名必昌。’於是帝辛介雀之德, 不修國政, 亢暴無極, 朝臣莫救, 外寇乃至, 殷國以亡。此即以己逆天時, 詭福反爲禍者也。又其先世殷王太戊之時, 道缺法圮, 以致夭蘖。桑穀於朝, 七日大拱, 占之者曰: ‘桑穀野木而不合生朝, 意者國亡乎! ’太戊恐駭, 側身修行, 思先王之政, 明養民之道。三年之後, 遠方慕義, 重譯至者, 十有六國。此即以己逆天時, 得禍爲福者也。故天災地妖, 所以儆人主者也; 寤夢徵怪, 所以儆人臣者也。災妖不勝善政, 寤夢不勝善行, 能知此者, 至治之極也, 唯明王達此。”公曰: “寡人不鄙固此, 亦不得聞君子之教也。”

13. Deception may have been built into the strategy required for the particular game in question.

14. Confucius plays on a double meaning of *junzi* here. The quoted poem (“Katydid,” #14, found today in the “Shao nan” section of the *Poems*), is a love poem, and *junzi* means something like “admirable man.” A colloquial translation to fit the context might be “my prince.” Confucius, understanding *junzi* in its later meaning of a person of high moral and social status, uses the poem to suggest that the people can and should feel a close personal bond with their leaders.

Duke Ai inquired of Confucius, "The good and ill that happen to states and families are truly designated by *tian* and are not just in the hands of people."

Confucius replied, "Good and ill lie in oneself alone. Omens in nature add nothing."

The duke said, "Well stated, sir, but can you give an example?"

Confucius responded, "Long ago, during the Shang dynasty when King Xin ruled, a large bird hatched out of a sparrow's egg in a corner of the city wall.[15] A prognostication was performed, and it was announced: 'When the small produces the large, the country shall thrive, and the king's glory shall spread.' And so, by virtue of the sparrow, King Xin neglected to reform the government and instead piled cruelty on top of cruelty. The court and its ministers were helpless, and then came the marauders from outside, and the state of Shang perished. This is how one asserts oneself against the course of *tian*, thwarting good fortune and turning it into disaster.

"In an earlier time, during the reign of the Shang King Tai Wu, corruption was so rampant that the king's rule was about to be cut short. And then one day, a mulberry sprout was found in the court. In seven days, its trunk grew to the span of a man's arms. A prognostication was performed, and it was announced: 'Mulberry trees should never be grown on the grounds of the court. It portends the end of the country.' Shocked, Tai Wu set out to reform himself, to contemplate the governments of the Ancient Kings, and to embark on a path of enlightened and nurturing rulership. After three years, people from far away so admired his *yi* that sixteen states came to express their esteem. This is how one asserts oneself against the course of *tian*, turning disaster into good fortune. Omens in nature and in dreams may be taken as warnings by rulers and officials, but they are no match for excellent government and excellent actions. If you can understand this, you can have the best government possible—but only an enlightened king can truly achieve it."

The duke said, "If I weren't so benighted, I wouldn't have had the opportunity to learn this teaching from you."

7.7

哀公問於孔子曰: "智者壽乎? 仁者壽乎?"孔子對曰: "然, 人有三死, 而非其命也, 行己自取也。夫寢處不時, 飲食不節, 逸勞過度者, 疾共殺之; 居下位而上干其君, 嗜慾無厭而求不止者, 刑共殺之; 以少犯衆, 以弱侮强, 忿怒不類, 動不量力者, 兵共殺之。此三者死非命也, 人自取之。若夫智士仁人, 將身有節, 動静以義, 喜怒以時, 無害其性, 雖得壽焉, 不亦可乎?"

15. A portion of this story appears in BA ("Di Xin"). It's probably not a coincidence that BA refers to Xin exclusively as Xin and that the only use of that name in the *Dialogues* is here. Elsewhere in the *Dialogues* he is referred to as Zhòu.

Duke Ai asked Confucius, "Do both wise people and *ren* people live long lives?"

Confucius replied, "Yes. There are three kinds of unnatural death that are brought on by one's own actions in comporting oneself. Living an irregular lifestyle, excessive eating or drinking, and overdoing it with regard to either idleness or labor—illness resulting from any of these can kill a person. Offending a superior or relentlessly pursuing an addiction—harsh punishment resulting from either of these can kill a person. Attacking a large number with a smaller number, or a stronger party with a weaker party; letting one's anger get out of hand; misjudging one's own strength—weapons used in any of these situations can kill a person. These are the three kinds of unnatural death brought on by one's own actions. Wise and *ren* people live well-regulated lives, acting or not acting in accordance with *yi*, expressing emotions at appropriate times, and never harming their own inner selves. Isn't it appropriate that they would live long lives due to these?"

8

Mind Wandering

Chapter 8 is the first appearance in the book of an *Analects*-like heterogeneous collection of brief dialogues and narratives. The loosely overarching theme seems to be a kind of pragmatism and flexibility founded on affectionate bonds: spend time with your parents when you have the opportunity; favor the practicality of education over immediate ambition, but realize that success lies in relationships, even though some people can be superficial; when faced with unique opportunities, don't stand on ceremony; and when carrying out the law, be fair. The chapter opens with an eloquent plea to beat swords into plowshares.

8.1

孔子北遊於農山，子路、子貢、顏淵侍側。孔子四望，喟然而嘆曰："於斯致思，無所不至矣。二三子各言爾志，吾將擇焉。"子路進曰："由願得白羽若月，赤羽若日，鐘鼓之音上震於天，旍旗繽紛下蟠于地。由當一隊而敵之，必也攘地千里，搴旗執聝。唯由能之，使二子者從我焉。"夫子曰："勇哉!"子貢復進曰："賜願使齊、楚合戰於漭瀁之野，兩壘相望，塵埃相接，挺刃交兵。賜著縞衣白冠，陳說其間，推論利害，釋國之患。唯賜能之，使夫二子者從我焉。"夫子曰："辯哉!"顏回退而不對。孔子曰："回，來！汝奚獨無願乎?"顏回對曰："文武之事，則二子者既言之矣，回何云焉?"孔子曰："雖然，各言爾志也，小子言之。"對曰："回聞薰、蕕不同器而藏，堯、桀不共國而治，以其類異也。回願得明王聖主輔相之，敷其五教，導之以禮樂，使民城郭不修，溝池不越，鑄劍戟以為農器，放牛馬於原藪，室家無離曠之思，千歲無戰鬥之患。則由無所施其勇，而賜無所用其辯矣。"夫子凜然曰："美哉德也!"子路抗手而對曰："夫子何選焉?"孔子曰："不傷財，不害民，不繁詞，則顏氏之子有矣。"

Confucius traveled north to Nong Mountain. Zilu, Zigong, and Yan Yuan accompanied him. Confucius looked out in all directions then sighed deeply, saying, "If you sit here and let your mind wander, it can go anywhere. Why don't each of you describe your ambitions, and I'll choose one."

Zilu stepped forward and said, "My ambition is to achieve wings[1] as white as the moon and as red as the sun, to have drums and cymbals that shake the hills right up to the heavens, and so many war banners that the longest trail across the ground. When I take my position as head of the army, in one swoop I would snatch up 250 miles of territory, capturing enemy flags and collecting ears as trophies. Only I would be able to do this, but you two may come along with me."

Confucius exclaimed, "Very brave!"

Then Zigong stepped forward, saying, "My ambition is to get the armies of Qi and Chu to meet on a broad battlefield, face to face in their formations, dust flying up in the air, swords drawn, then meeting in battle. I would be dressed in white clothes and cap, advising in the midst of the battle, strategizing about risks and benefits and how to spare the countries from harm. Only I would be able to do this, but you two may come along with me."

Confucius exclaimed, "Very eloquent!"

Yan Hui withdrew a step and remained silent.

Confucius said, "Come here, Hui! Are you the only one without ambitions?"

Yan Hui responded, "These two already spoke about military and diplomatic matters. What can I add?"

Confucius said, "It doesn't matter. Each is stating his ambitions. Let's hear yours, young man."

Yan Hui replied, "Just as you don't store fragrant and foul-smelling herbs in the same container, neither can a sage like Yao and a tyrant like Jie rule a country at the same time. All things belong to distinct categories. My ambition is to be a counselor to an enlightened sage-king, spreading the five transformative teachings,[2] advising about ritual and music, making it so that the people don't have to build city ramparts or cross over moats. Instead, I would have swords and spears melted down and made into farming tools, and I would put oxen and horses out to pasture. No wife would have to worry about an absent husband, and the ravages of warfare and strife would disappear for a thousand years. And so, both the bravery of Zilu and the eloquence of Zigong would be unnecessary."

Confucius said with gravity, "Beautiful! This is virtue!"

Zilu put his hands together and bowed, saying, "Which do you select, sir?"

Confucius said, "Not wasting money, not harming the people, spare in words—the son of Yan has it."

1. *Wings, yu* 羽: "feathers" or "wings," depending on context. Here, it is an evocative metaphor referring to military banners.

2. *Five transformative teachings, wu jiao* 五教: See "Five transformative teachings" in the glossary.

8.2

魯有儉嗇者，瓦鬲煮食，食之，自謂其美，盛之土型之器，以進孔子。孔子受之，歡然而悅，如受大牢之饋。子路曰："瓦甂，陋器也；煮食，薄膳也。夫子何喜之如此乎？"子曰："夫好諫者思其君，食美者念其親。吾非以饌具之爲厚，以其食厚而我思焉。"

A particularly frugal person of Lu once cooked a dish in a simple earthenware pot and on tasting it found it to be especially delicious. He then placed it on an earthenware platter and presented it to Confucius. Confucius was delighted to receive it, as if he had been given the best leftovers from a high sacrificial ceremony.

Zilu asked, "Earthenware is such a cheap material, and the food in it is flavorless. Why are you so pleased with it?"

Confucius replied, "Someone who favors advising a ruler always has the ruler in his thoughts. Someone who has the opportunity to eat delicious food thinks of his parents and how he would like to share it with them. It's not the cooking utensil that's meaningful; it's the fact that he thought of me when he made this dish."

8.3

孔子之楚，而有漁者而獻魚焉，孔子不受。漁者曰："天暑市遠，無所鬻也。思慮棄之糞壤，不如獻之君子，故敢以進焉。"於是夫子再拜受之，使弟子掃地，將以享祭。門人曰："彼將棄之，而夫子以祭之，何也？"孔子曰："吾聞諸，惜其腐餁而欲以務施者，仁人之偶也。惡有受仁人之饋而無祭者乎？"

Once when Confucius traveled to Chu, a fisherman offered him some fish. Confucius refused out of politeness. The fisherman said, "It's hot out, and the nearest market is a long way off, so I have no way to sell the fish. Better to give the fish to you than to throw them on the compost pile. That's why I dare to offer them to you."

So Confucius accepted the gift with gratitude, instructing his students to sweep the floor and perform a brief ceremony.

One of the students said, "He was just going to throw them away, and now you want to perform a ceremony over them? Why?"

Confucius said, "I have heard that in the past people didn't like food to go to waste and would prefer to give it to others than to let it spoil. These are people of *ren*. How could you receive a gift from a *ren* person and not perform some kind of ceremony?"[3]

3. A similar story appears in the *Xin xu* 新序, but instead of Confucius it is the king of Chu who receives a fish. The details in the two stories are quite different, but the moral is the same: a common, uneducated person can be a person of *ren*.

8.4

季羔爲衛之士師, 刖人之足。俄而, 衛有蒯聵之亂, 季羔逃之, 走郭門。刖者守門焉, 謂季羔曰: "彼有缺。"季羔曰: "君子不逾。"又曰: "彼有竇。"季羔曰: "君子不隧。"又曰: "於此有室。"季羔乃入焉。既而追者罷, 季羔將去, 謂刖者曰: "吾不能虧主之法而親刖子之足矣。今吾在難, 此正子之報怨之時, 而逃我者三, 何故哉?"刖者曰: "斷足, 固我之罪, 無可奈何。曩者君治臣以法, 令先人後臣, 欲臣之免也, 臣知; 獄決罪定, 臨當論刑, 君愀然不樂, 見君顏色, 臣又知之。君豈私臣哉? 天生君子, 其道固然。此臣之所以悦君也。"孔子聞之曰: "善哉爲吏, 其用法一也。思仁恕則樹德, 加嚴暴則樹怨, 公以行之, 其子羔乎?"

Ji Gao was a low official in Wei, in charge of meting out the common punishment of severing a felon's foot. During the Kuaikui Unrest[4] in Wei, Ji Gao had to flee the city for his own safety. On coming to the city gate, he saw that it was closed tight and the gatekeeper was missing a foot. The gatekeeper said, "There's a low point in the wall over there."

Ji Gao replied, "A *junzi* does not climb walls."

The gatekeeper said, "There's a hole in the wall over that way."

Ji Gao replied, "A *junzi* doesn't scramble through holes."

The gatekeeper said, "There's a room here that you can hide in." Ji Gao entered.

Later, his pursuers gave up, and when Ji Gao was about to leave he said to the gatekeeper, "Previously, I couldn't go against my superior's orders, and so I personally gave the order to cut off your foot. Just now was your chance to get back at me, and yet you offered me three routes of escape. Why?"

The felon said, "I lost my foot because of the crime I committed. It was unavoidable. At the time, when you handled my case, I noticed that you gave me a bit of a reprieve by putting me after the others. And after the verdict came down and you had to mete out the punishment, I could see how troubled you were by it. You had nothing personal against me and took no delight in it. You are a natural-born *junzi* who just follows the *dao*. This is why I helped you escape."[5]

Confucius caught wind of this story and commented, "A good official applies the law uniformly. With *ren* and compassion at the front of his mind, he engenders virtue. Severe or cruel intentions, on the other hand, engender resentment. Ji Gao is one who can carry out the law in a fair manner."

4. *Kuaikui Unrest*: See "Kuaikui Unrest" in the glossary.

5. *Escape, yue* 悦: interpreting *yue* 悦 (take delight in) as *tuo* 脱 (escape), following *Shuo yuan* 14.22.

8.5

孔子曰:"季孫之賜我粟千鍾也,而交益親;自南宫敬叔之乘我車也,而道加行。故道雖貴,必有時而後重,有勢而後行。微夫二子之貺財,則丘之道殆將廢矣。"

Confucius said, "Jisun once gave me a thousand bushels of grain[6] that I was able to distribute to others and from which I was able to build a base of good feelings. And it was only after Nangong Jingshu got me a carriage[7] that my path really began to open up. Although the *dao* is precious, one can only engage it seriously with the right timing, and one can only put it into effect under the right circumstances. Were it not for the gifts of these two, my own path was in danger of disappearing."

8.6

孔子曰:"王者有似乎春秋,文王以王季爲父,以太任爲母,以太姒爲妃,以武王、周公爲子,以太顛、閎夭爲臣,其本美矣。武王正其身以正其國,正其國以正天下,伐無道,刑有罪,一動而天下正,其事成矣。春秋致其時而萬物皆及,王者致其道而萬民皆治,周公載己行化,而天下順之,其誠至矣。"

Confucius said, "A ruler should be like the changing of the seasons. King Wen had King Ji for a father, Tai Ren for a mother, Tai Si for a wife, King Wu and the Duke of Zhou for sons, and Tai Dian and Hong Yao for ministers. They were the basis of his fine accomplishments.[8] King Wu set himself right as a way of setting his country right, and set his country right as a way of setting the whole land right. He attacked injustice, punished crimes, and in one move[9] he set the whole land right. This is how it all came to fruition. As the seasons change at due times, the flora and fauna thrive.

6. *Jisun . . . grain*: perhaps a reference to Confucius' first job as an official, which was as manager of the Jisun granary.

7. *Nangong Jingshu . . . carriage*: Perhaps a reference to Confucius' trip to Luoyang to see Laozi. In 11.1, it is Nangong who persuades the duke of Lu to give Confucius a carriage for his trip to Luoyang, and it was only upon his return to Lu that Confucius began attracting students. In the context of this episode, this and the above reference together suggest that Confucius saw these two events as pivotal in his career as an educator, and that without them he might never have succeeded to the extent that he did.

8. The point here is that King Wen had a vision of a Zhou dynasty, but it could never have come together without the cooperation of those around him.

9. King Wu laid the groundwork for conquering Shang by uniting his own people (the Zhou) and forming alliances with other peoples surrounding the Shang. Zhou attacked at a time when Shang was vulnerable, and a single battle resulted in complete victory.

When leaders achieve their *dao*, the people are orderly.[10] Then the Duke of Zhou put himself out there in his efforts to transform the people, and the whole world followed him. He expressed the ultimate sincerity."[11]

8.7

曾子曰:“入是國也,言信於群臣,而留可也;行忠於卿大夫,則仕可也;澤施於百姓,則富可也。”孔子曰:“參之言此,可謂善安身矣。”

Zengzi said, "On entering a country, if the speech of the sovereign[12] is trustworthy with respect to the officials in the government, you can feel good about staying there. If the behavior of the sovereign is conscientiousness toward high officials, you can feel good about taking up a position as an official there. If the benefits of all this are spread broadly among the people, you can feel good about accumulating wealth there."

10. The parallel structure of these two lines is worth noting:

春秋致其時而萬物皆及
王者致其道而萬民皆治

The syntactic similarities suggest a kind of structural metaphor—that just as nature comes to fruition in a spontaneous fashion through a web of interdependence, so people order themselves in a spontaneous fashion through a web of interdependence. The spontaneity of nature depends on the proper ordering of events. For example, an early spring or a late frost can devastate crops. The spontaneity of society depends on the leader's own well-ordered life. A leader with misplaced priorities leads to hardship, resentment, and unrest in the people.

11. Only a few years after vanquishing the Shang, King Wu passed away before his eldest son reached his majority. King Wu's younger brothers temporarily took the reins of government, with the Duke of Zhou playing the leadership role. The story that comes down to us is that the Duke of Zhou's sincerity was questioned, and he was suspected of usurping all the power for himself so that he could declare himself king. As a result, armies were raised against him. The Duke of Zhou personally led the strike against the revolting armies and won. When King Wu's son came of age, the Duke of Zhou installed him as king and continued to support him as an adviser and general. See "Duke of Zhou" and "Cai (person)" in the glossary.

12. *Sovereign*: The subjects of the verbs in this passage are implicit. Yang and Song (2013) understand there to be two subjects: an aspiring official traveling to a state, and the state's sovereign. Similarly, Kramers (1950) has the aspiring official but attributes the good actions in the state to the officials in the state. Henry (2022) understands there to be only one subject: the aspiring official. We follow Yang and Song. The interpretive difficulty also arises from the fact that the hierarchical virtues of *xin* and *zhong*, which are usually directed upward from officials to the sovereign, appear here to be directed downward from sovereign to officials. We take this at face value and understand it as having to do with the inherent flexibility in the terms, similar to 8.3, where Confucius attributes the hierarchical value *ren*, which usually runs in the doward direction, to a humble fisherman.

Confucius said, "These words of Shen can be understood as the way to excel at making a life for oneself."

8.8

子路爲蒲宰, 爲水備, 與其民修溝瀆。以民之勞煩苦也, 人與之一簞食、一壺漿。孔子聞之, 使子貢止之。子路忿然不悅, 往見孔子, 曰: "由也以暴雨將至, 恐有水災, 故與民修溝洫以備之, 而民多匱餓者, 是以簞食壺漿而與之。夫子使賜止之, 是夫子止由之行仁也。夫子以仁教而禁其行, 由不受也。"孔子曰: "汝以民爲餓也, 何不白於君, 發倉廩以賑之? 而私以爾食饋之, 是汝明君之無惠, 而見己之德美矣。汝速已則可, 不則汝之見罪必矣。"

When Zilu was the mayor of Pu, he once went out to help the people construct an overflow channel for flood prevention. He felt troubled by the hardships that the people were enduring and personally covered the expenses for each to have a basket of rice and a pot of broth. When Confucius heard about this, he sent Zigong to put a stop to it.

Incensed, Zilu went to confront Confucius, saying, "I'm afraid there may be a flood if we are hit by a large storm, so I helped the people construct a flood channel in preparation. But the people suffered from a lack of food, so I gave each a basket of rice and a pot of broth. Then you sent Zigong to put a stop to it. You are preventing me from putting *ren* into action. I refuse to accept that you will teach *ren* and then stop it from being put into action!"

Confucius responded, "If the people aren't getting enough to eat, why don't you tell your sovereign and have the granaries opened so that aid can get to them? By aiding them from your own resources, you are making it seem as if the sovereign doesn't care and as if you are the one with the glorious virtues. You have to stop it and quickly, otherwise your actions are bound to be seen as an offense to the ruler."

8.9

子路問於孔子曰: "管仲之爲人何如?"子曰: "仁也。"子路曰: "昔管仲說襄公, 公不受, 是不辯也; 欲立公子糾而不能, 是不智也; 家殘於齊而無憂色, 是不慈也; 桎梏而居檻車, 無慚心, 是無醜也; 事所射之君, 是不貞也; 召忽死之, 管仲不死, 是不忠也。仁人之道, 固若是乎?"孔子曰: "管仲說襄公, 襄公不受, 公之闇也; 欲立子糾而不能, 不遇時也; 家殘於齊而無憂色, 是知權命也; 桎梏而無慚心, 自裁審也; 事所射之君, 通於變也; 不死子糾, 量輕重也。夫子糾未成君, 管仲未成臣。管仲才度義, 管仲不死束縛而立功名, 未可非也; 召忽雖死, 過與取仁, 未足多也。"

Zilu asked Confucius, "What do you think of the way that Guan Zhong conducted himself?"

Confucius said, "He was *ren*."

Zilu said, "Guan Zhong tried to persuade Qi Duke Xiang to change his ways, but the duke refused. This shows that he was not good at rhetorical argument. He tried to install Prince Jiu but failed. This shows a lack of shrewdness. His own family was decimated in Qi,[13] and he didn't seem at all concerned. This shows a lack of sympathy. When he was arrested and brought in a paddy wagon shackled hand and foot, he didn't seem at all embarrassed.[14] This shows that he was shameless. His serving a ruler he once tried to assassinate shows a lack of devotion. Then Shao Hu took his own life, but Guan Zhong didn't.[15] This shows a lack of loyalty. Is this really the *dao* of a *ren* person?"

Confucius replied, "The duke's refusal to change his ways when Guan Zhong attempted to persuade him shows the duke's own failure to see clearly. Guan Zhong's failure to install Prince Jiu shows only that he didn't happen on the right circumstances at the right time. His lack of concern over his executed family shows his ability to evaluate unavoidable circumstances. His lack of embarrassment when shackled just shows his ability to see and judge events clearly for himself. His serving a ruler he once tried to assassinate shows his ability to change with the circumstances. The fact that he didn't take his own life when Jiu was killed shows that he knows what matters more and what less. Jiu's failure to achieve the throne also meant that Guan Zhong would not achieve a position as high minister. But Guan Zhong's sense of his own potential for achievement overrode his narrow sense of duty. You can't blame him for choosing to pursue achievements that eventually earned him fame over fetters. Shao Hu's taking of his own life was a forced, artificial kind of *ren*, not worth heaping praise on."

13. *His own family . . . in Qi*: There is no other record of this event. However, being a government official is an inherently dangerous affair when the ruler is corrupt. Guan Zhong held and lost several official posts before he became prime minister. Punishment for any one of these failures could have been met on his immediate family. And when he tried to persuade Duke Xiang to change his ways, that also could have been received poorly. On top of this, Guan Zhong once tried to assassinate the future Duke Huan. According to CQZZ, immediately after Duke Huan took the throne, the duke sent a military delegation to Lu, where Prince Jiu had taken refuge, forcing Lu to execute Jiu and extradite Guan Zhong. See "Guan Zhong" in the glossary.

14. *He was arrested . . . embarrassed*: When Guan Zhong was extradited to Qi from Lu, there was every expectation that he would be mercilessly punished. However, Bao Shuya knew Guan Zhong personally and recognized his potential as a leader. He convinced the duke to hire him instead of executing him. Still, Guan Zhong was hauled back like a common criminal.

15. Shao Hu also accompanied Guan Zhong to Lu with Prince Jiu. When Qi came after him in Lu for his role in competing for the throne, Shao committed suicide rather than face capture.

8.10

孔子適齊，中路聞哭者之聲，其音甚哀。孔子謂其僕曰："此哭哀則哀矣，然非喪者之哀矣。"驅而前，少進，見有異人焉，擁鐮帶索，哭者不衰。孔子下車，追而問曰："子何人也?"對曰："吾，丘吾子也。"曰："子今非喪之所，奚哭之悲也?"丘吾子曰："吾有三失，晚而自覺，悔之何及?"曰："三失可得聞乎？願子告吾，無隱也。"丘吾子曰："吾少時好學，周遍天下，後還，喪吾親，是一失也；長事齊君，君驕奢失士，臣節不遂，是二失也；吾平生厚交，而今皆離絶，是三失也。夫樹欲静而風不停，子欲養而親不待。往而不來者，年也；不可再見者，親也。請從此辭。"遂投水而死。孔子曰："小子識之！斯足爲戒矣。"自是弟子辭歸養親者十有三。

Once, on his way to Qi, Confucius heard someone weeping near the road. It was the sound of profound grief. Confucius said to his driver, "This is the sound of genuine sorrow, not just someone weeping for show at a funeral." He urged the driver closer and soon came upon a strange person carrying a scythe and a rope beside a river, weeping continuously.

Confucius stepped down from his carriage and approached the man, saying, "Who are you?"

The man replied, "I am Qiu Wuzi."

Confucius said, "There is no funeral here. What is the reason for your grief?"

The man replied, "I have suffered three losses and am realizing them only late in life. Now it's too late."

Confucius said, "May I inquire as to the three losses? I would appreciate it if you could be candid with me."

Qiu Wuzi said, "When I was younger, I loved to learn and so traveled all across the land. But when I returned home, I found that my parents had passed away in my absence. This is my first loss. Later, I worked for the sovereign of Qi. He was so extravagant that he lost the support of the officials. Although I tried to moderate his behavior, he didn't come around. This is my second loss. My whole life I've had deep friendships, but now my friends have all left and broken off relations with me. This is my third loss. A tree requires peace, but the wind won't stop. A man wants to take care of his elderly parents, but his parents have already passed away. The things that go and never return are the years. Those you'll never see again are your parents. With this, allow me to take my leave." Just then, the man leapt into the water and drowned.

Confucius said, "Students, pay attention. This should be a warning to all of us." Upon hearing this, thirteen of the students accompanying Confucius returned home to look after their parents.

8.11

孔子謂伯魚曰：“鯉乎，吾聞可以與人終日不倦者，其唯學焉！其容體不足觀也，其勇力不足憚也，其先祖不足稱也，其族姓不足道也。終而有大名，以顯聞四方、流聲後裔者，豈非學之效也？故君子不可以不學，其容不可以不飭，不飭無類，無類失親，失親不忠，不忠失禮，失禮不立。夫遠而有光者，飭也；近而愈明者，學也。譬之污池，水潦注焉，萑葦生焉，雖或以觀之，孰知其源乎？”

Confucius said to his son Boyu, "Li, I've heard that the only thing that can keep a person occupied all day without exhaustion is learning. One's[16] outward appearance, courage, lineage, or clan will never garner meaningful attention[17] from others. Isn't it true that the effects of learning are the only thing that in the end will earn fame that reaches the four corners of the land and extends even to one's descendants? So a *junzi* must study.

"At the same time, you must not neglect your outward appearance. If it is neglected, you won't fit in. If you don't fit in, you won't be able to form close relationships. Without close relationships, conscientiousness toward others will be impossible. To act unconscientiously is contrary to *li*. Without *li*, you won't be able to establish yourself or others.[18] That which shines from a distance is your outward appearance. That which increases in brightness[19] as others approach is your learning. It is like when a stagnant pond gets inundated from a torrential rain, the reeds and grasses begin to grow again. A passerby coming along won't be able to tell the origin of the water, will he?"[20]

8.12

子路見於孔子曰：“負重涉遠，不擇地而休；家貧親老，不擇祿而仕。昔者由也事二親之時，常食藜藿之實，爲親負米百里之外。親歿之後，南遊於楚，從車百乘，積粟萬鍾，累茵而坐，列鼎而食，願欲食藜藿，爲親負米，不可復得也。枯魚銜索，幾何不蠹？二親之壽，忽若過隙。”孔子曰：“由也事親，可謂生事盡力，死事盡思者也。”

16. *One's*: The subject is implicit. Yang and Song (2013) take the subject to be oneself—that is, a generic individual. Henry (2022) takes it to be study personified. We follow Yang and Song.

17. *Meaningful attention*: In the Chinese, each of the items from *outward appearance* to *clan* comes in a separate sentence, each sentence containing a distinct synonym for *attention*. We compress four sentences into one for rhetorical effect.

18. The direct objects of this sentence are implicit in the original.

19. *Brightness, ming* 明: In both the Chinese and English, this term has a double meaning of efflorescence and intelligence.

20. This analogy is a colorful expression of meritocracy. Your origins don't matter; education can bring anyone to prominence.

Meeting with Confucius, Zilu said, "When your burden is heavy and your path is long, you can't be choosy about where to stop and rest. When your family is poor and your parents are old, you can't be choosy about your salary or your official position. When I was taking care of my elderly parents, we often had to eat wild plants and weeds.[21] I would walk twenty-five miles to carry a sack of grain home for my parents. After my parents passed away, I traveled south to Chu, where I was in charge of a large fief. I was paid ten thousand bushels of grain, I had plush seats in my carriage, and I ate food from ornate bronze cauldrons. I would rather, however, still be eating wild plants and weeds and carrying grain for my parents. But there is no going back. After all, as with a string of dried fish, how often does decay not eventually set in? The lives of one's parents pass so quickly."[22]

Confucius said, "You did your best to take care of your parents when they were alive, and you do your best to remember them now that they have passed on."

8.13

孔子之郯，遭程子於塗，傾蓋而語，終日，甚相親。顧謂子路曰："取束帛以贈先生。"子路屑然對曰："由聞之，士不中間見，女嫁無媒，君子不以交，禮也。"有間，又顧謂子路。子路又對如初。孔子曰："由，《詩》不云乎：'有美一人，清揚宛兮。邂逅相遇，適我願兮。'今程子，天下賢士也。於斯不贈，則終身弗能見也。小子行之！"

On his way to the state of Tan, Confucius encountered Chengzi. They pulled their carriages alongside each other and began to chat. Their conversation continued for the whole day, as if they were long-lost family. Afterwards, Confucius turned to Zilu and said, "Select a bolt of silk to give to the gentleman."

With utmost respect, Zilu responded, "I have heard that two men meeting without proper introductions is like a woman marrying without the use of a matchmaker. It is *li* to avoid interacting with such a person."

There was a pause, then Confucius turned and repeated himself to Zilu.

Zilu then repeated himself to Confucius as before.

Confucius responded, "Zilu, isn't there a poem that says:

21. *Wild plants and weeds, lihuo zhi shi* 藜藿之實: *Li* 藜 refers to the plant *Chenopodium album*, a weedy plant that is sometimes eaten (the term also occurs in 38.12). *Hu* 藿 is a generic word for the leaves of bean plants, which are likewise eaten when other food is not available. Together, *lihuo* 藜藿 refers to coarse food eaten in impoverished circumstances. (Luo 1994; Kroll 2015)

22. The main sentiment of this moving passage about deceased parents eventually entered the lexicon as "the grief of plush seats" (*lei yin zhi bei* 累茵之悲). As adults progress through their careers and attain comforts not experienced as children, it is difficult to enjoy them while knowing that one's parents are no longer living. (Luo 1994)

There was a person I deemed so lovely,
Pure, uplifting, and gentle was she.
And when by chance we came to meet,
All past wishes came true for me.[23]

"This is Chengzi, one of the most capable and virtuous officials in all the land. If I can't give him a token of my appreciation now, I may never have the opportunity again. Get the silk, you scoundrel!"

8.14

孔子自衛反魯, 息駕於河梁而觀焉。有懸水三十仞, 圜流九十里, 魚鱉不能導, 黿鼉不能居。有一丈夫, 方將厲之。孔子使人並涯止之曰: "此懸水三十仞, 圜流九十里, 魚鱉黿鼉不能居也, 意者難可濟也。" 丈夫不以措意, 遂渡而出。孔子問之, 曰: "子巧乎? 有道術乎? 所以能入而出者, 何也?" 丈夫對曰: "始吾之入也, 先以忠信; 及吾之出也, 又從以忠信。忠信措吾軀於波流, 而吾不敢以用私, 所以能入而復出也。" 孔子謂弟子曰: "二三子識之, 水且猶可以忠信成身親之, 而況於人乎?"

When Confucius was on his way back to Lu from Wei, he stopped the carriage on a bridge over a river[24] to take in the view. A waterfall plunged down from 180 feet up, and fierce rapids ran for dozens of miles downriver. The water was too rough for fish or turtles to swim in or for alligators to linger in. A man appeared who was about to put himself in danger by jumping into the water to cross the river. Confucius told his students to rush to the shore and stop him, saying, "With the waterfall and the rapids, swimming across will be difficult." But without a second thought, the man swam across and came out on the other side.

Confucius asked the man, "You are very skillful. Do you have some certain method? How is it that you are able to go in and out of the water like that?"

23. These lines appear in the poem "Vines in the Wilderness" (#94) and can be found today in the "Zheng feng" section of the *Poems*. This brief love poem is written from the point of view of a man who has become smitten with a beautiful woman in an uncultivated area outside the city. It may be that the chance meeting or the uncultivated area suggests that the affair is illicit. Confucius seems to be suggesting that the circumstances make it no less legitimate, and that his chance meeting with Chengzi is both similarly outside the bounds of normal protocol and similarly acceptable.

24. *River, he* 河: In early texts, the word *he* (which means river) often refers specifically to the Yellow River. To get from Puyang (present-day location of the former capital of Wei) to Qufu (present-day location of the capital of Lu) does indeed require crossing the Yellow River. However, the Yellow River has changed course many times over the centuries, and in Confucius' day the river lay north of the Wei capital and so wouldn't have been crossed when traveling from Wei to Lu. For this reason, *he* is here translated as a generic "river." In 22.2, Confucius goes from the Wei capital toward Jin and encounters the Yellow River. (Tan 1996; Chen et al. 2012)

The man replied, “When I go underwater, I rely on single-mindedness and faith. And when I come out, I also rely on single-mindedness and faith. Single-mindedness and faith are what I entrust my body with in the waves. I can’t rely on just the work of self-preservation. That is how I can swim in and out like that.”

Confucius said to his students, “Pay attention, everyone. Single-mindedness and faith are required for controlling oneself in close proximity to water. Think how even more important they are for other people.”[25]

8.15

孔子將行，雨而無蓋。門人曰：“商也有之。”孔子曰：“商之爲人也，甚吝於財。吾聞與人交，推其長者，違其短者，故能久也。”

Confucius was about to go out into the rain, but his carriage didn’t have a canopy. One of his students said, “Shang has one.”

Confucius said, “Shang can be very stingy with his possessions. I’ve learned that the way to build lasting relationships is to promote the strong points of others and avoid their weak points.”

8.16

楚王渡江，江中有物大如斗，圓而赤，直觸王舟。舟人取之。王大怪之，遍問群臣，莫之能識。王使使聘于魯，問於孔子。子曰：“此所謂萍實者也，可剖而食之，吉祥也，唯霸者爲能獲焉。”使者反。王遂食之，大美。久之，使來，以告魯大夫。大夫因子游問曰：“夫子何以知其然乎?”曰：“吾昔之鄭，過乎陳之野，聞童謠曰：‘楚王渡江得萍實，大如斗，赤如日，剖而食之甜如蜜。’此是楚王之應也，吾是以知之。”

25. *Single-mindedness and faith, zhong* 忠 and *xin* 信: These are two key Confucian virtues, usually translated elsewhere in this book as conscientiousness and trustworthiness. The last sentence of the passage shows the usual interpersonal context in which the terms are used. The context of swimming stretches the meaning of the terms and challenges the reader to discover the relevance. The point of the passage seems to be that the meanings of these two virtues should be imbued also with the kinds of skill required to negotiate the fast-moving, swirling waters—perhaps, steadfastness, courage, and the ability to adjust quickly to changing conditions. A version of this episode appears in chapter 19 of the *Zhuangzi*. A similarity in the *Zhuangzi* version is that the swimmer disavows a concern for the self. A difference is that in the *Zhuangzi* version, the swimmer also disavows a particular method, saying that he merely goes in and out with the *dao* of the water. No mention is made of *zhong* or *xin*.

The king of Chu was crossing a river[26] when he saw something floating in the water. It was as big as a ladle, red, and round. It ran up against the king's boat, and someone reached down and grabbed it. The king was so fascinated by it that he asked all of his officials what it was, but none of them recognized it. The king then sent someone to Lu to ask Confucius. Confucius said, "It is the fruit of the *ping* plant.[27] Split open, it is edible and is considered an auspicious sign—only the leader of a superpower will find one." The messenger returned to the king. The king then ate the fruit and found it to be delicious. Eventually, the emissary returned to Lu and informed a high official.

The official met with Confucius through Ziyou and asked: "How did you know that?"

Confucius said, "Once when I was on my way to Zheng and passing through a field near Chen, I overheard a children's rhyme that went like this:

The king of Chu crossed a river
And found a fruit called *ping*
Big as a ladle
Red as the sun
Split it, eat it
Sweet as honey.

"It all came true. That's how I knew."

26. *River*: *jiang* 江. Like *he* above, *jiang* means river. Here, it could refer to the Yangtze River, but given the particulars of the situation, a smaller river would be more likely. (Luo 1994)

27. The term in Chinese (*ping* 萍) is difficult to make sense of in this context. The standard meaning is either duckweed or a member of the *Nymphaea* genus, such as waterlily or nuphar, but no known candidate has a fruit that fits the description in the passage. Henry (2022) renders the plant straightforwardly as "duckweed" but changes *fruit* (*shi* 實) to "bulb" (1087). The *Er ya* 爾雅, an early Chinese lexicon, glosses 萍 as follows: "*ping* 萍 means duckweed, but when large it refers to *ping* 蘋," which, when combined with *guo* 果 (fruit), means apple in later Chinese. However, an apple doesn't have to be split and does not thrive in the wet, humid climate of Spring and Autumn–period Chu. The description of the fruit could suggest a persimmon. The persimmon (*shi* 柿) is native to China, thrives in a warm environment, and does not appear in the textual record until the last centuries BCE, meaning that it might have been present but rare. It is described in the *Shuo wen jie zi* 說文解字 as a "red (*chi* 赤)" fruit, the same color as in the passage in question. It is usually peeled, and it does not have to be cut open to be eaten. The pomegranate is red and round and is eaten by splitting it open, but it is not thought to have reached China until the Han dynasty. If the fruit in question were the pomegranate, one would still wonder why it is called *ping* 萍. The persimmon and pomegranate do not usually float. Water caltrops, which some Chinese scholars suggest as the candidate fruit here, do float, but they are not round, red, or sweet. (Loewe and Shaughnessy 1999; Kroll 2015; Yang 2018)

8.17

子貢問於孔子曰: “死者有知乎? 將無知乎?”子曰: “吾欲言死之有知, 將恐孝子順孫妨生以送死; 吾欲言死之無知, 將恐不孝之子棄其親而不葬。賜欲知死者有知與無知, 非今之急, 後自知之。”子貢問治民於孔子。子曰: “懔懔焉若持腐索之扞馬。”子貢曰: “何其畏也?”孔子曰: “夫通達御之皆人也, 以道導之, 則吾畜也; 不以道導之, 則吾讎也。如之何其無畏也?”魯國之法, 贖人臣妾于諸侯者, 皆取金於府。子貢贖之, 辭而不取金。孔子聞之曰: “賜失之矣。夫聖人之舉事也, 可以移風易俗, 而教導可以施之於百姓, 非獨適身之行也。今魯國富者寡而貧者衆, 贖人受金則爲不廉, 則何以相贖乎? 自今以後, 魯人不復贖人於諸侯。”

Zigong asked Confucius, “Are people still conscious after they die?”

Confucius replied, “I would like to say that people are conscious after they die, but I fear that doing so would encourage very *xiao* people to go overboard and endanger their own lives during the mourning process. I would also like to say that people are not conscious after death, but I fear that doing so would encourage less *xiao* people to abandon their deceased parents without burying them. Zigong, your wanting to know whether or not people are still conscious after death is not an urgent matter. You will find out for yourself someday in the future.”

Zigong asked Confucius about governing the people. Confucius said, “One should be very careful, like leading a fearless horse with a frayed rope.”

Zigong said, “What is there to fear?”

Confucius replied, “Any seasoned charioteer knows[28] that if horses are treated well,[29] they will be tame livestock. If they are not treated well, then they will turn into enemies. What is not to fear?”

The state of Lu had a law that funds required for ransoming back a citizen of Lu enslaved[30] in another state could be sought from the Lu state treasury. Once when

28. *Seasoned charioteer knows*, 夫通達御之皆人也: The Chinese says something more like “the ones who know well how to control them are people.” Our phrasing gets the point across in English more naturally. Kramers (1950) interprets it in the opposite direction: the ones who are ridden as mounts are people.

29. *Treated well*, *you dao dao zhi* 有道導之: guided with *dao* 道.

30. *Enslaved*: The very notion of slavery is itself complex, and the history of slavery in ancient China is opaque. There was no equivalent in ancient China of the large-scale slavery that we see in ancient Greece or in early American history. However, there are records of people being held against their will and pressed into labor, as in the case of captured enemy soldiers (see 1.2; possibly part of the tribute in 41.6) and criminals, including records of them being bought and sold. There is even evidence that their enslaved state could be extended to their family and offspring. There also seems to have been a black market for kidnapped people who could be held against their will and for destitute people who sold themselves or a family member (such as a child) into a state resembling slavery (see 18.2). The mention of redeeming slaves in this passage may refer to people who were kidnapped or people who were sold and then repurchased. (Pulleyblank 1957; Yates 2001)

Zigong purchased the freedom of a citizen, he declined to accept funds from the Lu treasury.

Confucius heard about this and said, "This is a mistake on the part of Zigong. When a sage does something, he doesn't act simply on personal whims because his actions may change the customs of the day and his teachings may spread widely among the people. In Lu today, there are many poor people and few wealthy people. If it becomes unacceptable to seek funds from the state for purchasing the freedom of people, how can they be freed? From this day forward, the people of Lu will never again be able to free a Lu slave from another state."

8.18

子路治蒲，請見於孔子曰："由願受教於夫子。"子曰："蒲其何如？"對曰："邑多壯士，又難治也。"子曰："然，吾語爾，恭而敬，可以攝勇；寬而正，可以懷强；愛而恕，可以容困；温而斷，可以抑奸。如此而加之，則正不難矣。"

When Zilu was the mayor of Pu, he went to visit Confucius, saying, "I'm in need of instruction, sir."

Confucius said, "How are things in Pu?"

"It's difficult to govern because of all the local thugs."

Confucius said, "In that case, let me tell you something. A reverent attitude combined with respectful treatment of others can mollify boldness. A tolerant attitude combined with treating people with decency can placate brute force. A loving attitude combined with compassionate treatment can help you embrace people in dire straits. A warm attitude combined with decisiveness can help reduce the tendency to scheme. Put these into practice yourself and promote them among others, and reform will not be difficult."

9

Three *Shu*

Chapter 9 appears to be an extension of chapter 8, emphasizing substance over appearances. It also emphasizes self-cultivation that involves learning from things in our surroundings. Virtues discussed are *shu,* wisdom, *ren, xiao,* and devotion. But we also see the introduction of ideas that have echoes in the *Dao de jing*. Sections 9.3 and 9.11 present the common dilemma of whether and how to make positive contributions in a society that is unjust.

9.1

孔子曰:“君子有三恕。有君不能事,有臣而求其使,非恕也;有親不能孝,有子而求其報,非恕也;有兄不能敬,有弟而求其順,非恕也。士能明於三恕之本,則可謂端身矣。”

Confucius said, "A *junzi* understands three lessons of *shu.* (1) There is a minister who cannot[1] serve his sovereign but expects his subordinates to assist him—this is not a case of *shu.* (2) There is a child who cannot be *xiao* to his parents but expects his children to requite him—this is not a case of *shu.* (3) There is a younger brother who cannot show respect to his older brother but expects his own younger brother to be congenial to him—this is not a case of *shu.* When people with aspirations for office can understand the basis of *shu,* that is when they can be said to have set themselves right."

1. *Cannot, bu neng* 不能: This passage is particularly illustrative of the notion of *shu.* The use of *cannot* here, instead of *does not* or *refused to,* appears intentional (especially in light of Mencius' distinction (1A.7) between *cannot* (*bu neng*) and *does not* (*bu wei* 不爲). The gist of the passage is an emphasis on *shu* as sympathetic understanding: if you cannot do it and yet expect others to do it, you are not extending an understanding of your own situation to the possibility of a similar situation for others. If *does not* had been used instead, the emphasis would shift to refraining from hypocrisy—I refuse to do it and yet I expect you to do it—which is outside the typical semantic range of *shu.*

9.2

孔子曰："君子有三思，不可不察也。少而不學，長無能也；老而不教，死莫之思也；有而不施，窮莫之救也。故君子少思其長則務學，老思其死則務教，有思其窮則務施。"

Confucius said, "There are three future circumstances about which a *junzi* thinks carefully. You must not fail to examine them. If you do not study when young, you will be incapable as an adult. If you do not teach when old, you will not be remembered after death. If you do not share when you have something to share, you will not be helped when need arises. Thus, while still young, a *junzi* thinks carefully about his situation as an adult and so keeps learning. When old, he thinks carefully about what people will think of him after he dies and so teaches others. When well off, he thinks carefully about what might happen if he were ever in need and so spreads his wealth."[2]

9.3

伯常騫問於孔子曰："騫固周國之賤吏也，不自以不肖，將北面以事君子。敢問正道宜行，不容於世；隱道宜行，然亦不忍。今欲身亦不窮，道亦不隱，爲之有道乎？"孔子曰："善哉子之問也！自丘之聞，未有若吾子所問辯且說也。丘嘗聞君子之言道矣，聽者無察，則道不入；奇偉不稽，則道不信。又嘗聞君子之言事矣，制無度量，則事不成；其政曉察，則民不保。又嘗聞君子之言志矣，剛折者不終，徑易者則數傷，浩倨者則不親，就利者則無不弊。又嘗聞養世之君子矣，從輕勿爲先，從重勿爲後，見像而勿强，陳道而勿怫。此四者，丘之所聞也。"

Bochang Qian asked Confucius, "I have worked as a humble scribe for the Zhou government and don't consider myself to be incapable. I devote myself to serving my sovereign. What I'd like to ask you about is what to do if on one hand I try to properly practice *dao* publicly but it is not accepted by society, or on the other hand I try to practice *dao* privately but can't bear to do only that. If I don't wish to end up in trouble or to practice *dao* in seclusion, is there a *dao* for me?"

2. In this passage, the motivation is quite different from 9.1. Rather than sympathetic understanding (*shu*), there appears to be a transactional justification for self-improvement and moral action—you do it because you will get something out of it. Although there is no named interlocutor here, the most charitable reading would be that Confucius is speaking to a specific student who needs extra motivation beyond virtue for the sake of the greater good. Such a reading would be consistent with Confucius' views elsewhere. Although Confucius acknowledges that virtue unrewarded may still be worthwhile, he also understands that it can—and, under ideal circumstances, will—bring personal benefits. It is part of his practical outlook to use that belief in motivating others (see 8.11, for example).

"Great question!" exclaimed Confucius. "I've never had a question as discriminating and theory-laden as yours. Here are four things that I've learned. First, with regard to a *junzi* speaking about *dao*: If your interlocutor can't corroborate what you say, he won't accept it; and if your ideas are grand and inspiring but unverifiable, they won't be believed. Second, with regard to a *junzi* speaking about affairs of state: If the words are not put into effect in a measured way, they will not be successful; if the government is too intrusive in its governing, the people will not feel safe. Third, with regard to a *junzi* speaking about his own personal ambitions: Inflexibility won't last; impetuousness will be subject to repeated harm; pride will prevent the building of close relationships; focusing just on personal gain will ruin everything. Finally, with regard to a *junzi* getting along in the world: In small matters, don't rush to the front; in important matters, don't lag behind; be a model for others without forcing others to follow it; and don't contravene *dao* when trying to display it."[3]

9.4

孔子觀於魯桓公之廟, 有欹器焉。夫子問於守廟者曰: "此謂何器?"對曰: "此蓋爲宥坐之器。"孔子曰: "吾聞宥坐之器, 虛則欹, 中則正, 滿則覆。明君以爲至誡, 故常置之於坐側。"顧謂弟子曰: "試注水焉。"乃注之水, 中則正, 滿則覆。夫子喟然嘆曰: "嗚呼! 夫物惡有滿而不覆哉?"子路進曰: "敢問持滿有道乎?"子曰: "聰明睿智, 守之以愚; 功被天下, 守之以讓; 勇力振世, 守之以怯; 富有四海, 守之以謙。此所謂損之又損之之道也。"

Once when Confucius was visiting the Temple to Lu Duke Huan, there was a tilting cup[4] there. Confucius asked the caretaker, "What kind of vessel is this?"

He responded, "I believe this was a vessel placed at the duke's right-hand side."

3. Bochang Qian asks a complicated question, and Confucius gives a complicated answer. The question is about a moral dilemma commonly encountered by Confucians: whether to attempt to govern justly in an unjust world (thus compromising one's values) or whether to retire into seclusion until a more just time arrives (thus shirking one's responsibility to govern). Confucius implicitly rejects the basis of the dilemma, suggesting that what matters most is not *whether one should govern* but rather *how one conducts oneself.* He presents four levels of consideration from the grand and general to the increasing private and specific, and each stage is characterized by moderation in word and deed.

4. *Tilting cup, qi qi* 欹器: The second *qi* that is translated here as *cup* means more broadly *vessel.* It is not clear whether it was small, like a cup, or large, like a pitcher or pot. Though famous in lore, whether such an object ever existed is an open question. None has been handed down to posterity, and none has been found in an archaeological excavation. One theory is that the idea of the tilting cup was based on a burial find or a vague collective memory of a specific kind of Neolithic jar that was defunct by the time of Confucius. The jar was used for fermenting beverages. It was tapered from the center to

Confucius said, "I've heard that the so-called *vessel-to-the-right* leans to one side when empty, stands upright when half full, and tips over when completely full. An enlightened sovereign uses it as a cautionary reminder, and that is why it was kept at his side."

Confucius turned to his students and said, "Try putting some water in it."

One of them put some water in it, and it stood straight up when filled halfway, then tipped completely over when it was filled all the way up. Confucius let out a sigh, saying, "What doesn't tip over when full?"

Zilu stepped forward and said, "May I ask if there is a *dao* to maintaining fullness?"

Confucius said, "To safeguard wisdom and intelligence, use foolishness. To safeguard widespread accomplishments, use deference. To safeguard courageous strength that reverberates across the land, use timidity. To safeguard wealth enough for all within the four seas, use modesty. This is what is meant by the *dao* of reduction and further reduction."[5]

9.5

孔子觀於東流之水。子貢問曰: "君子所見大水必觀焉, 何也?"孔子對曰: "以其不息, 且遍與諸生而不爲也, 夫水似乎德: 其流也, 則卑下, 倨拘必修其理, 此似義; 浩浩乎無屈盡之期, 此似道; 流行赴百仞之溪而不懼, 此似勇; 至量必平之, 此似法; 盛而不求概, 此似正; 綽約微達, 此似察; 發源必東, 此似志; 以出以入, 萬物就以化潔, 此似善化也。水之德有若此, 是故君子見必觀焉。"

Confucius was observing a river flowing toward the east. Zigong asked, "Why is it said that a *junzi* never fails to stop and observe a large river?"

Confucius replied, "In that it ceaselessly spreads out to give life to all things, it doesn't do so actively; in this way, water resembles *de*. In flowing, it remains low and bends; this principle is worth cultivating in oneself; in this way, it resembles *yi*. When it flows with an unstoppable force, it resembles the *dao*. In how it fearlessly

---

the base and could not stand upright on its own; instead, loops on either side were used to suspend it. (Wei and Qian 2019)

5. This appears to be a transparent reference to the *Dao de jing*: 爲學日益, 爲道日損。損之又損, 以至於無爲, "Learning requires a daily increase, but acting in *dao* requires a daily reduction. Reduction and further reduction, all the way to nonaction" (chapter 48). In 8.5, we saw a reference to Confucius visiting Laozi before Confucius' teaching career took off. The story is also famous from SJ. Oddly, however, there is very little overlap in content between the *Analects* and the *Dao de jing*. If Laozi was Confucius' teacher and had such a profound influence on him, as the story goes, why do we not see more similarity in the written records? The *Dialogues* fills this gap. This passage and the following passage are examples. See also 15.8.

flows toward canyons hundreds of feet high, it resembles courageous behavior. In its remaining level while at rest, it resembles the law. When reaching capacity, it doesn't need to be leveled off; in this way, it resembles basic decency. In how it reaches minute places by virtue of its adaptability, it resembles the proper method of investigation. In how it always flows east[6] despite its distant origins, it resembles stalwart ambition. In how it cleanses all things that enter and exit it, it resembles transformation through excellence. The virtue of water is like this, and this is why a *junzi* never fails to stop and observe."

9.6

子貢觀於魯廟之北堂，出而問於孔子曰："向也賜觀於太廟之堂，未既輟，還瞻北蓋，皆斷焉，彼將有說耶？匠過之也？"孔子曰："太廟之堂，官致良工之匠，匠致良材，盡其功巧，蓋貴久矣。尚有說也。"

After visiting the north hall of the Lu ancestral temple, Zigong asked Confucius, "I went to visit the main hall of the Great Temple, and just before leaving I turned around and looked at the north gate, which had been assembled from shortened boards.[7] Is there an explanation for that, or is it just shoddy carpentry?"

Confucius said, "For the main hall of the Great Temple, the official in charge would have hired seasoned artisans. The artisans would have used high-quality materials and expert methods. The gate should, therefore, be a lasting masterpiece. There must be some explanation."[8]

6. Major rivers in China flow in a generally easterly direction.

7. *North gate . . . shortened boards, bei gai . . . duan* 北蓋 . . . 斷: It's not clear from the Chinese exactly what Zigong sees. The term *gai* 蓋, meaning cover or canopy, is commonly interpreted as a loan word for *he* 闔, meaning door—a single door of a double-door set. *Duan*, meaning shortened, cut-off, broken, truncated, and so on, is commonly understood to refer to the boards making up the door. We follow the common interpretations, but it is still unclear what the flaw in the door was. The building must have been one of the most august buildings in Lu at the time, its status akin to the Washington Monument or Lincoln Memorial in Washington, DC. Although it would have been five centuries old by that time, presumably it would have been well maintained. An ancestral temple was a walled compound, and from what we know, the "north hall," approached from the south, was likely the most important hall of all. Behind it would have been the "north gate," essentially a back door, perhaps reserved for use by the duke. (Though instead of "north gate," it could be "north door," referring to the back door of the north hall.) Zigong noticed that there was something off about the doors in the north gate: they were too short, formed from boards that had not been properly planed, or something like that. (Chen 2015; Hu 2020)

8. This passage seems to establish an implicit analogy between the seemingly flawed condition of the temple gate and some long-standing, difficult-to-understand custom of *li*. Just as there must be a

9.7

孔子曰:“吾有所耻,有所鄙,有所殆。夫幼而不能强學,老而無以教,吾耻之;去其鄉,事君而達,卒遇故人,曾無舊言,吾鄙之;與小人處而不能親賢,吾殆之。”

Confucius said, “From my perspective, there are some things that are shameful, some that are rude, and some that are disastrous. Failing to industriously study when young and then as a result having nothing to teach when old—I consider this shameful. To leave one’s hometown, take up a position serving one’s sovereign and achieve some accomplishments, and then, on meeting someone from your hometown, to act as if you have nothing in common to talk about—I consider this rude. To associate with small-minded people and as a result be unable to form close bonds with capable and virtuous people—I consider this to be disastrous.”

9.8

子路見於孔子。孔子曰:“智者若何?仁者若何?”子路對曰:“智者使人知己,仁者使人愛己。”子曰:“可謂士矣。”子路出,子貢入。問亦如之。子貢對曰:“智者知人,仁者愛人。”子曰:“可謂士矣。”子貢出,顏回入。問亦如之。對曰:“智者自知,仁者自愛。”子曰:“可謂士君子矣。”

Zilu met with Confucius.

Confucius asked, “What makes for a wise person? What makes for a *ren* person?”

Zilu replied, “A wise person causes others to understand oneself. A *ren* person causes others to care about oneself.”

Confucius said, “This is the response of someone who is on his way.”

Zilu departed, and Zigong entered.

Confucius asked the same question, and Zigong responded, “A wise person understands others. A *ren* person cares for others.”

Confucius said, “This is the response of someone who is on his way.”

Zigong left, and Yan Hui entered.

Confucius asked the same question, and Yan Hui said, “A wise person naturally understands. A *ren* person naturally cares.”[9]

---

reason for the use of the shortened boards in the gate, Confucius suggests, there must also be a reason that a custom of *li*—even if we don’t necessarily understand it—has persisted.

9. *Naturally understands, naturally cares, zi zhi, zi ai* 自知, 自愛: The Chinese here is usually interpreted as to understand oneself and to care for (love) oneself, but it is difficult to make sense of that interpretation in this context. The construction *zi zhi* occurs three other times in the *Dialogues*, in none of which does it mean to know oneself. Rather, it means to know for oneself, to come to understand something

Confucius said, "This is the response of someone who is on his way and who is a *junzi*."[10]

9.9

子貢問於孔子曰:"子從父命, 孝乎; 臣從君命, 貞乎。奚疑焉?"孔子曰:"鄙哉賜! 汝不識也。昔者明王萬乘之國, 有爭臣七人, 則主無過舉; 千乘之國, 有爭臣五人, 則社稷不危也; 百乘之家, 有爭臣三人, 則祿位不替; 父有爭子, 不陷無禮; 士有爭友, 不行不義。故子從父命, 奚詎爲孝? 臣從君命, 奚詎爲貞? 夫能審其所從, 之謂孝, 之謂貞矣。"

Zigong asked Confucius, "*Xiao* is following the orders of one's father. Devotion is following the orders of one's sovereign. How is there any doubt about this?"

Confucius said, "Ci, you are so crude. You don't understand at all. In the past, an enlightened king of a large state would have at least seven ministers of differing opinions to consult in order to avoid making serious errors in his conduct and actions. In a medium-size state, a ruler would have at least five ministers of differing opinions to consult in order to avoid putting his state in danger. In a small state, a ruler would have at least three ministers of differing opinions to consult in order to avoid having his throne usurped. A father would have sons with differing opinions in order to avoid descending into impropriety. An aspiring young man would have friends of differing opinions in order to avoid immoral behavior. So how can *xiao* mean for a son to merely follow the orders of his father? How can devotion mean for a minister to merely follow the orders of his sovereign? *Xiao* and devotion mean being able to thoroughly understand what one is following."

---

on one's own. A straightforward way of stating that same meaning in this context is to *naturally know*, a construction which can be extended to *ai*, in *naturally care for*. This interpretation preserves the traditional Confucian emphasis on spreading one's care in increasingly wider concentric circles as one ascends the moral and social hierarchy (see, for example, 17.1), and, in keeping with a Daoist bent in this chapter, expresses a Daoist-like emphasis on natural behavior.

10. *Someone who is on his way and who is a* junzi, *shi junzi* 士君子: The Chinese is somewhat confusing in how it combines what are normally understood as distinct levels of accomplishment: *shi* and *junzi*. The *Xunzi* depicts this episode and differs only in its terminology for the levels of accomplishment. Instead of *shi*, *shi*, and *shi junzi*, as seen here, it uses *shi*, *shi junzi*, and *ming* 明 (bright, enlightened) *junzi*. The term *shi junzi* is used repeatedly in the *Li ji*, where it appears to be interchangeable with *junzi*, and in the *Mozi*, where it appears to refer to the educated class. See "*Shi*" and "*Junzi*" in the introduction's philosophical lexicon.

9.10

子路盛服見於孔子。子曰:“由, 是倨倨者, 何也? 夫江始出於岷山, 其源可以濫觴; 及其至于江津, 不舫舟, 不避風, 則不可以涉。非唯下流水多耶。今爾衣服既盛, 顏色充盈, 天下且孰肯以非告汝乎?”子路趨而出, 改服而入, 蓋自若也。子曰:“由, 志之! 吾告汝: 奮於言者華, 奮於行者伐。夫色智而有能者, 小人也。故君子知之曰知, 言之要也; 不能曰不能, 行之至也。言要則智, 行至則仁。既仁且智, 惡不足哉?”

Zilu was all dressed up one day when he went to meet with Confucius.

Confucius said, “Zilu, why do you look so arrogant today? At the headwaters of the Yangtze River on Min Mountain, you can float a cup on the small stream. Further down at the ferry crossing, it’s not safe to cross except on a calm day with boats lashed together. This is not only because there is more water there.[11] Look at you in your fancy clothes with your nose up in the air. Who would dare approach you to caution you about any errors you might make?” Zilu hurried home to change and then went back to see Confucius, this time looking more like his usual self.

Confucius said, “Zilu, I’m going to tell you something that you need to remember. If you put all your energy into just your speech, it will end up flowery. If you put all your energy into just your outward behavior, you will appear arrogant. Someone who intentionally gives the impression of being capable and virtuous is in reality a small-minded person. For this reason, the crucial aspect of speaking is for a *junzi* to acknowledge to others what he knows.[12] And the ultimate form of behavior is acknowledging what you are unable to do. Wisdom lies in the crucial aspect of speaking and *ren* in the ultimate form of behavior. With both *ren* and wisdom, what is missing?”[13]

11. The analogy here seems to have to do with the relative safety of humility (the calm headwaters) vs. the relative danger of grandness (the fast-moving waters at the ferry crossing).

12. And, by extension, what he doesn’t know, which is stated explicitly in parallel passages in the *Xunzi* and *Shuo yuan*.

13. How can the description of Zilu at the beginning of this passage be squared with *Analects* 9.27, in which Zilu is praised by Confucius for giving little heed to the quality of his clothing in comparison with others? Zilu is described here as (1) possessing the wealth to acquire extravagant clothing and (2) exhibiting arrogance in Confucius’ presence. These characteristics are depicted separately in 8.12 and 19.1; this passage puts them together. Not feeling bad about one’s humble clothing does not preclude feeling good about one’s impressive clothing. We know that Zilu was prone to impulsiveness and arrogance and was not shy about revealing his true thoughts and feelings to Confucius. Thus, this passage seems perfectly in keeping with depictions of Zilu elsewhere.

9.11

子路問於孔子曰："有人於此，披褐而懷玉，何如?"子曰："國無道，隱之可也；國有道，則袞冕而執玉。"

Zilu asked Confucius, "Suppose someone were to hide a piece of jade inside his burlap robe.[14] What would you think about that?"

Confucius said, "When a government is thoroughly unjust, it is acceptable to go into seclusion. When a government is just, you need to don court vestments and reveal the jade."

14. As becomes apparent in the following line, this is a metaphor for someone who has the talent and wisdom to lead but declines to step forward. Compare *Analects* 9.13.

10

Valuing Life

Another collection of disparate events, chapter 10 covers familiar ground. The chapter opens and closes with depictions of wise and virtuous leaders who have the sage's nuanced abilities to exert a transformative influence on others, valuing life above all else. We're introduced to the *Changes* and treated to the *Poems* and their interpretive possibilities. And despite Confucius' common emphasis on *li,* we see that it is the substance and the feelings that give rise to li, rather than li's exterior manifestation, that are paramount.

10.1

魯哀公問於孔子曰:"昔者舜冠何冠乎?"孔子不對。公曰:"寡人有問於子,而子無言,何也?"對曰:"以君之問不先其大者,故方思所以爲對。"公曰:"其大何乎?"孔子曰:"舜之爲君也,其政好生而惡殺,其任授賢而替不肖,德若天地而静虛,化若四時而變物,是以四海承風,暢於異類,鳳翔麟至,鳥獸馴德,無他也,好生故也。君舍此道而冠冕是問,是以緩對。"

Duke Ai of Lu asked Confucius, "What kind of crown did Shun wear?"

Confucius didn't respond.

The duke said, "I asked you a question. Why don't you respond?"

Confucius said, "Your question does not prioritize important matters, so I need to think about how to respond."

The duke said, "What important matters?"

Confucius said, "When Shun was sovereign, in his governing he valued life and detested killing. In his hiring, he recruited men who were capable and virtuous and replaced the ones who weren't. His *de* matched the *de* of heaven and earth in his calm emptiness. His transformative powers matched the four seasons in his ability to usher in change. As a result, all within the four seas were affected by his powers, which flowed unimpeded to uncultured tribes.[1] *Feng* soared and *lin* appeared, and

1. *Uncultured tribes, yi lei* 異類: different kinds. We follow Wang Su in interpreting *yi lei* as uncultured tribes.

the birds and beasts followed their *de*. The one and only reason for all of this was his valuing of life. The reason I was slow to respond is that you set aside this *dao* to ask about crowns."

10.2

孔子讀史，至楚復陳，喟然嘆曰："賢哉楚王！輕千乘之國而重一言之信。匪申叔之信，不能達其義；匪莊王之賢，不能受其訓。"

One day when Confucius was reading history, he came across the story of Chu restoring Chen.[2] He sighed and said, "The king of Chu was a capable and virtuous leader! He ignored the might of being a superpower and focused on the trustworthiness of one adviser. If it weren't for Shenshu's trustworthiness, the king would never have been able to do the right thing. If it weren't for the king's wisdom and capability, he would never have been willing to listen to Shen's advice."

10.3

孔子常自筮其卦，得《賁》焉，愀然有不平之狀。子張進曰："師聞卜者得《賁》卦，吉也。而夫子之色有不平，何也？"孔子對曰："以其離耶。在《周易》，山下有火謂之《賁》，非正色之卦也。夫質也，黑白宜正焉。今得賁，非吾兆也。吾聞丹漆不文，白玉不雕。何也？質有餘，不受飾故也。"

2. From 685 to 591 BCE, China went through a period in which one state or another successively held sway over all the others. These leaders typically achieved superpower status for their states through internal reforms—levying taxes, hiring competent leaders, unifying measurements and currency, undertaking infrastructure projects, training the military, and so on (see "Superpower" in the glossary). King Zhuang of Chu was one of them. Confucius admired his ability for rational reform and admired the consistently good advice given by the king's minister Shenshu. The story referred to here is about Chu restoring a Zhou vassal state to its rightful status. Chen was a small but venerable state on Chu's northern border. Chen and Chu had engaged in many battles in the past, and Chu (like previous superpowers) had a history of absorbing smaller states. The story centers around the widowed wife of an official of Chen. She was known as Xia Ji 夏姬, and her son was Xia Zhengshu 夏徵舒. Xia Ji was extraordinarily beautiful. The ruler of Chen and two of his ministers earned a reputation for iniquity by throwing parties and sleeping with her. After one such party at Xia's own residence, Xia Zhengshu lay in wait for the duke outside and shot him dead with an arrow. The two ministers and the duke's sons fled to Chu, and Xia Zhengshu declared himself ruler of Chen. Although Xia had a just cause for punishing the Duke of Chen, he did not have a just claim to the throne, so the king of Chu had a pretext for attacking Chen and killing Xia, which he did. But the king went a step further and abolished Chen as a state. Shenshu is credited with giving good advice on at least two occasions in this story. First, when King Zhuang said he wanted Xia Ji for himself, Shenshu dissuaded him. Second, Shenshu convinced the king to restore the Chen heir apparent to his rightful place as ruler of Chen. See also 19.6. (CQZZ)

Confucius once did a divination with yarrow stalks,[3] resulting in the *bi* (ornamentation) hexagram. He suddenly got a worried look on his face.

Zizhang stepped forward and said, "I've heard that *bi* portends good fortune. Why did you get a worried look on your face?"

Confucius replied, "Doesn't it have *li* in it?[4] In the Changes, it says, '*Bi*—fire under mountain.'[5] It's not a clear-cut hexagram. The basic nature of something is as plain as black and white.[6] Getting *bi* is not necessarily a good omen for me. I've learned that red lacquerware doesn't need decoration and white jade doesn't require sculpting. Why is that? My reasoning is: If there is more than enough in the basic makeup of something, then decoration is unnecessary."[7]

10.4

孔子曰："吾於《甘棠》，見宗廟之敬甚矣。思其人，必愛其樹；尊其人，必敬其位，道也。"

Confucius said, "It was through the poem "Flowering Pear Tree"[8] that I came to really understand the respect displayed in ancestral temples. It is a natural principle

3. The traditional way to do a divination with the *Changes* was to use a bundle of dried stalks of the yarrow plant, separating them in a systematic way that, through random results, builds the six lines of one of the sixty-four hexagrams. See "Changes" and "Prognostication" in the glossary.

4. The Bi hexagram (䷕) is composed of the Li 離 (fire) trigram (☲) beneath the Gen 艮 (mountain) trigram (☶).

5. This passage identifying *bi* as fire under mountain appears in the Xiang 象 commentary to the *Changes*.

6. *Basic nature, zhi* 質: The word *zhi* 質 has a double meaning here. It means both basic makeup of something and to be plain, or undecorated.

7. Why does Confucius transition from the ambiguity of a hexagram to the basic nature of something? In giving advice to sovereigns, Confucius tried to keep the discussion to fundamental topics, but the sovereigns were often interested in other, frivolous things (see, for example, 10.1). This could be Confucius' worry here—that the distortion of ornamentation will take precedence in his life over the plain, unornamented fundamentals.

8. The entire poem goes like this:

> The lush and shady pear tree,
> Don't prune it, don't chop it;
> That's where the Earl of Shao lived.
> The lush and shady pear tree,
> Don't prune it, don't harm it;
> That's where the Earl of Shao rested.
> The lush and shady pear tree,
> Don't prune it, don't bend it;
> That's where the Earl of Shao sat.

This poem (#16) commemorates the Earl of Shao, brother of King Wu and the Duke of Zhou, and can be found in the "Shao nan" section of the *Poems*. See "Earl of Shao" in the glossary.

that, when you miss someone, you will cherish their special tree,[9] and when you have a special reverence for someone, you will display deep respect for their place in the temple."

10.5

子路戎服見於孔子，拔劍而舞之，曰："古之君子，以劍自衛乎？"孔子曰："古之君子，忠以爲質，仁以爲衛，不出環堵之室，而知千里之外，有不善則以忠化之，侵暴則以仁固之，何持劍乎？"子路曰："由乃今聞此言。請攝齊以受教。"

All decked out in military gear, Zilu met with Confucius.[10] Drawing his sword and putting on a display, he asked, "Did the *junzi* of the past use a sword mostly for self-defense?"

Confucius replied, "The *junzi* of the past took conscientiousness as their basic makeup and *ren* as their defense. Without leaving their humble cottages, they were known for hundreds of miles around. If there was some uncivil behavior, they would transform it with their conscientiousness. If there was violence, they would guard against it with their *ren*. What need was there to carry a sword?"

Zilu said, "Having heard your words, please allow me to humbly receive instruction from you."

10.6

楚恭王出遊，亡烏嗥之弓，左右請求之。王曰："止，楚王失弓，楚人得之，又何求之！"孔子聞之，曰："惜乎其不大也，不曰人遺弓，人得之而已，何必楚也。"

King Gong of Chu was out traveling and lost his Screeching Raven bow. His advisers suggested searching for it. The king replied, "Stop. The king of Chu loses a bow, and a person of Chu acquires it. Why search for it?"[11]

Confucius heard this story and commented, "Unfortunately, the king was not broad enough. He should have said: 'A person loses the bow, and another person acquires it.' Why say 'Chu'?"[12]

9. *Their special tree, shu* 樹: tree, as in the poem. Yang and Song (2013) interpret it as a tree that the person would stop to appreciate when passing. It could also be a tree planted in the person's memory or to mark the person's grave.

10. This story appears to be an account of Zilu's first meeting with Confucius. See also 19.1.

11. In other words, it's not lost at all; it once belonged to a Chu person and still belongs to a Chu person.

12. This story suggests a concern for narrow patriotism on the part of the king of Chu and a much broader concern for all of humanity on the part of Confucius. Another version of this story appears in the *Lü shi chunqiu*, in which Laozi is said to have heard the story and then suggested dropping the word

10.7

孔子爲魯司寇，斷獄訟，皆進衆議者而問之，曰：“子以爲奚若？某以爲何若？”皆曰云云如是，然後夫子曰：“當從某子，幾是。”

As minister of justice for Lu, Confucius would hear lawsuits. In each case, he would invite many different people in and ask them questions, such as, “What do you think happened? Why does this other person think it happened?” They would all speak, and then Confucius would say, “We should follow the view of this person, who is probably correct.”[13]

10.8

孔子問漆雕憑曰：“子事臧文仲、武仲及孺子容，此三大夫孰賢？”對曰：“臧氏家有守龜焉，名曰蔡。文仲三年而爲一兆，武仲三年而爲二兆，孺子容三年而爲三兆。憑從此之見，若問三人之賢與不賢，所未敢識也。”孔子曰：“君子哉，漆雕氏之子！其言人之美也，隱而顯；言人之過也，微而著。智而不能及，明而不能見，孰克如此？”

Confucius asked Qidiao Ping, “You have served under Zang Wenzhong, Zang Wuzhong, and Ru Zirong. Of these three high officials, which is the most capable and virtuous?”

Qidiao replied, “The Zang family has the plastron of a guardian turtle that all three have used for divination. It was given the name Cai. Wenzhong used it once in three years’ time, Wuzhong used it twice in three years, and Ru Zirong used it three times in three years. This says something about them, but it is beyond me to discern which of them is more or less capable and virtuous.”

Confucius said to the others present, “This son of Qidiao is a *junzi*! In speaking of the strengths and shortcomings of others, he is forthcoming but subtle. Who else is able to ascend this unreachable height of intelligence or achieve this boundless brilliance?”[14]

“person,” implying an even broader concern for the whole cosmos: A bow is lost, and it is found—why say “person”?

13. The generality of the language suggests that the people who would be invited included not only witnesses and experts but also advisers to help him think through the case. The point of this passage seems to be that Confucius was objectively fair, open to opinions from all sides, thorough in his investigation, and refrained from forcing his personal view on others.

14. In 18.4, Confucius makes it clear what he thinks about Zang Wenzhong and Zang Wuzhong. If that judgment is consistent with the judgment here, then the increasing number of prognostications (though still few in number over such a long time span) would demonstrate more wisdom and capability, and so Qidiao doesn’t have to say it directly. Being careful in one’s speech is an important virtue for Confucius, and Qidiao demonstrates that virtue here by expressing a definitive judgment of the three

10.9

魯公索氏將祭而亡其牲。孔子聞之，曰："公索氏不及二年將亡。"後一年而亡。門人問曰："昔公索氏亡其祭牲，而夫子曰不及二年必亡。今過期而亡，夫子何以知其然?"孔子曰："夫祭者，孝子所以自盡於其親。將祭而亡其牲，則其餘所亡者多矣。若此而不亡者，未之有也。"

A Lu man by the name of Gongsuo lost his sacrificial animal just before the ceremony to honor his deceased parents.

Confucius heard about this, and said, "Gongsuo will lose his life within two years' time." The following year, Gongsuo passed away.

One of Confucius' students asked, "Before, when Gongsuo lost his sacrificial animal, you said that he would lose his life within two years' time. Now he really has died. How did you know?"

Confucius said, "*Xiao* children will put their all into the ceremony to honor their deceased parents. Having lost his sacrificial animal just before the ceremony suggested that he would lose even more.[15] There has never been someone like this who hasn't himself soon died."

10.10

虞、芮二國爭田而訟，連年不決。乃相謂曰："西伯仁也，盍往質之?"入其境，則耕者讓畔，行者讓路；入其朝，士讓爲大夫，大夫讓爲卿。虞、芮之君曰："嘻！吾儕小人也，不可以履君子之庭。"遂自相與而退，咸以所爭之田爲閑田也。孔子曰："以此觀之，文王之道，其不可加焉。不令而從，不教而聽，至矣哉！"

The two states Yu and Rui both claimed a piece of land and quarreled over it for years. During a summit, one said to the other, "The Earl of the West is a *ren* man. Why not go there to see if he can help settle this?" On crossing the border into Zhou, the two rulers noticed that farmers deferred to each other where two fields shared a boundary. They noticed that in the streets, pedestrians yielded to each other as well. And in the courts, lower-level officials deferred to each other when vying for promotion, as did higher-up officials in vying for ministerial positions.

The rulers of Yu and Rui said to one another, "Sheesh, small-minded people like us aren't fit to set foot in the palace of such a *junzi*." And then they made up and departed, letting the disputed land sit idle.

---

men but in an indirect, tentative way. This combination is difficult to achieve and is what earns Confucius' unusually high praise.

15. In other words, this specific case of neglect in such an important matter suggests a general sense of neglect that will affect him in a serious way in the near future.

Confucius said, "It is apparent from this story that, already at this time, the *dao* of King Wen was not in any way deficient. People followed without being led and acted without being instructed. That's as good as it gets!"

10.11

曾子曰: "狎甚則相簡, 莊甚則不親。是故君子之狎足以交歡, 其莊足以成禮。"孔子聞斯言也, 曰: "二三子志之, 孰謂參也不知禮乎?"

Zengzi said, "Excessive familiarity can lead to impolite behavior. Excessive seriousness can lead to a loss of affection. For this reason, a *junzi* is just familiar enough to bring about happy interactions and just serious enough for proper *li*."

Confucius heard about this and said, "Remember this, everyone. Who would ever say that Shen doesn't understand *li*?"

10.12

哀公問曰: "紳、委、章甫, 有益於仁乎?"孔子作色而對曰: "君胡然焉? 衰麻苴杖者, 志不存乎樂, 非耳弗聞, 服使然也; 黼黻袞冕者, 容不褻慢, 非性矜莊, 服使然也; 介胄執戈者, 無退懦之氣, 非體純猛, 服使然也。且臣聞之, 好肆不守折, 而長者不爲市。竊夫其有益與無益, 君子所以知。"

Duke Ai asked Confucius, "Does wearing a Ruist belt or hat improve one's *ren*?"

Confucius' expression changed as he replied, "Why would your majesty ask such a question? Wearing funeral clothes and carrying a mourning staff, one has no mind for joyful music.[16] It's not that one's ears can't hear the music—rather, the attire sets the mood.[17] Wearing decorative formal vestments, one's expression is serious. It's

16. *Joyful music, yue* 樂: music. The word *music* alone doesn't make sense here, as one should be quite open to sad music during mourning. The character 樂 can also mean joy. Since there is an explicit reference to sound here, it makes most sense to put these two meanings together.

17. *Attire sets the mood, fu shi ran ye* 服使然也: attire makes/allows it thus. The meaning of *shi* is ambiguous here. Perhaps the first thought would be that it means to make, thus suggesting that the clothes are solely responsible for the emotional content. If this were so, it would go against many other passages in which Confucius says that the exterior is an expression of the interior (not the other way around). *Shi* can also mean to allow to happen or to indulge in. The broader range of meaning makes more sense in this context. Attire assists in the free flow of emotion. For example, black clothing at a funeral (in Western society) doesn't create sorrow, but it does lend to a sorrowful atmosphere that allows one to feel comfortable expressing sorrow. For Confucius, exterior manifestations of emotion (such as particular clothing) are what we might call emotional technologies. They assist in the proper interpersonal communication of emotion. The answer to the duke's question, then, would be: Yes, Ruist clothes

not that one is reverent by nature—the attire sets the mood. Wearing armor and carrying a weapon, one has the courage to fight. It's not that one is ferocity incarnate—the attire sets the mood. I've learned that, just as a keen businessman doesn't take a loss, so a virtuous elder doesn't set up a table in the market.[18] Thus, whether wearing a Ruist belt or hat improves one's *ren*—a *junzi* will know how to answer that."[19]

10.13

孔子謂子路曰: "見長者而不盡其辭, 雖有風雨, 吾不能入其門矣。故君子以其所能敬人, 小人反是。"

Confucius said to Zilu, "If I were to encounter an elder and fail to fully express deference[20] to him, I would be too ashamed to step inside his house, even if it were pouring rain outside. A *junzi* does his utmost in expressing respect for others. A small-minded person does the opposite."

10.14

孔子謂子路曰: "君子以心導耳目, 立義以爲勇; 小人以耳目導心, 不愻以爲勇。故曰退之而不怨, 先之斯可從已。"

Confucius said to Zilu, "A *junzi* uses the heart to lead the senses, establishing *yi* through courage. The small-minded person uses the senses to lead the heart, mistaking impertinence for courage. That's why it is said: Step back without complaint; take the lead and others will follow."[21]

(in that day and age) would help improve one's *ren*. They would act as a constant reminder of the virtues that a Ruist holds dear. They would also identify a person as a Ruist and thereby attract like-minded people. However, Confucius is not saying that Ruist clothes guarantee *ren* behavior; nor is he saying that *ren* behavior is impossible without Ruist clothes (see 8.3, for example).

18. The relevance of this sentence to the preceding message hinges on the belief that the market is a place where one must compromise one's ideals in order to do business successfully. In other words, the atmosphere of the market—its external aspect—influences one's internal attitude, like clothing does, and because the influence of the market is negative, it is best to avoid the market when possible.

19. See 7.1 for a description of *Ruist* clothing.

20. *Fully express deference, ci* 辭: *Ci* can mean to express in words and to politely decline. In this context, it seems to make the most sense to combine these meanings and extend them so that the translation is: *to fully express deference.*

21. For more on the relationship between courage and *yi*, see *Analects* 2.24 and 17.23–24.

10.15

孔子曰:“君子有三患。未之聞,患不得聞;既得聞之,患弗得學;既得學之,患弗能行。有其德而無其言,君子耻之;有其言而無其行,君子耻之;既得之,而又失之,君子耻之;地有餘,民不足,君子耻之;衆寡均而人功倍己焉,君子耻之。”

Confucius said, “A *junzi* has three worries: to not have the opportunity to hear something worth hearing about; having heard about it, to not have the opportunity to study it; having studied it, to not have the opportunity to put it into practice. There are five things of which a *junzi* is ashamed: to have virtues but be unable to put them into words; to have words for one's virtues but be unable to put them into practice; to lose one of these abilities after having once attained it; to see the people in want though the land provides enough; to see another's contributions exceed one's own, other things being equal.”

10.16

魯人有獨處室者,鄰之釐婦亦獨處一室。夜,暴風雨至,釐婦室壞,趨而托焉。魯人閉户而不納,釐婦自牖與之言:“何不仁而不納我乎?”魯人曰:“吾聞男女不六十不同居,今子幼,吾亦幼,是以不敢納爾也。”婦人曰:“子何不如柳下惠然?嫗不逮門之女,國人不稱其亂。”魯人曰:“柳下惠則可,吾固不可。吾將以吾之不可,學柳下惠之可。”孔子聞之曰:“善哉!欲學柳下惠者,未有似於此者。期於至善,而不襲其爲,可謂智乎!”

There was a man in Lu who lived alone. A neighboring widow lived alone as well. One evening when a heavy storm hit, the widow's house caved in. Seeking shelter, she fled to her neighbor's house. The Lu man locked the door and refused to let her in. From the window, the woman said, “Why can't you show a little *ren* and let me in?”

The Lu man said, “I've heard that single women and men under the age of sixty should not stay together. Because you and I are still young, I don't dare let you in.”

The widow said, “Then you are less of a man than Liuxia Hui. He used his body to warm a woman who couldn't make it out of the city gate in time, and no one criticized him.”[22]

22. Scholars offer two versions of how to interpret this story about Liuxia Hui. In both versions, Liuxia Hui spends time alone with a woman, and when word gets out he is not criticized for improper conduct. The different interpretations hinge on the phrase *bu dai men* 不逮門. The original has *bu jian men* 不建門. Yang and Song follow the SKQS, which corrects *jian* to *dai*. Under this interpretation (Yang and Song 2013), the woman, who lives outside the city, fails to leave the city before the gates close

The Lu man said, "So Liuxia Hui could do it, and I can't. I take my inability and imitate Liuxia Hui's ability."

Confucius said, "Excellent! There has never been anyone trying to learn from Liu Xiahui who has been able to achieve something like this. To aim for the greatest good without conforming to others' behavior—this is wisdom."[23]

10.17

孔子曰："小辯害義，小言破道。《關雎》興于鳥，而君子美之，取其雄雌之有別；《鹿鳴》興於獸，而君子大之，取其得食而相呼。若以鳥獸之名嫌之，固不可行也。"

Confucius said, "Petty arguments harm *yi*. Petty words destroy *dao*. In 'Chirp of the Osprey,'[24] the poet is inspired by the bird. A *junzi* appreciates the beauty of the poem and also learns about the natural distinctions of male and female. In 'Cry of the Deer,'[25] the poet is inspired by the animal. A *junzi* appreciates the grandeur of the poem and also learns about how deer communicate to share food. It does not do to reject these lessons just because they originate in birds and beasts."

(*bu dai men*) on a winter night. Liuxia lets her into his nearby home and, afraid that she is in danger of frostbite, holds her to his chest to keep her warm. In the less dramatic version (Yang and Chou 2020), Liuxia Hui merely houses an unmarried (*bu jian men*) woman for a period of time.

23. There are various ways to interpret the ending of this episode, especially the term *ke* 可 (which can mean not just to be able to but also to accept, or simply, acceptable/permissible) and the several pronouns. Confucius' emphasis seems to be that conforming to social standards is not the highest good. Instead, one should also be able to gauge one's own abilities when faced with moral dilemmas. Liu Xiahui understood his abilities and was able to preserve morality while transgressing social norms. And others were able to see this. The man in this episode, by contrast, understood that he himself was unable to do that. He imitated Liu in the sense that they both acted in accord with their abilities. Presumably, the woman could easily go to another neighbor's house and would not be left out in the storm.

24. The Australasian osprey has a loud, euphonious cry that is something between a chirp and a shriek. The first and most famous poem of the *Poems* begins with the sound of an osprey, out of reach on the sandbar of a river. The poem goes on to describe a beautiful young woman gathering edible plants in the slow-moving water. A young man is in love with her, but she, too, seems out of reach. The image of the osprey symbolizes both the difficulty of courtship and the enduring nature of romantic partnership, as ospreys are monogamous. The plants that the young woman is gathering are described repeatedly as patchy and sporadic, suggesting an unevenness among things that is at once natural and bountiful.

25. This poem (#161, found today in the "Xiao ya" section of the *Poems*) establishes a metaphor between deer who call to each other for mutual benefit and enjoyment and colleagues who gather for mutual benefit and enjoyment. Sika deer, native to China, are known to be quite vocal. See also 435n8.

10.18

孔子謂子路曰："君子而强氣，而不得其死；小人而强氣，則刑戮荐蓁。《豳詩》曰：'殆天之未陰雨，徹彼桑土，綢繆牖户，今汝下民，或敢侮余。'"孔子曰："能治國家之如此，雖欲侮之，豈可得乎？周自后稷，積行累功，以有爵土，公劉重之以仁。及至大王亶甫，敦以德讓，其樹根置本，備豫遠矣。初，大王都豳，翟人侵之。事之以皮幣，不得免焉；事之以珠玉，不得免焉。於是屬耆老而告之：'所欲吾土地。吾聞之，君子不以所養而害人。二三子何患乎無君？'遂獨與大姜去之，逾梁山，邑于岐山之下。豳人曰：'仁人之君，不可失也。'從之如歸市焉。天之與周，民之去殷，久矣，若此而不能王天下，未之有也。武庚惡能侮？《鄁詩》曰：'執轡如組，兩驂如儛。'"孔子曰："爲此詩者，其知政乎！夫爲組者，總紕於此，成文於彼。言其動於近，行於遠也。執此法以御民，豈不化乎？《竿旄》之忠告，至矣哉！"

Confucius said to Zilu, "An official who is inflexibly strident will not have a happy ending. A commoner who is inflexibly strident will incur frequent punishment. A Bin poem says:

> Dark clouds of a coming storm,
> Mulberry roots stripped for rope,
> Doors and windows lashed up tight,
> A peasant here and there
> May mock me if he dare."[26]

Confucius continued, "Is there anyone today who could rule a country under such circumstances and endure the mockery? From the time of Hou Ji, the Zhou made one accomplishment after another, receiving rewards in the form of titled fiefs. Lord Liu was known for stressing the importance of *ren*, straight through to the great King Dan Fu, who was generous in his *de* and deference, establishing firm roots and spreading contentment far and wide. At first, his capital was at Bin, which the Di people invaded. He placated them with furs and fabric, but they wanted more. He placated them with pearls and jade, but they wanted more. Then he gathered the elders and announced to them, 'What they really want is our land. I have learned that a *junzi* does not allow people to come to harm over a plot of land.[27] So, have no fear that you will be without a leader.' He then peacefully left all of his people and

26. The passage is from the poem "Owl" (#155, found today in the "Bin feng," or Bin-style, section of the *Poems*). One part of the *Poems* is divided into sections devoted to poems originating from specific states—thus, in the "style" of such-and-such a state. *Bin* refers to the early Zhou—before it conquered Shang—when it had its main site in the city of Bin. This part of the poem establishes a metaphor of long-term planning and preparation that Confucius builds on in the subsequent sentences, thus emphasizing the importance of long-term planning in good leadership.

27. *Over a plot of land, yi suo yang* 以所養: over that which nurtures.

his land to the invaders and secretly fled with Tai Jiang. They crossed Liang Mountain and established a new city at the foot of Qi Mountain.[28] The people back in Bin said to themselves, 'We can't lose this sovereign who is such a *ren* person.' So, they set out after him with the same excitement as if going to a fair.

"It has now been a long time since the people turned from the Shang to the Zhou, and there has never been an instance in which a person like these three has not been able to rule the land. How could Wugeng ever mock them? A Bei poem says:

> He wields the reins like tassels leading,
> The teams of horses move like dancing."[29]

Confucius continued, "This poet really understood governing! In crafting an official's tassels, you wind the threads at one end and a pattern appears at the other. In other words, when there is movement in one place, it spreads far and wide. Where are there people who cannot be transformed by employing a leadership method such as this? The conscientious declaration in the poem 'Pole Banners' expresses it exactly!"[30]

28. These areas lie to the north and west of present-day Xi'an. It is about a seven-mile trip on foot southwest from Bin to the plain at the southern foot of Qi Mountain via Liang Mountain. See "Bin" in the glossary.

29. *Bei poem*, 邶诗: *Bei* 邶 is an alternative character for *bei* 邶, the name of the state enfeoffed to Wugeng after the defeat of the Shang. In the "Bei feng" section of today's *Poems*, the poem "Clappers" (#38) contains the line "He wields the reins like tassels leading" but not the subsequent line. Both lines occur in the poem "Uncle in the Country 2" (#78), which occurs in the "Zheng 鄭 feng" section of today's *Poems*. Both poems extol a particular man's martial dancing and prowess. It could be that *zheng* 鄭 was miswritten as *bei* 邶 (in which case the prior reference to Wugeng would be irrelevant), that the lines were misremembered from one poem to another, or that the current version of the *Poems* differs from the version referred to by the author. To see the connection between leadership and dance, see "Dance" and "Music" in the glossary.

30. The poem "Pole Banners" (#53), which appears in the "Yong feng" section of today's *Poems*, depicts, under one interpretation, a charismatic leader attracting others to his side through a moving display of pageantry. After much showing of horses and banners, the reader is persuaded that something powerful is happening, that everyone watching is waiting with bated breath to hear what the leader has to say, until the poem ends with the question on everyone's mind: "What will you declare?"

11

Observing Zhou

Chapter 11 narrates Confucius' famous journey to the Zhou capital to visit Laozi. As we saw in 8.5, it occurred early in his career and was transformative for him. We learn of his being descended from Song nobility (and thus Shang royalty). Not many details of his encounter with Laozi are preserved in the chapter, but the inscription on the statue in the Zhou king's throne room resonates with ideas in the *Dao de jing*. The important conceptual links between *li* and the cosmic cycles of *dao* and *de*, introduced here, will be filled out in later chapters.

11.1

孔子謂南宮敬叔曰:“吾聞老聃博古知今, 通禮樂之原, 明道德之歸, 則吾師也。今將往矣。”對曰:“謹受命。”遂言於魯君曰:“臣受先臣之命云, ‘孔子, 聖人之後也, 滅於宋, 其祖弗父何始有國而授厲公, 及正考父, 佐戴、武、宣, 三命兹益恭。故其鼎銘曰:“一命而僂, 再命而傴, 三命而俯, 循墻而走, 亦莫余敢侮。饘於是, 粥於是, 以餬其口。”其恭儉也若此。臧孫紇有言:“聖人之後, 若不當世, 則必有明德而達者焉。”孔子少而好禮, 其將在矣。’屬臣曰:‘汝必師之。’今孔子將適周, 觀先王之遺制, 考禮樂之所極, 斯大業也, 君盍以乘資之? 臣請與往。”公曰:“諾。”與孔子車一乘, 馬二匹, 豎子侍御。敬叔與俱至周。問禮於老聃, 訪樂於萇弘, 歷郊社之所, 考明堂之則, 察廟朝之度。於是喟然曰:“吾乃今知周公之聖, 與周之所以王也。”及去周, 老子送之, 曰:“吾聞富貴者送人以財, 仁者送人以言。吾雖不能富貴, 而竊仁者之號, 請送子以言乎: 凡當今之士, 聰明深察而近於死者, 好譏議人者也; 博辯閎達而危其身, 好發人之惡者也。無以有己爲人子者, 無以惡己爲人臣者。”孔子曰:“敬奉教。”自周反魯, 道彌尊矣。遠方弟子之進, 蓋三千焉。

Confucius said to Nangong Jingshu, "I've heard that Lao Dan has a broad understanding of both ancient and modern knowledge, that he thoroughly understands the origins of *li* and music, and that he sees clearly the cycles of *dao* and *de*. These are why I would like to travel to study under him."

Nangong replied, "Yes, sir. I will do my best to help." Thereupon he said to the Lu sovereign, "My father once proclaimed his wishes, saying:[1]

> Confucius is the descendent of a sage.[2] Prior to his family leaving Song,[3] his ancestor Fu Fuhe had claim to the Song throne but gave it up for his younger brother, Duke Li.[4] His later Song ancestor, Zeng Kaofu held three appointments under three different dukes, each with a higher level of reverence. Thus, the inscription on the *ding* cauldron that was made for him said, "Nodding in my first appointment, bowing halfway in my second, bowing deeply in my third, creeping along walls,[5] no one dared criticize me. Whether the soup herein is thick or thin, it fills my stomach." Such was his level of reverence and humility. Zangsun He once said, "If society fails to install the descendant of a sage, his *de* will still shine brightly across the era." Confucius has been deeply fond of *li* since he was a child—perhaps he will be the one.

"My father continued, 'You must study under him.' Now Confucius wants to go to Zhou to observe the organizational structures passed down by the Ancient Kings and to study the greatest achievements of *li* and music. It is an important effort, and I recommend that you support him by providing a vehicle for his travels. I would like to accompany him."

The duke replied, "Granted," and provided Confucius with a carriage, two horses, and a driver. Confucius and Nangong traveled together to Zhou.[6]

Confucius studied *li* under Lao Dan and music under Chang Hong. He learned about the location of the Jiao and She sacrifices, and about all the various practices

1. The proclamation by Meng Xizi, Nangong's father, is also recorded in CQZZ ("Zhao" 7.12; 535 BCE). The two accounts closely match.

2. Confucius is said to have descended from nobility of the state of Song (see 39.1). When the Zhou empire was established, it settled the defeated Shang nobility in Song. The progenitor of the Shang was said to be the great sage Tang.

3. See 39.2 for the backstory.

4. The details of this period are murky. If Fu Fuhe had claim to the throne, as this account says, then he would have been the oldest son of a deceased duke. According to *Dialogues* 39.1, Fu Fuhe was the oldest son of Duke Xiang, who had assumed the throne after the death of his older brother, Duke Min. According to SJ ("Song Weizi shi jia"), Fu Fuhe's younger brother Fusi 鮒祀 murdered Duke Yang (宋煬公, dates unknown, brother of, and succeeded, Duke Min). Thus, Duke Xiang and Duke Yang appear to be different names, in different accounts, for the same person. One way of putting all of these pieces together is that after Fusi murdered his father, he attempted to install his brother (Fu Fuhe) as duke, but Fu Fuhe refused, and so Fusi assumed the throne. For more on Confucius' lineage, see 39.1.

5. *Creeping along walls, xun qiang er zou* 循墻而走: metaphor for trepidaciously reverential behavior—a reference to those who dared not criticize.

6. Drawing from a variety of early sources, such as CQZZ, BA, and the *Dialogues*, Yang Chaoming (2017) estimates the year of Confucius' trip to be 508 BCE, when he would have been forty-three years old.

and activities of the Zhou king in his court. Finally, he sighed out loud and said, "Now I really see the sageliness of the Duke of Zhou and the means by which the Zhou ruled the land."

When he departed Zhou, Laozi saw him off, saying, "I've heard that wealthy people send others off with expensive gifts, and *ren* people send others off with words of wisdom. I am not wealthy, and although I don't deserve the label of a *ren* person, I leave you with these words: Many people working their way up the ladder today have brilliant, perceptive, analytical minds, but because they enjoy criticizing others, they bring themselves perilously close to death. Many learned, well-spoken people endanger themselves because they enjoy exposing the misdeeds of others. The best child is one who is not self-centered; the best minister is one who does not engender spite in others."

Confucius said, "I will respectfully follow this advice." After returning to Lu from Zhou, Confucius' *dao* was well respected and spread quickly. Many students came from far away, and they eventually numbered three thousand.

11.2

孔子觀乎明堂，睹四門墉有堯舜之容、桀紂之象，而各有善惡之狀、興廢之誡焉。又有周公相成王，抱之負斧扆，南面以朝諸侯之圖焉。孔子徘徊而望之，謂從者曰："此周之所以盛也。夫明鏡所以察形，往古者所以知今。人主不務襲迹於其所以安存，而忽怠所以危亡，是猶未有以異於卻走而欲求及前人也，豈不惑哉！"孔子觀周，遂入太祖后稷之廟。廟堂右階之前，有金人焉。三緘其口，而銘其背曰："古之慎言人也，戒之哉！無多言，多言多敗；無多事，多事多患。安樂必戒，無所行悔。勿謂何傷，其禍將長；勿謂何害，其禍將大；勿謂不聞，神將伺人。焰焰不滅，炎炎若何？涓涓不壅，終爲江河；綿綿不絕，或成網羅；毫末不札，將尋斧柯。誠能慎之，福之根也。口是何傷？禍之門也。强梁者不得其死，好勝者必遇其敵。盜憎主人，民怨其上。君子知天下之不可上也，故下之；知衆人之不可先也，故後之。温恭慎德，使人慕之；執雌持下，人莫逾之。人皆趨彼，我獨守此；人皆或之，我獨不徙。内藏我智，不示人技。我雖尊高，人弗我害，誰能於此？江海雖左，長於百川，以其卑也。天道無親，而能下人。戒之哉！"孔子既讀斯文也，顧謂弟子曰："小子識之！此言實而中，情而信。《詩》曰：'戰戰兢兢，如臨深淵，如履薄冰。'行身如此，豈以口過患哉？"孔子見老聃而問焉，曰："甚矣，道之於今難行也。吾比執道，而今委質以求當世之君，而弗受也。道於今難行也。"老子曰："夫說者流於辯，聽者亂於辭，如此二者，則道不可以忘也。"

Once, when Confucius was observing the decor of the king of Zhou's throne room, he noticed that the wall near each of its four entrances had a portrait. The four portraits depicted, individually, the laudable Yao and Shun and the deplorable Jie and Zhòu, each with a cautionary phrase. And there was another painting depicting the Duke of Zhou as prime minister for King Cheng, embracing him, with their backs to a folding screen and facing south in the direction of the gathered nobility. Confucius paced back and forth looking at these, then said to those there with him, "This is why Zhou rose to ascendancy. Just as a mirror reflects what is in front of it, you can understand the present by looking at the past. It would show supreme confusion for a ruler to not follow the path of stability laid down by his ancestors and overlook the things that brought down earlier dynasties. This kind of failure would suggest that, though a ruler wished to be progressive, he instead preferred to run backward toward the same mistakes of the past."

After touring the Zhou court, he entered the Temple of Hou Ji, progenitor of the Zhou. In front of the stairs, on the right of the main hall, there was a bronze statue. Its mouth was bound with three cords, and on its back was the following inscription:

Here is a cautious speaker of old. Heed his warning!
Don't say too much. Many words mean many defeats.
Don't do too much. Many actions mean many disasters.

Even in happiness and stability, take precautions.
Don't do anything you will later regret.

Do not say, "What harm will it do?" for ruin will be large and lasting.
Say not that none hears, for the gods observe all.

Sparks do little damage, but what of the flames they grow into?
Streams that aren't dammed end in mighty rivers.
Vines left to grow form ensnaring nets.
If you don't pull the tiny sprout, soon you seek the handle of an axe.

The root of good fortune is a talent for discretion and integrity.
The damage the mouth can do is the doorway to disaster.

Violent bullies find their end in death
Just as the competitive eventually meet their match.

Thieves detest the wealthy, and the people resent their superiors.
A *junzi*, understanding the impossibility of lording over others, keeps below them;
Understanding the impossibility of leading others, keeps behind them.

Reverence and virtue inspire admiration.
Pliancy[7] and humility can never be surpassed.

7. *Pliancy, zhi ci* 執雌: to wield the feminine. A similar locution occurs in the *Dao de jing* (10, 28). The term *ci*, and another term (*pin* 牝) used in its place in excavated versions, refer to non-human animal females.

If others all rush over there, I alone stay over here.
If others all move to one place, I alone refuse to go.

I store my wisdom inside and don't reveal my talents.
Who is able to achieve high status without coming to harm at the hands of others?

Although rivers and seas stand low, they are fed by the many streams—all because of their humility.
The *dao* of *tian* has no favorites and prefers lying low.[8]
Heed these warnings!

When Confucius finished reading, he turned to his students and said, "Remember these! These words are truthful and accurate, precise and trustworthy. A poem says:

Fearful and cautious,
as if peering into a chasm
or treading on thin ice.[9]

If you live like this, how will your words ever bring you to ruin?"

Confucius then met with Lao Dan, saying, "Really, the *dao* is so difficult to put into practice. People like me possessing the *dao* offer our services to rulers, but our advice goes unheeded. The *dao* is so difficult to put into practice these days."

Laozi said, "Persuaders do their work through stirring arguments. Listeners are confused by eloquent speech. Facing these two facts, never forget the *dao*."

8. The many parallels of these lines with the *Dao de jing* are noteworthy. They demonstrate the close relationship in the *Dialogues* between Confucianism—following the *li* of the Zhou—and Daoism.

9. These are the final three lines of the poem "Narrow Sky" (#195), which can be found today in the "Xiao ya" section of the *Poems*. The poem laments the successful scheming of courtiers. A similar wording appears in the poem "Quite Small" (#196), lines from which appear in 17.5 below.

12

Student Conduct

Chapter 12 opens with an incisive description of Confucius' method of instruction, then immediately transitions into descriptions of Confucius' students. Along with the lists of Confucius' students in chapter 38 and in SJ, Zigong's appraisals here are an important source of information. The meritocratic ideal that was gaining momentum at the time of Confucius elevated the importance of being able to recognize potential leaders. Zigong modestly refrains from drawing conclusions about his fellow students but still provides valuable descriptions of them, along with appraisals, often couched in quotations from poems, that he had heard from Confucius. After Zigong's appraisals of Confucius' students, Confucius offers his own appraisals of important figures, most of whom were contemporaries or near contemporaries.

12.1

衛將軍文子問於子貢曰："吾聞孔子之施教也，先之以《詩》《書》，而道之以孝悌，説之以仁義，觀之以禮樂，然後成之以文德。蓋入室升堂者，七十有餘人。其孰爲賢？"子貢對以不知。

Wenzi, a Wei general, asked Zigong, "I've heard that Confucius' method of instruction is to lead his students in with poetry and history, to guide them with *xiao* and *ti*, to persuade them with *ren* and *yi*, and to model for them with *li* and music, culminating in cultured and virtuous individuals.[1] The number of students formally

1. Confucius is often recognized in China as the First Teacher, and the method of instruction here is worth noting. Confucius uses the *Poems* and the *Documents* as a literary and historical foundation for his students, providing them with a rich vocabulary and a palette of stories and metaphors with which to comprehend their world. The next step is a simple and straightforward guide to basic moral behavior: *xiao* and *ti* (see under "*Xiao*" in the introduction's philosophical lexicon). In the third step,

taking instruction under him probably exceeds seventy. Of these, who is the most capable and virtuous?"[2]

Zigong replied that he didn't know.

12.2

文子曰："以吾子常與學，賢者也，何爲不知？"子貢對曰："賢人無妄，知賢即難，故君子之言曰：'智莫難於知人。'是以難對也。"

Wenzi said, "You, my friend, are capable and virtuous and have spent so much time studying with the other students. Why wouldn't you know?"

Zigong replied, "A capable and virtuous person doesn't act with indiscretion. Discerning the capable and virtuous is difficult. There is a saying of the *junzi*: 'No form of knowledge is more difficult than understanding others.' That's why it is so difficult to reply."

12.3

文子曰："若夫知賢，莫不難。今吾子親遊焉，是以敢問。"子貢曰："夫子之門人，蓋有三千就焉。賜有逮及焉，未逮及焉，故不得遍知以告也。"

Wenzi said, "Since it is so hard to discern who is capable and virtuous, may I ask you to speak from your personal experience of having studied with them?"

Zigong replied, "In total, Confucius' students number about 3,000. Some of them I've interacted with and some I haven't, so I don't know them well enough to talk about them."

---

there is a transition from following simple moral guidelines to thinking through proper behavior by way of the virtues *ren* 仁 and *yi* 義 (see also in the philosophical lexicon, under separate entries). Achieving *ren* and *yi* are challenging. The notion of persuasion here is probably more internal than external. The idea seems to be that one must persuade oneself of the right thing to do through a process of self-reflection and consideration of others. The next step is to put one's virtues into action, which best occurs through adhering to established conventions. The significance Confucius places on human emotion can be found in his inclusion of music as a main avenue for expressing oneself morally. A person's education culminates in an individual who is highly cultivated, or cultured (*wen* 文), and who possesses the ultimate charismatic virtue (*de* 德) of a true leader—someone that others will admire and wish to emulate. For more on poetry, history, *li*, and music, see "Six Classics" in the glossary.

2. Wenzi seems to have a good grasp of Confucius' method of instruction but misses its significance in focusing on the number of students and their ranking.

12.4

文子曰："吾子所及者，請問其行！"子貢對曰："夫能夙興夜寐，諷誦崇禮，行不貳過，稱言不苟，是顏回之行也。孔子説之以《詩》曰：'媚兹一人，應侯慎德'，'永言孝思，孝思惟則。'若逢有德之君，世受顯命，不失厥名；以御于天子，則王者之相也。

Wenzi said, "Of those you have interacted with, please tell me about their behavior."[3]

Zigong replied, "As for Yan Hui's behavior, he rises early and retires late. He can recite the esteemed protocols of *li* from memory. He never makes the same mistake twice, and he always speaks conscientiously.

"Confucius described him, using a couple of passages from poems:

To be doted on by the chief,
The nobility must be vigilant in their *de*.

He so exemplifies the meaning of *xiao*,
The meaning of *xiao* comes only from him.[4]

"If he ever comes across a *de* sovereign, the world will see what has been conferred to him. It won't be an empty reputation. He is capable of acting as prime minister for the king.

12.5

"在貧如客，使其臣如借，不遷怒，不深怨，不録舊罪，是冉雍之行也。孔子論其材曰：'有土之君子也，有衆使也，有刑用也，然後稱怒焉。'孔子告之以《詩》曰：'靡不有初，鮮克有終。'匹夫不怒，唯以亡其身。

"As for the behavior of Ran Yong, although he comes from impoverished circumstances, he always maintains the propriety of a visiting guest, and when employing others, he does so courteously. He never transfers his anger, feels anger deeply, or holds grudges. Confucius described his character as follows: 'A *junzi* like him would

3. With the question phrased in terms of merely subjectively rating the quality of the other students, Zigong repeatedly declines. Only when the question is re-phrased as commenting on something more concrete and objective—namely, outward behavior—does Zigong finally answer the question. With this information Wenzi will, then, be free to decide for himself how to answer his original question.

4. These four lines (in a different order) come from the poem "Succession" (#243), which can be found today in the "Da ya" section of the *Poems*. The poem describes the loyalty and accomplishments of Kings Wu and Cheng, as successors of Zhou King Wen. Instead of the word *vigilant* (*shen* 慎), the *Poems* has *congenial* (*shun* 順).

express words of anger only once he had land, people to lead, and a system of rules and punishments.'

"Confucius praised him with these words from a poem:

All are good at first,
But few persist to the end.[5]

"Ordinary people fear getting angry because it is the rare occurrence when they lose self-control.[6]

12.6

"不畏强禦，不侮矜寡，其言循性，其都以富，材任治戎，是仲由之行也。孔子和之以文，説之以《詩》曰：'受小拱大拱，而爲下國駿庬。荷天子之龍'，'不戁不悚'，'敷奏其勇'。强乎武哉！文不勝其質。

"As for the behavior of Zhong You, he does not fear the powerful, he does not mistreat the widowed, he is straightforward in speech, any place he governs becomes prosperous, and he has the capacity to lead an army.

"Confucius pacified him with culture and praised him with the following passage from a poem:

Following rules major and minor,
Treats lower states magnanimously,
What favor from Heaven he deserves.
No fear or dread.
He spreads good policies courageously.[7]

5. These lines are from the poem "Dissolute" (#255), which can be found today in the "Da ya" section of the *Poems*. The poem is written from the perspective of King Wen, who condemns the dissolute behavior of Shang King Zhòu. Under one interpretation, this poem is a warning to a Zhou king (probably King Li 厲) to discontinue his dissolute behavior.

6. Confucius' point about anger in this passage is that anger can have a practical function. In an orderly system, you can use a few words of anger or impatience to chide and motivate, without harming yourself or harmonious relations with others. Anger, as a deeply felt emotion, on the other hand, that one irrationally transfers from one situation to another (from work to one's family, for example) is damaging both to oneself and to harmonious relations with others.

7. This is from the poem "Long Prosperity" (#304), which can be found today in the "Shang song" section of the *Poems*. The poem is about Tang, founder of the Shang dynasty. The order of the lines differs from the order in the current version of the *Poems*. The fuller context, with the lines ordered as in the current *Poems*, is:

Giving jades both large and small
To lower states for flair and decoration.

"A powerful fighter, his cultured embellishments will never obscure his true nature.

12.7

"恭老恤幼，不忘賓旅，好學博藝，省物而勤也，是冉求之行也。孔子因而語之曰：'好學則智，恤孤則惠，恭則近禮，勤則有繼。堯舜篤恭，以王天下。'其稱之也曰：'宜爲國老。'

"As for Ran Qiu's behavior, he is respectful to the old and tender to the young; he takes good care of traveling visitors; he is fond of learning and well-versed in the arts; plus, he is frugal and hard-working.

"About Ran Qiu, Confucius said, 'You can see his wisdom in his fondness for learning, his compassion in his tenderness toward orphans, his *li* in his reverence, and his progress from his hard work. Yao and Shun were able to rule the land due to their profound reverence.'

"Confucius also said of him, 'He is suitable to serve as an elder statesman.'

12.8

"齊莊而能肅，志通而好禮，擯相兩君之事，篤雅有節，是公西赤之行也。子曰：'禮經三百，可勉能也；威儀三千，則難也。'公西赤問曰：'何謂也？'子曰：'貌以儐禮，禮以儐辭，是謂難焉。'衆人聞之，以爲成也。孔子語人曰：'當賓客之事，則達矣。'謂門人曰：'二三子之欲學賓客之禮者，其於赤也。'

"As for the behavior of Gongxi Chi, he conveys dignity in his stateliness; he accomplishes what he sets his mind to and is fond of *li*; he can manage the intricate rituals of a diplomatic summit; and he is both tasteful and measured.

What blessings from heaven he deserves.
Not aggressive or rash,
Not rigid or lax,
He spreads good government with grace and ease,
And tribute comes from all around.
Following rules major and minor,
Treats lower states magnanimously.
What favor from Heaven he deserves.
He spreads good policies courageously,
Not vehement or reckless,
No fear or dread,
Tribute comes from everywhere.

The poem is also quoted in 12.15, 27.2, and 41.12.

"Confucius said, 'The three hundred rules of *li* can be learned with effort, but performing them three thousand times with due dignity and solemnity is truly difficult.'

"Gongxi Chi asked, 'Why is this?'

"Confucius answered, 'It is difficult because one's gestures and expression have to follow the solemnity of the ritual, while the ritual has to follow the solemnity of the recited words.'

"All those listening thought he had finished making his point, but he then said to everyone present, 'All of this can be accomplished through the simple act of attending well to a guest.'

"Then he said specifically to his students, 'If you want to learn the art of attending well to a guest, study with Chi.'

12.9

"滿而不盈，實而如虛，過之如不及，先王難之；博無不學，其貌恭，其德敦；其言於人也，無所不信；其驕大人也，常以浩浩，是以眉壽。是曾參之行也。孔子曰：'孝，德之始也；悌，德之序也；信，德之厚也；忠，德之正也。參中夫四德者也。'以此稱之。

"As for the behavior of Zeng Shen, he is proud without being conceited; solid but as if empty; and although he overachieves, he has the humility of an underachiever. Even the Ancient Kings would have had a hard time emulating him. His erudition was attained through his willingness to study anything. He is reverent in his demeanor and generous in his *de*. What he pledges to others is unfailingly trustworthy. His deep wellspring of noble confidence is the source of his longevity.

"Confucius praised him, saying, '*Xiao* is the genesis of *de*. *Ti*[8] is its next step. Trustworthiness is the profound expression of virtue. Conscientiousness is its precise manifestation. Shen gets each of these four virtues just right.'

12.10

"美功不伐，貴位不善，不侮不佚，不傲無告，是顓孫師之行也。孔子言之曰：'其不伐則猶可能也，其不弊百姓，則仁也。'《詩》云：'愷悌君子，民之父母。'夫子以其仁爲大。

"As for the behavior of Zhuansun Shi, although he accomplishes great things, he never boasts of them. Although he achieves high positions, he never appears self-satisfied. He is neither irreverent nor inconsiderate. He neither disdains the forsaken nor scorns the needy.

8. See under "*Xiao*" in the introduction's philosophical lexicon.

"Confucius said of him, 'His reticence to boast can be achieved by others, but his transparency toward the common people amounts to *ren*. A poem says:

Our leader, content and agreeable,
Parent of the people.[9]

"Confucius felt that Zhuansun Shi had made the greatest strides in *ren*.

12.11

"學之深，送迎必敬，上交下接若截焉，是卜商之行也。孔子説之以《詩》曰：'式夷式已，無小人殆。'若商也，其可謂不險矣。

"As for the behavior of Bu Shang, he is a deep learner. In his dealings with others, he is unfailingly respectful whether they are coming or going. He knows just what to do whether they are higher or lower.

"Confucius praised him with words from a poem:

Able to settle himself,
No danger from the small-minded man.[10]

There is no risk with Shang.

9. These lines appear in the poem "Distant Draw" (#251), which can be found today in the "Da ya" section of the *Poems*. The complete poem reads:

Draw from that distant flood,
Pour it into here,
It has its use for cooking.
Our leader, content and agreeable,
Parent of the people.
Draw from that distant flood,
Pour it into here.
It has its use for cleaning.
Our leader, content and agreeable,
Idol of the people.
Draw from that distant flood,
Pour it into here,
It has its use for farming.
Our leader, content and agreeable,
Refuge of the people.

This poem is also quoted in 13.9 and 27.2.

10. These lines appear in the poem "Lofty Nan Mountain" (#191), which can be found today in the "Xiao ya" section of the *Poems*. The poem is a lament about the disastrous governance of the top ministers under Zhou King You.

12.12

“貴之不喜，賤之不怒，苟利於民矣，廉於行己，其事上也以佑其下，是澹臺滅明之行也。孔子曰：‘獨貴獨富，君子耻之，夫也中之矣。’

“As for the behavior of Tantai Mieming, he is neither delighted when praised nor angry when disparaged. When he focuses on benefiting the people, he is irreproachable in how he comports himself. He assists the people as a way of serving his superiors.

“Confucius said, ‘A *junzi* would be ashamed to seek status and wealth for his own sake. Instead, he takes a middle path.’

12.13

“先成其慮，及事而用之，故動則不妄，是言偃之行也。孔子曰：‘欲能則學，欲知則問，欲善則詳，欲給則豫，當是而行，偃也得之矣。’

“As for the behavior of Yan Yan, he first thinks things through and then puts his plans into action at an opportune time. In this way, his actions are never haphazard.

“Confucius said, ‘Wishing to hone his talent, he studies; wishing to improve his understanding, he inquires; wishing to increase in excellence, he strives meticulously; wishing to be ready for anything, he anticipates everything. This is how it should be done, and Yan is able to do it.’

12.14

“獨居思仁，公言言義，其於《詩》也，則一日三復‘白圭之玷’，是宫縚之行也。孔子信其能仁，以爲異士。

“As for the behavior of Gong Tao, when alone, he contemplates *ren*; when in office, he promulgates *yi*. With respect to poetry, three times every day he recites the line:

> A flaw in a jade tablet.[11]

11. From the poem “Solemn” (#256), which can be found today in the “Da ya” section of the *Poems*. Surely, the listeners (and readers) would be able to complete the passage:

> A flaw in a jade tablet
> May be ground out,
> A flaw in one’s speech
> Can’t be undone.

A jade tablet (*bai gui* 白圭) was a symbol of authority entrusted to an official by a sovereign.

"Confucius had such confidence in his ability to effect *ren*[12] that he considered him a unique prospect.

12.15

"自見孔子，出入於户，未嘗越禮；往來過之，足不履影；啓蟄不殺，方長不折；執親之喪，未嘗見齒。是高柴之行也。孔子曰：'柴於親喪，則難能也；啓蟄不殺，則順人道；方長不折，則恕仁也。成湯恭而以恕，是以日臍。'

"As for Gao Chai's behavior, ever since becoming a student of Confucius he has never once transgressed *li*. In coming and going, he doesn't step on people's shadows.[13] He doesn't kill emerging insects in the spring or cut tall grasses in the summer.[14] And while mourning the death of his parents, he never once smiled.[15]

"Confucius said, 'In Chai's mourning for his parents, you can see his capacity for enduring hardship. In his unwillingness to kill emerging insects, you can see his following a humane way. In his unwillingness to cut tall grasses, you can see his *shu* and *ren*. The great reverence of Tang the Accomplished was made possible through his *shu*, and that's why his prominence "daily climbed."'[16]

12. *Ability to effect* ren, *neng ren* 能仁: see *neng le* 能樂 in 12.21 for a similar construction.

13. Popular spiritual concepts of the time included *po* 魄, a person's soul associated with the body, and *hun* 魂, a person's soul associated with one's *qi* (vital energy). These four entities (body, *qi*, *hun*, and *po*; also forces associated with *shen* 神 and *xue* 血) were seen as interacting in complex ways to account for a person's physical and mental health. A person's shadow was part of this mix, and stepping on it may have been seen as a causal factor in an associated affliction. See also 17.5. (Porkert 1978; Brashier 1996; Chen 2018)

14. This passage appears to show a concern for not interfering in the natural patterns of spontaneous development.

15. These three examples of Gao Chai not transgressing *li* show clearly that *li* is not about sticking steadfastly to sets of rules but about moving lightly and mindfully through the world. Whether or not Gao Chai himself believed that stepping on someone's shadow will harm them, he was still mindful of the custom. He didn't recklessly harm the flora and fauna around him in pursuing self-centered ambitions. And his grief at his parents' passing was so heavy and so thorough that he couldn't even experience a respite of lightheartedness during the long mourning period. Unfortunately, later Ruists, and even Ruists in Confucius' own day, misconstrued *li* as a practice of strict rule-following for the sake of rule-following.

16. Tang was the founder of the Shang dynasty. Here, the author ties Tang together with Gao Chai based on their nonviolence toward animals as a manifestation of their *shu*. *Shu* is best understood as an extension of one's feeling of self-care. In the same way that one would hope for and expect others to treat one with tenderness, civility, care, and respect, one also extends those feelings to others—and in this case, we see the extension not just to other people but to all flora and fauna. There is a story of Tang recorded in Liu Xiang's *Xin xu* (chapter 5). In it, Tang comes across a farmer setting up nets in all four

12.16

“凡此諸子，賜之所親睹者也。吾子有命而訊賜，賜也固，不足以知賢。”

“All that I’ve said just now about the behavior of these students of Confucius is based on my own personal experience. They are my answer to your persistent questioning, sir. But they still don’t amount to an answer as to which is the most capable and virtuous.”

12.17

文子曰：“吾聞之也，國有道則賢人興焉，中人用焉，乃百姓歸之。若吾子之論，既富茂矣。壹諸侯之相也，抑世未有明君，所以不遇也。”

Wenzi said, “I’ve heard it said that in a just society capable and virtuous people are brought to prominence. They are employed as leaders, and the people follow them. What you have said just now, sir, is plenty. All of these students seem capable of governing at the highest levels, but there are no enlightened sovereigns, and so they go unused.”

12.18

子貢既與衛將軍文子言，適魯，見孔子曰：“衛將軍文子問二三子之於賜，不壹而三焉。賜也辭不獲命，以所見者對矣，未知中否，請以告。”

After speaking with Wenzi, Zigong went to Lu and met with Confucius. He said, “The Wei general Wenzi asked me repeatedly about your students. I tried to politely refuse but ended up telling him things that I have personally witnessed. I don’t know if that was the suitable thing to do. I would appreciate some guidance.”

---

directions across his fields. Distressed by the impending carnage, Tang has three of the nets taken down. Spiders (nature’s builders of nets) construct only one at a time, he says. This shows Tang’s *shu*, but the story, as Confucius seems aware, doesn’t end there. The *Xin xu* goes on to say that by taking down three nets and leaving only one, Tang netted the allegiance of forty states, the leaders of which extrapolated Tang’s deep concern for the welfare of animals to a concomitant concern for the welfare of people. Confucius makes this extrapolation also, borrowing language of a Tang reference in the *Poems*:

> Tang’s descent right on time,
> His peerless merit daily climbed.

The poem is “Long Prosperity” (#304), which can be found today in the “Shang song” section of the *Poems*. The same poem is referenced in 12.6, 27.2, and 41.12. See “*Shu*” in the introduction’s philosophical lexicon.

12.19

孔子曰："言之乎。"子貢以其辭狀告孔子。子聞而笑曰："賜，汝次爲人矣。"子貢對曰："賜也何敢知人，此以賜之所睹也。"

Confucius replied, "Tell me what you said."

Zigong narrated the entire story. Confucius chuckled on hearing it and said, "Ci, you are good at evaluating people."

Zigong replied, "How can I presume to understand others? These were all just things that I witnessed."

12.20

孔子曰："然。吾亦語汝耳之所未聞，目之所未見者，豈思之所不至，智之所未及哉?"子貢曰："賜願得聞之。"

Confucius said, "Just so. I will tell you some things that you have neither seen nor heard before,[17] things that are probably even inconceivable to you."

Zigong replied, "I would like to hear them."

12.21

孔子曰："不克不忌，不念舊怨，蓋伯夷、叔齊之行也；思天而敬人，服義而行信，孝於父母，恭於兄弟，從善而不教，蓋趙文子之行也；其事君也，不敢愛其死，然亦不敢忘其身，謀其身不遺其友，君陳則進而用之，不陳則行而退，蓋隨武子之行也；其爲人之淵源也，多聞而難誕，内植足以没其世，國家有道，其言足以治，無道，其默足以生，蓋銅鞮伯華之行也；外寬而内正，自極於隱括之中，直己而不直人，汲汲於仁，以善自終，蓋蘧伯玉之行也；孝恭慈仁，允德圖義，約貨去怨，輕財不匱，蓋柳下惠之行也；其言曰：君雖不量於其身，臣不可以不忠於其君。是故君擇臣而任之，臣亦擇君而事之。有道順命，無道衡命。蓋晏平仲之行也；蹈忠而行信，終日言不在尤之内，國無道，處賤不悶，貧而能樂，蓋老子之行也；易行以俟天命，居下不援其上，其觀於四方也，不忘其親，不盡其樂，以不能則學，不爲己終身之憂，蓋介子山之行也。"

Confucius said, "You know of Boyi and Shuqi. They behaved in a way that was neither aggressive nor antagonistic, and they did not nurse grudges.[18]

17. By saying that he has provocative knowledge about historical figures that Zigong does not, Confucius seems to be suggesting that this is hearsay that has been conveyed to him by people in the know. Most of it concerns the state of Jin, Wei's neighbor to the west.

18. Zigong having detailed the behavioral characteristics of a number of Confucius' students in the preceding pages, now Confucius will do the same for a number of (mostly recent) figures. With

"More recently, there was Zhao Wenzi.[19] Contemplating the vagaries of fate,[20] he always showed respect for others. He served with *yi* and was trustworthy in his actions. He was *xiao* toward his parents[21] and reverential toward his brothers, and he selected the path of excellence without being taught to do so.

---

the exception of Boyi and Shuqi, these are people whom Confucius would have met in person (Qu Boyu and Yan Pingzhong) or who were major figures just before his time. He begins with two of his favorite heroes. According to SJ ("Boyi lie zhuan"), Boyi and Shuqi were two brothers and princes of a state called Guzhu that was aligned with the Shang dynasty just as the Shang was about to fall to the Zhou. The boys' father, the ruler of Guzhu, decided to pass the throne on to the third son, Shuqi, instead of to Boyi, the firstborn. After the father died, Shuqi refused the throne in deference to his older brother and fled, but Boyi, in deference to his father's wishes, also refused and fled. Having heard that King Wen of Zhou took good care of his people, the two brothers took up residence in Zhou. After King Wen passed away, King Wu made plans to attack Shang. The two brothers attempted to dissuade King Wu, for although they were in exile, they still identified as nobility of Guzhu, aligned with Shang. After King Wu defeated Shang King Zhòu, the two brothers refused to eat any food raised by the Zhou. Since Zhou now commanded the whole land, that left them little recourse. They left the city, found their way to Shouyang Mountain, and there foraged for edible ferns. Lacking sufficient sustenance but maintaining their principles come what may, the two brothers starved to death. Confucius' point in bringing up these two brothers as models of behavior, which he also does in the *Analects*, is less about loyalty to country and more about their refusal to bear grudges against either their father or King Wu. Confucius' view is that one is always free to choose the path of *ren* rather than surrender to the expediencies of an unjust society. Sometimes, when conditions are right, the path of *ren* will lead to a position of leadership, influence, and even glory and wealth. Other times, when conditions are not right, the path may lead to dire circumstances, including death. According to Confucius, a wise and capable person follows the path of *ren* in whichever direction it leads and does not fall back on the easy path of personal gain.

19. Zhao Wenzi (589–541 BCE) was a powerful member of the ruling family in the state of Jin. He controlled the Jin government when it was one of the most powerful states. In many ways, Zhao was the opposite of Boyi and Shuqi. Boyi and Shuqi were born to rule, but circumstances were against their doing it in an honorable way, and the only way for them to realize their ideal of *ren* was to flee society. By contrast, Zhao's entire family (save his mother) was exterminated when Zhao was just a baby, and so he was raised in seclusion, and yet eventually he rose to the heights of power. Zhao Wenzi was recognized as a major talent at a young age. He was acclaimed not only for his intelligence but also for being unusually handsome. However, while always involved in circles of power, his own influence waxed and waned. Regardless of his own status, he was said to be unfailingly polite and helpful to both political friends and rivals. In Confucius' eyes, then, just like Boyi and Shuqi, Zhao Wenzi kept his ambition to lead a *ren* life, but unlike Boyi and Shuqi, that life took him through the halls of power. (CQZZ; SJ; Zheng, Wu, and Yang 2000)

20. *Contemplating the vagaries of fate, si tian* 思天: to think of heaven/sky/nature.

21. Before Zhao was born, his family was powerful and influential. Not long after he was born, all of his relatives were killed, and the family was on the brink of annihilation. For Zhao to bring his family back to prominence was viewed as a continuous act of filial respect toward his family.

"There was also Sui Wuzi. He served his sovereign without concern for his own life or death, but did so without reckless disregard for his own safety. Further, in making his own way in the world, he never forsook his friends. When the sovereign showed promise, Sui made himself available for employment, but when the sovereign did not show promise, Sui slipped into seclusion.

"There was also Tongdi Bohua. He was broad-minded in his behavior; he was learned and thus difficult to fool; and he had a moral perseverance that he maintained to the end. When there was justice in society, his words were sufficient to govern, and when there was no justice, his silence was sufficient to ensure survival.

"There was also Qu Boyu. He was tolerant of others and demanding of himself; he reformed his own inner flaws; he preferred to correct himself rather than correct others; he felt an urgency about being *ren*; and he strove for excellence to the end of his days.

"There was also Liuxia Hui. He was *xiao*, reverent, compassionate, and *ren*. He trusted in *de* and planned on *yi*; he limited his material possessions and harbored no resentments; and having always looked down on wealth, he never felt he was lacking without it.

"There was also Yan Pingzhong. Someone once said, 'Although a sovereign may fail to take the measure of a minister, a minister must never fail to be conscientious toward the sovereign. And so not only does a sovereign select a minister to employ, but a minister also selects the sovereign to work for. If the sovereign is just, accept employment. If the sovereign is unjust, reject employment.'[22] This describes Yan Pingzhong.

"There is also Laozi. He walked the path of conscientiousness and trustworthiness; he could speak all day without making an error; and when society was unjust, he could serenely live an unassuming life and be happy in poverty.

"Finally, there was Jie Zishan. He adjusted his behavior in anticipation of determinations from *tian*; he remained in a lowly station instead of allowing himself to be pulled up; he was observant in all directions; he never forgot his parents; he didn't lose himself in revelry; he took ignorance as an opportunity to learn; and to the end of his days, he never let his own straits be a cause for anxiety."

12.22

子貢曰："敢問夫子之所知者，蓋盡於此而已乎？"孔子曰："何謂其然？亦略舉耳目之所及而矣。昔晋平公問祁奚曰：'羊舌大夫，晋之良大夫也。其行如何？'祁奚辭以不知。公曰：'吾聞子少長乎其所，今子掩之，何也？'祁奚對曰：'其少也恭而順，心有耻而不使其過宿；其爲大夫，悉善而謙其端；其爲輿尉也，信而好直其功；至於其爲容

22. *Reject employment, heng ming* 衡命: interpreting *heng* 衡 as *heng* 横 (to thwart), following Wang Su. Confucius' point here is that, if one chooses to work for someone, one must do so conscientiously. If that is not possible, then the proper thing to do is resign.

也，温良而好禮，博聞而時出其志。'公曰：'曩者問子，子奚曰不知也?'祁奚曰：'每位改變，未知所止，是以不敢得知也。'此又羊舌大夫之行也。"子貢跪曰："請退而記之。"

Zigong asked Confucius, "Is that everything you have to say about your understanding of the matter?"

Confucius replied, "How could that be everything? Like you, I am also just reporting what I have learned through my eyes and ears. Now for the behavior of the high official Yangshe. Back in the old days, Duke Ping of Jin asked his minister Qi Xi: 'Yangshe is one of our fine high officials of Jin. What do you think of his conduct?'

"Qi Xi demurred by saying he didn't know.

"The duke persisted, 'I heard that you grew up in his house. Why are you shielding him?'

"Qi Xi replied, 'When he was young, he was reverent and congenial. If he ever did anything for which he felt ashamed, he would correct it before the night was through. As a high official, he has an all-around excellence and yet is modest about his strengths. In his position as labor minister, he was trustworthy and seemed to enjoy taking his responsibilities head-on. As for his demeanor, he is gentle and pleasant and shows an interest in *li*. He is also widely knowledgeable and able to put his knowledge to use at opportune times.'

"The duke said, 'Just now when I asked you the first time, why did you say you didn't know?'

"Qi Xi replied, 'Positions tend to change, and I'm not even sure which one he is in now. So I didn't dare presume to be knowledgeable on the matter.'"

Zigong bowed[23] and said, "I'm going to go now and preserve this for posterity."[24]

23. Bowed, *gui* 跪: to kneel. Most likely, Zigong would have been sitting during this conversation. As the customary way to sit was on one's knees, leaning on one's heels, to kneel would mean to rise up off of your heels. However, the point isn't his movement, per se, but his demonstration of reverence. The *Shuo wen jie zi* glosses *gui* as to bow in reverence/respect (bai 拜).

24. *Preserved this for posterity*, *ji* 記: This term is usually interpreted as to commit to writing, but it can also mean to commit to memory. The translation here preserves the ambiguity of the original.

13

The Capable and Virtuous Sovereign

Chapter 13 continues the theme of recognizing virtue and talent. In conversations with students and several different rulers, Confucius explains the leadership virtues necessary to bring peace and prosperity to the people, which include: recognizing the capable and virtuous, humility, impartiality, not demanding much of the people, *li*, educating the people, reverence, respect, conscientiousness, and trustworthiness.

13.1

哀公問於孔子曰："當今之君，孰爲最賢？"孔子對曰："丘未之見也，抑有衛靈公乎？"公曰："吾聞其閨門之内無別，而子次之賢，何也？"孔子曰："臣語其朝廷行事，不論其私家之際也。"公曰："其事何如？"孔子對曰："靈公之弟曰公子渠牟，其智足以治千乘，其信足以守之。靈公愛而任之。又有士曰林國者，見賢必進之，而退與分其祿，是以靈公無遊放之士。靈公賢而尊之。又有士曰慶足者，衛國有大事則必起而治之，國無事則退而容賢。靈公悅而敬之。又有大夫史鰌，以道去衛，而靈公郊舍三日，琴瑟不御，必待史鰌之入而後敢入。臣以此取之，雖次之賢，不亦可乎。"

Duke Ai asked Confucius, "Of all the sovereigns today, which is the most capable and virtuous?"

Confucius replied, "I've yet to meet one, but if I had to choose, I would say Duke Ling of Wei."

The duke said, "I've heard that Duke Ling doesn't display proper respect for differences[1] in his own household. How can he rank as capable and virtuous?"

Confucius said, "I can't speak to the private matters of his household, only to matters of the court."

1. *Doesn't display proper respect for differences, wu bie* 無別: of status, gender, position, and so on. In CQZZ ("Ding" 14), at the request of Nanzi, Duke Ling invited Zizhao 子朝 of Song to Wei, presumably to be Nanzi's paramour. This is the kind of lack of proper respect for differences that Duke Ai references. This is the same Zhao (Chao) of Song that Confucius calls handsome in *Analects* 6.16.

Then Duke Ai asked, "And of those?"

Confucius replied, "Duke Ling's younger brother, Prince Qumou, has the wisdom to rule a large state and the trustworthiness to protect it. The duke employs and cherishes him. There is also an official named Lin Guo. Whenever he comes across someone capable and virtuous, he always recommends him to the duke. If that person is fired for cause, Lin surrenders his own salary to make up for the loss. As a result, Duke Ling has no worthless officials on the payroll because he recognized Lin as capable and virtuous and showed esteem for him. There is another official named Qing Zu. Whenever Wei has a crisis, Qing rises to the occasion to help resolve it; and when the crisis is over, he steps back and lets the other officials do their jobs. Duke Ling is delighted with Qing and esteems him. There is also a high official by the name of Shi Qiu, who left Wei on principle.[2] Duke Ling was so distressed at this that he camped on the outskirts of town for three days without any entertainment until Shi returned. These are examples of why I choose Duke Ling and rank him among the capable and virtuous. Wouldn't you agree?"[3]

13.2

子貢問於孔子曰: "今之人臣, 孰爲賢?"子曰: "吾未識也。往者齊有鮑叔, 鄭有子皮, 則賢者矣。"子貢曰: "齊無管仲, 鄭無子產?"子曰: "賜, 汝徒知其一, 未知其二也。汝聞用力爲賢乎? 進賢爲賢乎?"子貢曰: "進賢賢哉!"子曰: "然。吾聞鮑叔達管仲, 子皮達子產, 未聞二子之達賢己之才者也。"

Zigong asked Confucius, "Of the ministers working today, which is the most capable and virtuous?"

Confucius replied, "I don't know of any. In the past, there were Bao Shu in Qi and Zipi in Zheng. They were capable and virtuous."

Zigong said, "Not Guan Zhong in Qi, or Zichan in Zheng?"[4]

2. *On principle, yi dao* 以道: on the pretext of *dao*, meaning that there was something about the government that Shi strongly felt was contrary to *dao*.

3. Confucius seems to give a pass, probably on pragmatic grounds alone, to rulers who behave poorly in private, as long as they have competent ministers running the country. We see a similar attitude in Yanzi vis-à-vis Duke Jing of Qi.

4. As we've seen so far, it is not unusual for Confucius to refer to great men of the past as examples for today. If he is going to refer to great ministers of Qi and Zheng, Guan Zhong and Zichan are his favorite examples. Zigong seems to know this. And Confucius seems to anticipate that Zigong would expect him to refer to them. So here Confucius seems to take the opportunity to provide another lesson—that being able to recommend others is as important (or even more important) than achieving greatness on one's own. Perhaps he is building on the previous chapter, where Zigong showed a facility for being able to recognize talent. The next step is being able to bring that talent to prominence.

Confucius said, "Ci, you obviously don't know the whole story. You have heard of people who are capable and virtuous by virtue of their own efforts, but have you heard of those who are capable and virtuous by virtue of recommending others who are capable and virtuous?"

Zigong replied, "Yes, those who recommend the capable and virtuous are themselves capable and virtuous."

Confucius said, "Exactly. What I heard is that Bao Shu brought Guan Zhong to prominence and Zipi brought Zichan prominence. I have not heard that the people they brought to prominence were greater than they were."

13.3

哀公問於孔子曰:"寡人聞忘之甚者,徙而忘其妻,有諸?"孔子對曰:"此猶未甚者也,甚者乃忘其身。"公曰:"可得而聞乎?"孔子曰:"昔者夏桀貴爲天子,富有四海,忘其聖祖之道,壞其典法,廢其世祀,荒於淫樂,耽湎於酒;佞臣諂諛,窺導其心;忠士折口,逃罪不言。天下誅桀而有其國,此謂忘其身之甚矣。"

Duke Ai asked Confucius, "I've heard that there are men so forgetful that they move and forget to bring their own wives. Are there such people?"

Confucius replied, "That's not the most extreme case. Worse are those who forget even themselves."

The duke said, "Could you tell me about them?"

Confucius said, "Jie, the last king of the Xia dynasty, held the most esteemed position as king and was the richest person in all the land, and yet he forgot the *dao* of the sages and ancestors, he destroyed their models of good behavior, and decimated the sacrificial rites passed down to him. Instead, he lost himself in debauchery and soaked himself in liquor. Fast-talking ministers showered him with praise and manipulated him to their own ends. Conscientious officials were silenced or didn't dare speak honestly for fear of being persecuted. In the end, the whole land rose up, killed Jie, and took over. Wouldn't you say that his is a case of forgetting oneself in the extreme?"

13.4

顏淵將西遊於宋,問於孔子曰:"何以爲身?"子曰:"恭敬忠信而已矣。恭則遠於患,敬則人愛之,忠則和於衆,信則人任之。勤斯四者,可以政國,豈特一身者哉?故夫不比於數而比於疏,不亦遠乎?不修其中,而修外者,不亦反乎?慮不先定,臨事而謀,不亦晚乎?"

Before traveling west to Song, Yan Yuan asked Confucius, "How should I conduct myself properly?"

Confucius said, "Just be reverent, respectful, conscientious, and trustworthy. Reverence will keep disaster at bay. Others appreciate being respected. Conscientiousness helps you get along with others. Employers appreciate people who are trustworthy.[5] Be diligent in these four, and you'll be able to manage a whole country—why limit it to yourself alone? Associating with shifty people rather than steady[6] people is far off the mark. It is counter to your purposes to cultivate peripheral interests instead of your main interests. It is too late to wait for something to happen before reacting to it instead of planning ahead."

13.5

孔子讀《詩》，于《正月》六章，惕焉如懼，曰："彼不達之君子，豈不殆哉！從上依世則道廢，違上離俗則身危。時不興善，己獨由之，則曰非妖即妄也。故賢也既不遇天，恐不終其命焉。桀殺龍逢，紂殺比干，皆是類也。《詩》曰：'謂天蓋高，不敢不局。謂地蓋厚，不敢不蹐。'此言上下畏罪，無所自容也。"

One day when Confucius was reading poetry, he came to the sixth stanza in the poem "January"[7] and suddenly started trembling, as if with fear. He said, "Isn't it a tragedy when a *junzi* cannot achieve his ideals? Merely obeying the leadership and following along with the times destroys the *dao*. Disobeying the leadership and separating from society invites personal harm. When you try to do right in a world gone wrong, you are labeled deviant, if not downright monstrous. Not only can the capable and virtuous never meet the standards of *tian*, they may even lose

5. These four virtues are vintage Confucius, but notice that he doesn't refer to such virtues as *li*, *ren*, and *yi*. By referring to *zhong* and *xin* (virtues associated with life in an official capacity), Confucius may be giving Yan Hui a subtle push to seek employment in order to spread his virtue more broadly.

6. *Shifty . . . steady, cu* 數 *. . . shu* 疏: Tightly woven and loosely woven. The quality of the weave of fabric appears to be a metaphor for the quality of one's character.

7. The poem "January" (#192) can be found today in the "Xiao ya" section of the *Poems*. It is written from the perspective of a Zhou minister just before the fall of the Western Zhou dynasty, when the whole world seemed upside down. The sixth stanza reads in full:

They say the sky is high,
We dare but bow our heads.
They say the earth is thick,
We dare but mince our steps.
We're shouting out our words,
With reason and with purpose,
Now grieved that men have changed
To vile and poison serpents.

their lives for trying. That Jie killed Longpang and Zhòu killed Bigan is exactly what I'm talking about. This poem says:

They say the sky is high,
We dare but bow our heads.
They say the earth is thick,
We dare but mince our steps.

This means that people are afraid of offending anyone from top to bottom. There is no safe place."

13.6

子路問於孔子曰："賢君治國，所先者何？"孔子曰："在於尊賢而賤不肖。"子路曰："由聞晋中行氏尊賢而賤不肖矣，其亡何也？"孔子曰："中行氏尊賢而不能用，賤不肖而不能去。賢者知其不用而怨之，不肖者知其必己賤而讎之。怨讎並存於國，鄰敵搆兵於郊，中行氏雖欲無亡，豈可得乎？"

Zilu asked Confucius, "What is the first priority for a capable and virtuous leader ruling a country?"

Confucius said, "To esteem the capable and virtuous and disesteem the opposite."

Zilu said, "I heard that the Zhonghangs of Jin did just that, so what did they do wrong that they ended up eliminated for it?"

Confucius said, "The Zhonghangs esteemed the capable and virtuous but were unable to employ them. They disesteemed the unwise and incapable but were unable to dismiss them. A capable and virtuous person who goes unemployed will feel resentment, and an unwise and incapable person who is disesteemed will bear malice. When resentment and malice gain a foothold in a country, neighboring enemies will mass at the borders. The Zhonghangs didn't intend to be eliminated, but what could be done?"

13.7

孔子閑處，喟然而嘆曰："嚮使銅鞮伯華無死，則天下其有定矣。"子路曰："由願聞其人也。"子曰："其幼也，敏而好學；其壯也，有勇而不屈；其老也，有道而能下人。有此三者，以定天下也，何難乎哉？"子路曰："幼而好學，壯而有勇，則可也。若夫有道下人，又誰下哉？"子曰："由不知，吾聞以衆攻寡，無不克也；以貴下賤，無不得也。昔者周公居冢宰之尊，制天下之政，而猶下白屋之士，日見百七十人。斯豈以無道也？欲得士之用也。惡有道而無下天下君子哉？"

One day when Confucius was relaxing, he sighed and said, "Alas, if only Tongdi Bohua had not died, the world would be stable by now."

Zilu said, "I would like to hear about him."

Confucius said, "When he was a child, he was sharp and had a fondness for learning. After growing up, he was courageous and dauntless. In his old age, he was just and able to humble himself before others. With these three sets of characteristics, what difficulty would there be in bringing stability to the world?"

Zilu said, "I understand about the need for having a fondness for learning as a child and for courage when grown, but as for being just and humbling oneself before others, to whom would he need to humble himself?"

Confucius said, "Yóu, you don't understand. I've learned that anyone can be defeated by pitting the many against the few and that anything can be achieved when people of higher station humble themselves before people of lower station. In the past, when the Duke of Zhou held the esteemed position of prime minister and was controlling the reins of the government, he still humbled himself before ordinary people by meeting with 170 of them each day. Is there injustice in that? This is how he was able to hire the best people. Where is the just individual who is unable to humble himself before others?"[8]

13.8

齊景公來適魯，舍于公館，使晏嬰迎孔子。孔子至，景公問政焉。孔子答曰："政在節財。"公悅，又問曰："秦穆公國小處僻而霸，何也？"孔子曰："其國雖小，其志大，處雖僻，而其政中，其舉也果，其謀也和，法無私而令不愉。首拔五羖，爵之大夫，與語三日而授之以政。此取之，雖王可，其霸少矣。"景公曰："善哉！"

When Duke Jing of Qi came to Lu, he stayed at a state guesthouse and sent Yan Ying to invite Confucius for a visit. When Confucius arrived, the duke asked Confucius about governing. Confucius replied, "Good governing rests in prudently handling revenue."

The duke was delighted to hear this, then asked, "Why was Duke Mu of Qin, who had a small, out-of-the-way country, able to achieve the status of a superpower?

Confucius said, "Although his country was small, he had grand ambitions, and although his country was of little importance, his government was impartial. His policies had practical results, and his plans fit the circumstances. What's more, his legal system was unprejudiced, and his decrees were willingly followed. After ransoming Wugu and elevating him to high official, he spoke with him for three days

8. *Others, junzi* 君子: After saying that one should be able to humble oneself before others in the preceding lines, Confucius changes the locution to humbling oneself before a *junzi* at the end of the passage. He is probably lowering the bar for Zilu (it is easier to humble oneself before a *junzi* than before an ordinary person) while still implying that ideally one should be capable of humbling oneself not just before a *junzi* but also before ordinary people.

and then handed the government over to him. What we can get from all this is that not only was he qualified to be king, but becoming the leader of a superpower was not too much to expect."

The duke said, "Excellent!"

13.9

哀公問政於孔子。孔子對曰："政之急者，莫大乎使民富且壽也。"公曰："爲之奈何？"孔子曰："省力役，薄賦斂，則民富矣；敦禮教，遠罪疾，則民壽矣。"公曰："寡人欲行夫子之言，恐吾國貧矣。"孔子曰："《詩》云：'愷悌君子，民之父母。'未有子富而父母貧者也。"

Duke Ai asked Confucius about good governing. Confucius replied, "As for the crucial aspects of good government, nothing is more important than helping the people live long and prosper."

The duke said, "How can this be accomplished?"

Confucius said, "To help them prosper, use corvée labor sparingly and maintain a light tax burden. To help them live long, emphasize *li* and education and make harsh punishments few and far between."

The duke said, "I would like to put your words into action but am afraid it would impoverish the country."

Confucius said, "A poem says:

Our leader, content and agreeable,
Parent of the people.[9]

There has never been a prosperous child with impoverished parents."[10]

13.10

衛靈公問於孔子曰："有語寡人：'有國家者，計之於廟堂之上，則政治矣。'何如？"孔子曰："其可也。愛人者則人愛之，惡人者則人惡之。知得之己者，則知得之人。所謂不出環堵之室而知天下者，知反己之謂也。"

Duke Ling of Wei said to Confucius, "I was once told that a country whose leader makes plans in the court[11] will be well governed. How is this so?"

9. This poem is also quoted in 12.10 and 27.2.

10. In other words, a rising tide lifts all boats. The duke isn't really worried that the people won't be prosperous but that he won't be prosperous.

11. As opposed to making plans in some private place, where private interests may prevail.

Confucius said, "Yes, that makes sense.[12] Someone who cherishes others is cherished by others. Someone who despises others is despised by others. Someone who knows how to achieve through himself also knows how to achieve through others. The saying 'Able to understand the world without leaving a humble cottage' refers to understanding by examining oneself."

13.11

孔子見宋君。君問孔子曰: "吾欲使長有國而列都得之, 吾欲使民無惑, 吾欲使士竭力, 吾欲使日月當時, 吾欲使聖人自來, 吾欲使官府治理, 爲之奈何?"孔子對曰: "千乘之君, 問丘者多矣, 而未有若主君之問問之悉也。然主君所欲者, 盡可得也。丘聞之, 鄰國相親, 則長有國; 君惠臣忠, 則列都得之; 不殺無辜, 無釋罪人, 則民不惑; 士益之祿, 則皆竭力; 尊天敬鬼, 則日月當時; 崇道貴德, 則聖人自來; 任能黜否, 則官府治理。"宋君曰: "善哉! 豈不然乎! 寡人不佞, 不足以致之也。"孔子曰: "此事非難, 唯欲行之云耳。"

Confucius met with the sovereign of Song. The sovereign inquired, "I want to keep the entire country intact, including all of the cities currently within my borders. I want there to be no uncertainty among the people. I want government officials to work hard. I want the seasons and the weather to be regular. I want sages to choose to immigrate here. I want local governments to be well managed. How can all of this be accomplished?"

Confucius replied, "Many sovereigns of large countries like your own have asked me questions, but none as comprehensively as you. What you want is eminently possible. I have heard that a country can be kept intact by forming close relations with neighboring countries. Cities can be safeguarded within one's borders as long as the sovereign is munificent, and the ministers are conscientious. Uncertainty among the people can be prevented by not killing the innocent and not pardoning the guilty. Government officials can be encouraged to work hard by increasing their salaries. The seasons and weather can be kept regular by paying proper respect to *tian* and to ancestors. Sages can be attracted to immigrate by favoring *dao* and *de*. You can get local governments to run efficiently by hiring the capable and dismissing the corrupt."

The Song sovereign said, "Excellent! Why wouldn't this be correct?! But I'm afraid I am incapable of accomplishing it."

Confucius said, "It's not difficult to do. You just have to want to put your words into action, that's all."

12. *Makes sense, ke* 可: is admissible as a proposition.

14

Finer Points of Governing

Chapter 14 begins with a statement by Confucius that he tailors his answers to the questioner, explaining three distinct aspects of good governing. The rest of the chapter expands on various qualities and methods of a good leader, such as treating capable and virtuous men with *li*, avoiding dissolute pastimes, treating people with respect, being scrupulous and fair, and engaging in self-reflection.

14.1

子貢問於孔子曰："昔者齊君問政於夫子，夫子曰：'政在節財'；魯君問政於夫子，夫子曰：'政在諭臣'；葉公問政於夫子，夫子曰：'政在悅近而來遠'。三者之問一也，而夫子應之不同。然政在異端乎？"孔子曰："各因其事也。齊君爲國，奢乎臺榭，淫于苑囿，五官伎樂，不解於時，一旦而賜人以千乘之家者三，故曰'政在節財'。魯君有臣三人，内比周以愚其君，外距諸侯之賓以蔽其明，故曰'政在諭臣'。夫荆之地廣而都狹，民有離心，莫安其居，故曰'政在悅近而來遠'。此三者所以爲政殊矣。《詩》云：'喪亂蔑資，曾不惠我師！'此傷奢侈不節以爲亂者也；又曰：'匪其止共，惟王之邛。'此傷奸臣蔽主以爲亂也；又曰：'亂離瘼矣，奚其適歸？'此傷離散以爲亂者也。察此三者，政之所欲，豈同乎哉？"

Zigong inquired of Confucius, "In the past, the sovereign of Qi asked you about good government, and you answered, 'Good government lies in prudently handling revenue.'[1] The sovereign of Lu asked you about good government, and you said, 'Good government lies in managing one's vassals.'[2] The Duke of She asked about good government, and you said, 'Good government lies in pleasing those nearby and attracting those from farther away.'[3] Three people asked the same question, and you gave different answers to each. Does this mean that there are different paths to the same goal of good government?"

1. See 13.8.
2. This quotation is not recorded in any extant text.
3. See *Analects* 13.16.

Confucius said, "For each, I addressed their specific circumstances. The sovereign of Qi currently handles his country such that money is needlessly spent on terraces and towers and wasted on gardens and hunting reserves, and he spends all his time enjoying female entertainment. Three times in one morning, he bestowed a fief of a thousand chariots. So I said to him, 'Good government lies in prudently handling revenue.'

"The Lu sovereign has three main vassals.[4] Within the borders, they form cliques to keep the sovereign ignorant of what's going on around him. Beyond the borders, they reject all overtures from other nobility and keep him in the dark about what's going on in the other states. That's why I said to him, 'Good government lies in managing one's vassals.'

"Chu is a large country with a small capital. The people there are fractious. That's why I said, 'Good government lies in pleasing those nearby and attracting those from farther away.' These three each have different requirements when it comes to good government.

"A poem says:

Disorder that uses up all our resources
Has never been a boon for the people.[5]

This laments disorder resulting from wasteful spending.

"Another poem says:

Miscreants who cease all reverence
Are a particular distress for the king.[6]

This laments disorder resulting from corrupt vassals misleading their ruler.

"Another poem says:

Disorder and separation lead to affliction.
Where can I go for refuge?[7]

This laments disorder resulting from fractiousness and division. When looked at from these perspectives, can the requirements of good government always be the same?"

4. The Jisun, Shusun, and Mengsun families.

5. These lines are from the poem "Perverse" (#254), which can be found today in the "Da ya" section of the *Poems*. The poem is about the neglect of government by the ruler, the vain efforts of persuasion on the part of ministers, and subsequent hardship for the people.

6. These lines are from the poem "Clever Words" (#198), which can be found today in the "Xiao ya" section of the *Poems*. The poem is about the trouble in governing wrought by men with golden tongues.

7. These lines are from the poem "April" (#204), which can be found today in the "Xiao ya" section of the *Poems*. The poem is a bitter lament by a once prominent official on his way into exile in the south.

14.2

孔子曰:“忠臣之諫君,有五義焉:一曰譎諫,二曰戇諫,三曰降諫,四曰直諫,五曰風諫。唯度主而行之,吾從其風諫乎!”

Confucius said, “In regard to a conscientious minister advising a ruler, there are five ways that are broadly considered appropriate: deceptively,[8] bluntly,[9] authoritatively,[10] directly, and indirectly. Indeed, when it comes to figuring out how to get a ruler to act, I prefer the method of indirect advice.”

14.3

子曰:“夫道不可不貴也,中行文子倍道失義以亡其國,而能禮賢以活其身。聖人轉禍爲福,此謂是與!”

Confucius said, “The *dao* must be esteemed. Zhonghang Wenzi lost his country by violating the *dao* and abandoning *yi,* but he was able to save himself by treating capable and virtuous men with *li.* This is why it is said that a sage can turn disaster into good fortune.”

14.4

楚王將遊荊臺,司馬子祺諫,王怒之。令尹子西賀於殿下,諫曰:“今荊臺之觀,不可失也。”王喜,拊子西之背曰:“與子共樂之矣。”子西步馬十里,引轡而止,曰:“臣願言有道,王肯聽之乎?”王曰:“子其言之。”子西曰:“臣聞爲人臣而忠其君者,爵祿不足以賞也;諛其君者,刑罰不足以誅也。夫子祺者,忠臣也;而臣者,諛臣也。願王賞忠而誅諛焉。”王曰:“我今聽司馬之諫,是獨能禁我耳。若後世遊之何也?”子西曰:“禁後世易耳。大王萬歲之後,起山陵於荊臺之上,則子孫必不忍遊於父祖之墓以爲歡樂也。”王曰:“善!”乃還。孔子聞之,曰:“至哉,子西之諫也!入之於十里之上,抑之於百世之後者也。”

The king of Chu was about to go out to the Jing Terrace to enjoy himself[11] when Ziqi, the minister of security, advised against it, raising the king’s ire. The prime minister Zixi praised the king, offering advice of his own: “The views at Jing Terrace are not to be missed.”

8. *Deceptively, jue* 譎: fooling the ruler into doing the right thing.

9. *Bluntly, zhuang* 戇: This method borders on the tactless.

10. *Authoritatively, jiang* 降: coming from a position of superior knowledge, bordering on condescension.

11. See “*Tai*” in the glossary.

The king was delighted, wrapped an arm around Zixi and said, "Let's you and I go and enjoy the entertainment together."

Zixi drove the horses for about two miles, then reined them in and said to the king, "I would like to be straight with you.[12] Is your majesty willing to listen?"

The king said, "Go ahead."

Zixi said, "I've heard it said that no amount of salary is sufficient to repay the conscientiousness of a minister, and no amount of punishment is sufficient to penalize a minister intent on flattering his sovereign. Ziqi is a conscientious minister, and I am a flatterer. Better that you reward the conscientious and punish the flatterer."

The king said, "I can take the minister of security's advice, but it will be good only for me and won't stop my children and grandchildren from coming out here to have fun. What can I do about that?"

Zixi said, "That's easy. When you pass away—many, many years from now—have your tomb constructed at Jing Terrace. Your children and grandchildren won't dare seek entertainment on their ancestor's tomb."

The king said, "Excellent!" and returned to the city.

Confucius heard about this and said, "Zixi's way of advising was perfect! He turned two miles of slack into a hundred generations of restraint."[13]

14.5

子貢問於孔子曰："夫子之於子産、晏子，可爲至矣。敢問二大夫之所爲目，夫子之所以與之者。"孔子曰："夫子産，於民爲惠主，於學爲博物。晏子，於君爲忠臣，而行爲恭敏。故吾皆以兄事之，而加愛敬。"

Zigong asked Confucius, "Your approach to the high officials Zichan and Yanzi is to view them as very accomplished. What exactly is it about them that you so approve of?"[14]

Confucius said, "Zichan was a leader on behalf of the people, and his learning extended to many things. Yanzi was a conscientious minister for his sovereign, and

12. *Straight with you, yan you dao* 言有道: Speak in a way that presents the *dao*.

13. Unfortunately, archaeologists have not yet found the tomb of King Zhao, nor the remains of Jing Terrace.

14. Zichan and Yanzi were high ministers of Zheng and Qi, respectively, and both were broadly admired for their governing abilities. Interestingly, neither was known for being Ruist (a fact that may have motivated Zigong's question). Rather, they were known for being pragmatic reformers who eschewed superstition and the trappings of power, emphasizing instead a rational government that took good treatment of the people as its basis. Zichan, for example, was the first leader in Chinese history who put the penal code in writing and promulgated it widely to the populace. See "Zichan" and "Yanzi" in the glossary.

his behavior was both reverent and flexible. That's why I take them both as elders to learn from and why I admire and respect them so much."

14.6

齊有一足之鳥, 飛集於宮朝, 下止于殿前, 舒翅而跳。齊侯大怪之, 使使聘魯問孔子。孔子曰: "此鳥名曰商羊, 水祥也。昔童兒有屈其一脚, 振訊兩眉而跳且謠曰: '天將大雨, 商羊鼓舞。'今齊有之, 其應至矣。急告民趨治溝渠, 修堤防, 將有大水爲災。"頃之大霖雨, 水溢泛諸國, 傷害民人, 唯齊有備, 不敗。景公曰: "聖人之言, 信而有徵矣。"

A bird with just one leg flew into the Qi palace complex, landed in front of the main palace, and began hopping around with its wings outstretched. The Duke of Qi found this very odd and dispatched an emissary to Lu to ask Confucius about it. Confucius said, "This bird is a *shangyang* and is an omen of water. I once saw a child who bent one leg at the knee, pumped his eyebrows while jumping up and down, and chanted the following nursery rhyme:

When a big rain chances
The *shangyang* dances

With its arrival in Qi, there should be an appropriate response. To avoid disastrous flooding, immediately instruct the people to build sluicing channels and reinforce dikes."[15]

Soon it began to rain, and it continued for a long time. Waters rose and flooded several states, with many casualties among the people. Only Qi was prepared and so suffered no damage. Duke Jing said, "The words of a sage are trustworthy and can be substantiated."

14.7

孔子謂宓子賤曰: "子治單父, 衆悦, 子何施而得之也? 子語丘所以爲之者。"對曰: "不齊之治也, 父恤其子, 其子恤諸孤而哀喪紀。"孔子曰: "善。小節也, 小民附矣, 猶未足也。"曰: "不齊所父事者三人, 所兄事者五人, 所友事者十一人。"孔子曰: "父事三

15. This passage resembles 8.16. In both, Confucius relies on a past experience of listening to a children's rhyme to understand the present. While the main idea of each passage may be to display Confucius' wisdom, an indispensable aspect of each is that Confucius (1) is open to learning from a wide variety of sources—even children, and (2) sees the bottom-up direction of information transfer as significant. People often think of Confucianism as being primarily top-down and authoritarian. Such a conception is a mistake. For Confucius, wisdom originates with the ordinary people and then gets codified into pragmatically instrumentalized customs.

人，可以教孝矣；兄事五人，可以教悌矣；友事十一人，可以舉善矣。中節也，中人附矣，猶未足也。"曰："此地民有賢於不齊者五人，不齊事之而稟度焉，皆教不齊之道。"孔子嘆曰："其大者乃於此乎有矣！昔堯舜聽天下，務求賢以自輔。夫賢者，百福之宗也，神明之主也。惜乎不齊之以所治者小也。"

Confucius said to his student Fu Zijian, "Everyone is pleased with your governing in Shanfu. Please tell me what policies you have promulgated in order to accomplish this."

Fu replied, "In regard to my governing, if a father takes good care of his children, his children will take good care of the disadvantaged and attend properly to funerals."

Confucius replied, "Excellent. This is a fundamental measure that will apply well to the lower stratum of society. But that alone is not enough."

Fu said, "There are three people that I treat with the respect due to a father. There are five people I treat with the respect due to an elder brother. There are eleven people I treat with the respect due to a close friend."

Confucius said, "Your treating three people with the respect due to a father teaches by example the virtue of *xiao*. Your treating five people with the respect due to an elder brother teaches by example the virtue of *ti*. Your treating eleven people with the respect due to a close friend elevates excellence for all to see. These are more advanced measures that will apply well to the middle level of society. They are still not entirely sufficient, though."

Fu said, "There are five men in this area who are more capable and virtuous than me and whom I have appointed as my advisers. They all guide me along the *dao*."

Confucius breathed a sigh of relief and said, "Now you've come to the truly advanced stage. In former times, Yao and Shun were sure to solicit help from the capable and the virtuous. The capable and virtuous are the genesis of all good fortune, the captains of fate. It's just too bad that the area you govern is so small."

14.8

子貢爲信陽宰，將行，辭於孔子。孔子曰："勤之慎之，奉天子之時，無奪無伐，無暴無盜。"子貢曰："賜也少而事君子，豈以盜爲累哉？"孔子曰："汝未之詳也。夫以賢代賢，是謂之奪；以不肖代賢，是謂之伐；緩令急誅，是謂之暴；取善自與，是謂之盜。盜非竊財之謂也。吾聞之：知爲吏者，奉法以利民；不知爲吏者，枉法以侵民。此怨之所由也。治官莫若平，臨財莫如廉。廉平之守，不可改也。匿人之善，斯謂蔽賢；揚人之惡，斯爲小人。内不相訓而外相謗，非親睦也。言人之善，若己有之；言人之惡，若己受之。故君子無所不慎焉。"

Zigong accepted a post as mayor of the Chu city of Xinyang. Just before departing, he went to say goodbye to Confucius. Confucius said, "Work hard and be careful.

Carry out the king's annual calendar of projects. Do not expropriate from, assault, abuse, or rob others."

Zigong said, "I've been serving lords since I was young. How could I stoop to such things?"

Confucius said, "You don't understand exactly what I mean. To fire one capable and virtuous person just to hire another is akin to expropriation. To fire a capable and virtuous person in order to hire an unwise and incapable person is akin to assault. To be slow to issue edicts but quick to enforce them is akin to abuse. To take credit for the good deeds of others is robbery. Robbery isn't just the stealing of valuable things.

"I've learned the following: Someone who knows how to be an official benefits the people by respecting the law. Someone who is ignorant of how to be an official harms the people by perverting the law. Such is the genesis of resentment.

"When in charge of other officials, nothing is more important than fairness. When overseeing revenue, nothing is more important than scrupulousness. Whether to maintain fairness and scrupulousness is not open to question.

"To conceal someone else's excellence is called stifling the capable and virtuous. To make public the wrongdoing of others is to be a small-minded person oneself. You'll never form close relationships with others by disparaging them in public instead of correcting them in private.

"When mentioning people's virtues, see if you also possess them. When mentioning people's vices, see if the same criticism applies to you.

"In summary, a *junzi* is careful about everything."

14.9

子路治蒲三年，孔子過之。入其境，曰：“善哉！由也恭敬以信矣。”入其邑，曰：“善哉！由也忠信而寬矣。”至廷，曰：“善哉！由也明察以斷矣。”子貢執轡而問曰：“夫子未見由之政，而三稱其善，其善可得聞乎？”孔子曰：“吾見其政矣。入其境，田疇盡易，草萊甚辟，溝洫深治，此其恭敬以信，故其民盡力也；入其邑，墻屋完固，樹木甚茂，此其忠信以寬，故其民不偷也；至其庭，庭甚清閑，諸下用命，此其言明察以斷，故其政不擾也。以此觀之，雖三稱其善，庸盡其美乎？”

Zilu having been the mayor of Pu for three years, Confucius went to visit him. Crossing into the surrounding fields of Pu, he said, "Excellent! Yóu uses reverence and respect as a sign of his trustworthiness." Crossing through the city wall, he said, "Excellent! Yóu is conscientious, trustworthy, and broad-minded." Arriving at the city office building, he said, "Excellent! Yóu governs with a light hand."

Zigong pulled the reins and asked, "You haven't even seen Yóu's government, and yet you've already described it as excellent three times. What have you observed that allows you to proclaim its excellence?"

Confucius said, "I *have* seen his government. When we crossed into the surrounding fields, they were well tended, unused land was rare, and irrigation channels were deep and well-maintained. This shows that the people are working hard, in response to Yóu using reverence and respect as a sign of his trustworthiness. On entering the city, the exteriors of the walls and houses were in good condition, and the trees and plants were flourishing. These demonstrate that, in response to Yóu using conscientiousness and trustworthiness as a sign of his broad-mindedness, the people are not negligent. On arriving at the city office building, it was a clean and comfortable environment where everyone did their jobs. This demonstrates that he is decisive and governs with a light hand. From these perspectives, how can three exclamations of excellence fully express how commendable it is?"

15

Six Foundations

Chapter 15 is an eclectic mix of passages. Its title, like those of many of the chapters, comes from its opening episode and doesn't necessarily apply as an overarching theme, though it may resonate in different ways throughout. The chapter begins with the foundations of comporting oneself—that is, behaving in a way that expresses one's moral and sociopolitical ideals. The theme returns to, or finds resonance in, 15.3 (on declining undeserved payment), in 15.10 (on comporting oneself in a *xiao* way toward an abusive parent), in 15.13 (on counting one's blessings), in 15.14 (on practicing virtues), and in 15.17 (on modestly helping others). Sections 15.2 and 15.11 return to earlier themes of consultocracy. Sections 15.7, 15.15, 15.16, and 15.21 all touch on interpersonal influence and the importance of choosing one's associates wisely. Sections 15.4, 15.5, and 15.9 consider to what extent tradition should be questioned or accommodated. Sections 15.18–20 describe natural human psychological tendencies that a wise leader should be able to recognize in others. Section 15.8, echoing the *Dao de jing*, suggests that emptying oneself (loss) can be a crucial stage in learning how to effectively comport oneself.

15.1

孔子曰:“行己有六本焉,然後爲君子也。立身有義矣,而孝爲本;喪紀有禮矣,而哀爲本;戰陣有列矣,而勇爲本;治政有理矣,而農爲本;居國有道矣,而嗣爲本;生財有時矣,而力爲本。置本不固,無務農桑;親戚不悦,無務外交;事不終始,無務多業;記聞而言,無務多説;比近不安,無務求遠。是故反本修邇,君子之道也。”

Confucius said, "On the way to becoming a *junzi*, there are six foundations of personal comportment. (1) *Xiao* is the foundation of the *yi* in establishing oneself. (2) Grief is the foundation of the *li* in mourning customs. (3) Courage is the foundation of the formations used in warfare. (4) Agriculture is the foundation for organizing a well-managed government. (5) A concern for posterity is the foundation for the *dao* of a stable society. (6) Decisiveness is the foundation of timing in achieving prosperity. Do not engage in farming without well-planted roots. Do not engage in diplomacy without cordial relationships. Do not start new things until the previous project is finished. Do not spread rumors. Do not look into the distance without stability nearby. Therefore, it is the *dao* of the *junzi* to return to the fundamentals and cultivate the basics."

15.2

孔子曰:"良藥苦於口而利於病,忠言逆於耳而利於行。湯武以諤諤而昌,桀紂以唯唯而亡。君無争臣,父無争子,兄無争弟,士無争友,無其過者,未之有也。故曰:君失之,臣得之;父失之,子得之;兄失之,弟得之;己失之,友得之。是以國無危亡之兆,家無悖亂之惡,父子兄弟無失,而交友無絶也。"

Confucius said, "Medicine is bitter to the taste but beneficial to one's health. Conscientiously spoken words are hard to hear but beneficial to one's conduct. Tang and Wu thrived by listening to 'no, no,' and Jie and Zhòu died by listening to 'yes, yes.' There has never been a successful ruler who didn't have ministers of differing opinions to help him rectify his errors; likewise, for a father and his sons, an older brother and his younger brothers, and an up-and-comer and his friends. So, it is said that a ruler's errors are caught by his ministers; a father's errors are caught by his sons; an older brother's errors are caught by his younger brothers; one's own errors are caught by one's friends. When this occurs, countries remain whole, families remain harmonious, relations among father and sons and among brothers remain strong, and friendships remain solid."

15.3

孔子見齊景公,公悦焉,請置廩丘之邑以爲養。孔子辭而不受。入謂弟子曰:"吾聞君子當功受賞。今吾言於齊君,君未之有行,而賜吾邑,其不知丘亦甚矣。"於是遂行。

When Confucius met with Duke Jing of Qi, the duke was so delighted that he offered to confer on Confucius a city to provide support for him. Confucius declined the offer. Afterward, Confucius remarked to his students, "I've heard it said that a *junzi* accepts payment for services rendered. When I spoke with the Qi sovereign today, he refused my advice but offered to grant me a city. He really doesn't understand me." Thereupon, he departed.

15.4

孔子在齊，舍於外館，景公造焉。賓主之辭既接，而左右白曰：“周使適至，言先王廟災。”景公復問：“災何王之廟也？”孔子曰：“此必釐王之廟。”公曰：“何以知之？”孔子曰：“《詩》云：‘皇皇上天，其命不忒。天之以善，必報其德。’禍亦如之。夫釐王變文武之制，而作玄黄華麗之飾，宫室崇峻，輿馬奢侈，而弗可振也，故天殃所宜加其廟焉。以是占之爲然。”公曰“天何不殃其身而加罰其廟也？”孔子曰：“蓋以文武故也。若殃其身，則文武之嗣無乃殄乎？故當殃其廟，以彰其過。”俄頃，左右報曰：“所災者，釐王廟也。”景公驚起，再拜曰：“善哉！聖人之智，過人遠矣。”

When Confucius was in Qi, he stayed at a government guesthouse. Duke Jing came to visit. After the greeting, someone entered and said, "The Zhou has sent an emissary who says that a Zhou memorial temple has suffered a natural disaster."

Duke Jing asked in response, "The temple to which king of Zhou?"

Confucius said, "It has to be the temple to King Xi."

"How do you know that?" asked the duke.

Confucius replied, "A poem says:

Majestic, regal, lofty heaven,
Its ordinations never untoward.
When it deigns to grant a boon,
Ever merit-based reward.[1]

The same goes for disasters. King Xi changed the system begun by Kings Wen and Wu so that clothing insignia became colorful and ostentatious, palace halls became high-ceilinged, and horse carriages became ornate. These changes were irrevocable, and now heaven is inflicting this calamity on the king's memorial temple. This is my perspective."

The duke asked, "Why would heaven do this to his temple instead of to his person?"

Confucius said, "It probably has something to do with Wen and Wu. If it had happened to his person, it could have been the end of the line of succession for Wen and Wu. That's why the calamity struck the temple—to put Xi's errors on full display."

After a time, there was another report, which said, "The temple that was destroyed was the temple to King Xi."

Duke Jing was stunned and saluted Confucius, saying, "Outstanding! The wisdom of a sage, far surpassing others."[2]

1. This is the only surviving fragment of this poem.

2. Compare 16.6.

15.5

子夏三年之喪畢，見於孔子。子曰："與之琴，使之弦。" 侃侃而樂，作而曰："先王制禮，不敢不及。"子曰："君子也！"閔子三年之喪畢，見於孔子。子曰："與之琴，使之弦。" 切切而悲，作而曰："先王制禮[3]，弗敢過也。"子曰："君子也！"子貢曰："閔子哀未盡，夫子曰'君子也'；子夏哀已盡，又曰'君子也'。二者殊情而俱曰君子，賜也惑，敢問之。" 孔子曰："閔子哀未忘，能斷之以禮；子夏哀已盡，能引之及禮。雖均之君子，不亦可乎？"

After completing a three-year period of mourning, Zixia went to see Confucius. Confucius said, "Give him a zither and have him play a tune."

After strumming a joyful song, Zixia looked up and said, "I would never dare to not live up to the system of *li* arranged by the Ancient Kings."[4]

Confucius said, "You are a *junzi* indeed."

After completing a three-year period of mourning, Minzi went to see Confucius. Confucius said, "Give him a zither and have him play a tune."

After strumming a sad song, Minzi looked up and said, "I would never dare to violate the system of *li* arranged by the Ancient Kings."[5]

Confucius said, "You are a *junzi* indeed."

Zigong said, "Minzi's sorrow was not yet worked through, and you called him a *junzi*. Zixia's sorrow was entirely worked through, and you called him a *junzi* also. I'm confused that, although their emotional experiences were different, you labeled them both *junzi*. Could you explain?"

Confucius said, "Minzi's sorrow was not yet forgotten, and yet he was able to use *li* to control it. Zixia's sorrow was completely worked through, and yet he was able to use *li* to extend it. Despite the differences, is it not right to label them both *junzi*?"

15.6

孔子曰："無體之禮，敬也；無服之喪，哀也；無聲之樂，歡也。不言而信，不動而威，不施而仁，志。夫鐘之音，怒而擊之則武，憂而擊之則悲。其志變者，聲亦隨之。故志誠感之，通於金石，而况人乎？"

3. 不敢不及 . . . 先王制禮: This text was added, following SKQS and Tongwen editions.

4. Zixia, by playing a joyful song, has demonstrated that his sorrow naturally came to an end sometime before the end of the official mourning period. By saying he would not dare to not live up to the system of *li*, he is stating that he continued to maintain the rituals of the mourning period even though his sorrow had ended.

5. Minzi, by playing a sad song, has demonstrated that his sorrow has not yet come to a natural end even though the official mourning period has ended. By saying that he would not dare to violate the system of *li*, he is stating that, even though he has not yet worked through all of his sorrow, he has halted the mourning rituals in accord with *li*.

Confucius said, "Respect is *li* without the ceremony. Sorrow is mourning without the costume. Joy is music without the sound. To be trustworthy without being asked, to command respect without moving a muscle, to express *ren* without helping anyone—these are all thoughts and feelings. Consider the sound of orchestral bells and chimes. When played with fury, they emit a martial sound. When played in mourning, they emit a baleful sound. When one's thoughts and feelings change, the sound follows. If thoughts and feelings can be transferred in this way to metal and stone, how much more so can they be to people?"

15.7

孔子見羅雀者所得皆黄口小雀。夫子問之曰："大雀獨不得，何也？"羅者曰："大雀善驚而難得，黄口貪食而易得。黄口從大雀則不得，大雀從黄口亦不得。"孔子顧謂弟子曰："善驚以遠害，利食而忘患，自其心矣，而以所從爲禍福。故君子慎其所從。以長者之慮，則有全身之階；隨小者之戇，而有危亡之敗也。"

Confucius noticed that all the birds caught in a hunter's net were fledglings, and he asked the hunter, "Why aren't there any adult birds in your net?"

The hunter said, "Adult birds excel at staying alert and so are hard to catch. Fledglings are greedy for food and so are easy to catch. If the fledglings follow the adults, I can't catch them, and it is the same if the adults follow the fledglings."[6]

Confucius turned to his students and said, "Excelling at being alert keeps disaster at bay, while gluttony leads to neglecting danger. Both arise from one's feelings,[7] and that which you follow determines your fortune. Thus, a *junzi* is cautious about what he follows. If you live by the prudence of an elder, you stand to remain whole. If you live by the rashness of youth, you risk your life."

15.8

孔子讀《易》，至於《損》《益》，喟然而嘆。子夏避席問曰："夫子何嘆焉？"孔子曰："夫自損者必有益之，自益者必有决之，吾是以嘆也。"子夏曰："然則學者不可以益乎？"子曰："非道益之謂也。道彌益而身彌損。夫學者損其自多，以虛受人，故能成其

6. The point here seems to be that, if adult birds are involved, the fledglings will be safe. Analogically, as long as a well-cultivated elder is involved, youth will not come to harm. This analogy does not speak to the small-minded or otherwise uncultivated elder. The *Shuo yuan* contains a briefer version of this episode, and although the overall message is the same (be careful whom you follow), it says that if adults follow fledglings, they can be caught.

7. *Both arise from one's feelings, zi qi xin* 自其心: The Chinese does not contain the word "both." In fact, it's not clear in the Chinese whether this phrase applies to both preceding clauses or only to the immediately preceding clause. From context, inferring that it applies to both seems justified.

滿。博哉！天道成而必變。凡持滿而能久者，未嘗有也。故曰：'自賢者，天下之善言不得聞於耳矣。'昔堯治天下之位，猶允恭以持之，克讓以接下，是以千歲而益盛，迄今而逾彰。夏桀、昆吾自滿而無極，亢意而不節，斬刈黎民如草芥焉。天下討之如誅匹夫。是以千載而惡著，迄今而不滅。觀此，如行則讓長，不疾先；如在輿，遇三人則下之，遇二人則式之。調其盈虛，不令自滿，所以能久也。"子夏曰："商請志之，而終身奉行焉。"

When Confucius was reading the Changes and came to the hexagrams *sun* 損 (loss) and *yi* 益 (gain), he heaved a sigh. Zixia stood up and asked, "Why did you sigh, sir?"

Confucius said, "For someone who feels a personal loss (*sun* 損), there will inevitably be a gain (*yi* 益) from it; and for someone who feels a personal gain (*yi* 益), it will inevitably be cut short. This is why I sighed."

Zixia said, "But can't studying allow one to experience continual gain (*yi* 益)?"

Confucius said, "That's not how to speak of gain (*yi* 益) in relation to the *dao*. As there is an increase (*yi* 益) in one's *dao*, there is a loss (*sun* 損) of one's self. One loses (*sun* 損)[8] a sense of self-importance and uses the humility of emptiness to learn from others. That's how they attain fullness. This is far-reaching!

"Whenever the process of *tian dao* comes to maturity, it inevitably changes. There has never been a case when fullness was achieved and was able to stay that way. That's why it is said, 'A self-proclaimed capable and virtuous person is deaf to good advice.'

"When Yao governed, he indeed maintained it through humble reverence and was able to defer to those below him. This is why, after a thousand years, his name increases in splendor. Jie and Kunwu of Xia sought limitless fullness for themselves, were despotic without the least bit of self-restraint, and mowed down the common people like grass and weeds. The world now denounces them as common criminals. And so, after a thousand years, their vileness has not been extinguished. Looking at it from this perspective, one's conduct should consist in deferring to elders and not hurrying out in front of others. For example, if you are out in your carriage and you come across three acquaintances on the street, get down and greet them. If you come across two acquaintances, salute them by leaning on the front bar of the carriage. Longevity lies in adjusting one's level of emptiness and not striving for fullness."

Zixia said, "I am going to write down this teaching and follow it as a lifelong lesson."

8. There is a transition in this passage from *sun* (loss) and *yi* (gain) to the related terms *xu* 虛 (emptiness) and *man* 滿 (fullness). As in 9.4, where *sun* is translated "reduction," this passage seems to also reconcile Laozi's idea of emptiness with Confucius' exhortation to study. How can you have both without contradiction? The solution seems to be that there can be a gain in knowledge and understanding as long as there is a concomitant reduction in one's own sense of self-importance. In other words, humility counterbalances erudition.

15.9

子路問於孔子曰："請釋古之道而行由之意，可乎？"子曰："不可。昔東夷之子，慕諸夏之禮，有女而寡，爲内私婿，終身不嫁。不嫁則不嫁矣，亦非貞節之義也。蒼梧嬈娶妻而美，讓與其兄，讓則讓矣，然非禮之讓矣。不慎其初，而悔其後，何嗟及矣。今汝欲舍古之道，行子之意，庸知子意不以是爲非，以非爲是乎？後雖欲悔，難哉！"

Zilu asked Confucius, "Would it be acceptable to set aside the ancient ways and simply follow my own ideas?"

Confucius replied, "No. Once there was a man of the Eastern Yi people who greatly admired the Xia customs.[9] For his daughter, who was a widow, he brought in an unofficial husband to live with them, and they never married. This is not marrying, admittedly, but it violates the meaning of *faithfulness*.[10] More recently, a man named Rao of the Cangwu people married a beautiful woman and then, out of deference to his older brother, gave her to him. This is deference, true, but it is deference that violates *li*.[11] If you are not cautious in the beginning, you will regret it later, when it will be too late to make amends. If you set aside the ancient ways and follow your own ideas, how can you be sure that what you think is the right thing to do is not actually the wrong thing to do, and what you think is the wrong thing to do is not

9. In Confucius' time just as today, there were cultures within the geographical area of China that did not identify with the prevailing culture. The prevailing culture today is called Han. In Confucius' day it was called Zhou, after the dynastic power. Because it was understood that Zhou inherited the culture from Shang and that Shang inherited it from Xia, it was also identified variously with those terms. See "Xia" in the glossary.

10. *Faithfulness, zhen jie* 貞節: In other words, not remarrying is an expression of faithfulness (see 26.2 for Confucius' view on this, especially n2). To be married to a man in every way except formally does not express the faithfulness of not remarrying. This, by the way, is the earliest instance of *zhen jie* being associated with a woman's marriage situation. *Zhen*, which means loyalty/faithfulness/devotion, is often interpreted in the context of women's marriage situation in terms of her sexuality, as chastity or purity (e.g., in Kinney 2014), but there are many ways for a woman to be faithful. LNZ, in fact, lists a series of examples in an explanation of *zhen*. Kinney translates, "Once a woman drinks from the marriage cup, she does not waver. When her husband dies, she does not remarry. She manages hempen fibers, processes the silk cocoons, weaves silk fabric, and fashions cords to supply clothing and provide for her husband. She purifies the wine and prepares food in order to serve her father- and mother-in-law. She understands devotion to one [man] as purity" (33). The word "purity" is Kinney's translation of *zhen*. The final sentence (以專一為貞) could alternatively be translated, "She understands single-minded devotion as being faithful."

11. The point here seems to be that deference to one's elder brother is the right attitude to take, but deferring to the point of giving your own wife to him is taking it too far. Following *li*, Confucius seems to be saying, is a way to express our natural feelings and inclinations in ways that have proven successful over generations. By going it alone, one sacrifices this source of wisdom.

actually the right thing to do? Even if you realize later that you made a mistake, making amends will be difficult!"

15.10

曾子耘瓜，誤斬其根。曾皙怒，建大杖以擊其背。曾子仆地而不知人久之。有頃，乃蘇，欣然而起，進於曾皙曰："嚮也，參得罪於大人，大人用力教參，得無疾乎?"退而就房，援琴而歌，欲令曾皙而聞之，知其體康也。孔子聞之而怒，告門弟子曰："參來，勿內。"曾參自以爲無罪，使人請於孔子。子曰："汝不聞乎，昔瞽瞍有子曰舜。舜之事瞽瞍，欲使之，未嘗不在於側；索而殺之，未嘗可得。小棰則待過，大杖則逃走，故瞽瞍不犯不父之罪，而舜不失烝烝之孝。今參事父，委身以待暴怒，殪而不避。既身死而陷父於不義，其不孝孰大焉? 汝非天子之民也? 殺天子之民，其罪奚若?"曾參聞之，曰："參罪大矣。"遂造孔子而謝過。

Once when Zengzi was weeding around melons on the family farm, he mistakenly severed a melon vine. This angered his father, who hit him on the back with a large staff. Zengzi fell unconscious to the ground and lay there for a long time. Finally, he came to, rose with gladness, and approached his father. "I offended you, and it took all your strength to teach me a lesson. You didn't hurt yourself, did you?" Zengzi then returned to the house, where he got out his zither and sang, hoping that his father could hear it and so know that he hadn't been seriously injured.

Confucius heard about this and was upset, saying to his students, "When Shen comes, don't let him in." Believing he had done nothing wrong, Zengzi sent someone to ask Confucius about it. Confucius said: "Have you never heard of a man named Gusou who had a son named Shun? Whenever Gusou wanted him to do something, Shun was always by his side. Whenever Gusou sought Shun out to kill him, he couldn't find him. When Gusou hit him with a switch, Shun endured it. When Gusou tried to hit him with a staff, Shun ran away. In this way, Gusou was unable to commit the unfatherly offense of abusing him, and Shun was able to avoid violating pure *xiao*. Shen, on the contrary, let his father beat him to within an inch of his life. If he had died, he would have been letting his father sink into iniquity. What is worse than violating *xiao*? Aren't we all subjects of the king? Isn't it a crime to kill a subject of the king?"

Zengzi, on hearing Confucius' reply, said, "I made a grave error" and paid a visit to Confucius to admit his mistake.

15.11

荆公子行年十五而攝荊相事。孔子聞之，使人往觀其爲政焉。使者反，曰："視其朝，清淨而少事，其堂上有五老焉，其廊下有二十壯士焉。"孔子曰："合二十五人之智，以治天下，其固免矣，况荆乎?"

A prince of Chu[12] was fifteen years old when he stepped in to act as prime minister of Chu. When Confucius learned of this, he sent someone to Chu to observe how the crown prince governed. On returning, the messenger said, "Looking at the Chu court, it is orderly, with few incidents. In the main hall he has five elders advising him, and in the corridors he has twenty vigorous officials assisting him."

Confucius said, "With the combined wisdom of twenty-five people, you can rule the whole land and thoroughly avoid crises, let alone the state of Chu!"

15.12

子夏問於孔子曰:"顏回之爲人奚若?"子曰:"回之信賢於丘。"曰:"子貢之爲人奚若?"子曰:"賜之敏賢於丘。"曰:"子路之爲人奚若?"子曰:"由之勇賢於丘。"曰:"子張之爲人奚若?"子曰:"師之莊賢於丘。"子夏避席而問曰:"然則四子何爲事先生?"子曰:"居,吾語汝。夫回能信而不能反,賜能敏而不能詘,由能勇而不能怯,師能莊而不能同。兼四子者之有以易吾,弗與也。此其所以事吾而弗貳也。"

Zixia asked Confucius, "What do you think of Yan Hui's conduct?"

Confucius said, "Hui surpasses me in trustworthiness."

"What about Zigong's conduct?"

Confucius said, "Ci surpasses me in intelligence."

"What about Zilu's conduct?"

Confucius said, "Yóu surpasses me in bravery."

"What about Zizhang's conduct?"

Confucius said, "Shi surpasses me in seriousness."

Zixia stood up and said, "If this is so, then why are they your students?"

Confucius said, "Sit down and I'll tell you. Hui is very trustworthy but not so good at self-reflection. Ci is very intelligent but not so good at humbling himself. Yóu is very brave but not so good at backing down. Shi is very serious but not so good at getting along with others. If someone came to me with what these four possess and wanted to exchange with me, I wouldn't accept. This is why they don't consider it redundant to study with me."

15.13

孔子遊於泰山,見榮聲期行乎郕之野,鹿裘帶索,鼓瑟而歌。孔子問曰:"先生所以爲樂者,何也?"期對曰:"吾樂甚多,而至者三。天生萬物,唯人爲貴。吾既得爲人,是一樂也。男女之别,男尊女卑,故人以男爲貴。吾既得爲男,是二樂也。人生有不見日月,不免襁褓者,吾既以行年九十五矣,是三樂也。貧者,士之常;死者,人之終。處常得終,當何憂哉?"孔子曰:"善哉!能自寬者也。"

12. The unnamed prince of Chu may be Zixi (as in 14.4; see also in the glossary).

When Confucius took a trip to Tai Mountain, he ran into Rong Shengqi[13] in the wilderness outside the city of Cheng. He was dressed in deer furs with a rope for a belt, strumming a large zither and singing. Confucius asked, "Why are you singing so happily?"[14]

Rong Shengqi responded, "There are many reasons I sing happily, but there are three main reasons. First, of all the things of the world that nature has produced, people are preeminent, and I have the good fortune of being a person. Second, in the division of male and female, men are respected over women in our society, and I have the good fortune of being a man. Third, some people don't live long enough to see the sky or get out of their swaddling clothes, but I have walked this earth for ninety-five years. It is normal for a man to be poor, and death is the end of us all. Having achieved the norm and soon to reach the end, what do I have to worry about?"

Confucius said, "Fantastic! A master of self-contentment!"[15]

15.14

孔子曰: “回有君子之道四焉: 强於行義, 弱於受諫, 怵於待禄, 慎於治身。史鰌有君子之道三焉: 不仕而敬上, 不祀而敬鬼, 直己而曲人。”曾子侍, 曰: “參昔常聞夫子三言, 而未之能行也。夫子見人之一善而忘其百非, 是夫子之易事也; 見人之有善, 若己有之, 是夫子之不争也; 聞善必躬行之, 然後導之, 是夫子之能勞也。學夫子之三言而未能行, 以自知終不及二子者也。”

13. The name Rong Shengqi is not attested elsewhere. This story also appears in the *Shuo yuan* and the *Liezi* 列子, in both of which Confucius' interlocutor is named Rong Qiqi 榮啓期. Rong Qiqi also appears in *Huainanzi*, where he is identified as a master zither player.

14. *Singing so happily*. The one word *le/yue* 樂 means both to be happy and to make music.

15. *Master of self-contentment, zi kuan* 自寬: self-loosen. This term is pregnant with meaning. *Zi* means to do something of/to/for oneself. *Kuan* has a variety of meanings. As an adjective of things, it means broad, expansive. As an adjective of persons, it can mean broad-minded, tolerant, easygoing, indulgent. As a verb, it can mean loosen, excuse, relax, forgive, mitigate, be tolerant toward. *Zi kuan* could mean that Rong Shengqi is being self-indulgent, settling for a life outside of society when he should instead be striving for a better society. However, Confucius begins with *shan zai* 善哉, *fantastic*, indicating that he approves. A better interpretation seems to be that *zi kuan* here is about seeing the bigger picture and how one's life fits into that. Graham (1990a, 24) renders it "console himself" in his translation of a parallel passage in the *Liezi* (a Daoist text), but the notion of consolation does not work in a Daoist context. Consolation involves a judgment that some situation affecting you is negative and you must adjust your feelings to that negative situation. Daoists don't view hardship, poverty, illness, and so on, as negative, so there is no need for consolation. Confucius also had no problem with poverty. The meaning of *zi kuan*, therefore, seems to be something like: he is easy-going and nonjudgmental with regard to his own place in the world. We see Confucius approving of a similar kind of attitude in Zijian in 19.4.

Confucius said, "There are four ways in which Hui conducts himself in the *dao* of the *junzi*: he is aggressive when it comes to putting *yi* into practice; he is docile when accepting admonishment; he is guarded when it comes to expecting an official salary; and he is cautious when it comes to governing his own person.

There are three ways in which Shi Qiu conducts himself in the *dao* of the *junzi*: he respects his superiors even when not in office; he respects the spirits of his deceased ancestors even when not worshiping; he is strict with himself but lenient with others."

Zengzi was present and said to Confucius, "I am unable to put into practice three things that I once heard you say that you are able to do: (1) It is easy for you to be able to forget a hundred wrongs in a person just by witnessing one virtue[16] in them; (2) when you see a virtue in someone, you see if you also possess it, but without becoming competitive about it; and (3) you are able to diligently put into practice a virtue, once you have become aware of it, and afterward able to guide others in it. I've studied these three but have not been able to successfully put them into practice. Because of this, I realize that I will never be as good as Yan Hui or Shi Qiu."

15.15

孔子曰："吾死之後，則商也日益，賜也日損。"曾子曰："何謂也？"子曰："商也好與賢己者處，賜也好説不若己者。不知其子，視其父；不知其人，視其友；不知其君，視其所使；不知其地，視其草木。故曰：與善人居，如入芝蘭之室，久而不聞其香，即與之化矣；與不善人居，如入鮑魚之肆，久而不聞其臭，亦與之化矣。丹之所藏者赤，漆之所藏者黑。是以君子必慎其所與處者焉。"

Confucius said, "After I pass away, Shang will improve every day, and Ci will regress every day."

Zengzi said, "What makes you say this?"

Confucius said, "Shang likes to spend time with capable and virtuous people, whereas Ci likes to talk about people who are not as good as him. If you don't understand a son, observe his father. If you don't understand a person, observe his friends. If you don't understand a sovereign, observe his subordinates. If you don't understand an area of land, observe its flora. This is why it is said:

> Living with a good person is like entering a flower-scented room—after a while, you don't notice the fragrance, but you absorb it as your own. Living with a bad person is like entering a fish stall—after a while, you don't notice the stink, but you absorb it as your own.

16. *Virtue, shan* 善: merit, strength. The virtue of forgiveness is not prominent in early Chinese philosophy, but this seems to be an example of it.

Storage boxes for cinnabar turn red, and storage boxes for lacquer turn black. Based on the above, a *junzi* must be cautious about whom he spends time with."

15.16

曾子從孔子之齊，齊景公以下卿之禮聘曾子，曾子固辭。將行，晏子送之，曰："吾聞之，君子遺人以財，不若善言。今夫蘭本三年，湛之以鹿酭，既成，噉之，則易之匹馬。非蘭之本性也，所以湛者美矣。願子詳其所湛者。夫君子居必擇處，遊必擇方，仕必擇君。擇君所以求仕，擇方所以修道。遷風移俗者，嗜慾移性，可不慎乎？"孔子聞之，曰："晏子之言，君子哉！依賢者固不困，依富者固不窮。馬蚿斬足而復行，何也？以其輔之者衆。"

Zengzi accompanied Confucius to Qi, where Duke Jing offered Zengzi a position as an official.[17] Zengzi steadfastly refused.

When he was about to leave, the Qi prime minister Yanzi saw him off and said, "I've heard that it is better to leave someone with wise words than with a fancy gift. If you take a three-year-old root of the eupatorium plant and marinate it in venison broth, it will be so delicious that you could trade it for a horse. This is not due to the nature of the eupatorium but to the flavor of the marinade. It is my wish that you be particular about your own marinade. A *junzi* selects his place of residence, his area of recreation, and the sovereign he serves. He selects a sovereign as a way of serving. He selects an area as a way of cultivating *dao*. Someone who always changes with the customs has fickle tastes. Isn't it essential to be cautious?"

Confucius heard about this and said, "Yanzi's words are the words of a *junzi*! You won't get into trouble if you lean on a capable and virtuous person, just like you won't be poor if you lean on a wealthy person. Why can a millipede still walk after breaking a leg? Because it has so many more to make up for it."

17. There is a problem with the chronology of this story in that Zengzi was born in 505 BCE, Yanzi died in 500 BCE, and Duke Jing died in 497 BCE. From this fact, we can infer either that the story is a complete fabrication, or that the characters have been confused in the retelling—that it was a different student or a different ruler and minister. The part about a marinade can be found, with significantly different wording, in *Xunzi* (1), and the part about Yanzi seeing off Zengzi can be found in *Xunzi* (27). Parallels of these two parts can also be found in a wide variety of other, later works. These facts suggest that this passage was cobbled together from existing fragments in an attempt to restore a more complete narrative and that either the student in question was not Zengzi, or Zengzi's interlocutor was a different minister. We think the most likely scenario is that the original story mentioned an unnamed sovereign and prime minister of Qi, and that Duke Jing and Yanzi, being prominent in the time of Confucius, were added for color at a later date. Alternatively, it could be a variation of the story in 20.3. (Fang et al. 1994; Zheng, Wu, and Yang 2000)

15.17

孔子曰："以富貴而下人，何人不尊？以富貴而愛人，何人不親？發言不逆，可謂知言矣；言而衆嚮之，可謂知時矣。是故以富而能富人者，欲貧不可得也；以貴而能貴人者，欲賤不可得也；以達而能達人者，欲窮不可得也。"

Confucius said, "If you are affluent and esteemed and yet can humble yourself before others, who will not respect you? If you are affluent and esteemed and yet can extend loving care to others, who will not draw close to you? Someone whose speech is never perceived as derogatory can be said to understand how to speak well. Someone whose speech attracts others to gravitate toward him can be said to understand timing[18] well. Consider someone who is affluent and who helps others become affluent—this person couldn't become poor even if he wanted to. Consider someone who is esteemed and who esteems others—this person couldn't fall into disrepute even if he wanted to. Consider someone who is successful and who helps others become successful—he couldn't become destitute even if he wanted to."

15.18

孔子曰："中人之情也，有餘則侈，不足則儉，無禁則淫，無度則逸，從欲則敗。是故鞭扑之子，不從父之教；刑戮之民，不從君之令。此言疾之難忍，急之難行也。故君子不急斷，不急制，使飲食有量，衣服有節，宮室有度，畜積有數，車器有限，所以防亂之原也。夫度量不可不明，是中人所由之令。"

Confucius said, "The tendencies of the average person are as follows: surplus results in extravagance; scarcity results in thrift; unrestraint results in debauchery; immoderation results in dissipation; abandoning oneself to desires leads to ruin. And so, the son who gets whipped is the one who disobeyed the instruction of his father. The citizen who gets executed is the one who disobeyed the orders of his sovereign. This explains the difficulty of putting up with deleterious behavior and of dealing with rash behavior. Thus, in order to guard against the incipience of disorder, a *junzi* does not make hasty disciplinary judgments. Instead, he ensures that people eat and drink in moderation, are modest in dress, are decorous in their homes, have livestock that are not too numerous, and have limited vehicle accessories. Moderation must be elucidated, for it is the imperative from which the average person proceeds."

18. *Timing, shi* 時: The idea here is that knowing what to say and when to say it are crucial for successful communication. See also 23.5.

15.19

孔子曰:"巧而好度必攻,勇而好問必勝,智而好謀必成。以愚者反之。是以非其人,告之弗聽;非其地,樹之弗生。得其人,如聚砂而雨之;非其人,如會聾而鼓之。夫處重擅寵,專事妒賢,愚者之情也。位高則危,任重則崩,可立而待。"

Confucius said, "People who are clever and like to think will take the initiative. People who are courageous and inquisitive will prevail. People who are wise and enjoy planning will succeed. Replace each of the above virtues with *foolish* and you get the opposite. Therefore, people who are not ready will not listen to good advice, just as a tree planted on unprepared ground[19] will not thrive. People who are ready are like a mound of sand in the rain.[20] People who aren't ready are like deaf people having drums played for them. It is the tendency of foolish people to prefer being showered with favors when in a position of importance and to be jealous of the capable and virtuous when in charge of individual tasks. It can happen quickly that high positions become imperiled and heavy responsibilities collapse."

15.20

孔子曰:"舟非水不行,水入舟則沒;君非民不治,民犯上則傾。是故君子不可不嚴也,小人不可不整一也。"

Confucius said, "Without water, a boat can't go, but if water gets in, it will sink. Without the people, a leader can't govern, but if the people rise up, he will be toppled. Therefore, a *junzi* must be serious, and small-minded people must be brought in line."

15.21

齊高庭問於孔子曰:"庭不曠山,不直地,衣穰而提贄,精氣以問事君子之道,願夫子告之。"孔子曰:"貞以幹之,敬以輔之,施仁無倦。見君子則舉之,見小人則退之。去汝惡心,而忠與之,效其行,修其禮,千里之外,親如兄弟。行不效,禮不修,則對門不汝通矣。夫終日言,不遺己之憂;終日行,不遺己之患,唯智者能之。故自修者,必恐懼以除患,恭儉以避難者也。終日爲善,一言則敗之,可不慎乎!"

Gao Ting of Qi went to meet Confucius and said, "Having crossed mountains and plains, wearing simple clothes and bringing a small gift, I come to you with great enthusiasm to ask about the *dao* of serving a lord."

19. Like thick clay.
20. The water easily penetrates.

Confucius said, "Using devotion as your shield and respect as your brace, spread *ren* tirelessly. Meeting another *junzi,* elevate him. Meeting a small-minded person, avoid him. Eliminate ill will from your mind and replace it with conscientiousness. Of those who are a model of conduct for others and work to improve their *li,* become as close as brothers to all those within hundreds of miles. Of those who are not a model of conduct for others and who do not work to improve their *li,* do not connect with them even if they live across the street. Only someone of great wisdom is able to speak or act all day long without fear of saying or doing something he'll regret. Therefore, one who cultivates oneself will also be cautious, as a way of evading misfortune, and will be reverent, as a way of avoiding trouble. You can do good all day long only to ruin it with a single word. You must be careful!"

16

Reading Events

Episodes in this chapter[1] illustrate the perspicacity of Confucius, who is able to explain and provide historical context for unusual events, often involving rulers of various states, with echoes of 14.6 (in which the one-legged bird was explained) and 15.4 (in which the temple fire was explained). His ability to explain events rests on his understanding of cultural distinctions, mythology, and history, as well as his openness to learning from others, even from those outside the dominant culture.

16.1

季桓子穿井，獲如玉缶，其中有羊焉。使使問孔子曰："吾穿井於費，而於井中得一狗，何也?"孔子曰："丘之所聞者，羊也。丘聞之，木石之怪，夔、魍魎；水之怪，龍、罔象；土之怪，羵羊也。"

Once when Ji Huanzi was having a well dug, a covered wine container made of jade was found underground, and inside it was a goat.[2] He sent an emissary to ask Confucius, "When I was digging a well in Bi, I found a small dog[3] in the well. What should I think about that?"

1. The title of this chapter is "Reading Events" (*bian wu* 辯物). We use the word "reading" as it is often used in mantic contexts, like *reading palms* or *reading tea leaves*—that is, having the ability to interpret the hidden meaning of something.

2. The exact occurrence here is unclear. What is clear is that an antiquity was found underground while a well was being dug. What we would consider an accidental archaeological discovery (see 16.2 for another), they would consider an event of cosmic significance. The passage says that the container was like a *fou* 缶, which was used to hold liquid, such as an alcoholic beverage. Being made of jade, it would likely be small and so would not be large enough to hold a sacrificial goat (however, other versions of this story say the vessel was made of clay). Perhaps a sacrificial goat was near the *fou,* or perhaps it was a motif on the vessel itself. Or perhaps the story claims straightforwardly that a kind of magical goat was found living in a magical vessel underground. (Zheng, Wu, and Yang 2000)

3. In a childish ploy, Ji Huanzi appears to be trying to fool Confucius, calling it a dog instead of a goat, testing the extent of Confucius' perspicacity.

Confucius said, "From what I understand, it should be a goat. I have heard that the kind of beast associated with a strange occurrence near wood or stone is either the *kui*[4] or the *wangliang*. The kind of beast associated with a strange occurrence in water is either the dragon or the *wangxiang*. The kind of beast associated with a strange occurrence in the earth is a kind of goat called the *fen*."

16.2

吴伐越，隳會稽，獲巨骨一節，專車焉。吴子使來聘於魯，且問之孔子，命使者曰："無以吾命也。"賓既將事，乃發幣於大夫，及孔子，孔子爵之。既徹俎而燕，客執骨而問曰："敢問骨何如爲大？"孔子曰："丘聞之，昔禹致群臣於會稽之山，防風後至，禹殺而戮之，其骨專車焉，此爲大矣。"客曰："敢問誰守爲神？"孔子曰："山川之靈，足以紀綱天下者，其守爲神。諸侯，社稷之守爲公侯，山川之祀者爲諸侯，皆屬於王。"客曰："防風何守？"孔子曰："汪芒氏之君，守封嵎山者，爲漆姓，在虞夏商爲汪芒氏，於周爲長瞿氏，今曰大人。"有客曰："人長之極幾何？"孔子曰："焦僥氏長三尺，短之至也。長者不過十，數之極也。"

Once when the state of Wu attacked the state of Yue, there was a landslide on Kuaiji Mountain. A bone was found there that was as large as a wagon.[5] The ruler of Wu sent an emissary to Lu to ask about the bone but said, "Don't tell him I asked."

The emissary began by saying, "I have no particular mission," and after preliminary matters were settled, he distributed gifts to the high officials and to Confucius. Confucius toasted him. When the plates of sacrificial meat had been cleared away and the banquet had begun, the emissary held up a bone and asked respectfully, "What kind of bone counts as big?"

Confucius said, "I once learned that, in Yǔ's time, he gathered all of his vassals at Kuaiji Mountain. Fangfeng was late arriving, and Yǔ killed him, then put his bones on display.[6] He had bones that were as big as a wagon. That counts as big."

The guest said, "Who should be safeguarded as a god, if I may ask?"[7]

4. This and the subsequent creatures are members of the early Chinese bestiary of mythical animals. See the glossary for further explanation of *kui* and dragon. As for the others, the *fen* is mentioned elsewhere only in versions of this story, and the *wangxiang* and *wangliang* are mentioned in similar contexts elsewhere but not further elucidated. All of these creatures appear to have a spiritual significance. For further elucidation, see Boltz 1979; Harper 1985.

5. Large numbers of dinosaur fossils have been found in the general vicinity of Kuaiji Mountain, including those of sauropods. (Mannion et al. 2019)

6. BA records the story of Yǔ gathering his vassal lords at Kuaiji and killing Fangfeng. No details are given.

7. From this question and what follows, the issue seems to be whether the bone should be worshipped, and Confucius' answer is that it should not be because Fangfeng was just a large person, not a figure deserving of worship.

Confucius said, "Nature spirits, who bring rain regularly to all, should be safeguarded as gods. Of the aristocracy, sacrifices to the agricultural gods should be safeguarded by dukes, and sacrifices to nature gods by the lower aristocracy. All are under the purview of the king."

The guest said, "What of the safeguarding with respect to Fangfeng?"

Confucius said, "He was the sovereign of the Wangmang people[8] and safeguarded Feng and Yu Mountains. Of the surname Qi, they were referred to as the Wangmang people during the Yú, Xia, and Shang periods. Beginning in the Zhou dynasty, they became known as the Changqu people, who are recognized as giants today."

The guest said, "What is the tallest that a person can grow?"

Confucius said, "The Jiaoyao people grow to be two and a quarter feet tall, which is the lower limit.[9] The upper limit is no more than seven and a half feet tall."

16.3

孔子在陳，陳惠公賓之于上館。時有隼集陳侯之庭而死，楛矢貫之，石砮，其長尺有咫。惠公使人持隼，如孔子館而問焉。孔子曰："隼之來遠矣，此肅慎氏之矢。昔武王克商，通道于九夷百蠻，使各以其方賄來貢，而無忘職業。於是肅慎氏貢楛矢、石砮，其長尺有咫。先王欲昭其令德之致遠物也，以示後人，使永鑒焉，故銘其栝曰：'肅慎氏貢楛矢'，以分大姬，配胡公，而封諸陳。古者分同姓以珍玉，所以展親親也；分異姓以遠方之職貢，所以無忘服也，故分陳以肅慎氏貢焉。君若使有司求諸故府，其可得也。"公使人求，得之金櫝，如之。

When Confucius was in Chen, Duke Hui[10] put him up in a first-rate residence. One day, a falcon came to rest in the yard of the duke's palace and suddenly died. It had been pierced by a short, stone-tipped arrow with a shaft of *hu* wood.[11]

The duke had someone take the falcon to Confucius to ask him about it. Confucius said, "This thing in the falcon has come from far away. The arrow is from the Sushen people. After Zhou King Wu conquered the Shang, he built roads throughout

8. Outside of this story (which also appears in the *Shuo yuan* and *Guo yu*), the only early account of a Wangmang people is in the *Shuo wen jie zi* dictionary. Under its entry for Yu 嵎 Mountain, it says that it is between Chu and Wu in the state of Wangmang 汪芒. Wangmang also appears in the same dictionary (with a slightly different orthography 汪茫) as a lineage associated with the Fangfeng lineage.

9. The *Shuo wen jie zi* dictionary also mentions a Jiaoyao people as the lower limit of human height.

10. The Chen peerage level was actually marquis, but it was common to refer to a ruler after death with the honorific *duke*.

11. The arrow is more specifically described as being 1 *chi* 尺 and 1 *zhi* 咫 in length, about sixteen inches. A typical arrow used for a weapon during Confucius' time was two or more feet long, made of bamboo or birch, with a bronze tip. Nothing is known about the *hu* 楛 tree, except that according to the *Hanfeizi*, it grows about seven and a half feet in height. (Sui County Leigudun Archaeological Team 1979; Chen and Jin 2014)

the land to all the frontier peoples, encouraging them to send gifts to him as tribute, and these have not been forgotten. The Sushen people sent short, stone-tipped arrows with shafts of *hu* wood. In order to memorialize these gifts of tribute from afar for later generations to read, the king had the following inscribed on the arrow shafts: '*Hu* arrow tribute from the Sushen People.' He then sent the arrows along with his own daughter, whom he married to Duke Hu of Chen when the duke was enfeoffed. In ancient times, the gift given by the king to someone of the same surname was precious jade, demonstrating closeness among relations. The gift given by the king to someone of a different surname was a gift received from a distant land, as tribute to remind them not to forget their loyalty to the Zhou. So this gift of the Sushen people's tribute was given to Chen. If the sovereign wants to see if this is true, he can look in the state vaults. He should find more there."

The duke sent someone to look, and he found them there in a metal cabinet.[12]

16.4

郯子朝魯, 魯人問曰: "少昊氏以鳥名官, 何也?"對曰: "吾祖也, 我知之。昔黄帝以雲紀官, 故爲雲師而雲名。炎帝以火, 共工以水, 大昊以龍, 其義一也。我高祖少昊摯之立也, 鳳鳥適至, 是以紀之於鳥, 故爲鳥師而鳥名。自顓頊氏以來, 不能紀遠, 乃紀於近, 爲民師而命以民事, 則不能故也。"孔子聞之, 遂見郯子而學焉。既而告人曰: "吾聞之: '天子失官, 學在四夷。'猶信。"

The Viscount of Tan paid a state visit to Lu. A person of Lu asked him, "Why did Shao Hao name government posts after birds?"

The viscount replied, "Since I am a descendant, I know the answer. The Yellow Chief named government posts after clouds. That's why there was the 'cloud-general' and other 'cloud' names. Chief Yan using 'fire,' Gonggong using 'water,' and Tai Hao

12. There are two ways to interpret this story. The first and most straightforward way would take the first sentence to read: "This falcon has come from far away." Such an interpretation would depict a strange occurrence in which a falcon from far away suddenly appears in the duke's courtyard, and Confucius, from his vast historical knowledge, would identify the place of the falcon's origin. The problem with such an account is that the Sushen area borders present-day North Korea, some 1,300 miles from the state of Chen. It is highly unlikely that a falcon could fly that distance pierced by an arrow. It also does not account for the same kind of arrow being in the state vaults. A second and more plausible interpretation is a bit more complicated but accounts for all of the facts. Given the antipathy that often meets Confucius when he travels, due to the insecurity of local officials who fear for their own jobs if he is brought in (as we see in Chen in 20.1), the likely scenario is that someone highly placed in Chen wished to manufacture an ill omen (a dead falcon struck by a strange arrow) that would prompt the ruler to ask Confucius to leave. The plotters, who purloined one such arrow from the vaults, did not count on Confucius having the background knowledge that he had. Interpreting *du* 櫝 as *gui* 匱, following Wang Su.

using 'dragon' were all the same kind of thing. When my first ancestor Shao Hao ascended the throne, a *feng* bird appeared, and so he named government posts after birds; thus, there was the 'bird-general' and other 'bird' names. Since Zhuanxu, rulers stopped naming posts for things distant from daily life and instead named them for things more closely related to daily life, such as the 'people's general.' They named things after features of people's lives, and so things are not like they were before."

After Confucius heard about this, he paid a visit to the Viscount of Tan to learn from him. He then reported, "I have heard that when knowledge of our system of civil service was lost to us,[13] it was preserved in the Yi people. This is believable."

16.5

邾隱公朝于魯，子貢觀焉。邾子執玉高，其容仰。定公受玉卑，其容俯。子貢曰："以禮觀之，二君者將有死亡焉。夫禮，生死存亡之體，將左右、周旋，進退、俯仰，於是乎取之；朝、祀、喪、戎，於是乎觀之。今正月相朝，而皆不度，心以亡矣。嘉事不體，何以能久？高、仰，驕也；卑、俯，替也。驕近亂，替近疾。若爲主，其先亡乎？"夏五月，公薨，又邾子出奔。孔子曰："賜不幸而言中，是賜多言。"

When Duke Yin of Zhū paid a state visit to Lu, Zigong was in attendance. The duke lifted a piece of tribute jade high in their air and raised his face up respectfully. In humbly accepting the jade, Duke Ding lowered his head.

Later, Zigong remarked: "From the perspective of *li*, these two leaders will soon pass away, in keeping with what they've done. According to *li*, one's survival depends on proper movements, whether to left and right, turning around, forward and back, or facing up or down. State visits, sacrificial ceremonies, funerals, and military campaigns all take their cues from these. It is the first month of the year, and for them to have a state meeting and yet not follow the standard protocol shows that their sentiments are already a lost cause. When they don't have the wherewithal to get even a simple favorable affair right, how can they survive for long? Raising something high and looking up is a sign of arrogance. Taking on a humble demeanor and looking down is a sign of neglect. Arrogance is prone to chaos, and neglect to disaster.[14] Since our ruler is the host, I'm guessing that he will be the first to go."[15]

13. *Lost to us*: When Zhou King You was defeated, the Zhou capital was razed. When it was reestablished to the east in Luoyang, it was but a shell of its former self, with much institutional and textual knowledge lost forever.

14. Historically speaking, Duke Ding was, indeed, neglectful of the government. Rather than suggesting that one incidence of non-*li* behavior results in disaster, Zigong seems to be saying that the behavior here shows a pattern with predictable results.

15. This episode also appears in CQZZ ("Ding" 15.1) but with the subsequent proof of fact stated in future episodes rather than at the end of the passage.

In the fifth month of that year, Duke Ding passed away. Later, Duke Yin was forced into exile.

Confucius said, "Ci was right on the mark in discussing this unfortunate affair, but he said too much."

16.6

孔子在陳，陳侯就之燕遊焉。行路之人云："魯司鐸災，及宗廟。"以告孔子。子曰："所及者，其桓、僖之廟。"陳侯曰："何以知之?"子曰："禮，祖有功而宗有德，故不毀其廟焉。今桓、僖之親盡矣，又功德不足以存其廟，而魯不毀，是以天災加之。" 三日，魯使至，問焉，則桓、僖也。陳侯謂子貢曰："吾乃今知聖人之可貴。"對曰："君之知之，可矣，未若專其道而行其化之善也。"

Once when Confucius was in Chen, he and the duke went on an excursion. A passerby said, "A government office caught fire in Lu and it spread to ancestral temples." This was reported to Confucius.

Confucius said, "The temples it spread to were probably those of Huan and Xi."[16]

The duke asked, "How do you know that?"

Confucius said, "In the good done by *li*, there is merit that accrues to one's ancestors, which does not allow for the temples to them to be destroyed.[17] Dukes Huan and Xi were only distantly related to the Duke of Zhou,[18] and they did not do anything in their lifetimes to accumulate merit sufficient to keep their temples intact. Lu didn't destroy the temples. It took a natural disaster to do that."

Three days later, an emissary from Lu arrived. When asked about it, he responded that it was indeed the temples of Huan and Xi.

The duke said to Zigong, "Now I understand the esteem due a sage."

Zigong replied, "Better than understanding him would be spreading his *dao* and enacting his transformative excellence."[19]

16. A detailed account of the fire appears in CQZZ ("Ai" 3.2) but ends here, without an account of the subsequent discussion.

17. The separate terms *zu* 祖 and *zong* 宗, which are combined here and interpreted as ancestors are viewed by Kramers (1950) as technical terms for distinct ceremonies (as in those mentioned in the entry for "Five sacrificial ceremonies" in the glossary).

18. *Only distantly related to the Duke of Zhou, qin jin* 親盡: The Chinese is actually more direct than this, saying that the blood relation came to an end. The same locution occurs in 39.2 with respect to Confucius' ancestors and their distance from Song nobility. There is a long-standing belief in China that the obligations and merit related to blood relations do not extend beyond five generations. The meaning in this phrase is that because Dukes Huan and Xi are more than five generations after the Duke of Zhou (the founding ruler of Lu), then the spirit of the Duke of Zhou would not be there to protect their temples from disaster.

19. Compare 15.4.

16.7

陽虎既奔齊，自齊奔晉，適趙氏。孔子聞之，謂子路曰："趙氏其世有亂乎！"子路曰："權不在焉，豈能爲亂?"孔子曰："非汝所知。夫陽虎親富而不親仁，有寵於季孫，又將殺之，不克而奔，求容於齊。齊人囚之，乃亡歸晉。是齊、魯二國已去其疾。趙簡子好利而多信，必溺其説而從其謀。禍敗所終，非一世可知也。"

When Yang Hu fled Lu, he first went to Qi and then from Qi to Jin to meet with the Zhaos. When Confucius heard about this, he said to Zilu, "The Zhaos will soon come to ruin."

Zilu said, "But the Zhaos aren't in power. How can they come to ruin?"

Confucius said, "You don't understand. Yang Hu cozies up to wealth, not to *ren*. He was favored by Jisun, and when he tried to kill Jisun, he failed and had to flee. Then he sought refuge in Qi. Qi tried to jail him, and so he fled and sought refuge in Jin. Qi and Lu have now rid themselves of this disease. Zhao Jianzi is always looking to benefit himself and is trusting. No doubt he will fall under Yang Hu's influence. The disaster may reach across generations."[20]

16.8

季康子問於孔子曰："今周十二月，夏之十月，而猶有螽，何也?"孔子對曰："丘聞之，火伏而後蟄者畢。今火猶西流，司歷過也。"季康子曰："所失者，幾月也?"孔子曰："於夏十月，火既没矣。今火見，再失閏也。"

Ji Kangzi asked Confucius, "Right now it is the twelfth month according to the Zhou calendar and the tenth month according to the Xia calendar,[21] and yet there are still grasshoppers about. Why is that?"

Confucius replied, "I've learned that insects don't go completely into hibernation until after Antares disappears from the night sky. Antares is still in the night sky. The incongruity is the fault of the Keeper of the Calendar."

Ji Kangzi said, "How many months is it off?"

Confucius said, "Antares is supposed to be gone by the tenth month of the Xia calendar, but it's still visible.[22] We are behind two intercalary months."

20. Zhao Jianzi did indeed bring in Yang Hu and did come to power (see 22.2 and 41.15), and Zhao soon attacked and killed members of his own family. (Zheng, Wu, and Yang 2000)

21. In other words, late fall/early winter. For more information, see "Calendar" in the glossary.

22. At the latitude of Qufu (35.58°), Antares is visible in the southwestern sky at night during the fall. It gradually moves south until it is barely visible at dusk during the first week of November. ("Night Sky" 2022)

16.9

吴王夫差將與哀公見晋侯。子服景伯對使者曰：“王合諸侯，則伯率侯牧以見於王；伯合諸侯，則侯率子男以見於伯。今諸侯會，而君與寡君見晋君，則晋成爲伯也。且執事以伯召諸侯，而以侯終之，何利之有焉？”吴人乃止。既而悔之，遂囚景伯。伯謂大宰嚭曰：“魯將以十月上辛有事于上帝、先王，季辛而畢。何也世有職焉，自襄已來，未之改。若其不會，則祝宗將曰‘吴實然’。”嚭言於夫差，歸之。子貢聞之，見於孔子曰：“子服氏之子拙於説矣，以實獲囚，以詐得免。”孔子曰：“吴子爲夷德，可欺而不可以實。是聽者之蔽，非説者之拙也。”

King Fuchai of Wu was preparing to travel with Lu's Duke Ai for a summit called by the sovereign of Jin.[23] The Lu official Zifu Jingbo was in Jin and said to his counterpart there, “When the king convenes the nobles, they are led by one of their own. When a noble convenes nobles, a marquis leads the viscounts and barons. In our upcoming meeting with Jin, Jin plays the part of the noble convening nobles. What does it benefit your ruler to play the role of the marquis for the duration?”[24] Wu immediately put a stop to it but soon, coming to regret that decision, they captured and imprisoned Jingbo.

Jingbo said to Pi, the prime minister of Wu, “The auspicious day of the first week of the tenth month is coming up, when Lu will perform ceremonies to the high ancestors and the Ancient Kings, lasting until the auspicious day of the last week of the month.[25] My family has held our current position without interruption for many generations—since the time of Duke Xiang. If I am not present for the ceremony, the officiant will say that it is the fault of Wu.” Pi told Fuchai, who released Jingbo.

Zigong learned of this and said to Confucius: “This Zifu was an inept persuader. By telling the truth, he got himself jailed, and then he lied to get himself released.”

Confucius said, “The Wu follow a kind of barbarian virtue. With them, it is more effective to lie than to tell the truth. It was the benightedness of the listener, not the fault of the speaker.”[26]

23. The reason that Lu is associating itself with Wu is that Wu had asserted itself as a contender for superpower status, and Lu had paired with Wu against Qi, although it was a rocky relationship, as this episode shows. Following the chronology of CQZZ (“Ai” 13.4), where a version of this story also appears, this is the year 482, two years after a Lu-Wu alliance had defeated Qi in battle (see 37.2).

24. The ruler of Wu had declared himself king, so appearing to be anything lower would be embarrassing.

25. A week in premodern China was ten days long. Each month had three weeks. Each week had a rotating day that was considered more auspicious than the others. (Wilkinson 2022)

26. The version of this story that appears in CQZZ (“Ai” 13.4) provides more details but without Zigong's or Confucius' evaluations at the end.

16.10

叔孫氏之車士曰子鉏商，採薪於大野，獲麟焉，折其前左足，載以歸。叔孫以爲不祥，棄之於郭外，使人告孔子曰："有麕而角者，何也？"孔子往觀之，曰："麟也。胡爲來哉？胡爲來哉？"反袂拭面，涕泣沾衿。叔孫聞之，然後取之。子貢問曰："夫子何泣爾？"孔子曰："麟之至，爲明王也。出非其時而見害，吾是以傷焉。"

Shusun's driver, named Zichu Shang, was in Daye Marsh collecting firewood when he captured a *lin* with a broken left front leg. He hauled it back to the city. Shusun saw it as an unlucky omen and so released it outside the city wall and sent someone to ask Confucius: "It looks like a water deer but with antlers.[27] What is it?"

Confucius went to see for himself, then said, "It's a *lin*. Why has it come? Why has it come?" He rolled his sleeve back and wiped his face, the tears dampening the hem.

Shusun heard about this and had the *lin* brought back.

Zigong asked Confucius, "Why did you cry just then?"

Confucius said, "The arrival of a *lin* portends an enlightened king. But its injury suggests that it is not time yet. That's why I felt crestfallen."

27. Water deer is a species of deer native to China that has tusks, not antlers. The character translated as "antlers" is *jiao* 角, which can also mean horn. The number is not indicated. We default to the plural on the assumption that if there were just one, it would be indicated, as in the *Er ya* entry quoted under "*Lin*" in the glossary.

17

Duke Ai Asks about Governing

In an extended, intricate dialogue with Lu Duke Ai, Confucius explains that a theory of government extends beyond the civil service and straightforward political theory to include a wide spectrum of concerns, with moral cultivation of the individual at one end and the working of the cosmos at the other. Good government, Confucius says, ultimately depends on strong interpersonal relationships, founded on love and respect, within every level and among all the levels. Appended to this conversation is a conversation between Confucius and Zai Wo. As in chapter 23, Zai Wo's questions tend toward the esoteric, but here Confucius' explanation provides a reinforcement of the prior message in the chapter: in all of our relationships, and in the *li* that we use to navigate them, expressions of human emotion are the ultimate basis and motivation.

17.1

哀公問政於孔子。孔子對曰："文武之政，布在方策。其人存，則其政舉；其人亡，則其政息。天道敏生，人道敏政，地道敏樹。夫政者，猶蒲盧也，待化以成，故爲政在於得人。取人以身，修道以仁。仁者，人也，親親爲大；義者，宜也，尊賢爲大。親親之殺，尊賢之等，禮所以生也。禮者，政之本也。是以君子不可以不修身。思修身，不可以不事親；思事親，不可以不知人；思知人，不可以不知天。天下之達道有五，其所以行之者三。曰：君臣也，父子也，夫婦也，昆弟也，朋友也。五者，天下之達道。智、仁、勇三者，天下之達德也。所以行之者一也。或生而知之，或學而知之，或困而知之，及其知之，一也。或安而行之，或利而行之，或勉强而行之，及其成功，一也。"公曰："子之言，美矣至矣！寡人實固，不足以成之也。"孔子曰："好學近乎智，力行近乎仁，知耻近乎勇。知斯三者，則知所以修身；知所以修身，則知所以治人；知所以治人，則能成天下國家者矣。"

Duke Ai asked Confucius about governing.[1]

1. Most of the text in sections 17.1–17.3, minus the dialogue setting, appears nearly verbatim in section 20 (following Zhu Xi's arrangement) of the "Zhong yong" chapter of the *Li ji*, with a small part also appearing in the *Mencius*. Section 17.5, with some divergences, appears in the "Ji yi" chapter of the *Li ji*. Section 17.4 appears in no other extant text.

Confucius replied, "The governing of Kings Wen and Wu has been written down in books.[2] Anyone can come along and put it into effect. Without such a person, that kind of governing perishes.[3] The *dao* of *tian* promotes life; the *dao* of people promotes governing; the *dao* of the earth promotes growth. Governing is like a gourd—you have to wait for it to develop.[4]

"In the same way, good government depends on getting the right people. Selecting people depends on one's character, and cultivating oneself in *dao* depends on *ren*.[5]

"*Ren* has to do with people and relies on affection for one's parents and relatives[6] as its first priority. *Yi* has to do with appropriateness[7] and relies on respecting

2. *Books, fang ce* 方策: planks and slats. In Confucius' time, "books" were made of bamboo or wooden slats bound together with cords and rolled into scrolls for storage. Only a portion of what we would today call a book could be contained in a single scroll.

3. *Anyone . . . such a person, qi ren . . . qi ren* 其人 . . . 其人: Most translators and commentators take the pronouns here to refer either to Kings Wen and Wu or to people like them. It couldn't be a reference just to Kings Wen and Wu, though, because Confucius did not believe that their system perished with King Wu; to the contrary, he believed that the Duke of Zhou and King Cheng maintained it and extended it. Interpreting it to mean *people like them* neglects the previous sentence about the ideas of Kings Wen and Wu being recorded in books. We think that the pronouns refer to anyone who reads their books, making the paragraph more coherent and more relevant to Confucius and his time. Confucius promoted their "books" (the *Documents*) as a blueprint for good government, and it was often so closely studied that it was committed to memory.

4. *You have to wait for it to develop, dai hua yi cheng* 待化以成: This episode occurs almost verbatim in the "Zhong yong" (20), but without this phrase. Gourds had a wide variety of uses in ancient China and would have been familiar to the common person. To function, the gourd has to ripen and then be dried. If put to use before the process is complete, it loses its functionality. (Song 1993)

5. Whereas this sentence consists of two clauses, the parallel in the "Zhong yong" includes a clause between them that also ties them together, as follows: Selecting people depends on one's character, cultivating one's character depends on *dao*, and cultivating *dao* depends on *ren*. We added "oneself in" to the final clause to convey the more complete meaning.

6. *Affection for one's parents and relatives, qin qin* 親親: In the series of passages in this chapter, the term *qin qin* presents a challenge to the translator because in 17.3 (爵其能,重其祿 . . . 所以篤親親), the second *qin* clearly means relatives and not parents, and yet in 17.3 (同其好惡所以篤親親), 17.1 (*shi qin* 事親), and 17.4 (*xiao yu qin* 孝於親), it cannot refer to relatives broadly and can only refer to either parents or to parents and older relatives. Normally, we would translate differentially according to context, but the context here, where *qin qin* is used as a semantic unit, demands that it be translated uniformly. Most interpretations of the parallel passage in the "Zhong yong" do not contain the line with *xiao* in 17.4, ignore the danger of going along with the preferences of relatives broadly, and ignore the inherent directionality of *shi* in 17.1, rendering all instances of the second *qin* as "relatives." We instead translate it as "parents and relatives," with the understanding that in some contexts "relatives" means older relatives. Including the notion of parents in the translation maintains consistency throughout, preserves Confucius' repeated emphasis on *xiao*, and is consistent with *Analects* 1.2, which says that *xiao* and *ti* are the root of *ren*.

7. *People . . . appropriateness, ren . . . yi* 人 . . . 義: The Chinese for *people* and *appropriateness*, respectively, are pronounced *ren* and *yi*, so the Chinese says paronomastically: *ren* is *ren*, and *yi* is *yi*. In other

capable and virtuous people as its first priority. *Li* arises out of the hierarchy[8] of affection for one's parents and respecting capable and virtuous people. *Li* is the root of good governing. For this reason, a *junzi* cannot but cultivate himself.

"Cultivating oneself must involve serving one's parents and relatives. Serving one's parents and relatives must involve understanding others. Understanding others must involve understanding *tian*.[9]

"There are five ways in this world of achieving *dao*[10] and three ways of putting it into effect. The five ways are: lord-vassal, father-son, husband-wife, older brother-younger brother, and friend-friend.

"The three ways of achieving *de* in this world are: wisdom, *ren*, and courage. These ways of putting *de* into effect are unified in one overarching way. Some understand this from birth, some from study, and some from hardship, but in terms of understanding, they are the same. Some put it into effect in a serene way, some in a beneficial way, and some in a forced way, but in terms of having developed into the accomplishment, they are the same."

The duke replied, "Beautifully said and right on the mark! I am truly obstinate, however, and do not have the wherewithal to develop this."

Confucius said, "Having a fondness for learning is akin to wisdom. Working energetically is akin to *ren*. Having a sense of shame is akin to courage.[11] If you understand these three, then you understand how to cultivate yourself. If you understand how to cultivate yourself, then you understand how to govern others. If you understand how to govern others, then you can develop[12] a state renowned throughout the land."

---

words, the virtue *ren* is defined in terms of humanity, and the virtue *yi* is defined in terms of what is appropriate.

8. *Hierarchy*: Interpreting *sha* 殺 and *deng* 等 as synonyms meaning hierarchy. Instead of *sha*, the Tongwen edition has *jiao* 教, in which case the sentence would read: *Li* arises out of the teaching of affection for one's parents and the hierarchy of respecting wise and capable people.

9. We follow Ames and Hall (2001) in viewing *si* 思 as a syntactic particle with no semantic content.

10. *Achieving dao, da dao* 達道: This phrase is often interpreted in the "Zhong yong" as adjective-noun, viewing *da* as something like "all-pervading" or "universal." Such an interpretation is almost surely anachronistic. In other uses in early texts (e.g., *Zhuangzi*, *Huainanzi*), it is a verb/verbal-noun construction, as interpreted here. The same rationale applies to "achieving" *de* below.

11. *Sense . . . courage*: The connection here may not be obvious, but think of the example of peer pressure, and it begins to become clearer. Now extend that to working in a corrupt environment, where everyone is out for their own benefit, and you see how having a sense of shame can be akin to courage. Of course, the only peer pressure the duke experiences within his own state is from his own personal temptations, but the principle holds. To not give in to one's own desire for personal gain requires a sense of shame, which is akin to having the courage to do the right thing.

12. *Develop, cheng* 成: This entire episode hinges on the word *cheng*, which means to mature or to come to fruition. The episode begins with the metaphor of the gourd maturing. After Confucius has explained

17.2

公曰:“政其盡此而已乎?”孔子曰:“凡爲天下國家有九經,曰:修身也,尊賢也,親親也,敬大臣也,體群臣也,子庶民也,來百工也,柔遠人也,懷諸侯也。夫修身則道立,尊賢則不惑,親親則諸父、兄弟不怨,敬大臣則不眩,體群臣則士之報禮重,子庶民則百姓勸,來百工則財用足,柔遠人則四方歸之,懷諸侯則天下畏之。”

The duke said, "Applying oneself to these are all that is required for good governing?"

Confucius said, "There are nine requirements to become a state renowned throughout the land. They are: (1) cultivate yourself, (2) show reverence for capable and virtuous people, (3) be close to your parents and relatives, (4) respect high officials,[13] (5) understand the circumstances of the lower officials, (6) treat the common people like your own children, (7) attract artisans, (8) be accepting of people from distant places, (9) embrace nobility across the land.

"Cultivating yourself will allow the *dao* to be firmly established. Showing reverence for the capable and virtuous will help you solve problems. Being close to your parents and relatives will avert resentment from your uncles and brothers. Respecting high officials will prevent short-sightedness. Understanding the circumstances of lower officials will cause them to repay you with deeply felt *li*. Treating the common people as your own children will motivate them. Attracting artisans of all trades will bring sufficient revenue. Being accepting of people from distant places will cause people from the four directions to turn toward you. Embracing nobility across the land will cause the entire land to hold you in awe."

17.3

公曰:“爲之奈何?”孔子曰:“齊潔盛服,非禮不動,所以修身也;去讒遠色,賤財而貴德,所以尊賢也;爵其能,重其祿,同其好惡,所以篤親親也;官盛任使,所以敬大臣也;忠信重祿,所以勸士也;時使薄斂,所以子百姓也;日省月考,既廩稱事,所以來百工也;送往迎來,嘉善而矜不能,所以綏遠人也;繼絶世,舉廢邦,治亂持危,朝聘以時,厚往而薄來,所以懷諸侯也。治天下國家有九經,其所以行之者一也。凡事豫則立,不豫則廢,言前定則不跲,事前定則不困,行前定則不疚,道前定則不窮。在

what is required of a leader, the king says he does not have the wherewithal to *cheng*, to develop it, to bring it to fruition. In the final sentence, Confucius reiterates that what can be developed, what can come to fruition, if he just is willing to cultivate himself, is nothing less than a well-ordered state. See also 18.3.

13. What's the difference between items 2 and 4? As we see repeatedly in the *Dialogues*, showing reverence for the wise and capable means welcoming any person of wisdom and high capacity from any station in life into a role in the government. That role could be as a high minister, but it could also be as an occasional adviser. The point is to display a welcoming attitude, so that when their assistance is needed it will be available.

下位不獲于上，民弗可得而治矣。獲于上有道，不信于友，不獲于上矣；信于友有道，不順于親，不信于友矣；順于親有道，反諸身不誠，不順于親矣；誠身有道，不明于善，不誠于身矣。誠者，天之至道也；誠之者，人之道也。夫誠，弗勉而中，不思而得，從容中道，聖人之所以體定也；誠之者，擇善而固執之者也。"

The duke said, "How are all of these to be done?"

Confucius replied, "(1) The way to cultivate yourself is to engage in purifying fasts, to dress well, and not to engage in any activity that is contrary to *li*.

"(2) The way to show reverence for the capable and virtuous is to eschew slander, distance yourself from debauchery, disesteem wealth, and esteem virtue.

"(3) The way to really get close to your parents and relatives is to reward the capable, provide them with substantial income, and go along with their preferences.[14]

"(4) The way to respect high officials is to give them abundant human resources to carry out their responsibilities.

"(5) The way to encourage[15] lower officials is to reward conscientiousness and trustworthiness with substantial salaries.

"(6) The way to treat the common people as your own children is to conscript them to work on government projects only at appropriate times and to minimize the amount of taxes you collect.

"(7) The way to attract artisans of all trades is to provide daily oversight and monthly inspections and to match a person's income with that person's work.

"(8) The way to reassure people from distant places is to treat them hospitably, commend good behavior, and show sympathy for those of lesser ability.

"(9) The way to embrace nobility across the land is to restore broken lineages, revive destroyed states, suppress rebellions, take charge of crises, call the nobles to court at appropriate times, give them much, and expect little.

"The nine requirements for governing a state that is renowned throughout the land can be put into practice in a single way: in all affairs, preparation[16] yields

14. Rewarding capability applies to relatives, and going along with preferences applies to parents.

15. In 17.2 and 17.3, one would expect the key elements of the nine requirements to be the same: for example, cultivate the self . . . the way to cultivate the self; respect the wise and capable . . . the way to respect the wise and capable, and so on. In the *Dialogues*, there are two divergences from the first mention to the second. "Understanding" (*ti* 體) lower officials in the first becomes "encouraging" (*quan* 勸) them in the second. "Being accepting" (*rou* 柔) of people from distant places becomes "reassuring" (*sui* 綏) them. In the "Zhong yong," the verbs in requirements 2–7 all change to "encourage" (*quan* 勸) in the second mention. The emphasis in the "Zhong yong," then, is on instrumentalizing all relations, whereas in the *Dialogues* it remains on distinct ways of interacting in distinct relationships.

16. *Preparation, yu* 豫: *Xunzi* (27.24) defines this term as "contemplating disaster ahead of time."

success, and lack of preparation ends in failure. Decide beforehand what to say, and you won't get tripped up. Decide beforehand what to do, and you won't get trapped. Decide beforehand how to act, and you won't end up in grief. Decide beforehand how to put the *dao* into action, and your success will be limitless.[17]

"If those below do not feel supported by those above, the people will be impossible to govern. There is a *dao* for achieving support from those above—not being trusted by friends will result in not being supported by those above. There is a *dao* for being trusted by friends—not accommodating the wishes of one's parents will result in not being trusted by friends. There is a *dao* for accommodating the wishes of one's parents—not sincerely developing yourself upon introspection, you cannot accommodate the wishes of your parents. There is a *dao* for sincerely developing oneself—to not be clear about the good, one cannot sincerely develop oneself.

"Sincere development is the ultimate *dao* of *tian*. To sincerely develop something is the *dao* of people. To sincerely develop is to hit the mark without forcing it, to understand without overthinking, to effortlessly accord with the *dao*. It is how sages remain serene. Someone who acts on sincere development[18] selects the good and stubbornly maintains it."

17.4

公曰："子之教寡人備矣。敢問行之所始。"孔子曰："立愛自親始，教民睦也；立敬自長始，教民順也。教之慈睦，而民貴有親；教以敬，而民貴用命。民既孝於親，又順以聽命，措諸天下，無所不可。"公曰："寡人既得聞此言也，懼不能果行而獲罪咎。"

The duke said, "I fully accept your teachings. To put them into practice, where should I begin?"

Confucius said, "If you establish love by beginning with your own parents, you can teach the people to have strong relationships. If you establish respect by beginning with your own elders, you can teach the people to live amiably. Teach them to be kind and to build strong relationships, and the people will prioritize their parents.

17. In this sentence and the preceding three, there is a parallel structure: decide something beforehand, and you won't end up in a dire situation. This sentence is no different, except that the final negative *bu qiong* 不窮 has a dual meaning. Following the preceding three sentences, it could justifiably be rendered "you won't end up in dire straits." However, another common usage in other early texts, especially when associated with the functioning of the *dao*, is its meaning as unlimited, which we tentatively select here. There is no standard interpretation.

18. *Sincere development, cheng* 誠: The term *cheng* 誠 is discussed briefly in the introduction, just to say that it does not figure prominently in the *Dialogues*. Its use here is the first mention of it in these sections that overlap with the "Zhong yong," and yet in the "Zhong yong" it is the first of many mentions. Here, it seems to be closely related to *cheng* 成 (to develop) and we translate in that sense.

Teach them with respect, and the people will prioritize their duty to the state. As soon as the people treat their parents with *xiao*, live amiably, and perform their duty to the state, and these policies can emanate outward to the whole land, anything is possible."

The duke said, "Even though I've now heard your teachings, I fear that I cannot effectively put them into practice and will instead fall into error."

17.5

宰我問於孔子曰:“吾聞鬼神之名,而不知所謂,敢問焉。”孔子曰:“人生有氣有魄。氣者,神之盛也;魄者,鬼之盛也。夫生必死,死必歸土,此謂鬼;魂氣歸天,此謂神。合鬼與神而享之,教之至也。骨肉弊於下,化爲野土,其氣發揚于上者,此神之著也。聖人因物之精,制爲之極,明命鬼神,以爲民之則,而猶以是爲未足也,故築爲宮室,設爲宗祧,春秋祭祀,以别親疏,教民反古復始,不敢忘其所由生也。衆人服自此,聽且速焉。教以二端,二端既立,報以二禮:建設朝事,燔燎膻薌,所以報氣也;薦黍稷,羞肺肝,加以郁鬯,所以報魄也。此教民修本、反始、崇愛,上下用情,禮之至也。君子反古復始,不忘其所由生,是以致其敬,發其情,竭力從事,不敢不自盡也,此之謂大教。昔者,文王之祭也,事死如事生,思死而不欲生,忌日則必哀,稱諱則如見親,祀之忠也。思之深,如見親之所愛。祭欲見親之顏色者,其唯文王與!《詩》云:‘明發不寐,有懷二人。’則文王之謂與!祭之明日,明發不寐,有懷二人,敬而致之,又從而思之。祭之日,樂與哀半,饗之必樂,已至必哀,孝子之情也。文王爲能得之矣。”

Zai Wo asked Confucius, "I have heard of the terms *gui* and *shen*[19] but don't know what they mean. May I inquire about them?"

Confucius said, "In a human life, there are *qi* and *po*. *Qi* is the vitality of the *shen*, and *po* is the vitality of the *gui*. Death inevitably follows life and is inevitably returned to the soil. This is called *gui*. The *hun qi* returns to the sky. This is called *shen*. To bring *gui* and *shen* of the deceased together by offering a sacrifice is the ultimate achievement of proper instruction. As the bones and flesh rot underground and transform into soil, the *qi* dissipates upward. This is the radiance of the *shen*.[20]

19. The terms *gui* and *shen* often form a pair in Classical Chinese and are readily translated as "ghosts" and "spirits" (see, for example, 31.4 and 32.9). There was some question in Confucius' time and subsequent centuries about how seriously to take the metaphysics behind these ideas. In the *Analects* (6.22), for example, Confucius says to respect ghosts and spirits but keep one's distance. In *Analects* 11.12, Zilu asks about serving ghosts and spirits, and Confucius says, "Being unable to properly serve people, how can one speak of serving ghosts and spirits?" In *Analects* 8.21, Confucius praises Yǔ for his great *xiao* with respect to ghosts and spirits. The two terms together seem to refer to one's deceased relatives in the context of paying respect to them through sacrificial ceremony. Here, Zaiwo wants to know more about what exactly these spiritual things are, and Confucius obliges.

20. The gist of this paragraph seems to be that there are two spiritual aspects to the human being—the *hun*, which is associated with the spirit of a person and ascends to the sky after death, and the *po*,

"Setting standards in response to the nature of things, sages clearly established the terms *gui* and *shen* as guideposts for the people. And knowing that this alone would be insufficient, they also built temples and altars so that sacrifices could be made at appropriate times of the year, thereby distinguishing close relatives from distant ones and teaching the people to remember the past and return to their beginnings, reluctant to forget that from which they sprang.

"With these as a starting point, the people were able to quickly pick up on the ideas. When these two elements became firmly established in people's minds, they were manifested in the ritual of Bao, of which there were two kinds. They created a morning service involving the burning of mutton fat, which served as a way to *bao qi*. They also sacrificed millet and animal organs, with the addition of fragrant wine, which served to *bao po*.[21] These taught the people to foster the root, return to the beginning, and honor loved ones. Expressing feelings from top to bottom—that is the ultimate achievement of *li*.

"A *junzi* remembers the past and returns to his beginnings, never forgetting that from which he sprang. In this way, he expresses respect and proper emotion, giving his all in his service, always pushing himself to the limit. This is called the great teaching.

"In the past, when King Wen performed sacrifices, he served the dead just as if he were serving the living, he yearned for the dead as if he had no wish to go on living, he would inevitably be struck with grief on the anniversary of his parents' death, and when they were brought up in conversation it was as if they were right in front of him. This is an example of conscientious lineal sacrifice. The depth of his yearning was so profound that it was as if he could see his parents' favorite things. Surely, only King Wen was able to sacrifice with the fervent desire to see the very faces of his parents! A poem says:

> As the sun rises, I cannot sleep,
> For my parents are on my mind.[22]

This has to be talking about King Wen! On the day after the sacrifice, he couldn't sleep as the sun rose, having his parents on his mind. He reached out to them with respect, and his remembrance continued long afterward. On the day of the sacrifice, there is always a mixture of joy and sorrow. At the banquet, there is always joy, and when it ends there is always sorrow. These are the sentiments of a *xiao* child. King Wen would know all about it."

---

which is associated with the body of a person and descends to the earth after death. Thus, *hun* is associated with *shen* and *po* with *gui*. Among scholars, there is some uncertainty about the details and level of popularity of this belief. See also 12.15n14. (Brashier 1996)

21. See "Bao (ceremony)" in the glossary.

22. These lines are from the poem "Quite Small" (#196; found today in the "Xiao ya" section of the *Poems*), which is a lament about losing one's parents. It is probably not a coincidence that the rare term for gourd in 17.1 also appears in this poem.

18

Yan Hui

As the title suggests, this chapter is devoted to dialogues involving Yan Hui, Confucius' star pupil. His depicted role resembles that of a teacher offering advice, correcting the behavior of others, demonstrating discernment and perspicacity, and commenting on the qualities of prominent figures.

18.1

魯定公問於顏回曰："子亦聞東野畢之善御乎?"對曰："善則善矣。雖然，其馬將必佚。"定公色不悅，謂左右曰："君子固有誣人也。"顏回退。後三日，牧來訴之曰："東野畢之馬佚，兩驂曳，兩服入于廄。"公聞之，越席而起，促駕召顏回。回至，公曰："前日寡人問吾子以東野畢之御，而子曰善則善矣，其馬將佚，不識吾子奚以知之?"顏回對曰："以政知之。昔者，帝舜巧於使民，造父巧於使馬。舜不窮其民力，造父不窮其馬力，是以舜無佚民，造父無佚馬。今東野畢之御也，升馬執轡，銜體正矣；步驟馳騁，朝禮畢矣；歷險致遠，馬力盡矣，然而猶乃求馬不已。臣以此知之。"公曰："善！誠若吾子之言也。吾子之言，其義大矣，願少進乎。"顏回曰："臣聞之：鳥窮則啄，獸窮則攫，人窮則詐，馬窮則佚。自古及今，未有窮其下而能無危者也。"公悅，遂以告孔子。孔子對曰："夫其所以爲顏回者，此之類也，豈足多哉?"

Duke Ding of Lu asked Yan Hui, "Surely you have heard about Dongye Bi, who excels at charioteering?"

Yan Hui replied, "To excel is to excel. Despite his successes, his horses will one day flee."

Duke Ding took on a look of dissatisfaction and said to those around him, "You, sir, are slandering someone."

Yan Hui departed.

Three days later, the pasture manager reported: "Dongye Bi's horses have fled. The team's two outside horses jumped the fence and the two inside horses returned to the stable." When the duke heard this, he rose from his mat and hastily called for Yan Hui to return.

When Hui arrived, the duke said, "A few days ago, I asked you about Dongye Bi's charioteering and you said, 'To excel is to excel, but his horses will flee.' I don't see how you could have known that."

Yan Hui replied, "It can be known through the principles of governing. In the past, Shun had a knack for motivating[1] the people. Zaofu had a knack for motivating horses. Shun never pushed the people to their physical limit. Zaofu never pushed his horses to their physical limit. As a result, Shun never lost his people, and Zaofu never lost his horses. When Dongye Bi charioteers, he ascends the chariot and seizes the reins with the bit firmly in the horses' mouths to keep them in line. He presses them to gallop from start to finish, driving them long distances to the point of exhaustion. He keeps this up relentlessly. This is how I knew."

The duke exclaimed, "Excellent! Your words ring true, and they have a deeper meaning. I'd like to hear you say a little more."

Yan Hui said, "I've heard that, when pushed to the limit, birds peck, wild animals claw, people become treacherous, and horses flee. From ancient times to now, there has never been someone who pushed his subordinates to the limit and did not experience a crisis."

Overjoyed, the duke reported the conversation to Confucius.

Confucius replied, "Yan Hui is who he is because of things like this. Need more be said?"

18.2

孔子在衛, 昧旦晨興, 顔回侍側, 聞哭者之聲甚哀。子曰: "回, 汝知此何所哭乎?" 對曰: "回以此哭聲, 非但爲死者而已, 又有生離別者也。"子曰: "何以知之?"對曰: "回聞桓山之鳥, 生四子焉, 羽翼既成, 將分於四海, 其母悲鳴而送之, 哀聲有似於此, 謂其往而不返也。回竊以音類知之。"孔子使人問哭者, 果曰: "父死家貧, 賣子以葬, 與子長决。"子曰: "回也, 善於識音矣。"

One day in Wei, Confucius rose before dawn with Yan Hui attentively at his side. They heard the sound of anguished weeping.[2]

Confucius said, "Hui, can you discern the reason behind this person's crying?"

Yan Hui replied, "From the sound of it, the crying is not just on account of someone's death. It also has something to do with parting in this life."

Confucius said, "How can you tell?"

Yan Hui replied, "I've heard that the birds of Huan Mountain have a brood of four eggs, and after the chicks fledge they scatter to the four seas. Their mother sends

1. *Motivating, shi* 使: to drive, control, steer.

2. It is not unusual in traditional Chinese communities for houses to be built so close together that voices can be heard from one to the next.

them off with a baleful cry. That sound of sorrow resembles what we are hearing now—someone is departing and will not return. I've used the similarity in sound to discern the meaning."[3]

Confucius sent someone to inquire of the person crying.

Sure enough, he reported, "The family is destitute, so when the grandfather passed away, they had to sell the grandson[4] in order to bury the grandfather.[5] Father and son will be separated forever."

Confucius said, "Hui, you are very good at discerning sounds."

18.3

顏回問於孔子曰:"成人之行若何?"子曰:"達于情性之理,通於物類之變,知幽明之故,睹遊氣之原。若此可謂成人矣。既能成人,而又加之以仁義禮樂,成人之行也。若乃窮神知禮,德之盛也。"

Yan Hui asked Confucius, "What is the conduct of a fully developed[6] person like?"

Confucius said, "A fully developed person comprehends the order behind the tendencies and natures of things, the changes among species, the reasons behind the visible and the invisible, and the origins of the circulation of air.[7] The addition of *ren*, *yi*, *li*, and music make for the conduct of the developed person. What's more, the fullness of *de* lies in the total comprehension of both *li* and the mysterious subtleties of things."[8]

18.4

顏回問於孔子曰:"臧文仲、武仲孰賢?"孔子曰:"武仲賢哉!"顏回曰:"武仲世稱聖人,而身不免於罪,是智不足稱也;好言兵討,而挫銳於邾,是智不足名也。夫文仲其身雖歿,而言不朽,惡有未賢?"孔子曰:"身歿言立,所以爲文仲也。然猶有不仁者三,

3. This analogy may seem farfetched, but among social animals, convergent evolution can produce similar traits across species. Scientists have discovered, for example, that, like humans, dolphins raise the pitch of their voices when communicating with newborns.

4. The selling of a child by a destitute family could be into servitude (see note 8.17n30 on slavery) or, more benignly, to be raised as an heir in a childless family.

5. See 42.25 for Confucius' view of conserving funeral expenditures.

6. *Fully developed, cheng* 成: See 17.1.

7. This episode echoes passages in the *Xi ci* commentary to the *Changes*, one of which says, "Observing the patterns of the sky overhead and the earth below, one understands the origins behind the visible and the invisible 仰以觀於天文,俯以察於地理,是故知幽明之故." Another says, "The fullness of *de* lies in the total comprehension of the transformations and mysterious subtleties of things 窮神知化,德之盛也."

8. *Mysterious subtleties of things, shen* 神.

不智者三，是則不及武仲也。"回曰："可得聞乎？"孔子曰："下展禽，置六關，妾織蒲，三不仁；設虛器，縱逆祀，祠海鳥，三不智。武仲在齊，齊將有禍，不受其田，以避其難，是智之難也。夫臧武仲之智而不容於魯，抑有由焉，作而不順，施而不恕也夫。《夏書》曰：'念茲在茲，順事恕施。'"

Yan Hui asked Confucius, "Of Zang Wenzhong and Zang Wuzhong, which was more capable and virtuous?"[9]

Confucius said, "Wuzhong was!"

Yan Hui objected, "Wuzhong was known as a sage by society, but he could not avoid being convicted of a crime. This shows that he does not deserve to be called wise. He liked to talk about how to succeed in battle, but he was routed in Zhū.[10] This further shows that he does not deserve to be identified as wise. As for Wenzhong, although he is dead and gone, his words live on, so why can he not be considered capable and virtuous?"

Confucius responded, "Yes, Wenzhong is gone, and his words live on, but there were three cases of un-*ren* behavior and three cases of unwise behavior in him. These are why he was not as good as Wuzhong.

Hui said, "Can you tell me about them?"

Confucius said, "The three cases of un-*ren* behavior were: (1) he kept Zhan Qin down,[11] (2) he erected six toll stations, and (3) his concubines wove mats.[12] The three cases of unwise behavior were: (1) he created an extravagant ceremonial room,[13] (2) he recklessly put the positions in the ancestral sacrifice out of proper order,[14] and (3) he made a sacrificial offering to a sea bird.[15] When Wuzhong was in Qi,[16] he avoided disaster by refusing a gift of fields from the duke just prior to the duke's downfall,[17] demonstrating how he overcame a challenge to his wisdom. Despite his

9. Compare with Qidiao Ping's answer to a similar question in 10.8.

10. See 42.9.

11. In other words, he intentionally did not recommend Zhan Qin for a government post.

12. Apparently, the concubines were selling their handicrafts in the market, cutting into the income of people more in need of it. A saying later in Chinese officialdom captures the sentiment: do not compete with the people for profit 不要與民爭利.

13. We assume this is a reference to the episode in *Analects* 5.18 and translate accordingly.

14. According to CQZZ ("Wen" 2.5), Xiafu Fuqi (recorded there as *Xiafu Fuji* 夏父弗忌) placed Duke Xi 僖 (r. 659–627 BCE) ahead of Duke Min 閔 (r. 661–660 BCE) (Durrant, Li, and Schaberg 2016). According to *Dialogues* 42.8, Wenzhong is to blame for going along with it.

15. A passage in the *Guo yu* says that a seabird called *yuanju* stood for three days outside the eastern gate of Lu, and Wenzhong ordered the people to perform a sacrificial ceremony to it.

16. Although Wuzhong was raised in the Lu palace and once held the position of prime minister, he fell afoul of the Mengsun clan and was accused of plotting a coup. He had to flee for his life and went to Qi.

17. CQZZ ("Xiang" 23.8) records this event. The Duke of Qi was about to grant Zang Wuzhong lands, Wuzhong insulted the duke, and the duke did not go through with the offer. Following the passage, Confucius comments on Wuzhong's wisdom.

wisdom, there are reasons he was not accepted in Lu. He was not congenial in his work, nor was he sufficiently compassionate. The Xia shu[18] says, 'Stay mindful here and now. Be congenial and spread compassion.'"[19]

18.5

顏回問君子。孔子曰:"愛近仁, 度近智, 爲己不重, 爲人不輕, 君子也夫。" 回曰:"敢問其次。"子曰:"弗學而行, 弗思而得。小子勉之。"

Yan Hui asked about the *junzi*. Confucius said, "Love is akin to *ren*, and moderation is akin to wisdom. A *junzi* understands this and is someone who neither takes himself too seriously nor takes others lightly."

Hui said, "May I ask about the next level down?"

Confucius said, "To be able to do something without having to learn how, to understand something without having to think about it. Keep applying yourself!"

18.6

仲孫何忌問於顏回曰:"仁者一言而必有益於仁智, 可得聞乎?"回曰:"一言而有益於智, 莫如預; 一言而有益於仁, 莫如恕。夫知其所不可由, 斯知所由矣。"

Zhongsun Heji asked Yan Hui, "Could you tell me the one most important term a *ren* person would use that can help me improve *ren* and wisdom in myself?"

Hui said, "For wisdom, you can't do better than foresight. For *ren*, you can't do better than *shu*. When you know what not to do, then you know exactly what to do."

18.7

顏回問小人, 孔子曰:"毀人之善以爲辯, 狡訐懷詐以爲智, 幸人之有過, 耻學而羞不能, 小人也。"

18. Xia shu 夏書: a section of the *Documents* in its current form. It may have circulated as an independent text before being incorporated into a complete *Documents* text.

19. The second sentence does not occur in the *Documents* as we have it today. Yang and Song (2013) believe it may be a lost fragment. Alternatively, the quotation may end after the first sentence (there being no equivalent of quotation marks in the classical language), and the subsequent sentence may be an explanation, which is how Durrant, Li, and Schaberg (2016) interpret it in a related passage in CQZZ ("Xiang" 23.8). The sentence, which has two instances of the pronoun *zi* 茲 (this, here) is translated according to the *Dialogues* context, not according to the original Documents context.

Yan Hui asked about the concept of the small-minded person. Confucius said, "A small-minded person thinks that ad hominem attacks count as proper disputation, thinks that indiscretion and malevolent scheming count as wisdom, is pleased when others make errors, looks down on learning, and ridicules those of lesser ability."

18.8

顏回問子路曰: "力猛於德而得其死者鮮矣, 盍慎諸焉?"孔子謂顏回曰: "人莫不知此道之美, 而莫之御也, 莫之爲也。何居? 爲聞者盍日思也夫?"

Yan Hui suggested to Zilu, "It is rare to see someone who favors strength over virtue and who comes to a good end. Maybe this is something you should be more concerned about."

Confucius said to Yan Hui, "Everyone understands the attractiveness of this *dao*, but none can set it in motion or put it into effect. So how can one do it? Once one has learned it, why not reflect on it daily?"[20]

18.9

顏回問於孔子曰: "小人之言有同乎君子者, 不可不察也。"孔子曰: "君子以行言, 小人以舌言。故君子於爲義之上相疾也, 退而相愛; 小人於爲亂之上相愛也, 退而相惡。"

Yan Hui observed to Confucius, "When the words of a small-minded person match those of a *junzi*, one must look into it."

Confucius said, "A *junzi* speaks with his actions. A small-minded person speaks with his tongue. And so a *junzi* may agitate people when advancing a cause of *yi* but otherwise treats them with loving concern. A small-minded person may attend lovingly to people when advancing a cause of unrest but otherwise treats them with hostility."

18.10

顏回問朋友之際如何, 孔子曰: "君子之於朋友也, 心必有非焉, 而弗能謂'吾不知', 其仁人也。不忘久德, 不思久怨, 仁矣夫。"

Yan Hui asked about forming friendships. Confucius said, "The way a *junzi* treats friends is that, when he knows in his heart that a friend has done something wrong,

20. Perhaps this is Confucius' indirect admonition to Yan Hui. In 15.12, Confucius says that self-reflection is a weakness of Yan Hui. (Thanks to Amy Gardner for making this connection.)

he cannot say, 'I didn't realize.' Such is a *ren* person. You have achieved *ren* when you never forget past favors and never dwell on past slights."[21]

18.11

叔孫武叔見[22]於顏回，回曰："賓之。"武叔多稱人之過，而己評論之，顏回曰："固子之來辱也，宜有得於回焉。吾聞諸孔子曰：'言人之惡，非所以美己；言人之枉，非所以正己。'故君子攻其惡，無攻人惡。"

Once when Shusun Wushu met with Yan Hui, Yan Hui had him treated like an honored guest.[23]

Wushu repeatedly brought up the transgressions of others and added his own criticisms.

Yan Hui said, "Your reason for coming to my humble home must be that you want something from me. I have heard Confucius say the following: 'Discussing the misdeeds of others does not better oneself; discussing the scandals of others does not improve oneself.' Thus, a *junzi* attacks his own faults, not the faults of others."[24]

18.12

顏回謂子貢曰："吾聞諸夫子：'身不用禮而望禮於人，身不用德而望德於人，亂也。'夫子之言，不可不思也。"

Yan Hui said to Zigong, "I once heard our teacher say, 'It is contradictory to expect others to be *li* without being *li* oneself, or to expect others to be virtuous without being virtuous oneself.' One must reflect on these words of our teacher."

21. Confucius is making a fine point here. Friends don't help friends cover up their faults and instead help them improve. Confucius sees a circle of friends as a valuable community on the path to self-improvement. At the same time, he clarifies: friends don't dwell on the flaws of friends, even those that have affected you personally.

22. After *jian* 見, SBCK and other editions have *wei shi* 未仕, but these characters appear excrescent. We follow Yang and Song (2013) in deleting them.

23. In *Analects* 19.23 and 19.24, Shusun Wushu speaks ill of Confucius. If that event preceded this event, Yan Hui would have reason to resent Shusun, and yet he still treats him respectfully. See also 43.15.

24. From *Analects* 12.21.

19

Zilu's First Meeting

Two dialogues between Zilu and Confucius open this chapter, and Zilu returns in the seventh episode.[1] The other episodes are apparently loosely collected here under the five virtues itemized in the second episode: perseverance, hard work, conscientiousness, trustworthiness, and reverence. Themes include standing on principle when appropriate (19.3, 19.6, 19.7), maintaining a positive outlook (19.4), and making correct value discriminations (19.5, 19.8, 19.9, 19.10).

19.1

子路見孔子。子曰："汝何好樂？"對曰："好長劍。"孔子曰："吾非此之問也，徒謂以子之所能，而加之以學問，豈可及乎？"子路曰："學豈益也哉？"孔子曰："夫人君而無諫臣則失正，士而無教友則失聽。御狂馬不釋策，操弓不反檠。木受繩則直，人受諫則聖。受學重問，孰不順哉？毀仁惡士，必近於刑。君子不可不學。"子路曰："南山有竹，不揉自直，斬而用之，達于犀革。以此言之，何學之有？"孔子曰："括而羽之，鏃而礪之，其入之不亦深乎？"子路再拜曰："敬而受教。"

Zilu met with Confucius. Confucius said, "What kind of diversions do you enjoy?"

Zilu replied, "I enjoy the long sword."

Confucius said, "That's not what I was asking. I was asking what ability you have that could be brought to a higher level through study."

Zilu asked, "How can study improve a skill?"

Confucius said, "Without advice from ministers, a leader of people will be unable to govern. Without guidance from friends, an up-and-comer will be unable to make good judgments. It's like trying to ride a wild horse without a crop or trying to shape a bow without a frame.[2] Wood receiving rope becomes straight, and a

1. The first passage in this chapter is widely understood as an account of Zilu's first meeting with Confucius, hence the title. See also 10.5.

2. When a bow in ancient times was unstrung for a long period of time, it was restricted by a frame that would maintain its shape. (Peng 2019)

person receiving advice becomes a sage. When does accepting and valuing instruction not go well? Destroying *ren* and despising up-and-comers leads only to criminal punishment. A *junzi* cannot but study."

Zilu said, "In the southern mountains, there is a kind of bamboo that is straight without being shaped, and when split and used as an arrow, it can penetrate rhino-skin armor. From this perspective, what is the use of study?"

Confucius asked, "But won't it penetrate deeper if you add feathers to the shaft and sharpen its tip?"

Zilu bowed and said, "I respectfully accept instruction."

19.2

子路將行, 辭於孔子。子曰: "贈汝以車乎? 贈汝以言乎?"子路曰: "請以言。"孔子曰: "不强不達, 不勞無功, 不忠無親, 不信無復, 不恭失禮。慎此五者而矣。"子路曰: "由請終身奉之。敢問親交取親若何? 言寡可行若何? 長爲善士而無犯若何?"孔子曰: "汝所問, 苞在五者中矣。親交取親, 其忠也; 言寡可行, 其信乎; 長爲善士而無犯, 其禮也。"

When Zilu was going away, he stopped by to bid farewell to Confucius. Confucius said, "What should I send you away with—a carriage or some advice?"

Zilu said, "I would prefer some advice."

Confucius said, "Be cautious about five things: (1) There is no accomplishment without perseverance; (2) there is no success without hard work; (3) building close relationships does not happen without conscientiousness; (4) you do not win allegiance without being trustworthy; and (5) lack of reverence leads to impropriety.

Zilu said, "I will follow these to the end of my days.

"May I also ask: In forming new relationships, how can I build close ties? How can I speak little but carry into action those words that I do say? How can I endure as a good official without offending others?"

Confucius replied, "The answers to your questions are in the five items just mentioned. It is conscientiousness that allows you to build close ties in new relationships. It is trustworthiness that allows you to carry through on your words, though speaking little. And it is *li* that allows you to endure as a good official without offending others."

19.3

孔子爲魯司寇, 見季康子, 康子不悦。孔子又見之。宰予進曰: "昔予也常聞諸夫子曰: '王公不我聘, 則弗動。'今夫子之於司寇也日少, 而屈節數矣, 不可以已乎?"孔子曰: "然。魯國以衆相陵, 以兵相暴之日久矣, 而有司不治, 則將亂也。其聘我者, 孰大於是哉?"魯人聞之, 曰: "聖人將治, 何不先自遠刑罰?"自此之後, 國無争者。孔子謂宰予曰: "違山十里, 蟪蛄之聲, 猶在於耳, 故政事莫如應之。"

When Confucius became minister of justice for Lu, he met with Ji Kangzi. Ji Kangzi was not pleased. Confucius met with him again.

Zai Yu approached and said, "I have heard you say in the past, 'If a ruler does not hire me, I do not take the initiative.' You have been minister of justice for only a brief period, and you've already endured humiliation several times. Can't you resign?"

Confucius replied, "Yes, but for a long time now, factions in Lu have used mobs and weapons to oppress and harass, and yet those in charge have ignored it. If allowed to continue, it will lead to chaos. Now that I have been hired, what is more important than this?"

When the people of Lu heard about this exchange, they said, "With a sage on the way, why not steer clear of punishment?" Afterwards there were no more power struggles within the state.

Confucius said to Zai Yu, "Even at a distance of two miles, the sound of mountain cicadas is right at your ear. Likewise, in governing, nothing is better than responsiveness."

19.4

孔子兄子有孔篾者，與宓子賤偕仕。孔子往過孔篾，而問之曰："自汝之仕，何得何亡?"對曰："未有所得，而所亡者三。王事若龍，學焉得習，是學不得明也；俸禄少，饘粥不及親戚，是以骨肉益疏也；公事多急，不得弔死問疾，是朋友之道闕也。其所亡者三，即謂此也。"孔子不悅，往過子賤，問如孔篾。對曰："自來仕者無所亡，其有所得者三。始誦之，今得而行之，是學益明也；俸禄所供，被及親戚，是骨肉益親也；雖有公事，而兼以弔死問疾，是朋友篤也。"孔子喟然謂子賤曰："君子哉若人！魯無君子者，則子賤焉取此。"

Confucius' older brother had a son named Kong Mie, who worked as a bureaucrat alongside Fu Zijian.

Confucius went to visit Kong Mie, asking, "Since you have started working as a bureaucrat, what have you gained and what have you lost?"

Kong Mie said, "I haven't gained anything, but I have lost three things. I'll tell you what they are: (1) Working in government is repetitive. I can't practice anything that I've learned, and what I've learned on the job is utterly unenlightening. (2) The salary is small, not providing for enough food to feed my parents and extended family, and so my relations with them are becoming strained. (3) Many matters in the office are of such an urgent nature that I have little time to get out and visit the sick or attend funerals. As a result, relations with my friends are strained as well."

Displeased, Confucius went to visit Zijian, asking him the same question he had asked Kong Mie.

Zijian said, "Since working as a bureaucrat, I haven't lost anything, but I have gained three things. (1) Previously I just memorized things, but now I can put into practice what I've learned, and so my learning is becoming clearer by the day. (2)

I am able to give my salary to my parents and extended family, and so my relations with them have become closer. (3) Despite my work in the office, I still have time to visit the sick and attend funerals, so my relations with friends have deepened.

Confucius heaved a sigh and said of Zijian, "Here is a *junzi*! If there were no *junzi* in Lu, where would Zijian have learned this?"

19.5

孔子侍坐於哀公，賜之桃與黍焉。哀公曰：“請食。”孔子先食黍而後食桃。左右皆掩口而笑。公曰：“黍者所以雪桃，非爲食之也。”孔子對曰：“丘知之矣。然夫黍者，五穀之長，郊禮宗廟以爲上盛。果屬有六而桃爲下，祭祀不用，不登郊廟。丘聞之，君子以賤雪貴，不聞以貴雪賤。今以五穀之長，雪果之下者，是從上雪下，臣以爲妨於教，害於義，故不敢。”公曰：“善哉！”

Once when Confucius was sitting in attendance on Duke Ai, the duke gave him some peaches and millet, saying, "Try some." Confucius ate the millet first, then a peach. Others nearby began snickering.

The duke said, "The millet is to help with wiping off the peach fuzz, not for eating."

Confucius replied, "I realize that, but millet is the first of the five grains and is placed in ritual vessels in ancestral temples during the Jiao ceremony. There are six main fruits, and the peach is the least of them. It is not used for sacrificial ceremonies at all, certainly not for the Jiao ceremony. I've heard that a *junzi* uses lowly things to clean esteemed things, not esteemed things to clean lowly things. To use the first of the five grains to clean the least of the fruits is to use the esteemed to clean the lowly. For me to do so would be to hamper transformative instruction and harm *yi*, and so I dare not."[3]

The duke exclaimed, "Excellent!"

19.6

子貢曰：“陳靈公宣淫於朝，泄冶正諫而殺之。是與比干諫而死同，可謂仁乎？”子曰：“比干於紂，親則諸父，官則少師，忠報之心，在於宗廟而已，固必以死爭之，冀身死之後，紂將悔寤，其本志情在於仁者也。泄冶之於靈公，位在大夫，無骨肉之親，懷寵不去，仕於亂朝，以區區之一身，欲正一國之淫昏，死而無益，可謂狷矣。《詩》云：‘民之多僻，無自立辟。’其泄冶之謂乎。”

3. The method of using millet to clean peach fuzz is unknown. Perhaps after dipping the peach in thin millet congee, a cloth was used to wipe the fuzz off the peach. Sacrificial millet could be cooked or uncooked, but uncooked millet would not be served as food. (Fong 1980)

Zigong said, "When Duke Ling of Chen engaged in dissolute behavior in court, Xie Ye advised against such behavior and was killed for it.[4] This is similar to how Bigan died. Can it be considered *ren* behavior?"

Confucius said, "Bigan was both related to Zhòu, in being his uncle, and was an official, in being junior preceptor. He harbored the intention of conscientiously repaying the king and of perpetuating the royal line. He used his death as a way of exhortation, hoping that, after he was gone, the king would come to regret his error and reform. His intentions were fundamentally *ren*.

"Xie Ye was a high official, not related by blood to the duke. He was shown special favor and was thus reluctant to leave, and so he stayed and tried to serve a dysfunctional court. Sacrificing his own insignificant self to reform the concupiscent benightedness of an entire state did not really help matters and can be called obstinacy. A poem says:

> When most are corrupt,
> Do not interrupt.[5]

This is what we can say about Xie Ye."[6]

19.7

孔子相魯。齊人患其將霸，欲敗其政，乃選好女子八十人，衣以文飾而舞容璣，及文馬四十駟，以遺魯君。陳女樂、列文馬於魯城南高門外。季桓子微服往觀之再三，將受焉，告魯君爲周道遊觀。觀之終日，怠於政事。子路言於孔子曰："夫子可以行矣。"孔子曰："魯今且郊，若致膰於大夫，則是未廢其常，吾猶可以止也。"桓子既受女樂，君臣淫荒，三日不聽國政，郊又不致膰俎。孔子遂行，宿於郭屯。師已送，曰："夫子非罪也。"孔子曰："吾歌可乎?"歌曰："彼婦人之口，可以出走；彼婦人之請，可以死敗。優哉游哉，聊以卒歲。"

When Confucius worked in the Lu government, Qi feared that he would be so effective in leading the country that Lu would become a superpower. Seeking to ruin

4. The story is told in CQZZ ("Xuan" 9.6). The duke and two of his high officials were wearing the "intimate garments of [the same lover] under their robes, bantering about them in court" (Durrant, Li, and Schaberg 2016, 627; brackets added). After Xie Ye advised the duke against such behavior, Xie Ye was killed for it. For more on this story, see 10.2n2.

5. These lines are from the poem "Perverse" (#254). See 14.1n5.

6. After CQZZ ("Xuan" 9.6) relates the story of Xie Ye's death, it provides Confucius' comment via the lines from the poem as seen in this episode of the *Dialogues*, but nothing else. The brief criticism by Confucius of Xie Ye in the CQZZ has been controversial down through the ages because it seems to dissuade officials from fulfilling their duty to attempt to correct the wrong behavior of their superiors. This episode in the *Dialogues* provides a rationale for Confucius' criticism of Xie Ye that is not found elsewhere.

the government from within, Qi sent eighty beautiful women in decorative clothes and jewelry to dance a popular dance and forty teams of horses, as gifts for Lu. They displayed them outside Lu's high Southern Gate.

Ji Huanzi put on some everyday clothes and went to inspect the gifts several times. Before formally accepting them, he announced to the Lu sovereign that he had to go away on an inspection tour.[7] He then neglected government affairs for days on end.

Zilu said to Confucius, "I think it would be a good time to leave now."

Confucius said, "It's time for Lu's Jiao ceremony. If they go through with it and sacrificial meat is duly given to the high officials, that will indicate that current standards have not been totally ruined and we can refrain from leaving."

Huanzi formally accepted the female entertainment, sovereign and vassal indulged in dissolute abandonment, and for three days they did not attend to affairs of state. After the Jiao ceremony, sacrificial meat was not distributed to the high officials. Thereupon, Confucius left the capital, staying the night in a village near the outer wall.

Shi Yi came to see him off, saying, "You did nothing wrong."

Confucius said, "Do you mind if I sing a tune?" Then he sang:

The lips of those ladies
Have us fleeing the city.
The presence of those women
Portend death and destruction.
Free now, free and clear
To while away the years.

19.8

澹臺子羽有君子之容，而行不勝其貌。宰我有文雅之辭，而智不充其辯。孔子曰："里語云：'相馬以輿，相士以居，弗可廢矣。'以容取人，則失之子羽；以辭取人，則失之宰予。"

Tantai Ziyu had the face of a *junzi*, but his conduct was no match for his appearance. Zai Wo had elegant speech, but his wisdom was no complement to his rhetoric.

Confucius said, "There is a saying that goes, 'In judging a horse, look at how it pulls a chariot; in judging a man, look at what he abides in.' This should not be forgotten. If

7. The likely scenario here is that Ji Huanzi, who was in control of the government, accepted the gifts on behalf of the duke and then publicly announced to the duke that he would be going away for an inspection tour of Lu, while actually debauching with the women from Qi. The public announcement was a way of keeping up appearances.

one were to select a man based on his face, one would err in Ziyu. If one were to select a man based on his eloquence, one would err in Zai Yu."

19.9

孔子曰:"君子以其所不能畏人,小人以其所不能不信人。故君子長人之才,小人抑人而取勝焉。"

Confucius said, "A *junzi* admires people for abilities that exceed his own. A small-minded person mistrusts people for abilities that exceed his own. Thus, a *junzi* encourages the talents of others, while a small-minded person seeks to get the best of others by suppressing their talents."

19.10

孔篾問行己之道。子曰:"知而弗爲,莫如勿知;親而弗信,莫如勿親。樂之方至,樂而勿驕;患之將至,思而勿憂。"孔篾曰:"行己乎?"子曰:"攻其所不能,補其所不備。毋以其所不能疑人,毋以其所能驕人。終日言,無遺己憂;終日行,不遺己患。唯智者有之。"

Kong Mie asked about the *dao* of comporting oneself.[8]

Confucius said, "Better to not know than to know but not act. Better to not be close to someone than to be close but not trust them. When joy is on the horizon, revel without being smug. When disaster is imminent, think carefully without feeling anxious."

Kong Mie asked, "That's what it is to comport oneself?"

Confucius said, "Conquer your inabilities and supplement your deficiencies. Don't let your own inabilities make you doubt others, and don't let your own abilities make you feel superior to others. Only a wise person can speak all day without bringing himself worries, or function all day without causing himself trouble."

8. *Comport oneself, xing ji* 行己: This is an uncommon locution, which simply means to act as oneself, with an apparent emphasis on individuality, and, for Confucius, it is assumed that the behavior would be proper behavior. Thus, the question seems to be: what is the proper way to act as an individual in society but within the bounds of propriety? The locution occurs twice in the *Analects*. In *Analects* 5.16, Confucius says that Zichan comported himself with reverence. In *Analects* 13.20, Zigong asks about the behavior of an up-and-comer, and part of Confucius' response is that one should comport oneself with a sense of shame. The text with the highest number of uses of this locution is the *Dialogues* itself, with occurrences in five episodes: 7.7, 12.12, 15.1,37.1, and this episode. In each, the advice is different, and we see in 7.7 that doing so wrongly can even lead to one's death.

20

Trapped

The incident of Confucius and his retinue being trapped between Chen and Cai is a common point of reference in Warring States texts. Here, in the first and final episodes, we are provided details of the incident. In the first, which resembles 8.1 and 9.8 in cycling through Zilu, Zigong, and Yan Hui, Confucius offers his opinion on the independence of a *junzi* and how a visionary does not back down in the face of danger. In the final episode, he devises a clever plan to test Yan Hui's integrity. The second episode echoes the first in its theme of the comportment of a *junzi* under stress, and the third resonates with the fourth in its theme of incorruptibility.

20.1

楚昭王聘孔子，孔子往拜禮焉，路出于陳、蔡。陳、蔡大夫相與謀曰："孔子聖賢，其所刺譏，皆中諸侯之病。若用於楚，則陳、蔡危矣。"遂使徒兵距孔子。孔子不得行，絕糧七日，外無所通，藜羹不充，從者皆病。孔子愈慷慨講誦，弦歌不衰。乃召子路而問焉，曰："《詩》云：'匪兕匪虎，率彼曠野。'吾道非乎，奚爲至於此？"子路慍，作色而對曰："君子無所困。意者夫子未仁與，人之弗吾信也？意者夫子未智與，人之弗吾行也？且由也昔者聞諸夫子：'爲善者，天報之以福；爲不善者，天報之以禍。'今夫子積德懷義，行之久矣，奚居之窮也？"子曰："由未之識也，吾語汝：汝以仁者爲必信也，則伯夷、叔齊不餓死首陽；汝以智者爲必用也，則王子比干不見剖心；汝以忠者爲必報也，則關龍逢不見刑；汝以諫者爲必聽也，則伍子胥不見殺。夫遇不遇者，時也；賢不肖者，才也。君子博學深謀而不遇時者衆矣，何獨丘哉！且芝蘭生於深林，不以無人而不芳。君子修道立德，不爲窮困而改節。爲之者人也，生死者命也。是以晉重耳之有霸心，生於曹、衛；越王勾踐之有霸心，生於會稽。故居下而無憂者，則思不遠；處身而常逸者，則志不廣。庸知其終始乎？"子路出。召子貢，告如子路。子貢曰："夫子之道至大，故天下莫能容夫子，夫子盍少貶焉？"子曰："賜，良農能稼，不必能穡；良工能巧，不能爲順。君子能修其道，綱而紀之，不必其能容。今不修其道，而求其容。賜，爾志不廣矣，思不遠矣！"子貢出。顏回入，問亦如之。顏回曰："夫子之道至大，天下莫能容，雖然，夫子推而行之，世不我用，有國者之醜也。夫子何病焉？不容，然後見君子。"孔子欣然嘆曰："有是哉，顏氏之子，使爾多財，吾爲爾宰。"

King Zhao of Chu hired Confucius. When Confucius was on his way to pay his respects to the king, his road passed between the states of Chen and Cai.

High officials in Chen and Cai conspired together, saying, "Confucius is a capable and virtuous sage. All of his pointed criticisms are aimed at the defects of noblemen of the various states. If he is employed in Chu, it will mean danger for Chen and Cai." And so they sent soldiers to block Confucius' path.

Unable to advance, Confucius went without food for seven days. He had no way of communicating with the outside world and no way to supplement his supply of food. Those traveling with him took ill. Confucius, however, became increasingly energetic, tirelessly speaking, reciting poems, playing the zither, and singing.

He called Zilu over and posed a question. "A poem says:

Neither rhino nor tiger
Yet led through the wilderness.[1]

Is there something wrong with my *dao* that it has come to this?"

Uncomfortable, Zilu blanched and replied, "A *junzi* never feels troubled. Does it mean that you have not been *ren* toward others that these people don't trust us? Does it mean that you have not been wise toward others that these people will not let us go on our way? I once heard you say, 'Those who do good, *tian* repays with good fortune; those who do bad, *tian* repays with misfortune.' For a long time now, you have laid up virtue and borne *yi* in your breast. Why are we in such dire straits?"

1. From the poem "What Grasses Never Yellow" (#234), which can be found today in the "Xiao ya" section of the *Poems*. The poem is a soldier's lament on being driven to war through the wilderness. The full poem is as follows:

What grasses never yellow?
When does the sun not fly?
What people never march?
Making camp at the ends of the earth.
What grasses never die?
What people never collapse?
Our poor soldiers on the march,
The most pitiful of our people.
Neither rhino nor tiger
Yet led through the wilderness.
Our poor soldiers on the march,
Resting neither night nor day.
Foxes in a thicket
Led through deep grasses.
Wagons on a precipice
Walk winding routes.

Confucius said, "Yóu, you don't quite understand yet. Let me tell you. If a person of *ren* were always trusted, Boyi and Shuqi would never have starved to death at the foot of Shouyang Mountain.[2] If a wise person were always employed, Prince Bigan would never have had his heart cut out. If conscientiousness were always rewarded, Guan Longpang would not have been punished. If advisers were always listened to, Wu Zixu would not have been killed.

"What happens to someone depends on timing. How great one is depends on one's abilities. There have been many knowledgeable and visionary *junzi* who have not met with the right timing. How could I be the only one?

"Angelica and orchids grow deep in the forest and waft out their fragrance without waiting for people to come. Having cultivated himself and established a moral foundation, a *junzi* does not alter his standards because of hard times.

"One's behavior is a matter of one's own; one's life and death are a matter of circumstance. Thus, the superpower ambitions of Jin's Chonger were born out of his conflict with Cao and Wei.[3] The superpower ambitions of King Goujian of Yue were born out of his defeat at Kuaiji. And so someone who lives a modest, worry-free life will never be a visionary; someone who spends their life running away will never have broad ambitions—how would we ever hear their stories?"[4]

Zilu exited.

Confucius called in Zigong, beginning the same way he began with Zilu.

Zigong replied, "Your *dao* is too expansive to be accepted by this world. Why not narrow it a little?"

Confucius said, "Ci, a farmer who is especially skilled at cultivating crops need not be especially skilled at harvesting them.[5] A craftsman who is especially skilled at his craft need not be especially attentive to his customer's whims. Likewise, a *junzi* who is especially skilled at cultivating the *dao*, with strong mainstays and supporting principles, need not be accepted by everyone. You are suggesting that we stop cultivating the *dao* in order to be accepted by others. Ci, neither are your ambitions broad nor your thoughts visionary."

Zigong exited.

Yan Hui entered and was posed the same question.

2. For the story of Boyi and Shuqi, see 12.21n19. It is not clear from the little we have of them how being trusted fits into the their narrative.

3. When the future Jin Duke Wen was bouncing from one state to the next during his nearly two decades in exile, he was poorly received in Cao and Wei. See "Jin Duke Wen" in the glossary.

4. The *Xunzi* (28) version of this episode begins without mentioning Confucius' being hired by the king of Chu and ends here, omitting the conversations with Zigong and Yan Hui.

5. The focus should be on the cultivation of the crops. Whether exigencies beyond one's control (pestilence, drought, etc.) affect the harvest should not be the focus of one's attention.

Yan Hui said, "Your *dao* is too expansive to be accepted by the world. Despite this, you practice and promote it. That the world does not accept it is an embarrassment for every ruler. Why feel bad about it? Not being accepted is a sign of being a *junzi*."

Confucius sighed happily, saying, "That's right. This son of Yan—if you were wealthy, I'd become your household manager."

20.2

子路問於孔子曰: "君子亦有憂乎?"子曰: "無也。君子之修行也, 其未得之, 則樂其意; 既得之, 又樂其治。是以有終身之樂, 無一日之憂。小人則不然, 其未得也, 患弗得之; 既得之, 又恐失之。是以有終身之憂, 無一日之樂也。"

Zilu asked Confucius, "Does a *junzi* experience anxiety like everyone else?"

Confucius said, "No. A *junzi* cultivates himself, and before he encounters success he delights in the prospect of success. When he succeeds, he delights in the governing. In this way, a *junzi* is joyful his whole life, without a single day of anxiety.

"A small-minded person is different. Before success, he worries that it won't come. After success, he frets that he'll lose it. In this way, a small-minded person is anxious his whole life, without a single day of joy."

20.3

曾子弊衣而耕於魯, 魯君聞之而致邑焉。曾子固辭不受。或曰: "非子之求, 君自致之, 奚固辭也?"曾子曰: "吾聞受人施者常畏人, 與人者常驕人。縱君有賜, 不我驕也, 吾豈能勿畏乎?"孔子聞之曰: "參之言, 足以全其節也。"

Zengzi worked in the fields of Lu wearing tattered clothes. The sovereign of Lu heard about this and offered him a fief. Zengzi adamantly refused.

Someone asked, "It's not something you asked for, and the sovereign offered the gift of his own initiative, so why did you adamantly refuse?"

Zengzi said, "I have heard that those who receive gifts from others end up fearing them, and those who give them end up acting imperious. Even if the sovereign does not act imperious toward me for having given me the gift, how could I still not fear him?"

Confucius heard about this and said, "These words of Shen are sufficient to preserve his moral integrity."

20.4

孔子厄於陳、蔡, 從者七日不食。子貢以所賫貨, 竊犯圍而出, 告糴於野人, 得米一石焉。顔回、仲由炊之於壞屋之下, 有埃墨墮飯中, 顔回取而食之。子貢自井望見之, 不悦, 以爲竊食也。入問孔子曰: "仁人廉士, 窮改節乎?"孔子曰: "改節即何稱於仁廉哉?"子貢曰:"若回也,其不改節乎?"子曰:"然。"子貢以所飯告孔子。子曰:"吾信回之爲仁久矣,雖汝有云,弗以疑也,其或者必有故乎?汝止,吾將問之。"召顏回曰:"疇昔予夢見先人,豈或啓佑我哉?子炊而進飯,吾將進焉。"對曰:"向有埃墨墮飯中,欲置之,則不潔;欲棄之,則可惜,回即食之。不可祭也。"孔子曰:"然乎,吾亦食之。"顏回出,孔子顧謂二三子曰:"吾之信回也,非待今日也。"二三子由此乃服之。

When Confucius was trapped between Chen and Cai, those accompanying him went hungry for seven days. Zigong gathered together some of the supplies they had brought with them, snuck out through the encirclement, and traded with the locals for some grain, getting five and a half gallons in exchange. While Yan Hui and Zhong You were cooking the grain in a dilapidated shed, a bit of ash fell into the pot. Yan Hui scooped it out and ate it.

Coming from the well, Zigong saw Yan Hui eating out of the pot. He was displeased, because he thought that Yan Hui was secretly eating rations. He entered and asked Confucius about it, saying, "A person of *ren* is incorruptible. Can dire straits alter one's moral integrity?"

Confucius said, "If one's moral integrity can be altered, how can one be called incorruptibly *ren*?"

Zigong said, "Take Hui, for instance: he wouldn't alter his moral integrity, right?"

Confucius said, "That's right."

Then Zigong told Confucius about the food.

Confucius said, "I have always trusted Hui's *ren*. Despite what you have said—not that I am doubting it—could there not be an explanation? Wait a moment, and I'll ask."

He called in Yan Hui, saying, "Just recently I dreamt of the ancestors. Could they be wanting to give us a sign or protect us? Bring in some of the cooked food so that I can make an offering to them."

Yan Hui replied, "Just now a bit of ash fell into the pot. I thought of letting it stay there, but that would be unsanitary. I thought of throwing it out, but that would be a waste. So I ate it. It is not fit for a sacrificial ceremony."

Confucius said, "Is that so? I would have eaten it too."

Yan Hui exited, and Confucius turned to his students saying, "It's not just because of what happened today that I trust Hui."

After this, the other students regained their trust of Yan Hui.

21

Entering Government

Chapter 21 is an eloquent summary of Confucius' theory of governing. It begins in the official who hollows himself out, maintains a simple lifestyle, governs impartially, and is not demanding of the people. He observes and works with the natural inclinations and emotions of the people, understanding that they are the ultimate basis of the government. He models ideal behavior in his own person so that others may follow and allows the people to achieve their own ends.

21.1

子張問入官於孔子。孔子曰:“安身取譽爲難。”子張曰:“爲之如何?”孔子曰:“己有善勿專,教不能勿怠,已過勿發,失言勿掎,不善勿遂,行事勿留,君子入官,有此六者,則身安譽至而政從矣。且夫忿數者,官獄所由生也;距諫者,慮之所以塞也;慢易者,禮之所以失也;怠惰者,時之所以後也;奢侈者,財之所以不足也;專獨者,事之所以不成也。君子入官,除此六者,則身安譽至而政從矣。

Zizhang asked Confucius about taking a job as an official in the government.

Confucius said, "The hard parts are finding a stable position and earning a good reputation."

Zizhang asked, "How can those be done?"

Confucius said, "On taking an official position in the government, a *junzi* who does the following six things will find a stable position and earn a good reputation such that those who are governed will follow along: (1) When something favorable happens to you, don't monopolize it. (2) If your transformative instruction to the people doesn't immediately bear fruit, don't let up. (3) Don't make the same mistake twice. (4) If you misspeak, don't sidestep it. (5) If you encounter bad behavior, don't follow it. (6) In your duties, don't linger on any one thing.

"On taking an official position in the government, a *junzi* who eliminates the following six things will find a stable position and earn a good reputation such that those who are governed will follow along: (1) A short temper, which invites official censure.

(2) Rejecting advice out of hand, which is how the flow of thinking comes to a stop. (3) Discourtesy, which is where *li* is lost. (4) Indolence, which makes one lag behind. (5) Extravagance, which is the root of scarcity. (6) Imperiousness, which is an obstacle to development.

21.2

"故君子南面臨官，大域之中而公治之，精智而略行之，合是忠信，考是大倫，存是美惡，進是利而除是害，無求其報焉，而民之情可得也。夫臨之無抗民之惡，勝之無犯民之言，量之無佼民之辭，養之無擾於其時，愛之無寬於刑法。若此，則身安譽至而民得也。

"Thus, when a *junzi* takes an august position as an overseeing official in this great land, you must govern with impartiality and keen wisdom, with a unity of conscientiousness and trustworthiness, a pledge of integrity, and a sense of right and wrong. You must advance benefit and eliminate harm without heed to repayment for yourself. This is how to win the favor of the people.

"Oversee the people without the defect of being inflexible toward them. Win them over without offending them through frank speech. Take their measure without deceiving them through rhetoric. Nurture them without disturbing their regular calendar. Care for them without being too lenient in punishments. By doing these things, your position will be stable, your reputation will be made, and you will have earned the allegiance of the people.

21.3

"君子以臨官，所見則邇，故明不可蔽也；所求於邇，故不勞而得也。所以治者約，故不用衆而譽立。凡法象在內，故法不遠而源泉不竭，是以天下積而本不寡。短長得其量，人志治而不亂政。德貫乎心，藏乎志，形乎色，發乎聲。若此，而身安譽至，民咸自治矣。是故臨官不治則亂，亂生則争之者至，争之至，又於亂。明君必寬裕以容其民，慈愛優柔之，而民自得矣。

"As overseeing official, the *junzi*'s gaze is not obstructed, and you are able to see all things as if they were up close. What you wish to have near, you acquire without effort. You govern with simplicity and so make your reputation without the need for conscripting the masses.

"When the normative model[1] has been internalized, it is never far away, like a natural spring that never ceases flowing. In this way, benefits will accumulate across the land, and the source will not be diminished.

1. *Normative model, fa xiang* 法象: see "*Fa xiang*" in the glossary.

"When right and wrong are correctly recognized, people set their minds on good governing, eliminating disorder. *De* is habituated in your mind and concealed in your intentions, revealed in your exterior, and expressed through your voice. By doing these things, your position will be stable, your reputation will be made, and the people will be self-governed.

"Without governing by an overseeing official, there will be disorder. When disorder arises, there will be strife. Strife gives rise to even more disorder.

"An intelligent ruler is always tolerant in dealing with the people. Through love and tenderness toward them, the people will be able to achieve their own ends.

21.4

"行者，政之始也。説者，情之導也。善政行易而民不怨，言調説和則民不變。法在身則民象之，明在己則民顯之。若乃供己而不節，則財利之生者微矣；貪以不得，則善政必簡矣；苟以亂之，則善言必不聽也；詳以納之，則規諫日至。言之善者，在所日聞；行之善者，在所能爲。故君上者，民之儀也；有司執政者，民之表也；邇臣便僻者，群僕之倫也。故儀不正則民失，表不端則百姓亂，邇臣便辟，則群臣污矣。是以人主不可不敬乎三倫。

"Governing begins in actions, but people's emotions are guided by words. Under good government, it's easy to take action and the people don't complain. When speech is mild, persuasion is agreeable and the people don't resist. When you model proper behavior in your own person, the people will follow. When you act intelligently yourself, the people will do the same.

"If, however, you indulge yourself without restraint, the sources of your wealth will shrink; and when you can't get what you lust after, your government will fall into neglect. And when disorder results, no amount of colorful persuasion will be listened to.

"Conversely, if you are open to counsel from others, good advice will come daily. The good of speech is in the daily hearing of it; the good of action is in the ability to carry it out.

"Thus, the sovereign is a guidepost for the people; the officials holding the reins of government are standards for the people; the officials who surround the sovereign are the moral exemplars for all government servants. If the guidepost is not correct, the people will be lost; if the standard is not proper, the populace will fall into disorder; if surrounding officials are mere sycophants, other officials will be corrupted. For these reasons, the sovereign must respect this three-tiered hierarchy.

21.5

"君子修身反道，察里言而服之，則身安譽至，終始在焉。故夫女子必自擇絲麻，良工必自擇完材，賢君必自擇左右。勞於取人，佚於治事。君子欲譽，則必謹其左右。爲上者，譬如緣木焉，務高而畏下滋甚。六馬之乖離，必於四達之交衢。萬民之叛道，必於君上之失政。上者尊嚴而危，民者卑賤而神。愛之則存，惡之則亡。長民者必明此之要。故南面臨官，貴而不驕，富而能供，有本而能圖末，修事而能建業，久居而不滯，情近而暢乎遠，察一物而貫乎多，治一物而萬物不能亂者，以身本者也。

"From beginning to end, the way for the *junzi* to have a stable position and a good reputation is to cultivate yourself, return to the *dao*, and adhere to opinions of commoners[2] after having evaluated them.

"A woman must select just the right fabric, an artisan must select just the right material to work with, and a capable and virtuous leader must select just the right people to surround himself with. If you labor over selecting people, you can relax in doing your work.

"A *junzi* seeking a good reputation, therefore, must be careful about those he surrounds himself with. Being on top is like climbing a tree. The higher you climb, the greater your fear of falling. If a six-horse carriage team separates, it will be at a crossroads going in all directions. If the people rebel, it will be due to the leaders' error in governing.

"Those above are reverent and stern, which makes them forebidding. The people may be lowly and common by comparison, but they possess a mysterious power. If you love and care for them, you will survive. If you detest them, you will perish. To cultivate the people, you must clearly understand this essential factor.

"Thus, the overseeing official has status but is not overbearing, has wealth but is able to share it. Possessing the root, you are able to plan for the tips of the branches. By meticulously taking care of affairs, you are able to establish a career. If you are consistent in this way, affairs will flow without obstruction. When you are sensitive and responsive to those nearby, policies can smoothly extend far and wide. Looking into one thing, you can extrapolate to many things. When you govern each thing well, nothing will fall into disorder. You accomplish these things by taking yourself as the root.

21.6

"君子莅民，不可以不知民之性而達諸民之情。既知其性，又習其情，然後民乃從命矣。故世舉則民親之，政均則民無怨。故君子莅民，不臨以高，不導以遠，不責民之所不爲，不强民之所不能。廓之以明王之功，不因其情，則民嚴而不迎；篤之以累年之業，不因其力，則民引而不從。若責民所不爲，强民所不能，則民疾，疾則僻矣。

2. *Opinions of commoners, li yan* 里言: *Li* is a neighborhood or a hamlet. It appears by synecdoche to refer to people who live in ordinary circumstances. In the early corpus, there is one other occurrence of this phrase—in CQZZ ("Zhuang" 14.2). Durrant, Li, and Schaberg translate it as "news" (2016, 173). Throughout chapter 21 there is an emphasis on unity with the common people.

"In supervising the people, *junzi* must understand their natural inclinations and attend to their emotions. When officials understand the inclinations of the people and work with their emotions, the people will be able to follow edicts. Thus, when society is flourishing, the people will feel a close bond with the leader, and when governing is equitable, the people will be without complaint. Therefore, in supervising the people, the *junzi* doesn't reach too high, doesn't stretch too far, doesn't demand what the people can't do, and doesn't force the people to accomplish the impossible.

"If you attempt to enlarge the people's opportunities in order to accomplish great things on behalf of an enlightened king but do not consider their emotions, they will be standoffish and unwelcoming. If you attempt to deepen their opportunities in order to establish a long career but do not consider their abilities, they will not follow your lead. If you require the people to do what they can't or force them to do the impossible, the people will grow hostile; hostile, they will break away.

21.7

"古者聖主冕而前旒，所以蔽明也；紘紞充耳，所以掩聰也。水至清則無魚，人至察則無徒。枉而直之，使自得之；優而柔之，使自求之；揆而度之，使自索之。民有小罪，必求其善，以赦其過；民有大罪，必原其故，以仁輔化；如有死罪，其使之生，則善也。是以上下親而不離，道化流而不蘊。故德者，政之始也。政不和，則民不從其教矣；不從教，則民不習；不習，則不可得而使也。

"In ancient times, the strings of beads on the front of the king's *mian* crown symbolically obstructed his vision, and the hanging bead on each side of the crown symbolically obstructed his hearing. Water that is completely pure cannot sustain fish; people who look into everything have no adherents.[3]

"When crooked people must be set straight, make it so they achieve it of their own accord. When the worried require comfort, make it so they seek it of their own accord. When the immoderate require moderation, make it so they find it of their own accord.

"If a commoner commits a minor offense, look for the good in it and pardon the wrongdoing. If a commoner commits a serious offense, seek the reason, and use *ren* to help them reform. If it is an offense that is punishable by death, allowing them to live is still preferable. In this way, the upper and lower levels of society will maintain close ties and not become estranged. The transformative powers of the *dao* will continue to flow without obstruction. Thus, governing begins in *de*.

3. The point in this paragraph is that moral probity has its limits. One should not be too strident, lest it alienate others.

"If governing is not harmonious, the people will not follow its instruction. If the people don't follow instruction, they cannot be worked with. If they cannot be worked with, you cannot achieve anything.

21.8

"君子欲言之見信也，莫善乎先虛其內；欲政之速行也，莫善乎以身先之；欲民之速服也，莫善乎以道御之。故雖服必強，自非忠信[4]，則無可以取親於百姓者矣。內外不相應，則無可以取信於庶民者矣。此治民之至道矣，入官之大統矣。"子張既聞孔子斯言，遂退而記之。

"If as a *junzi* you wish your speech to be treated as trustworthy, nothing is better than hollowing yourself out. If you wish your policies to be swiftly put into practice, nothing is better than exhibiting them in your own person first. If you wish the people to swiftly follow along, nothing is better than leading them with *dao*. Therefore, if obedience must be forced, neither conscientiousness nor trustworthiness will ensue and the common people will not feel close to you. If interior and exterior do not resonate, the common people will not trust you.

"This is the ultimate way to govern the people, a primer for the person entering officialdom."

After hearing what Confucius said, Zizhang departed and preserved it for posterity.

4. It is difficult to make sense of this sentence in the current context. We have done the best we can with it. It makes more sense in the context of the parallel passage in the *Da Dai li ji*: 不以道御之，雖服必強矣。故非忠信，則無可以取親于百姓矣。

22

A Pledge under Duress

Chapter 22 continues the theme of Confucius on the road, taking its title from the ninth episode, in which Confucius violates a pledge made under duress. We return to the hardship between Chen and Cai, and he travels to Wei and to Zheng, encountering some sort of difficulty in each. Music is held up as a solace for hardship, and we see further discussion of non-violence in the second episode. Section 22.7 resembles the *Dao de jing*'s exhortation to place oneself beneath others. Section 22.3 reiterates claims from elsewhere in the *Dialogues* that one's own personal achievement also depends on others. And the final episode depicts a moving example of a faithful minister who continues to give advice even after death. The chapter begins with Confucius demonstrating a virtuosic command of the classic poems, eloquently convincing Zigong that industriousness in life is an inescapable imperative.

22.1

子貢問於孔子曰："賜倦於學，困於道矣，願息於事君，可乎？"孔子曰："《詩》云：'溫恭朝夕，執事有恪。'事君之難也，焉可息哉！"曰："然則賜願息而事親。"孔子曰："《詩》云：'孝子不匱，永錫爾類。'事親之難也，焉可以息哉！"曰："然賜請願息於妻子。"孔子曰："《詩》云：'刑于寡妻，至于兄弟，以御于家邦。'妻子之難也，焉可以息哉！"曰："然賜願息於朋友。"孔子曰："《詩》云：'朋友攸攝，攝以威儀。'朋友之難也，焉可以息哉！"曰："然則賜願息於耕矣。"孔子曰："《詩》云：'晝爾于茅，宵爾索綯，亟其乘屋，其始播百穀。'耕之難也，焉可以息哉！"曰："然則賜將無所息者也？"孔子曰："有焉。自望其廣，則睪如也；視其高，則填如也；察其從，則隔如也。此其所以息也矣。"子貢曰："大哉乎死也！君子息焉，小人休焉，大哉乎死也！"

Zigong asked Confucius, "I am tired of studying and feel perplexed about the *dao*. How about if I just rest and serve our sovereign?"

Confucius replied, "A poem says:[1]

Attentive and respectful morning and night,
Scrupulous in a position of service.[2]

Such is the difficulty of serving one's sovereign. How can you rest?"

Zigong said, "Then I would like to rest and serve my parents."

Confucius replied, "A poem says:

A *xiao* son is lacking in nothing,
Always giving like this.[3]

Such is the difficulty of serving one's parents. How can you rest?"

Zigong said, "Then I would like to rest and be with my wife."[4]

Confucius replied, "A poem says:

Be a model for your wife,
Extending to your brothers,
Thereby leading families and countries.[5]

Such is the difficulty of being with one's wife. How can you rest?"

Zigong said, "Then I would like to rest and be with my friends."

Confucius replied, "A poem says:

The way friends help each other,
They help by being impressive and dignified.[6]

1. This delightful and instructive episode shows Confucius' masterful grasp of poetry and his ability to always have an appropriate quotation at the ready. It appears almost verbatim in *Xunzi* 27.

2. These lines appear in the poem "Many" (#301), which can be found today in the "Shang song" section of the *Poems*. It extols the devotion of ancestors who carried on the custom of sacrificing to Tang, the founder of the Shang dynasty.

3. These lines appear in the poem "Already Drunk" (#247), which can be found today in the "Da ya" section of the *Poems*. It extols the virtues of a host who is demonstrating his largesse through a banquet.

4. *Wife*, *qizi* 妻子: This term could be understood as *qizi* (wife) or as *qi* and *zi* (wife and children). From context, it appears to be the former, a term that goes back as far as the *Poems*, as in the lines 妻子好合, 如鼓瑟琴 (With wife in harmony / Two zithers strumming), from the poem "Cherry Tree" (#164) in the "Xiao ya" section of the *Poems*.

5. These lines appear in the poem "Solemn" (#240), which can be found today in the "Da ya" section of the *Poems*. It underscores the importance of Tai Ren, Tai Jiang, and Tai Si (King Wen's mother, grandmother, and wife, respectively) in King Wen's success. The pronouns in the translation (merely implied in the original) are tailored to the context.

6. As above, these lines also appear in the poem "Already Drunk" (#247).

Such is the difficulty of friendship. How can you rest?"

Zigong said, "Then I would like to rest and tend to the fields."

Confucius replied, "A poem says:

In the daytime you work with thatch,
At night you weave ropes,
Hurry to mend the roof,
Then it's time to sow the grains.[7]

Such is the difficulty of tending to fields. How can you rest?"

Zigong asked, "Then there is no way for me to rest?"

Confucius replied, "There is. Let us observe from here out into the distance. It looks as if there is a high mound. Observe the high mound. It looks as if it is being filled. Observe the people gathered there. It looks as if they are setting up ritual vessels. That is where you may rest."

Zigong said, "Great is death, where *junzi* and small-minded people alike may rest. Great is death."

22.2

孔子自衛將入晋, 至河, 聞趙簡子殺竇犨鳴犢及舜華, 乃臨河而嘆曰: "美哉水, 洋洋乎! 丘之不濟此, 命也夫!"子貢趨而進曰: "敢問何謂也?"孔子曰: "竇犨鳴犢、舜華, 晋之賢大夫也。趙簡子未得志之時, 須此二人而後從政。及其已得志也, 而殺之。丘聞之, 刳胎殺夭, 則麒麟不至其郊; 竭澤而漁, 則蛟龍不處其淵; 覆巢破卵, 則鳳凰不翔其邑, 何則? 君子違傷其類者也。鳥獸之於不義尚知避之, 况於人乎?"遂還, 息於鄒, 作《槃操》以哀之。

Confucius was leaving Wei and about to enter Jin, arriving at the Yellow River.[8] Just then, he got news that Zhao Jianzi had killed Dou Chou Mingdu and Shun Hua.

He approached the river and sighed, saying, "The water is beautiful as it flows along! It is fate that I don't cross here."

Zigong approached and said, "May I ask why you say that?"

Confucius said, "Dou Chou Mingdu and Shun Hua were capable and virtuous high officials of Jin. Before Zhao Jianzi achieved power, he needed these two, and through them he was able to govern. Now that he has achieved power, he has had them killed. I have heard that a *qilin* will not frequent the outskirts of a city where

7. These lines appear in the poem "Seventh Month" (#154), which can be found today in the "Bin feng" section of the *Poems*. The poem depicts the hardships of life for men and women who farm.

8. The capital of Jin was some 200 miles to the west. The Yellow River was about twenty-five miles from the Wei capital.

young and innocent creatures are harmed; a dragon will not abide the depths where shallows are drained for the purpose of catching fish; a *fenghuang* will not fly over areas where bird nests are overturned and eggs broken—how could they? A *junzi* abhors those who harm his kind. If even birds and beasts know enough to avoid those whose behavior is improper, how much more so should people?"

And so he turned back, stopping in Zou,[9] where he wrote the song "Pan Cao"[10] to lament the situation.

22.3

子路問於孔子曰: "有人於此, 夙興夜寐, 耕芸樹藝, 手足胼胝, 以養其親, 然而名不稱孝, 何也?"孔子曰: "意者身不敬與? 辭不順與? 色不悅與? 古之人有言曰: '人與己與, 不汝欺。'今盡力養親而無三者之闕, 何謂無孝之名乎?"孔子曰: "由, 汝志之! 吾語汝, 雖有國士之力, 而不能自舉其身, 非力之少, 勢不可矣。夫內行不修, 身之罪也; 行修而名不彰, 友之罪也; 行修而名自立。故君子入則篤行, 出則交賢, 何謂無孝名乎?"

Zilu asked Confucius, "Suppose there is the following kind of person. He rises at dawn and works late into the night. He plows and weeds and plants seeds and sprouts. He works until his hands and feet are callused. He does all of this for the purpose of supporting his parents, and yet he is not known as a *xiao* son. Why?"[11]

Confucius said, "Let's see. Could it be that he is not respectful in his person, or that his words are disagreeable, or that his facial expression is unpleasant? The ancients said, 'According with others accords to oneself. Such a principle will never betray you.'"

Zilu asked, "He expends all his effort in supporting his parents, and he is not guilty of any of the three things you mentioned. So why does he not have a reputation for being *xiao*?"

Confucius said, "Yóu, pay attention, and I will tell you. Even the strongest person in the country cannot lift himself entirely off the ground. Not because his strength is insufficient but because it is simply impossible. If you do not cultivate your own inner person, that is your own fault. But if you do cultivate yourself and your name is not spread, that is the fault of your friends. Cultivate yourself, and your name will

9. Geographically, Confucius' return route is not clear. Either he returned to Lu and stopped in Zou, near the Lu capital, on the way; or he returned to Wei, and this is a different, elsewhere unattested, Zou.

10. According to Wang Su, this is the name of a song written for the zither.

11. A question may arise in the readers' mind as to why Zilu would care so much about whether a person has a reputation for *xiao* as long as it is being accomplished. Is this not shallow of him? A reputation for *xiao* was a valuable commodity in ancient China and could make (or break, if un-*xiao*) one's career, not unlike how being known as a "family man" could help one's career in America in the not-so-distant past.

naturally be established. Therefore, if a *junzi* is generous and kind at home and makes capable and virtuous friends outside, how could he not earn a reputation as *xiao*?"[12]

22.4

孔子遭厄於陳、蔡之間，絶糧七日，弟子餒病，孔子弦歌。子路入見曰："夫子之歌，禮乎？"孔子弗應，曲終而曰："由，來！吾語汝，君子好樂，爲無驕也；小人好樂，爲無懾也。其誰之子，不我知而從我者乎？"子路悦，援戚而舞，三終而出。明日，免於厄。子貢執轡曰："二三子從夫子而遭此難也，其弗忘矣！"孔子曰："善，惡何也？夫陳、蔡之間，丘之幸也。二三子從丘者，皆幸也。吾聞之，君不困不成王，烈士不困行不彰。庸知其非激憤厲志之始於是乎在？"

When Confucius was trapped between Chen and Cai and ran out of grain for seven days, his students suffered from hunger. Confucius played the zither and sang.

Zilu entered and asked, "Is it in accord with *li* for you to sing?"

Confucius did not respond and instead finished his song. Then he said, "Yóu, come here and I will tell you. While a small-minded person may enjoy music for the purpose of reducing fear, a *junzi* enjoys music for the purpose of reducing arrogance. Do you follow me without really understanding me?"

Zilu was delighted by this, grabbed a spear, and danced to several songs before leaving.

The next day, they were released.

Zigong, holding the reins, said, "All of you followers of our teacher, don't forget the difficulty we encountered here!"

Confucius said, "Yes, but was it all bad? Being between Chen and Cai could be a stroke of luck for me and for all those who follow me. I have heard it said:

A king without hardship will never reign
A hero without hardship will never shine

"Who knows but that the experience will spur the beginning of our own will and determination? And it all started here!"

22.5

孔子之宋，匡人簡子以甲士圍之。子路怒，奮戟將與戰。孔子止之曰："惡有修仁義而不免世俗之惡者乎？夫《詩》《書》之不講，禮、樂之不習，是丘之過也。若以述先王、好古法而爲咎者，則非丘之罪也，命之夫。由，歌，予和汝。"子路彈琴而歌，孔子和之，曲三終，匡人解甲而罷。

12. This episode appears almost verbatim in *Xunzi* 29.

Confucius went to Song, and on the way Jianzi of Kuang surrounded him with armored soldiers. Enraged, Zilu leapt up with a polearm and was about to engage them in battle.

Confucius stopped him, saying, "How is it that you have cultivated *ren* and *yi* and yet cannot overcome the faults of a commoner? If I had not studied poetry and history or had not practiced *li* and music, this would all be my fault. If I, having inherited the ways of the Ancient Kings and favoring the ancient exemplars, still incur disaster, that is not an error on my part but is due to circumstance.

"Yóu, begin singing, and I will follow."

Zilu strummed the zither and sang. Confucius followed along in song.

After several songs, the Kuang people removed their armor and left.[13]

22.6

孔子曰："不觀高崖，何以知顛墜之患？不臨深泉，何以知没溺之患？不觀巨海，何以知風波之患？失之者其不在此乎？士慎此三者，則無累於身矣。"

Confucius said, "How can you understand the danger of a fall if you have not peered over a cliff's edge? How can you understand the danger of drowning if you have not encountered deep waters? How can you understand the danger of wind and waves if you have not stood at the ocean's shore? Are these not reasons people make such errors? An up-and-comer who is cautious about these three will not bring them upon himself."

22.7

子貢問於孔子曰："賜既爲人下矣，而未知爲人下之道，敢問之。"子曰："爲人下者，其猶土乎。汨之[14]深則出泉，樹其壤，則百穀滋焉，草木植焉，禽獸育焉，生則出焉，死則入焉。多其功而不意，弘其志而無不容。爲人下者以此也。"

Zigong asked Confucius, "I have begun putting myself below others but don't fully understand the *dao* of putting oneself below others. Could you please tell me?"

Confucius said, "Putting yourself below others is like the soil. Dig down, and you find fresh water. Plant seedlings, and all kinds of grains come to life. Trees and plants grow in soil; birds and beasts breed in it. Things come out of it at the beginning of

13. This passage provides context for two references in the *Analects* (9.5, 11.23) in which Confucius is vaguely said to encounter trouble in Kuang.

14. After *zhi* 之, SBCK has another *zhi* 之. SKQS and Tongwen editions do not. We follow Yang and Song (2013) in removing it, as it appears excrescent.

life and go into it at death. You can amplify its accomplishments, but it will pay no heed. You can praise its ideals, but it won't stop embracing everything. To put yourself below others is to do these things."

22.8

孔子適鄭, 與弟子相失, 獨立東郭門外。或人謂子貢曰: "東門外有一人焉, 其長九尺有六寸, 河目隆顙, 其頭似堯, 其頸似皋繇, 其肩似子產, 然自腰已下, 不及禹者三寸, 纍然如喪家之狗。"子貢以告, 孔子欣然而嘆曰: "形狀末也, 如喪家之狗, 然乎哉! 然乎哉!"

Confucius went to Zheng and got separated from his students. He stood alone outside the eastern wall.

Someone inquired of Zigong: "There is someone outside the eastern wall. He is seven feet two inches tall, with long, even eyes and a high forehead. His head resembles that of Yao, his neck that of Gao Yao, his shoulders those of Zichan. But from the waist down, he is a few inches shorter than Yǔ.[15] He appears disillusioned to the point that he resembles a lost puppy."

When Zigong told Confucius about this, Confucius smiled and sighed, "My physical features are neither here nor there, but as for looking like a lost puppy, that is exactly right, exactly right!"

22.9

孔子適衛, 路出于蒲, 會公叔氏以蒲叛衛, 而止之。孔子弟子有公良儒者, 爲人賢長, 有勇力, 以私車五乘從夫子行, 喟然曰: "昔吾從夫子遇難于匡, 又伐樹於宋, 今遇困於此, 命也夫! 與其見夫子仍遇於難, 寧我鬥死。"挺劍而合衆, 將與之戰。蒲人懼, 曰: "苟無適衛, 吾則出子。"以盟孔子, 而出之東門。孔子遂適衛。子貢曰: "盟可負乎?" 孔子曰: "要我以盟, 非義也。"衛侯聞孔子之來, 喜而於郊迎之。問伐蒲, 對曰: "可哉!"公曰: "吾大夫以爲蒲者, 衛之所以恃晉、楚也。伐之, 無乃不可乎?"孔子曰: "其男子有死之志, 吾之所伐者, 不過四五人矣。"公曰: "善!"卒不果伐。他日, 靈公又與夫子語, 見飛雁過而仰視之, 色不悅。孔子乃逝。

When Confucius was en route to the Wei capital and just departing the Wei town of Pu, he was stopped by one Gongshu, who was heading up a Pu rebellion against the Wei leadership. Confucius' student Gongliang Ru was with Confucius.

15. This is one of the few descriptions in early literature of the appearance of Confucius. The comparisons to the features of other historical figures are untraceable, but it is generally accepted that he was exceptionally tall and striking in appearance without being particularly handsome.

Gongliang had the bearing of a capable and virtuous leader, was courageous and strong, and had brought along five of his own carriages. He called out, "I was with you when we encountered trouble in Kuang,[16] when the tree was uprooted in Song,[17] and now we're trapped here as well. It must be destiny! I would rather fight to the death than see my teacher encounter difficulty!" He drew his sword, united the others, and was about to engage the opposition in battle.

Alarmed, the leader of the Pu rebellion said, "We will set you free if you don't go to the Wei capital."

He made the deal with Confucius, and they were allowed to depart through the east wall.

Confucius immediately went in the direction of the Wei capital.

Zigong said, "Is it okay to violate an agreement?"

Confucius said, "Coercing my assent violated *yi*."

The Wei ruler was delighted to hear that Confucius was coming and went outside the city walls to greet him. He asked whether he should attack the rebels in Pu.

Confucius replied, "Yes!"

The duke said, "My advisers say that Pu is Wei's best defense against Jin and Chu. Would attacking it not be counterproductive?"

Confucius said, "The ordinary men of Pu are willing to die rather than participate in the rebellion. What I mean by attacking them is that you can target just a handful of their men."

The duke said, "Excellent." In the end, however, no soldiers were sent to attack Pu.

Another day, when Duke Ling and Confucius were talking, the duke, with an expression of displeasure on his face, raised his eyes and gazed at a flock of geese flying overhead.

Confucius left Wei.

22.10

衛蘧伯玉賢而靈公不用, 彌子瑕不肖, 反任之。史魚驟諫而不從。史魚病將卒, 命其子曰: "吾在衛朝, 不能進蘧伯玉, 退彌子瑕, 是吾爲臣不能正君也。生而不能正君, 則死無以成禮。我死, 汝置尸牖下, 於我畢矣。"其子從之。靈公弔焉, 怪而問焉。其子以其父言告公。公愕然失容, 曰: "是寡人之過也。"於是命之殯於客位, 進蘧伯玉而用之, 退彌子瑕而遠之。孔子聞之, 曰: "古之列諫之者, 死則已矣。未有若史魚死而尸諫, 忠感其君者也, 可不謂直乎?"

Qu Boyu of Wei was a capable and virtuous man and yet was not employed by Duke Ling. Mi Zixia was neither wise nor capable but was employed. Shi Yu advised otherwise several times but was not heeded.

16. See 22.5.

17. For this incident, see under "Huan Tui" in the glossary.

Shi Yu fell ill, and on his deathbed he instructed his son: "In the Wei court, I have been unable to have Qu Boyu hired and Mi Zixia fired. As a minister I have failed in reforming my sovereign. Unable to reform my sovereign while alive, I do not deserve the proper *li* in death. When I die, simply place my body beneath the window and be done with me."

His son complied.

Duke Ling went to pay his respects. Taken aback, he asked about the situation.

The son told him what his father had said. The duke blanched in astonishment, saying, "It is my fault." He then ordered Shi's body to be placed in a coffin and given favored treatment. He also hired Qu Boyu, putting him in a position of influence, and fired Mi Zixia, keeping him at a distance.

Confucius heard about this and said, "For the heroes of the past who were able to advise their sovereigns, they stopped at death. There has never been the like of Shi Yu, whose dead body continued giving advice. His faithfulness moved his sovereign. Can this not be considered upright behavior?"

23

De of the Five Chiefs

In this chapter, Confucius narrates biographies of China's first cultural heroes, whom he esteemed as models for his own day. They were inventive, visionary, virtuous, gentle, competent, caring, practical, and in tune with nature. They created a culture, Confucius believed, that allowed for the security, flourishing, and prosperity of the people, a culture that therefore deserved to be preserved and expanded.

23.1

宰我問於孔子曰:“昔者吾聞諸榮伊曰:‘黃帝三百年。’請問黃帝者人也,抑非人也?何以能至三百年乎?”孔子曰:“禹、湯、文、武、周公,不可勝以觀也,而上世黃帝之問,將謂先生難言之故乎?”宰我曰:“上世之傳,隱微之說,卒采之辯,闇忽之意,非君子之道者,則予之問也固矣。”孔子曰:“可也,吾略聞其說。黃帝者,少典之子,曰軒轅。生而神靈,弱而能言,幼齊睿莊,敦敏誠信,長聰明。治五氣,設五量,撫萬民,度四方。服牛乘馬,擾馴猛獸,以與炎帝戰于阪泉之野,三戰而後剋之。始垂衣裳,作爲黼黻。治民以順天地之紀,知幽明之故,達生死存亡之說。播時百穀,嘗味草木,仁厚及於鳥獸昆蟲。考日月星辰,勞耳目,勤心力,用水火財物以生民。民賴其利,百年而死;民畏其神,百年而亡;民用其教,百年而移。故曰‘黃帝三百年’。”

Zai Wo asked Confucius, "I once heard Rong Yi say, 'Three centuries of the Yellow Chief.'[1] Was the Yellow Chief really a person? How could he have lived for three hundred years?"

Confucius said, "We can't get a full picture of Yǔ, Tang, Wen, Wu, or the Duke of Zhou, and yet you ask about the Yellow Chief, who lived in an even earlier age. Isn't this why it is such a difficult question to answer?"[2]

1. *Chief, di* 帝: often translated as *emperor*. The position of these leaders is understood in the tradition as being more like tribal chief—and forerunner of later kings and emperors—than ruler of vast empire. See "Emperor" in the glossary.

2. In this chapter, Confucius attempts to make sense of some common stories about legendary figures. For equivalents from our own culture, think of Methuselah's living for hundreds of years or King Arthur's

Zai Wo said, "Legends from earlier ages, vague and indistinct theories, debates about things that have come and gone, obscure and hazy ideas—these are not the *dao* of a *junzi*. It is callous of me to pose the question."

Confucius said, "That's fine. I have learned a little bit about it.

"The Yellow Chief was the son of Shao Dian and was also called Xuanyuan. He was born with special capacities. He was articulate at a very young age. He was bright when small and grew into a wise young man. He was generous, compassionate, sincere, and trustworthy. As an adult, he was very perceptive. He classified the five *qi*, established the five units of measurement, took leadership over the populace, and traversed the four directions. He tamed the ox and broke the horse. He domesticated wild beasts. He fought with Chief Yan in the fields outside Banquan, defeating him after three battles. He started the custom of wearing draped clothing and embroidering patterns with distinctive insignia. He governed the people in line with the cycles of nature. He understood the reasons behind mysterious events and the theories about life and death. He made sure that grains were planted according to the season and personally tasted the various plants and herbs. He extended his *ren* and care to the birds, the beasts, and the bugs. He studied astronomy and developed the use of water, fire, and other natural resources, devoting all of his energy to fostering a flourishing populace. For the century of his lifetime, people came to depend on the benefits he brought them. For a century after his death, people paid respect to his spirit. For still another century after that, people maintained his teachings. This is why it is said, 'Three centuries of the Yellow Chief.'"

23.2

宰我曰:"請問帝顓頊。"孔子曰:"五帝用說, 三王有度, 汝欲一日遍聞遠古之說, 躁哉! 予也。"宰我曰:"昔予也聞諸夫子曰:'小子毋或宿。'故敢問。"孔子曰:"顓頊, 黃帝之孫, 昌意之子, 曰高陽。淵而有謀, 疏通以知遠, 養財以任地, 履時以象天, 依鬼神而制義, 治氣性以教衆, 潔誠以祭祀, 巡四海以寧民。北至幽陵, 南暨交趾, 西抵流沙, 東極蟠木, 動静之類, 小大之物, 日月所照, 莫不底屬。"

Zai Wo said, "Could you tell me about Chief Zhuanxu?"

Confucius said, "All we know about the Five Chiefs are legends, unlike the Three Kings, for which we have history.[3] You want to hear about all the legends in one day? Yu, you are too impatient!"

---

pulling the sword from the stone. Notice that Confucius interprets the stories in terms of the good that each of these figures has done for society. Sima Qian, looking at this same issue from the perspective of a historian, cites the contents of this chapter, which appears elsewhere only in the *Da Dai li ji*.

3. *History, du* 度: standards, something more rigorous than just legends.

Zai Wo said, "I once heard you say, 'Students should never wait for another day.' That's why I dare to ask."

Confucius said, "Zhuanxu was the grandson of the Yellow Chief and the son of Changyi. He is also known as Gao Yang. Far-thinking and good at planning, he knew what was off in the future by looking at events in the past; he put land to good use by nurturing natural resources; he modeled himself after *tian* by aligning with temporal cycles; he established a system for appropriate actions grounded in ancestors and spirits; he instructed the masses in how to regulate their inner selves; he performed proper sacrifices with purity and integrity; and he brought peace to the people by traveling all across the land. He went as far as Youling in the north, Jiaozhi in the south, the deserts in the west, and Panmu in the east. Whether restive or tranquil, large or small, wherever the sun and moon shone all came to subordinate themselves to him."

23.3

宰我曰："請問帝嚳。"孔子曰："玄枵之孫，喬極之子，曰高辛。生而神異，自言其名。博施厚利，不於其身。聰以知遠，明以察微。仁以威，惠而信，以順天地之義。知民所急，修身而天下服，取地之財而節用焉，撫教萬民而誨利之，歷日月之生朔而迎送之，明鬼神而敬事之。其色也和，其德也重，其動也時，其服也哀。春夏秋冬，育護天下。日月所照，風雨所至，莫不從化。"

Zai Wo said, "Could you tell me about Chief Ku?"

Confucius said, "The grandson of Xuanxiao and the son of Jiaoji, he is also known as Gao Xin. From the day he was born, he had unique abilities, such as being able to say his name. He spread his vast knowledge widely and was generous in benefiting others, never considering himself. He was perceptive with regard to both distant events and subtle events at hand. He was *ren* and dignified, wise and trustworthy, with *yi* that came from being in tune with heaven and earth. He understood the anxieties of the people, and people complied with him because of his high level of self-cultivation. He harvested natural resources but used them sparingly. He touched the people through his instruction, benefiting them greatly. He established a calendar so that the movements of the sun and moon could be predicted. He understood ancestors and spirits and demonstrated respect for and service to them. He was mild in his facial expressions, solid in his *de*, timely in his actions, and sincere in his mourning. He nurtured and protected the whole land in every season of the year. Wherever the sun and moon shone, wherever wind and rain blew, everyone was transformed by him."

23.4

宰我曰：“請問帝堯。”孔子曰：“高辛氏之子，曰陶唐。其仁如天，其智如神。就之如日，望之如雲。富而不驕，貴而能降。伯夷典禮，夔、龍典樂，舜時而仕，趨視四時，務先民始之，流四凶而天下服。其言不忒，其德不回。四海之內，舟輿所及，莫不夷說。”

Zai Wo said, "What about Chief Yao?"

Confucius said, "The son of Gao Xin, he is also known as Taotang. He was as *ren* as the heavens and as all-knowing as spirits. Approaching him was like approaching the sun. Seeing him was like watching clouds. He was affluent but not arrogant, high up but able to come down. He had Boyi to manage *li* for him and Kui and Long to manage music. Shun was brought on at the right time to work as his minister. He paid close attention to the four seasons and put the needs of the people first. After he had exiled the four villains,[4] people across the land paid allegiance to him. His speech was never untoward, his *de* never insincere. Wherever boats and wagons went within the four seas, everyone flourished."

23.5

宰我曰：“請問帝舜。”孔子曰：“喬牛之孫，瞽瞍之子也，曰有虞。舜孝友聞於四方，陶漁事親。寬裕而溫良，敦敏而知時，畏天而愛民，恤遠而親近。承受大命，依于二女。睿明智通，爲天下帝，命二十二臣，率堯舊職，躬己而已。天平地成，巡狩四海，五載一始。三十年在位，嗣帝五十載，陟方岳，死于蒼梧之野而葬焉。”

Zai Wo said, "What about Chief Shun?"

Confucius said, "The grandson of Jiaoniu and son of Gusou, he is also known as Youyu. Shun's *xiao* and amiability were famous throughout the land. He made ceramics and fished to support his parents. He was magnanimous, warmhearted, sincere, and astute, and he understood timeliness. He held *tian* in awe and cared for the people. He empathized with those far away and attended to those nearby. He was able to handle great responsibility and often relied on his two women.[5] He was sagacious and intelligent, wise in all things. As chief of the land, he commanded twenty-two ministers, followed the organization established by Yao, and was respectful and nothing more.[6] With the heavens peaceful and the earth fruitful, he toured the

4. According to the *Documents*, Shun (after Yao's time) exiled four obscure legendary figures, each to an obscure distant place. According to CQZZ ("Wen" 18.7), Shun (under Yao) exiled the vile rulers of four obscure peoples.

5. Shun was married to two daughters of Yao.

6. This resonates with *Analects* 15.5, which says that Shun was a model for ruling through *wu wei* by simply being respectful.

country once every five years. He initially held a position in the government for thirty years[7] and then sat on the throne for fifty. While touring the country he passed away in rural Cangwu and was buried there."

23.6

宰我曰："請問禹。"孔子曰："高陽之孫，鯀之子也，曰夏后。敏給克齊，其德不爽，其仁可親，其言可信。聲爲律，身爲度，亹亹穆穆，爲紀爲綱。其功爲百神之主，其惠爲民父母。左準繩，右規矩，履四時，據四海。任皋繇、伯益，以贊其治，興六師以征不序，四極之民，莫敢不服。"

Zai Wo said, "What about Yǔ?"[8]

Confucius said, "The grandson of Gao Yang and son of Gun, he is also known as Xia Hou. He was sharp, articulate, disciplined, and nimble. His *de* was error-free, his *ren* was approachable, and his speech was trustworthy. His voice set the standard, and his person was the measure. Tirelessly respectful, he was the moral norm for all. His practical accomplishments were so great that they set him as leader of even the hundred spirits. His compassion made him the parent of the people. To his left was the carpenter's measuring line, to his right the compass and square. He followed the seasons in everything he did and occupied all of the land within the four seas. He employed Gao Yao and Bo Yi as ministers to assist him in governing. He led six armies to invade recalcitrant territories, reaching all people within the four directions, until none dared defy him."

23.7

孔子曰："予！大者如天，小者如言，民悅至矣。予也非其人也。"宰我曰："予也不足以戒敬承矣。"他日，宰我以語子貢，子貢以復孔子。子曰："吾欲以顏狀取人也，則於滅明改之矣；吾欲以言辭取人也，則於宰我改之矣；吾欲以容貌取人也，則於子張改之矣。"宰我聞之，懼，弗敢見焉。

Confucius said, "Their minor aspects were as I've said, and their greatness was like that of the heavens. The people could not have been happier. Yu, you are not on the same level with those men."

Zai Wo said, "I am inadequate to receive your instruction."

7. As minister under Yao.

8. The title of the chapter is "*De* of the Five Chiefs," and yet here we have a sixth figure. Yǔ is not usually categorized as one of the Five Chiefs.

Another day, Zai Wo told Zigong about what had happened, who then repeated it to Confucius. Confucius said, "I used to judge people based on their appearance, but Mieming cured me of that. I used to judge people based on what they said, but Zai Wo cured me of that. I used to judge people based on their facial expressions, but Zizhang cured me of that."

When Zai Wo heard about this, he was struck with anxiety and didn't dare meet with Confucius because of it.

24

The Five "Chiefs"

The five "chiefs" in this chapter are a metaphor for the so-called five elemental phases—water, fire, metal, wood, and earth—which, in addition to being raw materials and resources, were also viewed as physical substrates and perhaps as metaphysical powers in their own right.

24.1

季康子問於孔子曰:"舊聞五帝之名,而不知其實,請問何謂五帝?"孔子曰:"昔丘也聞諸老聃曰:'天有五行:水、火、金、木、土。分時化育,以成萬物,其神謂之五帝。'古之王者,易代而改號,取法五行。五行更王,終始相生,亦象其義。故其爲明王者,而死配五行。是以太皞配木,炎帝配火,黄帝配土,少皞配金,顓頊配水。"

Ji Kangzi asked Confucius, "For a long time, I've heard the term five "chiefs," but I don't know what it really means. May I ask what is meant by five "chiefs"?

Confucius said, "I also once asked Lao Dan about this, and he said that in nature, there are five elemental phases: water, fire, metal, wood, and earth. Depending on timing, they transform all things in the world, fostering them to maturity. Their spiritual aspects are called the five 'chiefs.' Ancient kings changed their dynastic periods following the model of the elemental phases. The alternation of moving from one king to another is like the changing of the phases. It is a dynamic cycle, with each giving rise to the next, and there is a symbolic meaning to it. Therefore, enlightened kings of the past were matched at death with one of the elemental phases. Tai Hao was matched with wood, Chief Yan was matched with fire, the Yellow Chief was matched with earth, Shao Hao was matched with metal, and Zhuanxu was matched with water."[1]

1. These five overlap with the Five Chiefs in the previous chapter only in the cases of the Yellow Chief and Zhuanxu.

24.2

康子曰："太皞氏其始之木何如?"孔子曰："五行用事，先起於木。木東方，萬物之初皆出焉。是故王者則之，而首以木德王天下，其次則以所生之行轉相承也。"

Kangzi said, "What does it mean that Tai Hao begins in wood?"

Confucius said, "In how the five elemental phases correspond to events, the beginning is in wood. Wood corresponds to the east, where all things get their start.[2] Beginning with the power of wood to rule the land, kings follow in the same order, the next phase being generated from that and taking its place."

24.3

康子曰："吾聞勾芒爲木正，祝融爲火正，蓐收爲金正，玄冥爲水正，后土爲土正，此則五行之主而不亂，稱曰帝者，何也?"孔子曰："凡五正者，五行之官名。五行佐成上帝，而稱五帝。太皞之屬配焉，亦云帝，從其號。昔少皞氏之子有四叔，曰重、曰該、曰脩、曰熙，實能金、木及水。使重爲勾芒，該爲蓐收，脩及熙爲玄冥。顓頊氏之子曰黎，爲祝融。共工氏之子曰勾龍，爲后土。此五者，各以其所能業爲官職，生爲上公，死爲貴神，别稱五祀，不得同帝。"

Kangzi said, "But I have heard that Goumang was the wood reformer, Zhurong was the fire reformer, Rushou was the metal reformer, Xuanming was the water reformer, and Houtu was the earth reformer.[3] These are leaders associated with the five elemental phases, and by which they prevented chaos. Why are they called chiefs?"

Confucius said, "The official titles that adopt the names of the five phases can be applied to any five reformers. The five phases are known as the five 'chiefs' because of the way that they assisted the high chiefs in their accomplishments. That which matches Tai Hao is also called a 'chief' and is used as a byname. Shao Hao had four uncles,[4] called Chong, Gai, Xiu, and Xi, who were skilled with metal, wood, and water. The arrangement was such that Chong was Goumang, Gai was Rushou, and Xiu and Xi were Xuanming. The name of Zhuanxu's son was Li; he was Zhurong.

2. As in the start of a day, with the sun rising in the east.

3. Each of the five figures here are associated in the early literature with the elemental phases as mentioned by Ji Kangzi and are often elevated to the status of gods—each the appropriate deity to supplicate for relevant reasons. This explains why Confucius goes on to say that it is best to refer to them in terms of sacrificing rather than as chiefs.

4. *Uncles*: The Chinese has *zhi zi you shu* 之子有叔: his children had uncles. CQZZ ("Zhao" 29.4) contains a similar passage but without the *zhi zi* (his children), suggesting that it may be excrescent. Yang Bojun (2016) agrees with the *Dialogues* account. We follow CQZZ.

The name of the son of Gonggong was Goulong; he was Houtu.[5] The working capacity of each one of these became his official position. During their lives, they held the most exalted positions, and in death they were revered as gods. Another reference to them is the term *five sacrificial ceremonies*. They are not the same as chiefs."

24.4

康子曰："如此之言，帝王改號，於五行之德，各有所統，則其所以相變者，皆主何事?"孔子曰："所尚則各從其所王之德次焉。夏后氏以金德王，色尚黑，大事斂用昏，戎事乘驪，牲用玄；殷人用水德王，色尚白，大事斂用日中，戎事乘翰，牲用白；周人以木德王，色尚赤，大事斂用日出，戎事乘騵，牲用騂。此三代之所以不同。"康子曰："唐、虞二帝，其所尚者何色?"孔子曰："堯以火德王，色尚黃。舜以土德王，色尚青。"

Kangzi said, "From what you say, then, the names of the 'chiefs' are related to the powers of the elemental phases, with each dynasty using it in some way to rule. In what kinds of things were they used?"

Confucius said, "What was elevated was the power that was exploited for ruling. The sequence was as follows: The Xia people used metal for their ruling power; their color was black—the black of dusk for mourning, black horses for war, and black animals for sacrifices. The Shang leaders used water for their ruling power; their color was white—the white of the noon sun for mourning, white horses for war, and white animals for sacrifices. The Zhou leaders use wood for their ruling power; their color is red—the red of dawn for mourning, red horses for war, and red animals for sacrifices. These are the differences among the three dynasties."

Kangzi said, "What colors did the chiefs Yao and Shun use?"

Confucius said, "Yao used fire for his ruling power; his color was yellow. Shun used earth for his ruling power; his color was green."

24.5

康子曰："陶唐、有虞、夏后、殷、周獨不配五帝，意者德不及上古耶？將有限乎?"孔子曰："古之平治水土，及播殖百穀者衆矣，唯勾龍氏兼食於社，而棄爲稷神，易代奉之，無敢益者，明不可與等。故自太皞以降，逮于顓頊，其應五行而王，數非徒五，而配五帝，是其德不可以多也。"

5. *Shao Hao ... Hou Tu* (four sentences): CQZZ ("Zhao" 29.4) contains a version of this story, but rather than being spoken by Confucius, it is in the mouth of an otherwise unknown official of Cai, who is originally asked to explain the appearance of a dragon. That passage ends by explaining how the figures mentioned are associated with the Sheji sacrifices. The names of the uncles are not attested elsewhere.

Kangzi said, "Is it the case that Taotang, Youyu, Xia Hou,[6] Shang, and Zhou didn't match the five 'chiefs,' and does that suggest that their *de* was inferior to that of their ancient predecessors? Is there a limit as time passes?"

Confucius said, "There were many in the most ancient time who successfully cultivated grain by managing water and soil, but only Goulong was installed as a god in temples to the soil, and only Hou Ji was known as the god of grain. In successive eras since then, they were sacrificed to, and none presumed to improve upon them, demonstrating that none was their equal. Since the time of Tai Hao through Zhuanxu, the number of those who ruled through responsiveness to the five elemental phases was more than just five, but of those who matched the five 'chiefs,' their *de* could not surpass them."

6. Taotang, Youyu, and Xia Hou refer to Yao, Shun, and Yǔ, respectively, the final three figures of the previous chapter.

25

Controlling the Bit

Chapter 25 comes in two distinct parts. In the first two episodes we have a lengthy disquisition by Confucius on the centrality of virtue and norms to governing, in which the emphasis is on managing the emotions and behavior of the people in the same way that one would manage the emotions and behavior of a team of horses. It requires care, coordination, and a light hand. In the two episodes constituting the second half of the chapter, we have a lengthy disquisition from Zixia on numerology and a quaint explanation of certain natural phenomena. Perhaps these two episodes are what Kong Anguo meant when he called some of the content of the *Dialogues* "baseless, confused, and dispensable."

25.1

閔子騫爲費宰, 問政於孔子。子曰: "以德以法。夫德法者, 御民之具, 猶御馬之有銜勒也。君者, 人也; 吏者, 轡也; 刑者, 策也。夫人君之政, 執其轡策而已。"子騫曰: "敢問古之爲政。"孔子曰: "古者天子以内史爲左右手, 以德法爲銜勒, 以百官爲轡, 以刑罰爲策, 以萬民爲馬, 故御天下數百年而不失。善御馬者, 正銜勒, 齊轡策, 均馬力, 和馬心, 故口無聲而馬應轡, 策不舉而極千里; 善御民者, 壹其德法, 正其百官, 以均齊民力, 和安民心, 故令不再而民順從, 刑不用而天下治。是以天地德之, 而兆民懷之。夫天地之所德, 兆民之所懷, 其政美, 其民而衆稱之。今人言五帝三王者, 其盛無偶, 威察若存, 其故何也? 其法盛, 其德厚, 故思其德必稱其人, 朝夕祝之, 升聞於天, 上帝俱歆, 用永厥世, 而豐其年。不能御民者, 棄其德法, 專用刑辟, 譬猶御馬, 棄其銜勒而專用棰策, 其不制也, 可必矣。夫無銜勒而用棰策, 馬必傷, 車必敗; 無德法而用刑, 民必流, 國必亡。治國而無德法, 則民無脩, 民無脩則迷惑失道。如此上帝必以其爲亂天道也。苟亂天道, 則刑罰暴, 上下相諛, 莫知念患, 俱無道故也。今人言惡者, 必比之於桀紂, 其故何也? 其法不聽, 其德不厚, 故民惡其殘虐, 莫不吁嗟, 朝夕祝之, 升聞于天。上帝不蠲, 降之以禍罰, 災害並生, 用殄厥世。故曰德法者, 御民之本。

When Min Ziqian was mayor of Bi, he asked Confucius about governing. Confucius said, "Use virtue and norms. Virtue and norms are tools for controlling the behavior of the people, like a bit and bridle for controlling the behavior of a horse.[1] The ruler is the rider, government officials are the reins, and punishments are the riding crop. Governing by a ruler lies simply in handling the reins and the crop."

Ziqian said, "May I ask about government in ancient times?"

Confucius said, "In ancient times, the king took his court advisers as his left and right hands, took virtue and norms as bit and bridle, took all the various officials as reins, took criminal punishments as riding crop, and took the people as the horse, guiding the world for hundreds of years without error. Someone who excels at driving a horse keeps the bit and bridle steady and is nimble in his use of the reins and crop, maintaining the horse at an even pace and steadying the horse's emotions. As a result, the horse responds to the reins without a sound from its mouth and reaches hundreds of miles without the use of the crop.

"Someone who excels at guiding the people is consistent in virtues and norms, keeps the various officials in line, nimbly keeps the people's lives at an even pace, and keeps the people's emotions steady. As a result, people follow instructions without needing them repeated, and the entire land remains orderly without the need for criminal punishments. And so nature looks on him with *de,* and the people embrace him. The reason nature looks on him with *de* and the people embrace him is that his governing is commendable and the masses esteem him.

"What was the reason that there was an unparalleled abundance under the Five Chiefs and Three Kings and such a high level of awe for them? Their norms were superb, and their virtue was profuse. Thus, people remembering their virtue inevitably praised them, such that they were sacrificed to, with reputations reaching the heavens, the high ancestors all delighting in them, enduring across generations, abundant in their years.

"Someone who cannot guide the people abandons virtue and norms, using only criminal punishments. To analogize with driving a horse, it is like abandoning the bit and bridle and using only the whip and crop—undoubtedly the horse cannot be controlled in this way. If the whip and crop are used without the bit and bridle, the horse will be injured and the carriage will be lost.

"If only criminal punishments are used, without virtue or norms, the people will flee and the country will be lost. If a country is governed without virtue or norms, the people will have no self-discipline. If the people have no self-discipline, they will be confused and lose their way. The high ancestors would certainly view this as disrupting the *dao* of *tian*. If the *dao* of *tian* is disrupted, the use of criminal punishments will soar, both upper and lower levels of society will resort to flattery, none will recognize the danger, and all will lack *dao*.

1. *Horse, ma* 馬: Number is not a lexical feature in classical Chinese, and so this could also be plural, as in 25.2 below.

"Nowadays when people speak of someone with bad behavior, they inevitably compare the person to Jie and Zhòu. Why is this? Because their norms were not worth following, nor was their virtue profuse, and so people despised their cruelty and neglect. Everyone was exasperated. Day and night, prayers were made, rising up to the heavens, but the high ancestors refused them and sent disasters down instead, and these, combined with man-made catastrophes, cut short their lineages.

"Therefore, it is said that virtues and norms are the basis of controlling the behavior of the people.

25.2

"古之御天下者, 以六官總治焉: 冢宰之官以成道, 司徒之官以成德, 宗伯之官以成仁, 司馬之官以成聖, 司寇之官以成義, 司空之官以成禮。六官在手以爲轡, 司會均仁以爲納, 故曰: 御四馬者執六轡, 御天下者正六官。是故善御馬者, 正身以總轡, 均馬力, 齊馬心, 回旋曲折, 唯其所之, 故可以取長道、可赴急疾。此聖人所以御天地與人事之法則也。天子以內史爲左右手, 以六官爲轡, 已而與三公爲執六官, 均五教, 齊五法, 故亦唯其所引, 無不如志, 以之道則國治, 以之德則國安, 以之仁則國和, 以之聖則國平, 以之禮則國定, 以之義則國義, 此御政之術。過失, 人之情莫不有焉, 過而改之, 是爲不過。故官屬不理, 分職不明, 法政不一, 百事失紀, 曰亂。亂則飭冢宰。地而不殖, 財物不蕃, 萬民饑寒, 教訓不行, 風俗淫僻, 人民流散, 曰危。危則飭司徒。父子不親, 長幼失序, 君臣上下乖離異志, 曰不和。不和則飭宗伯。賢能而失官爵, 功勞而失賞祿, 士卒疾怨, 兵弱不用, 曰不平。不平則飭司馬。刑罰暴亂, 奸邪不勝, 曰不義。不義則飭司寇。度量不審, 舉事失理, 都鄙不脩, 財物失所, 曰貧。貧則飭司空。故御者同是車馬, 或以取千里, 或不及數百里, 其所謂進退緩急異也; 夫治者同是官法, 或以致平, 或以致亂者, 亦其所以爲進退緩急異也。古者, 天子常以季冬考德正法, 以觀治亂。德盛者治也, 德薄者亂也。故天子考德, 則天下之治亂, 可坐廟堂之上而知之。夫德盛則法修, 德不盛則飭法, 與政咸德而不衰。故曰: 王者又以孟春論吏之德及功能, 能德法者爲有德, 能行德法者爲有行, 能成德法者爲有功, 能治德法者爲有智。故天子論吏而德法行, 事治而功成。夫季冬正法, 孟春論吏, 治國之要。"

"Those who guided the land in ancient times used the six ministers to govern all. The prime minister succeeded by way of *dao*. The minister of education succeeded by way of *de*. The minister of ceremony succeeded by way of *ren*. The minister of security succeeded by way of sageliness. The minister of justice succeeded by way of *yi*. And the minister of public works succeeded by way of *li*.[2] With the six ministers as reins in his hands, the examiner[3] used even distribution of *ren* as the stabilizing

2. It is interesting that *ren* is assigned to the minister of ceremony, while *li* is assigned to the minster of public works.

3. *Examiner, si kuai* 司會: In SBCK, this term was mistakenly relegated to commentary. Following Yang and Song (2013), we have restored it to the main text based on the SKQS and Tongwen editions. It also occurs in the *Da Dai li ji* version of this passage.

reins.[4] And so it is said, 'Just as guiding four horses requires holding six reins,[5] so guiding the land requires maintaining the correctness of the six ministers.'

"Someone who excels at driving horses sits upright and gathers the reins, maintaining the horses' pace and keeping their emotions even. He can wind this way and that, going in whichever direction he wishes. He can run them for long distances and break into a sprint when necessary. This is the method for how a sage guides the world and manages human affairs. The king takes his court advisers as his left and right hands, the six ministers as reins. With his three top advisers, he wields the six ministers, spreads the five transformative teachings, and promotes the five norms.[6] And so he can lead in whichever direction he wishes. With his *dao*, the country is well governed; with his *de*, the country is steady; with his *ren*, the country is harmonious;[7] with his sageliness, the country is at peace; with his *li*, the country is stable; with his *yi*, the country is *yi*. This is the art of guiding the country. It is human nature to make mistakes, and to correct them is like not having made them in the first place.

"Turmoil occurs when the official lines of command are not well ordered, when responsibilities are not clearly assigned, when policies and laws are not consistent, and when there is no sequence to how things are undertaken. In times of turmoil, correct the prime minister.

"Crisis occurs when the soil is not cultivated, when finances are not ample, when the people are hungry and cold, when teachings and trainings are not circulated, when customs are perverted, or when the people emigrate. In times of crisis, correct the minister of education.

"Disharmony occurs when parents and children are not close, when proper ordering is lost among the different age groups, and when the sovereign and ministers are not in harmony. In times of disharmony, correct the minister of ceremony.

"Disquiet occurs when the capable and virtuous lose their positions of leadership, when accomplishments are not rewarded, when there are incessant complaints from lower-level bureaucrats, and when soldiers are not at the ready. In times of disquiet, correct the minister of security.

4. In a team of four horses, the two inner horses are attached to the carriage crossbar with stabilizing reins, one per horse.

5. Two each from the two outside horses and one each from the two inner horses.

6. Five norms: *wǔ fǎ* 五法: This is not a common locution, and the exact reference is unclear. Wang Su says it refers to *ren*, *yi*, *li*, wisdom, and trustworthiness. However, a passage in the *Li ji* ("Shen yi") says the five norms are associated with the costume of government officials and identified as the compass, square, cord, weight, and balance bar and signify specific virtues of governing. The compass and square signify impartiality, the cord (hanging vertically) signifies uprightness, the weight and balance bar (forming a scale) signify a calm and steady mind.

7. *Stable . . . harmonious, an . . . he* 安 . . . 和: This use of *an* and *he* may tie back to the emotional steadying (*he an* 和安) of 25.1.

"Injustice occurs when criminal punishments surge and when misbehavior in society cannot be checked. In times of injustice, correct the minister of justice.

"Poverty occurs when units of measure are not precise, when bureaucratic duties are not regularized, when city walls are not repaired, and when finances are not properly distributed. In times of poverty, correct the minister of public works.

"Even if all drivers were the same in their horses and carriages, some would be able to cover hundreds of miles while others couldn't even go dozens of miles. The difference would lie in how they handle their direction and speed. Even if all leaders were the same in their officials and laws, some would achieve peace while others would end in turmoil. The difference would lie in how they handle their direction and speed.

"In ancient times, the king took the last month of the year to assess virtues and reform norms for the purpose of evaluating whether things were tending in the direction of order or disorder. If virtue was in abundance, then order would prevail. If virtue was lacking, disorder would prevail. He could achieve all of this by just sitting in the ancestral temple.

"If virtue is abundant, that means norms are well honed. If virtue is not abundant, then reform the norms, by which you can bring all virtues to government without decline. And so it is said, 'A ruler takes the first month of the year to evaluate the virtues, accomplishments, and capacities of his officials.'

"An official who is capable of virtue and normative behavior is considered to have *de*. An official who is capable of acting according to virtues and norms is considered to have proper behavior. An official who is capable of bringing virtue and norms to full development is considered to have accomplishments. An official who is able to govern with virtue and norms is considered to have wisdom. Therefore, by evaluating the virtues, norms, and behavior of his officials, a leader ensures that things are put in order and accomplishments are made. It is essential that norms be reformed in the last month of the year and officials be evaluated in the first month of the year."

25.3

子夏問於孔子曰:"商聞易之生人及萬物、鳥獸、昆蟲, 各有奇耦, 氣分不同。而凡人莫知其情, 唯達德者能原其本焉。天一、地二、人三, 三三如九。九九八十一, 一主日, 日數十, 故人十月而生; 八九七十二, 偶以從奇, 奇主辰, 辰爲月, 月主馬, 故馬十二月而生; 七九六十三, 三主斗, 斗主狗, 故狗三月而生; 六九五十四, 四主時, 時主豕, 故豕四月而生; 五九四十五, 五爲音, 音主猿, 故猿五月而生; 四九三十六, 六爲律, 律主鹿, 故鹿六月而生; 三九二十七, 七主星, 星主虎, 故虎七月而生; 二九一十八, 八主風, 風爲蟲, 故蟲八月而生。其餘各從其類矣。鳥、魚生陰而屬於陽, 故皆卵生。魚遊於水, 鳥遊於雲, 故立冬則燕雀入海化爲蛤; 蠶食而不飲, 蟬飲而不食, 蜉蝣不飲不食, 萬物之所以不同。介鱗夏食而冬蟄, 齕吞者八竅而卵生, 齟嚼者九竅而胎生, 四足者無羽翼, 戴角者無上齒, 無角無前齒者膏, 無角無後齒者脂。晝生者類父，夜生者似母，是以至陰主牝，至陽主牡。敢問其然乎?”孔子曰：“然，吾昔聞諸老聃亦如汝之言。”

Zixia posed a long question to Confucius: "I have heard that in the *Changes* it says that each kind of living thing—people, birds, beasts, bugs—has its own even or odd number, which matches its original allotment of *qi*. Most people don't understand this. Only those who have achieved a high level of *de* are able to get to the root of it.

"The sky corresponds to the number one,[8] earth to two, and people to three. Three threes equal nine.

"Nine nines equal eighty-one. The number one is chiefly represented by daylight, and the number chiefly associated with a day is ten.[9] Therefore, people are born at ten months.[10]

"Eight nines equal seventy-two. Even numbers follow odd numbers. Odd numbers are chiefly represented by the stations of the zodiac. The stations of the zodiac are associated with the moon,[11] and the moon is chiefly represented by the horse.[12] Therefore, horses are born at twelve months.

"Seven nines equal sixty-three. The number three is chiefly represented by the dipper,[13] and the dipper is chiefly represented by the dog. Therefore, dogs are born at three months.

8. To make sense of this passage, one has to understand a little about the traditional Chinese system of numerological and calendrical counting. According to this system, the bare structure of which appears as early as the oracle bones, there are ten "sky stems" (*tian gan* 天干) and twelve "earth branches" (*di zhi* 地支). Each stem signifies a single day, and all ten successively signify one ten-day week. Each branch signifies a month, and all twelve successively signify one year. Each branch can also signify one of the twelve zodiac stations in the night sky. The stems and branches are also used as numerals that are paired to name years, a full cycle of which is complete after sixty successive pairings—sixty years. In addition, the first item of the ten stems and twelve branches, as well as each alternate item, is considered an odd number and the others are considered even numbers. Odd and even can be said to correspond to *yin* and *yang* respectively. See also under "Calendar" in the glossary. (Hua 1993; Loewe and Shaughnessy 1999; Zheng, Wu, and Yang 2000)

9. There are, for example, ten sky stems and ten days in a traditional week.

10. The association here links an important aspect of human life with an important aspect of the cosmos, in an attempt to explain astrological causal influence. Each of the subsequent sentences does the same for different animals of the Chinese zodiac. Why is the period of human gestation ten months rather than nine months? See under "Counting custom" in the glossary.

11. The moon passes through the stations of the zodiac.

12. The seven kinds of animal mentioned here belong to the twelve animals of the Chinese zodiac, although the deer mentioned here is commonly replaced by the snake in the zodiac, and the bug mentioned here is commonly replaced by the dragon.

13. The Big Dipper, the primary constellation.

"Six nines equal fifty-four. The number four is chiefly represented by the seasons, and the seasons are chiefly represented by the pig. Therefore, pigs are born at four months.

"Five nines equal forty-five. The number five signifies the notes of the musical scale,[14] and the notes of the musical scale are chiefly represented by the monkey. Therefore, monkeys are born at five months.

"Four nines equal thirty-six. The number six signifies the six pitches in music,[15] and the pitches in music are chiefly represented by the deer. Therefore, deer are born after six months.

"Three nines equal twenty-seven. The number seven is chiefly represented by stars, and stars are chiefly represented by the tiger. Therefore, tigers are born after seven months.

"Two nines equal eighteen. The number eight is chiefly represented by the wind, and the wind is chiefly represented by bugs. Therefore, bugs come to life at eight months.

"Other animals also behave according to their kind. Birds and fish are born in dark places but belong to the light. Thus, they are oviparous. Fish flow through water, and birds flow through the clouds. At the beginning of winter, small birds fly to the sea and metamorphose into shellfish.

"Silkworms eat but don't drink. Cicadas drink but don't eat. Mayflies neither eat nor drink. This is how the various creatures in the world differ.

"Animals with shells or scales feed in the summer and hibernate in the winter. Animals that swallow without chewing[16] have eight orifices[17] and are oviparous. Animals that have teeth for chewing have nine orifices[18] and are viviparous. Animals with four limbs don't have feathers. Animals with antlers or horns[19] don't have upper incisors. Those without antlers or horns and without incisors[20] produce lard.[21] Those without antlers or horns and without back teeth produce fat.

"Animals born in the daytime will take after their fathers, and those born in the nighttime will be like their mothers. This is because maximal *yin* (dark) governs the female and maximal *yang* (light) governs the male.

14. The Chinese pentatonic scale: *gong* 宫, *shang* 商, *jue* 角, *zhi* 徵, *yu* 羽.

15. The odd-numbered notes on the following twelve-note Chinese harmonic scale: *huangzhong* 黄鐘, *dalü* 大吕, *taicu* 太蔟, *jiazhong* 夾鐘, *guxi* 姑洗, *zhonglü* 仲吕, *ruibin* 蕤賓, *linzhong* 林鐘, *yize* 夷則, *nanlü* 南吕, *wuyi* 無射, *yingzhong* 應鐘. (Luo 1994)

16. Birds, reptiles, amphibians, fish.

17. Seven for the five senses plus one for reproduction and excretion.

18. Seven for the five senses, one for reproduction and excretion, and another for excretion.

19. The word *jiao* 角 can refer to both antlers and horns. The reference here is probably to bovines, deer, and goats.

20. This may be a reference to pigs, the front teeth of which are pointed rather than flat and so may not have counted to the early Chinese as incisors per se.

21. *Lard*, *gao* 膏: interpreting the animal referred to here as a pig.

"Is this correct?"

Confucius said, "Yes. I once heard Lao Dan say much the same."

25.4

子夏曰："商聞《山書》曰：'地東西爲緯，南北爲經；山爲積德，川爲積刑；高者爲生，下者爲死；丘陵爲牡，谿谷爲牝；蚌蛤龜珠，與日月而盛虛。'是故堅土之人剛，弱土之人柔，墟土之人大，沙土之人細，息土之人美，耗土之人醜。食水者善遊而耐寒，食土者無心而不息，食木者多力而不治，食草者善走而愚，食桑者有緒而蛾，食肉者勇毅而捍，食氣者神明而壽，食穀者智惠而巧，不食者不死而神。故曰：羽蟲三百有六十，而鳳爲之長；毛蟲三百有六十，而麟爲之長；甲蟲三百有六十，而龜爲之長；鱗蟲三百有六十，而龍爲之長；倮蟲三百有六十，而人爲之長。此乾坤之美也，殊形異類之數。王者動必以道，靜必順理，以奉天地之性，而不害其所主，謂之仁聖焉。"子夏言終而出，子貢進曰："商之論也何如？"孔子曰："汝謂何也？"對曰："微則微矣，然則非治世之待也。"孔子曰："然，各其所能。"

Zixia said, "I learned that the *Book of Mountains*[22] says the following: 'East and west overland is latitude; north and south is longitude. Mountains represent accumulated *de*; rivers represent repeated disfigurement. Heights represent life; depths represent death. Hills represent male; valleys represent female. Shellfish, turtles, and pearls wax and wane with the sun and moon.' It follows that people raised on firm soil are tough; people raised on loose soil are gentle; people raised on hilly soil are large; people raised on sandy soil are small; people raised on rich soil are beautiful; people raised on depleted soil are ugly.

"Those that[23] subsist on water are good at swimming and resistant to cold. Those that subsist on dirt lack a heart and do not breathe air.[24] Those that subsist on trees are energetic and unruly. Those that subsist on grasses are good runners but stupid. Those that subsist on the mulberry tree produce silk and transform into moths.[25] Those that subsist on meat are bold, ruthless, and aggressive. Those that subsist on air are spiritual, perceptive, and long-lived.[26] Those that subsist on grains are intelligent and skillful. Those that don't eat are long-lived spirits.

"Thus, it is said: Of the 360 kinds of feathered creatures, the *feng* is the leader. Of the 360 kinds of furred creatures, the *lin* is the leader. Of the 360 kinds of shelled

22. This book is not attested elsewhere.

23. There is a switch here from people to an indeterminate pronoun. Most items in this series appear to be references to non-human creatures, except for the last three.

24. This appears to be a reference to worms, which have neither hearts nor recognizable respiratory systems.

25. A reference to silkworms, which subsist almost exclusively on the leaves of mulberry trees.

26. There was a belief that the most spiritually accomplished sages could subsist on nothing but air.

creatures, the turtle is the leader. Of the 360 kinds of scaled creatures, the dragon is the leader. Of the 360 kinds of nude creatures, the human is the leader.

"This is the beauty of *qian* and *kun*,[27] the calculation of different shapes and kinds. A king must work with the *dao* when active and flow with the natural order when inactive. If he defers to the tendencies of heaven and earth, without harming that over which he has dominion, he can be recognized as a *ren* sage."

When he finished speaking, Zixia departed, and Zigong entered, saying, "What did you think of Shang's theory?"

Confucius said, "What did you think?"

Zigong replied, "Although it was subtle, it is not what is required for governing society."

Confucius said, "Yes, each according to his abilities."

27. The two primary hexagrams in the *Changes*. They are often equated with *yang* and *yin*, respectively, and here represent natural processes conceived as a result of their combination and alterations.

26

Understanding Original Destiny

Chapter 26 continues the previous chapter's discussion of biological phenomena—this time in the words of Confucius, but still of little philosophical import. What readers may find interesting is the brief discussion at the end about the origins of the three-year mourning period.

26.1

魯哀公問於孔子曰:"人之命與性何謂也?"孔子對曰:"分於道,謂之命;形於一,謂之性;化於陰陽,象形而發,謂之生;化窮數盡,謂之死。故命者,性之始也;死者,生之終也。有始,則必有終矣。人始生而有不具者五焉:目無見,不能食,不能行,不能言,不能化。及生三月而微煦,然後有見;八月生齒,然後能食;三年顋合,然後能言;十有六而精通,然後能化。陰窮反陽,故陰以陽變;陽窮反陰,故陽以陰化。是以男子八月生齒,八歲而齔;女子七月生齒,七歲而齔,十有四而化。一陽一陰,奇偶相配,然後道合化成。性命之端,形於此也。"

Duke Ai of Lu asked Confucius, "What is meant by human *fate* and human *inborn nature*?"

Confucius replied, "Differences in *dao* are called fate. Sameness in form is called inborn nature.

"Reproduction through *yin* and *yang* and development of form is called life. The exhaustion of the stages of development is called death. And so fate is the origin of inborn nature, and death is the end of life. Anything that has an origin also has an ending.

"There are five possible disabilities in human development: the inability to see, to eat, to walk, to speak, and to reproduce.

"At three months, the eyes begin to move voluntarily and then there is vision. At eight months, teeth start to erupt and there is the ability to eat. In the third year, the jaws come together and there is the ability to speak. In the sixteenth year, semen circulates and there is the ability to reproduce.

"When *yang* reaches its end, it reverts to *yin*; and so *yang* changes into *yin*. When *yin* reaches its end, it reverts to *yang*; and so *yin* transforms into *yang*. Through this process, boys get their milk teeth in their eighth month and their adult teeth in their eighth year, while girls get their milk teeth in their seventh month and their adult teeth in their seventh year, and are able to reproduce in their fourteenth year. One *yang*, one *yin*, the matching of odd and even—thereupon *dao* is unified and reproduction achieved.

"The budding of inborn nature and fate takes shape in this way."

26.2

公曰:"男子十六精通, 女子十四而化, 是則可以生民矣。而禮, 男子三十而有室, 女子二十而有夫也, 豈不晚哉?"孔子曰:"夫禮言其極, 不是過也。男子二十而冠, 有爲人父之端; 女子十五許嫁, 有適人之道。於此而往, 則自婚矣。群生閉藏乎陰, 而爲化育之始。故聖人因時以合偶男女, 窮天數也。霜降而婦功成, 嫁娶者行焉; 冰泮而農桑起, 婚禮而殺於此。男子者, 任天道而長萬物者也。知可爲, 知不可爲; 知可言, 知不可言; 知可行, 知不可行者。是故審其倫而明其别, 謂之知, 所以效匹夫之聽也。女子者, 順男子之教而長其理者也。是故無專制之義, 而有三從之道: 幼從父兄, 既嫁從夫, 夫死從子。言無再醮之端, 教令不出於閨門, 事在供酒食而已。無閫外之非儀也, 不越境而奔喪。事無擅爲, 行無獨成, 參知而後動, 可驗而後言, 晝不遊庭, 夜行以火, 所以效匹婦之德也。"

The duke said, "The semen of males begins to circulate in the sixteenth year, and females are able to reproduce in their fourteenth year; and thus the people are propagated. And yet according to *li*, men begin a household in their thirtieth year and women have a husband in their twentieth year. Is this not late?"

Confucius said, "*Li* speaks to the upper limit. It is not to be exceeded.

"Males have their capping ceremony in their twentieth year. This is when they may begin to father children. Females are permitted to marry in their fifteenth year. This suits the human *dao*. From this age forward, they marry as they may.

"All forms of life hibernate in winter, making it the beginning of the process of rearing. Thus, sages, staying within natural limits, paired up men and women according to proper timing. When the first frost comes[1] and women finish their work for the season, wedding preparations begin. By the time the ice is melting and silk farming is starting up, wedding ceremonies come to an end.

"Following the *dao* of *tian*, men nurture the things in the world. They understand when to act and when not to act, when to speak and when not to speak, when to put things into motion and when not to put things into motion. For this reason, they examine relationships and understand relevant differences. This is called understanding, and it is how the average man expresses his *de*.

1. *First frost comes, shuang jiang* 霜降: These characters may also refer to a specific fall day of the twenty-four periods of the annual calendar. (Luo 1994)

"Women follow the instructions from men and grasp the reasoning. Thus, instead of narrow concerns of their own, there are three compliances: When young, they comply with their fathers and older brothers; when married, they comply with their husbands; if their husbands die, they comply with their sons. This means that there is no new toasting ceremony.[2] Their sphere of responsibility does not extend beyond the women's quarters; their service is merely in providing food and drink. They don't do anything untoward outside the house or cross borders to attend funerals. In serving, they don't decide for themselves; in putting things into effect, they don't try to do everything themselves; they consult with others before making a move; they speak only about what is verified; they don't wander in the courtyard during the day, and they walk with a light at night. This is how the average woman expresses her virtue."[3]

26.3

孔子遂言曰："女有五不取：逆家子者，亂家子者，世有刑人子者，有惡疾子者，喪父長子者。婦有七出、三不去。七出者：不順父母出者，無子者，淫僻者，嫉妒者，惡疾者，多口舌者，竊盜者。三不去者：謂有所取無所歸，與共更三年之喪，先貧賤後富貴。凡此，聖人所以順男女之際，重婚姻之始也。"

Confucius continued, saying, "There are five kinds of women not to marry: those who have seriously defied their family; those who have seriously disrupted their family; those with recent felons in the family; those with deformities or serious communicable diseases;[4] those who are an eldest child with a deceased father.

"There are seven grounds for divorce and three conditions that should not lead to abandonment. The seven are: disobeying in-laws, infertility, adultery, jealousy, deformity or serious communicable disease, talkativeness, and theft. The three conditions that should not lead to abandonment are: married on proper grounds and with no home to which to return; having performed three years of mourning with her husband; being wealthy after having come from poverty.

"These are how the sages created smooth relationships between a man and a woman, stressing the beginning of a marriage."

2. A ceremony with the future in-laws that precedes a wedding. In other words, widows do not remarry.

3. This passage and the passages related to numerology and related topics seem to be the most timebound. Contemporary Confucians quickly move past them as tied to ancient customs rather than as reflective of core principles.

4. *Deformity or serious communicable disease, e ji* 惡疾: glossed variously as blindness, deafness, syphilis, and leprosy.

26.4

孔子曰:“禮之所以象五行也,其義四時也,故喪禮有舉焉,有恩有義,有節有權。其恩厚者其服重,故爲父母斬衰三年,以恩制者也。門内之治恩掩義,門外之治義掩恩。資於事父以事君而敬同。尊尊貴貴,義之大也。故爲君亦服衰三年,以義制者也。三日而食,三月而沐,期而練,毀不滅性,不以死傷生;喪不過三年,齊衰不補,墳墓不修;除服之日鼓素琴,示民有終也。凡此以節制者也。資於事父以事母而愛同。天無二日,國無二君,家無二尊,以治之。故父在爲母齊衰期者,見無二尊也。百官備,百物具,不言而事行者,扶而起;言而後事行者,杖而起;身自執事行者,面垢而已。此以權制者也。親始死,三日不怠,三月不懈,期悲號,三年憂,哀之殺也。聖人因殺以制節也。”

Confucius said, “The manifestations of *li* take after the five elemental phases, and its *yi* lies in the four seasons. We can take the *li* of mourning as an example. Involved are: fondness, *yi*, austerity, and contingency.

“A child with deep fondness for his parents displays it in mourning apparel, wearing simple, rough clothing for three years on their behalf. This custom stems from fondness. In the conduct of a household, fondness outweighs *yi*.

“Outside the home, *yi* outweighs fondness. The resourcefulness that one brings to respecting one's father one should also bring to respecting one's sovereign. Respecting those who deserve respect and esteeming those who deserve to be esteemed are the best way to be *yi*. And so, one wears simple, uncomfortable clothes for three years in mourning one's sovereign. This custom stems from *yi*.

“The following are examples in which custom stems from austerity: to not eat until the third day after a funeral and to not wash one's hair until the third month after a funeral, to conduct a one-year anniversary ceremony,[5] to not harm oneself or others from grief over the death, to not extend the mourning beyond the three-year period, to not mend one's clothes during the period of mourning or complete the grave mound,[6] and finally, when the mourning period comes to an end, to announce it to others by strumming a plain zither.

“The resourcefulness that one brings to displaying love for one's father one should also bring to displaying love for one's mother. However, just as there are not two suns in the sky nor two sovereigns in a country, so there are not two highest seats of

5. A small-scale ceremony to commemorate the one-year anniversary of a parent's death, distinct for its costume of white silk.

6. *Not complete the grave mound, fen mu bu xiu* 墳墓不修: Interpreting this phrase depends on how one parses *fen mu* 墳墓. If separated, then the current interpretation holds. If combined, the phrase would be: to not tend to the grave. The latter interpretation would point to a later dating of the passage, because this disyllabic term, like a number of other disyllabic terms, seems to have evolved during the Han dynasty. This is the only occurrence in the *Dialogues* of *fen* and *mu* together.

respect in the household. Govern your household in this way. To demonstrate that there are not two seats of respect in the household, mourn your mother for only one year if your father is still alive.

"In one kind of funeral, the full range of government officials attend, and all funeral items are put into use; the whole affair is conducted without any instructions given; and mourners are given helping hands. In another kind of funeral, instructions must be given, and mourners support themselves on mourning staffs. In a third type of funeral, everything is prepared by the family themselves, and faces are merely kept unwashed.[7] These customs stem from contingency.

"Abatement of sorrow follows a pattern. When a parent has first died, you can't stop crying for three days. You can't stop feeling sorrow for three months. After a year, you're liable to still break into tears. After three years, you still miss them. The sages created the customs of mourning according to this pattern of abatement of sorrow."

7. According to Wang Su, these three kinds of funeral are for (1) the king and other nobility, (2) officials of all levels, and (3) ordinary people, respectively.

27

On *Li*

Chapter 27 presents the first of several essays in the *Dialogues* dedicated to the topic of *li*, explaining that *li* permeates every facet of life. In contemporary terms, we would say that there are norms informing all of our interpersonal relations, some formal, or explicit, others informal, or implicit. A complete command of *li*, Confucius suggests, amounts to competence in any matter because it allows for properly handling the ins and outs and ups and downs of any situation. The second episode, and second half of the chapter, is a brief but important exposition on the centrality of culture to governing, involving the roles of *li*, poetry, and music in the so-called five manifestations, three absences, three starting points, and three impartialities.

27.1

孔子閑居, 子張、子貢、言游侍, 論及於禮。孔子曰: "居! 汝三人者, 吾語汝, 以禮周流, 無不遍也。" 子貢越席而對曰: "敢問如何?" 子曰: "敬而不中禮, 謂之野; 恭而不中禮, 謂之給; 勇而不中禮, 謂之逆。" 子曰: "給奪慈仁。" 子貢曰: "敢問將何以爲此中禮者?" 子曰: "禮乎! 夫禮, 所以制中也。" 子貢退。言游進曰: "敢問禮也, 領惡而全好者與?" 子曰: "然。" 子貢問: "何也?" 子曰: "郊社之禮, 所以仁鬼神也; 禘嘗之禮, 所以仁昭穆也; 饋奠之禮, 所以仁死喪也; 射饗之禮, 所以仁鄉黨也; 食饗之禮, 所以仁賓客也。明乎郊社之義、禘嘗之禮, 治國其如指諸掌而已。是故, 居家有禮, 故長幼辨; 以之閨門有禮, 故三族和; 以之朝廷有禮, 故官爵序; 以之田獵有禮, 故戎事閑; 以之軍旅有禮, 故武功成。是以宮室得其度, 鼎俎得其象, 物得其時, 樂得其節, 車得其軾, 鬼神得其享, 喪紀得其哀, 辯說得其黨, 百官得其體, 政事得其施。加於身而措於前, 凡衆之動, 得其宜也。" 言游退。子張進曰: "敢問禮何謂也?" 子曰: "禮者, 即事之治也, 君子有其事, 必有其治。治國而無禮, 譬猶瞽之無相, 倀倀乎何所之? 譬猶終夜有求於幽室之中, 非燭何以見? 故無禮則手足無所措, 耳目無所加, 進退揖讓無所制。是故, 以其居處, 長幼失其別, 閨門三族失其和, 朝廷官爵失其序, 田獵戎事失其策, 軍旅武功失其勢, 宮室失其度, 鼎俎失其象, 物失其時, 樂失其節, 車失其軾, 鬼神失其享, 喪紀失其哀, 辯說失其黨, 百官失其體, 政事失其施。加於身而措於前, 凡動之衆失其宜。如此, 則無以祖洽四海。" 子曰: "慎聽之, 汝三人者! 吾語汝, 禮猶有九焉, 大饗有四焉。苟知此矣, 雖在畎畝之中, 事之, 聖人矣。兩君相見, 揖讓而入門, 入門而懸興;

揖讓而升堂，升堂而樂闋；下管《象》舞，《夏》籥序興；陳其薦俎，序其禮樂，備其百官。如此而後，君子知仁焉。行中規，旋中矩，鑾和中《采薺》，客出以《雍》，徹以《振羽》。是故，君子無物而不在於禮焉。入門而金作，示情也；升歌《清廟》，示德也；下管《象》舞，示事也。是故，古之君子，不必親相與言也，以禮樂相示而已。夫禮者，理也；樂者，節也。無理不動，無節不作。不能《詩》，於禮謬；不能樂，於禮素；薄於德，於禮虛。"子貢作而問曰："然則夔其窮與?"子曰："古之人與！上古之人也，達於禮而不達於樂，謂之素；達於樂而不達於禮，謂之偏。夫夔達於樂而不達於禮，是以傳於此名也。古之人也。凡制度在禮，文爲在禮，行之其在人乎！"三子者既得聞此論於夫子也，煥若發矇焉。

Once when Confucius was seated in leisure, Zizhang, Zigong, and Yan You were sitting in attendance. Their conversation turned to *li*.

Confucius said, "Stay. Let me tell the three of you about *li*, which is circulating everywhere, spreading to every corner of the land."

Zigong crossed over the mat and replied, "May I ask how that happens?"

Confucius said, "To show respect without getting *li* just right is to be uncouth. To show reverence without getting *li* just right is to flatter. To show courage without getting *li* just right is to be contrary."

Confucius continued, "Flattery is the theft of compassion and *ren*."

Zigong said, "May I ask how we can get *li* just right?"

Confucius said, "*Li*! *Li* is the system for getting things just right."

Zigong stepped back.

Yan You stepped forward and said, "May I ask if *li* is something that can prevent misbehavior and guarantee good behavior?"

Confucius said, "Yes."

Zigong asked, "How?"

Confucius said, "The *li* of the Jiao and She sacrifices are how *ren* is expressed to the recently deceased. The *li* of the Di and Chang sacrifices are how *ren* is expressed to the ancestral line. The *li* of laying out food offerings are how *ren* is expressed at a funeral. The *li* of *xiang* archery banquets are how *ren* is expressed to one's neighbors around town and extended family. The *li* of informal banquets are how *ren* is expressed to one's guests at home. By understanding the meaning and practice of these ceremonies, one can rule the country as if holding it in the palm of one's hand.

"Therefore, if you maintain *li* in your household, there will be clear divisions between elder and younger. Extended to the *li* of the inner quarters, three generations will live in harmony. If extended to the *li* of the court, each member of the nobility and officialdom will know their place. If extended to the *li* of going after wild game, hunting will be done skillfully. If extended to the *li* of military expeditions, battles will be successful.

"This is how moderation is achieved in the palace, how the arrangement of ceremonial implements is properly handled, how the needs of everything are met at the proper times, how music achieves its modulation, how vehicles achieve standard axle lengths, how gods and spirits achieve satisfaction, how funeral rites achieve a proper expression of sorrow, how debate and persuasion achieve a proper level of partiality, how the various officials complete their duties, and how governmental policies are properly promulgated. When it is applied to one's self and prioritized in life, people achieve appropriateness in every action they take."

Yan You stepped back.

Zizhang stepped forward and said, "May I ask, what exactly is this thing called *li*?"

Confucius said, "*Li* is the managing of affairs. For every affair that a person has, there is a method of managing it. To try to manage a country without *li* is like the inability of the blind to see—what can they do by just groping around? It's like being kept in a dark room for the whole night—how can one see without a light? Without *li*, the hands and feet don't know what to do, the eyes and ears don't know what to attend to, and there is no system for how to engage politely with others.

"And so, without *li* in the household, differences between elder and younger will be lost; in the inner quarters, harmony among the three generations will be lost; in the court, members of the nobility and officialdom will not know their place; in going after wild game, hunting will lose its tactics; in military expeditions, battles will lose their strategic advantage; in the palace, moderation will be lost; the arrangement of ceremonial implements will not be properly handled; the needs of things will not be met at the proper times; music will not achieve its modulation; vehicles will not achieve standard axle lengths; gods and spirits will not achieve satisfaction; funeral rites will not achieve a proper expression of sorrow; debate and persuasion will not win over allies; the various officials will not fulfill their duties; and governmental policies will not be properly promulgated. If this kind of neglect is applied to one's self and prioritized in life, people will not achieve appropriateness in the actions they take. Thus, there will be no way to unify people within the four seas."

Confucius said, "Listen carefully, you three. Let me tell you, there are still nine basic items of *li* relevant here, and four of them are involved in the Grand Xiang ceremony. If only these are understood, even if someone who works in the fields were to implement them, he would be revered as a sage. When two sovereigns meet, they salute and then enter. When they enter, the music of the bells and chimes resonates. They salute again and ascend to the hall. When they reach the hall, the music ends. Then *guan*-flutes play the Xiang dance, followed by the Xia dance on the panpipes.

"Display each ritual item correctly, keep each step of *li* and music in proper order, and have all the various officials present—from these, a *junzi* comes to understand *ren*. Every step has its rule; every turn has its guideline. When the carriage bells marking the arrival of your guest are heard, play the song 'Collecting Herbs.' When the guest is on the way out, play the song 'Affable.'[1] As the guest drives off into the distance, play the song 'Flapping Wings.' Thus, there is nothing in a *junzi*'s life for which there is not *li*.

1. Compare *Analects* 3.2, where the three usurping families of Lu are implicitly criticized for having this song performed.

"To express feelings, have the chimes played during an entrance. To express *de*, have the song 'Pure Temple' sung during the ascension to the hall. To express the sentiment of service, have the Xiang dance played on the *guan*-flute. The *junzi* of old thus did not need to personally use words to express these; they expressed them to others through *li* and music.

"*Li* is order; music is modulation. If something is not well ordered,[2] don't do it. If something is not well modulated, don't undertake it. *Li* performed without an understanding of poetry will be error-prone. *Li* performed without an understanding of music will be flat. *Li* performed from meager *de* will be vacuous."

Zigong gestured and asked, "What about Kui? Could he be thorough in *li*?"

Confucius said, "Ah, the ancients! Those ancients who were thoroughly versed in *li* but not in music were called flat. Those who were thoroughly versed in music but not in *li* were called partial. Kui was thoroughly versed in music but not in *li*, and so his name has come down to us as such. These were the ancients. *Li* is where we find system and measure, where we find civility and good behavior, but actually putting *li* into effect is up to each individual."

When the three students heard this, it was as if their eyes had been opened for the first time.

27.2

子夏侍坐於孔子, 曰: "敢問《詩》云'愷悌君子, 民之父母', 何如斯可謂民之父母?" 孔子曰: "夫民之父母, 必達於禮樂之源, 以致五至而行三無, 以橫於天下。四方有敗, 必先知之。此之謂民之父母。" 子夏曰: "敢問何謂五至?" 孔子曰: "志之所至, 詩亦至焉; 詩之所至, 禮亦至焉; 禮之所至, 樂亦至焉; 樂之所至, 哀亦至焉。詩禮相成, 哀樂相生, 是以正明目而視之, 不可得而見; 傾耳而聽之, 不可得而聞。志氣塞于天地, 行之充于四海。此之謂五至矣。" 子夏曰: "敢問何謂三無?" 孔子曰: "無聲之樂, 無體之禮, 無服之喪, 此之謂三無。" 子夏曰: "敢問三無何詩近之?" 孔子曰: "'夙夜基命宥密', 無聲之樂也; '威儀逮逮, 不可選也', 無體之禮也; '凡民有喪, 扶伏救之', 無服之喪也。" 子夏曰: "言則美矣大矣! 言盡於此而已乎?" 孔子曰: "何謂其然? 吾語汝, 其義猶有五起焉。" 子夏曰: "何如?" 孔子曰: "無聲之樂, 氣志不違; 無體之禮, 威儀遲遲; 無服之喪, 內恕孔悲。無聲之樂, 所願必從; 無體之禮, 上下和同; 無服之喪, 施及萬邦。既然, 而又奉之以三無私而勞天下, 此之謂五起。" 子夏曰: "何謂三無私?" 孔子曰: "天無私覆, 地無私載, 日月無私照。其在《詩》曰: '帝命不違, 至于湯齊。湯降不遲, 聖敬日躋。昭假遲遲, 上帝是祇, 帝命式于九圍。' 是湯之德也。" 子夏蹶然而起, 負墻而立, 曰: "弟子敢不志之?"

Zixia was sitting in attendance on Confucius and said, "A poem says:

Our leader, content and agreeable,
Parent of the people.[3]

2. Following SKQS, which has *li* 理 instead of *li* 禮.

3. This poem is also quoted in 12.10 and 13.9.

What is meant by 'parent of the people'?"

Confucius said, "A parent of the people will have reached the source of *li* and music and thereby have achieved the five manifestations and the three absences, spreading them all across the land. Any disaster in the land can be known ahead of time. This is what it is to be called the parent of the people."

Zixia said, "What are the five manifestations, if I may ask?"

Confucius said, "Where thoughts and feelings[4] manifest,[5] poetry follows. Where poetry manifests, *li* follows. Where *li* manifests, joy follows. Where joy manifests, sorrow follows.[6]

4. *Thoughts and feelings, zhi* 志: The term *zhi* occurs four times in the passage. Twice we render it *thoughts and feelings,* as it refers to what one might express in poetry. It also occurs twice with the term *qi,* once following it and once preceding it. The second pairing is one of the instances above of *thoughts and feelings.* The first pairing we render *the* qi *of aspiration.* The final time comes in the very last sentence, where we translate it as *never forget.* One general meaning of *zhi* is to record for posterity, either in one's memory or in writing, so the final usage is the most straightforward one, although the exact nature of it is still ambiguous. It is also fairly straightforward that it refers to the content of what is recorded as it originates in a person's psyche—that is, thoughts and feelings. The Shanghai Museum "Parent of the People" manuscript version of this passage complicates the interpretation in many places. The two pairings of *zhi* and *qi,* for example, are expressed in different graphs in the "Parent of the People" manuscript. In the first use, *zhi* and *qi* are both ambiguous, and Shaughnessy (2006) interprets them as completely different graphs, rendered "virtue already" (48). Another complication is that the character in the "Parent of the People" manuscript that corresponds to the first uses of the term *poetry* in the *Dialogues* passage is this very same *zhi.*

5. *Manifests, zhi* 至: This term is particularly difficult to fully understand and hence to translate. The general Chinese trend follows Zheng Xuan's interpretation of the parallel passage in the *Li ji.* He understands *zhi* 志 as the compassion that a leader has for the people and when this is fully expressed to the extent that it reaches (*zhi* 至) the people, poetry (by or about) the leader ensues (J. Wu 2015). However, more recent evaluations stemming from the Shanghai Museum manuscripts draw different conclusions. Huang Huaixin (2009) interprets it in terms of a metaphorical point of arrival, but with the people as the initial subject: the people's thoughts and feelings arrive at a certain point, and then the leader's follow. Wu Jianwei (2015) shares Huang's interpretation but shifts the subject back to the leader: the leader, thinking of the people, arrives as certain thoughts and feelings, and poetry, and so on also arrive there. Shaughnessy (2006) renders *zhi* as "to reach": for example, "where ritual reaches, music also reaches there" (46), suggesting a spatial metaphor rather than a temporal process. Richter (2013) renders it "presence," as in, "Where intentions are fully present, there will also be present rites" (50). *Zhi* 至 fundamentally means to arrive, temporally and/or spatially. However, to say that thoughts and feelings *arrive* or that poetry *arrives* is awkward in English. The underlying meaning seems to have more to do with manifestation—when one has thoughts about something, they can manifest in the language of poetry and the rituals of *li.* These can lead to outward manifestations of joy.

6. What does it mean for sorrow to follow joy? For the prior items in the series, there is a causal, synchronic sense. To have thoughts and feelings manifest is to prompt a poetic response. The culmination of *li* results in joy. The relationship between joy and sorrow is more likely a diachronic

"Poetry and *li* are mutually informing; joy and sorrow are mutually generating. Opening your eyes wide to look, it cannot be seen; tilting your ears to listen, it cannot be heard. Rather, the *qi* of aspiration fills the space between heaven and earth, traveling in every direction. These are the five manifestations."[7]

Zixia said, "What are the three absences, if I may ask?"

Confucius said, "The three absences are: music without the sound, *li* without the ceremony,[8] and mourning without the costume."

Zixia said, "May I ask how the three absences are expressed in poetry?"

Confucius said:

Day and night pursuing the mission with passion and care.[9]

This is music without the sound.[10]

My pride and dignity
Won't yield so easily.[11]

This is *li* without the ceremony.

If people are about to drown,
Rush to pull them out.[12]

---

one—meaning that though we may feel joy today, sorrow is likely just around the corner because everything comes in cycles. See, for example, 24.1 and 32.10.

7. *Five manifestations, wu zhi* 五至: There are five items here (aspiration, poetry, *li*, joy, and sorrow), each reaching an apogee.

8. *Ceremony, ti* 體: body, embody. While Richter (2013) renders *ti* literally as "embodiment," Shaughnessy (2006) prefers the more abstract "form." The gist of the passage seems to be that it is the spirit of *li* that matters, not the form. In other words, you can have the meaningfulness of *li* without the ceremonial form of it. Hence our translation: *li* without the ceremony.

9. This line appears in the poem "Great Heaven Has a Mission for Me" (#271), which can be found today in the "Zhou song" section of the *Poems*. The brief poem is about King Cheng and expresses his dedication to continuing the work of his predecessors in establishing a virtuous state.

10. Rapid, diligent, focused movements, like a percussionist playing bells and chimes, but absent the sound.

11. These lines appear in the poem "The Cypress Boat." For a description of the poem, see 2.1n3. The full stanza reads:

My heart is not a stone;
It can't be flipped over.
My heart is not a mat;
It can't be rolled up.
My pride and dignity
Won't yield so easily.

12. These lines appear in the poem "Valley Winds" (#35), which can be found today in the "Bei feng" section of the *Poems*. The poem is a wife's lament on being abandoned by her husband. The poem tells the story of a wife and husband who come from difficult circumstances to build a prosperous life, at

This is mourning without the costume."

Zixia said, "What important words, and so eloquently put! Is that all there is to say?"

Confucius said, "How could that be all? Let me tell you, there is still more to the meaning, namely, the three[13] starting points."

Zixia said, "What are those?"

Confucius said, "They are as follows: In silent music, thoughts and feelings are never violated; in *li* without ceremony, pride and dignity march on; in costume-less mourning, the heart opens in compassion. In silent music, let wishes lead the way; in non-ceremonial *li*, upper and lower levels achieve harmony; in costume-less mourning, the feeling is spread to all states. Having achieved these, they can be given

---

which time the husband suddenly divorces the wife. The stanza from which the quotation originates sets up an extended metaphor of crossing a river to analogize the challenges that a husband and wife face in building their lives. The full stanza reads:

> If the water is deep,
> Take a boat across.
> If the water is shallow,
> You can swim.
> If any encounter danger,
> Others rush to help.
> If people are about to drown,
> Rush to pull them out.

A difference, albeit insignificant, between the wording of this quotation and the wording of the *Poems* as it comes down to us is in the second line. Where the quotation has *fufu* 扶伏 (to help someone up who is prostrate), the line in the *Poems* has *pufu* 匍匐 (to drag someone [out]). This poem also appears in 42.10.

13. The Chinese has the number 5, which is problematic because it is not apparent that there are five items in the subsequent passage. We can think of three possible ways to make sense of it. First, it could be a copyist error for the number 3: 三 = 五. Each has three horizontal lines, making it so that one can be mistaken for the other (see 38.10n5 for a similar case). Another way of making sense of it is provided by Pang Pu (Pang 2004). He notes that the construction 3X5Y, or 5X3Y, is common in the early corpus and that the three and five items are not always discretely three and five. Hence, both numbers can be interpreted as a few or several. A third way of making sense of it is that in the versions of this passage available in the Shanghai Museum manuscripts and the *Li ji*, the three items (silent music, non-ceremonial *li*, and costume-less mourning) are cycled through five times with five different elaborations. Those could be the five starting points. Since the first two possibilities both allow for a substitution of 3 for 5 (perhaps meaning few), and since the cycle of five does not appear in this passage, we settle on 3 as the best interpretation here.

as a gift of accomplishment, like the three impartialities, to the whole land.[14] These are what are called the three starting points."

Zixia said, "What are the three impartialities?"

Confucius said, "The sky covers impartially. The earth carries impartially. The sun and moon shine impartially. We can see these in a poem, which says:

The lord's command not defied,
Tang's reforms had arrived.
Tang's descent right on time,
His peerless merit daily climbed.
Shining down far and wide,
Giving praise to the lord on high,
His order to the nine environs.[15]

Such was the *de* of Tang."

Zixia leapt to his feet, stood with his back to the wall, and said, "I will never forget what you have said."

14. From Zixia asking the question at the beginning of the passage down to this point in the text, there is significant overlap with the Shanghai Museum "Parent of the People" manuscript. The similarities and differences have caused an outpouring of research that is too voluminous even to list (see Qi 2012 for a summary of some of it). One area of agreement is that the excavated text confirms that at least this part of the *Dialogues* is very early—earlier even than *Mencius* and *Zhuangzi*—and (along with other excavated texts) reflects the earliest purported record of Confucius yet unearthed. Another general point of agreement is that, if it is indeed a genuine record of Confucius' thought, it sheds light on Confucius' political philosophy. Finally, there is general consensus that, because of terminology like *qi* 氣 and *wu* 無 (absence/without), it throws the long-standing barrier between Daoism and Confucianism into doubt—at least at the earliest stages of their respective development. See Shaughnessy (2006) for a translation of the Shanghai Museum version and a comparison with the transmitted versions. See Richter (2013) for a book-length study of the Shanghai Museum version.

15. This passage appears in the poem "Long Prosperity" (#304). See 12.6n7 for a description of the poem. "Nine environs" refers to the nine provinces of the Shang dynasty—in other words, to the whole land. The poem is also quoted in 12.15 and 41.12.

28

Observing a Village Archery Event

In chapter 4, the Grand Wedding serves as a microcosm for the role of *li* in governing. Chapter 28, as a complement to that, takes the *xiang* ceremonial banquet as a microcosm of governing. The former is a ritual particular to the ruler, and the latter is a common ceremony that all sectors of society would have experienced. In both, distinctions are made clear, emotions are channeled, and all levels of society are either invited or implicated.

28.1

孔子觀於鄉射, 喟然嘆曰: “射之以禮樂也, 何以射? 何以聽? 循聲而發, 而不失正鵠者, 其唯賢者乎? 若夫不肖之人, 則將安能以求飲?《詩》云: ‘發彼有的, 以祈爾爵。’祈, 求也。求所中, 以辭爵。酒者, 所以養老, 所以養病也。求中以辭爵, 辭其養也。是故士使之射而弗能, 則辭以病, 懸弧之義。” 於是, 退而與門人習射於矍相之圃, 蓋觀者如墻堵焉。試射至於司馬, 使子路執弓矢, 出列延, 謂射之者曰: “奔軍之將, 亡國之大夫, 與爲人後者, 不得入, 其餘皆入。”蓋去者半。又使公罔之裘、序點揚觶而語曰: “幼壯孝悌, 耆老好禮, 不從流俗, 修身以俟死者, 在此位。”蓋去者半。序點又揚觶而語曰: “好學不倦, 好禮不變, 耄期稱道而不亂者, 在此位。”蓋僅有存焉。射既闋, 子路進曰: “由與二三子者之爲司馬, 何如?”孔子曰: “能用命矣。”

After observing a village archery event, Confucius sighed and said, “Archery is related to *li* and music, so how should one shoot, and how should one listen? Isn’t it only a capable and virtuous person who is able to shoot in rhythm with the music without missing the bull’s-eye? How would an unwise or incapable person be able to hit the target? A poem says:

> Shoot to hit the target,
> Pray for him to drink.[1]

1. This passage appears in the poem “Guests Arrived and Seated” (#220), which can be found today in the “Xiao ya” section of the *Poems*. The poem discusses the proper and improper uses of liquor, especially at a banquet for an archery event.

Pray means to seek. You seek to hit the target in order to beg off drinking yourself.[2] Alcohol can act as an elixir for the aged and the sick. To seek to hit the target in order to beg off from drinking is to beg off from taking the elixir for yourself. The reason people hang a bow in their house is to remind them of the obligation to shoot;[3] if they are unable, they should beg off on the pretext of illness."

Confucius exited and went with his students to practice shooting at the Juexiang target range. A crowd as broad as a city wall gathered outside. Zilu was handed a bow and arrows and put in charge of selecting the people to be invited in to participate. He said to the prospective archers, "Those who may not enter are defeated generals, high officials of annihilated states, and those who attempt to act as heirs.[4] Everyone else may enter." Half of the people remained outside.

Then Gongwang Zhiqiu and Xu Dian were asked to raise a cup and said to those present, "The following people, please come over here: youths who are good to their elders, elders who have shown a fondness for *li* into old age, those who do not go along with what is fashionable, and those who plan on cultivating themselves right up to their time of death." About half were thus excluded.

Then Xu Dian raised his cup again and said to those present, "Come to the target area only if you never tire of learning, if you never swerve from *li*, or if you have remained true to the *dao* to the age of eighty or above." Only a handful stepped forward.

When the archery ended, Zilu approached Confucius and asked, "The others and I were in charge today. How did we do?"

Confucius said, "You can be put to work."

2. We see here that the village archery event was like a contemporary drinking game, in which the loser of a competition is "penalized" by being required to take a drink of alcohol. In the subsequent sentences, Confucius rationalizes the apparent selflessness of winning, saying how it allows the loser to enjoy the restorative properties of the alcohol. See "Alcohol" in the glossary for more details.

3. According to Wang Su, it was a custom to hang a bow in the house upon the birth of a boy.

4. *Those who attempt to act as heirs, yu wei ren hou zhe* 與爲人後者: Zhou dynasty China was a patrimonial system of primogeniture, meaning that status and wealth were handed down from father to the first-born son of the wife (see "Wife" in the glossary), but as we've seen, this system was occasionally disrupted when a father selected a different son to be heir, which could lead to turmoil. Because an upper-class man might have many sons from his wife and concubines, it would not be unusual for more than one of them to vie to be his successor. Zilu is here weeding out those seeking to be illegitimate heirs.

28.2

孔子曰："吾觀於鄉，而知王道之易易也。主人親速賓及介，而衆賓從之，至於正門之外，主人拜賓及介，而衆賓自入，貴賤之義別矣。三揖至於階，三讓，以賓升。拜至，獻，酬，辭讓之節繁。及介升，則省矣。至于衆賓，升而受爵，坐祭，立飲，不酢而降，隆殺之義辯矣。工入，升歌三終，主人獻賓。笙入三終，主人又獻之。間歌三終，合樂三闋，工告樂備而遂出。一人揚觶，乃立司正，焉知其能和樂而不流也。賓酬主人，主人酬介，介酬衆賓，少長以齒，終於沃洗者，焉知其能弟長而無遺矣。降，脱屨，升坐，修爵無算。飲酒之節，旰不廢朝，暮不廢夕。賓出，主人迎送，節文終遂，焉知其能安燕而不亂也。貴賤既明，降殺既辯，和樂而不流，弟長而無遺，安燕而不亂。此五者，足以正身安國矣，彼國安而天下安矣。故曰：'吾觀於鄉，而知王道之易易也。'"

Confucius said, "When I observe the *xiang* ceremonial banquet, I realize how simple the *dao* of ruling really is. The host personally welcomes the guest of honor and his second, then all the other guests follow their lead. It occurs first outside the main entrance, where the host welcomes the guest of honor and his second, then the other guests enter on their own. The places of higher and lower status have thereby been distinguished.

"At the bottom of the steps, the host salutes the guest of honor three times with clasped hands, and three times the guest of honor politely declines, then the guest of honor ascends the steps. With the welcoming complete, the host offers him liquor and toasts him, and there is much restraint shown through polite declining. Next, the second ascends, and a briefer interaction ensues. Then it is time for the other guests to enter. They ascend, accept a toast from the host, sit for a ceremonial offering, then stand to drink. They descend without toasting the host. The places of importance have thereby been differentiated.

"The singers enter, ascend, and sing three songs. The host then passes liquor to the guest of honor. The *sheng* mouth-organ players enter, play three songs, and then the host again passes liquor. Then the singers and the musicians alternate three songs and then play three songs together. Then singers and musicians exit. Someone raises a cup and nominates a master of ceremonies to lead the drinking. In this, we see how they are able to be convivial without going overboard.

"The guest of honor toasts the host. The host toasts the second. The second toasts the other guests. The other guests drink in order by age, right down to those tasked with cleaning up. In this, we see how young and old alike are able to partake and no one is left out.

"They then descend, remove their straw sandals, take their seats, and toast each other without keeping score. They remain restrained in their drinking, however, ready to attend to morning or afternoon affairs as necessary. The guest of honor departs, and the host sees him off. The ceremony thereby comes to an end. In this, we see that they are all able to remain calm and orderly.

"Places of higher and lower status are made clear, places of importance distinguished, conviviality without going overboard, young and old alike partaking with no one left out, calm and orderly—these five are sufficient to set oneself right and bring peace to the country, to other states, and to the whole land. And so I said, 'When I observe the *xiang* ceremonial banquet, I realize how simple the *dao* of ruling really is.'"[5]

28.3

子貢觀於蜡。孔子曰："賜也，樂乎？" 對曰："一國之人皆若狂，賜未知其爲樂也。"孔子曰："百日之勞，一日之樂，一日之澤，非爾所知也。張而不弛，文武弗能；弛而不張，文武弗爲。一張一弛，文武之道也。"

Zigong observed the Zha festival. Confucius said, "Ci, are you enjoying yourself?"

Zigong replied, "It's as if everyone in the country has gone crazy. I don't understand why they are celebrating so."

Confucius said, "After working for so many days in a row, they get this one day for enjoyment. One day for fun—it's not something you would understand.[6] Even Wen and Wu were incapable of being intense all the time without relaxing.[7] They were also incapable of being relaxed all the time without some intensity. The *dao* of Wen and Wu is to be sometimes intense, sometimes relaxed."

5. According to 30.1, the *xiang* banquet can help reduce criminal behavior.

6. Zigong was wealthy from his business ventures. (Zheng, Wu, and Yang 2000)

7. *Intense* and *relaxed*, *zhang* 張 and *chi* 弛: terms for the state of a bowstring when pulled and not pulled, respectively.

29

Questions about the Jiao Sacrifice

The Jiao ceremony was an important regular sacrificial ceremony in Confucius' time, conducted by the ruler himself. As described here, it is a public demonstration of the ruler's involvement in affairs and is a crucial link in the cosmic cycles, with society and nature (including the spirit realm) being understood as intricately intertwined.

29.1

定公問於孔子曰:"古之帝王,必郊祀其祖以配天,何也?"孔子對曰:"萬物本於天,人本乎祖。郊之祭也,大報本反始也,故以配上帝。天垂象,聖人則之,郊所以明天道也。"

Duke Ding asked Confucius, "In performing the Jiao sacrifice, why did rulers in ancient times worship their ancestors along with *tian*?"

Confucius replied, "Creatures of the world find their origins in *tian*. People find their origins in their ancestors. The Jiao sacrifice is about expressing gratitude for our origins and reflecting on our beginnings. That is why the ancestors were worshipped alongside Shang Di. In imitation of *tian*'s suspended[1] features, sages illuminated the *dao* of *tian* through the Jiao sacrifice."

29.2

公曰:"寡人聞郊而莫同,何也?"孔子曰:"郊之祭也,迎長日之至也。大報天而主日,配以月,故周之始郊,其月以日至,其日用上辛;至於啓蟄之月,則又祈穀于上帝。此二者,天子之禮也。魯無冬至大郊之事,降殺於天子,是以不同也。"公曰:"其言郊,何也?"孔子曰:"兆丘於南,所以就陽位也,於郊,故謂之郊焉。"曰:"其牲器何如?"孔子曰:"上帝之牛角繭栗,必在滌三月,后稷之牛唯具,所以別事天神與人鬼也。牲用

1. *Suspended, chui*垂: *Chui* means hanging or suspended and was an idiomatic way of referring to astronomical phenomena.

騂，尚赤也；用犢，貴誠也。掃地而祭，於其質也。器用陶匏，以象天地之性也。萬物無可稱之者，故因其自然之體也。"

The duke said, "I have heard that the Jiao sacrifice isn't always the same. Why is that?"

Confucius said, "The Jiao sacrifice welcomes the arrival of the lengthening of days. It displays great gratitude toward *tian* and gives the sun a place of prominence alongside the moon. Therefore, when the Zhou first began the Jiao, they selected the month of the winter solstice and the first auspicious day of that month. Then, in the month when hibernation ends,[2] they prayed to Shang Di for grain. These two sacrificial times were the prerogative of the king. Lu didn't have a large Jiao sacrifice on the winter solstice because Lu is a step below the king. That's why there is a difference."

The duke said, "Why is it called Jiao?"

Confucius said, "The sunny side[3] of an auspicious hill south of the city was selected for the place of sacrifice. Because it lay on the outskirts (*jiao* 郊) of the city, it was called the Jiao sacrifice."

The duke said, "Which sacrificial items were used?"

Confucius said, "The ox used for sacrificing to Shang Di was so small that it still had nubs for horns, so it was first housed in the sacrificial stables for three months. The ox used for sacrificing to Hou Ji merely had to have the standard qualities. This is how they differentiated serving the god of *tian* from serving the ancestors.[4] In sacrificial animals, oxen with a reddish coat were chosen because the color red was prized. Calves were chosen because demeanor was prized. The ground was cleared before the sacrifice because of its basic substance. Pottery and gourd ware were used as sacrificial implements because they symbolize the basic nature of heaven and earth. Nothing compares to them, and so their natural bodies were emulated."[5]

29.3

公曰："天子之郊，其禮儀可得聞乎？"孔子對曰："臣聞天子卜郊，則受命于祖廟，而作龜于禰宮，尊祖親考之義也。卜之日，王親立于澤宮，以聽誓命，受教諫之義也。既卜，獻命庫門之內，所以誡百官也。將郊，則天子皮弁以聽報，示民嚴上也。郊之

2. The beginning of spring, the first month of the lunar calendar.

3. That is, the south side.

4. In other words, the animal used to sacrifice to the god of *tian* must be very special, but the animal sacrificed to human ancestors must merely meet the minimal standards of sacrificial quality.

5. This sentence gives an interesting perspective on Confucius' view of the early Zhou. We know now that the Zhou inherited sophisticated bronze technology from the Shang. In Neolithic times, gourds were used very early, and some of the earliest earthenware vessels were modeled on the gourd shape. Some later bronzes perpetuated such shapes. (Zhao 1993; He 1996; Yao and Wang 2019)

日，喪者不敢哭，凶服者不敢入國門，氾掃清路，行者必止，弗命而民聽，敬之至也。天子大裘以黼之，被袞象天，乘素車，貴其質也。旂十有二旒，龍章而設以日月，所以法天也。既至泰壇，王脫裘矣，服袞以臨燔柴，戴冕，璪十有二旒，則天數也。臣聞之，誦《詩》三百，不足以一獻；一獻之禮，不足以大饗；大饗之禮，不足以大旅；大旅具矣，不足以饗帝。是以君子無敢輕議於禮者也。"

The duke said, "Could you tell me about the ceremony of the king's Jiao sacrifice?"

Confucius replied, "I have heard that the king does a *bu* prognostication for the Jiao sacrifice, whereby he receives his mission from the ancestral temple, and he does a *gui* prognostication[6] at his father's temple to get the opinion of his revered ancestors and his loving father. On the day of the prognostication, the king personally stands at the royal archery range, where he receives his mission, in order to show that he can listen to advice. After the prognostication, the results are posted inside the outer gate as exhortations to the various officials. As the day of the Jiao sacrifice approaches, the king dons his fur *bian* hat to listen to reports, in order to demonstrate to the people the importance of following instructions from above. On the day of the Jiao sacrifice, people in mourning dare not cry, people in mourning attire dare not enter the city gates, the streets are cleaned, pedestrians keep their distance, people obey orders without being told, and reverence is maintained all around. The king dons a fur coat with axe patterns—the fur symbolizing *tian*[7]—and rides in an unadorned coach, prizing its basic nature. Banners fly, each decorated with dragons and twelve streamers, as prominent as the sun and moon, taking after heaven itself. Arriving at the Peace Altar, the king removes his furs and dons his imperial robe, for the purpose of supervising the sacrificial pyre, and a *mian* crown with twelve beads, to be in line with the numerology of *tian*.

"I have learned that having the ability to recite 300 poems is not sufficient for being able to perform the offering at a sacrificial ceremony. Being able to perform the *li* of an offering of a sacrificial ceremony does not mean one has the ability to perform the Grand Xiang ceremony. Being able to perform the *li* of the Grand Xiang ceremony does not mean one has the ability to perform the Grand Lü ceremony. Being able to perform the Lü ceremony does not mean one is able to perform the Xiang ceremony to Di. Therefore, a *junzi* dares not lightly enter into discussions about ceremonial *li*."

6. See "Prognostication" in the glossary.

7. According to commentators, the simplicity of nature is reflected in the simplicity of the fur. To the Chinese, furs were considered a primitive style of dress.

30

Explicating Criminal Punishment

This chapter continues the theme of *li* but in the context of legal punishment of wrongdoers. As elsewhere in the *Dialogues,* Confucius favors prevention of crime over punishment. In a sophisticated analysis, he examines five causes of criminal behavior and says that addressing the causes is preferable to punishing crimes. His remedy hinges on clarifying and promulgating *li.*

30.1

冉有問於孔子曰:“古者三皇五帝不用五刑,信乎?”孔子曰:“聖人之設防,貴其不犯也;制五刑而不用,所以爲至治也。凡民之爲奸邪、竊盜、靡法、妄行者,生於不足。不足生於無度。無度則小者偷盜,大者侈靡,各不知節。是以上有制度,則民知所止,民知所止則不犯。故雖有奸邪、賊盜、靡法、妄行之獄,而無陷刑之民。不孝者,生於不仁。不仁者,生於喪祭之無禮也。明喪祭之禮,所以教仁愛也。能教仁愛,則服喪思慕,祭祀不解,人子饋養之道。喪祭之禮明,則民孝矣。故雖有不孝之獄,而無陷刑之民。殺上者,生於不義。義,所以別貴賤、明尊卑也。貴賤有別、尊卑有序,則民莫不尊上而敬長。朝聘之禮者,所以明義也。義必明,則民不犯。故雖有殺上之獄,而無陷刑之民。鬥變者,生於相陵。相陵者,生於長幼無序而遺敬讓。鄉飲酒之禮者,所以明長幼之序而崇敬讓也。長幼必序,民懷敬讓,故雖有鬥變之獄,而無陷刑之民。淫亂者,生於男女無別。男女無別,則夫婦失義。禮聘享者,所以別男女、明夫婦之義也。男女既別,夫婦既明,故雖有淫亂之獄,而無陷刑之民。此五者,刑罰之所以生,各有源焉。不豫塞其源,而輒繩之以刑,是謂爲民設阱而陷之。刑罰之源,生於嗜欲不節。夫禮度者,所以禦民之嗜欲,而明好惡,順天之道。禮度既陳,五教畢修,而民猶或未化,尚必明其法典,以申固之。其犯奸邪、靡法、妄行之獄者,則飭制量之度;有犯不孝之獄者,則飭喪祭之禮;有犯殺上之獄者,則飭朝覲之禮;有犯鬥變之獄者,則飭鄉飲酒之禮;有犯淫亂之獄者,則飭婚聘之禮。三皇五帝之所化民者如此,雖有五刑之用,不亦可乎?”孔子曰:“大罪有五,而殺人爲下。逆天地者罪及五世,誣文武者罪及四世,逆人倫者罪及三世,謀鬼神者罪及二世,手殺人者罪及其身。故曰大罪有五,而殺人爲下矣。”

Ran You asked Confucius, "Is it believable that the Three Founders[1] and Five Chiefs did not resort to punishment for criminals?"[2]

Confucius said, "In devising a way to prevent criminality, a sage seeks to ensure that violations do not occur. He institutes a system of criminal punishment, but the highest achievement in governing is never having to use it. The cause of fraud, thievery, lawlessness, and recklessness is scarcity. The cause of scarcity is immoderateness, which occurs when those above engage in extravagant spending and those below engage in stealing, neither understanding restraint. Therefore, when the leaders on top have a system of moderation, the people will understand when to stop and thus will not commit crimes. So although there may be statutes against fraud, thievery, lawlessness, and recklessness, the people will not fall into the trap of criminal punishment by committing such crimes.

"An absence of *xiao* behavior is caused by an absence of *ren* behavior, which in turn is caused by impropriety in mourning ceremonies. Clarifying the *li* of mourning ceremonies is how to instruct people in *ren* and love, which in turn will cause people to don mourning attire and lament the deceased. To not slack in performing the sacrifices is the child's *dao* of attending to deceased parents. When the *li* of mourning ceremonies is clear, the people will be *xiao*. So, although there may be statutes against not being *xiao*, the people will not risk corporal punishment by committing such a crime.

1. *Three Founders, san huang* 三皇: The three earliest legendary progenitors of Chinese culture: Fu Xi 伏羲, Shen Nong 神農, and a third, identified variously as the Yellow Chief, Nü Wa 女媧, or Sui Ren 燧人, all five of whom were celebrated as cultural innovators and inventors. (Luo 1994)

2. *Punishment for criminals, wu xing* 五刑: The five criminal punishments: tattooing the forehead, excising the nose, amputating a foot, sterilizing the person, and execution. This chapter and the following chapter should be read in light of two key passages in the *Documents*, with which the reader in Confucius' time would have been familiar. The first occurs in the "Da Yǔ mo" chapter, in which Shun (one of the Five Chiefs) is conversing with his successor Yǔ (legendary founder of the Xia dynasty and one of the Three Kings) and his minister of justice Gao Yao about the judicial system. Shun compliments Gao Yao for being able to get the people to live moderate lives without the use of criminal punishments. Gao Yao returns the compliment, saying that Shun goes easy on the people, giving the benefit of the doubt in favor of lesser punishments and greater reward and hesitancy to punish the innocent even at the risk of more crime. Shun's *de*, Gao Yao says, has permeated the minds of the people. The second relevant passage from the *Documents* occurs in the "Lü xing" chapter, in which Zhou King Mu discussing the judicial system with his ministers and nobles. King Mu recounts a story of the distant past in which the people were subject to extremely harsh punishments and suffered greatly from them, until Yao (one of the Five Chiefs) came along and transformed them through his *de*. Then his minister Boyi was able to institute laws and criminal punishments, "using transformative teachings and reverencing *de*." The king explains that when his ministers preside over the judicial system, they should be like Boyi and not like the ruthless forebears. See also "Five transformative teachings" in the glossary.

"Disrespect for higher-ups is caused by an absence of *yi*. *Yi* is how distinctions of status and worth are made and maintained. When distinctions of status and worth are made and maintained, the people will respect their superiors and revere their elders. The *li* of vassals meeting their lord is how *yi* is made clear. *Yi* must be made clear, and then the people will not transgress. And even though there may be statutes against disrespect, the people will not fall into the trap of criminal punishment by committing such a crime.

"Civil strife is caused when people disregard each other's boundaries, which is caused by the loss of deference when the proper ordering of elder and younger is not maintained. The *li* of the *xiang* ceremonial banquet is how proper ordering of elder and young is made clear and how the people come to value deference.[3] Elder and younger must be properly distinguished, and the people must value deference. Thus, although there may be statutes against civil strife, the people will not fall into the trap of criminal punishment by committing such a crime.

"Licentious sexual behavior occurs when the sexes are not differentiated into separate spheres, which leads to a loss of *yi* between husband and wife. Betrothal and wedding ceremonies are how the separate spheres of the sexes are maintained and how the *yi* of husband and wife is clarified. When the separate spheres of the sexes are maintained and the *yi* of husband and wife is clear, although there may be statutes against fornication, the people will not fall into the trap of criminal punishment by committing such a crime.

"These five are the reasons that there is criminal punishment, each having its own causes. If you don't proactively prevent the cause and instead always try to directly restrain the behavior through punishment, this is called setting traps for the people to fall into. The origin of criminal punishment lies in a failure to restrain sensual desires. Achieving moderation through *li* is how to control the people's sensual desires, influence their tastes, and flow with the *dao* of *tian*. If moderation through *li* has been put on full display, and the five transformative teachings have been taught in their entirety, and yet the people falter and fail to reform, you must clarify the laws, promulgate them, and enforce them.

"If people are breaking statutes against fraud, thievery, lawlessness, or recklessness, reform the system of moderation. If people are breaking statutes against being *xiao*, reform the *li* of mourning ceremonies. If people are breaking statutes against disrespect for higher-ups, reform the *li* of audiences with the sovereign. If people are breaking statutes against civil strife, reform the *li* of village banquets. If people are breaking statutes against sexual promiscuity, reform the *li* of wedding and betrothal ceremonies. Is it not admissible to say that the Three Kings and the Five Chiefs transformed the people in this way, even though criminal punishment was there for them to use?"

3. See 28.2.

Confucius continued, "There are five heinous crimes, and murder is the least of them. Punishment for crimes that violate natural cycles[4] will impact one's family for five generations.[5] Punishment for crimes that slander Wen and Wu will impact one's family for four generations. Punishment for crimes that violate fundamental human relations will impact one's family for three generations. Punishment for crimes that plot against ancestors and gods will impact one's family for two generations. Punishment for murdering someone by one's own hand affects only oneself. This is why I say that murder is the least of the five kinds of heinous crime."

30.2

冉有問於孔子曰: "先王制法, 使刑不上於大夫, 禮不下於庶人。然則大夫犯罪, 不可以加刑; 庶人之行事, 不可以治於禮乎?" 孔子曰: "不然。凡治君子, 以禮御其心, 所以屬之以廉耻之節也。故古之大夫, 其有坐不廉污穢而退放之者, 不謂之不廉污穢而退放, 則曰'簠簋不飭'; 有坐淫亂男女無別者, 不謂之淫亂男女無別, 則曰'帷幕不修'也; 有坐罔上不忠者, 不謂之罔上不忠, 則曰'臣節未著'; 有坐罷軟不勝任者, 不謂之罷軟不勝任, 則曰'下官不職'; 有坐干國之紀者, 不謂之干國之紀, 則曰'行事不請'。此五者, 大夫既自定有罪名矣, 而猶不忍斥然正以呼之也。既而爲之諱, 所以愧耻之。是故大夫之罪, 其在五刑之域者, 聞而譴發, 則白冠氂纓, 盤水加劍, 造乎闕而自請罪, 君不使有司執縛牽掣而加之也; 其有大罪者, 聞命則北面再拜, 跪而自裁, 君不使人捽引而刑殺之也, 曰: '子大夫自取之耳, 吾遇子有禮矣。'以刑不上大夫, 而大夫亦不失其罪者, 教使然也。所謂禮不下庶人者, 以庶人遽其事而不能充禮, 故不責之以備禮也。" 冉有跪然免席, 曰: "言則美矣! 求未之聞。"退而記之。

Ran You asked Confucius, "Is the following correct? In the legal systems of the Ancient Kings, punishments were not applied to high officials and *li* was not expected of common people. And so if high officials committed crimes they were not punished, and the affairs of common people were not managed through the application of *li*."

4. Violate natural cycles, *ni tian di* 逆天地: go against the flow of *tian* and earth. There is a sense here of going against the natural order, and since *tian* could have been understood by Confucius as connoting divinity, there may be a sense of apostasy—hence its primacy in the hierarchy of crimes.

5. It's not clear what is meant by a crime impacting a family over multiple generations or even what examples of the crimes might be. There have been infamous punishments in which multiple generations and branches of one's family were implicated (see the note on Zhao Wenzi in 12.21, for example), but the locution is different (e.g., *san shi* 三世 vs. *san zu* 三族). Similarly, it may be another reference to the "Da Yǔ mo" chapter of the *Documents*, in which Gao Yao says that Shun's punishments do not extend to one's descendants (*yan yu shi* 延于世) but his rewards do. The extension to descendants may be an extension of shame in the case of punishment and esteem in the case of reward.

Confucius said, "No, that is not correct. Any governing *junzi* controls his own mind through *li*, and thereby acquires restraint through a sense of shame. Thus, high officials in ancient times who were guilty of corrupt and immoral behavior and then exiled were not called corrupt and immoral and then exiled;[6] they were called 'disordered platters.'[7] Those who were guilty of licentiously disrupting the separate spheres of the sexes were not named as licentiously disrupting the separate spheres of the sexes; they were called 'unpulled curtains.' Those who were guilty of disloyally deceiving their superiors were not named as disloyally deceiving their superiors; they were called 'incomplete in their duties.' Those who were guilty of being feeble and incompetent were not named as being feeble and incompetent; they were called 'functionaries without portfolio.' Those who were guilty of violating the norms of governing were not named as violating the norms of governing; they were called 'unauthorized administrators.'

"Although the high officials themselves created terms for each of these five kinds of crimes, they could not bear to apply them directly to their colleagues. The euphemisms were sufficient to induce shame. Thus, although the crimes committed by high officials may have been within the realm of criminal punishment, once they became known, the official would 'don a white cap with ribbons'[8] and 'place a sword atop a basin of water.'[9] If he did something wrong, instead of being arrested and dragged to the court in ropes, he would voluntarily admit his guilt.

"For very serious crimes, instead of being dragged by his hair and then executed, the official would accept his fate and be willing to bow twice to the north,[10] kneel, and then commit suicide. The sovereign, instead of having him dragged away and executed, would say, 'Because you have chosen to come here of your own accord, I grant you this *li*.'

"Corporal punishment was not applied to high officials because high officials did not attempt to escape their punishment—and this is all because of proper education.

6. The English syntax retains the ambiguity in the Chinese as to whether the person was exiled or not.

7. In formal *li*, whether in sacrifices or in dining occasions, food platters and wine goblets were arranged in specific order according to the status of the relevant persons. To refer to a person as disordered platters appears to mean that the person intentionally disrupts social order for his own gain.

8. Commentators suggest that this refers to funeral attire. White was the color of mourning. It seems to suggest an outward admission of guilt and thus a means of humiliation.

9. The meaning of this idiom is unclear. One possible interpretation is that the level state of water in a basin is a metaphor for fairness in the justice system, and the sword is a reference to punishment. Another interpretation is that both the sword and the basin of water were implements used in the bloodletting of sacrificial animals and are in this sense metaphors for punishment.

10. *North*: The ruler always sat facing south, so a reference to facing north means facing the ruler.

"What is meant by saying that *li* is not expected of the common people is that the common people are so busy with their daily affairs that they are unable to be complete in their *li*. And so they were not expected to attend to every facet of *li*."

Ran You bowed and left the mat, saying, "What beautiful words. Beyond my expectations." He left, and what had been said he preserved for posterity.

31

Criminal Punishment in Governing

Chapter 31, as the title indicates, continues the theme of criminal punishment, in an extended dialogue between Zhonggong and Confucius. Here, the conversation shifts from historical and philosophical concerns to practical matters. Some of the claims are easily recognizable: guilt should be established beyond doubt, some cases deserve to be heard again by a higher authority in the system, felons should be denied some privileges, and possible exculpatory factors should be considered.

31.1

仲弓問於孔子曰:“雍聞至刑無所用政, 至政無所用刑。至刑無所用政, 桀、紂之世是也; 至政無所用刑, 成、康之世是也。信乎?”孔子曰:“聖人之治化也, 必刑政相參焉。太上以德教民, 而以禮齊之; 其次以政焉導民, 以刑禁之, 刑不刑也。化之弗變, 導之弗從, 傷義以敗俗, 於是乎用刑矣。顓五刑必即天倫。行刑罰則輕無赦。刑, 侀也; 侀, 成也, 壹成而不可更, 故君子盡心焉。”

Zhonggong asked Confucius, “I have heard the following and I wonder, is it believable? In a brutal regime, there is no place for good governing. In the best governments there is no place for criminal punishment. The times of Jie and Zhòu were examples of brutal regimes with no place for good governing. The times of Cheng and Kang were examples of ideal governing with no place for criminal punishment.”

Confucius said, “The transformational government of the sage requires the interplay of both criminal punishment and good governing. The highest form of governing uses virtue to teach the people and *li* to keep them well ordered. The next form down uses good governing to guide the people and criminal punishment to prevent bad behavior—punishing violators. Criminal punishment is used in cases where a person refuses to reform through instruction, refuses to follow guidance, or harms *yi* by destroying moral norms. Criminal punishment is necessary to maintain the natural moral order. When applying a punishment, even minor infractions should not be pardoned.[1] To punish is to shape; to shape is to bring to full development; and once something has been brought to full development, it cannot be easily altered. Thus, a *junzi* applies himself to properly seeing to criminal punishment."

31.2

仲弓曰："古之聽訟，尤罰麗於事，不以其心。可得聞乎?"孔子曰："凡聽五刑之訟，必原父子之情，立君臣之義，以權之；意論輕重之序，慎測淺深之量，以別之；悉其聰明，正其忠愛，以盡之。大司寇正刑明辟以察獄，獄必三訊焉。有指無簡，則不聽也；附從輕，赦從重；疑獄則泛與衆共之，疑則赦之，皆以小大之比成也。是故爵人必於朝，與衆共之也；刑人必於市，與衆棄之也。古者公家不畜刑人，大夫弗養也，士遇之塗，以弗與之言，屏諸四方，唯其所之，不及與政，弗欲生之也。"

Zhonggong said, "When legal cases were heard in the past, punishments were determined depending on the facts of the case and not according to personal feelings. Could I hear more about this?"

Confucius said, "In hearing criminal punishment cases, decisions were weighed in favor of leniency toward a father-and-son relationship and maintaining the *yi* of the vassal-and-lord relationship. Differentiations were made that involved discussing the gradient of severity and estimating the extent of the wrongdoing. And all efforts were made to obtain eyewitness accounts and to maintain conscientiousness and concern.

"When a minister of justice investigated a case for the purpose of clarity and applying the correct punishment, he always undertook 'three interrogations.' (1) If indications were that there was nothing there, the case was not heard. (2) He tended toward the light punishment rather than the stern. (3) If there was some doubt about a case, people were canvassed far and wide for information. If doubt persisted, the suspect was exonerated. In all such cases, he came to a decision by comparing all factors large and small.

"Just as someone who is enfeoffed as nobility is always done so at court so that everyone can acknowledge the achievement, so someone who was punished was always punished in the market so that everyone could renounce him. In the past, a felon was not eligible for public assistance, high officials would not materially support a felon, and lower officials would avoid a felon in public. A felon would be scorned across the land, and wherever he ended up, to avoid providing him a living, he would not be allowed to work in the government."[2]

1. See 41.12 for a discussion of balancing leniency and strictness in punishment.

2. Compare 43.8, in which outlaws are reformed.

31.3

仲弓曰："聽獄，獄之成，成何官？"孔子曰："成獄成於吏，吏以獄成告於正。正既聽之，乃告大司寇。聽之，乃奉於王。王命三公卿士參聽棘木之下，然後乃以獄之成疑于王。王三宥之，以聽命而制刑焉，所以重之也。"

Zhonggong said, "What was the proper judicial process for criminal cases? Which officials were involved?"

Confucius said, "A criminal case would first be handled by a low official, who reported it to the head of his office. The head of the office heard the case and then reported to the minister of justice. The minister of justice heard the case and then presented it to the king. The king would order officials at all levels to hear cases belonging to their own jurisdictions and to report any cases that remained doubtful up to the king. To demonstrate the seriousness with which he handled cases, the king would also take into account the three exculpatory factors[3] in deciding a case and setting the punishment."

31.4

仲弓曰："其禁何禁？"孔子曰："巧言破律，遁名改作，執左道與亂政者，殺；作淫聲，造異服，設伎奇器，以蕩上心者，殺；行偽而堅，言詐而辯，學非而博，順非而澤，以惑衆者，殺；假於鬼神、時日、卜筮，以疑衆者，殺。此四誅者，不以聽。"

Zhonggong said, "What was absolutely prohibited?"

Confucius said, "People were severely penalized[4] for (1) throwing the government into turmoil by using rhetorical subtleties to bend laws, by secretly having officeholders switch duties, or by promoting heterodox *dao*; (2) perturbing the minds of superiors by playing licentious music, by creating deviant fashions, or by using newfangled or nonstandard ritual vessels; (3) confusing the masses by fabricating and steadfastly maintaining falsehoods, by tricking people with sophistry, by pretending to be broadly educated but spreading false learning, or by doing wrong and obscuring or validating it through generosity to others; and (4) sowing doubt among the masses by spreading false claims about ancestors, spirits, auspicious

3. According to the *Zhou li* and the *Han shu*, they are ignorance, accident, and forgetfulness.

4. *Severely penalized, sha* 殺: The most intuitive rendering of *sha* is "to kill," but it can also mean to exile. Because of Confucius' reluctance to execute people outright (chapter 2) and because the meaning here is uncertain, we keep it vague.

dates, or prognostications. These four serious crimes[5] were not adjudicated at the jurisdictional level."[6]

31.5

仲弓曰："其禁盡於此而已?"孔子曰："此其急者，其餘禁者十有四焉：命服命車，不粥於市；珪璋璧琮，不粥於市；宗廟之器，不粥於市；兵車旍旗，不粥於市；犧牲秬鬯，不粥於市；戎器兵甲，不粥於市；用器不中度，不粥於市；布帛精粗不中數，廣狹不中量，不粥於市；奸色亂正色，不粥於市；文錦珠玉之器，雕飾靡麗，不粥於市；衣服飲食，不粥於市；果實不時，不粥於市；五木不中伐，不粥於市；鳥獸魚鱉不中殺，不粥於市。凡執此禁以齊衆者，不赦過也。"

Zhonggong said, "Are those all of the things that were prohibited?"

Confucius said, "Those are the most crucial ones, but there were fourteen more. They were prohibitions against selling certain items in the public market. The prohibited items were: royal or noble vestments and carriages; jade implements with ritual and burial uses; ritual implements used in ancestral temples; military vehicles and banners; animals and liquor used for sacrificial ceremonies; weapons and armor; vessels that were of nonstandard measures; fabric that was of nonstandard fineness or length; nonstandard colors that could disrupt the standard color system; decorated jewelry and jades with wildly ornate patterns; ready-made clothing and prepared food and drinks; unseasonal fruit; lumber taken out of season; and fish and game taken out of season. In order to govern evenly, no one possessing such contraband would be let off."

5. *Serious crimes, zhu* 誅: behavior worth denouncing. See 2.1n2.

6. *Not adjudicated at the jurisdictional level, bu yi ting* 不以聽: The original wording appears to mean that the case was not heard at one of the levels noted above—that is, at the jurisdictional level or at a level of appeal. We interpret it as meaning that, given the serious nature of the crimes, the cases would go immediately to a higher level. Alternatively, however, it could mean that the crimes were so severe that they deserved immediate punishment and so were not open to appeal.

32

Li in Motion

One of the most important chapters of the *Dialogues,* chapter 32 proposes a comprehensive system of government that is rooted in spontaneous cosmic fecundity and productivity. The sources are (1) the Great Inchoate, which separates into heaven and earth, the four seasons, gods and spirits, the five elemental phases, and *de,* and (2) human nature, which involves unlearned preferences and aversions, along with cultivated virtues. This fecundity and productivity is, ideally, exploited by the sage and the civil leadership. In chapter 21, we saw how the leadership hollowed itself out and regulated itself so as to build close bonds with the people and allow the people to pursue their own ends. Here, the emphasis is on the sage ruler, who proceeds from *li* and *yi,* ever mindful of human nature and the propensities of the people. The people, by deferring to the sovereign, model themselves after his example. These interactions result in the Grand Congeniality—communication, movement, and connection among all levels, in which emotions are well managed, needs are met, and strong relations are forged.

32.1

孔子爲魯司寇, 與於蜡。既賓事畢, 乃出遊於觀之上, 喟然而嘆。言偃侍, 曰: "夫子何嘆也?"孔子曰: "昔大道之行, 與三代之英, 吾未之逮也, 而有記焉。大道之行, 天下爲公, 選賢與能, 講信修睦。故人不獨親其親, 不獨子其子, 老有所終, 壯有所用, 矜寡孤疾, 皆有所養。貨惡其棄於地, 不必藏於己; 力惡其不出於身, 不必爲人。是以奸謀閉而不興, 盗竊亂賊不作, 故外户而不閉。謂之大同。

When Confucius was Lu minister of justice, he attended the Zha festival. As soon as his duties as guest of honor were complete, he left and climbed a watchtower, where he heaved a sigh. Yan Yan, who was in attendance, said, "Why did you sigh?"

Confucius said, "I was born too late to spend time with the heroes of the Three Dynasties when the great *dao* flourished. Nevertheless, there are records. When the great *dao* flourished, impartiality reigned, capable and virtuous people were selected to lead, people were trustworthy, and strong relations were forged. Thus, people didn't have feelings only for their own parents and didn't look out only for their own children. Old people came to a proper end, young people had proper employment, and compassion was shown to widows, orphans, and the sick, who all received proper care. People disliked seeing goods discarded in the street but at the same time did not hoard for themselves. People disliked when effort was not put forth but at the same time did not act only to please others. And so, deviant machinations were closed off and not given the chance to flourish, and thieves and rebels did not appear. As a result, there was no need to bar outer doors. We can call this period the Grand Unity.

32.2

"今大道既隱，天下爲家，各親其親，各子其子，貨則爲己，力則爲人，大人世及以爲常，城郭溝池以爲固。禹、湯、文、武、成王、周公由此而選，未有不謹於禮。禮之所興，與天地並。如有不由禮而在位者，則以爲殃。"

"These days, the great *dao* is obscured, and the entire land belongs to one family.[1] People have feelings only for their own parents and look after only their own children. People hoard goods for themselves and put in effort to please others. Power is passed down only through family lines, and walls and moats are made secure. Yǔ, Tang, Wen, Wu, King Cheng, and the Duke of Zhou obtained

1. *One family, jia* 家: There is a parallel structure between this phrase and a phrase in the preceding section, as follows:

tianxia wei gong 天下爲公
tianxia wei jia 天下爲家

We render these respectively as:

impartiality reigned
the entire land belongs to one family

This interpretation is consistent with Legge's (1885) and Yang and Song's (2013) and distinguishes between a world of public-spiritedness, as Legge says, and a world of self-interest. Michael Ing translates the same lines from the *Li ji* as follows:

everything under the heavens was commonly shared
everything under the heavens became the property of individual families. (Ing 2012, 105–106)

Although Ing's focus is on personal property, his emphasis in the second passage is also on self-interest.

power this way, but they also earnestly performed *li*.[2] *Li* flourishes in concert with nature. If someone is in power without proceeding from *li*, it will lead to calamity."

32.3

言偃復問曰:"如此乎, 禮之急也?"孔子曰:"夫禮, 先王所以承天之道, 以治人之情, 列其鬼神, 達於喪祭、鄉射、冠婚、朝聘。故聖人以禮示之, 則天下國家可得以禮正矣。"

Yan Yan inquired again, "Is this why *li* is so urgent?"

Confucius said, "*Li* is how the Ancient Kings inherited the *dao* of *tian*, how they governed people's emotions, how they maintained proper rankings of ancestors and gods, and how they performed proper funerals, village archery events, coming-of-age ceremonies, weddings, and audiences with the sovereign. Thus, when the *li* of sages is properly displayed, states and families throughout the world are able to achieve order through *li*."

32.4

言偃曰:"今之在位莫知由禮, 何也?"孔子曰:"嗚呼, 哀哉! 我觀周道, 幽、厲傷也。吾捨魯何適? 夫魯之郊及禘皆非禮, 周公其已衰矣。杞之郊也禹, 宋之郊也契, 是天子之事守也, 天子以杞、宋二王之後。周公攝政致太平, 而與天子同是禮也。諸侯祭社稷宗廟, 上下皆奉其典, 而祝嘏莫敢易其常法, 是謂大嘉。

Yan Yan asked, "Why is it that those in power today don't understand that they should proceed from *li*?"

Confucius said, "Ugh. When I look back at the *dao* of the Zhou, it was under Kings You and Li that it was harmed. If we were to leave Lu, where would we go?[3]

2. There is a tension in Confucius' philosophy between loyalty to the ruler as a person and loyalty to the ruler as a virtuous head of state. This tension gets fleshed out in *Mencius*, where regicide of tyrannical rulers is condoned. The tension arose with Yǔ's passing the crown on to his son and beginning the Xia dynasty, the first imperial dynasty. Prior to that, each of the Five Chiefs passed the crown on to the man they thought was most capable (there may be an exception in Ku, who passed it down to his son, but we don't know the ranking among the sons). The tension is resolved in the virtuous ruler, and so Confucius states that although his heroes (Yǔ, Tang, Wen, Wu, King Cheng, and the Duke of Zhou) all perpetuated the dynastic system, they were also virtuous leaders, guiding through the use of *li*. For more about the early rulers and the tension between meritocratic and hereditary rule, see Allan (2015, 2016).

3. Presumably, what's left of the Zhou *li* is most well preserved in Lu, so looking for better circumstances elsewhere would be pointless.

That the Jiao and Di sacrifices in Lu violate *li* shows that the system of the Duke of Zhou is in decline.[4] When the Qǐ state conducts the Jiao ceremony, it does so on behalf of its founder, Yǔ. When the Song state conducts the Jiao ceremony, it does so on behalf of its founder, Xie. This is the Zhou king maintaining his heritage[5] and recognizing the descendants of the founding kings of Qǐ and Song.[6] When the Duke of Zhou brought peace to the land by taking the reins of government, he used this same *li* in concert with the king. When the nobility held agrarian and ancestral sacrifices, those at each level made offerings to their forebears, and the performer of the rite dared not alter the long-standing norms. We can call this the Grand Celebration.

32.5

"今使祝嘏辭説，徒藏於宗祝巫史，非禮也，是謂幽國；醆斝及尸君，非禮也，是謂僭君；冕弁兵車，藏於私家，非禮也，是謂脅君；大夫具官，祭器不假，聲樂皆具，非禮也，是爲亂國；故仕於公曰臣，仕於家曰僕。三年之喪，與新有婚者，期不使也。以衰裳入朝，與家僕雜居齊齒，非禮也，是謂臣與君共國；天子有田以處其子孫，諸侯有國以處其子孫，大夫有采以處其子孫，是謂制度。天子適諸侯，必舍其宗廟，而不以禮籍入，是謂天子壞法亂紀；諸侯非問疾弔喪而入諸臣之家，是謂君臣爲謔；夫禮者，君之柄，所以別嫌明微，儐鬼神，考制度，列仁義，立政教，安君臣上下也。故

4. The theme of Lu's transgressions of *li* is continued in the subsequent section. In the subsequent lines in this section, an account is given of how *li* is properly performed.

5. The text diverges at this point from its parallel in the "Li yun" chapter of the *Li ji*. In the *Li ji* version, a clear distinction is established, with the prerogative of worshipping heaven and earth (understood as implying the Jiao ceremony in the previous sentences) reserved for the Zhou king, and the Sheji ceremony left to the leaders of the various states. Such a distinction is also implied in *Dialogues* 32.12, although a close inspection of the text will reveal that the situation is actually more complicated than just saying that the king has the exclusive privilege and so other states cannot perform the ceremony. The *Li ji* view can also be shoehorned into an interpretation of the passage here. Section 29.2 also says something about Jiao being the prerogative of the king, but that appears to be a reference to specific dates, not to the ceremony itself. Historically, we see about a dozen references in CQZZ to the Jiao ceremony performed in Lu. It is technically true that the Jiao ceremony is the exclusive privilege of the king, but since Qǐ, Song, and Lu (by virtue of the Duke of Zhou's special status) carry on the traditions of the kings of the three ancestral states (see note 6), they were also granted the right of performing the ceremony. So the infraction against *li* is not in the performing of the ceremony itself but in other aspects, such as the time of year it is performed or other details of the ceremony. For a detailed argument similar to the perspective given here, see Q. Wang (2005).

6. After Zhou conquered Shang, the remains of Shang's ruling house were settled in Song, where the tradition of venerating the Shang ancestors continued. The first ruler of Qǐ was said to be descended from the Xia line and continued the tradition of venerating the Xia ancestors. The Zhou viewed itself as heir and successor to the Xia and Shang and made a point of perpetuating the veneration of the Xia and Shang ancestral lines (in Qǐ and Song), which, according to Confucius, was the right thing to do.

政不正則君位危，君位危則大臣倍、小臣竊，刑肅而俗弊則法無常，法無常則禮無別，禮無別則士不仕、民不歸，是謂疵國。

"It is contrary to *li* to leave the recitations of sacrificial ceremonies in the hands only of the minister of ceremony, diviners, and astrologers, as is done today. Such a practice can be called benighted.[7]

"It is contrary to *li* to offer the *zhan* and *jia* vessels[8] to the surrogate of the deceased sovereign. Such a practice can be called arrogating the privileges of the sovereign.

"It is contrary to *li* to store extra ceremonial vestments, weapons, and chariots in one's private residence. Such a practice can be called threatening the sovereign.[9]

"It is contrary to *li* for one official to possess the authority of all other official posts, to not borrow sacrificial implements, or to have a complete set of ritual musical instruments. Such a practice can be called disrupting the state.[10]

"One who serves a sovereign is known as a vassal; one who serves a household is known as a servant. Do not send on a traveling assignment someone who is newly married or in a three-year mourning period. It is contrary to *li* to enter the court in mourning attire or to mix indiscriminately with servants. Such practices can be called sovereign and vassal both ruling the country.

"The king has the royal domain,[11] which he bequeaths to his descendants; noble lords have states, which they bequeath to their descendants; officials have fiefs, which they bequeath to their descendants; this is called an organized system. When

7. Confucius' point seems to be that sacrificial ceremonies should not be left only to specialists, in which case they would just be technical affairs. Rather, the descendants themselves should be involved, making them personally meaningful. Personal relations are what matter, not technical protocol.

8. *Zhan and jia vessels, zhan jia* 醆斝: The exact references of *zhan* 醆/盞 and *jia* 斝 in Confucius' time are not clear. In the Shang and early Zhou dynasties, the term *jia* referred to a specific kind of bronze cup/decanter used to hold liquor. It was distinctive for its three legs and for its two vertical knobs that were used to suspend it over a flame. According to the archaeological record, this kind of bronze had gone out of use by the time of Confucius. The *zhan* during Confucius' time was a bronze food container, but the term *zhan* seems to have been confined to Chu. In Confucius' region, the same item was called *dun* 敦. In the Warring States period, the term *zhan* referred largely to an oil lamp, and later it took on its now more common meaning of a drinking cup (see Yang Xiong's 楊/揚雄 *Fang yan* 方言). (Peng 2008)

9. These are all instruments of power, and by accumulating them for oneself, one can wield them against the sovereign to influence his decisions.

10. This sentence also has to do with the appropriate allotment of power. The authority of any official or nobleman is partial. Only aristocrats at a certain level had the authority to manufacture their own bronze ritual vessels. Their lower relatives had to borrow vessels from them. No one but the ruler could possess a full set of bronze musical instruments, which were used for performance at ceremonies. See 41.20 for a successful attempt at arrogation of this power by a clever nobleman.

11. *Royal domain*: reading *tian* 田 as *dian* 甸 or *ji* 畿.

the king travels to the state of a noble lord, if it is imperative that he lodge in the ancestral temple,[12] but if he does not follow the recorded instructions of the temple, it would be called destroying the ancestral system.[13] If a nobleman visits the home of a minister but enters without first inquiring about whether anyone is ill or in mourning, this would be called frivolity between lord and vassal.

"*Li* is the lever[14] by which the ruler brings order to disorder, elucidates the arcane, honors the deceased, confirms the organized system, asserts *ren* and *yi*, establishes good government and education, and stabilizes the different levels of society. If the government is not set right, the position of the ruler will be precarious. If the position of the ruler is precarious, high ministers may turn on him, lower ministers steal, punishments turn grave, and customs be lost, disrupting the norms. If norms are disrupted, the differentiations upon which *li* is based will be lost. If such differentiations are lost, officials will no longer serve and the people will no longer submit; such a country can be called defective.

32.6

"是故夫政者，君之所以藏身也，必本之天，效以降命。命，降於社之謂效地，降於祖廟之謂仁義，降於山川之謂興作，降於五祀之謂制度。此聖人所以藏身之固也。聖人參於天地，並於鬼神，以治政也。處其所存，禮之序也；翫其所樂，民之治也。天生時，地生財，人其父生而師教之。四者君以政用之，所以立於無過之地。

"And so, the execution of good government is how the sovereign stands in reserve,[15] rooting himself in nature and bringing it to fruition through issuing decrees. Decrees applied to altars to the soil are modeled after the earth. Those applied to ancestral temples have to do with *ren* and *yi*. Those applied to the natural landscape promote flourishing. Those applied to the five sacrificial ceremonies regulate and moderate.

12. The exact layouts and uses of ancestral temples in Confucius' time have not come down to us. We do have hints, however, from bronze inscriptions and transmitted texts. There appears to have been a building (*qin* 寢) in the back of ancestral temples that was used as lodging quarters for a ruler. Lodging there would provide a head start for a busy day of ceremonial hosting. (Hu 2020)

13. The point of this sentence seems to be that established traditions in a locale should not be tampered with willy-nilly, not even by a king.

14. *Lever*: *bing* 柄: handle, haft. This is a term common in the *Han Feizi* 韓非子 for the levers of power used by the absolute monarch; but rather than *li*, Han Fei advocates reward and punishment. The term appears again in 32.10, where it is translated "handle," and in 32.14, where it is translated "haft."

15. *Stands in reserve, cang shen* 藏身: conceals/stores himself. *Cang* here has a sense of storage for later use, as in a treasury that stores money to be distributed as needed. The association of *cang* with the ruler is another instance of resonance with the *Han Feizi*, but, again, with a different connotation. Thanks to Joshua Caine-Welch for suggesting this English wording.

This is the stability achieved when the sage stands in reserve. To achieve good government, the sage participates with heaven and earth and cooperates with the ancestors. The sequencing of *li* lies in placing things properly. The governing of the people lies in allowing for their amusement. Seasons come from the heavens and resources from the earth. Our bodies come from our fathers and instruction from our teachers. By making good use of these four things in governing, the sovereign establishes himself without error.

32.7

“君者, 人所明, 非明人者也; 人所養, 非養人者也; 人所事, 非事人者也。夫君者, 明人則有過, 養人則不足, 事人則失位。故百姓明君以自治, 養君以自安, 事君以自顯, 是以禮達而分定。人皆愛其死, 而患其生, 是故用人之智去其詐, 用人之勇去其怒, 用人之仁去其貪。國有患, 君死社稷爲之義, 大夫死宗廟爲之變。凡聖人能以天下爲一家, 以中國爲一人, 非意之, 必知其情, 從於其義, 明於其利, 達於其患, 然後爲之。

“People follow the example of the sovereign, not the other way around. People support the sovereign, not the other way around. People serve the sovereign, not the other way around. If the sovereign tries to take others as an example, he’ll misstep. If he tries to support others, there will be scarcity. If he tries to serve others, he’ll lose his influence.[16]

“Thus, the common people govern themselves by virtue of modeling after the sovereign, achieve stability for themselves by supporting the sovereign, and bring themselves to prominence by serving the sovereign. This is how *li* is achieved and everyone’s place decided.

“Because people prefer a good death and fear trouble in life, a ruler exploits the people’s own intelligence to rid them of deviousness, exploits their own bravery to rid them of rage, and exploits their own *ren* to rid them of greed.

“When calamity is imminent, a sovereign willingly dies on behalf of his country in accord with *yi*. A high official willingly dies on behalf of his clan in accord with what is proper.

“Whenever a sage is able to form the whole world into one family, to form the whole country into one person, it doesn’t occur just by thinking about it. One must understand people’s feelings, proceed from *yi* accordingly, be clear about both the benefits and harms to them, and only then take action.

16. Again, we see a resonance in this paragraph with the *Han Feizi*, in which the king must jealously safeguard his power, and each official and bureaucrat in the government must be careful not to overstep his bounds. The texts diverge in the subsequent paragraph. In the *Han Feizi*, self-government was considered workable only in former times, but not workable in the present time.

32.8

"何謂人情？喜、怒、哀、懼、愛、惡、欲七者，弗學而能；何謂人義？父慈、子孝、兄良、弟悌、夫義、婦聽、長惠、幼順、君仁、臣忠十者，謂之人義；講信修睦，謂之人利；争奪相殺，謂之人患。聖人之所以治人七情，脩十義，講信脩睦，尚辭讓，去争奪，舍禮何以治之？飲食男女，人之大欲存焉；死亡貧苦，人之大惡存焉。欲、惡者，人之大端。人藏其心，不可測度，美、惡皆在其心，不見其色，欲一以窮之，舍禮何以哉？

"What is meant by *human feelings?*[17] Delight, anger, sorrow, fear, preference, aversion,[18] and desire—these seven are unlearned abilities.

"What is meant by *human yi*? Love on the part of a father, *xiao* on the part of a son, helpfulness on the part of an older brother, solicitude on the part of a younger brother, *yi* on the part of a husband, coordination[19] on the part of a wife, mentoring on the part of an elder, congeniality on the part of a younger person, *ren* on the part of a sovereign, conscientiousness on the part of a minister—these ten refer to human *yi*.

"What is beneficial to people are trustworthiness and forging strong relations. What is disastrous for people are contentiousness and fighting. Other than through *li*, how can a sage govern such that the seven emotions are managed, the ten *yi* are cultivated, trustworthiness is promoted and strong relations are forged, deference is inculcated, and contentiousness is eliminated? He must be mindful of the primary desires for food, drink, and sex, and of the primary aversions to death, poverty, and hardship. Desires and aversions are the two primary human motivations. They are concealed in people's hearts and unfathomable. With pleasure and aversion in

17. *Human feelings, ren qing* 人情: This term has received a significant amount of analysis and explanation (see, for example, Bruya 2001; Eifring 2004).

18. *Preference, aversion, ai* 愛, *wu* 惡: On the surface these terms may appear to mean to love and to hate, as they tend to mean in Modern Chinese, but they don't mean to love in a sense of romantic love or to hate in a sense of deep enmity or resentment. Rather, they have a sense of desire to associate oneself with or separate oneself from. There is room for thinking more about these, however. Notice that, at the end of the paragraph, rather than the typical pairing of *ai* and *wu*, *wu* is paired first with *yu* 欲 (desire) and then with *mei* 美 (pleasure).

19. Yi *on the part of a husband, coordination on the part of a wife*: The term translated "coordination" is *ting* 聽, which means to listen or to obey. One has to make sense of this in light of the overall passage. *Yi* is defined in five pairs of directional virtues pertaining to five binary hierarchical relationships. The person of broader or greater responsibility cares for or mentors the person with narrower or less responsibility, and the person with narrower or less responsibility readily returns the favor. *Ting*, therefore, refers not to blind obedience but to managing household affairs in coordination with the wishes of the husband, who proceeds, himself, from undefined *yi*. It's as if the *yi* of the husband is a crystallization of the other four virtues—care, helpfulness, mentoring, and *ren* all together.

people's hearts but not visible in their expressions, absent *li*, how can they best be channeled?[20]

32.9

"故人者, 天地之德, 陰陽之交, 鬼神之會, 五行之秀。天秉陽, 垂日星; 地秉陰, 載山川。播五行於四時, 和四氣而後月生。是以三五而盈, 三五而缺, 五行之動, 共相竭也。五行、四氣、十二月, 還相爲本; 五聲、五律、十二管, 還相爲宫; 五味、六和、十二食, 還相爲質; 五色、六章、十二衣, 還相爲主。故人者, 天地之心, 而五行之端, 食味、别聲、被色而生者也。

"And so, as for people, there are the *de* of heaven and earth, the interaction of *yin* and *yang*, the convening of deceased ancestors, and the fruition of the five elemental phases.

"By virtue of *yang*, the heavens suspend the sun and stars. By virtue of *yin*, the earth carries the mountains and rivers. They distribute the phases out among the four seasons and harmonize the four climatic conditions,[21] from which the months are created. And so, the waxing and waning of the moon each lasts fifteen days, propelled by the exhaustive interactions of the elemental phases.

"The five phases, the four climatic conditions, the twelve months—their interactions form the primary divisions of the calendar.

"The five sounds, the six tones, the twelve notes of the panpipe—their interactions form the primary division of the musical scale.[22]

"The five flavors,[23] the six blends, the twelve foods—their interactions form the primary divisions of the palate.

"The five colors,[24] the six patterns, the twelve articles of clothing—their interactions form the primary divisions of fashion.

20. *Channeled:* The verb *channeled* in this sentence is implicit.

21. *Four climatic conditions, si qi* 四氣: The general climatic conditions associated with each of the four seasons. (Luo 1994)

22. This is the second sentence of four sentences that are parallel in structure: five X, six/four Y, twelve Z—their interactions form the [primary term]. This sentence is specific in mentioning *gong* 宫 (the primary divisions of musical notes) as the primary term. The other three sentences use only synonyms for *primary*. The specificity of the primary term in this sentence suggests that the primary terms in the other sentences (i.e., *calendar, palate,* and *fashion*) are implied and so have been added in the translation for clarity.

23. *Five flavors*: The five flavors are sour, sweet, bitter, pungent (spicy hot), and salty. (Luo 1994)

24. *Five colors*: The five colors are green (specifically, aquamarine, ranging from pale green to dark blue), red (specifically, cinnabar), white, black, and yellow. (Luo 1994)

"Thus, people are the heart of heaven and earth, the germination of the elemental phases, and the reason for the generation of flavors of food, musical notes, and fabric dyes.

32.10

"聖人作則，必以天地爲本，以陰陽爲端，以四時爲柄，以日星爲紀，月以爲量，鬼神以爲徒，五行以爲質，禮義以爲器，人情以爲田，四靈以爲畜。以天地爲本，故物可舉；以陰陽爲端，故情可睹；以四時爲柄，故事可勸；以日星爲紀，故業可別；月以爲量，故功有藝；鬼神以爲徒，故事有守；五行以爲質，故事可復也；禮義以爲器，故事行有考；人情以爲田，故人以爲奧；四靈以爲畜，故飲食有由。[25]

"In creating guides for behavior, the sage necessarily takes heaven and earth as the root, *yin* and *yang* as the sprout, the four seasons as the handle, the sun and stars as the mainstays, the moon as the measure, deceased ancestors as companions, the five elemental phases as constituents, *li* and *yi* as implements, human feelings as fertile ground, and the four auspicious creatures[26] as domestic animals.

"With heaven and earth as the root, things can be nurtured. With *yin* and *yang* as the sprout, circumstances can be observed. With the four seasons as handle, affairs can be facilitated. With the sun and stars as guidelines, enterprises can be differentiated. With the moon as measure, labor will fall within rhythms. With deceased ancestors as companions, affairs will have a safeguard. With the five phases as constituents, affairs can fall into cycles. With *li* and *yi* as implements, there will be confidence in the execution of affairs. With human feelings as fertile ground, there will be leadership. With the four auspicious creatures as domestic animals, food and drink will have a reliable source.[27]

32.11

"何謂四靈？麟、鳳、龜、龍謂之四靈。故龍以爲畜，而魚鮪不諗；鳳以爲畜，而鳥不翅；麟以爲畜，而獸不狘；龜以爲畜，而人情不失。先王秉蓍龜，列祭祀，瘞繒，宣祝嘏辭說，設制度，故國有禮，官有御，事有職，禮有序。

25. The phrases 故人以爲奧 and 故飲食有由 do not appear in SBCK. Following Yang and Song (2013), they were added based on SKQS.

26. *Four auspicious creatures*: See 32.12 and 25.4.

27. Of the ten sentences in this paragraph, five end with possibilities, and five with eventualities. The reasons behind such distinctions deserve exploration. They may have something to do with a simple grammatical distinction between passive and active voice, but the connection is not obvious. In the parallel sentences in the "Li yun" chapter of the *Li ji*, Legge (1885) changes one eventuality to a possibility. Yang and Song (2013) interpret them all as possibilities.

"What are the four auspicious creatures? The four auspicious creatures are the *lin*, *feng*, turtle, and water dragon.

"When the water dragon is domesticated, fish won't feel alarm.[28] When the *feng* is domesticated, birds won't take wing. When the *lin* is domesticated, wild animals won't bound away. When the turtle is domesticated, public sentiment won't get away.[29]

"By using yarrow stalks and turtle shells for divination, the Ancient Kings were able to set up sacrificial ceremonies, create ceremonial vestments, propagate the recitations of sacrificial ceremonies, and establish a system of moderation. As a result, the country was civil, officials were in control, affairs were handled by the appropriate offices, and *li* was well ordered.

32.12

"先王患禮之不達於下, 故饗帝于郊, 所以定天位也; 祀社於國, 所以列地利也; 禘祖廟, 所以本仁也; 旅山川, 所以儐鬼神也; 祭五祀, 所以本事也。故宗祝在廟, 三公在朝, 三老在學, 王前巫而後史, 卜筮瞽侑, 皆在左右, 王中心無爲也, 以守至正。是以禮行于郊, 而百神受職; 禮行於社, 而百貨可極; 禮行於祖廟, 而孝慈服焉; 禮行於五祀, 而正法則焉。故郊社、宗廟、山川、五祀, 義之脩而禮之藏。

"Fearing that *li* would not reach to all levels of society, the Ancient Kings made offerings to Di on the outskirts of the towns in order to establish the status of *tian*.[30] They instituted She ceremonies in each state in order to bring benefits to the soil everywhere. They instituted Di sacrifices at ancestral temples in order to establish *ren* as the root. They sacrificed to mountains and rivers in order to express reverence to gods and spirits. They performed the five sacrificial ceremonies in order to institute a foundation of service.

"And so, with the minister of ceremony in temples, the three high ministers in court, the three elders in schools, with a shaman in front of the king and the official historian behind him, with overseers of divination, court music, and advisers to his left and right, the king takes a position of nonaction in the center, safeguarding the supreme order.

"Thus, with *li* properly performed on the outskirts of towns, each of the hundred spirits receives its official position. With *li* performed in the She ceremony, there is a wide variety of plentiful goods. With *li* performed in ancestral temples, *xiao* and

28. In other words, they won't swim away and so can easily be caught and used for food.

29. Turtles are among the set of magical animals because their shells were used for divination. One thing they divined was public sentiment, *renqing* 人情. See "Prognostication" in the glossary. (Bruya 2001)

30. *Status of* tian, *tian wei* 天位: This could also be interpreted as the king's status under *tian*.

parental love are expressed. With *li* performed in the five sacrificial ceremonies, norms are set right.

"Thus, when leaders perform the Jiao and She, worship their ancestors, worship along mountains and rivers, and perform the five sacrificial ceremonies, it marks the cultivation of *yi* and the storing up of *li*.

32.13

"夫禮必本於太一，分而爲天地，轉而爲陰陽，變而爲四時，列而爲鬼神。其降曰命，其官於天也，協於分藝。其居於人也曰養，所以講信修睦，而固人之肌膚之會、筋骸之束者；所以養生送死、事鬼神之大端；所以達天道、順人情之大竇。唯聖人爲知禮之不可以已也，故破國、喪家、亡人，必先去其禮。

"*Li* must root itself in the Great Inchoate,[31] which separates into heaven and earth, transforms into *yin* and *yang*, changes into the four seasons, and splits into the gods and spirits.

"Its issuing is called a decree, its authority lies in *tian*, and it harmonizes natural talents. When it resides within people, it is called cultivation, by which one becomes trustworthy in speech and forges strong relations. It also keeps one's skin and muscles together and one's sinews strong. It is the primary starting point for living life and sending off the dead, as well as for serving gods and spirits. It is the broad way of attaining the *dao* of *tian* as well as flowing along with human emotions.

"Only sages fully understand that *li* must not be dispensed with. If one wishes to destroy a country, annihilate a family, or put an end to a person, first eliminate *li*.

32.14

"禮之於人，猶酒之有櫱也，君子以厚，小人以薄。聖人脩義之柄、禮之序，以治人情。人情者，聖王之田也，修禮以耕之，陳義以種之，講學以耨之，本仁以聚之，播樂以安之。故禮者，義之實也，協諸義而協則禮，雖先王未有，可以義起焉；義者，藝之分，仁之節。協於藝，講於仁，得之者强，失之者喪；仁者，義之本，順之體，得之者尊。故治國不以禮，猶無耜而耕；爲禮而不本於義，猶耕之而弗種；爲義而不講於學，猶種而弗耨；講之以學而不合之以仁，猶耨而不穫；合之以仁而不安之以樂，猶穫而弗食；安之以樂而不達於順，猶食而不肥。四體既正，膚革充盈，人之肥也；父子篤，兄弟睦，夫婦和，家之肥也；大臣法，小臣廉，官職相序，君臣相正，國之肥也；

31. *Great Inchoate, tai yi* 太一: Great One. This term occurs in other early Chinese texts but is rarely elucidated as it is here. Two other elucidations are in the *Lü shi chunqiu* and the excavated Guodian document "Tai yi sheng shui." All three appear mutually consistent, although the *Dialogues* version adds a perspective on its relation to human physiology and its association with *li*. (Henricks 2000)

天子以德爲車，以樂爲御，諸侯以禮相與，大夫以法相序，士以信相考，百姓以睦相守，天下之肥也。是謂大順。順者，所以養生送死、事鬼神之常也。故事大積焉而不苑，並行而不謬，細行而不失。深而通，茂而有間，連而不相及，動而不相害，此順之至也。明於順，然後乃能守危。

"*Li* is to people as malt is to beer[32]—in the *junzi* it is strong and in small-minded persons weak. The sage directs the haft of *yi* and the ordering of *li* to govern human emotions.

"Human emotions are the fertile ground of sages and kings, who plow it by developing *li,* plant in it by displaying *yi,* weed it by teaching, bring a feeling of community through creating a foundation of *ren,* and create an atmosphere of stability through playing ceremonial music. Thus, *li* is the realization of *yi.*

"*Li* harmonizes different *yi,* and in the very harmonizing shows itself to be *li.* Even if the Ancient Kings had not existed, we could still take *yi* as the starting point.

"*Yi* is the differentiation of norms and the regulation of *ren.* With it, there can be harmony among the norms and attention paid to *ren.* Strength comes with its achievement and demise with its loss. *Ren* is the root of *yi* and the embodiment of congeniality.[33] Respect is accorded to those who achieve it.

"Thus, governing a country without using *li* is like farming without plowing. Trying to enact *li* without rooting it in *yi* is like trying to farm without planting. Trying to enact *yi* without paying due attention to education is like sowing but not weeding. To pay attention to education but not match it with *ren* is like weeding but not harvesting. To match education with *ren* but not create a comfortable atmosphere through ceremonial music is like harvesting but not eating. To create a comfortable atmosphere but one that does not achieve congeniality is like eating but getting no nourishment.

"Healthy limbs and full cheeks are a sign that people are getting adequate nourishment. Devotion between father and son, consideration between siblings, and harmony between spouses are signs that a family is getting adequate nourishment. Major officials following the law, minor officials minding their duties, official posts in good order, and sovereign and ministers improving each other are signs that a state is getting adequate nourishment. When the king takes *de* as his chariot and ceremonial music as the driver, when lords across the land treat each other with *li,* when high officials use the law to keep themselves in order, when low officials use trustworthiness to keep each other in line, and when common people protect each

32. See "Alcohol" in the glossary. The oblique analogy here is that as alcohol raises one's spirits, so does *li.*

33. Congeniality, *shun* 順: *Shun* is a key term of political philosophy. Its basic meaning is to move smoothly along with the current. We see it used above in 1.3 to refer to women's behavior under Confucius' effective governing, and in 12.22 to refer to Yangshe's behavior when young. See "Congeniality" in the introduction's philosophical lexicon.

other through mutual consideration, those are signs that the whole land is getting adequate nourishment. This is the Grand Congeniality.

"Congeniality is how one nurtures the living and sends off the dead, the standard for serving gods and spirits. When affairs multiply to a high degree, congeniality means that there is no stagnation, they can be conducted simultaneously without error and in minuscule detail without loss. With congeniality, communication can be maintained across gulfs, space can be opened up in thick growth, connection can be made without friction, and there can be movement without collision. Only by clearly understanding congeniality can one safeguard against crisis.

32.15

"夫禮之不同，不豐不殺，所以持情而合危也。山者不使居川，渚者不使居原；用水、火、金、木，飲食必時；冬合男女，春頒爵位，必當年德，皆所順也，用民必順。故無水旱昆蟲之災，民無凶饑妖孽之疾。天不愛其道，地不愛其寶，人不愛其情，是以天降甘露，地出醴泉，山出器車，河出馬圖，鳳凰麒麟，皆在郊掫，龜龍在宮沼，其餘鳥獸及卵胎，皆可俯而窺也。則是無故，先王能循禮以達義，體信以達順。此順之實也。"

"Neither increased nor decreased, the differentiation inherent in *li* allowed for emotions to be supported and crises averted.

"People who lived in the mountains were not forced to move to the riverside. People who lived along shorelines were not forced to move to the plains. Putting to use water, fire, metal, and wood for the sake of meals required proper timing. Unions between women and men were created in the winter, and noble ranks were conferred in the spring, each according to appropriate age and contributions. These are all examples of making things congenial.

"Congeniality is the only way to work with the people. This prevents natural disasters, such as floods, droughts, and insect pestilence. It also prevents human tragedies, like plagues and famine.

"*Tian* did not stint its *dao*; the earth did not stint its treasures; and people did not stint their emotions. As a result, heaven gave sweet dew, the earth gushed forth spring water, mountains produced resources for tools and carriages,[34] rivers produced the equine chart,[35] *fenghuang* and *qilin* flourished in the countryside marshes, turtles

34. According to Yang and Song (2013), it was believed that in utopian times the trunks of trees growing on hillsides would be so perfectly round that they could be formed directly into wheels, without being worked.

35. It was believed that in utopian times, a numerological chart would appear from river water. In *Analects* 9.9, Confucius laments that the river has not produced a chart. In the *Documents* ("Gu ming"), one of the precious items put on display after the death of King Cheng was a river chart (*he tu* 河圖). In his commentary on the *Documents*, Kong Anguo glosses "river chart," explaining that during the

and water dragons flourished in palace ponds, and the offspring of all of the other birds and beasts could be glimpsed just by looking down. There was no particular cause. It was just that the Ancient Kings were able to follow *li* and achieve *yi*, to embody trustworthiness and achieve congeniality. Such is the realization of congeniality."

time of Fu Xi (at the very beginning of Chinese civilization), a "dragon horse" emerged from the Yellow River with the patterns of the eight trigrams on it.

33

The Capping Ceremony Ode

Like chapters 4, 28, and 29, this chapter is dedicated to the topic of a single kind of ceremony—in this case, the coming-of-age rite called the capping ceremony. The ceremony, Confucius says, does not change according to rank. Its purpose is to position the young man in the social fabric of the family, including his ancestry, thereby inspiring emotions of reverence and humility and carrying forward the intentions and industriousness of his forebears.

33.1

郱隱公既即位，將冠，使大夫因孟懿子問禮於孔子。子曰："其禮如世子之冠。冠於阼者，以著代也，醮於客位，加其有成，三加彌尊，導喻其志。冠而字之，敬其名也。雖天子之元子，猶士也，其禮無變，天下無生而貴者故也。行冠事必於祖廟，以祼享之禮以將之，以金石之樂節之。所以自卑而尊先祖，示不敢擅。"

Duke Yin of the state of Zhū had just assumed the throne at the same time that he was preparing for his coming-of-age capping ceremony. He asked a high official to go through Meng Yizi to ask Confucius about the *li* of it.

Confucius said, "The *li* of it is like the coming-of-age ceremony for any firstborn son[1] of a lord.

"The capping is done at the east staircase,[2] which highlights the transmission from one generation to the next. The host stands on the guest side of the hall and makes a toast, wishing success. Then three hats are donned in succession, each performed with more solemnity than the previous, fostering appropriate aspirations in

1. *First-born son, shizi* 世子: This more specifically refers to the eldest son of the wife (not of a concubine)—in other words, to the first person in the main line of descent from the father.

2. *East staircase*: See 5.2n2. Holding the ceremony on the east side indicates that the boy, in coming of age, is preparing to assume the role of the master of the household.

the son.[3] At the capping, the boy takes on a *zi* to show due respect for his given name.[4]

"Whether for the crown prince or an average up-and-comer, the *li* does not change, the reason being that for all born in this world, none is superior by birth.

"The capping ceremony must be held at one's ancestral temple and is introduced through a *li* of formal wine offering and modulated with the music of metal and stone chimes. In this way, one shows reverence for the ancestors by putting oneself in an inferior position, demonstrating that one does not dare go off on one's own."

33.2

懿子曰:"天子未冠即位, 長亦冠也?"孔子曰:"古者王世子雖幼, 其即位則尊爲人君。人君, 治成人之事者, 何冠之有?"懿子曰:"然則諸侯之冠異天子與?"孔子曰:"君薨而世子主喪, 是亦冠也已。人君無所殊也。"懿子曰:"今邾君之冠非禮也?"孔子曰:"諸侯之有冠禮也, 夏之末造也, 有自來矣, 今無譏焉。天子冠者, 武王崩, 成王年十有三而嗣立。周公居冢宰, 攝政以治天下。明年夏六月, 既葬, 冠成王而朝于祖, 以見諸侯, 示有君也。周公命祝雍作頌曰:'祝王達而未幼。'祝雍辭曰:'使王近於民, 遠於年, 嗇於時, 惠於財, 親賢而任能。'其頌曰:'令月吉日, 王始加元服。去王幼志, 服衮職, 欽若昊命, 六合是式。率爾祖考, 永永無極。'此周公之制也。"

Yizi said, "The king assumes the throne before his capping ceremony. Can an adult still go through with the capping ceremony?"

Confucius said, "In the past, even young crown princes assumed the throne and were respected as sovereign rulers—sovereign rulers who governed the affairs of adults. What would be the purpose of having a capping ceremony for them?"

Yizi said, "Well then, is the capping ceremony of the noble lords any different from that of the king?"

Confucius said, "When a sovereign passes away, the crown prince presides over the funeral, which also functions as a capping ceremony. The sovereign is not special in this regard."

Yizi said, "Is holding a capping ceremony for the Zhū sovereign at this time in violation of *li*?"

3. The details of the ceremony have not come down to us. One plausible commentarial reconstruction is as follows: One cap was made of black fabric, one was made of deer hide, and one, indicating noble rank, came in various shapes and was black or red. The first cap is worn by an official and represents the aspiration to govern; the second cap is worn by a soldier and represents the aspiration to defend the crown; and the third cap is worn by the nobility for sacrificial ceremonies and represents the aspiration to take a position of responsibility in the family. See also "Capping ceremony" in the glossary. (Zheng, Wu, and Yang 2000)

4. See "Naming convention" in the glossary.

Confucius said, "The capping ceremony among nobility was begun at the end of the Xia dynasty and has continued on its own ever since, so there is no reason to repudiate it now.

"There is the case of the capping ceremony of King Cheng, who was still a minor when his father, King Wu, passed away. King Wu's brother, the Duke of Zhou, assumed the position of prime minister, handling the government across the land. In the sixth month of the following year, after the king had been buried, the Duke of Zhou conducted a capping ceremony for King Cheng, facing the ancestors and in front of the noble lords to announce his rulership. Ordering Zhu Yong[5] to write an ode, the Duke of Zhou said, 'Commemorate that the king has arrived and is no longer a child.'

"Zhu Yong first prayed, 'May the king be close to the people, far away from the end of his years, thrifty in his use of time, and wise in his use of resources, and may he frequent the company of men of ability and virtue and employ them.' Then he chanted:

Good month, propitious day
The king's inaugural cap
May he discard childish thoughts.
Assuming the vestments of noble office,
May he obey the decree of *tian*,
Become a model for the six directions,
And follow the ways of the ancestors,
Always and without end.

Such was the system of the Duke of Zhou."

33·3

懿子曰:"諸侯之冠，其所以爲賓主，何也?"孔子曰:"公冠則以卿爲賓，無介，公自爲主，迎賓揖，升自阼，立于席北。其醴也，則如士，饗之以三獻之禮。既醴，降自阼階。諸侯非公而自爲主者，其所以異，皆降自西階，玄端與皮弁異。朝服素畢，公冠四，加玄冕祭。其酬幣于賓，則束帛乘馬。王太子、庶子之冠擬焉，皆天子自爲主，其禮與士無變，饗食賓也皆同。"

Yizi said, "In the capping ceremonies of the noble lords, how should the host and guest act?"

Confucius said, "In the capping ceremony of a duke, a high minister should act as the guest, with no second, and the duke himself acts as the host, welcoming the

5. *Zhu Yong* 祝雍: *Zhu* can be interpreted as a surname or as the official position of cantor. This person is not attested elsewhere.

guest with hands clasped together and a slight bow. He ascends by the east steps and stands on the north side of the mat. In raising the cup of sweet liquor, he does so like an official at a local banquet, with the *li* of saluting with three toasts. After the sweet liquor, he descends by the east stairs.

"Noble lords other than the duke also play the host themselves, and the way they differ is that they descend by the western stairs. They also differ in their dark attire and leather cap.

"The court robes are understated throughout. The duke has four hats, with the addition of the dark crown ceremony, and his gifts to the guest are silk and horses.

"The capping ceremonies of the crown prince and children of the king's concubines are otherwise alike. The king acts as host himself, and the *li* of this is unchanged right down to low officials. The offering of food to the guests is also the same."

33.4

懿子曰："始冠必加緇布之冠，何也？"孔子曰："示不忘古。太古冠布，齋則緇之，其緌也，吾未之聞。今則冠而幣之可也。"懿子曰："三王之冠，其異何也？"孔子曰："周弁，殷冔，夏收，一也。三王共皮弁素緌。委貌，周道也；章甫，殷道也；毋追，夏后氏之道也。"

Yizi said, "Why must the black fabric cap be included in the beginning of the capping ceremony?"

Confucius said, "To demonstrate our not forgetting the ancients. In high antiquity, the cap was made of bast fabric, and it was dyed black after preparatory purification. I am not aware of their having tassels (as today). Nowadays, people prefer a silk cap for capping."

Yizi said, "How was the capping ceremony in the times of the Three Kings different?"

Confucius said, "The *bian* of the Zhou, the *xu* of the Shang, and the *shou* of the Xia, which were equivalent. They all had leather *bian* with plain tassels. The *weimao* hat is used in the way of the Zhou, the *zhangfu* hat is used in the way of the Shang, and the *wuzhui* hat is used in the way of the Xia."[6]

6. There is much speculation about the distinctions between the different hats mentioned in this passage. Unfortunately, the archaeological record is silent. The early Chinese hat began in the Neolithic period as a head ornament with the practical function of binding long hair, and it retained this function as it evolved over the centuries. (Tian 2001; Zhang and Zhang 2015)

34

The Temple System

This brief chapter outlines the ancestral system of worship and the responsibilities of different levels of society. The main thrust of the chapter seems to be veneration in light of important contributions. Those ancestors who made great contributions deserve lasting veneration. Others are permitted to fall by the wayside as time passes. This sentiment is consistent with stories in the *Dialogues* in which the temples to less illustrious rulers are destroyed by fire.

34.1

衛將軍文子將立先君之廟於其家，使子羔訪於孔子。子曰：“公廟設於私家，非古禮之所及，吾弗知。”子羔曰：“敢問尊卑上下立廟之制，可得而聞乎？”孔子曰：“天下有王，分地建國，設祖宗，乃爲親疏貴賤多少之數。是故天子立七廟，三昭三穆，與太祖之廟七。太祖近廟，皆月祭之。遠廟爲祧，有二祧焉，享嘗乃止。諸侯立五廟，二昭二穆，與太祖之廟而五，曰祖考廟，享嘗乃止。大夫立三廟，一昭一穆，與太廟而三，曰皇考廟，享嘗乃止。士立一廟，曰考廟。王考無廟，合而享嘗乃止。庶人無廟，四時祭於寢。此自有虞以至于周之所不變也。凡四代帝王之所謂郊者，皆以配天；其所謂禘者，皆五年大祭之所及也。應爲太祖者，則其廟不毀；不及太祖，雖在禘郊，其廟則毀矣。古者祖有功而宗有德，謂之祖宗者，其廟皆不毀。”

Wenzi, a general of Wei, was about to build a temple to the former rulers of Wei on his land[1] and sent Zigao to ask Confucius about it. Confucius said, “Building a state temple on private land is not a part of the ancient *li*. I don’t know anything about it.”

Zigao said, “Perhaps I could ask about the hierarchical system of reverence in establishing a temple.”

Confucius said, “When a single kingdom was first established across the land, and the land was divided into separate states, locations were established to worship

1. Wenzi was a descendent of the Wei rulers but not in the direct line of descent, so building a temple to them was not a proper thing to do.

each founding ruler and his ancestors and to track the proximity of the relations and their positions of honor.

"And so the king established seven temples. Three for the closest even-numbered ancestors, three for the closest odd-numbered ancestors, and one to the first ancestor make seven. Services were held monthly at the temple to the first ancestor and at temples to direct descendants.

"Temples to more distantly related ancestors were called *Tiao*, of which there were two, and where sacrifices were made seasonally.

"Rulers of the states each established five temples. Two for the closest even-numbered ancestors, two for the closest odd-numbered ancestors, and one to the first ancestor make five. The temple to the first ancestor was called the *Zukao* Temple, and sacrifices were made seasonally.

"High officials established three temples. One for the father, one for the grandfather, and one to the first ancestor make three. This last was called the *Huangkao* Temple, and sacrifices were made seasonally.

"Lower officials established one temple, called the *Kao* Temple, for the father. Their grandfather did not have his own temple. He was placed in the father's temple, where sacrifices were made seasonally.

"Commoners did not have ancestral temples and instead worshipped seasonally in their homes.

"This system began with Yú and persisted unchanged down to the Zhou.

"In the Jiao ceremonies of the chiefs and kings of all the four dynasties, the ancestors were worshipped alongside *tian*. They were also worshipped in what is called the Di ceremony once every five years. Temples dedicated to the first ancestor are never to be destroyed. Temples to ancestors whose contributions do not live up to the first ancestor, even though they fall within the scope of the Jiao or Di ceremonies, may be destroyed. Venerable ancestors of old were venerated on account of their accomplishments and great *de*, and none of their temples has been destroyed."[2]

34.2

子羔問曰:"祭典云:'昔有虞氏祖顓頊而宗堯, 夏后氏亦祖顓頊而宗禹, 殷人祖契而宗湯, 周人祖文王而宗武王。'此四祖四宗, 或乃異代, 或其考祖之有功德, 其廟可也。若有虞宗堯, 夏祖顓頊, 皆異代之有功德者也, 亦可以存其廟乎?"孔子曰:"善, 如汝所聞也。如殷周之祖宗, 其廟可以不毀, 其他祖宗者, 功德不殊, 雖在殊代, 亦可以無疑矣。《詩》云:'蔽芾甘棠, 勿翦勿伐','邵伯所憩'。周人之於邵公也, 愛其人, 猶敬其所舍之樹, 況祖宗其功德而可以不尊奉其廟焉?"

2. Kramers (1950, 148) views this entire paragraph as drawing a distinction between Zu and Zong sacrifices (as in the "Five sacrificial ceremonies" entry in the glossary).

Zigao asked, "The ritual manuals say that the people of the Youyu clan recognized Zhuanxu and Yao as ancestors. The Xia also recognized Zhuanxu as ancestor and Yǔ as well. The Shang recognized Xie and Tang as their ancestors. The Zhou recognize Kings Wen and Wu. It was acceptable to build temples to these four different ancestral lines, because even though the ancestors may have been of different lineages, they are the ones who had accomplishments and *de*. For example, it is true that the Youyu and Xia recognized Yao and Zhuanxu, respectively, as their ancestors in order to acknowledge their accomplishments and *de*, despite being of different lineages. Is it also acceptable that their temples be preserved?"

Confucius said, "Good. Yes, it is as you have heard. The temples to the ancestors of Shang and Zhou should be preserved and not destroyed. As for the purported ancestors of the others, their accomplishments and *de* were no different, so even though they may have been of different lineages, they may unquestionably remain. A poem says:

> The lush and shady pear tree,
> Don't prune it, don't chop it . . .
> That's where the Earl of Shao rested.[3]

Look at the reverence of the Zhou people for the Earl of Shao. They loved him and especially revered the tree under which he rested. Compare that to the accomplishments and *de* of other venerable ancestors. Could they not be worshipped in their own temples?"

3. See 10.4n8 for more about this poem.

35

Understanding the Finer Points of Music

Chapter 35 focuses on music and dance, topics that have come up already at various points, often connected to *li*, education, and the transmission of emotion. With a zither master, we see Confucius as an unusually focused student, plumbing the meaning of a particular song that he concludes must have to do with his hero, King Wen. Another hero, King Wen's son King Wu, is the topic of another episode, where King Wu is the subject of a dance. Here, we see Confucius providing a nuanced artistic interpretation. We also see Confucius discussing the qualities of music in two different geographical regions, assessing their suitability to education and self-cultivation.

35.1

孔子學琴於師襄子。襄子曰: "吾雖以擊磬爲官, 然能於琴。今子於琴已習, 可以益矣。" 孔子曰："丘未得其數也。"有間，曰："已習其數，可以益矣。"孔子曰："丘未得其志也。"有間, 曰: "已習其志, 可以益矣。"孔子曰: "丘未得其爲人也。"有間, 孔子有所繆然思焉, 有所睪然高望而遠眺, 曰: "丘迨得其爲人矣。黮而黑, 頎然長, 曠如望羊, 奄有四方, 非文王其孰能爲此?"師襄子避席葉拱而對曰: "君子聖人也, 其傳曰《文王操》。"

Confucius studied the zither with Shi Xiangzi.

Xiangzi said, "Although I am the official in charge of ceremonial music, I am also able to play the zither. You are well-practiced at playing the zither, but there are more songs to learn."

Confucius said, "I don't yet grasp the technique for playing this particular song."

After a period of time, Xiangzi said, "You have now mastered the technique for playing this song. There are more songs to learn."

Confucius said, "I don't yet grasp the ideas in this song."

After a period of time, Xiangzi said, "You have now mastered the ideas in this song. There are more songs to learn."

Confucius said, "I don't yet know who this song is about."

For a time, Confucius sat pensively looking off into the distance. He then said, "I finally know who this song is about. Somber and dark, tall and imposing, expansive like a vista, extending in the four directions. Who but King Wen was like this?"

Shi Xiangzi rose from his mat, gestured admiringly, and replied, "You are a sage. By tradition it is called King Wen's Tenacity."

35.2

子路鼓琴，孔子聞之，謂冉有曰："甚矣！由之不才也。夫先王之制音也，奏中聲以爲節，流入於南，不歸於北。夫南者，生育之鄉；北者，殺伐之域。故君子之音温柔居中，以養生育之氣。憂愁之感，不加于心也；暴厲之動，不在于體也。夫然者，乃所謂治安之風也。小人之音則不然，亢麗微末，以象殺伐之氣。中和之感，不載於心；温和之動，不存于體。夫然者，乃所以爲亂之風。昔者舜彈五弦之琴，造《南風》之詩，其詩曰：'南風之薰兮，可以解吾民之慍兮；南風之時兮，可以阜吾民之財兮。'唯脩此化，故其興也勃焉，德如泉流，至于今，王公大人述而弗忘。殷紂好爲北鄙之聲，其廢也忽焉，至于今，王公大人舉以爲誡。夫舜起布衣，積德含和，而終以帝。紂爲天子，荒淫暴亂，而終以亡，非各所修之致乎？由，今也匹夫之徒，曾無意于先王之制，而習亡國之聲，豈能保其六七尺之體哉？"冉有以告子路，子路懼而自悔，静思不食，以至骨立。夫子曰："過而能改，其進矣乎！"

Once when Zilu was strumming the zither, Confucius heard it and said to Ran You, "Really! Yóu [Zilu] is so untalented.

"When the Ancient Kings created our system of music, mild sounds were performed for the purpose of self-moderation.

"The tradition was transmitted south and never returned north. The south is a place of vitality and nurturance. The north is a place of war and death. Thus, the music of a *junzi* is gentle and mild, possessing a sense of vitality and nurturance. There is no anxious confusion in the heart nor violent movements in the body. Such music belongs to the so-called style of *creating order*.

"The music of a small-minded person is different. It is intense and shrill, possessing only a sense of war and death. There is no feeling of moderation or harmony in the heart nor gentle movements in the body. Such music is thus said to be in the style called *breeding unrest*.

"In the past, Shun, playing the five-string zither, created a poem called 'The Southern Wind.' It goes:

The soft blowing of the southern wind
Can ease the tension of our people.

The timeliness of the southern wind
Can increase the prosperity of our people.[1]

Indeed, by cultivating this music for the purpose of educating the people, his rise was rapid. His *de*, which gushed like spring water, flows right down to today. Royalty, nobles, and leaders have never forgotten and still extol it.

"Zhòu of the Shang dynasty preferred the sound of the northern cities. It was vapid and frenetic. Right through to today, royalty, nobles, and leaders have used it as an object lesson in what to avoid.

"Shun started out as a commoner, and through accumulating *de* and possessing inner harmony, he ended as chief. Zhòu started out as king, and through depravity and tyranny he ended up losing everything. Is this difference not due to their different paths of cultivation?

"Now, Yóu is a commoner and has expressed no interest in the musical system of the Former Kings, preferring instead the sound of a lost kingdom. How will he be able to preserve his six-foot frame?"

Ran You told Zilu what Confucius had said. Zilu turned fearful and regretful. He sat in silent thought without eating until he was all skin and bones.

Confucius said, "To be able to recognize one's error is already progress."

35·3

周賓牟賈侍坐於孔子。孔子與之言，及樂，曰："夫《武》之備誡之以久，何也?"對曰："病疾不得其衆。""詠嘆之，淫液之，何也?"對曰："恐不逮事。""發揚蹈厲之已蚤，何也?"對曰："及時事。""《武》坐致右而軒左，何也?"對曰："非《武》坐。""聲淫及商，何也?"對曰："非《武》音也。"孔子曰："若非《武》音，則何音也?"對曰："有司失其傳也。"孔子曰："唯，丘聞諸萇弘，亦若吾子之言是也。若非有司失其傳，則武王之志荒矣。"賓牟賈起，免席而請曰："夫《武》之備誡之以久，則既聞命矣。敢問遲矣而又久立於綴，何也?"子曰："居，吾語爾。夫樂者，象成者也。總干而山立，武王之事也。發揚蹈厲，太公之志也。《武》亂皆坐，周、邵之治也。且夫《武》，始成而北出，再成而滅商，三成而南反，四成而南國是疆，五成而分陝，周公左、邵公右，六成而復綴，以崇其天子焉。衆夾振焉而四伐，所以盛威於中國。分陝而進，所以事蚤濟。久立於綴，所以待諸侯之至也。""今汝獨未聞牧野之語乎？武王克殷而反商之政，未及下車，則封黃帝之後於薊，封帝堯之後於祝，封帝舜之後於陳；下車又封夏后氏之後於杞，封殷之後於宋，封王子比干之墓，釋箕子之囚，使人行商容之舊，以復其位，庶民弛政，庶士倍祿。既濟河西，馬散之華山之陽而弗復乘，牛散之桃林之野而弗復服，車甲則釁之而藏之諸府庫以示弗復用。倒載干戈而包之以虎皮，將率之士使爲諸侯，命之曰鞬櫜，然後天下知武王之不復用兵也。散軍而修郊射，左射以《狸

1. Although this poem is mentioned by name in several other early texts, this is the only surviving fragment. It does not appear in the *Poems*.

首》，右射以《騶虞》，而貫革之射息也；裨冕搢笏，而虎賁之士脫劍；郊祀后稷，而民知尊父焉；配明堂，而民知孝焉；朝覲，然後諸侯知所以臣；耕籍，然後民知所以敬親。六者，天下之大教也。食三老五更於太學，天子袒而割牲，執醬而饋，執爵而酳，冕而總干，所以教諸侯之弟也。如此，則周道四達，禮樂交通。夫《武》之遲久，不亦宜乎？”

Binmou Gu of Zhou was sitting in attendance on Confucius.

Confucius spoke with him, touching on the topic of music, and said, "There is an arresting moment of drumming at the opening[2] of the Wu dance.[3] Do you know why?"

Binmou replied, "It depicts Wu's tremulous fear that he may not be able to win the support of the masses."

Confucius asked, "It is drawn out and sustained. Why is that?"

Binmou replied, "It depicts the fear that he cannot measure up."

Confucius asked, "Why put such an intense dance so early in the performance?"

Binmou replied, "The time for action had arrived."

Confucius asked, "He sits[4] with his right knee down and his left knee up. Why is that?"

Binmou replied, "Actually, there should be no such scene of Wu sitting."

Confucius asked, "The withering tone of the *shang* note is drawn out. Why is that?"

Binmou replied, "Actually, there should be no such note."

Confucius asked, "If there should be no such note, why is it there?"

Binmou replied, "This part of the tradition was once lost to the official in charge."

Confucius said, "Yes, I have heard the same thing from Chang Hong. Suppose it is not true that the tradition was lost to the official in charge. Then the interpretation of Wu's feeling would be wildly wrong."

Binmou Gu rose, stepped off the mat, and invited Confucius to continue, saying, "As for the arresting moment of drumming at the opening of the Wu dance, I've done as you wished and given my interpretation. May I be so bold as to ask: After the drawn-out beginning, why do the performers stand so long in place?"

Confucius said, "Sit, and I will tell you. The musical performance is a depiction of accomplishment. As leader, standing solid as a mountain with his shield upraised—this is a depiction of the task that King Wu has to accomplish. The intense dance depicts the feelings of the Grand Duke. In the coda of the Wu dance, they all

2. *Arresting moment of drumming at the opening, bei jie* 備誡: following Wang Su, who likely follows Zheng Xuan commenting on the same passage in the *Li ji*.

3. A dance that depicts the victory of King Wu.

4. The customary way to sit was with both knees on the ground, resting on one's heels.

sit, which is a depiction of the orderly government of the Duke of Zhou and Earl of Shao. The opening section of the Wu dance depicts the northern campaign. The next section depicts the destruction of Shang. The third section depicts the return south. The fourth section depicts setting the borders of the southern kingdoms. The fifth section depicts the division at Shan, with the Duke of Zhou in the east and the Earl of Shao in the west.[5] In the sixth section, they return to their places, depicting their honoring the king. Then as a mass, they gather in the center, lunging in the four directions to depict complete authority over the central states. Advancing out from the division at Shan depicts the rapid success of the conquest. The extended period of standing in place depicts them awaiting the arrival of the noble lords.

"Have you not heard the story of Muye?[6] King Wu conquered Shang, overturned their government, and, before alighting from his chariot, enfeoffed the descendants of the Yellow Chief at Ji, enfeoffed the descendants of Chief Yao at Zhù, and enfeoffed the descendants of Chief Shun at Chen.

"After alighting, he enfeoffed the descendants of the Xia dynasty at Qǐ, enfeoffed the remnants of the Shang royalty at Song, posthumously enfeoffed Prince Bigan, freed the Viscount of Ji from prison, sent people to scour the Shang ruins for Shang Rong and restored him to his position, freed the people from the government, and doubled the salaries of low officials alike.

"After crossing the Yellow River and turning west, he dispersed the horses to the south side of Hua Mountain, not to be ridden again. He dispersed the oxen to the countryside outside of Tao Forest, not to be yoked again. He consecrated the chariots and armor with blood and put them away in storage, not to be used again. He dumped out the weapons and stored them in tiger hide. Then he installed his generals as lords across the country.

"This whole process was called 'the quiver,' and afterward the world knew that King Wu would not be raising an army again.

"Discharged soldiers studied archery ceremony on the outskirts of cities. On the east side of a city, the 'Li Shou' song was used. On the west side of a city, the 'Zouyu'[7]

5. The early Western Zhou had an unofficial east/west division, with the border being Shan 陝 (present-day Shan 陝縣, Henan). The Duke of Zhou was in charge of keeping the peace among the noble lords on the eastern side of the country, and the Earl of Shao was in charge of keeping the peace among the noble lords to the west. For a depiction of the Earl of Shao's role based on inscriptions on excavated bronzes, see Shaughnessy (1997).

6. The Battle of Muye was the decisive victory of Zhou over Shang. This event is mentioned in inscriptions on contemporaneous bronzes (Shaughnessy 1997).

7. The "Li shou" and "Zouyu" were probably hunting songs. The "Li shou" (head of the raccoon dog) is unknown, but the "Zouyu" is in the *Poems* (#25, in the "Shao nan" section) and goes like this:

In burgeoning reeds,
One release, five sows.

song was used. Archery that involved piercing armor was put to an end. Ceremonial clothes were donned, official tablets were tucked into robes, and warriors shed their swords.

"Through the king's performing the Jiao sacrifice to Hou Ji, the people learned to revere their fathers. Through the king's communicating with ancestors in court ceremonies, the people learned to be *xiao*. By having formal audiences with the king, the noble lords learned how to be proper vassals. Through the king's ceremonial planting, the people understood how to respect their parents. These six[8] were the major forms of education.

"Elders from across the land were feted in the High Academy,[9] where the king pushed up his sleeves, carved the sacrificial meat, personally served the food, raised toasts after the meal, and performed a shield dance in a ceremonial cap. In this way, the noble lords were taught how to act as proper younger siblings.

"This is how the way of the Zhou reached the four directions and *li* and music became so common. Is it not appropriate that the Wu dance goes on so long?"

Woo hoo, the *Zouyu*.
In burgeoning weeds,
One release, five shoats.
Woo hoo, the *Zouyu*.

The song seems to depict a hunting party delightedly bringing down game. For such a brief, seemingly straightforward hunting song, the exact references to the terms are hotly debated, not least of which is the term *zouyu*, which, we are told, refers either to a game warden or a mythical beast resembling a white tiger. Overall, however, the poem is taken to be a metaphor for a leader who presides over a flourishing society. (Yuan and Tang 1983; Pei 1998; Shaughnessy 2021; Taiwan Academic Network 2021)

8. The preceding four items are numbers three through six. Numbers one and two are the two steps of the quiver—installing royal descendants and dispersing his army—from which people learned that there would be no need to raise an army again.

9. *High Academy, tai xue* 太學: Outside of the *Dialogues*, the earliest record we have of a High Academy, using this specific terminology, is in the Western Han. We know very little about the educational systems during the Zhou dynasty. The terms *da* 大 and *tai* 太 were often used interchangeably, and the term *da xue* 大學 occurs prominently as the title of a famous Warring States–period text attributed to Zengzi.

36

Question about Jade

Chapter 36 continues the theme of art and its relation to education and self-cultivation. Jade is used as an analogy for the cultivated *junzi* and is thus prized. Confucius says that different classic texts offer educational opportunities along distinct dimensions. *Li* and music need not be overthought.

36.1

子貢問於孔子曰:“敢問君子貴玉而賤珉，何也?爲玉之寡而珉多歟?”孔子曰:“非爲玉之寡故貴之，珉之多故賤之。夫昔者君子比德於玉:温潤而澤，仁也;縝密以栗，智也;廉而不劌，義也;垂之如墜，禮也;叩之，其聲清越而長，其終則詘然，樂矣;瑕不掩瑜，瑜不掩瑕，忠也;孚尹旁達，信也;氣如白虹，天也;精神見于山川，地也;珪璋特達，德也;天下莫不貴者，道也。《詩》云:‘言念君子，温其如玉。’故君子貴之也。”

Zigong asked Confucius, "Why does a *junzi* prize jade but not other semiprecious stones? Is it because jade is rare and other stones are not?"

Confucius said, "Jade is not prized for its rarity, nor are other semiprecious stones spurned for being abundant. In the past, *junzi* analogized virtue to jade. To be agreeable, polished, and illustrious was to be *ren*. To be solid through being substantial was to be wise. To be sharp without cutting was to be *yi*. To be well-draped was to be *li*. If you tap a jade chime, the sound is clear and resonant but ends abruptly—a *junzi*'s joyful harmoniousness was like this. To have flaws unconcealed by luster and luster unconcealed by flaws was to be conscientious. To shine in all directions was to be trustworthy. To be as bright as the sky was to be stellar. To have the spirit of the landscape was to be earthy. To be stately and glorious was to be *de*. To be prized by all was to be *dao*. A poem says:

Missing my gentleman,

Agreeable as jade.[1]

This is why a *junzi* prizes it."

36.2

孔子曰:“入其國,其教可知也。其爲人也,温柔敦厚,《詩》教也;疏通知遠,《書》教也;廣博易良,《樂》教也;潔静精微,《易》教也;恭儉莊敬,《禮》教也;屬辭比事,《春秋》教也。故《詩》之失,愚;《書》之失,誣;《樂》之失,奢;《易》之失,賊;《禮》之失,煩;《春秋》之失,亂。其爲人也,温柔敦厚而不愚,則深於《詩》者矣;疏通知遠而不誣,則深於《書》者矣;廣博易良而不奢,則深於《樂》者矣;潔静精微而不賊,則深於《易》者矣;恭儉莊敬而不煩,則深於《禮》者矣;屬辭比事而不亂,則深於《春秋》者矣。天有四時者,春夏秋冬,風雨霜露,無非教也。地載神氣,吐納雷霆,流形庶物,無非教也。清明在躬,氣志如神,有物將至,其兆必先。是故,天地之教與聖人相參。其在《詩》曰:‘嵩高惟岳,峻極于天。惟岳降神,生甫及申。惟申及甫,惟周之翰。四國于蕃,四方于宣。’此文、武之德。‘矢其文德,協此四國。’此文王之德也。凡三代之王,必先其令問。《詩》云:‘明明天子,令問不已。’三代之德也。”

Confucius said, "You can tell a country's level of education as soon as you enter. If the behavior of the people is warm and sincere, they've been educated in the Poems.[2] If they are knowledgeable and forward thinking, they've been educated in the Documents. If they are broad-minded and kind, they've been educated in the Music. If they are pure and their thinking subtle and precise, they've been educated in the Changes. If they are reverent and respectful, they've been educated in the Li. If they are eloquent and historically aware, they've been educated in the Spring and Autumn.

"However, if the Poems are studied superficially, people tend to be naive. If the Documents are studied superficially, people tend to scheme. If the Music is studied superficially, people tend to be extravagant. If the Changes is studied superficially, people tend to be dishonest. If the Li is studied superficially, people tend to be convoluted. If the Spring and Autumn is studied superficially, people tend to be rebellious.

1. From "The Light Chariot" (#128), which can be found today in the "Qin feng" section of the *Poems*. The poem is a wife's lament on missing her husband who has gone off to war.

2. This passage describes the crucial role of the Six Classics in Confucius' view of education. Since Confucius is said to have sifted, organized, edited, and provided commentary for the individual volumes of the Six Classics toward the end of his life (39.3), he is probably not referring to the finished works here but to the original material that circulated in various fragments and editions. See "Six Classics" in the glossary.

"In their behavior, if people are warm and sincere but not naive, they have a profound understanding of the Poems. If they are knowledgeable and forward-thinking without scheming, they have a profound understanding of the Documents. If they are broad-minded and kind without being extravagant, they have a profound understanding of the Music. If they are pure and their thinking subtle and precise without being malicious, they have a profound understanding of the Changes. If they are reverent and respectful without being convoluted, they have a profound understanding of the Li. If they are eloquent and historically aware without being rebellious, they have a profound understanding of the Spring and Autumn.

"There are four seasons—spring, summer, fall, and winter—with wind, rain, frost, and dew; all are instructive. Weather patterns flow across the land—winds rise and thunder claps, affecting every creature on earth; all are instructive.

"Pure and modest in his person, with a godlike determination—when an event associated with a sage is imminent, it will always be preceded by an omen. Thus, the instructions of nature are intertwined with the sage. We see this in the Poems:

Lofty mountain peaks
Reaching to the sky;
Spirits peaks send down,
The likes of Fu and Shēn.
Shēn and Fu
Helped Zhou to soar;
The states now grow and thrive,
Their fame spreads far and wide.[3]

This passage speaks to the *de* of Kings Wen and Wu.

"The Poems say:

Spread his culture and *de*
To states across the land.[4]

This passage speaks to the *de* of King Wen.

"For all the kings of the Three Dynasties, their fame preceded them. The Poems say:

3. These lines appear in the poem "Lofty"(#259), which can be found today in the "Da ya" section of the *Poems*. The poem was a gift to the Earl of Shēn on the occasion of King Xuan 周宣王 (d. 782 BCE) enfeoffing Shēn in gratitude for his assistance.

4. From the poem "Yangtze and Han Rivers" (#262), which can be found today in the "Da ya" section of the *Poems*. The poem was written to commemorate the victory of Duke Mu of Shao 召/邵穆公 (fl. 841 BCE) in suppressing an uprising in the south during the reign of King Xuan. Duke Mu of Shao was a descendent of the Earl of Shao. (Zheng, Wu, and Yang 2000)

Assiduous king,
Reputation everlasting.[5]

This speaks to the *de* of the Three Dynasties."

36. 3

子張問聖人之所以教。孔子曰:"師乎, 吾語汝。聖人明於禮樂, 舉而措之而已。"子張又問。孔子曰:"師, 爾以爲必布几筵, 揖讓升降, 酌獻酬酢, 然後謂之禮乎? 爾以必行綴兆, 執羽籥, 作鐘鼓, 然後謂之樂乎? 言而可履, 禮也; 行而可樂, 樂也。聖人力此二者, 以躬己南面。是故天下太平, 萬民順伏, 百官承事, 上下有禮也。夫禮之所以興, 衆之所以治也; 禮之所以廢, 衆之所以亂也。目巧之室則有隩阼, 席則有上下, 車則有左右, 行則並隨, 立則有列序, 古之義也。室而無隩阼, 則亂於堂室矣; 席而無上下, 則亂於席次矣; 車而無左右, 則亂於車上矣; 行而無並隨, 則亂於階塗矣; 列而無次序, 則亂於著矣。昔者明王聖人, 辯貴賤長幼, 正男女内外, 序親疏遠近, 而莫敢相逾越者, 皆由此塗出也。"

Zizhang asked about how sages teach.

Confucius said, "Shi, let me tell you about it. A sage merely clarifies *li* and music, brings them to public attention, then implements them."

Zizhang asked again.

Confucius said, "Shi, you think that promulgating *li* requires spreading sitting mats around, or bowing and ascending a platform, or pouring liquor and toasting? You think that music requires musicians in rows, holding instruments or batons, playing bells and drums?

"*Li* is merely words that can be put into action. Music is merely behavior that can be enjoyed. A sage accomplishes these two things by positioning himself facing south. As a result, the world is at peace, the people are cooperative, the officials perform their duties, and there is *li* between higher and lower stations. The way for *li* to flourish is the way to govern the people. The way that *li* collapses is the way that people fall into disarray.

"In a well-designed house, there are inner quarters for family life and an eastern staircase for welcoming guests. A mat allows for positioning superior and subordinate. A carriage allows for positioning left and right. In walking with others, there is room for walking side by side or single file. In standing with others, there is an order to it. These are all the *yi* of the ancients.

"Without inner quarters for family life or an eastern staircase for welcoming guests, relations in a house would be in disarray. Without allowing for positioning superior and subordinate, relations on mats would be in disarray. Without

5. These lines precede the two lines above in the poem "The Yangtze and Han Rivers."

allowing for left and right positioning, relations among carriages would be in disarray. Without allowing for walking side by side or in single file, relations on stairs and walkways would be in disarray. Without allowing for standing in order, relations among those standing together would be in disarray. Because enlightened kings and sages of the past distinguished honor and age, reformed gender and location with men outside the home and women inside, and ordered family relations from close relative to distant, no one stepped outside the bounds of acceptable behavior. All enlightened kings and sages navigated this path."

37

Understanding What It Means to Stoop to Indignities

Chapter 37 is organized around the topic of suffering indignities, sometimes on purpose. There are times, Confucius says, when you must put your dignity aside. We see in the examples of this chapter that this may be necessary to save a country from attack, to prove an important point to a superior, and to help a friend.

37.1

子路問於孔子曰:“由聞丈夫居世,富貴不能有益於物,處貧賤之地而不能屈節以求伸,則不足以論乎人之域矣。”孔子曰:“君子之行己,期於必達於己,可以屈則屈,可以伸則伸。故屈節者所以有待,求伸者所以及時。是以雖受屈而不毀其節,志達而不犯於義。”

Zilu asked Confucius, “I have heard that there are certain ways a proper man behaves in this world. If in fame and fortune he cannot lend assistance, and in poverty and disrepute he cannot stoop to indignities to get ahead, then he is not worth counting among the realm of the human.”

Confucius said, “In comporting himself, a *junzi* achieves his ideals within himself. When it is allowable to stoop to indignities, then stoop. When it is allowable to get ahead, then get ahead. Thus, a person stooping to indignities does it with expectations in mind, and a person attempting to get ahead capitalizes on opportunities. A person can suffer indignities without destroying his integrity, and he can achieve his ambitions without offending against *yi*.”

37.2

孔子在衛,聞齊國田常將欲爲亂,而憚鮑、晏,因欲移其兵以伐魯。孔子會諸弟子而告之曰:“魯,父母之國,不可不救,不忍視其受敵。今吾欲屈節於田常以救魯,二三子誰爲使?”於是子路曰:“請往齊。”孔子弗許。子張請往,又弗許。子石請往,又弗許。

三子退，謂子貢曰："今夫子欲屈節以救父母之國，吾三人請使而不獲往。此則吾子用辯之時也，吾子盍請行焉？"子貢請使，夫子許之。遂如齊，説田常曰："今子欲收功於魯，實難，不若移兵於吴，則易。"田常不悦。子貢曰："夫憂在內者攻强，憂在外者攻弱。吾聞子三封而三不成，是則大臣不聽令。戰勝以驕主，破國以尊臣，而子之功不與焉，則交日疏於主，而與大臣爭。如此，則子之位危矣。"田常曰："善！然兵甲已加魯矣，不可更，如何？"子貢曰："緩師，吾請於吴，令救魯而伐齊，子因以兵迎之。"田常許諾。子貢遂南，説吴王曰："王者不滅國，霸者無强敵。千鈞之重，加銖兩而移。今以齊國而私千乘之魯，與吴爭强，甚爲王患之。且夫救魯以顯名，以撫泗上諸侯，誅暴齊以服晋，利莫大焉。名存亡魯，實困强齊，智者不疑。"吴王曰："善！然吴常困越，越王今苦身養士，有報吴之心。子待我先越，然後乃可。"子貢曰："越之勁不過魯，吴之彊不過齊，而王置齊而伐越，則齊必私魯矣。王方以存亡繼絶之名，棄齊而伐小越，非勇也。勇者不避難，仁者不窮約，智者不失時，義者不絶世。今存越，示天下以仁，救魯伐齊，威加晋國，諸侯必相率而朝，霸業盛矣。且王必惡越，臣請見越君，令出兵以從，此則實害越而名從諸侯以伐齊。"吴王悦，乃遣子貢之越。越王郊迎，而自爲子貢御，曰："此蠻夷之國，大夫何足儼然辱而臨之？"子貢曰："今者，吾説吴王以救魯伐齊，其志欲之，而心畏越，曰：'待我伐越而後可。'則破越必矣。且無報人之志而令人疑之，拙矣；有報人之意而使人知之，殆乎；事未發而先聞者，危矣。三者，舉事之患矣。"勾踐頓首曰："孤嘗不料力而興吴難，受困會稽，痛於骨髓，日夜焦唇乾舌，徒欲與吴王接踵而死，孤之願也。今大夫幸告以利害。"子貢曰："吴王爲人猛暴，群臣不堪，國家疲弊，百姓怨上，大臣內變，申胥以諫死，大宰嚭用事，此則報吴之時也。王誠能發卒佐之，以邀射其志，而重寶以悦其心，卑辭以尊其禮，則其伐齊必矣。此聖人所謂屈節求其達者也。彼戰不勝，王之福；若勝，則必以兵臨晋。臣還北請見晋君共攻之，其弱吴必矣。鋭兵盡於齊，重甲困於晋，而王制其弊焉。"越王頓首許諾。子貢返五日，越使大夫文種頓首言於吴王曰："越悉境內之士三千人以事吴。"吴王告子貢曰："越王欲身從寡人，可乎？"子貢曰："悉人之率衆，又從其君，非義也。"吴王乃受越王卒，謝留勾踐。遂自發國內之兵以伐齊，敗之。子貢遂北見晋君，令承其弊。吴、晋遂遇於黄池。越王襲吴之國，吴王歸與越戰，滅焉。孔子曰："夫其亂齊存魯，吾之始願。若能强晋以弊吴，使吴亡而越霸者，賜之説之也。美言傷信，慎言哉！"

When Confucius was in Wei, he heard that Qi's Tian Chang, desiring to instigate a rebellion but afraid of Qi's high ministers Bao and Yan, moved his troops into position to attack Lu.

Confucius called his students together and said to them, "As Lu is our mother country, we cannot bear to see it attacked by an enemy and must go to its rescue. I wish to stoop to indignities under Tian Chang in order to save Lu. Which one of you will act as my emissary?"

Zilu said, "Allow me to go to Qi."

Confucius denied his request.

Zizhang volunteered and was also denied.

Zishi volunteered and was also denied.

Stepping back, the three of them said to Zigong, "Our teacher wants to stoop to indignities on behalf of his mother country, and none of the three of us is allowed to go in his place. This is a time for someone with rhetorical skills to step forward. Why don't you go?"

Zigong volunteered and was allowed.

Subsequently, he arrived in Qi and attempted to persuade Tian Chang, saying, "You are trying to earn merit by winning a military victory over Lu, but it will be more difficult than you think. It would actually be easier to move your troops to the border with Wu."

Tian Chang expressed displeasure.

Zigong said, "Someone experiencing domestic threats attacks a strong neighbor. Someone experiencing foreign threats attacks a weak neighbor. I've heard that three times you were in line to be enfeoffed and each time failed because the other ministers disobeyed the order. If a war is won, it will be the ruler who feels proud, and if another state is destroyed, it will be other ministers who win respect—with no credit going to you. So you would grow only more distant from the ruler and have to contend with the other ministers. From this perspective, your position is precarious."

Tian Chang said, "Good. But my soldiers have already been sent to Lu, and that can't be changed. What can be done?"

Zigong said, "Please slow them down. I will go to Wu and plead with the king to invade Qi on the pretext of saving Lu. You can lie in wait for them."

Tian Chang gave his word, whereupon Zigong went south to attempt to persuade the king of Wu.

Zigong said to the king of Wu, "A true king does not allow a country to be destroyed, and a superpower does not allow for a strong rival. Adding a couple of ounces to a hundredweight can tip the scales. With Qi attempting to compete with Wu by taking a neighboring state for itself, becoming a stronger rival of Wu, I fear deeply that your highness may be in danger. There would be no greater benefit for you than to bolster your fame by saving Lu, placating the noble lords along the Si River, punishing upstart Qi, and cowing Jin into submission. No intelligent person would doubt that, on the pretext of saving Lu, you can prevent Qi from strengthening itself."

The king of Wu said, "Good. However, we previously defeated Yue,[1] and right now, the king of Yue is toiling to raise manpower to get his revenge on us. Wait for me to first deal with Yue, then I will be with you."

Zigong said, "The power of Yue does not exceed that of Lu, and the strength of Wu does not exceed that of Qi, and so you wish to set Qi aside and attack Yue, in

1. According to the CQZZ ("Ai" 1.2), Wu defeated Yue in 494 BCE. Against the advice of his adviser, Wu King Fuchai did not kill Yue King Goujian at Kuaiji or annex Yue. King Fuchai would come to regret these decisions.

which case Qi will certainly take Lu for itself. Your highness wishes to earn fame saving endangered states and noble lineages, but it is not brave to unleash Qi or attack tiny Yue. A brave person does not avoid difficulty. A *ren* person does not allow others to fall into traps. A wise person does not miss an opportunity. A *yi* person does not terminate a lineage. Allowing Yue to survive demonstrated your *ren* to the world. If you save Lu by attacking Qi, and in doing so overawe Jin, the noble lords will submit to you and visit your court to pay their respects. That will mark your triumph as the leader of a superpower. No doubt your highness detests Yue. Allow me to go meet with the sovereign of Yue and get him to send soldiers to follow you into battle. On the pretext of rallying the noble lords to punish Qi, it will actually do damage to Yue."

The king of Wu was delighted and sent Zigong to Yue.

The king of Yue welcomed Zigong on the outskirts of the capital and personally acted as his driver on the way in. He said to Zigong, "Why would a gentleman like yourself deign to visit a backward country such as this?"

Zigong replied, "I am in the process of persuading the king of Wu to save Lu by attacking Qi. Although he wishes to do it, he also fears Yue. He said, 'Wait for me to first deal with Yue, then I will be with you.' So he definitely plans to destroy Yue.

"If you have no ambition to get back at Wu but lead him to believe that you do, it would be clumsiness on your part. If you do plan to get back at Wu but let him know ahead of time, you would be in peril. It would also be dangerous to divulge your plan before setting it in motion. These are three dangers of your uprising against Wu."

Goujian bowed to Zigong and said, "I once overestimated my strength and got into difficulty by raising arms against Wu and was defeated on Kuaiji Mountain. It was painful right through to my marrow. Since then, I have dwelt on it day and night. All I've wanted to do is destroy him in a suicidal attack. This has been my obsession. Fortunately, you have come to remind me of the true danger."

Zigong said, "The king of Wu is a violent man. His ministers cannot tolerate him. His country is worn down. The people resent the government. There is dissent among the high ministers. Shen Xu died for admonishing the king. His prime minister Pi[2] is put in charge of things. This is the time to get back at the king of Wu. If your highness can really send troops to assist him, thereby feeding his ambition, and send a hefty treasure to appease him, deprecating yourself and showing respect to him, it is a sure thing that he will attack Qi. This is what sages call stooping to indignities for the sake of success. If he loses the war, it will be to your advantage. If he wins, he will send troops to the vicinity of Jin. I will return to the north to meet with the Jin sovereign and help him prepare for the attack. This will definitely weaken Wu. He will exhaust his vanguard against Qi, and then his soldiers in heavy armor will get trapped in Jin. Your Highness can then subdue his spent forces."

2. According to Wang Su, Pi was a flattering toady.

The king of Yue agreed with a bow.

Five days after Zigong returned to Wu, Yue sent the high official Wenzhong to the king of Wu to submissively say, "Yue will send the 3,000 soldiers within its borders to serve Wu."

The king of Wu said to Zigong, "The king of Yue wants to personally follow me into battle. Should I allow it?"

Zigong said, "It would not be *yi* to take all of the soldiers and have the sovereign follow you as well."

The king of Wu accepted the soldiers, thanked Goujian, and allowed him to stay. Subsequently, he launched an attack of his own against Qi and defeated them.[3]

Zigong went north to meet with the Jin sovereign, advising him to take advantage of Wu's weakness.

Jin and Wu met at Huangchi, and Yue launched a surprise attack against the Wu territory.[4] The king of Wu returned, went to war with Yue, and was destroyed.

Confucius said, "It was my original intention to merely sow disorder in Qi as a way of saving Lu. Due to Ci's persuasive rhetoric, however, Jin has been strengthened by the weakened Wu, Wu has been destroyed, and Yue has become a superpower. Eloquent words can undermine trustworthiness. Be careful what you say!"

37.3

孔子弟子有宓子賤者, 仕於魯, 爲單父宰。恐魯君聽讒言, 使己不得行其政, 於是辭行, 故請君之近史二人, 與之俱至官。宓子戒其邑吏, 令二史書。方書輒掣其肘, 書不善則從而怒之, 二史患之, 辭請歸魯。宓子曰: "子之書甚不善, 子勉而歸矣。" 二史歸報於君曰: "宓子使臣書而掣肘, 書惡而又怒臣, 邑吏皆笑之。此臣所以去之而來也。" 魯君以問孔子, 子曰: "宓不齊, 君子也。其才任霸王之佐, 屈節治單父, 將以自試也。意者以此爲諫乎?" 公寤, 太息而嘆曰: "此寡人之不肖。寡人亂宓子之政而責其善者, 非矣。微二史, 寡人無以知其過; 微夫子, 寡人無以自寤。" 遽發所愛之使, 告宓子曰: "自今已往, 單父非吾有也, 從子之制, 有便於民者, 子決爲之。五年一言其要。" 宓子敬奉詔, 遂得行其政, 於是單父治焉。躬敦厚, 明親親, 尚篤敬, 施至仁, 加懇誠, 致忠信, 百姓化之。齊人攻魯, 道由單父。單父之老請曰: "麥已熟矣, 今齊寇至, 不及人人自收其麥。請放民出, 皆穫傅郭之麥, 可以益糧, 且不資於寇。" 三請而宓子不聽。俄而, 齊寇逮于麥。季孫聞之, 怒, 使人以讓宓子曰: "民寒耕熱耘, 曾不得食, 豈不哀哉? 不知猶可, 以告者而子不聽, 非所以爲民也。" 宓子蹴然曰: "今茲無麥, 明年可樹。若使不耕者穫, 是使民樂有寇。且得單父一歲之麥, 於魯不加强, 喪之不加弱。若使民有自取之心, 其創必數世不息。" 季孫聞之, 赧然而愧曰: "地若可入, 吾豈忍見宓子

3. According to CQZZ ("Ai" 11.3), in 484 BCE, Wu attacked Qi in defense of Lu and defeated them (see also 41.2), but there is no mention of Zigong's involvement. CQZZ ("Ai" 12) does, however, record Zigong in successful interstate negotiations involving Wu in 483 BCE.

4. According to CQZZ ("Ai" 13), these two events occurred in 482 BCE.

哉!"三年, 孔子使巫馬期往觀政焉。巫馬期陰免衣, 衣弊裘, 入單父界。見夜漁者, 得魚輒舍之。巫馬期問焉, 曰: "凡漁者爲得, 何以得魚即舍之?"漁者曰: "魚之大者名爲鱄, 吾大夫愛之; 其小者名爲鱦, 吾大夫欲長之。是以得二者, 輒舍之。"巫馬期返, 以告孔子曰: "宓子之德至, 使民闇行若有嚴刑於旁。敢問宓子何行而得於是?"孔子曰: "吾嘗與之言曰: '誠於此者刑乎彼。'宓子行此術於單父也。"

One of Confucius' students was Fu Zijian. He held an official position in Lu as mayor of Shanfu. Afraid that the Lu sovereign was listening to slander, thereby affecting Fuzi's[5] ability to govern, Fuzi decided to make a trip to the capital to consult with the duke. When returning to Shanfu, Fuzi invited along two scribes close to the duke to come and work with him.

Once, when Fuzi was admonishing his own city's officials, he had his scribes there recording. As one of them was writing, Fu Zijian intentionally grabbed him by the elbow to stop him from writing, then expressed anger on account of him writing poorly as he was bumped. Afraid for themselves, the two scribes expressed the wish to excuse themselves and return to the capital. Fuzi said, "Your writing is awful. You should return to the capital and try harder."

The two scribes reported back to the sovereign, saying, "Fuzi asked us to act as scribe but grabbed my elbow to prevent me from writing. He angrily accused me of writing poorly. His officials then laughed at us. This is why we left there and returned."

The sovereign of Lu asked Confucius about this.

Confucius said, "Fu Buqi is a *junzi*, who is capable of acting as adviser to the leader of a superpower. He suffers indignities in acting as mere mayor of Shanfu. He wanted to give it a try as a way of testing himself. I think he is using this episode to make a point."

The duke suddenly understood, heaved a great sigh, and said, "This is my fault. It was wrong of me to interfere in his governing and to find fault with the good that he has done. If it hadn't been for the two scribes, I wouldn't have realized this error, and if not for you, I wouldn't have been able to come to my senses."

Thereupon, he sent his beloved scribes with a message for Fuzi: "Henceforward, I will no longer interfere in Shanfu. I will follow your system there. Whatever is for the convenience of the people, your decisions are final. You need only report key events to me every five years."

Fuzi followed the duke's order and gained complete control of his government. Shanfu was subsequently well governed. He personally acted honestly and sincerely, he clarified the importance of being close to one's parents, he elevated kindness and respect, he spread *ren* far and wide, he spurred sincere integrity, and he acted with

5. Fuzi 宓子: In the customary way, the suffix *zi* 子 is added to a surname as an honorific. See "Naming convention" in the glossary.

utmost conscientiousness and trustworthiness. The people were transformed by him.

Qi invaded Lu, and their route passed through Shanfu.[6] The elders of Shanfu approached Fuzi, saying, "The wheat is already ripe, but the Qi marauders are arriving, and there is no time for everyone to go out and harvest as they normally would. We suggest that you let the people out so they can all harvest the wheat near the wall. This will increase our supply of grain and deprive the marauders of resources."

Three such requests were made to Fuzi, but Fuzi did not accept them.

Not long after, the Qi marauders seized the wheat.

Jisun caught wind of this and was angered by it. He sent someone to reprimand Fuzi, saying, "The people work the land through cold weather and hot and now they won't get to eat. Have you no pity? I don't know how you find it acceptable. You were advised but did not listen. This is not acting on behalf of the people."

Fuzi respectfully replied, "If we go without wheat this year, we can plant more next year. But if we let people harvest what they did not sow, they will be happy to have marauders come through in the future. One year's supply of grain from Shanfu will not make Lu stronger, and losing it will not make Lu weaker. If I make the people feel that they can take things at will, the harm will last for generations."

When Jisun heard this, he felt embarrassed and sheepishly said, "If only I could sink into the earth. How will I bear to face Fuzi again?"

Three years later, Confucius sent Wuma Qi to observe the government in Shanfu.[7] Wuma Qi crossed into Shanfu incognito, disguised in burlap. He came across a man fishing at night and saw him immediately release the fish he had netted.

Wuma Qi asked him, "People fish for the purpose of getting fish. Why are you letting them go?"

The fisherman said, "The big ones were *chou*, which our high officials love. The small ones were *ying*,[8] which our high officials want to allow to grow bigger. That's why after catching them I immediately threw them back."

6. Shanfu lies on the opposite side (southwest) of the Lu capital from the Qi capital (to the northeast) and so may seem an unlikely place for Qi to attack Lu. And yet, by the Warring States period, Qi had taken a wide swath of land west of Lu, including Shanfu. (Tan 1996; Zheng, Wu, and Yang 2000)

7. There are three stories in 37.3, all having to do with Fu Zijian's governing of Shanfu. In the first, Fu struggles because the duke is interfering. In the second, he has gained control of Shanfu but has not yet transformed the people. In the third, his transformation of the people is in full effect.

8. The characters used for the names of both of these fish are virtually unknown elsewhere. Perhaps this is a literary device to indicate that these fish would be unknown to the visitor and therefor in need of description, or that the fisherman's actions are beyond gainsaying by the reader, or perhaps they are simply records of the local dialect.

Wuma Qi returned and reported to Confucius, saying, "Fuzi's *de* has had its effect. The people act in private as if the executioner were by their side. May I ask how Fuzi has accomplished this?"

Confucius said, "I once said to him, 'If sincerity is nearby, punishment will be far away.' Fuzi put this method into effect in Shanfu."

37·4

孔子之舊曰原壤, 其母死, 夫子將助之以沐椁。子路曰: "由也昔者聞諸夫子曰: '無友不如己者, 過則勿憚改。'夫子憚矣, 姑已若何?"孔子曰: "'凡民有喪, 匍匐救之'。況故舊乎? 非友也。吾其往。"及爲椁, 原壤登木曰: "久矣, 予之不託於音也。" 遂歌曰: "狸首之班然, 執女手之卷然。"夫子爲之隱, 佯不聞以過之。子路曰: "夫子屈節而極於此, 失其與矣, 豈未可以已乎?"孔子曰: "吾聞之, 親者不失其爲親也, 故者不失其爲故也。"

Confucius had an old friend named Yuan Rang, whose mother passed away. Confucius was about to help prepare the coffin.

Zilu said, "I once heard you say, 'Have no friend not better than yourself; and when you make a mistake, do not shy away from correcting it.' You seem to be shying away. How about pausing for a moment?"[9]

Confucius said:

"When someone suffers a death in the family
Rush to help them out.[10]

Even more so for an old friend, wouldn't you say? Even if he weren't a friend, I would still go."

When it was time to take care of the coffin, Yuan Rang climbed on top of it and said, "It has been a long time since I put my feelings to music." Then he broke into song, singing:

As dazzling as the spots on a raccoon dog's head
Like holding a girl's tender hand.

9. Zilu's attitude toward Yuan Rang can be explained by the one passage from the *Analects* that features Yuan Rang, for whom there is no other account: "Yuan Rang was squatting and waiting. Confucius said, 'Only a rascal is immodest and rude when young, fails to mentor as an adult, and refuses to die when old.' Confucius then rapped him on the shin with his cane" (14.43).

10. See 27.2n12 on the passage "If any are about to drown / Others pull them out." The lines of poetry here are identical in the Chinese (except for the use of *pufu* 匍匐 for *fufu* 扶伏) but interpreted and translated according to the context of the *Dialogues* passage.

Confucius tried to conceal his own embarrassment, pretending not to hear and letting it pass.

Zilu said, "You have suffered indignities enough, and this exceeds everything. You've lost every reason to interact with him. Is it not time to break it off?"

Confucius said, "I have heard that:

Family never forget that they are family
Friends never forget that they are friends."[11]

11. This passage may throw an entirely different light on *Analects* 14.43. Absent this passage, the event recounted in the *Analects* makes one think that Yuan Rang is a boorish lout and Confucius an officious prig. With this context, however, the *Analects* event looks more like two old friends (one a well-meaning ne'er-do-well and the other an ambitious striver) playfully giving each other a hard time, in which case Zilu comes off as the priggish one. Alternatively, perhaps the truth lies somewhere in between, with Confucius eager to help a friend who doesn't want to be helped and feeling exasperated when reminded of his friend's failure and thus his own failure in attempting to help him.

38

Understanding the Seventy-Two Students

Chapter 38 is an important record of Confucius' students. Although the total number of students stated in the title and at the end is seventy-two, seventy-six individuals are listed. The first ten match the names of those in *Analects* 11.3, in a slightly different order. There is a large overlap with the seventy-seven students listed in SJ.

38.1

顏回，魯人，字子淵，少孔子三十歲。年二十九而髮白，三十一早死。孔子曰："自吾有回，門人日益親。"回之德行著名，孔子稱其仁焉。

Yan Hui was a native of Lu. His *zi*[1] was Ziyuan. He was thirty years Confucius' junior. His hair went gray at the age of twenty-nine. He died at only thirty-one.[2] Confucius said, "From the time I accepted Hui, my students became closer to me on a daily basis." Hui was known for his virtuous behavior. Confucius used the term *ren* to describe him.

1. To understand the naming customs used in this chapter, see "Naming convention" in the glossary.

2. Wang Su notes that this age raises a chronological conflict. In *Analects* 11.8, it says that Confucius' son Kong Li (see "Boyu" in the glossary) had already passed away when Yan Hui passed away, but *Dialogues* 39.2 puts Kong Li's death after Yan Hui's. According to this passage (38.1), Yan Hui passed away in 490 BCE (Confucius was born in 551 BCE, Yan Hui was born thirty years later (521 BCE) and died thirty-one years after that). According to *Dialogues* 39.2, Kong Li passed away seven years later, in 483 BCE (he was born when Confucius was twenty years old (532 BCE by the traditional way of counting) and died at the age of fifty (551 – 68 = 483). Yang and Song (2013) speculate that the *thirty-one* recorded here as Yan Hui's age at death is a scribal error for *forty-one*.

38.2

閔損，魯人，字子騫，少孔子五十歲。以德行著名，孔子稱其孝焉。

Min Sun was a native of Lu. His *zi* was Ziqian. He was fifty years Confucius' junior. He was known for his virtuous behavior. Confucius used the term *xiao* to describe him.

38.3

冉耕，魯人，字伯牛。以德行著名。有惡疾，孔子曰："命也夫！"

Ran Geng was a native of Lu. His *zi* was Boniu. He was famous for his virtuous behavior. He suffered from a serious illness. Confucius said, "It must be fate."[3]

38.4

冉雍，字仲弓，伯牛之宗族。生於不肖之父。以德行著名。

Ran Yong's *zi* was Zhonggong. He was of the same lineage as Ran Boniu. He was born to a derelict father but was himself famous for virtuous behavior.

38.5

宰予，字子我，魯人。有口才著名。

Zai Yu's *zi* was Ziwo, and he was a native of Lu. He was known for his eloquence.

38.6

端木賜，字子貢，衛人，少孔子三十一歲。有口才著名。

Duanmu Ci's *zi* was Zigong, and he was a native of Wei. He was thirty-one years Confucius' junior. He was known for his eloquence.

38.7

冉求，字子有，仲弓之族，少孔子二十九歲。有才藝，以政事著名。

3. *It must be fate*: In other words, it is not his own fault; he is blameless.

Ran Qiu's *zi* was Ziyou, and he was of the same clan as Zhonggong. He was twenty-nine years Confucius' junior. He was talented and known for his governing.

38.8

仲由, 卞人, 字子路, 一字季路, 少孔子九歲。有勇力才藝, 以政事著名。

Zhong You was a native of the Lu city of Bian. His *zi* was Zilu, or Jilu.[4] He was nine years Confucius' junior. Brave, strong, and talented, he was known for his governing.

38.9

言偃, 魯人, 字子游, 少孔子三十五歲。時習於禮, 以文學著名。

Yan Yan was a native of Lu. His *zi* was Ziyou. He was thirty-five years Confucius' junior. He regularly rehearsed *li* and was known for his cultural learning.

38.10

卜商, 衛人, 字子夏, 少孔子四十四歲。習於《詩》, 能通其義, 以文學著名。爲人性不弘, 好論精微, 時人無以尚之。嘗返衛, 見讀史志者云: "晋師伐秦, 三豕渡河。"子夏曰: "非也! '己亥'耳。"讀史志者問諸晋史, 果曰"己亥"。於是衛以子夏爲聖。孔子卒後, 教於西河之上。魏文侯師事之, 而諮國政焉。

Bu Shang was a native of Wei. His *zi* was Zixia. He was forty-four years Confucius' junior. He was well-versed in the *Poems*, fully understanding their meanings. He was known for his cultural learning. In his character, he was not broad-minded, preferring to focus on subtle topics. No one at the time could surpass him in that respect. Once on returning to Wei, he met someone reading a history book, who read the line, "The Jin army attacked Qin. Three pigs crossed the Yellow River." Zixia said, "That's incorrect. It should be 'In the *jihai* year,[5] they crossed the Yellow River.'" The other person asked a Jin historian, who indeed confirmed that it should

4. As explained under "Naming convention" in the glossary, the term *zi* 子 was often added to a name. It is essentially an aesthetic addition to the main part of the name, which in this case is *lu* 路. Zilu was also known as Jilu. The addition of the character *ji* 季 signified that he was one of the younger sons of his family.

5. Jihai 己亥 was the thirty-sixth year of the sexagenary cycle. The person reading the book did not recognize it as a calendar reference and instead interpreted each character on its face. *Hai* 亥, as one of the twelve branches making up the sexagenary cycle, is associated with the pig. The

be read *jihai*. Subsequently, Zixia was recognized as a sage in Wei. After Confucius passed away, Zixia taught on the bank of the West River.[6] Marquis Wen of Wei treated him with the respect due a teacher and consulted with him on government affairs.[7]

38.11

顓孫師，陳人，字子張，少孔子四十八歲。爲人有容貌資質，寬冲博接，從容自務，居不務立於仁義之行，孔子門人友之而弗敬。

Zhuansun Shi was a native of Chen. His *zi* was Zizhang. He was forty-eight years Confucius' junior. Physically, he was naturally good-looking. His generosity of spirit earned him many friends. He was leisurely and marched to his own drummer. He did not go out of his way to behave in a manner of *ren* and *yi*, and although he was befriended by other followers of Confucius, he was not particularly respected by them.

38.12

曾參，南武城人，字子輿，少孔子四十六歲。志存孝道，故孔子因之以作《孝經》。齊嘗聘，欲與爲卿而不就，曰："吾父母老，食人之祿，則憂人之事，故吾不忍遠親而爲人役。"參後母遇之無恩，而供養不衰。及其妻以藜烝不熟，因出之。人曰："非七出也。"參曰："藜烝，小物耳。吾欲使熟，而不用吾命，況大事乎？"遂出之，終身不取妻。其子元請焉，告其子曰："高宗以後妻殺孝己，尹吉甫以後妻放伯奇。吾上不及高宗，中不比吉甫，庸知其得免於非乎？"

Zeng Shen was a native of the city of Nanwu in Lu. His *zi* was Ziyu. He was forty-six years Confucius' junior. He was always mindful of the way of *xiao*, and it was on account of him that Confucius created the *Classic of Xiao*. Qi once sought to employ him as a high minister, but Zeng Shen declined, saying, "My parents are aged. To earn a salary from someone means to worry over their affairs. I can't bear to leave my parents to labor for someone else."

---

association between *ji* 己 and *three* (*san* 三) is likely orthographic. Each has three primary horizontal lines, and in certain early forms the two characters can resemble each other (see 27.2n13 for a similar case).

6. *On the banks of the West River, Xi He zhi shang* 西河之上: present-day location unknown.

7. There is an interesting discrepancy here with SJ ("Zhongni dizi lie zhuan"). While the *Dialogues* says merely that Marquis Wen treated Zixia with the respect due a teacher, SJ says that Marquis Wen took Zixia as his teacher. If the more modest narrative is the earlier narrative, as is often assumed by scholars, then this passage would point to the *Dialogues* being earlier than SJ.

Shen's stepmother responded to his assistance without gratitude, and yet he looked after her all the same, even to the point that he divorced his wife after she served his stepmother undercooked greens.[8]

Others said, "This is not one of the seven grounds for divorce."[9]

Shen responded, "Cooking greens is a small thing. I wanted her to cook the leaves thoroughly, and she disregarded me. How would she respond in a larger matter?"[10]

After divorcing her, he never remarried. His son Yuan beseeched him to remarry, but he said to his son, "It was because of their second wives that King Gaozong of Shang killed Xiaoji and Yin Jifu banished Boqi.[11] I could never reach the heights of Gaozong nor even the middling realm of Jifu, so how could I know that I could avoid such an error with a second wife?"

38.13

澹臺滅明，武城人，字子羽，少孔子四十九歲。有君子之姿，孔子嘗以容貌望其才。其才不充孔子之望，然其爲人公正無私，以取與去就以諾爲名，仕魯爲大夫也。

Tantai Mieming was a native of the Lu city of Wǔ. His *zi* was Ziyu. He was forty-nine years Confucius' junior. He had the bearing of a *junzi*. Confucius once remarked on his appearance, with hope for his talent. Although his talent did not entirely live up to Confucius' expectations, he was fair and impartial. He was known for keeping his promises whether in giving or seeking. He worked as a high official in the Lu government.

38.14

高柴，齊人，高氏之別族，字子羔，少孔子四十歲。長不過六尺，狀貌甚惡。爲人篤孝而有法正。少居魯，知名於孔子之門。仕爲武城宰。

8. *Undercooked greens, li zheng bu shu* 藜烝不熟: The greens are of the lambsquarters plant (a kind of amaranth), considered an inferior food that, unless picked young, needs to be thoroughly cooked to be palatable. The term also occurs in 8.12.

9. See 26.3.

10. When a woman married into a multi-generation household, as was the custom in those times, she was under an obligation to be compliant with her husband, who was under an obligation to be *xiao* to his parents. If his mother (or stepmother, in this case) did not fulfil her own obligation to be kind and caring, life for the young wife could be difficult.

11. This passage fills in two historical lacunae. Xiaoji and Boqi both appear in later Confucian sources as models of *xiao*, but their stories do not appear in the earliest historical records. BA records only that King Gaozong's son Xiaoji died in the wilds in the twenty-fifth year of the king's reign. Zengzi's offhand way of referring to them suggests that the stories were already widespread by this time.

Gao Chai was a native of Qi. He belonged to a minor branch of the Gao clan, and his *zi* was Zigao. He was forty years Confucius' junior. He was under five-and-a-half feet tall[12] and was unappealing in appearance. He was deeply *xiao* in his behavior and punctilious in his affairs. He resided in Lu as a child and became well known as a student of Confucius. He later served as mayor of the city of Wu.

38.15

宓不齊，魯人，字子賤，少孔子四十九歲。仕爲單父宰。有才智，仁愛百姓，不忍欺。孔子大之。

Fu Buqi was a native of Lu. His *zi* was Zijian. He was forty-nine years Confucius' junior. He served as mayor of Shanfu. He was talented, was caring toward the people, and found dishonesty unbearable. Confucius praised him.

38.16

樊須，魯人，字子遲，少孔子四十六歲。弱仕於季氏。

Fan Xu was a native of Lu. His *zi* was Zichi. He was forty-six years Confucius' junior. He served in the Jisun household from the age of twenty.

38.17

有若，魯人，字子有，少孔子三十六歲。爲人强識，好古道也。

You Ruo was a native of Lu. His *zi* was Ziyou. He was thirty-six years Confucius' junior. Among his personal traits, he was very knowledgeable and favored the ancient *dao*.

38.18

公西赤，魯人，字子華，少孔子四十二歲。束帶立朝，閑賓主之儀。

Gongxi Chi was a native of Lu. His *zi* was Zihua. He was forty-two years Confucius' junior. He was always dressed for court and was well-versed in the guest-host protocols.

12. His height may be commented on because his surname *Gao* means tall, highlighting the irony of a short person named Tall.

38.19

原憲，宋人，字子思，少孔子三十六歲。清凈守節，貧而樂道。孔子爲魯司寇，原憲嘗爲孔子宰。孔子卒後，原憲退隱，居于衛。

Yuan Xian was a native of Song. His *zi* was Zisi. He was thirty-six years Confucius' junior. He had a pure heart and was steadfastly moderate. He was poor and yet delighted in the *dao*. When Confucius was minister of justice for Lu, Yuan Xian worked as Confucius' household manager. After Confucius died, Yuan Xian went into seclusion in Wei.

38.20

公冶長，魯人，字子長。爲人能忍耻。孔子以女妻之。

Gongye Chang was a native of Lu. His *zi* was Zichang. Among his personal traits, he was capable of enduring humiliation. Confucius gave his daughter in marriage to Zichang.

38.21

南宫韜，魯人，字子容。以智自將，世清不廢，世濁不污。孔子以兄子妻之。

Nangong Tao was a native of Lu. His *zi* was Zirong. He was astute at looking out for himself. In just times, he stepped forward and didn't waste his talents. In corrupt circumstances, he was not tarnished by the corruption. Confucius gave his niece in marriage to Nangong Tao.

38.22

公析哀，齊人，字季沉。鄙天下多仕於大夫家者，是故未嘗屈節人臣。孔子特嘆貴之。

Gongxi Ai was a native of Qi. His *zi* was Jichen. He felt it was beneath the many men who took jobs as household managers for high officials. Thus, he always refused to suffer the indignities that come with working for someone else. Confucius valued him highly.

38.23

曾點，曾參父，字子皙。疾時禮教不行，欲修之。孔子善焉。《論語》所謂"浴乎沂，風乎舞雩之下"。

Zeng Dian was the father of Zeng Shen. His *zi* was Zixi. He felt bad that *li* teachings were not followed in his time and desired to rectify the situation. Confucius praised that in him. He is the one who says in the *Analects*, "Bathe in the Yi and air-dry beneath Wuyu."[13]

38.24

顔由，顔回父，字季路。孔子始教學於闕里，而受學。少孔子六歲。

Yan You was the father of Yan Hui. His *zi* was Jilu. He began studying with Confucius when Confucius first began teaching at Queli. He was six years Confucius' junior.

38.25

商瞿，魯人，字子木，少孔子二十九歲。特好《易》，孔子傳之，志焉。

Shang Qu was a native of Lu. Hi *zi* was Zimu. He was twenty-nine years Confucius' junior. He had a special interest in the *Changes*. Confucius transmitted his knowledge of the *Changes* to Shang, who recorded it.

38.26

漆雕開，蔡人，字子若，少孔子十一歲。習《尚書》，不樂仕。孔子曰："子之齒可以仕矣，時將過。"子若報其書曰："吾斯之未能信。"孔子悅焉。

Qidiao Kai was a native of Cai. His *zi* was Ziruo. He was eleven years Confucius' junior. He was well-versed in the *Documents*. He was not interested in working as an official. Confucius said, "You are old enough to work as an official now. Soon it will be too late." Ziruo replied in writing, "I am not sure that I am adequate to it."[14] Confucius was pleased at this response.

38.27

公良儒，陳人，字子正。賢而有勇，孔子周行，常以家車五乘從。

13. This is a reference to an incident recorded in *Analects* 11.26, in which Confucius asks several students what they would wish to do, and after other students give grand answers, this is Zeng Dian's modest response (except that the *Analects* does not have the word for *beneath*). The Yi 沂 River can still be found south of the city of Qufu, and the Wuyu 舞雩 Terrace just north of that.

14. Following Roger Ames and Henry Rosemont Jr.'s translation (1998) of a parallel passage in the *Analects*. The *Analects* (5.6) passage is absent the mention of putting it in writing.

Gongliang Ru was a native of Chen. His *zi* was Zizheng. He was capable, virtuous, and brave. He accompanied Confucius on his travels around the states, bringing five of his own carriages.

38.28

秦商，魯人，字不慈，少孔子四歲。其父堇父，與孔子父叔梁紇俱力聞。

Qin Shang was a native of Lu. His *zi* was Buci. He was four years Confucius' junior. Like Confucius' father Shuliang He, Qin's father Jinfu was known for his physical strength.

38.29

顏刻，魯人，字子驕，少孔子五十歲。孔子適衛，子驕爲僕。衛靈公與夫人南子同車出，而令宦者雍梁參乘，使孔子爲次乘，遊過市。孔子耻之。顏刻曰："夫子何耻之？"孔子曰："《詩》云：'覯爾新婚，以慰我心。'"乃嘆曰："吾未見好德如好色者也。"

Yan Ke was a native of Lu. His *zi* was Zijiao. He was fifty years Confucius' junior. When Confucius visited Wei, Zijiao was his driver. Once when Duke Ling of Wei and his wife Nanzi went out together in their carriage, the duke ordered his servant Yong Liang to come along and had Confucius ride in the carriage behind them. They traveled through the marketplace. Confucius felt ashamed by this. Yan Ke said, "Why do you feel ashamed by this?" Confucius said, "A poem says:

> Meeting you at our wedding,
> My heart is comforted."[15]

Sighing, he continued, "I have yet to meet someone who is as enamored of *de* as he is of beauty."[16]

38.30

司馬黎耕，宋人，字子牛。牛爲性躁，好言語。見兄桓魋行惡，牛常憂之。

15. These are the last two lines of the poem "The Carriage Linchpin" (#218), which can be found today in the "Xiao ya" section of the *Poems*. It relates the excitement of a groom greeting his bride on their wedding day. Confucius seems to be using the genuine feeling of love in the poem as a contrast to the superficial attraction to beauty exhibited by the king and the onlookers as the carriage passes by.

16. *I have . . . of beauty*: This passage occurs twice in the *Analects*, in 9.18 and 15.13, but both times without any context.

Sima Ligeng was a native of Song. His *zi* was Ziniu. Niu had an anxious personality and was talkative. He often worried over the misdeeds of his older brother Huan Tui.

38.31

巫馬期，陳人，字子期，少孔子三十歲。孔子將近行，命從者皆持蓋。已而，果雨。巫馬期問曰："旦無雲，既日出，而夫子命持雨具。敢問何以知之？"孔子曰："昨暮月宿畢，《詩》不云乎：'月離於畢，俾滂沱矣。'以此知之。"

Wuma Qi was a native of Chen. His *zi* was Ziqi. He was thirty years Confucius' junior. Once when Confucius was about to go on an excursion to a nearby area, Confucius told his followers to carry umbrellas.[17] Not long after, it in fact started to rain. Wuma Qi asked, "There were no clouds this morning, and yet you told us to carry rain gear when we were leaving. May I ask how you knew this?"

Confucius said, "Last night, the moon was at the Net[18] constellation. Doesn't a poem say the following:

Moon beside the Net,
Downpour immanent.[19]

This is how I knew."

38.32

梁鱣，齊人，字叔魚，少孔子三十九歲。年三十，未有子，欲出其妻。商瞿謂曰："子未也。昔吾年三十八無子，吾母爲吾更取室。夫子使吾之齊，母欲請留吾。夫子曰：'無憂也。瞿過四十，當有五丈夫。'今果然。吾恐子自晚生耳，未必妻之過。"從之，二年而有子。

Liang Zhan was a native of Qi. His *zi* was Shuyu. He was thirty-nine years Confucius' junior. At the age of thirty, he still didn't have a son, so he wished to divorce his wife.

17. *Umbrella, gai* 蓋: cover. Umbrella-like rain and sun protectors (also variously translated as canopies, parasols, and baldachins), whether held in the hand or mounted, appear to be very early in origin. A chariot-mounted canopy appears in the archaeological record as early as the Western Zhou (Wang and Huang 1984). Perhaps the earliest reference (*shi* 冟, interpreted as *mi* 冪) is in the Mao Gong Ding 毛公鼎 Inscription, dating to about 800 BCE (Shi 2016). The *Chu ci* mentions the Umbrella (*hua gai* 華蓋) constellation (see also Allred 2003), and the *Zhou li*'s "Kao gong ji" 考工記 section describes the fabrication of a chariot canopy (*gai* 蓋) (see also Needham and Ling 1965). The mention here of Confucius' students carrying hand-held umbrellas may be the earliest such mention.

18. Equivalent to the constellation Hyades.

19. From the poem "Steep Rocks" (#232), which can be found today in the "Xiao ya" section of the *Poems*. The poem describes the difficult conditions of an army on the march.

Shang Qu said to him, "Don't do it yet. At the age of thirty-eight, I still did not have any sons. My mother arranged for me to remarry. Confucius sent me to Qi, and my mother wanted Confucius to let me stay there. Confucius said, 'Don't worry. After the age of forty, you will have five little men.' And that's exactly what happened. I suspect that you are just someone who naturally has children late and that it is no fault of your wife." Liang Zhan took his advice, and two years later he had a son.

38.33

琴牢，衛人，字子開，一字張。與宗魯友。聞宗魯死，欲往弔焉。孔子弗許，曰："非義也。"

Qin Lao was a native of Wei. His *zi* was Zikai, recorded also as Zhang. He was friends with Zong Lu, and when he learned that Zong Lu had died, he wished to go and pay his respects. Confucius didn't allow it, saying, "It would be contrary to *yi*."[20]

38.34

冉儒，魯人，字子魚，少孔子五十歲。

Ran Ru was a native of Lu. His *zi* was Ziyu. He was fifty years Confucius' junior.

38.35

顏辛，魯人，字子柳，少孔子四十六歲。

Yan Xin was a native of Lu. His *zi* was Ziliu. He was forty-six years Confucius' junior.

38.36

伯虔，字楷，少孔子五十歲。

Bo Qian's *zi* was Kai. He was fifty years Confucius' junior.

38.37

公孫寵，衛人，字子石，少孔子五十三歲。

Gongsun Chong was a native of Wei. His *zi* was Zishi. He was fifty-three years Confucius' junior.

20. See 43.18 for why Confucius would be opposed.

38.38

曹邮，少孔子五十歲。

Cao Xu was fifty years Confucius' junior.

38.39

陳亢，陳人，字子亢，一字子禽，少孔子四十歲。

Chen Gang was a native of Chen. His *zi* was Zigang, also recorded as Ziqin. He was forty years Confucius' junior.

38.40

叔仲會，魯人，字子期，少孔子五十歲。與孔琁年相比。每孺子之執筆記事於夫子，二人迭侍左右。孟武伯見孔子而問曰："此二孺子之幼也於學，豈能識於壯哉?"孔子曰："然！少成則若性也，習慣若自然也。"

Shuzhong Hui was a native of Lu. His *zi* was Ziqi. He was fifty years Confucius' junior, about the same age as Kong Xuan. Every time there were children taking notes from Confucius, these two would take turns helping out. Meng Wubo once asked Confucius, "These two are such young students. How do you know what they will be like when they are grown?"

Confucius said, "Good question. Beginning the process of education when still young is like creating inborn nature. Habits are like the unfolding of nature itself."

38.41

秦祖，字子南。奚蒧，字子偕。公祖兹，字子之。

Qin Zu's *zi* was Zinan.

Xi Dian's *zi* was Zixie.

Gongzu Zi's *zi* was Zizhi.

38.42

廉潔，字子曹。公西輿，字子上。宰父黑，字子黑。

Lian Jie's *zi* was Zicao.

Gongxi Yu's *zi* was Zishang.

Zaifu Hei's *zi* was Zihei.

38.43

公西減，字子尚。穰駟赤，字子從。冉季，字子産。

Gongxi Jian's *zi* was Zishang.
Rangsi Chi's *zi* was Zicong.
Ran Ji's *zi* was Zichan.

38.44

薛邦，字子從。石處，字里之。懸亶，字子象。

Xue Bang's *zi* was Zicong.
Shi Chu's *zi* was Lizhi.
Xuan Dan's *zi* was Zixiang.

38.45

左郢，字子行。狄黑，字哲之。商澤，字子秀。

Zuo Ying's *zi* was Zixing.
Di Hei's *zi* was Zhezhi.
Shang Ze's *zi* was Zixiu.

38.46

任不齊，字子選。榮祈，字子祺。顏噲，字子聲。

Ren Buqi's *zi* was Zixuan.
Rong Qi's *zi* was Ziqi.
Yan Kuai's *zi* was Zisheng.

38.47

原忼，字子籍。公肩定，字子仲。秦非，字子之。

Yuan Kang's *zi* was Ziji.
Gongjian Ding's *zi* was Zizhong.
Qin Fei's *zi* was Zizhi.

38.48

漆雕從，字子文。燕伋，字子思。公夏守，字子乘。

Qidiao Cong's *zi* was Ziwen.
Yan Ji's *zi* was Zisi.
Gongxia Shou's *zi* was Zisheng.

38.49

勾井疆，字子疆。步叔乘，字子車。石子蜀，字子明。

Gou Jingjiang's *zi* was Zijiang.
Bushu Sheng's *zi* was Ziche.
Shi Zishu's *zi* was Ziming.

38.50

邽選，字子飲。施之常，字子常。申績，字子周。

Gui Xuan's *zi* was Ziyin.
Shi Zhichang's *zi* was Zichang.
Shen Ji's *zi* was Zizhou.

38.51

樂欣，字子聲。顏之僕，字子叔。孔弗，字子蔑。

Yue Xin's *zi* was Zisheng.
Yan Zhipu's *zi* was Zishu.
Kong Fu's *zi* was Zimie.

38.52

漆雕侈，字子斂。懸成，字子横。顏相，字子襄。

Qidiao Chi's *zi* was Zilian.
Xuan Cheng's *zi* was Ziheng.
Yan Xiang's *zi* was Zixiang.

38.53

右夫子弟子七十二人，皆升堂入室者。

The above are the seventy-two students of Confucius who achieved a notable level of mastery.

39

Original Surname

This chapter is an important record of Confucius' ancestry. The account here overlaps and is consistent with the accounts appearing in CQZZ "Yin" 3, "Huan" 1–2, and "Zhao" 7.

39.1

孔子之先，宋之後也。微子啓，帝乙之元子，紂之庶兄。以圻内諸侯，入爲王卿士。微，國名；子，爵。初，武王剋殷，封紂之子武庚於朝歌，使奉湯祀。武王崩，而與管、蔡、霍三叔作難。周公相成王，東征之。二年，罪人斯得，乃命微子於殷後，作《微子之命》，由之與國于宋，徙殷之子孫。唯微子先往仕周，故封之賢。其弟曰仲思，名衍，或名泄，嗣微子後，故號微仲，生宋公稽。胄子雖遷爵易位，而班級不及其故者，得以故官爲稱。故二微雖爲宋公，而猶以微之號自終，至于稽乃稱公焉。宋公生丁公申，申生緍公共及襄公熙，熙生弗父何及厲公方祀，方祀以下，世爲宋卿。

Confucius' ancestors were the descendants of the state of Song. Viscount Qi of Wei was the oldest son of King Yi of the Shang dynasty and the older half-brother of the Shang King Zhòu. He was a noble lord inside the capital city, where he acted as high minister to the king. Wei is the name of a state. Viscount is a noble title. When Zhou King Wu first conquered the Shang, he enfeoffed Zhòu's son Wugeng at Zhaoge and put him in charge of sacrificing to Tang. When King Wu passed away, his three younger brothers, enfeoffed at Guan, Cai, and Huo, respectively, instigated a rebellion. The Duke of Zhou, acting as prime minister for Cheng, led an eastern expedition. After two years, the rebels were subdued, the Viscount of Wei was named the heir of the Shang, the Duke of Zhou announced the Declaration to Viscount Wei whereby the state of Song was established, and the Viscount of Wei became the leader of the descendants of the Shang. As a capable and virtuous man, he was enfeoffed because he was the first of the Shang to pay allegiance to Zhou.[1] His younger brother was called Zhongsi. His name was Yan, or some say Xie. Having inherited the title Viscount of Wei, he was called Viscount Weizhong. He was the father of Duke Ji of Song. Although the oldest son changed noble rank and it was never as high as previously,[2] he held on to the previous title, and so although the two Weis became Dukes of Song, they maintained the title Viscount of Wei for the rest of their lives. Then Ji adopted the title of duke. This Duke of Song was the father of Duke Ding (given name Shen). Shen was the father of Duke Min (given name Gong) and Duke Xiang (given name Xi). Xi was the father of Fu Fuhe and Duke Li (given name Fangsi).[3] After Fangsi, future generations were high ministers of Song.

39.2

弗父何生宋父周，周生世子勝，勝生正考甫，考甫生孔父嘉。五世親盡，别爲公族，故後以孔爲氏焉。一曰孔父者，生時所賜號也，是以子孫遂以氏族。孔父生子木金父，金父生睪夷，睪夷生防叔，避華氏之禍而奔魯。防叔生伯夏，伯夏生叔梁紇。曰："雖有九女，是無子。"其妾生孟皮，孟皮一字伯尼，有足病。於是乃求婚於顔氏。顔氏有三女，其小曰徵在。顔父問三女曰："陬大夫雖父祖爲士，然其先聖王之裔。今其人身長十尺，武力絶倫，吾甚貪之，雖年長性嚴，不足爲疑，三子孰能爲之妻？"二女莫對，徵在進曰："從父所制，將何問焉？"父曰："即爾能矣。"遂以妻之。徵在既往，廟見，以夫之年大，懼不時有男，而私禱尼丘之山以祈焉。生孔子，故名丘，字仲尼。孔子三歲而叔梁紇卒，葬於防。至十九，娶于宋之并官氏。一歲而生伯魚。魚之生也，魯昭公以鯉魚賜孔子。榮君之貺，故因以名曰鯉，而字伯魚。魚年五十，先孔子卒。

Fu Fuhe was the father of Songfu Zhou. Zhou's eldest male descendant was Sheng. Sheng was the father of Zheng Kaofu. Kaofu was the father of Kongfu Jia. After these five generations, the family connection to the sovereign came to an end, and descendants thereafter took the surname Kong. One account says that Kongfu was an appellation that Kongfu Jia received at birth, and so his descendants took that as their surname. Kongfu was the father of Mu Jinfu. Jinfu was the father of Gaoyi. Gaoyi was the father of Fangshu, who fled to Lu to escape the Hua disaster.[4] Fangshu was the father of Boxia. Boxia was the father of Shuliang He. It is said that although he

1. The story of the Wugeng rebellion and enfeoffment of the Viscount of Wei is recounted in CQZZ and the *Documents*, the latter of which contains the chapter "Declaration to Viscount Wei."

2. This must be a reference to the fact that being an immediate member of the royal family represents a higher rank than being the ruler of a vassal state.

3. *Fusi*: See Fangsi as an alternative name for Fusi in 11.1n4.

4. According to CQZZ ("Huan" 2.1), Kongfu Jia was murdered by Huafu Du 華父督, a minister of Song, in the year 710 BCE. CQZZ ("Huan" 1.5) implies that Huafu desired Kongfu Jia's wife for himself. Through generous bribes, Huafu maintained his position. That Kongfu's great grandson still felt he was

had nine daughters, he was without a son. His concubine then gave birth to a son, Mengpi, also called Boni, who had a foot or leg malady. Shuliang He then sought a second marriage from the Yan family, who had three daughters, the youngest of whom was called Zhengzai. Yan asked his three daughters, "Although this high official of Zou is from a lineage of officials, he is actually the descendant of a sage king. He is very tall and unsurpassed in strength. I very much want him for you. Although he is older and has a solemn character, he should not be underestimated. Which of you three would like to be his wife?"[5]

Two of them did not respond, but Zhengzai stepped forward saying, "I will follow father's decision. What more is there to ask?"

Her father replied, "Then you will be the one." And so he married her to him.

Zhengzai went, and after three months she was worried that, because of his advanced age, she might not be able to give him a son in a timely fashion, and so she secretly went to Ni Hill (*qiu*) to pray. She gave birth to Confucius, who is thus named Qiu. His *zi* was Zhongni. Shuliang He passed away when Confucius was three years old and was buried at Fang. At the age of nineteen, he married a daughter of the Bingguan family of Song. One year later, his son Boyu was born. At his birth, Lu Duke Zhao sent a carp as a gift. Confucius felt honored by this and named his son Li (carp). His *zi* was Boyu. Boyu passed away at the age of fifty[6]—preceding Confucius in death.

39.3

齊太史子與適魯, 見孔子。孔子與之言道。子與悅, 曰: "吾鄙人也, 聞子之名, 不睹子之形久矣。而求知之寶貴也。乃今而後知泰山之爲高, 淵海之爲大。惜乎, 夫子之不逢明王, 道德不加于民, 而將垂寶以貽後世。"遂退而謂南宮敬叔曰: "今孔子先聖之嗣, 自弗父何以來, 世有德讓, 天所祚也。成湯以武德王天下, 其配在文。殷宗以下, 未始有也。孔子生於衰周, 先王典籍, 錯亂無紀, 而乃論百家之遺記, 考正其義, 祖述堯舜, 憲章文武, 刪《詩》述《書》, 定《禮》理《樂》, 制作《春秋》, 贊明《易》道, 垂訓後嗣, 以爲法式, 其文德著矣。然凡所教誨, 束脩已上, 三千餘人。或者天將欲與素王之乎, 夫何其盛也!"敬叔曰: "殆如吾子之言, 夫物莫能兩大, 吾聞聖人之後, 而非繼世之統, 其必有興者焉。今夫子之道至矣, 乃將施之無窮。雖欲辭天之祚, 故未得耳。"子貢聞之, 以二子之言告孔子。子曰: "豈若是哉? 亂而治之, 滯而起之, 自吾志, 天何與焉?"

---

under threat from Huafu's family suggests that the affair had not been settled. Perhaps a cross-generational feud had ensued.

5. That the word "wife" is used here suggests that the original wife had either died or been divorced.

6. See 38.1n6 for a discussion of the chronology of the deaths of Kong Li and Yan Hui.

Zi Yu, the court archivist of Qi, travelled to Lu and paid a visit to Confucius. Confucius discussed the *dao* with him. Delighted, Zi Yu said, "I'm just a simple person who has long heard about your fame but has never had the opportunity to meet you in person. Now I know, and will always know, that the value of seeking wisdom from you is as high as Tai Mountain and as deep as the sea. It is a pity that you have not met an enlightened king who would allow you to spread your *dao* and *de* to all the people. However, your teachings, like precious heirlooms, will be handed down to later generations."

After leaving Confucius, he said to Nangong Jingshu, "Confucius is heir to the former sages. Ever since Fu Fuhe, he is the one of *de* and deference, the one favored by *tian*. Tang the Accomplished ruled the land with martial virtues and matched them with culture. The Shang lineage has never since seen anything like him. Confucius was born into a declining Zhou, with the books of the Ancient Kings all disorganized and out of order, and so he selected the transmitted records of the great thinkers, checking and analyzing their content. Following in the footsteps of Yao and Shun, and modeling himself after Kings Wen and Wu, he compiled the *Poems,* retold the *Documents,* set the form of the *Li,* organized the *Music,* wrote the *Spring and Autumn,* and clarified the *dao* of the *Changes*—all in order to preserve them for later generations as norms and models. His refinement and *de* are thus visible to all. As for the transmission of these teachings, the number of people for whom he is officially their teacher is over 3,000. Perhaps *tian* wants to designate him as uncrowned king. Why else would he be so popular?"

Jingshu said, "Yes, it is probably as you've said. No one can accomplish everything. I've heard that if the descendants of a sage do not become rulers, they will end up flourishing anyway. Now that the *dao* of Confucius has reached its ultimate expression, it will be spread without limit. Even if he wanted to beg off from the favor of *tian,* it is too late for that now."

When Zigong heard about this, he conveyed the dialogue to Confucius, who said, "How could that be true? My ambition is simply to bring order to the disordered and free up stagnation. How can *tian* help with that?"

40

Record of the End

Chapter 40 narrates Confucius' final days, his funeral and burial arrangements, and the formation of the community that developed around his legacy.

40.1

孔子蚤晨作, 負手曳杖, 逍遥於門, 而歌曰: “泰山其頽乎! 梁木其壞乎! 哲人其萎乎!”既歌而入, 當户而坐。子貢聞之, 曰: “泰山其頽, 則吾將安仰? 梁木其壞, 吾將安杖? 哲人其萎, 吾將安放? 夫子殆將病也。”遂趨而入。夫子嘆而言曰: “賜, 汝來何遲? 予疇昔夢坐奠於兩楹之間。夏后氏殯於東階之上則猶在阼, 殷人殯於兩楹之間即與賓主夾之, 周人殯於西階之上則猶賓之。而丘也即殷人。夫明王不興, 則天下其孰能宗余? 余殆將死。”遂寢病, 七日而終, 時年七十二矣。哀公誄曰: “昊天不弔! 不憖遺一老, 俾屏余一人以在位, 煢煢余在疚, 於乎哀哉, 尼父! 無自律。”子貢曰: “公其不沒於魯乎! 夫子有言曰: ‘禮失則昏, 名失則愆。失志爲昏, 失所爲愆。’生不能用, 死而誄之, 非禮也; 稱一人, 非名。君兩失之矣。”

One day, Confucius was up early, sauntering leisurely outside his door, hands clasped behind him, singing:

Shall Tai Mountain never split?
Shall a crossbeam never rot?
Shall a wise man never wilt?

After finishing, he entered and sat facing the door.

Zigong heard him and said:

If our Tai Mountain were to split, whom would we adulate?
If our crossbeam were to rot, whom would we lean against?
If our wise man were to wilt, whom would we emulate?

"I'm afraid you are ill, sir." He then politely shuffled in.

Confucius sighed, saying, "Ci, why are you so late? Last night I dreamed that I was sitting between two pillars accepting offerings. A Xia descendant lay in a coffin atop the east staircase—that is, in the place of the host. A Shang person lay in a coffin between two pillars—that is, between the host and guest. A Zhou person lay in a coffin atop the west staircase—that is, in the place of the guest. I was the Shang person. Without an enlightened king guiding the world, who in this world will carry on my teachings after my death? I think I am dying." He was soon bedridden with illness, and he passed away after seven days. He was seventy-two years old.

Duke Ai eulogized him, saying, "Pitiless *tian* above! Unwilling to let the old man stay, I am left behind, alone on the throne, brotherless and bereft. Oh, the sorrow, Father Ni![1] I cannot contain myself!"

Zigong said, "I'm afraid you will not end your days in Lu, Your Highness. Our teacher once said, 'Darkness comes to those who forsake *li*. Grave error comes to those who fall into infamy. *Darkness* means to be thwarted. *Grave error* means losing one's position.' It is contrary to *li* for you to say you miss him now, never having employed him while he was still alive. To say you are 'alone on the throne' is also not fitting.[2] You err on both counts."[3]

40.2

既卒, 門人疑所以服夫子者。子貢曰: "昔夫子之喪顏回也, 若喪其子而無服, 喪子路亦然。今請喪夫子如喪父而無服。"於是弟子皆弔服而加麻。出有所之, 則由經。子夏曰: "入宜經可居, 出則不經。"子游曰: "吾聞諸夫子: 喪朋友, 居則經, 出則否; 喪所尊, 雖經而出, 可也。"孔子之喪, 公西赤掌殯葬焉。唅以疏米三貝, 襲衣十有一稱, 加朝服一, 冠章甫之冠, 珮象環, 徑五寸而綦組綬, 桐棺四寸, 柏棺五寸, 飭廟置翣。設披, 周也; 設崇, 殷也; 綢練、設旐, 夏也。兼用三王禮, 所以尊師, 且備古也。葬於魯城北泗水上, 藏入地, 不及泉。而封爲偃斧之形, 高四尺, 樹松柏爲志焉。弟子皆家于墓, 行心喪之禮。既葬, 有自燕來觀者, 舍於子夏氏。子貢謂之曰: "吾亦人之葬聖人, 非聖人之葬人。子奚觀焉? 昔夫子言曰: '見吾封若夏屋者, 見若斧矣。從若斧者也, 馬鬣封之謂也。'今徒一日三斬板而以封, 尚行夫子之志而已。何觀乎哉!"二三子三年喪畢, 或留或去, 惟子貢廬於墓六年。自後群弟子及魯人處於墓如家者, 百有餘家, 因名其居曰孔里焉。

After he died, his students wondered how they should dress for mourning. Zigong said, "When Yan Hui died, Confucius treated him like his own son for the funeral but without dressing that way. He did the same for Zilu. I suggest that we treat him

1. *Father Ni*: A reference to Confucius, whose *zi* was Zhongni and who was old enough to be Duke Ai's father.

2. According to Wang Su, "to be alone on the throne" was a saying reserved for the Zhou king. It was not fitting for a duke to refer to himself this way.

3. CQZZ ("Ai" 16.3) records Confucius' death in 479 BCE and relates the dialogue between Duke Ai and Zigong. Durrant, Li, and Schaberg (2016) render the duke's eulogy in verse.

as our father for the funeral but without dressing that way." And so the students all wore burlap belts atop their mourning vestments for the funeral and wore the belts atop their regular clothes for the remainder of the mourning period.

Zixia said, "It is appropriate to wear the belt at home, but not outside the home."

Ziyou said, "I have heard our teacher say, 'For the death of a friend, wear a mourning belt at home but not outside the home. For the death of an elder, the mourning belt can be worn outside as well.'"

Gongxi Chi was in charge of preparing the body for burial. He placed some polished rice and three cowrie shells in Confucius' mouth.[4] He dressed Confucius in eleven sets of clothing, plus his court robes. He adorned Confucius' head with his favorite Ruist hat from the state of Song and the Shang dynasty before that. And he decorated him with an ivory disk five inches in diameter, attached by a gray silk cord.

The inner coffin was made of four-inch-thick paulownia wood and the outer coffin of five-inch-thick cypress wood. The coffin was placed in a decorated temporary wooden pavilion, and a fan-shaped screen was erected. For the burial items, they followed the Zhou. For the pennants draped over the coffin, they followed the Shang. For the white silk flying as banners in the procession, they followed the Xia. They showed deference for their teacher and covered all the bases of the ancients by drawing from the *li* of the Three Kings.

Confucius was buried north of the Lu city along the banks of the Si River, interred in the earth above the water table. The burial mound was three feet high and in the shape of an upright axe blade. Pine and cypress trees were planted to mark the spot. His students made the area their home and did their mourning *li* there. As soon as he was buried, visitors from Yan arrived hoping to observe. They were put up at Zixia's home. Zigong said to them, "We are common people burying a sage, not sages burying a common person. What is there to observe? Confucius once said, 'I have seen burial mounds shaped like a Xia house and shaped like an axe blade. Make mine the shape of an axe blade.'[5] Some call it the shape of a horse's mane. Just today, we used three beams of rammed earth to shape the mound, trying to follow Confucius' wishes. What is there to observe?"

When the three-year mourning period was complete, some students stayed and some left. Zigong alone remained in a cottage by the grave for six years. Later, the students and people of Lu who made their homes near the grave numbered over one hundred families, and the area where they lived came to be called Kong Village.

4. The custom of placing items symbolizing food or wealth in the mouth of the deceased dates back to Neolithic times and was still common during the Western Zhou. It gradually fell out of favor during the Eastern Zhou, and during the Han dynasty, jade cicadas (symbolizing rebirth) were preferred. (Wang 2001; S. Li 2015)

5. Regarding the practice of burial mounds, see 42.27n24 and 44.3.

41

Understanding Good Governance

Unlike in other chapters, where we see aspects of a comprehensive theory of governance,[1] here we are treated to various fascinating accounts of Confucius confronting specific issues of governance, from which he, or we, may generalize. There are questions of the role of historians in recounting events of governance, utilitarian calculations regarding whether an individual should enter government, and the value of eloquence in government and diplomacy; indirect advice; impartiality; free speech; promoting the welfare of the people; modesty; frugality; and so on.

41.1

孔子在齊，齊侯出田，招虞人以旌，不進，公使執之。對曰："昔先君之田也，旌以招大夫，弓以招士，皮冠以招虞人。臣不見皮冠，故不敢進。"乃舍之。孔子聞之曰："善哉！守道不如守官。君子韙之。"

When Confucius was in Qi, the lord of Qi went hunting. Using a colorful banner, he summoned the game warden, but the warden didn't come forward. The duke then sent someone to bring him by force. The game warden said to the duke, "In the past, when sovereigns went hunting, they would use a colorful banner to summon high officials, an archery bow to summon low officials, and a leather hat to summon the game warden. I did not see a leather hat, and that's why I dared not come forward." The duke then let him go.

1. The title of this chapter is "Understanding *Zheng* 正." *Zheng* means to correct, to reform, to be upright. It can also stand for its homophone *zheng* 政. This *zheng* means to govern, which is clearly the intended meaning in the title of this chapter about good governing.

Confucius heard about this and said, "Excellent! Adhering to one's office is even better than adhering to the *dao*.[2] A *junzi* would approve."[3]

41.2

齊國書伐魯，季康子使冉求率左師禦之，樊遲爲右。師不逾溝，樊遲曰："非不能也，不信子。請三刻而逾之。"如之，衆從之。師入齊軍，齊軍遁。冉有用戈，故能入焉。孔子聞之曰："義也。"既戰，季孫謂冉有曰："子之於戰，學之乎？性達之乎？"對曰："學之。"季孫曰："從事孔子，惡乎學？"冉有曰："即學之孔子也。夫孔子者，大聖，無不該，文武並用兼通。求也適聞其戰法，猶未之詳也。"季孫悅。樊遲以告孔子。孔子曰："季孫於是乎可謂悅人之有能矣。"

Guo Shu, a high minister of Qi, attacked Lu.[4] Ji Kangzi sent Ran Qiu as lead general to defend against the attack, with Fan Chi as second in command. When Ran Qiu's troops hesitated at a waterway, Fan Chi said to Ran Qiu, "It's not that they are unable but that they do not have confidence in you. I suggest that you call out your order three times, and then ford it yourself." Ran Qiu did what Fan Chi suggested, and the troops followed him. When the troops entered battle with the Qi army, the Qi army turned and fled. Ran You was able to attack at will with his dagger-axe.

Confucius heard about this and said, "This is *yi*."

After the battle, Jisun asked Ran You, "Is warfare something you learned, or do you just have a natural ability?"

Ran You replied, "It is learned."

Jisun asked, "As a follower of Confucius, how is it that you learned about warfare?"

2. This statement is perfectly consistent with *Analects* 12.11, which says that a king should act like a king and a minister should act like a minister. It seems strange, however, that Confucius puts acting within one's role in opposition to acting according to the *dao*, since they should be the same for him—to act according to one's role is acting in accord with the *dao*. It may be significant that Confucius is speaking of the actions of a lower official, not a high official. According to Confucius' view, lower officials should take their cues from their leaders. It's not that they should be unthinking, like a functionary in *Han Feizi*, but that they should act within their purview, under the positive influence of a leader (see, e.g., 21.4). The game warden is deserving of high praise in this episode exactly because his leaders are such awful exemplars, acting neither according to their roles nor according to the *dao*. Confucius' compliment toward him is simultaneously a criticism of the Qi duke.

3. CQZZ ("Zhao" 20.7) places this episode in the year 522 BCE.

4. According to CQZZ ("Ai" 11.1), this episode occurs in the year 484 BCE. Lu gets revenge for this incursion later in the year when they team up with Wu in a counterattack (see 37.2 and CQZZ "Ai" 11.3).

Ran You said, "Indeed, I learned it under Confucius, who is a great sage. There is nothing that he does not comprehend, whether civil or martial. I only learned about the fighting strategy by happenstance. I still don't know the finer points."[5]

Jisun was delighted by this response. Fan Chi told Confucius about it.

Confucius said, "Because of this, we can finally say that Jisun appreciates people for their abilities."

41.3

南容説、仲孫何忌既除喪，而昭公在外，未之命也。定公即位，乃命之。辭曰："先臣有遺命焉，曰：'夫禮，人之幹也，非禮則無以立。'囑家老，使命二臣必事孔子而學禮，以定其位。"公許之。二子學於孔子。孔子曰："能補過者，君子也。《詩》云：'君子是則是效。'孟僖子可則效矣。懲己所病，以誨其嗣。《大雅》所謂'詒厥孫謀，以燕翼子'，是類也夫。"

Nan Rongyue and Zhongsun Heji finished mourning their deceased father. At the time, Lu Duke Zhao[6] was away, and so they could not yet receive their new commissions. As soon as Duke Ding ascended the throne,[7] he commissioned them. They declined, saying, "Our father left instructions to us, saying, '*Li* is a person's support. Without it, one cannot establish oneself.' He sent us to study *li* under Confucius in order to establish our position." The duke permitted this. The two brothers studied with Confucius.

Confucius said, "A *junzi* is someone who makes up for his errors. A poem says:

A *junzi* is the rule and the model.[8]

"Your father Meng Xizi is worth taking as a rule and a model. Learn from your own mistakes and use them to teach your descendants. It's as the Da ya says:

5. Ran You is only slightly exaggerating. Despite Confucius' explicit disavowal of having studied military tactics (41.17; *Analects* 15.1), he believed that getting the broad principles of his philosophy correct would have its impact even on military success. See, for example, 3.2, 16.5, and 27.1.

6. Duke Zhao got caught up in a dispute between two powerful families, and after siding with one was defeated in a battle by the other's allies (one of whom was Zhongsun Heji) and forced to flee the country. Duke Zhao's younger brother was installed in his place as Duke Ding. (CQZZ "Zhao" 25)

7. This passage fulfills a prediction in CQZZ ("Zhao" 7.12). On his deathbed (535 BCE), Meng Xizi predicted that a sage named Confucius would appear and instructed his household managers to have his two sons study with him.

8. This is from the poem "Cry of the Deer" (#161), which can be found today in the "Xiao ya" section of the *Poems*. It is written from the perspective of King Wu, who is holding a victory banquet for his new family of noblemen after their defeat of the Shang. This line points to his aspirations for the new leaders to act as moral models for the people. *Junzi* in this context means noble lord. See also 216n25.

He bequeathed his plans to posterity
To support and protect his descendants."[9]

41.4

衛孫文子得罪於獻公，居戚。公卒，未葬，文子擊鐘焉。延陵季子適晋，過戚，聞之，曰："異哉！夫子之在此，猶燕子巢于幕也，懼猶未也，又何樂焉？君又在殯，可乎？"文子於是終身不聽琴瑟。孔子聞之，曰："季子能以義正人，文子能克己服義，可謂善改矣。"

Sun Wenzi of Wei was in exile in the city of Qi, having offended Wei Duke Xian. After the duke died but before he was buried, Wenzi had bells played. Jizi of Yanling, passing through Qi on his way to Jin, heard about this. He said to Wenzi, "Strange! Living here, you are like a swallow that built its nest atop a tent. If something were to happen, you wouldn't even have time to be terrified. How can you play music? And is it really permissible with the duke still lying in state?" After this, Wenzi never again listened to music.[10]

Confucius heard about this and said, "Jizi was able to correct people with *yi*. Wenzi was able to discipline himself and follow *yi*. Both can be called correcting errors."

41.5

孔子覽《晋志》，晋趙穿殺靈公，趙盾亡，未及山而還。史書"趙盾弒君"。盾曰："不然。"史曰："子爲正卿，亡不出境，返不討賊，非子而誰？"盾曰："嗚呼！'我之懷矣，自詒伊戚'，其我之謂乎！"孔子嘆曰："董狐，古之良史也，書法不隱。趙宣子，古之良大夫也，爲法受惡。惜也，越境乃免。"

Confucius was reading in a history of Jin about how Zhao Chuan of Jin assassinated Jin's Duke Ling. At the time, Zhao Chuan's older cousin Zhao Dun, who had been the Jin

9. This quotation is from the poem "The Voice of King Wen" (#244), which can be found today in the "Da ya" section of the *Poems*. The poem extols the merits of Kings Wen and Wu in establishing the Zhou dynasty.

10. *Music*: Zither music. The meaning here seems to be that Wenzi wouldn't listen to any music at all, even zither music, a kind of very personal music. The sense is that Wenzi deeply regretted what he had done, putting himself and his whole family in danger and refused, as a kind of disciplinary reminder, to listen to music. Wenzi's city of Qi was in the territory of Wei, but according to CQZZ ("Xiang" 26.2), due to vicious animosity between Wenzi and the Wei ruler, the city was under the military protection of Jin. Nevertheless, it had recently been attacked by Wei, during which one of Wenzi' son's died fighting. For the backstory to this passage, see "Jizi of Yanling" and "Sun Wenzi" in the glossary.

prime minister, was heading out of the country into self-exile. Before Zhao Dun reached the mountains on the border, he heard the news and turned around. In recording the event, Dong Hu, Jin's official historian, wrote, "Zhao Dun committed regicide."

Zhao Dun said to Dong Hu, "That's not what happened."

The historian replied, "You were the prime minister and were heading off into self-exile. Before reaching the border, you returned, and you have not yet punished the perpetrator. If it wasn't you, who was it?"

Zhao Dun said, "Oh, my! Doesn't the following refer to my situation?

My heartfelt feelings,
Distress self-made."[11]

Confucius sighed and said, "Dong Hu was one of the great historians. His method was to hide nothing. Zhao Dun was one of the great high officials. His own methods brought him ignominy, which is regrettable. If he had just crossed the border, he would have escaped blame."[12]

41.6

鄭伐陳，入之，使子產獻捷于晉。晉人問陳之罪焉，子產對曰："陳亡周之大德，介恃楚衆，馮陵弊邑，是以有往年之告。未獲命，則又有東門之役。當陳隧者，井堙、木刊，弊邑大懼。天誘其衷，啓弊邑心，知其罪，授首於我，用敢獻功。"晉人曰："何故侵小？"對曰："先王之命，惟罪所在，各致其辟。且昔天子一圻，列國一同，自是以衰，周之制也。今大國多數圻矣，若無侵小，何以至焉。"晉人曰："其辭順。"孔子聞之，謂子貢曰："《志》有之：'言以足志，文以足言。'不言，誰知其志？言之無文，行之不遠。晉爲伯，鄭入陳，非文辭不爲功。小子慎哉！"

11. From the poem "The Valiant Pheasant" (#33), which can be found today in the "Bei feng" section of the *Poems*. It uses migrating pheasants as an analogy for the separation of a wife and her husband, who is going away on a military expedition. The husband, in the voice of the pheasant says: My heartfelt feelings, leaving distance between her 我之懷矣，自詒伊阻. The *Dialogues* version substitutes *qi* 戚 (distress) for *zu* 阻 (between). The semantic flexibility of the other words allows for the different contextual interpretation.

12. This story, including Confucius' remarks, appears in CQZZ ("Xuan" 2.3). In their introduction to their translation, Durrant, Li, and Schaberg (2016) comment on its centrality in understanding historiography during Confucius' time. They also wonder about Confucius' intentions because this passage has been criticized over the centuries for appearing to promote disloyalty. In the *Dialogues* generally, Confucius' loyalty is clearly to the people, not to the ruler, so although he would in principle be opposed to regicide as disrupting the hierarchy (see 41.18, where, indeed, he would be willing to go to war in opposition to regicide), he could conceivably sympathize with it if the ruler were a brutal tyrant, such as Jie of the Xia and Zhòu of the Shang, and as Jin Duke Ling was reputed to be.

After Zheng attacked Chen and penetrated their defenses, Zheng sent Zichan to Jin to offer spoils of war as tribute.[13] Jin asked what offense Chen had committed.[14] Zichan replied, "Chen neglected the great *de* of the Zhou by capitalizing on its close relationship with its large neighbor Chu to encroach on our territory, which we complained about to you before, but you did not respond. And then there was the Battle at the East Gate.[15] When Chen was on the march, they stopped up our wells and chopped down our trees, striking fear into our townspeople. *Tian* was moved by this and raised the spirits of our people. Chen, realizing their guilt, accepted punishment from us, and now we present to you the fruits of our victory."

Jin said, "Why invade a smaller state?"

Zichan replied, "According to the rule of the Ancient Kings, each state would be punished according to its crime. In the Zhou system, the king had a domain of 1,000 square *li*[16] and the highest-ranked noble lords had domains of 100 square *li*, with the sizes decreasing according to rank. Now, most large states[17] are several thousand square *li*. If there were no invasions of smaller states, how could it have come to this?"

Jin said, "That sounds about right."

Confucius heard about this and said to Zigong, "It has been written that when you have intentions to express, use speech adequate to the intentions, and eloquence adequate to the speech. Without speech, who could know your intentions? Without eloquence, actions cannot be taken very far. When Jin held the position of eldest

13. See in the last paragraph that Jin, an ally of Zheng, was in the position of influence.

14. Battles in the Zhou were generally understood as justifiable if the attacking side were righting a wrong, often on a pretext of maintaining the Zhou system.

15. Chu attacked Zheng, and there was a battle outside the East Gate. See CQZZ "Xiang" 24.8.

16. We retain the *li* unit of length here to make the proportions clear. The Chinese term *qi* 圻 is glossed by Wang Su as "land in a square of 1,000 *li* (*di fang qian li* 地方千里)." The terminology is ambiguous—it could mean a perimeter of 1,000 *li*, or it could mean 1,000 square *li*. The most likely interpretation of a land measurement using the term *fang* 方 is to view it as an "area measurement" (Wu 1984, 94), meaning 1,000 square *li*, which equals about 62.5 square miles, about the size of a small US city such as Richmond, Virginia. That makes a Zhou state capital about 6.25 square miles. We have evidence of the city walls of only two early Zhou states. The Lu state's walls measure about 3.4 square miles, but the dating is in question and may not date back to the early Zhou (Chen, Sun, and Liu 2020), and the Yan state's wall was even smaller, at 0.1 square mile (Kong 2020). (By comparison, Vatican City is 0.19 square miles and Monaco 0.77 square miles.) All of this sheds light on the passage in 3.2, which refers to an early Zhou capital city as 50 *li* (which we take to mean 50 square *li*) and a state as 100 *li*. The precision (the size of Lu's capital matches the stated size of an early Zhou city in 3.2) and imprecision (it is half the size stated in 41.6) may have to do with the changing uses and meanings of words for *state* and *capital* in early texts: *bang* 邦, *guo* 國, and *du* 都.

17. Such as Jin.

brother[18] and Zheng invaded Chen, Zheng would never have succeeded without Zichan's eloquence. Pay attention to such things!"[19]

41.7

楚靈王汰侈。右尹子革侍坐，左史倚相趨而過。王曰："是良史也，子善視之。是能讀《三墳》《五典》《八索》《九丘》。"對曰："夫良史者，記君之過，揚君之善。而此子以潤辭爲官，不可爲良史。"曰："臣又乃嘗聞焉，昔周穆王欲肆其心，將過行天下，使皆有車轍並馬迹焉。祭公謀父作《祈昭》，以止王心，王是以獲殁於文宮。臣聞其詩焉而弗知，若問遠焉，其焉能知。"王曰："子能乎?"對曰："能，其詩曰：'祈昭之愔愔乎，式昭德音。思我王度，式如玉，式如金。刑民之力，而無有醉飽之心。'"靈王揖而入，饋不食，寢不寐，數日，則固不能勝其情，以及於難。孔子讀其志，曰："古者有志：'克己復禮爲仁。'信善哉！楚靈王若能如是，豈期辱於乾谿？子革之非左史，所以風也，稱詩以諫，順哉。"

King Ling of Chu led an extravagant lifestyle. Once when the high official Zige was sitting in attendance, the associate historian Yixiang shuffled past. The king said, "This one is a good historian. Look after him well. He can recite obscure books."[20]

Zige replied, "A good historian both records the errors and exalts the excellences of a sovereign. A man like this, who earned his position by embellishing, cannot be considered a good historian."

He continued, "In addition, I have heard that once when King Mu of Zhou[21] wished to indulge his desires in a tour across the land, and had already left horse and carriage tracks in many places, Zhaigong Moufu composed the poem 'Royal Music' to reform him. Because of this, the king died a good death in his own home. I once asked Yixiang if he knew this poem, and he didn't. If you were to ask him about even more distant events, how could he know?"

The king asked Zige, "Do you know it?"

He replied, "Yes. The poem goes like this:

18. Relationships among states at this time assumed a familial order, with the Zhou acting in the position as father, and the other states as brothers. The most powerful state acted in the position of the eldest brother.

19. A version of this story, including Confucius' comment, appears in CQZZ ("Xiang" 25.10).

20. *Obscure books*: The titles of several histories are mentioned. If any such books once existed, they are now lost. The king is praising the historian's erudition for being able to recite them.

21. King Mu was the fourth king after King Wu. The first two after Wu were Cheng and Kang, who are generally regarded as fine rulers. Zhao was the third. Both he and Mu are considered to have lived lives of extravagance, with little concern for proper governing.

Royal music, quiet and serene,
Enough to radiate *de*.
I imagine my king's moderation,
A model like jade,
A model like bronze.
The people's strength is sapped,
But the king is never sated."

King Ling saluted and entered his chambers. He was unable to eat or sleep for several days. Incapable of overcoming his urges, however, he ultimately suffered disaster.

Confucius read about this and said, "There is a record from ancient times that says, '*Ren* is overcoming oneself and returning to *li*.'[22] Very true. If King Ling had been able to do this, he would not have ended up disgraced at Qianxi.[23] Because Zige was not the associate historian, he did just right by using the indirect method of a poem to advise the king."

41.8

叔孫穆子避難奔齊，宿於庚宗之邑。庚宗寡婦通焉，而生牛。穆子返魯，以牛爲内豎，相家。牛讒叔孫二子，殺之。叔孫有病，牛不通其饋，不食而死。牛遂輔叔孫庶子昭而立之。昭子既立，朝其家衆曰："豎牛禍叔孫氏，使亂大從，殺適立庶，又被其邑，以求舍罪，罪莫大焉，必速殺之。"遂殺豎牛。孔子曰："叔孫昭子之不勞，不可能也。周任有言曰：'爲政者不賞私勞，不罰私怨。'《詩》云：'有覺德行，四國順之。'昭子有焉。"

Shusun Muzi, encountering trouble, fled to Qi, and on his way he stayed in the city of Gengzong. A widow of Gengzong slept with him and subsequently gave birth to Niu. Later, back in the Lu capital, Shusun employed Niu as a servant in charge of household responsibilities. Shusun had two sons by his own wife. Niu slandered them, which led to their deaths. Shusun fell ill. Niu refused to feed him, and Shusun starved to death. Niu then helped Zhao, Shusun's son by a concubine, to become head of the family.

Zhao called the family together and said, "The servant boy Niu has brought disaster to the Shusun lineage by inciting disorder and disharmony. He killed the sons by the wife and installed the son of a concubine. He then gave away their cities to be

22. This line appears in 12.1 of the *Analects* as Confucius' own words.

23. King Ling made a military expedition to Qianxi to attack the state of Xu. While he was away from the capital, the king's younger brother murdered the king's son and usurped the throne. King Ling's soldiers and officers all deserted him. Even the local people wouldn't provide food for him. (CQZZ "Zhao" 12.11, 13.2)

pardoned for his crimes.[24] No crimes are worse than these. He must be killed immediately." They then killed Niu the servant boy.

Confucius said, "Shusun Zhaozi's not viewing Niu's helping him as a favor is beyond most people's abilities. Zhou Ren once said, 'In government, a leader should never reward someone for a personal favor nor punish someone out of personal resentment.' A poem says:

Realize *de* behavior,
And other states will follow.[25]

Zhao did this."

41.9

晋邢侯與雍子争田，叔魚攝理，罪在雍子。雍子納其女於叔魚，叔魚弊獄邢侯。邢侯怒，殺叔魚與雍子於朝。韓宣子問罪於叔向，叔向曰："三奸同坐，施生戮死，可也。雍子自知其罪而賂以置直，鮒也鬻獄，邢侯專殺，其罪一也。己惡而掠美爲昏，貪以敗官爲默，殺人不忌爲賊。《夏書》曰：'昏、默、賊，殺。'咎陶之刑也。請從之。"乃施邢侯，而尸雍子、叔魚於市。孔子曰："叔向，古之遺直也。治國制刑，不隱於親。三數叔魚之罪，不爲末，或曰義，可謂直矣。平丘之會，數其賄也，以寬衛國，晋不爲暴；歸魯季孫，稱其詐也，以寬魯國，晋不爲虐；邢侯之獄，言其貪也，以正刑書，晋不爲頗。三言而除三惡，加三利，殺親益榮，由義也夫。"

Marquis Xing of Jin had a dispute over lands with Yongzi. Shu Yu was the acting magistrate and initially found Yongzi in the wrong. Yongzi then gave his daughter to Shu Yu, and Shu Yu promptly found the marquis guilty and attempted to jail him. Enraged, the marquis murdered both Shu Yu and Yongzi in the court. Han Xuanzi referred the case to Shu Xiang, who said, "All three miscreants are guilty. It is thus permissible to punish the one who is still alive and humiliate the dead ones. Yongzi knew that he had committed a crime and so bribed an official to get off; Shu Yu put imprisonment up for sale; and Marquis Xing committed murder. Their crimes are equivalent. It is corruption to appropriate a good name despite one's guilt; it is fraud to fail in one's duties because of greed; and it is lawlessness to murder someone without flinching. The Xia shu[26] says, 'Corruption, fraud, and lawlessness are to be severely punished.'[27] Such was Gao Yao's penal code. I suggest you follow him." So

24. These events are conveyed in more detail in CQZZ "Zhao" 4.8 and 5.1.

25. A passage from the poem "Solemn" (#256), which is an extended tirade about how not to act in government office. For more about this poem, see 12.14n12.

26. Xia shu: A section of the *Documents* in its current form.

27. This passage does not appear in the extant editions of the *Documents*.

Marquis Xing received punishment, and the bodies of Yongzi and Shu Yu were put on display in the central marketplace.[28]

Confucius said, "History has bequeathed to us Shu Xiang as one of the great upright officials. He governed the state and administered the penal system without covering up for his family. He found Shu Yu in the wrong three times and never went easy on him. Some say this is *yi*. It could also be called upright.[29] First, at the Pingqiu summit, he called out Shu Yu's extortion of Wei, thereby exonerating Wei.[30] As such, Jin was not belligerent. Second, he put the blame for deception on Shu Yu, which allowed Jisun to return to Lu,[31] thereby exonerating Lu of any blame. As such,

28. There is an apparent contradiction in this passage related to the punishment of Marquis Xing (he should be *shi* 施, he should be *sha* 殺, and, again, he was *shi*). The text uses two distinct and, on first glance, mutually incompatible terms, in three instances, to describe one action that was applied to the marquis. *Shi* is a polysemic word, and commentators generally rely on its meanings of to exert and to set up to interpret it in this context as *deemed guilty and arrested*. In fact, Luo (1994) identifies this passage as the locus classicus for this meaning. But how to reconcile this meaning with *sha*, which commonly means to kill, if only one action was taken against the marquis? Yang and Song (2013) render the first *shi* as *to punish*, *sha* as *to execute*, and the second *shi* as *to execute*. This approach resolves the contradiction but introduces an inconsistency in the interpretation of *shi*. Yang and Chou (2020) render the two instances of *shi* as *to convict* and *sha* as *to execute*, solving the problem by keeping the punishment of the marquis vague—he was convicted, which could mean that he was also executed. Durrant, Li, and Schaberg (2016), in the CQZZ parallel ("Zhao" 14.7), interpret *shi* as to execute and expose the corpse, solving the problem but introducing a new problem—namely, how exposing the corpse of the marquis differs from displaying the corpses of Yongzi and Shu Yu in the marketplace. In the first use, the Chinese says *shi* for the marquis and *lu* 戮 for the Yongzi and Shu Yu—*lu* meaning to put on public display for the purpose of humiliation. In the second use, *shi* is used for the marquis, and for Yongzi and Shu Yu, it says they were *shi* 尸 in the marketplace—*shi* 尸 meaning to lay out a corpse (in a neutral sense). Durrant, Li, and Schaberg combine the two verbs (*shi* 施 and *shi* 尸) into one, translating, "exposed [the marquis'] corpse and the corpses of Yongzi and [Shu Yu] in the marketplace" (1519). This is a clever and plausible way to solve the problem. We take a different route that relies on the polysemic nature of *sha*, which we've seen already in notes 2.1n2, 17.1n8, and 31.5n4. We translate *sha* as *to severely punish*, which easily solves the problem (he should be punished [*shi*], he should be severely punished [*sha*], he was punished [*shi*]), although, admittedly, as with Yang and Chou's solution, it does not tell us exactly what the punishment was.

29. This looks like a direct challenge to *Analects* 13.18, in which Confucius refers to an upright (*zhi* 直) person as someone who covers up (*yin* 隱) for his family. It is worth pondering why Confucius would favor covering up for one's father in the case of a stolen sheep and favor denouncing one's younger brother in the case of Shu Yu's three misdeeds.

30. Jin, the reigning superpower, called an interstate summit after Lu invaded two neighboring states. Han Xuanzi, the prime minister of Jin, put Shu Yu in charge of the large number of troops sent to the summit. On the road there, Shu Yu passed through Wei and attempted to use his military force to extort wealth from Wei. Wei refused. Shu unleashed his troops, decimating Wei crops. Wei finally relented.

31. At the end of the summit, Jisun Yiru (Ji Pingzi), who held power in Lu, was arrested and held in Jin as scapegoat, so that Lu was not punished. According to Confucius, Shu Xiang was responsible for freeing him by putting the blame on Shu Yu.

Jin was not antagonistic. Third, by calling out the corruption of Shu Yu and jailing Marquis Xing, he reformed the penal system. As such, Jin was not biased. Three times Shu Xiang spoke and each time corrected a wrong, while also fostering three benefits. Increasing honor by killing one's own family—it comes from *yi*."

41.10

鄭有鄉校，鄉校之士非論執政。鬷明欲毀鄉校。子產曰："何以毀爲也？夫人朝夕退而遊焉，以議執政之善否。其所善者，吾則行之；其所否者，吾則改之。若之何其毀也？我聞忠言以損怨，不聞立威以防怨。防怨猶防水也，大決所犯，傷人必多，吾弗克救也。不如小決使導之，不如吾所聞而藥之。"孔子聞是言也，曰："吾以是觀之，人謂子產不仁，吾不信也。"

Zheng had a public school, the graduates of which would gather to critique government officeholders.[32] Zong Ming wished to abolish the school.

Zichan said, "Why abolish it? Mornings and evenings, people retreat to the school as a diversion and spend time talking about what's right and what's wrong in the government. What they approve of, we try to put into practice. What they disapprove of, we try to reform. What reason is there to destroy it? I've heard that conscientious speech reduces resentment among the people. I've never heard of a show of force blocking resentment. Blocking resentment is like damming a river—a large breach will harm many people, and there is little that can be done about it in the moment. It's better to have smaller outflows and channel them. It's better for me to hear about the ills so that I can treat them."

Confucius heard this statement and said, "From this exchange, it's hard for me to believe people when they say that Zichan was not *ren*."

41.11

晋平公會諸侯于平丘，齊侯及盟。鄭子產争貢賦之所承，曰："昔日天子班貢，輕重以列，列尊貢重，周之制也。卑而貢重者，甸服。鄭伯，南也，而使從公侯之貢，懼弗給也，敢以爲請。"自日中争之，以至於昏，晋人許之。孔子曰："子產於是行也，是以爲國基也。《詩》云：'樂只君子，邦家之基。'子產，君子之於樂者。"且曰："合諸侯而藝貢事，禮也。"

32. *Graduates of the school, xiang xiao zhi shi* 鄉校之士: people from the school who are up-and-comers, who had achieved some minor level of status in society, or who at least see themselves as having something to contribute to the intellectual conversation of the day—in other words, quasi-intellectuals. The term *shi* may be used somewhat facetiously here. In the CQZZ ("Xiang" 31.11) version of this episode, "men of Zheng (*Zheng ren* 鄭人)" gathered at the *xiao* 校, which Durrant, Li, and Schaberg render "the village meeting places" (2016, 1287).

Duke Ping of Jin held an interstate summit in Pingqiu, which the Duke of Qi attended. Zichan of Zheng disputed the ranking of the tribute gifts that were brought, saying, "In the Zhou system, the king established tributes of greater and lesser value, with higher-ranked states offering gifts of greater value. However, a low-ranked state near the domain of the capital is also required to present a very valuable tribute gift. The ruler of Zheng, though low-ranked, resides just south of the capital,[33] and so is required to prepare a gift of a higher rank. However, we fear that he will be unable to provide it, and we pray for leniency." This argument was made at midday, and by sunset the Jin duke had allowed it.

Confucius said, "Zichan built a firm foundation for his state by acting this way. A poem says:

> Happy are the princes
> With foundations such as these.[34]

Zichan is the delight of his prince."

He also said, "To convene the noble lords and standardize tribute gifts is in accord with *li*."

41.12

鄭子産有疾，謂子太叔曰："我死，子必爲政。唯有德者能以寬服民，其次莫如猛。夫火烈，民望而畏之，故鮮死焉；水濡弱，民狎而翫之，則多死焉，故寬難。"子産卒，子太叔爲政，不忍猛，而寬，鄭國多掠盜。太叔悔之曰："吾早從夫子，必不及此。"孔子聞之，曰："善哉！政寬則民慢，慢則糾於猛。猛則民殘，民殘則施之以寬。寬以濟猛，猛以濟寬，寬猛相濟，政是以和。《詩》曰：'民亦勞止，汔可小康。惠此中國，以綏四方。'施之以寬。'毋縱詭隨，以謹無良。式遏寇虐，憯不畏明。'糾之以猛也。'柔遠能邇，以定我王'，平之以和也。又曰：'不競不絿，不剛不柔。布政優優，百祿是遒。'和之至也。"子産之卒也，孔子聞之，出涕曰："古之遺愛。"

Zichan of Zheng was ill. He said to Zitaishu, "After I die, you will take over the government. Only a *de* person can win the people's allegiance through leniency. The alternative is coercion. Consider the ferocity of fire. Because people view it with fear and respect, few people die from it. Water is more welcoming, and so people get comfortable with it and even play in it, and then people end up drowning. This is why leniency is difficult."

33. The Zheng capital (present-day Xinzheng) was about ninety-three miles southeast of the Zhou capital (present-day Luoyang).

34. From the poem "Sedge in the Southern Hills" (#172), which can be found today in the "Xiao ya" section of the *Poems*. The poem describes the mirth of the leading noblemen in times of plenty.

Zichan passed away, and Zitaishu took over the government. Finding coercive governing intolerable, he favored leniency, and crime increased in Zheng. Regretful, Taishu said, "If only I had listened to Zichan, it would not have come to this."

Confucius heard about this, and said, "Excellent! Under a lenient government, the people become shiftless. Shiftlessness leads to the need for coercive restraint. But coercion can lead to cruelty, which then has to be corrected with leniency. Leniency remedies coercion, and coercion remedies leniency. With leniency and coercion balancing each other out, harmony in governing can be achieved.[35] A poem says:

Beleaguered are the people,
A respite will bring relief—
A kindness to the central states,
A way to pacify the whole land.[36]

This is showing leniency.

Follow not the panderers,
Guard against the heartless.
Prevent vile brutality,
Fear not their cunning ways.

This is remediation through severity.

Gentleness attracts the distant
And secures the king's position.

This is bringing peace through harmony.

Another poem says:

Not aggressive or rash,
Not rigid or lax,
He spreads good government with grace and ease,
And tribute comes from all around.[37]

This is the ultimate in harmony."

35. See 31.1 for details about how to create harmony by balancing coercion and leniency.

36. These four lines and the following six make up the first stanza of the poem "Beleaguered People" (#253), which can be found today in the "Da ya" section of the *Poems*. This poem is believed to describe the difficult conditions of the people under Zhou King Li, who exploited the people to maintain a debauched lifestyle.

37. These lines are from the poem "Long Prosperity" (#304). The poem is also quoted in 12.6, 12.15, and 27.2

When Confucius learned of Zichan's death, he wept, saying, "He had the love bequeathed by the ancients."

41.13

孔子適齊，過泰山之側，有婦人哭於野者而哀。夫子式而聽之，曰："此哀一似重有憂者。"使子貢往問之。而曰："昔舅死於虎，吾夫又死焉，今吾子又死焉。"子貢曰："何不去乎?"婦人曰："無苛政。"子貢以告孔子。子曰："小子識之：苛政猛於暴虎。"

On his way to Qi, Confucius passed by Tai Mountain, where a woman in deep sorrow was crying at the edge of a field. He leaned forward in the carriage to listen and then said, "This one exhibition of grief appears compounded by multiple worries." He sent Zigong to inquire.

The woman said, "First my father-in-law was killed by a tiger, then my husband, and now my son."

Zigong asked, "Then why don't you leave?"

The woman said, "At least the government is not oppressive."

Zigong reported this to Confucius, who said, "Remember this. An oppressive government is worse than a vicious tiger."

41.14

晋魏獻子爲政，分祁氏及羊舌氏之田，以賞諸大夫及其子成，皆以賢舉也。又謂賈辛曰："今汝有力於王室，吾是以舉汝。行乎，敬之哉，毋墮乃力。"孔子聞之曰："魏子之舉也，近不失親，遠不失舉，可謂義矣。"又聞其命賈辛，以爲忠："《詩》云：'永言配命，自求多福'，忠也。魏子之舉也義，其命也忠，其長有後於晋國乎。"

When Wei Xianzi held the reins of government in Jin, he split up the fiefs of the Qi and Yangshe clans[38] to reward the high officials and his son Cheng, all of whom were promoted on account of their ability and virtue.[39] He also said to Jia Xin, one of the promoted officials, "I promoted you because you have been helpful to the royal family.[40] Take the job seriously, work hard, and don't slack off."

Confucius heard about this and said, "Weizi's way of promoting people, neither losing those close to him nor losing the opportunity to elevate those who were

38. See 41.15n42 for an explanation of why he would break up the clans' territory.

39. According to CQZZ ("Zhao" 28.3), Wei divided the Qi clan's territory into seven districts and the Yangshe clan's territory into three districts and installed a particular named person in each.

40. Jia Xin helped restore the Zhou royal house after a rebellion. (CQZZ "Zhao" 22.5)

strangers to him, can be considered *yi*." And when he heard how Wei had hired Jia Xin, he considered it in line with conscientiousness, saying, "A poem says:

> Hire the right match
> And fortune will come.[41]

This is conscientiousness. Weizi's promoting people was *yi*, and his hiring Jia was conscientiousness. His lineage will endure in Jin."

41.15

趙簡子賦晋國一鼓鐘，以鑄刑鼎，著范宣子所爲刑書。孔子曰："晋其亡乎！失其度矣。夫晋國將守唐叔之所受法度，以經緯其民者也。卿大夫以序守之，民是以能遵其道而守其業，貴賤不愆，所謂度也。文公是以作執秩之官，爲被廬之法，以爲盟主。今棄此度也，而爲刑鼎，銘在鼎矣，何以尊貴？何業之守也？貴賤無序，何以爲國？且夫宣子之刑，夷之蒐也，晋國亂制，若之何其爲法乎？"

Zhao Jianzi collected a large amount[42] of iron in taxes in the state of Jin and used it to cast a "penal cauldron," inscribing it with the penal code created by Fan Xuanzi. Confucius remarked, "Jin is not long for this world, for they have lost their measure! The state of Jin once took the models that act as a measure received from Tang Shu and used them to guide the people. As ministers and high officials maintained the system one after the other, the people were able to safeguard their livelihoods by respecting the civic order. Not bringing disorder to differences in station is considered the measure. For this reason, Duke Wen created offices with specific duties, created the Beilu Law, and sponsored a summit. But now the measure has been abandoned. In making the penal cauldron and inscribing it, where is the respect for status? How can livelihoods be safeguarded? Without order among

41. From the poem "King Wen" (#235), which can be found today in the "Da ya" section of the *Poems*. This poem extols the Zhou for conquering the Shang and suggests that the way for peace to reign is for the Zhou house to rule virtuously and for the remains of the Shang house to accept their fate.

42. *Large amount, gu zhong* 鼓鐘: *gu* is a measure of volume. Accounts of its size differ. Wang Su says that one *gu* equals 4 *dan* 石, or about 22 gallons. *Zhong* can refer either to a bell or to a measure of volume (about 7 gallons [Qiu 1992]), which would bring the total to about 29 gallons of ingots, approximately enough to make the equivalent of the largest *ding* in the archaeological record. Instead of *zhong*, the CQZZ ("Zhao" 29.5) version of this story has *tie* 鐵 (iron), which we adopt here. According to Liangcheng Lu (2005), "The use of iron was already relatively common among the people of the state of Jin" (p. 206) in the late sixth century BCE.

stations, how can there even be a state? Fan Xuanzi's penal code was a response to the troop review in Yi.[43] How can Jin's chaotic system be used as a model or law?"[44]

41.16

楚昭王有疾，卜曰："河神爲祟。"王弗祭，大夫請祭諸郊。王曰："三代命祀，祭不越望。江、漢、沮、漳，楚之望也。禍福之至，不是過乎？不穀雖不德，河非所獲罪也。"遂不祭。孔子曰："楚昭王知大道矣，其不失國也，宜哉。《夏書》曰：'維彼陶唐，率彼天常，在此冀方。今失厥道，亂其紀綱，乃滅而亡。'又曰：'允出兹在兹'，由己率常，可矣。"

43. The episode in 41.15 about the penal cauldron, according to CQZZ ("Zhao" 29.5), occurred in Jin in the year 513 BCE, the year after the immediately preceding episode (41.14) about the splitting of territories in Jin. Confucius praises the prime minister Wei Xianzi in the first and then criticizes the high minister Zhao Jianzi in the second. Why such different attitudes toward what was essentially the same government only one year apart? There is much happening beneath the surface that informs this praise and criticism. Confucius favors a government that is run by a virtuous and visionary ruler who hires wise and capable officials, all of whom can act as models for those lower on the hierarchy. As far as this kind of ideal government applies to Jin, it helps to think of it in terms of a high point and a low point. The high point (on par with the virtuous beginning of Jin under Tang Shu) was in 633 BCE, when the once exiled Chonger had consolidated power as Duke Wen of Jin. Confucius says, "Duke Wen created offices with specific duties, created the Beilu Law, and sponsored a summit." We don't know the details of the so-called Beilu Law, but there is a reference to it in CQZZ in the year 633, which also involves hiring a man who "is delighted by *li* and music and is well-versed in the *Poems* and *Documents*, which are treasuries of *yi*. *Li* and music are the standards of *de*, and *de* and *yi* are the root of benefit" ("Xi" 27.4). This is just the kind of government favored by Confucius. A few years later, in 621, the Jin minister Zhao Dun instituted governmental reforms that systematized ritual roles to make the government fairer and more harmonious and which became "enduring standards" (CQZZ "Wen" 6.1). This occurred at the troop review in Yi, mentioned at the end of 41.15. However, by this time, Duke Wen had already passed away, and for Confucius, a system of government is only as good as those who implement it. In the middle of the sixth century BCE, the Jin high minister Fan Xuanzi apparently recorded Zhao Dun's penal reform, and that was what was inscribed in the penal cauldron of 513. Jin was then in full decline, with greedy families controlling various aspects of the government. Two powerful families (but not the most powerful families) were Qi and Yangshe. A story in CQZZ ("Zhao" 28.2) tells of how the leaders of Qi and another family shared their wives and concubines with each other and of the corruption involved in trying to prosecute them for it. So in 41.14, when Wei Xianzi essentially destroys Qi and Yangshe (who was also implicated) by splitting up their territories, he is also rooting out iniquity and corruption. The decimation of the families is praised by Confucius because it is reducing corruption and iniquity and replacing them with wise and capable local officials. The following year, the penal cauldron is criticized by Confucius because the Jin central government is still controlled by greedy families (such as Zhao Jianzi's) and so the legal reform is really just window dressing. See Ames (1983) for other perspectives on Confucius' attitude toward this incident and penal law more generally.

44. *Model or law*, *fa* 法: The word *fa* means norm. Since norms can be soft, as in a model, or hard, as in a law, *fa* is translated in this passage as both *model* and *law*. See entry for "*Fa*" in the introduction's philosophical lexicon.

King Zhao of Chu fell ill. A prognosticator said, "The illness is a disaster brought on by the spirit of the Yellow River."

The king had not performed a ceremonial sacrifice, and his high officials pleaded with him to perform a sacrifice on the outskirts of the capital.

The king said, "According to the rules of sacrifice handed down by the founders of the Three Dynasties, one does not sacrifice beyond the purview of one's kingdom. The rivers within Chu's purview are the Yangtze, the Han, the Ju, and the Zhang.[45] If good or ill fortune occurs, surely it will not have crossed over these. Even if I were lacking in *de*, it's not the Yellow River that would punish me." And so he refused to sacrifice.

Confucius said, "King Zhao of Chu understood the general *dao*. It is fitting that he did not lose his state.[46] The Xia shu says:

There was once Taotang
Who followed the customs of *tian*
Right here in the Central Plains.
Now we've lost his *dao*,
Corrupted his moral standards,
And brought ourselves to ruin.[47]

It is also said, 'To offer up what is near at hand.'[48] It is permissible to follow the common standard proceeding from one's own particular circumstances."

45. The four major rivers are likely the present-day Yangtze, Han, Qu, and Zhang. At the time of Chu King Zhao, the capital of Chu was either Ying 郢, which was in the area of present-day Jiangling County, Hubei, on the Yangtze River (until 506 BCE; see note 45) or Ruo 鄀, which was in present-day Yicheng County, Hubei, along the Han River, about 125 miles north of Ying. The Yangtze spanned the breadth of Chu, running west to east. The other major river was the Han, running from the far northwest of Chu in a southeast direction, and emptying into the Yangtze downriver from Ying in the area of present-day Wuhan. To the north of Ying, the Qu and Zhang rivers ran a roughly parallel course from north to south, below the Han, conjoined, then emptied into the Yangtze just upriver from Ying. The Yellow River is hundreds of miles to the north, well outside the borders of Chu. (Tan 1996; Zheng, Wu, and Yang 2000)

46. Likely a reference to the 506 BCE Battle of Boju, in which Wu routed Chu and laid waste the Chu capital. King Zhao managed to escape and later to return. (Zheng, Wu, and Yang 2000)

47. From the poem "Song of the Five Sons," which can be found today in the "Xia shu" section of the *Documents*. This poem is a lament, spoken from one perspective of each of the five brothers, after their oldest brother, Xia king Taikang 太康, was overthrown for having paid attention only to hunting rather than to the affairs of government. The wording here differs somewhat from the wording the *Documents* of today, but the meaning is equivalent.

48. This is from the essay "Plans of the Great Yǔ" (Da Yǔ mo), which appears today in the "Yao dian" section of the *Documents*. The section is a conversation among Shun (the ruler) and his two ministers Gao Yao and Yǔ. Shun says that Yǔ is the man to succeed him due to his many abilities. Yǔ demurs and nominates Gao Yao. In this context, the line would read: I put him out of my mind, yet he remains in my thoughts.

41.17

衛孔文子使太叔疾出其妻，而以其女妻之。疾誘其初妻之娣，爲之立宮，與文子女，如二妻之禮。文子怒，將攻之。孔子舍蘧伯玉之家，文子就而訪焉。孔子曰："簠簋之事，則嘗聞學之矣。兵甲之事，未之聞也。"退而命駕而行，曰："鳥則擇木，木豈能擇鳥乎？"文子遽自止之曰："圉也豈敢度其私哉？亦訪衛國之難也。"將止，會季康子問冉求之戰。冉求既對之，又曰："夫子播之百姓，質諸鬼神而無憾，用之則有名。"康子言於哀公，以幣迎孔子，曰："人之於冉求，信之矣，將大用之。"

Kong Wenzi of Wei ordered Taishu Ji to divorce his wife, giving his own daughter in marriage to him.[49] Taishu Ji then lured back his former wife's younger half-sister, who had originally been given to him as a gift during the first marriage, built a mansion for her, and, along with Wenzi's daughter, it was as if he had fulfilled the *li* of having two wives. This angered Wenzi,[50] who as a result was about to send armed men to attack Taishu Ji. Confucius was staying at the home of Qu Boyu in Wei when Kong Wenzi stopped by to visit him.

Confucius said, "I have studied how to conduct ceremonial sacrifices. I have not studied how to engage in armed conflict."[51] He exited, called for a carriage, and began to depart, saying, "A bird selects the tree. Where is the tree that selects the bird?"

Kong Wenzi stopped him and said, "I am doing this not for my own personal benefit but to prevent trouble in Wei."[52]

As Confucius was deciding whether to stay in Wei, there was a meeting in Lu, in which Ji Kangzi asked Ran Qiu about warfare. Ran Qiu replied to him and then added, "Confucius' teachings have spread to the common people such that they can now approach the spirit world without confusion. Hiring him would improve your reputation."

Ji Kangzi, recommending that they invite Confucius with a substantial payment, said to Duke Ai, "People trust Ran Qiu, so let's put Confucius to use in a big way."

49. Kong Wenzi's motivation is unclear and also not explained in the CQZZ ("Ai" 11.6) version of this story, although there is a hint. Taishu Ji had to flee Wei for Song, where he married the daughter of one Zizhao of Song. Zizhao, was later invited to Wei by Duke Ling to be paramour of his own wife, Nanzi. It was when Zizhao departed Wei (after the death of Duke Ling) that Kong Wenzi demanded the divorce, perhaps to free Taishu Ji of his association with the disgraced Zizhao.

50. See "Wife" in the glossary for an explanation of why Wenzi would have been angry about this.

51. A differently worded version of this passage appears in *Analects* 15.1, but without the context and with Duke Ling of Wei as the interlocutor instead of Kong Wenzi. Also compare 41.2.

52. In other words, it is better for the people of Wei that I eliminate Taishu Ji while he is abroad than to wait for him to raise an army and come back and battle me here in Wei.

41.18

齊陳恒弒其君簡公，孔子聞之，三日沐浴而適朝，告於哀公曰：“陳恒弒其君，請伐之。”公弗許。三請，公曰：“魯爲齊弱久矣，子之伐也，將若之何？”對曰：“陳恒弒其君，民之不與者半。以魯之衆，加齊之半，可克也。”公曰：“子告季氏。”孔子辭，退而告人曰：“以吾從大夫之後，吾不敢不告也。”

Chen Heng of Qi murdered his sovereign, Duke Jian. Hearing of it, Confucius did three days of purificatory bathing and then went to the court to report it to Duke Ai, saying, “Chen Heng murdered his sovereign. I suggest we attack him.” The duke did not allow it.

Confucius pleaded with him repeatedly, but the duke said, “Lu has been weaker than Qi for a long time. What will happen if we follow your advice and attack?”

Confucius replied, “Half of the people in Qi disapprove of Chen Heng's murder of the sovereign. With Lu's numbers and half of Qi, we could beat them.”

The duke said, “Report it to Ji Kangzi.” Confucius left.

Afterward, he explained to someone, “Because I had once been a high official, I had to speak up.”

41.19

子張問曰：“《書》云：‘高宗三年不言，言乃雍’。有諸？”孔子曰：“胡爲其不然也？古者天子崩，則世子委政於冢宰三年。成湯既没，太甲聽於伊尹；武王既喪，成王聽於周公，其義一也。”

Zizhang asked, “The Documents says, ‘For three years, Gaozong did not speak. When he did finally speak, all was in harmony.’[53] Did this really happen?”

Confucius said, “Why should we think otherwise? When the ruler died in ancient times, the crown prince might hand the government over to the prime minister for three years. When Tang passed away, Taijia deferred to Yi Yin.[54] When King Wu's

53. The passage in question that appears in the edition of the *Documents* that has come down to us does not exactly say that. It says that Gaozong was in mourning for three years, and when he came out of it, he did not speak. His ministers, as a result, were anxious (see the “Shuo ming” 説命 section in the “Shang shu” 商書 chapter). However, later in the text, the Duke of Zhou comments on this passage, saying explicitly that Gaozong did not speak for three years, and when he finally did, all was in harmony (using the exact words that Zizhang quotes). Zizhang's particularly incisive question, then, is whether the Duke of Zhou's commentary is correct. *To speak* means to speak of government affairs, which is an idiom for handling government affairs—in other words, to govern.

54. Taijia was the grandson and successor of Tang. According to the *Documents* (“Taijia 1”), Taijia's behavior was not fit for a king, and so the prime minister Yi Yin put him under house arrest during the mourning period, where he was kept in silence. After that, the story continues, he was “truly *de*.”

mourning period began, King Cheng deferred to the Duke of Zhou.[55] The appropriate actions were the same in each."[56]

41.20

衛孫桓子侵齊，遇，敗焉。齊人乘之，執。新築大夫仲叔于奚以其衆救桓子，桓子乃免。衛人以邑賞仲叔于奚，于奚辭，請曲懸之樂，繁纓以朝。許之，書在三官。子路仕衛，見其故，以訪孔子。孔子曰："惜也！不如多與之邑，惟器與名，不可以假人，君之所司。名以出信，信以守器，器以藏禮，禮以行義，義以生利，利以平民，政之大節也。若以假人，與人政也。政亡，則國家從之，不可止也。"

Sun Huanzi of Wei invaded Qi but was met with resistance and defeated. Qi pursued and captured him. The high official Zhongshu Yuxi of Xinzhu used his own people to rescue Huanzi, and so Huanzi escaped disaster. The Duke of Wei wanted to reward Zhongshu Yuxi with a city, but Yuxi demurred, requesting instead a rack of ceremonial bells and chimes and an insignia on his horse that would allow him to enter court. The duke agreed, and it was recorded at the highest levels of government. When Zilu was working as an official in Wei, he read about this incident and asked Confucius his opinion.

Confucius said, "It's a pity. It would have been better to have given him an extra city. Ceremonial implements and titles must not be given indiscriminately and should be kept in the firm control of the sovereign. Titles convey trustworthiness. Trustworthiness is symbolized in ceremonial implements. Ceremonial implements symbolize *li*. *Li* brings about *yi*. *Yi* produces benefits. Benefits devolve to the common people. Such are the workings of the government. To confer one part of this indiscriminately is to relinquish the government. If the government is lost, the state follows, and it will be too late to save it."[57]

55. It may not be immediately apparent that this example is relevant, since the Duke of Zhou assumed control of the government because King Cheng had not yet come of age, and the Duke of Zhou controlled the government for seven years, not three. However, BA says that King Cheng made his first appearance in a battle during his third year on the throne and that he made his first appearance at the ancestral temple as king during his fourth year. The BA narrative, along with Confucius' use of King Cheng as an example (Confucius may have been privy to information that we don't have), suggest that King Cheng indeed fits the formula of a new ruler who hands the government over to his ministers while he mourns his deceased father.

56. The gist of this passage, as is clear from another telling in *Analects* 14.40, is that it is appropriate for a ruler to not attend to government affairs during the mourning period for a deceased parent.

57. This explanation is an expansion on the statement in 32.5 about ceremonial implements as symbols of power. Commenting on a parallel passage in CQZZ ("Cheng" 2.2), Durrant, Li, and Schaberg (2016) explain that the kind of rack mentioned signifies a status higher than the minister should have been allowed.

41.21

公父文伯之母紡績不解，文伯諫焉。其母曰：“古者王后親織玄紞，公侯之夫人加之紘綖，卿之内子爲大帶，命婦成祭服，列士之妻加之以朝服。自庶士已下，各衣其夫。社而賦事，烝而獻功，男女紡績，愆則有辟，聖王之制也。今我寡也，爾又在下位，朝夕恪勤，猶恐忘先人之業，况有怠墮，其何以避辟？”孔子聞之曰：“弟子志之，季氏之婦，可謂不過矣。”

The mother of Gongfu Wenbo was always weaving. Wenbo admonished her for it. His mother replied, "In the past, queens personally wove the black stopper cords for the crown. The wives of noble lords added chin straps. The wives of the high ministers made pendant cords. The wives of senior officials[58] made ceremonial robes. The wives of lower officials added court robes. The wives of all lower people clothed their husbands. The system of the sage kings was such that the She ceremony marked the beginning of the year's agricultural and sericultural activities, and the Zheng ceremony was for sacrificial offerings.[59] Both men and women made contributions and would be punished for failing to participate. I am a widow now and you are in a relatively low position, working hard day and night. We can only fear forgetting the industriousness of our forebears. If we become lazy, how will we avoid punishment?"[60]

Confucius heard about this and said to his students, "Remember this. There is no fault in this woman of the Ji family."

41.22

樊遲問於孔子曰：“鮑牽事齊君，執政不撓，可謂忠矣，而君刖之，其爲至闇乎？”孔子曰：“古之士者，國有道則盡忠以輔之，國無道則退身以避之。今鮑莊子食於淫亂之朝，不量主之明暗，以受大刖，是智之不如葵，葵猶能衛其足。”

Fan Chi asked Confucius, "When Bao Qian served the Qi sovereign, he handled his office unflinchingly. Can we say that he was conscientious, while the duke, who punished him by cutting off his feet, was entirely benighted?"[61]

58. *Wives of senior officials, ming fu* 命婦: titled women. We follow Wang Su, who glosses the term as "wife of senior official" (*dafu zhi qi* 大夫之妻).

59. Of the grain and silk that resulted from the agriculture and sericulture.

60. *Forgetting* (*wang* 忘) in the previous sentence in some versions appears as *losing* (*wang* 亡), but *forgetting* makes it consistent with the idea of punishment here, which would presumably come from one's forebears for forgetting their customs and, by extension, forgetting them. The parallel in LNZ ("Lu Ji jing Jiang") also has *wang* 忘.

61. According to CQZZ ("Cheng" 17.6), in the year 574 BCE, while the Qi Duke Ling was away at a summit, Bao Qian witnessed the minister Qing Ke 慶克 sneaking into the women's palace apartments dressed in women's clothing to have an affair with Duke Ling's mother, Shengmengzi 聲孟子. Bao

Confucius said, "Aspiring officials of the past worked conscientiously for the government when it was just but retired to avoid trouble when it was unjust. Here, Bao got caught up in a nasty palace affair without first gauging whether it was a sufficiently enlightened place to work and ended with the serious punishment of having his feet severed. His wisdom was no match for the *kui* plant, for at least the *kui* plant can protect its feet."[62]

41.23

季康子欲以一井田出法賦焉，使訪孔子。子曰："丘弗識也。"冉有三發，卒曰："子爲國老，待子而行，若之何子之不言？"孔子不對，而私於冉有曰："求，汝來。汝弗聞乎，先王制土，藉田以力，而底其遠近；賦里以入，而量其有無；任力以夫，而議其老幼。於是鰥、寡、孤、疾、老者，軍旅之出則徵之，無則已。其歲收，田一井出稯禾、秉芻、缶米，不是過，先王以爲之足。君子之行，必度於禮，施取其厚，事舉其中，斂從其薄。若是其已，丘亦足矣。不度於禮，而貪冒無厭，則雖賦田，將有不足。且子孫若以行之而取法，則有周公之典在。若欲犯法，則苟行之，又何訪焉？"

Ji Kangzi wanted to levy a new tax on landholdings and sent someone to ask Confucius' opinion. Confucius said, "I don't know anything about this kind of thing."

Ran You was then sent repeatedly to Confucius, and finally said, "You are an elder statesman, and the country's leaders are waiting to hear your opinion before acting. Why don't you say something?"

Confucius still didn't answer the question, but he said to Ran You privately, "Qiu, come with me. Haven't you learned that, in the land reform undertaken by the Ancient Kings, they taxed landholdings according to capability and took into account distance from the city? In urban areas, they took into account a person's total assets. In estimating a farmer's capabilities, they took into account his age. As a result, old widowers, widows, orphans, the ill, and senior citizens were exempt from taxation unless there was a military expedition. Each year, one *jing* of land would pay forty bundles of unthreshed grain, nine bushels of fodder, and nine gallons of hulled grain. It would never exceed this amount, for it was sufficient for the Ancient Kings. In his behavior, a leader must achieve measure through *li*, be magnanimous in giving and

---

reported it to Guo Zuo. Guo admonished Qing, who complained to Shengmengzi. When the duke returned, Shengmengzi accused Bao Qian of plotting a coup, for which the duke punished Bao by cutting off his feet.

62. About the *kui* plant, Durrant, Li, and Schaberg say: "This *kui* . . . is an edible vegetable mentioned often in ancient texts. *Kui* leaves were picked carefully so that the roots remained behind to produce more leaves—hence these lines from an ancient poem: 'Pick the *kui* without injuring its roots. / Injure its roots and the *kui* will not live' 採葵不[*sic*]傷根，傷根葵不生. 'Not suffering injury in the roots' is here compared to 'being able to protect one's feet'" (2016, 856n396).

receiving, be moderate in managing affairs, and be spare in collecting taxes from the masses. If such were the case today, taxes from just sixteen *jing* would be sufficient. Instead, the measure is not found in *li*. Rather, there is relentless greed, so even if there were a new tax on fields, it would not be enough. If Jisun wants a method for taxation, the Zhou example is right there for him to follow. If he wants to go against it and act carelessly, why ask for my advice?"

41.24

子游問於孔子曰："夫子之極言子產之惠也，可得聞乎？"孔子曰："惠在愛民而已矣。"子游曰："愛民謂之德教，何翅施惠哉？"孔子曰："夫子產者，猶衆人之母也，能食之，弗能教也。"子游曰："其事可言乎？"孔子曰："子產以所乘之輿濟冬涉者，是愛無教也。"

Ziyou asked Confucius, "You have praised Zichan's magnanimity in the highest terms. May I learn more?"

Confucius said, "Magnanimity goes no further than loving and caring for the people."

Ziyou said, "Loving and caring for the people is best done through moral instruction. Why do you put it just in terms of spreading magnanimity?"

Confucius said, "Zichan was like a mother. He was able to feed the people but not to give them formal instruction."

Ziyou said, "Can you speak about what he did?"

Confucius said, "For example, he used his own carriage to help people cross a river during the winter. This is love and care, not formal instruction."

41.25

哀公問於孔子曰："二三大夫皆勸寡人，使隆敬於高年，何也？"孔子對曰："君之及此言，將天下實賴之，豈唯魯哉！"公曰："何也？其義可得聞乎？"孔子曰："昔者，有虞氏貴德而尚齒，夏后氏貴爵而尚齒，殷人貴富而尚齒，周人貴親而尚齒。虞、夏、殷、周，天下之盛王也，未有遺年者焉。年者，貴於天下久矣，次于事親。是故朝廷同爵而尚齒。七十杖於朝，君問則席；八十則不仕朝，君問則就之，而悌達乎朝廷矣。其行也，肩而不並，不錯則隨，斑白者不以其任於道路，而悌達乎道路矣；居鄉以齒，而老窮不匱，强不犯弱，衆不暴寡，而悌達乎州巷矣；古之道，五十不爲甸役，頒禽隆之長者，而悌達乎蒐狩矣；軍旅什伍，同爵則尚齒，而悌達乎軍旅矣。夫聖王之教，孝悌發諸朝廷，行於道路，至於州巷，放於蒐狩，循於軍旅，則衆感以義，死之而弗敢犯。"公曰："善哉，寡人雖聞之，弗能成。"

Duke Ai asked Confucius, "Several high officials have advised me that more respect should be paid to older people. Do you know why?"

Confucius replied, "If you were to do what was advised, then the whole land would put their trust in you, not just Lu."

The duke said, "But why is it so important?"

Confucius said, "In the past, the founder of the Youyu esteemed virtue and age. The Xia founder esteemed nobility and age. The Shang founder esteemed wealth and age. The Zhou founders esteemed parents[63] and age. None of the glorious kings of Youyu, Xia, Shang, and Zhou failed to esteem elders. Elders were esteemed throughout the land for a very long time, second only to one's parents.

"And so, where there were nobles of the same rank in the court, the elder was held in highest esteem. When a man of seventy entered the court carrying a staff, if the king wished to seek advice from him, the king would lay out a mat for him to be seated. A man who was eighty need not even come into the court; the king would go to him to seek advice. This was the achievement of respect for elders in the court.

"In walking, one would not walk side by side with an elder but one step over and one step back or directly behind. People with gray hair would not be left carrying burdens on the streets. This was the achievement of respect for elders on the street.

"As for elders living in villages, the impoverished elderly would lack nothing, the strong would not take advantage of the weak, nor would the many harass the few. This was the achievement of respect for elders in villages.

"The way of the ancients was that men over fifty would not work for the hunt, and yet old people would be given a share of the game. This was the achievement of respect for elders during hunting seasons.

"In those of the same rank among a company of soldiers, the elders would be esteemed. This was the achievement of respect for elders in the military.

"In the instruction of the sage kings, respect for elders inside and outside the family was promulgated starting from the palace to pedestrians on the street, to villages, to hunting parties, to the military. In this way, everyone felt it to be the *yi* thing to do, and no one would dare violate it their whole lives."

The duke said, "Excellent, but now that I understand it, I'm afraid I won't be able to successfully bring it about."

41.26

哀公問於孔子曰:"寡人聞東益不祥,信有之乎?"孔子曰:"不祥有五,而東益不與焉。夫損人自益,身之不祥;棄老而取幼,家之不祥;釋賢而任不肖,國之不祥;老者不教,幼者不學,俗之不祥;聖人伏匿,愚者擅權,天下不祥。不祥有五,東益不與焉。"

63. *Parents, qin* 親: This *qin* could be interpreted more broadly as family or relatives. The Zhou founders emphasized the importance of family relations.

Duke Ai asked Confucius, "I've heard that it is bad luck to build an addition to one's residence toward the east. Should I believe this?"

Confucius said, "There are five kinds of bad luck, and building an addition toward the east is not one of them. Harming someone else for personal gain is bad luck for one's person. Forsaking the old in favor of the young is bad luck for one's household. Employing the incapable and unwise instead of the capable and wise is bad luck for the state. Elders who refuse to teach and youth who refuse to learn are bad luck for society. Sages hiding away and imbeciles taking power are bad luck for the entire land. These are the five kinds of bad luck, and expanding one's residence to the east is not one of them."

41.27

孔子適季孫, 季孫之宰謁曰: "君使求假於田, 將[64]與之乎?" 季孫未言, 孔子曰: "吾聞之, 君取於臣, 謂之取; 與於臣, 謂之賜。臣取於君, 謂之假; 與於君, 謂之獻。" 季孫色然悟曰: "吾誠未達此義。" 遂命其宰曰: "自今已往, 君有取之, 一切不得復言 '假' 也。"

Confucius went to visit Jisun. Just then, the manager of Jisun's household asked Jisun, "The sovereign sent someone here to borrow the use of a field. Should we lend it to him?"

Before Jisun could reply, Confucius said, "I've heard that the word for a sovereign acquiring something from a vassal is *acquire*. The word for a sovereign giving something to a vassal is *confer*. The word for a vassal acquiring something from a sovereign is *borrow*. The word for a vassal giving something to a sovereign is *tribute*."

Jisun's expression showed that he had a sudden realization, and he said, "I've never really understood the meanings of these words."

He immediately gave instructions to his household manager, saying, "From now on, whenever the sovereign wants something from me, never use the word *borrow*."

64. For *jiang* 將, SBCK has *te* 特. SKQS and Tongwen editions have *jiang*. We follow Yang and Song (2013), emending to *jiang*.

42

Zigong Asks about the Finer Points of *Li*

The final three chapters of the *Dialogues* are entitled *Qu li* 曲禮, translated "finer points of *li*." According to Kong Anguo's preface, they were added to the collection after it was solicited by the government, having been dispersed among private collectors. It is interesting that this chapter begins with a discussion of historiography rather than *li* per se. This topic, and many others in the chapter, suggest the very wide scope of Confucius' conception of *li*. It is really the proper way of doing virtually anything in life, taking full account of people's natural tendencies and how to act in a way that helps all concerned to join in creating a peaceful and prosperous society. The question that should be at the front of the reader's mind while reading these chapters is: What is the relation between an individual's personal actions and the people in the individual's immediate environment? And then: Can a general principle be extracted? Sometimes a general principle seems elusive, which is in keeping with Confucius' emphasis on the importance of taking particular circumsntances into account. And yet other times Confucius provides a general principle—for example, in 42.7, where he concludes: "A *junzi* should not make a superior feel threatened or a subordinate feel pressured."

42.1

子貢問於孔子曰: "晉文公實召天子, 而使諸侯朝焉。夫子作《春秋》, 云: '天王狩于河陽.' 何也?" 孔子曰: "以臣召君, 不可以訓。亦書其率諸侯事天子而已。"

Zigong asked Confucius, "Duke Wen of Jin once called the Zhou king to a summit and had all of the noble lords swear allegiance. In recording this incident in the

Spring and Autumn, you wrote, 'The king went for a hunt in Heyang.'[1] Why did you do that?"

Confucius said, "Having a vassal calling a king to him is not a good model for instruction. I wrote only that he led the other noble lords to swear allegiance to the king, that's all."[2]

42.2

孔子在宋，見桓魋自爲石椁，三年而不成，工匠皆病。夫子愀然曰："若是其靡也，死不如速朽之愈。"冉子僕，曰："禮，凶事不豫，此何謂也？"夫子曰："既死而議謚，謚定而卜葬，既葬而立廟，皆臣子之事，非所豫屬也，况自爲之哉？"

When Confucius was in Song, he saw that Huan Tui was having a stone coffin made for himself. After three years, it still wasn't finished and the artisans were exhausted from the work. A distressed look appeared on Confucius' face and he said, "If someone is going to be this extravagant, it would be better for him to quickly decay after death."

Ranzi, who was driving, said, "Why is it said that, according to *li,* one should not prepare ahead of time for one's funeral?"

Confucius said, "One's posthumous name is determined right after one's death. After that, the proper time of burial is calculated. After one's burial, the memorial shrine is built. All of these are done by one's auxiliaries and children and cannot be predicted ahead of time, let alone performed by oneself."

42.3

南宮敬叔以富得罪於定公，奔衛。衛侯請復之，載其寶以朝。夫子聞之，曰："若是其貨也，喪不若速貧之愈。"子游侍，曰："敢問何謂如此？"孔子曰："富而不好禮，殃也。敬叔以富喪矣，而又弗改，吾懼其將有後患也。"敬叔聞之，驟如孔氏，而後循禮施散焉。

1. Heyang is near present-day Mengzhou 孟州, Henan, just outside Luoyang (the Zhou capital) and about seventy-one miles west of Jiantu 踐土 (present-day Yuanyang 原陽, Henan), where the summit was held. Heyang belonged to Jin, and Jiantu to Zheng. Confucius' point here is that he did not record that the Jin sovereign called the king to a summit, as that was not a proper thing to do. The king did go, however. So, Confucius says he recorded that the king went on a hunting trip to the vicinity of where the summit was held. (Zhang, Lin, and Gao 1980; Tan 1996; Liu and Chi 2002)

2. The *Spring and Autumn* is traditionally attributed to Confucius, whose rationale for writing it (on the interpretation in the *Dialogues*) was to instruct later generations, in that it would help them learn how to act properly. On this view, history is not an objective recording of facts but an opportunity to learn from the past. As in this episode, one may even rewrite the past. The CQZZ ("Xi" 28.9) version of this episode leaves the authorship of the *Spring and Autumn* passage ambiguous.

For reasons having to do with his wealth, Nangong Jingshu offended Duke Ding and fled to Wei. The Duke of Wei petitioned Duke Ding to permit him to return, and Nangong returned with a load of jewels for the palace. When Confucius heard about this, he said, "With wealth such as this, it would be better to quickly be made poor than merely to lose his noble rank."[3]

Ziyou, who was in attendance, said, "May I ask why?"

Confucius said, "Wealth absent a love for *li* leads to an early demise. Jingshu's wealth led to the loss of his position and still he didn't change. I fear there will be dire consequences to come." When Jingshu caught wind of this, he rushed to Confucius. Subsequently, he followed *li* and distributed his wealth accordingly.

42.4

孔子在齊，齊大旱，春饑。景公問於孔子曰："如之何？"孔子曰："凶年則乘駑馬，力役不興，馳道不修，祈以幣玉，祭祀不懸，祀以下牲。此賢君自貶以救民之禮也。"

When Confucius was in Qi, Qi suffered a drought, resulting in a famine during the spring. Duke Jing asked Confucius, "What should I do?"

Confucius said, "During a bad year, ride a nag; halt all corvée labor; do not repair roads; in supplication ceremonies, use silk and jade for offerings;[4] do not use bells and chimes during sacrificial ceremonies; and when animals are offered in sacrifice, use second-rate animals. This is the *li* of how a capable and virtuous ruler humbles himself in order to save the people."

42.5

孔子適季氏，康子晝居內寢。孔子問其所疾，康子出見之。言終，孔子退。子貢問曰："季孫不疾，而問諸疾，禮與？"孔子曰："夫禮，君子不有大故，則不宿於外；非致齊也，非疾也，則不晝處於內。是故夜居外，雖弔之，可也；晝居於內，雖問其疾，可也。"

Confucius went to see Ji Kangzi, who had retired to his inner chambers during the daytime. Confucius inquired about his illness, and Kangzi came out to greet him. After they spoke, Confucius departed.

Zigong asked, "Jisun was not ill, and yet you asked about his illness. Is that in accordance with *li*?"

3. *Lose one's noble rank, sang* 喪: What exactly is in danger of being lost is not specified in the text. We follow interpreters who take it to be referring to noble rank, presumably the rank Nangong Jingshu lost when he was forced to flee.

4. Instead of offering grains or animals. Silk and jade can be reused and are therefore more frugal.

Confucius said, "According to *li*, a *junzi* does not sleep away from home at night except in exceptional circumstances. And unless he is fasting for a sacrificial ceremony or ill, he does not remain in his inner chambers during the day. If someone sleeps away at night, it is permissible to go so far as to offer sympathy; and if someone spends daylight hours in the inner chambers, it is permissible to inquire after his illness."

42.6

孔子爲大司寇，國廄焚。子退朝而之火所，鄉人有自爲火來者，則拜之，士一，大夫再。子貢曰："敢問何也?"孔子曰："其來者，亦相弔之道也。吾爲有司，故拜之。"

When Confucius was minister of justice, the state stables caught fire. He left the court and went to the burning building. Some local officials came of their own initiative on behalf of those putting out the fire, and Confucius bowed to thank them—once to lower officials and twice to higher officials. Zigong asked, "Can you explain that to me?"

Confucius said, "The officials who came followed the *dao* of expressing gratitude for services rendered. As a state officer, it was proper for me to bow in thanks[5] to them."

42.7

子貢問曰："管仲失於奢，晏子失於儉。與其俱失矣，二者孰賢?"孔子曰："管仲鏤簋而朱紘，旅樹而反坫，山節藻梲。賢大夫也，而難爲上。晏平仲祀其先祖，而豚肩不揜豆，一狐裘三十年。賢大夫也，而難爲下。君子上不僭下，下不逼上。"

Zigong asked, "Guan Zhong erred in extravagance, and Yanzi erred in frugality. Though both erred, which of them was the more capable and virtuous?"

Confucius said, "Guan Zhong had *gui* bronze vessels with openwork designs[6] and hats with red cords. He put up decorative screens and placed a courtesy dais[7] in his mansion. He had his interlocking roof supports carved with designs of mountains and his vertical roof supports painted with designs of water plants. He was a capable

5. *Bow in thanks, bai* 拜: *Bai* means to bow as a way of conveying the deeply held emotion of the moment: reverence, grief, commiseration, and so on. In this case the emotion was gratitude.

6. Bronze openwork designs reached their full artistic potential during the era in which Guan Zhong lived and could be particularly complex and ornate, as these *gui* must have been. A *gui* is a squat round vessel used for food offerings. On Guan Zhong's lack of frugality, see *Analects* 3.22. (Zhou and Huang 2015)

7. *Decorative screen* and *courtesy dais, lü shu* 旅樹 and *fan dian* 反坫: See *Analects* 3.22, where both of these items are described as something belonging to a sovereign, making it seem an extravagance or a privilege that Guan Zhong arrogates to himself.

and virtuous high official, but he made it difficult for his superior. When Yan Pingzhong sacrificed pork shoulder[8] to his ancestors, it was too small to fill the *dou* ritual vessel. He wore the same fox-fur robe for thirty years. He was a capable and virtuous high official, but he made it difficult for his subordinates. A *junzi* should not make a superior feel threatened or a subordinate feel pressured."

42.8

冉求曰：“昔文仲知魯國之政，立言垂法，于今不亡，可謂知禮矣。”孔子曰：“昔臧文仲安知禮？夏父弗綦逆祀而不止，燔柴於竈以祀焉。夫竈者，老婦之所祭，盛於甕，尊於瓶，非所柴也。故曰禮也者，由體也。體不備，謂之不成人。設之不當，猶不備也。”

Ran Qiu said, "When Zang Wenzhong managed the government of Lu, he left behind written models of excellent speech that are still with us. He can be considered to have understood *li*."

Confucius said, "How can Zang Wenzhong have understood *li*? When Xiafu Fuqi violated ceremonial protocol, Zang didn't stop him.[9] And he allowed a pyre sacrifice to be performed on a stove. The stove is where old ladies sacrifice using earthenware jars and bottles and is not a place for a pyre sacrifice. And so it is said: *Li* is like the human body. If the body is not yet complete, then one is not fully mature. If a sacrificial ceremony is inappropriate in some way, it might as well be incomplete."

42.9

子路問於孔子曰：“臧武仲率師與邾人戰于狐鮐，遇，敗焉，師人多喪而無罰。古之道然與？”孔子曰：“凡謀人之軍，師敗則死之；謀人之國邑，危則亡之，古之正也。其君在焉者，有詔則無討。”

Zilu asked Confucius, "When Zang Wuzhong led troops to battle against Zhū in Hutai, he suffered defeat. Although many men were killed in battle, he was not punished. Is this the way of the ancients?"

Confucius said, "Any leader of an army who lost a battle was expected to commit suicide. Any leader of a city that experienced a revolt was expected to flee into exile. This was the system of the ancients. However, if the sovereign was implicated, then there would be a reprimand but no punishment."[10]

8. *Pork shoulder, tun jian* 豚肩: According to a similar passage in the *Li ji* ("Li qi"), pork shoulder was considered an inferior cut of meat.

9. See 18.4n14.

10. The record in CQZZ ("Xiang" 4.8) of the defeat of Wuzhong by Zhū at Hutai does not directly mention interference by the duke, but it does say that the people blamed the duke for sending Wuzhong.

42.10

晋將伐宋，使人覘之。宋陽門之介夫死，司城子罕哭之哀。覘者反，言於晋侯曰：“陽門之介夫死，而子罕哭之哀，民咸悦。宋殆未可伐也。”孔子聞之，曰：“善哉，覘國乎！《詩》云：‘凡民有喪，匍匐救之。’子罕有焉。雖非晋國，其天下孰能當之？是以周任有言曰：‘民悦其愛者，弗可敵也。’”

Jin was about to attack Song and sent out a reconnaissance agent. A guard at Song's main gate had just died, and Zihan, the minister of public works, wept in sorrow. The agent returned and said to the Jin duke, "A guard at the main gate has just died, and Zihan is weeping in sorrow. All the people are pleased with his reaction. This may not be a good time to attack them."

Confucius heard about this and said, "This reconnaissance agent was excellent! A poem says:

> If any are about to drown,
> Others pull them out.[11]

Zihan was in this position. Not just Jin, but what other country could have taken on Song at that moment? This is why Zhou Ren once said, 'The people are pleased with those who love and care for them. Such a leader is invincible.'"

42.11

楚伐吴，工尹商陽與陳棄疾追吴師。及之，棄疾曰：“王事也，子手弓而可。”商陽手弓。棄疾曰：“子射諸！”射之，斃一人，韔其弓。又及，棄疾謂之。又及，棄疾復謂之。斃二人。每斃一人，輒掩其目。止其御，曰：“吾朝不坐，燕不與，殺三人亦足以反命矣。”孔子聞之曰：“殺人之中，又有禮焉。”子路怫然進曰：“人臣之節，當君大事，唯力所及，死而後已。夫子何善此？”子曰：“然，如汝言也。吾取其有不忍殺人之心而已。”

Chu attacked Wu. Shang Yang, the minster of labor for Chu, and the prince Chen Qiji were pursuing the Wu army. When they caught up to them, Qiji said, "We're on a mission from the king. Take up your bow." Shang Yang took up his bow.

Qiji said, "Shoot at them!" Shang Yang shot, and one man fell dead. He then put his bow away.

They caught up again, and Qiji said the same thing as before. Again they caught up, and again Qiji did the same as before. Now two more people had fallen dead. Each time someone fell dead, Shang Yang covered his eyes.

He stopped the driver and said, "I do not have a high enough position to have a seat at court or attend ministerial banquets, so killing three people should be sufficient for me to report back."

11. For information about this poem, see 27.2n12.

Confucius heard about this and said, "There is *li* even in killing others."

Indignant, Zilu stepped forward and said, "When a well-disciplined vassal undertakes one of the great affairs of his sovereign, he puts all his effort into it, even unto death. Why do you praise this behavior?"

Confucius said, "What you say is correct. I was just talking about how he couldn't bear to kill others."

42.12

孔子在衛，司徒敬之卒，夫子弔焉。主人不哀，夫子哭不盡聲而退。蘧伯玉請曰："衛鄙俗，不習喪禮，煩吾子辱相焉。"孔子許之。掘中霤而浴，毀竈而綴足，襲於床。及葬，毀宗而躐行也，出于大門。及墓，男子西面，婦人東面，既封而歸，殷道也。孔子行之。子游問曰："君子行禮，不求變俗，夫子變之矣。"孔子曰："非此之謂也，喪事則從其質而已矣。"

When Confucius was in Wei, Situ Jingzhi passed away. Confucius went to pay his respects. The master of ceremonies displayed no sorrow, and Confucius left without having let out wails of grief. Qu Boyu said to him, "Lacking proper education in *li*, Wei has crude customs. Could I trouble you to take over?" Confucius agreed. He conducted the proceedings according to Shang-dynasty custom. In the center of the room, he had a hole dug, over which the body was washed. He had bricks removed from the hearth and bound to the feet, then had the body placed on a bed and clothed. When it was time for the burial, they made a chink in the wall of the ancestral temple for the spirit of the roads to pass through, then they all departed through the main gate. At the gravesite, men gathered facing west and women facing east. After sealing the grave, they returned.

Ziyou asked, "When a *junzi* acts according to *li*, he should not alter custom, and yet you changed it."

Confucius said, "I wouldn't say that. A funeral ceremony is conducted according to what is most fundamental, and that's all there is to it."[12]

42.13

宣公八年六月辛巳，有事于太廟，而東門襄仲卒，壬午猶繹。子游見其故，以問孔子曰："禮與?"孔子曰："非禮也，卿卒不繹。"

On the *xinsi* day in the sixth month of the eighth year of Duke Xuan's reign, there was an event at the duke's ancestral temple during which the high official Dongmen

12. In other words, what matters is that there is an opportunity for mourning, not the details of the ceremony.

Xiangzhong suddenly passed away. The next day, things went on as before. Seeking the reason for this, Ziyou asked Confucius, "Was this in accord with *li*?"

Confucius said, "No. When a high official dies, things should not go on as before."[13]

42.14

季桓子喪，康子練而無衰。子游問於孔子曰："既服練服，可以除衰乎？"孔子曰："無衰衣者，不以見賓，何以除焉？"

Ji Huanzi passed away. On the one-year anniversary, Kangzi held the memorial ceremony but without wearing the customary burlap apron. Ziyou asked Confucius, "Is it permissible to wear mourning attire that doesn't include a burlap apron?"

Confucius said, "One cannot greet guests without wearing a burlap apron, so how could one do without it?"

42.15

邾人以同母異父之昆弟死，將爲之服，因顏克而問禮於孔子。子曰："繼父同居者，則異父昆弟從爲之服；不同居，繼父且猶不服，況其子乎？"

The younger half-brother of a man of Zhū passed away. The two had had different fathers, and in preparing for the funeral the man was unsure of whether he should wear mourning attire. Through Yan Ke, he asked Confucius about the proper *li*. Confucius said, "If you lived under the same roof with your stepfather, then you would wear mourning attire for his funeral, but not if you didn't live with him. Wouldn't that go even more so for his son?"

42.16

齊師侵魯，公叔務人遇人入保，負杖而息。務人泣曰："使之雖病，任之雖重，君子弗能謀，士弗能死，不可也。我則既言之矣，敢不勉乎？"與其鄰嬖童汪錡乘往，奔敵死焉。皆殯，魯人欲勿殤童汪錡，問於孔子，曰："能執干戈，以衛社稷，可無殤乎！"

A Qi army invaded Lu. Gongshu Wuren met a man entering the fortress leaning on his staff and out of breath. In tears, Wuren said, "We exhaust them with labor and burden them with taxes. It is impermissible for a *junzi* to not participate, for an

13. Dongmen died in 601 BCE, well before Confucius or Ziyou had been born, so Ziyou is asking about a past event. Dongmen played an ignominious role in Lu history. After the death of Duke Wen, he had two legitimate successors murdered and installed Duke Xuan, and it was under Duke Xuan that ruling authority shifted to the Three Huans. So, it is with some irony, but not without cosmic justice, that Dongmen was not honored by Duke Xuan and the Three Huans upon his death.

official to not be willing to die. This being the case, dare I shrink from battle?" At that, he and his beloved servant boy Wang Yi rode forth on a chariot, rushed the enemy, and died in battle.

In preparation for the funeral, the people of Lu, wishing to not give Wang Yi the funeral of merely a minor, asked the advice of Confucius.

Confucius said, "Anyone who can carry a weapon and shield into battle to defend the homeland altars may be given the funeral of an adult!"[14]

42.17

魯昭公夫人吴孟子卒，不赴于諸侯。孔子既致仕，而往弔焉。適于季氏，季氏不絰，孔子投絰而不拜。子游問曰："禮與?"孔子曰："主人未成服，則弔者不絰焉，禮也。"

Wu Mengzi, wife of Lu Duke Zhao passed away. No notices were sent to the noble lords of the other states. Although Confucius was already retired at the time, he went to pay his respects. When he saw that Jisun[15] was not wearing a mourning belt, he removed his own, and he declined to kneel in reverence. Ziyou asked him about this, "Was this in accord with *li*?"

Confucius said, "It is in accord with *li* for a mourner to not wear a mourning belt if the host is not properly dressed in mourning attire."[16]

42.18

公父穆伯之喪，敬姜晝哭；文伯之喪，晝夜哭。孔子曰："季氏之婦，可謂知禮矣! 愛而無私，上下有章。"

At the funeral for Gongfu Mubo of the Jisun clan, Mubo's wife Jingjiang wept all day long. At the funeral of her son Wenbo, she wept all day and all night.

Confucius said, "This wife of Jisun truly understands *li*. Full of love and selflessness, she makes the perfect display up and down the hierarchy."[17]

14. According to CQZZ ("Ai" 11.1), this episode occurred in 484 BCE and is part of a longer story, some of which can also be found in *Dialogues* 41.2.

15. As head of the government, Jisun would have been the officiant and should have been dressed in some form of mourning attire.

16. Although Confucius seems to be concerned with outward niceties here, his point seems to be that a funeral ceremony is a communal activity more for the living than for the dead, and that if even the officiant cannot muster the appropriate emotional response, then the occasion is spoiled for everyone else.

17. This sentence emphasizes the emotional rather than dogmatic or rule-following aspect of *li*. Jingjiang makes just the right display of sorrow—long for her husband and even longer for her son—not out of calculation but out of selfless abandon.

42.19

南宫縚之妻，孔子兄之女。喪其姑，而誨之髽，曰："爾毋從從爾，毋扈扈爾。蓋榛以爲笄，長尺，而總八寸。"

The daughter of Confucius' older brother was the wife of Nangong Tao. When her mother-in-law passed away, Confucius instructed her on how to wear her mourning topknot: "It should be neither too casual nor too restrained.[18] Use a pin of hazelnut wood nine inches long, with ribbons hanging down seven inches."

42.20

子張有父之喪，公明儀相焉。問啓顙於孔子，孔子曰："拜而後啓顙，頹乎其順；啓顙而後拜，頎乎其至也。三年之喪，吾從其至也。"

Gongming Yi acted as officiant at the funeral of Zizhang's father. He asked Confucius about kowtowing. Confucius said, "To kneel[19] first and then kowtow[20] is reverent and keeping with expectations. To kowtow first and then kneel is to express profound devotion and is the ultimate in expressiveness. To begin the three-year mourning period, I prefer the route of ultimate expressiveness."

42.21

孔子在衛，衛之人有送葬者，而夫子觀之，曰："善哉，爲喪乎！足以爲法也。小子識之！"子貢問曰："夫子何善爾？"曰："其往也如慕，其返也如疑。"子貢曰："豈若速返而虞哉？"子曰："此情之至者也。小子識之！我未之能也。"

While Confucius was in Wei, he witnessed a funeral mourner and said to his students, "An excellent mourner. He can act as a model. Remember this one!"

18. *Casual . . . restrained, congcong* 从从 . . . *huhu* 扈扈: These two terms are unusual locutions. *Congcong* appears in only one other place in the literature of the time—in the *Chu Ci*, where it is set in parallel structure with *rongrong* 容容, by dint of which it seems to clearly mean something like leisurely (even though commentators generally focus on a preceding phrase and gloss it as the sound of a bell). However, commentators say that here *congcong* means high or tall (apparently because of its phonetic resemblance to *chong* 崇, high/tall). As for *huhu*, commentators, without explanation, say it means wide. As a single term, *hu* means restrained, moderate. Though a reduplicated term often means more of the same, *huhu* appears elsewhere in SJ, *Han shu*, and *Hou Han shu* 後漢書, where it clearly means something like bright, and in the *Han Shi* 韓詩, where it is glossed as lovely (*mei* 美). Here, it seems that it could mean either restrained or ostentatious. (Zhang, Lin, and Gao 1980)

19. To express gratitude to the attendees.

20. To express devotion to one's deceased parents.

Zigong asked, "What was so excellent about him?"

Confucius said, "On the way to the burial, you could see how he missed the deceased. On the way back, you could see how he faltered."

Zigong said, "Is this better than hurrying back to perform the customary sacrificial ceremony?"

Confucius said, "It is the ultimate expression of sincere emotion. Remember this. It is something I have not yet mastered."

42.22

卞人有母死而孺子之泣者, 孔子曰: "哀則哀矣, 而難繼也。夫禮, 爲可傳也, 爲可繼也。故哭踊有節, 而變除有期。"

At the funeral for his mother, a man of Bian wept like a child. Confucius said, "In sorrow, there is sorrow, but it is difficult to pass on. *Li* is such that things can be transmitted; they can be passed on. And so there is measure to bouncing in grief on one's haunches, and a time for removing mourning attire."

42.23

孟獻子禫, 懸而不樂, 可御而不處內。子游問於孔子曰: "若是則過禮也?"孔子曰: "獻子可謂加於人一等矣。"

For the ceremony marking the last day of the three-year mourning period for one of his parents, Meng Xianzi had a rack of ceremonial bells and chimes placed but did not have them played. It was permissible for him to have sex again, but he did not enter his inner chambers. Ziyou asked Confucius, "Were these transgressions of *li*?"

Confucius said, "Xianzi can be considered to be a step above most people."

42.24

魯人有朝祥而暮歌者, 子路笑之。孔子曰: "由! 爾責於人終無已。夫三年之喪, 亦以久矣。"子路出, 孔子曰: "又多乎哉! 逾月則其善也。"

Zilu ridiculed a man of Lu for singing at night when that very morning he had just held the ceremony marking the last day of the three-year mourning period for one of his parents. Confucius said, "Yóu! You're always blaming others. Three years is a long time to mourn."

Zilu left, and Confucius said, "How much longer should he have waited? Actually, a month would be ideal."

42.25

子路問於孔子曰:“傷哉貧也!生而無以供養,死則無以爲禮也。”孔子曰:“啜菽飲水,盡其歡心,斯爲之孝乎。斂手足形,旋葬而無椁,稱其財,斯謂之禮,貧何傷乎?”

Zilu inquired of Confucius, "Poverty is so harmful. One is unable to care for one's parents while they are alive and unable to afford a proper ceremony when they pass on."

Confucius said, "It is *xiao* enough to make one's parents happy by serving them beans to eat and water to drink. It is *li* enough to prepare the body for burial and expeditiously bury it according to one's means, absent an outer coffin. What is so harmful about poverty?"[21]

42.26

吴延陵季子聘于上國,適齊。於其返也,其長子死於嬴、博之間。孔子聞之,曰:“延陵季子,吴之習於禮者也。”往而觀其葬焉。其斂以時服而已;其壙掩坎,深不至於泉;其葬無盟器之贈。既葬,其封廣輪揜坎,其高可肘隱也。既封,則季子乃左袒,右還其封,且號者三,曰:“骨肉歸于土,命也!若魂氣則無所不之,則無所不之!”而遂行。孔子曰:“延陵季子之禮,其合矣。”

Jizi of Yanling was sent by Wu as an emissary to build relations with the Upper States[22] and had gone to Qi. On his way back, his oldest son, who was with him, died between the towns of Ying and Bo.[23] Confucius heard about this and said, "Jizi of Yanling is someone who is well-versed in the *li* of Wu."

He went to observe the funeral. Preparing the corpse consisted only of dressing it in seasonal clothing. The burial pit was just big enough for the coffin and above

21. It may be worth noting here that Confucius was no stranger to poverty himself (see 43.27, for example).

22. This is a reference to the states of the central plains vis-à-vis the states to the south. However, it is probably just a coincidence that such a reference aligns with our standard map orientation, as there was no standard map orientation in ancient China. It could be a reference to status levels on the Zhou hierarchy, as the central states were viewed as superior, and the earliest reference appears to be by a central state with reference to Wu (see CQZZ "Cheng" 7.5). More likely, though, it is a reference to perceived geographic elevation. Major rivers in China tend to flow from the west or northwest to the east or southeast, so the commonly perceived geological alignment in China approximately tracks modern map alignment. For example, there is a reference in CQZZ ("Zhao" 14.3) of the Chu king sending someone to inspect the troops of the upper state, and the exact location is a city further up the Yangtze, to the northwest. The other main rivers of the Chu capital run to the capital from due north. (Yee 1994; Tan 1996)

23. Ying and Bo lie on a likely route between the Lu and Qi capitals, so Jizi was probably returning to Wu via Lu. (Tan 1996)

the water table. No burial items were left as offerings. The mound on top of the grave fit the parameters of the grave and was built high enough to lean on. After the tomb was sealed, Jizi bared the left half of his torso and circled the mound to his right, shouting three times, "Flesh and bones return to the earth! Such is fate, but your soul can go anywhere! It can go anywhere!"

He then departed.

Confucius said, "The *li* of Jizi of Yanling was fitting."[24]

42.27

子游問喪之具。孔子曰："稱家之有亡焉。"子游曰："有亡惡於齊?"孔子曰："有也，則無過禮。苟亡矣，則斂手足形，還葬，懸棺而封。人豈有非之者哉? 故夫喪亡，與其哀不足而禮有餘，不若禮不足而哀有餘也；祭祀，與其敬不足而禮有餘，不若禮不足而敬有餘也。"

Ziyou asked about implements used during funerals. Confucius said, "They should depend on the means of the family."

Ziyou said, "How does one know where to draw the line?"

Confucius said, "A family of means should not transgress *li*. A poor family can prepare the body and then simply lower the coffin into a narrow grave with ropes, immediately sealing it. What more is necessary beyond that? In a funeral, it is better to have an excess of sorrow and a lack of *li* than to have an excess of *li* and a lack of sorrow. In a sacrificial ceremony, it is better to have an excess of reverence and a lack of *li* than to have a lack of reverence and an excess of *li*."

42.28

伯高死於衛，赴於孔子。子曰："吾惡乎哭諸? 兄弟，吾哭諸廟；父之友，吾哭諸廟門之外；師，吾哭之寢；朋友，吾哭之寢門之外；所知，吾哭之諸野。今於野則已疏，於寢則已重。夫由賜也而見我，吾哭於賜氏。"遂命子貢爲之主，曰："爲爾哭也來者，汝拜

24. This passage is especially interesting for how closely it coheres with the archaeological record. There is archaeological evidence that the practice of building mounds over very large tombs belonging to royalty and nobility diffused into the Central Plains from the south during the Spring and Autumn period. Among the earliest in the south is in Shucheng, Anhui, less than 200 miles west of Yanling, Jiangsu. This passage seems to depict one aspect of how exposure to the practice (on a smaller scale) might have occurred. The prevalence of smaller-scale mounds in the time of Confucius, for which there is sporadic evidence going as far back as the Neolithic, is still a matter of debate among scholars. While there is little direct evidence, scholars like Yin Qun (2001) say that the precise layout of cemeteries over long periods of time suggests that graves were easily visible from the surface, and that mounds are the best explanation, but that the mounds have since been eroded or destroyed. See also 44.3. (Yin 2001; Falkenhausen 2006; Suo 2020)

之；知伯高而來者，汝勿拜。”既哭，使子張往弔焉。未至，冉求在衛，攝束帛、乘馬而以將之。孔子聞之，曰：“異哉！徒使我不成禮於伯高者，是冉求也。”

Confucius' acquaintance Bo Gao passed away in Wei, and Confucius received the funeral notice in Lu. Confucius said, "Where should I go to weep for him? For a brother, I would weep in the ancestral temple. For the friend of my father, I would weep outside the gate of the ancestral temple. For a teacher, I would weep at the deathbed. For a friend, I would weep outside the door of the bedchamber. For an acquaintance, I would weep in an open space. If I weep in an open space in this case, it would seem too distant, and to weep at the bedchamber would seem excessive. Since it was Zigong who introduced him to me, I should weep at Zigong's house."

He made Zigong into the officiant, saying, "If anyone comes to weep with you, kneel in a display of gratitude. If anyone comes just on behalf of Bo Gao, don't kneel." After weeping, he sent Zizhang to Wei to extend his respects. Before arriving, Ran Qiu, who was already in Wei, had given a bolt of silk and a team of four horses on Confucius' behalf.

Confucius heard about this and said, "Bizarre! Leave it to Ran Qiu to make me commit an error of *li* toward Bo Gao."[25]

42.29

子路有姊之喪，可以除之矣，而弗除。孔子曰：“何不除也？”子路曰：“吾寡兄弟，而弗忍也。”孔子曰：“行道之人皆弗忍。先王制禮，過之者俯而就之，不至者企而及之。”子路聞之，遂除之。

After mourning the death of his older sister, the time came when Zilu could remove his mourning attire, and yet he didn't. Confucius said, "Why don't you remove it?"

Zilu said, "I don't have many siblings, and I just can't bear it."

Confucius said, "Everyone practicing the *dao* has times when they can't bear something. When the Ancient Kings established the system of *li*, those who exceeded the standards had to cut back, and those who couldn't achieve them had to try harder." After hearing this, Zilu removed his mourning attire.[26]

42.30

伯魚之喪母也，期而猶哭。夫子聞之曰：“誰也？”門人曰：“鯉也。”孔子曰：“嘻！其甚也，非禮也。”伯魚聞之，遂除之。

25. Compare 43.13, where Confucius leaves two of his horses after the funeral of an old acquaintance. The main difference in the two scenarios seems to be Confucius' sudden upwelling of emotion in 43.13.

26. Although emotion has priority over *li* (42.27), *li* has the function of giving us practical limits.

Boyu's mother died, and he was still crying after the mourning period. Confucius heard the sound and said, "Who's crying?"

An attendant said, "Boyu."

Confucius said, "Sheesh. He's overdoing it and violating *li*." When Boyu heard what his father said, he stopped mourning.

42.31

衛公使其大夫求婚於季氏，桓子問禮於孔子。子曰："同姓爲宗，有合族之義，故繫之以姓而弗别，綴之以食而弗殊。雖百世，婚姻不得通，周道然也。"桓子曰："魯、衛之先，雖寡兄弟，今已絶遠矣。可乎？"孔子曰："固非禮也。夫上治祖禰，以尊尊之；下治子孫，以親親之；旁治昆弟，所以教睦也。此先王不易之教也。"

The Duke of Wei sent a high official to Lu, seeking the hand of a Ji woman in marriage. Ji Huanzi asked Confucius about the *li* of it.[27] Confucius said, "People of the same surname share an ancestor, meaning that they are of the same clan. And so people are connected by their surname and thereby indivisible. If they need to help each other, they provide food without distinction. And even over one hundred generations they must not intermarry. Such is the *dao* of the Zhou."

Huanzi said, "The progenitors of Lu and Wei were brothers, but since today the families are entirely separate, is it permissible?"

Confucius said, "It is still in violation of *li*. We keep order with respect to the ancestors by paying due reverence to them according to their position in the family hierarchy. We keep order with respect to our descendants by building close ties with them. It is up to our generation to instruct in the ways of harmony. It is an instruction from the Former Kings that cannot be altered."[28]

27. Ji 季 Huanzi was a descendant of the Lu ducal line, which was descended from the Zhou royal line, which had the surname Ji 姬. The Wei ducal line was also descended from the Zhou royal line and had the same Ji 姬 surname. Ji Huanzi knew that it was against *li* for two people of the same lineage to intermarry, but he went to Confucius to see if there was a way to accommodate it in this case.

28. There are medical reasons that all human societies have taboos against incest, but how the taboo is implemented varies widely. In premodern Europe, the near familial limit was no closer than first cousin, which even still could result in genetic abnormalities. Here, Confucius carries the custom to the other extreme. His reasoning lies in the well-ordering of the family hierarchy. Records were kept for many generations following the male bloodline, and ancestors were afforded a level of reverence according to their distance from the present head of the line. Because the woman's bloodline was not recorded, it did not need to enter into such calculations, but if a woman of the same surname intermarried, there would be an ancestral connection, severely complicating the hierarchical calculations, not just for the present but for all future generations. This concern could upset family harmony, which is Confucius' overriding concern.

42.32

有若問於孔子曰:“國君之於百姓,如之何?”孔子曰:“皆有宗道焉。故雖國君之尊,猶百世不廢其親,所以崇愛也。雖以族人之親,而不敢戚君,所以謙也。”

You Ruo asked Confucius, “What is the relationship between a sovereign and his distant relatives?”

Confucius said, “The system of ancestral lineage is always there. Although the sovereign is in an exalted position, he demonstrates his love and respect for his relatives by not disclaiming them even after a hundred generations. And even though the sovereign’s distant relatives may be related to him, they demonstrate their humility by not daring to get too close to him.”

43

Zixia Asks about the Finer Points of *Li*

Here again, a chapter that is ostensibly about *li* begins with a passage that is not about *li* at all and is instead about avenging murdered parents. The chapter ends with a passage about a makeshift shroud for burying a dog. In between are a variety of passages discussing the ins and outs of *li* behavior, with Confucius depicted as an authority. As above, the reader is challenged to extrapolate generalities from the specific circumstances. How should one fully express *li* in one's own life?

43.1

子夏問於孔子曰: "居父母之仇, 如之何?"孔子曰: "寢苫枕干, 不仕, 弗與共天下也。遇於朝市, 不返兵而鬥 。"曰: "請問居昆弟之仇, 如之何?"孔子曰: "仕, 弗與同國, 銜君命而使, 雖遇之不鬥。"曰: "請問從昆弟之仇如之何?"曰: "不爲魁, 主人能報之, 則執兵而陪其後。"

Zixia asked Confucius, "How should one avenge a parent's murder?"[1]

Confucius said, "Sleep on a reed mourning mat with your shield as a pillow.[2] Do not work in the government, and do not be satisfied living under the same sky with the murderer. Carry a weapon with you, and when you encounter this person in the court or in the marketplace, attack."

Zixia asked, "How should one avenge a brother's death?"

Confucius said, "Go ahead and work in the government, but not in the same state as him. If you are sent to his state on a government mission, do not attack."

Zixia said, "How should one avenge a cousin's death?"

Confucius said, "Do not take the lead. If the head of the family wishes to seek revenge, follow behind with weapon in hand."

1. *Avenge a parent's murder, fu mu zhi chou* 父母之仇: parent's vendetta. The severity of Confucius' response to each of Zixia's questions in this episode suggests (1) that the family member in question has died innocently by another's hand and (2) that legal recourse has failed.

2. In other words, he should be prepared at all times to take revenge. This is the locus classicus for this phrase, which later became an idiom.

43.2

子夏問："三年之喪既卒哭，金革之事無避，禮與？初有司爲之乎？"孔子曰："夏后氏之喪三年，既殯而致事，殷人既葬而致事，周人既卒哭而致事。《記》曰：'君子不奪人之親，亦不奪故也。'"子夏曰："金革之事無避，非與？"孔子曰："吾聞諸老聃曰：'魯公伯禽有爲爲之也。'今以三年之喪從利者，吾弗知也。"

Zixia asked, "Is it in accord with *li* to stop excusing oneself from going to war after the ten-day mark[3] of the three-year mourning period for one's parents? Was there originally a government policy about this?"

Confucius said, "For the three-year mourning period during the Xia dynasty, one officially resigned one's office after the body was encoffined.[4] During the Shang, one officially resigned after the funeral. For the Zhou, one officially resigns after the ten-day mark. It is written: 'A sovereign does not deprive people of the opportunity to care for their parents or mourn their death.'"

Zixia asked, "So it is not a violation to stop excusing oneself from going to war?"

Confucius said, "Lao Dan told me that the Lu founder Bo Qin did it under special circumstances.[5] What I don't understand is all the people who try to benefit themselves during the three-year mourning period."

43.3

子夏問於孔子曰："《記》云：周公相成王，教之以世子之禮。有諸？"孔子曰："昔者成王嗣立，幼，未能莅阼，周公攝政而治，抗世子之法於伯禽，欲王之知父子、君臣之道，所以善成王也。夫知爲人子者，然後可以爲人父；知爲人臣者，然後可以爲人君；知事人者，然後可以使人。是故抗世子法於伯禽，使成王知父子、君臣、長幼之義焉。凡君之於世子，親則父也，尊則君也，有父之親，有君之尊，然後兼天下

3. *Ten-day mark, zu ku* 卒哭: According to commentaries, *zu ku* was the time during the three-year mourning period for one's parents when one would stop being liable to break into tears at any time of the day.

4. The inferential link between resigning from office and excusing oneself from going to war has to do with the deep mourning that is presumed to occur upon the death of a parent. It was customary to not work during the three-year mourning period, but immediately after the death of one's parent, one would be so incapacitated with grief as to even be unable to officially resign one's duties. The question here has to do with the length of that period of incapacitation. When it is over, could a person then go to war? The financial hardship of being out of work during the mourning period could be significant, as could the amount earned in a successful battle.

5. According to the *Documents*, Bo Qin, the first duke of Lu, took up arms to deal with an uprising of the Rong people. Since the story is in the *Documents*, Confucius wouldn't need Laozi to tell him about it. The part that Laozi presumably provided is that Bo Qin did this after the ten-day mark of the mourning period for his mother.

而有之，不可不慎也。行一物而三善皆得，唯世子齒於學之謂也。世子齒於學，則國人觀之，曰：'此將君我，而與我齒讓，何也？'曰：'有父在，則禮然。'然而衆知父子之道矣。其二曰：'此將君我，而與我齒讓，何也？'曰：'有君在，則禮然。'然而衆知君臣之義矣。其三曰：'此將君我，而與我齒讓，何也？'曰：'長長也，則禮然。'然而衆知長幼之節矣。故父在斯爲子，君在斯爲臣，居子與臣之位，所以尊君而親親也。在學，學之爲父子焉，學之爲君臣焉，學之爲長幼焉。父子、君臣、長幼之道得，而後國治。語曰：'樂正司業，父師司成。一有元良，萬國以貞。'世子之謂。聞之曰：'爲人臣者，殺其身而有益於君則爲之。'况于其身以善其君乎？周公優爲也。"

Zixia asked Confucius, "It is written that the Duke of Zhou acted as regent for King Cheng and taught him the *li* of the crown prince. Is this true?"

Confucius said, "At the time that King Cheng acceded to the throne, he was still a child and so unable to assume oversight of the government. The Duke of Zhou assumed this responsibility and also made clear the succession of his own state of Lu to his son Bo Qin, with the wish that the king could understand the *dao* of father–son and sovereign–minister relationships, for the purpose of fostering virtue in King Cheng. It is only by understanding how to be a son that one can be a good father. It is only by understanding how to be a minister that one can be an effective sovereign. It is only by understanding how to serve others that one can effectively lead others. Thus, by making clear the succession of his own state of Lu to his son Bo Qin, he helped King Cheng understand the *yi* of the relationships of father–son, sovereign–minister, and elder–youth.

"In the case of a sovereign and his crown prince, affection is directed toward the father and reverence toward the sovereign. Only when the crown prince feels and expresses love toward his father and reverence for his sovereign can such feelings become common throughout the land. One cannot neglect this. One correct act can have three positive consequences. This is how a crown prince learns.

"When a crown prince learns well, the people of the country see it, and someone may ask, 'This person will be my sovereign in the future—why does he defer to me based on age?' Someone may answer, 'This is how *li* is when a father is present.' In this way, everyone learns the *dao* of the father–son relationship.

"Someone else may ask, 'This person will be my sovereign in the future—why does he defer to me based on age?' Someone may answer, 'This is how *li* is when a sovereign is present.' In this way, everyone learns the *yi* of the sovereign–minister relationship.

"Someone else may ask, 'This person will be my sovereign in the future—why does he defer to me based on age?' Someone may answer, 'This is how *li* is when there is respect for elders.' In this way, everyone learns the etiquette of the elder–youth relationship.[6]

6. Confucius' point here seems to be that deference based on rank is the easy—and expected—case. After all, rank often goes along with power, and it is in a person's self-interest to defer to the powerful.

"While the father is still alive, he is a son; while the sovereign is still alive, he is a minister. Being in the positions of son and minister allows him to show reverence for a sovereign and affection toward a parent. In this way, he learns to be both a father and a son, to be both a sovereign and a minister, to be both an elder and a youth. With the roles of father and son, sovereign and minister, elder and youth, the state will be well-governed.

"Someone once said, 'His teacher and mentor manage his learning and development. With a beginning in goodness, all states will show devotion.'[7] This refers to a crown prince.

"I've heard it said, 'A minister is willing to sacrifice himself for the benefit of his sovereign.' Isn't it even better if you can improve the sovereign and also come out ahead yourself? The Duke of Zhou excelled at doing this."

43.4

子夏問於孔子曰："居君之母與妻之喪，如之何？"孔子曰："居處、言語、飲食衎爾。於喪所，則稱其服而已。""敢問伯母之喪，如之何？"孔子曰："伯母、叔母疏衰期，而踊不絶地。姑、姊、妹之大功，踊絶於地。若知此者，由文矣哉。"

Zixia asked Confucius, "When the sovereign's mother or wife passes away, what should we do?"

Confucius said, "In your daily life, in your speech, and in your eating habits, be your normal, contented self. Near the mourning area, wear suitable attire. That's all."

"What about when a paternal uncle's wife dies?"

Confucius said, "For women who married into the family, wear your second-degree mourning attire for one year, and when you are weeping at the funeral, rise up from your haunches but don't leap off the ground. For women born into the family, wear your third-degree mourning attire, and when you are weeping at the funeral, rise up from your haunches and leap clear of the ground. Such is the civil way to behave."[8]

Deference based on age, however, is more difficult to carry out but also more admirable and important. In a virtuous society, people care for and respect their elders, whether or not they have power.

7. This sentence is a near verbatim quotation of a passage from the "Taijia 3" chapter of the *Documents*, in which the king's trusted prime minister advises him that if one person (i.e., the king) is good, the whole land will follow suit.

8. Traditionally, there are five degrees of mourning attire and corresponding periods of mourning. The first degree has the coarsest fabric and longest period and is for those who are closest and one rung above on the hierarchy. As relations grow more distant, the mourning fabric becomes less coarse and the mourning period becomes shorter. Each degree is purported to reflect the degree of one's grief. There is an interesting inconsistency in this passage. One expresses more grief in dress for women who marry into the family than for women born into the family, but the degree of expression is the opposite

43.5

子夏問於夫子曰："凡喪小功已上，虞、祔、練、祥之祭皆沐浴？於三年之喪，子則盡其情矣？"孔子曰："豈徒祭而已哉？三年之喪，身有瘍則浴，首有瘡則沐，病則飲酒食肉。毀瘠而病，君子不爲也。毀則死者，君子爲之無子，則祭之沐浴，爲齊潔也，非爲飾也。"

Zixia asked Confucius, "To fully express one's feelings during the three-year mourning period for one's parents, one should bathe and wash one's hair only prior to each of the four ceremonies for which one wears fourth-degree mourning attire or above. Is that correct?"

Confucius replied, "Why only for these ceremonies? During the three-year mourning period, bathe when the skin becomes inflamed, and wash your hair when the scalp becomes inflamed. If you fall ill, resume taking meat and alcohol. A *junzi* does not mourn to the point of illness or emaciation. If one ends up dying, there will be no descendants. Thus, bathing with respect to sacrificial ceremonies is for purification and cleanliness, not for vanity."

43.6

子夏問於孔子曰："客至無所舍，而夫子曰：'生，於我乎館。'客死無所殯矣，夫子曰：'於我乎殯。'敢問禮與？仁者之心與？"孔子曰："吾聞諸老聃曰：'館人，使若有之，惡有有之而不得殯乎？'夫仁者，制禮者也。故禮者不可不省也。禮不同不異，不豐不殺，稱其義以爲之宜。故曰：'我戰則剋，祭則受福'，蓋得其道矣。"

Zixia asked Confucius, "If a visitor comes and cannot find a place to stay, I have heard you say, 'I'll put you up.' If a visitor passes away and there is no place to lay out the body, I have heard you say, 'Use my place to lay him out.' Did you say these things because they are the things to do according to *li* or because of your feelings of *ren*?"

Confucius said, "I once heard Lao Dan say, 'When putting someone up, they should feel at home.' How could it be that someone is staying in his own home but is not laid out for a funeral when he dies? *Ren* is what guides *li*. Thus, one must look inside oneself for *li*. For *li*, there is no guide to follow or deviate from; there is no absolute excess or deficiency. You simply follow *yi* and do what is appropriate. That is why it is said, 'I stand to gain victory only by fighting, and stand to gain good fortune only by performing sacrificial ceremonies.' This seems to capture the *dao* of it."

---

when it comes to actual weeping. In fact, it seems to be the point of this passage that although women marry out of one's household and are thus of less economic and practical value, there is still a strong emotional attachment.

43·7

孔子食於季氏, 食祭, 主人不辭。不食亦不飲而飡。子夏問曰: “禮也?”孔子曰: “非禮也, 從主人也。吾食於少施氏而飽, 少施氏食我以禮, 吾食祭, 作而辭曰: ‘疏食, 不足祭也。’吾飡, 而作辭曰: ‘疏食, 不敢以傷吾子之性。’主人不以禮, 客不敢盡禮; 主人盡禮, 則客不敢不盡禮也。”

Confucius was dining at the home of Jisun. After the premeal offering, the host did not speak the customary words. Confucius complimented the meal but neither ate nor drank. Zixia asked, “Is this in accordance with *li*?”

Confucius said, “Whether or not it is in accordance with *li* all depends on the host. Once when I dined at the home of Shaoshi, I ate my fill because Shaoshi treated me with *li*. When I rose to perform the premeal offering, he said, ‘Such coarse food is not worthy of being offered.’ To my host, I complimented the food, and then he rose and said to me, ‘I dare not harm your body with such coarse food.’ If a host does not lead with *li*, a guest will not wholeheartedly express *li*. If a host wholeheartedly expresses *li*, how could a guest dare not wholeheartedly express *li*?”

43·8

子夏問曰: “官於大夫, 既升於公, 而反爲之服, 禮與?”孔子曰: “管仲遇盜, 取二人焉, 上之爲公臣, 曰: ‘所以遊, 僻者, 可人也。’公許。管仲卒, 桓公使爲之服。官於大夫者爲之服, 自管仲始也, 有君命焉。”

Zixia asked, “Suppose one works in the household of a high official and later is elevated to a government position. When the high official dies, would it be in accord with *li* to observe a period of mourning for him?”

Confucius said, “Guan Zhong once selected two former bandits to work in his household and later recommended them for posts in the government, saying, ‘They became outlaws because they got mixed up with the wrong crowd. They can be made into good people.’ The duke agreed. After Guan Zhong passed away, Duke Huan ordered that they observe a period of mourning for him. It was with Guan Zhong that former employees of high officials began observing mourning periods—because it had been decreed by a sovereign.”

43·9

子貢問居父母喪。孔子曰: “敬爲上, 哀次之, 瘠爲下, 顏色稱情, 戚容稱服。”曰: “請問居兄弟之喪。”孔子曰: “則存乎書筴已。”

Zigong asked about mourning one’s own parent.

Confucius said, "The most important thing is reverence. Sorrow is second to that. Becoming all emaciated is the least important. Your emotions should match your expression, and your expression should match your attire."

Zigong said, "What about mourning one's brother?"

Confucius said, "This is all written down in relevant books."[9]

43.10

子貢問於孔子曰："殷人既窆而弔於壙，周人反哭而弔於家，如之何？"孔子曰："反哭之弔也，喪之至也。反而亡矣，失之矣。於斯爲甚，故弔之。死，人卒事也。殷以慤，吾從周。殷人既練之明日而祔于祖，周人既卒哭之明日祔于祖。祔，祭神之始事也。周以戚，吾從殷。"

Zigong asked Confucius, "During the Shang, people grieved at the graveside after the coffin was lowered into the ground. Now, in the Zhou, people return weeping and grieve at home. What should we do?"

Confucius said, "It is the ultimate in mourning to return weeping and grieve at home. Returning and recognizing that the deceased is gone, one misses the deceased. The feeling is intense, and so one grieves for the deceased. Death is the final affair in our lives. The Shang were too scrupulous immediately after the funeral, so I follow the Zhou. The Shang performed the *fu* ceremony of inducting the deceased into the ancestral temple the day after the anniversary of the beginning of the three-year mourning period. The Zhou did this on the 101st day of the three-year mourning period. The *fu* ceremony is the beginning of worshipping the deceased as an ancestor. The Zhou are rushed in this, so I follow the Shang."

43.11

子貢問曰："聞諸晏子，少連、大連善居喪，其有異稱乎？"孔子曰："父母之喪，三日不怠，三月不解，期悲哀，三年憂。東夷之子，達於禮者也。"

Zigong asked, "I heard from Yanzi that Lian junior and Lian senior excelled at mourning their parents. Did they do something different from others?"

Confucius said, "In mourning their parents, for the first three days they didn't rest. For the first three months they didn't slack off. During the first year, they experienced constant sorrow. After three years, they still felt troubled. These sons of the Eastern Yi[10] achieved the *li* of it."[11]

9. Such manuals contain suggestions—guidelines—rather than hard-and-fast rules.

10. Apparently Lian junior and Lian senior were Eastern Yi. Nothing else is known of them.

11. It may be significant that there is no mention of ceremonial details here but only of affective states.

43.12

子游問曰："諸侯之世子，喪慈母如母，禮與?"孔子曰："非禮也。古者男子外有傅父，內有慈母，君命所使教子者也。何服之有？昔魯孝公少喪其母，其慈母良。及其死也，公弗忍，欲喪之。有司曰：'禮，國君慈母無服，今也君爲之服，是逆古之禮，而亂國法也。若終行之，則有司將書之，以示後世，無乃不可乎?'公曰：'古者，天子喪慈母，練冠以燕居。'遂練以喪慈母。喪慈母如母，始則魯孝公之爲也。"

Ziyou asked, "Would it be in accordance with *li* for the child of nobility to observe a mourning period for a motherly figure in his life?"

Confucius said, "It would be in violation of *li*. In ancient times, a son of nobility had a mentor outside the household and a motherly figure inside the household who were designated to teach the child. How is it that he would observe a period of mourning for them?

"However, Duke Xiao of Lu lost his mother when he was small, and a motherly figure was very good to him as he grew up. When she passed away, it was unbearable for the duke, and he wanted to observe a period of mourning. The official in charge said, 'According to *li*, a sovereign does not observe a mourning period for a motherly figure in his life. If you go through with it, it would be in violation of the ancient *li* and upend the state's role as a model of behavior. It would also be recorded by state officials and passed down to posterity. Do you really think you should do it?' The duke said, 'In ancient times, the king mourned a motherly figure by wearing a second-year mourning cap at home.' He then donned his second-year mourning cap and mourned the motherly figure in his life. The practice of mourning a motherly figure as one would mourn one's own mother began with Duke Xiao doing this."

43.13

孔子適衛，遇舊館人之喪，入而哭之哀。出，使子貢脫驂以贈之。子貢曰："於所識之喪，不能有所贈。贈於舊館，不已多乎?"孔子曰："吾向入哭之，遇一哀而出涕。吾惡夫涕而無以將之。小子行焉。"

Once when Confucius went to Wei, a person who had previously given him lodging had just passed away. Confucius attended the funeral and grieved in sorrow. Upon leaving, he told Zigong to untie two of the horses from his team of four and give them as a gift to the man's family.

Zigong said, "According to the *li* of mourning acquaintances, giving a gift is not allowed. And even if you want to give a gift to someone who once put you up, isn't this too much?"

Confucius replied, "When I went in to grieve him, I was suddenly moved to tears. I hate it when someone is moved to tears and yet does not leave a gift. Please do as I said."[12]

43.14

子路問於孔子曰:"魯大夫練而杖,禮也?"孔子曰:"吾不知也。"子路出,謂子貢曰:"吾以爲夫子無所不知,夫子亦徒有所不知也。"子貢曰:"子所問何哉?"子路曰:"由問:'魯大夫練而杖,禮與?'夫子曰:'吾不知也。'"子貢曰:"止,吾將爲子問之。"遂趨而進,曰:"練而杖,禮與?"孔子曰:"非禮也。"子貢出,謂子路曰:"子謂夫子而弗知之乎?夫子徒無所不知也。子問非也。禮,居是邦,則不非其大夫。"

Zilu asked Confucius, "Is it in accord with *li* for a high official of Lu to still carry a mourning staff after the first year of a three-year mourning period?"

Confucius said, "I don't know."

Zilu departed and told Zigong, "I thought our teacher knew everything, but just now he said there's something he doesn't know."

Zigong said, "What did you ask him?"

Zilu said, "I asked him if it is in accord with *li* for a high official of Lu to still carry a mourning staff after the first year of a three-year mourning period.' He said, 'I don't know.'"

Zigong said, "Hold on. I'll ask again on your behalf." Then he politely shuffled in and asked, "Is it in accord with *li* to still carry a mourning staff after the first year of a three-year mourning period?"

Confucius said, "It is in violation of *li*."

Zigong departed and said to Zilu, "You said there was something our teacher doesn't know? Actually, there isn't. You just asked it wrong. As for *li*, one should not reproach high officials in the state in which one lives."

43.15

叔孫武叔之母死,既小斂,舉尸者出户,武孫從之,出户,乃袒,投其冠而括髮。子路嘆之。孔子曰:"是禮也。"子路問曰:"將小斂則變服,今乃出户,而夫子以爲知禮。何也?"孔子曰:"由,汝問非也。君子不舉人以質士。"

The mother of Shusun Wushu passed away, and the body was laid out. When it was carried out of the bedroom, Wushu followed, and when he was out, he removed his upper clothing and hat and tied up his hair with a burlap cord. Zilu sighed in disapproval.

Confucius said, "This is in accord with *li*."

12. Compare 42.28.

Zilu asked, "One should change clothes before the body is laid out. He didn't change until he left the bedchamber. Why do you say he understands *li*?"

Confucius said, "Zilu, you are not asking it right. A *junzi* does not judge an aspiring young man by typical standards."[13]

43.16

齊晏桓子卒，平仲粗衰斬，苴絰、帶、杖，以菅屨，食粥，居傍廬，寢苫枕草。其老曰："非大夫喪父之禮也。"晏子曰："唯卿大夫。"曾子以問孔子。孔子曰："晏平仲可謂能遠害矣。不以己之是駁人之非，愻辭以避咎，義也夫。"

Yan Huanzi of Qi passed away. His son, Pingzhong, began the three-year mourning period wearing burlap clothing, a burlap sash around his head, a burlap cord around his waist, and straw shoes. He leaned on a mourning staff, ate congee, and lived in a grass hut, slept on a reed mat, and used straw for a pillow. An elder of his remarked, "This is not the *li* of a high official mourning his father."

Yanzi said, "I am merely an official."[14]

Zengzi asked Confucius about this.

Confucius said, "Yan Pingzhong was capable of distancing himself from trouble. Instead of insisting that you are correct when another says you are wrong, it is better to simply use self-deprecating language to avoid trouble. It is the *yi* thing to do."[15]

43.17

季平子卒，將以君之璵璠斂，贈以珠玉。孔子初爲中都宰，聞之，歷級而救焉，曰："送而以寶玉，是猶曝尸於中原也，其示民以奸利之端，而有害於死者，安用之？且孝子不順情以危親，忠臣不兆奸以陷君。"乃止。

13. See 18.11n23 for more about Confucius and Shusun Wushu.

14. *Official, qing dafu* 卿大夫: Yan Pingzhong seems to be using this locution, which would typically mean ministers and high officials, to mean all levels of officials, hinting that he does not deserve to be ranked as a "high" official.

15. Scholars have debated the particular meaning of this passage. Speculation is that although Confucians held (and Yan Pingzhong also, seemingly) that funeral rites for parents should be uniform across classes, higher officials and nobility had distinct practices during Yan Pingzhong's time. Yan Pingzhong was criticized for not following the practices of the upper classes (since he was one of them). The point of the passage is that instead of Yan pointing out that others of his class were doing it wrong (which would have exposed him to further criticism), he redirected the topic to himself, suggesting that he wasn't worthy of his elevated status. This episode also appears in CQZZ ("Xiang" 17.7). There are two significant differences. First, the passage ends with Yan's retort. Second, Yan's retort is different. In CQZZ, he says, 唯卿為大夫, which Durrant, Li, and Schaberg translate as "Only ministers can be considered high officials" (2016, 1049). Interestingly, the *Yanzi chunqiu*, which purports to be a record of Yan Pingzhong and his times, contains both the CQZZ wording and Confucius' commentary.

When Ji Pingzi passed away, they laid out the body with a kind of precious jade piece usually reserved for the sovereign, and they intended to bury him with other precious jewels and jades as well.

At the time, Confucius had just assumed the position as mayor of Zhongdu. When he heard about this, he rushed over to stop them, saying, "To bury a body with precious jewels is akin to laying it out in the middle of a field.[16] It invites the people to resort to nefarious means for their own benefit, and it harms the deceased. Why do it? A *xiao* son does not follow his emotions if it means harming his parents, just as a conscientious minister does not engage in unseemly acts that would harm his sovereign."

They did not go through with it.[17]

43.18

孔子之弟子琴張，與宗魯友。衛齊豹見宗魯於公子孟縶，孟縶以爲參乘焉。及齊豹將殺孟縶，告宗魯，使行。宗魯曰："吾由子而事之，今聞難而逃，是僭子也。子行事乎，吾將死以事周子，而歸死於公孟，可也。"齊氏用戈擊公孟，宗魯以背蔽之，斷肱，中公孟、宗魯，皆死。琴張聞宗魯死，將往弔之。孔子曰："齊豹之盜，孟縶之賊也，汝何弔焉？君子不食奸，不受亂，不爲利病於回，不以回事人，不蓋非義，不犯非禮，汝何弔焉？"琴張乃止。

Confucius' student Qin Zhang was friends with Zong Lu. Qi Bao of Wei introduced Zong Lu to the prince Meng Zhi, who put him to work as bodyguard. Later, Qi Bao plotted to assassinate Meng Zhi.[18] Qi Bao communicated his plan to Zong Lu and advised him to flee. Zong Lu said, "I am here to serve Meng Zhi on account of you. It would be disloyal of me toward you to flee in the face of danger. Go ahead and do it. I am willing to die with Meng Zhi as a way of fully serving you."

When Qi swung at Meng with his dagger-axe, Zong Lu protected Meng with his back, resulting in his upper arm being severed. Both Meng and Zong were killed in the attack.

When Qin Zhang heard about Zong Lu's death, he planned to go and pay his respects. Confucius said, "He was behind Qi Bao's revolt and Meng Zhi's death. Why go pay your respects? A *junzi* does not accept support from people who engage in nefarious acts, does not participate in inciting disorder, does not profit from evil deeds, does not serve others for illicit purposes, does not cover up behavior that

16. Because it invites grave robbers.

17. A version of this episode also occurs in CQZZ ("Ding" 5.4), in which Yang Hu is named as the person wanting to adorn the corpse with jade. One Zhongliang Huai prevents him. Yang Hu subsequently removes Ji Pingzi's successor from power and sets the stage for open rebellion.

18. As part of an attempted coup against Duke Ling that ultimately failed (CQZZ "Zhao" 20.4).

violates *yi*, and does not commit behavior that violates *li*. Why go and pay your respects?"

And so Qin Zhang did not go through with it.

43.19

郕人子蒲卒，哭之，呼滅。子游曰："若是哭也，其野哉！孔子惡野哭者。"哭者聞之，遂改之。

Zipu of Cheng passed away. In grieving for him, a family member cried out, "Take me, too!"

Ziyou said, "Grieving in this way is uncouth. Confucius dislikes uncouth grieving." When the mourner heard this, he changed his behavior.

43.20

公父文伯卒，其妻妾皆行哭失聲。敬姜戒之曰："吾聞好外者，士死之；好內者，女死之。今吾子早夭，吾惡其以好內聞也。二三婦人之欲供先祀者，請無瘠色，無揮涕，無拊膺，無哀容，無加服，有降服，從禮而靜，是昭吾子也。"孔子聞之，曰："女智無若婦，男智莫若夫。公父氏之婦，智矣。剖情損禮，欲以明其子爲令德也。"

After Gongfu Wenbo passed away, his wife and concubines grieved with loud wails until they were hoarse. His mother Jingjiang discouraged them, saying, "I have heard that of men who favor public life, their officials are willing to die for them. Of men who favor the inner quarters, their women are willing to die for them. I would hate that my son who has died young would get a name as someone who favored the inner quarters. If you women wish to be people who perform rites of offering appropriately, you will not take on an emaciated appearance, will not constantly wipe away tears, will not pound your chest, will not look overcome with sorrow, will not overdo it with mourning attire, will remove mourning attire at the appropriate time, and will maintain composure in accordance with *li*. Acting in this way will reflect well on my son."

Confucius heard about this and said, "Wisdom in women comes with age, just as it does in men. Gongfu's mother was wise. After analyzing human behavior, she curtailed the overexpression of *li* with the intention of illuminating her son's *de* behavior."

43.21

子路與子羔仕於衛，衛有蒯聵之難。孔子在魯，聞之，曰："柴也其來，由也死矣。"既而衛使至，曰："子路死焉。"夫子哭之於中庭。有人弔者，而夫子拜之。已哭，進使者而問故，使者曰："醢之矣。"遂令左右皆覆醢，曰："吾何忍食此！"

Zilu and Zigao both held posts in Wei during the Kuaikui disturbance. Confucius heard about it in Lu and said, "Zigao will have escaped, and Zilu will have perished."

Just then, an emissary from Wei arrived and said, "Zilu passed away there." Confucius wept for him in the great hall. When people arrived to pay their respects, Confucius saluted them.[19] When he was done weeping, he invited the emissary in and asked what had happened.

The emissary said, "Meat sauce."[20]

Confucius then had his students dump out all the meat sauce in his house, saying, "How could I bear to eat it!"

43.22

季桓子死，魯大夫朝服而弔。子游問於孔子曰："禮乎？"夫子不答。他日，又問。夫子曰："始死則矣，羔裘、玄冠者，易之而已，汝何疑焉？"

After Ji Huanzi passed away, high officials of Lu paid their respects wearing court robes.[21] Ziyou asked Confucius, "Is this in accord with *li*?" Confucius did not respond.

Another day, Ziyou asked again.

Confucius said, "After a person has just died, those close to him who normally wear lambskin and black silk caps should change clothes, that's all. Why is there even a question?"

43.23

孔子有母之喪，既練，陽虎弔焉，私於孔子曰："今季氏將大饗境內之士，子聞諸？"孔子答曰："丘弗聞也。若聞之，雖在衰絰，亦欲與往。"陽虎曰："子謂不然乎？季氏饗士，不及子也。"陽虎出，曾點問曰："語之何謂也？"孔子曰："己則衰服，猶應其言，示所以不非也。"

When Confucius was observing the mourning period for his mother and it was the one-year ceremony, Yang Hu came to pay his respects and said privately to Confucius, "Have you heard that Jisun is holding a large banquet for all Lu officials?"

19. This may indicate that Confucius assumed the role of officiant.

20. After Zilu was killed in Wei, the Duke apparently ordered that he be given one of the more gruesome punishments—namely, being turned into meat sauce to be eaten as a garnish, presumably by the duke and his cohorts. This macabre detail is not in the CQZZ ("Ai" 15.5) account.

21. An expression of grief through one's attire should involve coarse fabric, not refined apparel.

Confucius said, "No, I have not heard that. Had I heard it, I would wish to attend, even though I am in mourning."

Yang Hu said, "You think so? Jisun invited everyone but you" and then left.

Zeng Dian asked, "What did you mean by that, sir?"

Confucius said, "I spoke with him even though I'm in mourning and let it be known that I lay no blame."[22]

43.24

顏回死，魯定公弔焉，使人訪於孔子。孔子對曰：“凡在封內，皆臣子也。禮，君弔其臣，升自東階，向尸而哭，其恩賜之施，不有笇也。”

After Yan Hui passed away, Lu Duke Ding[23] paid his respects, and he sent a representative to confer about it with Confucius. Confucius replied, "Everyone inside the border is the duke's vassal. According to *li,* whenever the duke pays respects to a deceased vassal, he should ascend by the eastern steps and grieve facing the corpse. The magnanimity he extends by doing so is incalculable."

43.25

原思言於曾子曰：“夏后氏之送葬也，用盟器，示民無知也；殷人用祭器，示民有知也；周人兼而用之，示民疑也。”曾子曰：“其不然矣，夫以盟器，鬼器也；祭器，人器也。古之人胡爲而死其親也？”子游問於孔子，曰：“之死而致死乎，不仁，不可爲也；之死而致生乎，不智，不可爲也。凡爲盟器者，知喪道也。有備物而不可用也。是故竹不成用，而瓦不成膝，琴瑟張而不平，笙竽備而不和，有鐘磬而無簨簴。其曰盟器，神明之也。哀哉！死者而用生者之器，不殆而用殉也。”

Yuan Si said to Zengzi, "The fact that in the Xia they buried people with spirit items demonstrates that they did not believe people are sentient after death. That the Shang used sacrificial items demonstrates that they believed that people are sentient after death. That the Zhou follow both customs shows that Zhou people are ambivalent on this matter."

Zengzi said, "It's not like that. Spirit items are meant for spirits, whereas sacrificial items are for people's use. Why would the ancients think that[24] about their dead relatives?"

22. Yang Hu was very rude to Confucius by bringing this up. Confucius responded in a way that would not lay blame on Yang Hu.

23. The chronology here with regard to the time of Yan Hui's death differs from that of SJ. In SJ, Yan Hui passes away a few years later, during the reign of Duke Ai.

24. That they are insentient.

When Ziyou asked Confucius about it, he said, "It is not *ren* to think that a dead person is completely dead. You mustn't do this. And it is not wise to think that a dead person is entirely living. You mustn't do this, either. To use spirit items is to understand the *dao* of funerals. They are to be prepared but are not intended for actual use. Those made of bamboo are unfinished. Those made of clay are unpainted. Zithers are only loosely strung. Wind instruments are not made to tune. Bells and chimes are not hung on racks. They are called spirit items because they are given to the spirits of the recently deceased. It is sad when items meant for the living are buried with the dead. Isn't it almost as bad as using human beings as burial items?"[25]

43.26

子罕問於孔子曰:"始死之設重也,何爲?"孔子曰:"重,主道也,殷主綴重焉,周人徹重焉。""請問喪朝。"子曰:"喪之朝也,順死者之孝心,故至於祖考廟而後行。殷朝而後殯於祖,周朝而後遂葬。"

Zihan asked Confucius, "After a person dies, why do we place a double of the commemorative tablet?"

Confucius said, "A double is part of the practice of the ancestral tablet.[26] The Shang attached the double to the permanent tablet. The Zhou replaced the double with the permanent one."

25. An unfinished item, or an item made of cheap material, and without practical utility, buried with the dead, counts as a *spirit item*. Yuan Si expresses the view that burying these with the dead displays a belief that the dead are not sentient after death. A *sacrificial item* is an item that is used in daily life—ritual vessels, musical instruments, weapons, dogs, horses, humans—and then buried with the dead. To bury sacrificial items with the dead, according to Yuan Si, displays a belief that the dead are sentient after death. Yuan Si is surely right about this latter point, but spirit items, because they were believed to also have efficacy in the next life, display the same belief. Yuan Si is partly correct about early religious beliefs and partly correct about the chronology of burial practices. Although both spirit items and sacrificial items can be found in tombs from the Neolithic right through to the end of the Zhou dynasty, the proportion shifted over time. Spirit items are relatively rare in Neolithic tombs and tombs of the Shang and Western Zhou, which contained numerous sacrificial items, but by the end of the Warring States period, it was the opposite, with spirit items predominating and sacrificial items rare. The time of Confucius was a time of transition, from sacrificial to spirit items, understandably prompting the issue discussed in this passage. The issue is also raised in 44.4 but from another perspective. (Loewe and Shaughnessy 1999; Y. Zhang 2002; Falkenhausen 2006; Wu 2006)

26. After a member of the upper classes passed away, it was common practice to have a small wooden tablet made and inscribed with the name of the deceased. That tablet was placed in proper lineal order at the ancestral temple, where ceremonies were held for all of the ancestors on a regular basis. Following the logic of this passage, the tablet was not made in advance, and while it was being made (immediately after the person's death), a cheap double was used in its place. Perhaps it took time

Zihan asked, "Can you explain why we go to the ancestral temple to sacrifice just before a burial?"

Confucius said, "This is something that a person who feels *xiao* does naturally after a person passes away. One takes the body to the temple and only then proceeds to the burial. During the Shang, after the body was brought to the temple, it remained laid out there for a time. Now in the Zhou, after the body is brought to the temple, it goes straight to the burial."

43.27

孔子之守狗死，謂子貢曰："路馬死，則藏之以帷，狗則藏之以蓋。汝往埋之。吾聞弊幃不棄，爲埋馬也；弊蓋不棄，爲埋狗也。今吾貧，無蓋。於其封也，與之席，無使其首陷於土焉。"

After Confucius' guard dog passed away, he said to Zigong, "When a transport horse[27] dies, it is buried wrapped in a shroud. When a dog dies, it is buried inside a chariot canopy. I would like you to bury the dog. I've heard that one should not dispose of a worn curtain because it can be used as a shroud for burying a horse, nor should one dispose of a chariot canopy because it can be used for burying a dog. I am quite poor, however, and have no canopy. When you bury it, wrap it in a reed mat, not letting its head rest on the dirt."

---

to determine the deceased's posthumous name and make other such arrangements. Zihan's question seems to be targeted at the need for the double.

27. A horse belonging to the aristocracy, used for transportation rather than labor or warfare. (Zhang, Lin, and Gao 1980)

44

Gongxi Chi Asks about the Finer Points of *Li*

Chapter 44 is a brief continuation of the previous two chapters. The most salient episode is 44.3, in which Confucius is depicted as making a grievous error in arranging for the burial of his parents, resulting in the collapsing of the grave itself.

44.1

公西赤問於孔子曰:"大夫以罪免,卒,其葬也,如之何?"孔子曰:"大夫廢其事,終身不仕,死則葬之以士禮。老而致仕者,死則從其列。"

Gongxi Chi asked Confucius, "Regarding a high official who was once fired because he committed a crime, how should he be buried?"

Confucius replied, "A high official who was once fired and never rehired should be buried according to the *li* of a common official. An official who dies after a normal retirement should be buried according to his rank."

44.2

公儀仲子嫡子死,而立其弟。檀弓問子服伯子曰:"何居?我未之前聞也。"子服伯子曰:"仲子亦猶行古人之道。昔者文王捨伯邑考而立武王,微子捨其孫腯,立其弟衍。"子游以問諸孔子,子曰:"否!周制立孫。"

Gongyi Zhongzi's oldest son by his wife passed away, and he named the next oldest son as his heir.[1] Tangong asked Zifu Bozi, "What? I've never heard of such a thing before."

1. The context here is almost certainly that Gongyi is an elderly nobleman with a title to pass on. The practice since the beginning of the Zhou in China (as Confucius says at the end of the passage)

Zifu Bozi said, "Zhongzi is behaving according to ancient *dao*. King Wen selected King Wu as his heir over Boyikao,[2] and Viscount Qi selected his younger brother Yan over his grandson Tu."[3]

When Ziyou asked Confucius about this, he said, "No. According to the Zhou system, the grandson is the heir."

44.3

孔子之母既喪，將合葬焉，曰："古者不祔葬，爲不忍先死者之復見也。《詩》云：'死則同穴。'自周公已來，祔葬矣。故衛人之祔也，離之，有以間焉。魯人之祔也，合之，美夫！吾從魯。"遂合葬於防。曰："吾聞之，古者墓而不墳。今丘也，東西南北之人，不可以弗識也。吾見封之若堂者矣，又見若坊者矣，又見覆夏屋者矣，又見若斧形者矣。吾從斧者焉。"於是封之，崇四尺。孔子先反虞，門人後，雨甚至，墓崩，修之而歸。孔子問焉，曰："爾來何遲？"對曰："防墓崩。"孔子不應，三云，孔子泫然而流涕，曰："吾聞之，古不修墓。"及二十五月而大祥，五日而彈琴不成聲，十日過禫而成笙歌。

After Confucius' mother's funeral, he wanted to bury her with his father and said, "The reason people didn't do joint burials in ancient times was that they couldn't bear to see their deceased parent again. A poem says:

> The same grave at death.[4]

Joint burials began at the time of the Duke of Zhou. In a Wei joint burial, the coffins are separated, creating a distance between them. In Lu, they are placed together, which is the more charming way to do it. I follow Lu." He then buried them jointly at Fang.[5]

---

was that in principle a title would go to the oldest son by the wife (not by a concubine), and if the oldest son died prematurely and had a son of his own, then his son would become the heir. (Loewe and Shaughnessy 1999)

2. Boyikao was the oldest son of King Wen. There is no early record of the reason King Wen passed over Boyikao. One grim story from a later commentator is that Boyikao, while a political hostage in Shang, was boiled into soup and fed to his father. This does not, however, support the "passed over" theory. In order to be passed over, he would have to have had a son to pass over, and there is also no record of Boyikao's descendants. In addition, political hostages were usually minors or unmarried. (Zhang, Lin, and Gao 1980; Sima 1981)

3. Viscount Qi of Wei was the older brother of the last Shang king, and although he lived under the Zhou system, it would not be unexpected for him to follow the Shang system, in which the throne was regularly passed to the next oldest brother. See his story in 39.1. (Loewe and Shaughnessy 1999)

4. The line is from the poem "Big Wagon" (#73), which can be found today in the "Wang feng" section of the *Poems*. The poem is written from the point of view of a young woman who wants to run away with a wagon driver. She laments that she may have to settle for merely sharing the same grave.

5. According to the archaeological record, joint burial of spouses can be found as far back as the Neolithic but was not common. As for whether spouses were buried in the same grave or in adjacent

Confucius said, "I have heard that the ancients did not build mounds over graves. Because I am often away, I must mark the spot. I've seen mounds piled in the shape of a hall, a dike, and an inverted Xia house. I've also seen mounds in the shape of an axe blade. I prefer the axe shape."[6] He then had one built four feet high.[7]

Confucius returned for the regular sacrificial ceremony, while some students remained at the grave site. Then a heavy rain came, and the grave collapsed. The students repaired it and then returned. Confucius asked them, "What took you so long?"

They replied, "The grave collapsed."

Confucius did not respond.

They repeated themselves several times, whereupon Confucius expressed great sorrow and broke into tears, saying, "I've heard that the ancients did not build on their graves."[8]

Confucius held the end-of-mourning ceremony after twenty-five months. Five days later, he resumed playing the zither but could not put together a complete song. Ten days after removing his mourning attire, he resumed playing the *sheng* mouth organ and could finally play a tune.

44.4

子游問於孔子曰："葬者塗車芻靈，自古有之。然今人或有偶，是無益於喪。"孔子曰："爲芻靈者善矣，爲偶者不仁，不殆於用人乎？"

---

graves, it was most common for them to be buried in adjacent graves (including examples found in Wei), probably for practical purposes. Evidence for Lu is inconclusive but suggests that (as for the rest of Zhou China) spouses were generally not buried in the same grave unless the deaths occurred within the same time frame. (Ota 1989; Yin 2001)

6. According to Zheng Xuan, the shape of a hall was a cube, the shape of a dike was thinner and tapered somewhat upward, and the Xia house was squat. For more on burial mounds, see 42.26n24.

7. Comparing this passage with the related passage in the beginning of Chapter 1 reveals something important about the philosophy of Confucius with respect to *li*. Many people, when thinking of the norms of *li*, view them as rules that must not be broken. For Confucius, however, they are better viewed as suggestions of best practice—ways of living that have been honed over multiple generations so that they are the right thing for most people under normal circumstances. Sometimes, however, circumstances dictate a divergence from the norm. Here, Confucius refers to his propensity to travel, making it difficult for him to regularly return to the gravesite to maintain it, even to remember its location. Therefore, it makes sense for him to go against common practice and mark it with a mound. However, see note 8 below.

8. In other words, maybe the ancients were right for not building mounds on their graves. This is another revealing aspect of *li*—that as a practice is honed over generations, the explicit rationale for it may be lost, but not necessarily its significance.

Ziyou asked Confucius, "In the past, people used toy carts and straw figurines as burial items. Now, people use lifelike earthenware and wooden statues.[9] It doesn't seem to be an improvement in burial practices."

Confucius said, "Using the straw figurines is best. It is not *ren* to use lifelike statues. Doesn't it too closely resemble using real human beings?"

44.5

顏淵之喪，既祥，顏路饋祥肉於孔子。孔子自出而受之，入，彈琴以散情，而後乃食之。

After the ceremony marking the end of the mourning period for Yan Hui, Yan Lu sent the meat used in the sacrifice as a gift to Confucius. Confucius went to the gate personally to receive it, then he went back into the house, played a song on the zither to ease his emotions, and finally ate the meat.

44.6

孔子嘗，奉薦而進，其親也慤，其行也趨趨以數。已祭，子貢問曰："夫子之言祭也，濟濟漆漆焉。今夫子之祭，無濟濟漆漆，何也?"孔子曰："濟濟者，容也遠也；漆漆者，自反。容以遠，若容以自反，夫何神明之及交?必如此，則何濟濟漆漆之有?反饋樂成，進則燕俎，序其禮樂，備其百官，於是君子致其濟濟漆漆焉。夫言豈一端而已哉?亦各有所當也。"

When Confucius was performing the Chang sacrifice, he carried the offerings forward with great earnestness, shuffling his feet at a rapid pace. After the sacrifice, Zigong asked, "When you have spoken about sacrificial ceremonies, you have said there has to be a dignified and solemn appearance. When you performed the ceremony just now, why did you not have a dignified and solemn appearance?"

Confucius said, "By 'dignified,' I meant that one has to give an appearance of distance. By 'solemn,' I meant that one has to give an appearance of self-reflection. But if one is distant and introspective, how can one interact with one's deceased family member? That being the case, what is the point in being dignified and solemn? At a grand state ceremony, when the dignitaries have eaten and the entertainment has ended, it is time for the sequence of *li* and music to begin and for the various officials to take their places. There, a *junzi* assumes a dignified and solemn

9. As opposed to 43.25, where the distinction is between sacrificial and spirit items, here, the distinction is between less lifelike spirit items and more lifelike spirit items. Ziyou's chronology is not reflected in the archaeological record.

appearance throughout. Can one speak only of one side of it? Each has its own behavior appropriate to it."

44.7

子路爲季氏宰。季氏祭，逮昏而奠，終日不足，繼以燭。雖有强力之容，肅敬之心，皆倦怠矣。有司跛倚以臨事，其爲不敬也大矣。他日，子路與焉。室事交于户，堂事當于階。質明而始行事，晏朝而徹。孔子聞之，曰："以此觀之，孰謂由也而不知禮?"

Zilu worked as Jisun's household manager. Normally when Jisun held a sacrificial ceremony, it would begin before dawn, and the whole day was not sufficient to complete it, continuing under torchlight. Even those of energetic appearance and deep feelings of reverence were exhausted by it. The official in charge would be leaning to support himself, which was itself a great irreverence. Then Zilu took over. Now, for the rites in the private quarters, items change hands at the doorway. For the public rites in the hall, they are placed at the top of the stairs.[10] As a result, a ceremony begun at dawn is finished by nightfall.

Confucius heard about this and said, "Considering him from this perspective, who could say Zilu does not understand *li*?"

10. The point in these two sentences appears to be that although Jisun tended to make an enormous number of offerings in a ceremony, Zilu was able to organize the process so that items were handled in an efficient manner.

APPENDIX 1

Postface

KONG ANGUO[1]

THE *DIALOGUES OF CONFUCIUS* contains discussions in which noblemen, officials at all levels, and the seventy-two main students of Confucius seek counsel and converse with him. Some students subsequently recorded their conversations, dating to the same period as the *Lun yu* [*Analects*] and *Classic of Xiao*. The students selected the items they felt were most authentic and sensible and separated them off into the *Lun yu*. The items left over were collected into their own volume, which was named *Kongzi jia yu* [*Dialogues of Confucius*]. Of debatable passages, some have been determined through examination and comparison to reflect the original thoughts of Confucius. Others belong to a lesser category—baseless, confused, and dispensable. And yet, because the seventy-two students individually and jointly narrated them from beginning to end, they were polished despite their limitations, and that's what we have today.

Confucius passed away, and his subtle utterances came to an end. After his seventy-two students themselves passed away, his central ideas were distorted, and during the Six States period[2] the way of Ruism dissolved as sophists traveled around dispensing nonsense. Only Meng Ke 孟軻[3] and Sun Qing 孫卿[4] kept to the original lessons. In the time of King Zhao of Qin 秦昭王, Xun Qing traveled to Qin, where the king inquired about the arts of the Ru. Xun Qing gave him over 100 chapters of the dialogues of Confucius, his interactions in the various states, and the words of

1. Kong Anguo's name is not directly attached to this postface in the Chinese, but the description of the author's situation fits Kong, and the second postface makes the direct attribution.

2. Another name for the Warring States period, from the perspective of Han dynasty authors. Toward the end of the Warring States period, only six states remained standing against Qin: Qi, Chu, Yan, Han, Zhao, and Wei.

3. Meng Ke: Mencius (c. 372–289 BCE). (Zheng, Wu, and Yang 2000)

4. *Sun Qing* 孫卿: more commonly written as Xun Qing 荀卿, Xunzi (c. 313–238 BCE). (Zheng, Wu, and Yang 2000)

the seventy-two students. From this point forward, it was Qin that had the full collection. When Li Si 李斯 burned the books during the time of the First Emperor, the *Dialogues of Confucius* was grouped among the books of the Masters and so escaped destruction.[5] After Han Emperor Gaozu 漢高祖 conquered the Qin, the entire collection was acquired and transferred to bamboo strips two-*chi* 尺 long, with many archaic characters. When the Lü[6] clan defeated the Han, they acquired the bamboo manuscripts, and when they themselves lost power and were executed,[7] the compilation was dispersed into the hands of private collectors. Well-meaning people made additions and subtractions to the wording, such that the same event might be recorded in different terms. In the last year of the reign of Emperor Jing, there was a call across the land for all writings related to *li* 禮, and as educated men sent in manuscripts to the officials in charge, the Lü clan copy of the *Dialogues of Confucius* was reacquired. However, it became mixed up with events of the various states and the words of the seventy-two students, and it became impossible to tell them apart. It was turned over to the official archivist, who combined it with a group of strips entitled "Finer Points of *Li*" and stored in the imperial archives.

In the Yuanfeng reign period [110–105 BCE] of Han Emperor Wu 漢武帝, when I held an official post in the capital, I worried that the works of our forebears would vanish once and for all, and so I made private solicitations to noblemen and to

5. The point here is a bit confusing. The books of the Masters were philosophical texts (of Mencius, Xunzi, etc.), and according to SJ were commanded by the First Emperor of Qin to be collected from across the land and burned. If the *Dialogues* had been grouped among the Masters texts, then it would have been destroyed, too. However, not all such books were destroyed. SJ says that copies in the imperial archives and copies owned by imperial scholars were exempt. Another wrinkle to this episode is that the SJ account is not the only account we have of this event, and Kong Anguo was an older contemporary of Sima Qian, author of SJ. Thus, it is possible that Kong Anguo, rather than settling for the SJ account about the burning of the books incident, may have had access to the same or a similar set of resources as Sima Qian, which may have had differing accounts of the incident that have now been lost. Perhaps this passage suggests a different narrative, and that Masters books were not after all subjected to burning. There is a mention in SJ's account of an interest in banning histories other than the Qin's official version. Perhaps the reality is that those were the books that were burned by Qin and not the Masters books. Or perhaps there was no book burning at all. Scholars today question the extent of damage caused by such an event; however, one catastrophe did do extensive damage to an enormous number of texts, namely the destruction of the Qin capital (and imperial archives) in 207 BCE. If the *Dialogues* escaped a destructive event, perhaps that was the event.

6. Reference to the family of Lü Zhi 呂雉 (241–180 BCE), wife of Emperor Gaozu (Liu Bang 劉邦; 256–195 BCE), the founding emperor of the Han dynasty. She ruled as sole regent and then as sole sovereign for fifteen years. (X. Huang 1997)

7. Empress Lü had installed relatives of hers into positions of power during her reign, and after her death it is said that they had conspired to depose the royal Liu clan to form a new dynasty under the Lü clan. The entire Lü clan was subsequently exterminated.

officials high and low for their assistance. I acquired the entire collection and then set about putting it into order by topic, ending up with a collection of forty-four chapters. There was also one chapter called "Zengzi Inquires about *Li,*" which belongs to the book *Zengzi's Inquiries,* and so I did not duplicate it here.[8] With regard to all possible sayings of Confucius that were recorded by his students, I did not add any that were recorded elsewhere and not already here. All *junzi* will want to study this collection.

8. In retrospect, perhaps leaving it out was an error, since no chapter of that name survives.

APPENDIX 2

Postface Following Kong Anguo's

KONG ANGUO's *zi* was Ziguo 子國.[1] He was a twelfth-generation descendant of Confucius. Confucius fathered Boyu 伯魚. Boyu fathered *Zisi* 子思, whose given name was Ji 伋. Ji encountered trouble in Song, where he wrote the "Zhong yong 中庸" in forty-seven chapters. He continued the enterprise of the sage, taking on Meng Ke among his several hundred students. He passed away at the age of sixty-two. Zisi fathered Zishang 子上, whose given name was Bai 白 and who passed away at the age of forty-seven. Just as Shuliang He[2] divorced his wife and Boyu divorced his wife, so did Zisi, and they are together known as the three generations of Kongs who divorced their wives.[3]

Zishang fathered Zijia 子家, whose given name was Ao 傲, later byname Yong 永, and who passed away at the age of forty-five. Zijia fathered Zizhi 子直, whose given name was Gai 槛,[4] and who passed away at the age of forty-six. Zizhi fathered Zigao 子高, whose given name was Chuan 穿. He wrote a book in twelve chapters on dialogues of Confucians called *Jian yan* 讕言 and passed away at the age of fifty-seven. Zigao fathered Wu 武, whose *zi* was Zishun 子順, given name Wei 微, and later byname Bin 斌. He held a post as prime minister for King Wen of Wei 魏文王 and passed away at the age of fifty-seven. Ziwu 子武 fathered Ziyu 子魚, whose given name was Fu 鮒; Zixiang 子襄, whose given name was Teng 騰; and Ziwen 子文, whose given name was Fu 祔. Ziyu's later byname was Jia 甲. Zixiang loved the classics and was well-read. In fear of the draconian laws of Qin, he hid his family's copies of the *Classic of Xiao*, the *Classic of Documents*, and the *Analects* inside a wall of his home. Ziyu

1. In the transmitted editions where this document appears, it is attached to the first postface as the second part of a single two-part document. Yang and Song (2013), acknowledging that they are likely authored by different people, separated them into two distinct documents. We follow Yang and Song.

2. Confucius' father.

3. The speculation here that three generations of the Kong family divorced their wives appears to rest on questionable assumptions and possible misreadings of the classics. (Yang 2009; Liu 2018)

4. This character is not recorded in any available dictionary. The pinyin transcription is an approximation.

was employed as Academician and tutor to King Chen She 陈王涉[5] and died with him. He fathered Yuanlu 元路, whose *zi* was Yuansheng 元生, given name Yu 育, and later byname Sui 随.

Ziwen fathered Zui 冣, whose *zi* was Zichan 子産. Zichan followed Han Emperor Gaozu as his general, and behind Han Xin 韓信 defeated Chu 楚 at Gaixia 垓下. For his contributions, he was given the noble title of Marquis Liao 蓼. He passed away at the age of fifty-three and was given the posthumous title Marquis Yi 夷. His oldest son Mie 滅 was heir and held the high office of Tai Chang 太常. His second son, Xiang 襄, *zi* Zishi 子士, and later byname Rang 讓, held the post of Academician under Emperor Xiaohui 孝惠 and was later promoted to Imperial Preceptor to the Prince of Changsha 長沙. He passed away when he was fifty-seven. He fathered Jizhong 季中, whose given name was Yuan 員, and who passed away at the age of fifty-seven. He was father to Wu 武 and Ziguo 子國.[6]

When Ziguo was young, he studied the *Poems* with Shen Gong 申公 and received tutelage in the *Documents* under Fu Sheng 伏生. As an adult, he read extensively in the classics and their commentaries without any fixed instructor. At the age of forty, he assumed the post of *Jianyi Dafu* 諫議大夫 and was subsequently promoted to *Sizhong* 侍中 and then Academician. After the Tianhan 天漢 reign period (100–97 BCE), when Prince Gong of Lu 魯恭王 demolished the old residence of Confucius, the *Poems* and the *Documents* were recovered inside a wall, and both were returned to Ziguo. With the tadpole script[7] originals from the wall, Ziguo analyzed the ancient script in comparison with the contemporary script, and after considering the opinions of many teachers, edited the *Ancient Script Analects* in eleven chapters, the *Classic of Xiao* in two chapters, and the *Documents* in fifty-eight chapters. He also collected and compiled the *Dialogues of Confucius* in forty-four chapters. At the time it was completed, the Black Magic Scandal occurred, and he set it aside without circulating it. Ziguo was promoted from Academician to Prefect of Linhuai 臨淮, where he remained for six years, until he was granted sick leave. He passed away in his home at the age of sixty. Later, Emperor Xiaocheng 孝成 delegated the *Guanglu Dafu* 光祿大夫 Liu Xiang 劉向 to edit the classics, and in his *Bie lu* 別録 he recorded the titles of all the selected works, including those in ancient and contemporary script. When Ziguo's grandson Yan 衍 held the post of Academician, he composed a memorial to make a case in favor of the book. It read as follows:

> I have heard that enlightened kings do not conceal people's contributions, nor do great sages ignore good deeds done by others, and this is how they get to be

5. King Chen She: Chen Sheng 陳勝 (his *zi* was She 涉), a rebel who rose up in the waning days of the Qin dynasty and proclaimed himself king. (Zheng, Wu, and Yang 2000)

6. Ziguo: Kong Anguo.

7. A version of Zhou dynasty script in which the shape of the brushstrokes resembles tadpoles.

enlightened and sagely. Your Majesty issued an enlightened edict that Confucians should be consulted and books should be collected from across the land, leaving none out, and that learned scholars should edit them for clarity so that the writings from distant ages, the texts that underpin our culture, may be made available to the present day. Making it so that the words set down by the scholars of the past never fade is following in the footsteps of the enlightened kings of the past and revering the precedents set by the great sages. Besides the brilliance of Emperor Tang and the illustriousness of the Zhou kings, nothing compares to this apogee. Of the scholars who will write about this event, all will delight in estimating the significance of this for maintaining important human relationships.

My grandfather Anguo, who was once Prefect of Linhuai, who entered service under Emperor Xiaowu, earned a name for himself because of his scholarship, earned an official position because of his educated refinement, promoted justice, and was known for these in the prior reigns. When Prince Gong of Lu obtained the ancient tadpole script *Documents, Classic of Xiao,* and *Analects* while demolishing the former home of Confucius, people of the time were unable to decipher them. Anguo transcribed them into contemporary script, and wrote commentaries on their meaning. He also collected and compiled the *Dialogues of Confucius*. Just as he concluded this work, the Black Magic Scandal broke out, and so each was abandoned without being circulated. And yet their elegance and authenticity cannot be compared to anything else circulating today. Because they had not been circulated by the time of *Guanglu Dafu* Xiang, the *Documents* was not recorded in his *Bie lu,* nor the *Analects* listed under famous thinkers. May I be so bold as to express my regrets. Every chapter and verse of the hundred schools[8] is recorded, and so how much more should the books from Confucius' home, which are in ancient script and authentic, be recorded; and yet instead they are under suspicion! On top of this, Dai Sheng, a minor scholar of modern times, believing the "Finer Points of *Li*" chapters to be insufficient on their own, selected random parts of the *Dialogues of Confucius* and supplemented them with writings from Zisi, Mencius, and Sun Qing, then called it the *Li ji*. Now people want to take the passages that are in the *Li ji* and eliminate them from the *Dialogues,* where they were originally. This is eliminating the roots to protect the branches, and isn't it a tragedy? From my limited perspective, I find it fitting that the examples above be given their own separate entries. Thus, I brazenly bring this to your attention.

The memorial was submitted, and the emperor permitted it. However, before it could be put into effect, the emperor passed away. Xiang also died of illness, and so it never came to fruition.

8. The various schools of thought during the Warring States period.

APPENDIX 3

Preface

WANG SU 王肅

IT HAS BEEN fifty years now that the teachings of Zheng[1] have been circulating. When I set my mind on learning as a youth, I studied the Zheng teachings. However, after critically examining the texts and analyzing everything from top to bottom, I find the reasoning wanting; also, there are numerous departures and errors. Therefore, I felt forced to make revisions. And yet people misunderstood my sincere intentions and instead accused me of contradicting my teachers in an attempt to stand out among others. And so I heaved a deeply felt sigh and said, "Why would I enjoy such hardship? I did it because I had no choice." The gateway to sagehood is lately obstructed, and the path of Confucius is covered with brambles. Shouldn't it be opened up? It is not my fault if nobody follows. Thus, I edited the classics of *li*, clarifying the meanings, including defending my opinion in the imperial court. These are all my personal views.

Kong Meng 孔猛 is a twenty-second-generation descendant of Confucius, and in his home were writings from previous generations. Once when we were studying together, he went back home and returned with some documents. He told me there was some overlap in them with what I had been saying. Confucius once said, "Since the passing of King Wen, is culture not right here? If *tian* had wanted to exterminate it, it would have been unavailable for those who came after. Since *tian* has not exterminated it, what can the people of Kuang do to me?"[2] Speaking of *tian* exterminating this culture, I have been chosen to transmit it to the world. It seems that *tian* does not yet want to disrupt it and so caused Kong Meng to study with me and thereby enabled me to acquire the text from him in order to present its clear perspective in a way that does not violate the House of Confucius. It contains authentic ideas of

1. Zheng Xuan 鄭玄 (127–200).

2. See *Analects* 9.5.

the sage; afraid that they might be lost, I made a point of adding explanations for the sake of interested readers.

There is a passage in the *Analects* that says, "Lao 牢 stated, 'Confucius said, "Because I have never been employed as an official, I have other skills."'" No one knows who the speaker is, and so there have been many frivolous theories. Among the students listed in the *Dialogues of Confucius* is one Qin Zhang 琴張,[3] whose given name is Lao 牢, whose *zi* was Zikai 子開, also recorded as Zhang 張, and who was a native of Wei. According to the passage, when Zong Lu passed away, he wanted to pay his respects, but Confucius stopped him.

There is a passage in the *Chunqiu wai zhuan* 春秋外傳 that says, "In the past, Yao ruled the people through five." The prevailing theory about this is that Yao undertook an inspection tour every five years. An inspection tour every five years is not the same as ruling through five. There is a reference in the classics to "inspection tours every five years,"[4] but it is a reference to Shun, not to Yao. In the *Dialogues*, however, Confucius explains the "five chiefs," each with different capacities. With regard to Shun, he says, "he toured the country once every five years."[5] As for Yao's inspection tours, we don't know the yearly interval. The Zhou kings did it every twelve years, so would it be preferable to say that the Zhou ruled the people by twelve? Confucius said that Yao used fire for his power of ruling the land, and his color was yellow.[6] Yellow is the *de* of earth, and five is the number for earth—hence the meaning of ruling the people through five.

3. See 38.33.

4. See the "Shun dian" section of the *Documents*.

5. See 25.3.

6. See 24.4.

GLOSSARY

Notes

- Persons referred to by more than one name in different episodes are listed under the name that is most commonly used in the *Dialogues,* with cross-references from the other names.
- All persons with noble rank and personal (posthumous) name are listed as "[polity] [noble rank] [name]," as in "Zhou Duke Wu." If there is no concomitant name, the person is listed as "[noble rank] of [polity]," as in "Earl of Shao."
- Personal names that appear only once in the *Dialogues* and for whom there is no other relevant historical or personal information have been omitted.
- The term *surname* refers to *xìng* 姓 or *shì* 氏 interchangeably. For distinctions between *xìng* and *shì,* see Durrant, Li, and Schaberg (2016).
- Many geographic locations are parenthetically placed relative to Qūfù, the hometown of Confucius, in order to give a sense of felt distance from the points of view of Confucius and his students. Transportation in Confucius' day was generally conducted at a walking pace (human, ox, or horse) over a system of local and interstate roadways. Estimating a pace of roughly twenty miles per day allows distances to be calculated in temporal terms. For example, Dìqiū, the capital of Wèi, where Confucius spent three years, was about 120 miles northwest of Qūfù, or a six-day walk. Zībó, the capital of Qí, Lǔ's large neighbor to the northeast, was about the same distance, as was the capital of Sòng, Lǔ's neighbor to the west and ancestral home of Confucius. By contrast, the city of Bì, home base of the powerful Jìsūn clan of Lǔ, was about half that distance but still a good three-day walk from the capital. Some locations, such as the capital of Lǔ, have been determined from archaeological excavations (Chen, Sun, and Liu 2020); others have been inferred by scholars from textual evidence. Distances in this glossary were calculated using present-day locations via the app *Bǎidù Dìtú* 百度地圖 and are approximate.
- For primary sources, we give priority to the *Documents*, the *Poems*, CQZZ, and BA (Loewe 1993), while referring to other sources (such as SJ, *Guo yu,* and LNZ) where they provide illumination not available in the others. We also rely on peer-reviewed secondary sources and standard tertiary sources. Going so far back in time, with scarce sources of often questionable

reliability, one's claims to truth must be modest. The best way to get at a semblance of truth surrounding events and material conditions of the time of Confucius and earlier is a combination of archaeological, paleographic, and textual scholarship (Loewe and Shaughnessy 1999). Because the record with respect to these is far from complete, however, claims in the glossary should be taken as best approximations according to current scholarship.

- For clarity, pinyin tone marks are included throughout the glossary, except in the headwords, which are exactly as shown in the main body of the text. A small number of proper-noun headwords have pinyin tone marks for the sake of distinguishing one homonym from another: for example, Zhòu (distinguished from Zhou) and Qǐ (distinguished from Qi). The tone marks are for current Mandarin pronunciation and should not be misconstrued as marks of precision. The precise pronunciations and tones of the standard dialect (if any) during the time of Confucius have been the subjects of valuable research (e.g., Baxter and Sagart 2014) but will not be touched on here. For terms already common in nonstandard spellings, such as Confucius, Mencius, and Yangtze, we diverge from standard Pinyin orthography. For words and phrases of four characters or less, we provide *pinyin* transcription throughout.
- Abbreviations: R., r. = reigned; D., d. = died; Fl., fl. = flourished.

Weights and Measures

Exact units of weights and measures in the Spring and Autumn period are unknown, and although archaeological finds have allowed scholars to determine precise units of Warring States weights and measures, such units were not uniform across localities. We approximate from the best data available.

The early Chinese system of weights and measures had similarities to many traditions around the world in that it used body parts as standards (see, e.g., 3.2), but it was also in part a decimal system. For example, a *cùn* is 1/10 of a *chǐ*. In 22.8, Confucius' height is given as 9 *chǐ* and 6 *cùn*, which converts to 7 feet, 2 inches—very close to what Confucius says (in 16.2) is the human maximum of 7.5 feet (i.e., 10 *chǐ*; which, by the way, is given as his father's height in 39.2).

Weights and measures can be challenging to render across languages. Sometimes a measure and its amount are meant to be specific and sometimes to merely give a general sense of magnitude. In the main body of the text, we translate according to context.

Length

Cùn 寸: Inch-like unit. 1/10 of a *chǐ*. 0.9 inch. (Zeng 1964) *1.1, 3.2, 22.8, 40.2, 42.19*

Zhǐ 咫: Foot-like unit, but shorter than a *chǐ*. 8 *cùn*. (This measure exists only in the transmitted textual record and has not been confirmed in the archaeological record; Zeng 1964.) *16.3*

Chǐ 尺: Foot-like unit. 10 *cùn*. 9 inches. (Chen 1964; Zeng 1964; Qiu 1992) *2.2, 3.2, 16.2, 16.3, 22.8, 35.2, 38.14, 39.2, 40.2, 42.19, 44.3*

Bù 步: Yard- or meter-like unit. Length of two strides. 6 *chǐ*. 5½ feet. *3.2*

Rèn 仞: Measurement unit for vertical distance. Precise length is unknown, and sources vary in their stated equivalences, including 8 *chǐ*; 7 *chǐ*; 5 *chǐ*, 6 *cùn*; and 4 *chǐ*. We follow Wang Su, who specifies 8 *chǐ*. 6 feet. (Hua 1993; Luo 1994) *2.2, 8.14, 9.5*

Shù 束: Bolt-like unit for fabric. 5 *pǐ* 匹.[1] 50 yards. *8.13, 33.3, 42.28*

Lǐ 里: Standard unit of measurement for geographical distance. 300 *bù*, 1,800 *chǐ*. About 1,350 feet, ¼ of a mile. *3.1, 3.2, 8.1, 8.12, 8.14, 10.5, 14.4, 15.21, 19.3, 25.1, 25.2*

Area

Jing, jǐng 井: Standard unit of measurement for an area of land. One square *li*. About 42 acres. (Zheng, Wu, and Yang 2000) *41.23*

Capacity

Dàn 石: Bushel-like unit. 10 *dǒu* 斗.[2] 5.5 gallons. (Liu, Wang, and Lu 2019; Qiu 1992) *20.4*

Fǒu 缶: 16 *dǒu* 斗. 8.75 gallons. *41.23*

Bǐng 秉: 16 *dàn* 石. 87.5 gallons or 9.4 bushels.[3] *41.23*

Alcohol: *Jiǔ* 酒 was a common term in early China for alcoholic beverages, which were essentially beer in that they were made of malted grain. Beer nowadays in the West is generally made with barley for the malt, hops as a bittering agent, and yeast for fermentation. In early China, actually going back thousands of years into at least the middle Neolithic period, according to archaeological evidence, beer was made from millet, broomcorn millet, barley, wheat, or rice, with various herbs added, and fermentation agents that contained fungi other than yeast. Alcohol production was a major part of life even in Neolithic times, playing an important role in both religious sacrifices and community feasts. Its role was even larger in the highly stratified Shang dynasty, where we find the first written records, which include many words involving alcohol, and even a government position known as the minister of malt (*xiǎo niè chén* 小蘖臣). According to these earliest records, if beer was made from rice, it was called *yǐ* 酏. If it was made from millet and had a sweet taste and a low alcohol content, it was called *lǐ* 醴. If it was

1. 1 *pǐ* = 4 *zhàng* 丈; 1 *zhàng* = 10 *chǐ* 尺. (Hua 1993)
2. *Dǒu* 斗: peck-like unit. 10 *shēng* 升 (cup-like unit). 2.1 lit., 0.55 gal.
3. 1 bushel = 9.31 gallons. (Judson 1976)

made from broomcorn millet and a fragrant herb, it was called *chàng* 鬯. These last two are mentioned in the *Dialogues*—in the context of the capping ceremony, for toasting (33.3); in the context of the earliest cultural innovations of the sages (6.2); and in the context of religion (17.5, 31.5). *Jiǔ* may have been a catchall term for all such kinds of beer, or it may have referred to a filtered version with a higher alcohol content. *Jiǔ*, probably in thick, unfiltered form brewed with herbs, was also seen as medicinal and nutritive (see, for example, 28.1 and 43.5). The *Dialogues* (6.2, on prehistoric cultural innovations) mentions three further varieties of alcoholic drinks: (1) *xuánjiǔ* 玄酒, an unknown drink that is usually glossed as "water" or "diluted beer"; (2) *jìtí* 粢醍, said to be a filtered beer, reddish in color; and (3) *lào* 酪, a beverage made from fermented rice or millet. Although H. T. Huang (2000) makes a strong case for generally translating *jiǔ* as "wine," the variety of terms and usages in the *Dialogues* demands a more nuanced approach. We variously use the terms *beer, wine, alcohol, drink, liquor*, and so on, according to context. See Huang (2000) for a thorough historical, culinary, and technological treatment. (Huang 2000; McGovern et al. 2004; Zhao et al. 2008; Wang et al. 2016; Liu et al. 2018, 2019; Liu, Wang, and Di 2020) *6.2, 7.1, 13.3, 17.5, 26.2, 28.1, 28.2, 30.1, 31.5, 32.14, 33.3, 43.5*

Ancient Kings, *xiān wáng* 先王: Great sage-kings of the past, including Yáo 堯, Shùn 舜, King Wǔ, and King Wén. *7.6, 11.1, 12.9, 15.5, 16.9, 22.5, 30.2, 32.3, 32.11, 32.12, 32.14, 32.15, 35.2, 39.3, 41.6, 41.23, 42.29, 42.31*

Angelica and *eupatorium*, *zhī lán* 芝蘭: Two fragrant plants that have come to symbolize capable and virtuous officials willing to enter government. *Zhī*, *Angelica dahurica*, is a fragrant perennial that grows in wetlands and resembles Queen Anne's lace in appearance. The *eupatorium* is probably *Eupatorium fortunei* (*lancao* 蘭草 / *peilan* 佩蘭), which was cultivated for its lavender-like fragrance and used as a perfume. In 15.15, *zhī lán* is translated as *flower-scented*. (Zhao et al. 1992; Luo 1994; Dong and Yuan 2013; Kroll 2015; Yu et al. 2024) *15.15, 20.1*

Baili Xi, Bǎilǐ Xī 百里奚(傒): Fl. 647 BCE. Bǎilǐ Xī appears in only one brief passage of the CQZZ ("Xī" 13.4), where he is depicted as an adviser to Qín Duke Mù. According to SJ ("Qín běn jì"), Bǎilǐ Xī was a senior official in the state of Yú 虞. When Jìn conquered Yú in 655 BCE, Bǎilǐ Xī was captured, then sent as a servant to Qín as part of a princess' dowry. On the way there he escaped, but he was later captured by Chǔ. Duke Mù of Qín, having heard of Bǎilǐ Xī's brilliance, ransomed him from Chǔ for the price of the pelts of five black sheep. Bǎilǐ Xī and the duke spoke together for three days, and the duke was so pleased that he handed over the government to him and named him Senior Official Wǔgǔ 五羖 (Five Black Sheep). Already past the age of seventy at the time, he worked as a general and senior official in the government, where he played a pivotal role in Qín's becoming one of the five superpowers of the Spring and Autumn period. *13.8*

Banquan, Bǎnquán 阪泉: Prehistoric settlement, location unknown. One proposed site is modern-day Zhuōlù 涿鹿縣, Héběi (440 mi. NNW of Qūfù). (Luo 1994; Zheng, Wu, and Yang 2000) *23.1*

Banquet: See ***xiang*****.**

Bao (ceremony), Bào 報: A ceremony of gratitude involving reporting one's well-being to one's ancestors and acknowledging them through a demonstration of reverence and remembrance. Cf. 29.1, 29.2. (Liu 1989) *17.5*

Bao (surname), Bào 鮑: A leading family of Qí during the Spring and Autumn period. See, for example, Bao Qian (41.22) and Bao Shu (13.2). See also **Chen Heng.** *37.2, 41.22*

Bao Shu, Bào Shū 鮑叔: Also known as Bào Shūyá 鮑叔牙. Minister of Qí who played a pivotal role in the rise and success of Duke Huán of Qí, the first Spring and Autumn superpower. According to CQZZ ("Zhuāng" 9–10), when Qí Duke Xiāng was acting erratically, there was fear of rebellion, and so two princes in line for succession fled, Xiǎobái 小白 to Jǔ 莒 and Jiū 糾 to Lǔ. Bào Shū accompanied Xiǎobái to Jǔ, and Guǎn Zhòng accompanied Jiū to Lǔ. After Duke Xiāng was killed, a Lǔ army escorted Jiū to Qí to install him as duke but was defeated by Qí. Bào then led Qí's troops to Lǔ. Lǔ executed Jiū at the behest of Bào and handed Guǎn Zhòng over as prisoner. Bào, who had such high regard for Guǎn Zhòng's talent, recommended him to Xiǎobái (the newly installed Duke Huán), and Guǎn Zhòng eventually became prime minister. *8.9n14, 13.2*

Bao Shuya: See **Bao Shu.**

Bi, Bì 費: City in Lǔ. Home base of the Jìsūn clan. Present-day Fèi 費縣, Shāndōng (68 mi. ESE of Qūfù). (Luo 1994; Tan 1996) *1.3, 16.1, 25.1*

Bian, Biàn 卞: Near present-day Miáoguǎn 苗館鎮 along the eastern Sì River 泗水 (about 25 mi. E of Qūfù). (Tan 1996) *42.22*

Bigan, Bǐgān 比干: Paternal uncle of, and high minister to, Shāng King Zhòu. According to BA ("Dì Xīn" 51), Bǐgān was killed by Zhòu. In Zhōu and Hàn literature, Bǐgān became the key symbol of the loyal minister who is killed by a despotic ruler despite giving sound advice. According to SJ ("Yīn běn jì"), Zhòu, the last king of the Shāng dynasty, was tyrannical and dissolute. His adviser Bǐgān insistently tried to change his behavior. Zhòu responded, "I've heard that a sage has seven orifices in his heart," then had Bǐgān's heart removed to see for himself. According to the *Documents* ("Wǔ chéng"), Bǐgān was memorialized by Zhōu King Wǔ. Confucius praises him as one of three *ren* officials of the last Shāng reign (Analects 18.1), which he further explains in *Dialogues* 19.6. *13.5, 19.6, 20.1, 35.3*

Bin, Bīn 豳: Polity in prehistoric times. Present-day Bīnzhōu 彬州市, Shǎnxī. Name later changed to Zhōu 周. Founded by Lord Liú. See also **Lord Liu.** *10.18*

Bo, Bó 博: City along the Wèn 汶 River, just southeast of present-day Tài'ān (about 45 mi. NNW of Qūfù). (Tan 1996) *42.26*

Bo Qin, Bó Qín 伯禽: Surname Jī 姬, *zì* Bó Qín 伯禽. Eldest son of the Duke of Zhōu and founder of the state of Lǔ at Qūfù after his father declined the position in order to remain at the Zhōu capital to assist in construction of the new government. (Zheng, Wu, and Yang 2000) *43.2, 43.3*

Bo Yi, Bó Yì 伯益 (cf. Boyi): According to 23.6, he was, along with Gāo Yáo, a trusted minister under Yǔ. In the *Documents* ("Shùn diǎn"), he is also minister under Yǔ's predecessor Shùn 舜. In BA ("Dì Qǐ"), he is identified as Marquis of Bì (Bì Hóu 費侯). *23.6*

Bochang Qian, Bócháng Qiān 伯常騫: Bócháng Qiān appears elsewhere only in the *Zhuāngzǐ* (where he is depicted as a historian) and in the *Yànzǐ Chūnqiū*, where he is depicted as a diviner. *9.3*

Bolt: See "Weights and Measures" at the beginning of the glossary.

Boyi, Bóyí 伯夷 (cf. Bo Yi): (1) Prince of the state of Gūzhú. For his story, see 12.21n19. *12.21, 20.1* (2) Minister under Yáo. *23.4, 30.1n2*

Boyu, Bóyú 伯魚: 532–483 BCE. Surname Kǒng, given name Lǐ 鯉, *zì* Bóyú 伯魚. Only son of Confucius. Bóyú's name is scarce in the textual record and appears in only two passages of the *Analects* (16.13, 17.10) and three passages of the *Dialogues*. In three of these five passages Confucius exhorts him to study, and in another he blames him for excessive emotional expression. If it is true that Confucius targets his advice to the needs or shortcomings of a student, then Bóyú would appear to have been in need of more learning, a more refined outward appearance, and greater moderation—in other words, he may have resembled a typical teenager. Bóyú predeceased Confucius, living only to the age of fifty. See 39.2 for details of his naming, which is the locus classicus for the story. (Taiwan Academic Network 2021) *8.11, 39.2, 42.30*

Bu, Bù 步: See "Weights and Measures" at the beginning of the glossary.

Bu Shang: See **Zixia.**

Cai (person), Cài 蔡: Also known as Càishū 蔡叔. Surname Jī 姬, given name Dù 度. According to accounts in the *Documents* and SJ (see also 39.1 for a brief account), King Wén of Zhōu had ten sons, many of whom were instrumental in helping overthrow the Shāng. The eldest son, Bóyìkǎo, was passed over, and the second son, the future King Wǔ, was selected as heir. When Wǔ passed away and his son and heir, King Chéng, had not yet reached adulthood, King Wén's fourth son, known to posterity as the Duke of Zhōu, named himself regent and took control of the government. The third and fifth sons had been enfeoffed respectively at Guǎn 管 and Cài 蔡; being uncles of King Chéng, they are known to posterity by the names of their respective states, or as Guǎnshū 管叔 and Càishū 蔡叔 (Uncle Guan and Uncle Cai).[4] Before Guǎn and Cài could take control of

4. The birth order of the sons of King Wen is a contested topic. See Yang (1998) for an alternative view.

their respective domains, they were sent to Sòng to supervise Wǔgēng, the heir of the Shāng, who had been enfeoffed at Sòng. Guǎn (who was apparently the ringleader) and Cài suspected the Duke of Zhōu's motives and coerced Wǔgēng to conspire with them in spreading a rumor that the Duke of Zhōu was not working for the benefit of King Chéng. They then mounted an uprising. The Duke of Zhōu led an expedition east to suppress the rebellion, which took three years, after which he punished Guǎn, executed Wǔgēng, and freed Cài, who died shortly thereafter. *2.1, 39.1*

Cai (state), Cài 蔡: State enfeoffed by Zhōu. After the original ruler rebelled, his son was enfeoffed as ruler at present-day Shàngcài 上蔡 (270 mi. SW of Qūfù). See also **Cai (person).** *20.1, 20.4, 22.4, 38.26*

Calendar: Agricultural societies like ancient China depended on an accurate calendar for the timing of spring plantings. Such societies tended to rely on the phases of the moon as a temporal anchor for their calendar and on the sun as a temporal anchor for the agricultural seasons. Because twelve cycles of the moon (354 days) do not quite match up with the 365¼ days of the solar year, an extra month (called an intercalary month) was added to the Chinese calendar every few years to bring the two cycles back into sync. (The problem is solved today by disengaging the length of a month from the cycles of the moon altogether.) Different calendrical systems were used in different periods in China, and in the *Dialogues* we see Confucius referring to both the Xià and Zhōu calendars. Calendars were so important that there was a government position called Keeper of the Calendar, *sī lì* 司曆. A sexagenary system, called the "stems and branches" (*tiān gān dì zhī* 天干地支), was used to keep track of years, months, and days. There were ten individually named stems and twelve individually named branches. Each item being tracked was given the name of one stem and one branch, and the next in the series was named after the subsequent stem and branch. The cycle would be complete after sixty pairings, after which it would begin again. In 42.13, for instance, the *xīnsì* day is mentioned. *Xīn* is the eighth stem, and *sì* is the sixth branch; as a pair, they mark the eighteenth day of the cycle. See also 25.3n8. (Yu 1992; Loewe and Shaughnessy 1999) *16.8, 21.2, 23.3, 25.3n8, 29.2n2, 32.9, 38.10n5*

Cangwu, Cāngwú 蒼梧: Cāngwú is mentioned multiple times in the textual record, typically as the place where Shùn died or was buried. Cāngwú is probably the name of a non-Han minority. They are mentioned as being in the area of present-day Dōnghǎi, Jiāngsū, and in the area where present-day Húnán, Guǎngdōng, and Guǎngxī meet. They are thought to be a branch of the Yuè 越 people who may have emigrated. Cāngwú is often associated with present-day Jiǔyí Mountain 九嶷山, Húnán. (Chen 1987; Pan 2005; Shi, Zheng, and Zhu 2005; Xu 2012) *15.9, 23.5*

Cao, Cáo 曹: State enfeoffed by the Zhōu to Jī Zhènduó 姬振鐸, younger brother of King Wǔ. Capital city Táoqiū, north of present-day Dìngtáo, Shāndōng (about 100 mi. WSW of Qūfù). Absorbed by Sòng in 487 BCE. (Luo 1994; Zheng, Wu, and Yang 2000) *20.1*

Capping ceremony, *guàn* 冠: The capping ceremony is the traditional coming-of-age ceremony for young men in premodern China. According to 26.2, it occurs in the twentieth year, or at age nineteen (an analogous hairpin [*ji* 笄] ceremony was held for young women, at the age of fifteen [He 2012]). See 33.1 for a description; see also 33.2–33.4. *26.2, 32.3, 33.1, 33.2, 33.3, 33.4*

Chang, Cháng 嘗: A major sacrificial ceremony, likely developed during the late Western Zhōu, associating the autumnal harvest with the ancestors. According to passages in CQZZ, it could occur during the eighth month and eleventh month (but was not necessarily restricted to these) and upon the death of a ruler, and it was associated with the Zhēng 烝 and Dì 禘 sacrifices. In the *Poems*, it is dedicated to the Ancient Kings and is associated with the Yuè 礿 and Zhēng 烝 sacrifices. The focus in 27.1 on ancestral lines appears consistent with these passages. See also **Di (ceremony).** (Liu 1989; Loewe 1993) *27.1, 44.6*

Chang Hong, Cháng Hóng 萇弘: Cháng Hóng appears in a number of textual sources, but the accounts vary. They largely agree that he was a brilliant diviner for the Zhōu king, but his vast knowledge could not keep him from finally being executed. The *Dialogues* depicts him as also knowledgeable in music. *11.1, 35.3*

Changes, *Yì* 易 or *Yì jīng* 易經 or *Zhōu Yì* 周易: The *Changes* (or *Classic of Changes, Book of Changes, I Ching*) is a composite text composed of layers that include sixty-four hexagrams, a judgment about each hexagram, and a statement about each line of each hexagram. Later layers include ten distinct commentaries. Traditionally, the hexagrams are attributed to the prehistoric sage Fú Xī, the judgments on the hexagrams to King Wén, the line statements to the Duke of Zhōu, and editing of the text as well as composition of the commentaries to Confucius. Without the ten commentaries, the work is sometimes referred to as the *Zhōu Yì* 周易 (*Changes of Zhōu*). The purpose of the *Changes* is prognostication. Each hexagram represents a type of situation, and differences in the lines represent the dynamics of change from one situation to the next. While there is no definitive reference to the *Changes* in the *Analects*,[5] there are several in the *Dialogues*. The *Changes* was recognized in the Hàn dynasty as one of the Five Classics of Confucianism. Italicized, the name refers in this translation to a single, edited collection created either by Confucius or sometime after, editions of which have been passed down to us today. When not italicized, it refers to whatever relevant collections of related divination documents existed during the time of Confucius, prior to their arrangement into a single collection. See also **Six Classics.** *10.3, 15.8, 36.2, 38.25, 39.3*

5. There is one mention of *yi* 易 ("change"; 7.17), which some scholars believe refers to the *Changes* while others disagree. Peimin Ni (2016) identifies several passages in the *Analects* that he argues can be traced to the *Changes*.

Chen, Chén 陳: State enfeoffed by the Zhōu at the level of Marquis. Founder Guī Mǎn 嬀满. Capital city Wǎnqiū 宛丘 (present-day Huáiyáng 淮陽, Hénán (about 190 mi. SW of Qūfù). Chén was a small state that remained small; however, because the rulers were considered direct descendants of the sage Shùn, the state always held a special status, and it survived until it was absorbed by Chǔ in 478 BCE. See also 10.2n2. (Zheng, Wu, and Yang 2000; Liu and Chi 2002) *8.16, 10.2, 16.3, 16.6, 20.1, 20.4, 22.4, 35.3, 38.11, 38.27, 38.31, 38.39, 41.6*

Chen Duke Hu, Chén Hú Gōng 陳胡公: Surname Guī 嬀, given name Mǎn 満. Said to be a direct ancestor of Shùn. Founding duke of Chén 陳. (Huang and Zhao 1997) *16.3*

Chen Duke Hui, Chén Huì Gōng 陳惠公: R. 529–506 BCE. Chén had been conquered and destroyed by Chǔ in 534 BCE, but in order to curry favor with leaders of other states after engineering a coup in Chǔ, King Píng of Chǔ restored Chén and installed Duke Huì, the former duke's grandson. (Zheng, Wu, and Yang 2000) *16.3*

Chen Duke Ling, Chén Líng Gōng 陳靈公: R. 613–599 BCE. Infamous for his dissolute, arbitrary behavior. See also under **Xie Ye.** (Zheng, Wu, and Yang 2000) *10.2n2, 19.6*

Chen Heng, Chén Héng 陳恒: Surname Chén (or Tián 田), given name Héng (or Cháng 常). In 481 BCE, Chén Héng mounted a successful rebellion in Qí, deposing and murdering Duke Jiǎn, installing his own successor, and eliminating the powerful Bào 鮑 and Yàn 晏 families. Thereafter, his family controlled the levers of power in Qí. See 37.2 for the prelude to the rebellion and 41.18 for its aftermath. (Zheng, Wu, and Yang 2000) *37.2, 41.18*

Cheng (person): See **Zhou King Cheng.**

Cheng (state), Chéng 郕: City-state enfeoffed by Zhōu. Founder Jī Shūwǔ 姬叔武, younger brother of King Wǔ. Location, present-day Níngyáng 寧陽, Shāndōng (18 mi. NW of Qūfù). (Zheng, Wu, and Yang 2000) *15.13, 43.19*

Chengzi, Chéngzǐ 程子: In the early corpus, Chéngzǐ appears elsewhere only in the *Mòzǐ* ("Gong Meng"), where he defends Ruism and Confucius. *8.13*

Chi, Chǐ 尺: See "Weights and Measures" at the beginning of the glossary.

Chief: See **Emperor.**

Chief Yan, Yán Dì 炎帝: Also known as Shén Nóng 神農. Legendary prehistoric ruler. Surname Jiāng 姜. Son of Shào Diǎn 少典 and half-brother of the Yellow Chief. Defeated by the Yellow Chief. (Luo 1994; Taiwan Academic Network 2021) *16.4, 23.1, 24.1*

Chief Yao: See **Yao.**

Chonger: See **Jin Duke Wen.**

Chu, Chǔ 楚: State enfeoffed by Zhōu King Chéng at the level of viscount. Founder Mǐ Xióngyì 芈熊繹, great-grandson of Yùxióng 鬻熊, a general for Kings Wǔ and Wén. Initially founded in the region of Jīng 荆 Mountain (present-day Nánzhāng

南漳, Húběi), hence also known historically as the state of Jīng. Major capital was at Yǐng 郢 (present-day Jīngzhōu 荆州, Hubei, about 540 mi. SW of Qūfù). Chǔ grew steadily into the largest of the Zhōu-era states, but with its own distinct cultural aspects, it viewed itself as somewhat non-Zhōu, or non-Xià. During the time of Confucius, it extended from Hénán in the north to Ānhuī in the east, south to Dòngtíng Lake and west to Shǎnxī. Chǔ reigned as one of the Five Superpowers of the Spring and Autumn period and was one of the seven states left standing toward the end of the Warring States period. It suffered a major defeat by Wú in 506 BCE. See also 10.2n2. (Huang and Zhao 1997; Loewe and Shaughnessy 1999; Zheng, Wu, and Yang 2000; Shi, Zheng, and Zhu 2005; Durrant, Li, and Schaberg 2016) *10.2, 42.11*

Rulers of Chǔ in the *Dialogues*

King Zhuāng	r. 613–591 BCE
King Gōng	r. 590–560 BCE
King Líng	r. 540–529 BCE
King Píng	r. 528–516 BCE
King Zhāo	r. 515–489 BCE

Chu King Gong, Chǔ Gōng (Gòng) Wáng 楚恭(共)王: R. 590–560 BCE. Son of King Zhuāng. He made temporary peace with Jìn, but when hostilities broke out again in 575 BCE, Chǔ was defeated by Jìn. (Zheng, Wu, and Yang 2000) *10.6*

Chu King Ling, Chǔ Líng Wáng 楚靈王: R. 540–529 BCE. Son of King Gōng. He initially served as prime minister, then assumed the throne after assassinating the king (who was also his nephew). He engaged in warfare near and far. After a decade of turmoil he was ousted by his younger brother, whereupon he committed suicide. See also 41.7n23. (Zheng, Wu, and Yang 2000) *41.7*

Chu King Ping, Chǔ Píng Wáng 楚平王: R. 528–516 BCE. Youngest son of King Gōng. He launched a revolt in 529 while King Líng was on a campaign, assassinated the crown prince and placed his older brother on the throne, then took the position of minister of security. After King Líng committed suicide, the future King Píng forced his older brother the king to commit suicide and then assumed the throne himself. See also **Wu Zixu.** (Zheng, Wu, and Yang 2000)

Chu King Zhao, Chǔ Zhāo Wáng 楚昭王: Son of King Píng. R. 515–489 BCE. See also 41.16n44. (Zheng, Wu, and Yang 2000) *20.1, 41.16*

Chu King Zhuang, Chǔ Zhuāng Wáng 楚莊王: R. 613–591 BCE. After reforming the government, improving water infrastructure, and promoting commerce, King Zhuāng rapidly expanded Chu's territory by pacifying other ethnic peoples and conquering other states. In 598 BCE, he conquered and then restored Chén, installing Duke Chéng. The following year, he achieved superpower status by defeating Zhèng and Jìn in separate battles. (Yuan, Li, and Qi 1990; Zheng, Wu, and Yang 2000) *10.2n2*

Ci: See **Zigong.**

Coming-of-age ceremony: See **Capping ceremony.**

Confucius, Kǒng Qiū 孔丘: 551–479 BCE. Surname Kǒng 孔, given name Qiū 丘, *zì* Zhòngní 仲尼. For his family history, see 39.1–3. (Fang et al. 1994)

Counting custom: In the West, when counting units of time, we generally use cardinal numbers at the completion of each unit. For example, we count one year in age at the completion of the first year after birth. The ancient Chinese sometimes seem to have instead used ordinal numbers to count at the initial threshold of the unit of time. For example, for the age of a person, they counted one immediately after birth. A newborn was one *suì* 歲. (Each subsequent change in age occurred at the New Year, regardless of the date of birth.) We see something similar in the counting of the mourning period. The longest mourning period was traditionally "three years," which meant not thirty-six months but instead only two years plus one month into the third year—that is, twenty-five months. Similarly, in *Dialogues* 25.3, the human gestation period is said to be ten months. Since the length of human gestation is 280 days on average, or 9.33 months (assuming thirty days in a month), a child is born during the tenth month of gestation. Thus, the length of gestation is deemed to be ten months.

Crown: A crown in Zhōu-dynasty China, rather than being a metal ring with vertical efflorescences, was a ceremonial cap (*guān* 冠) worn by the sovereign and high officials. A *guān* that is referred to as *miǎn* 冕 was especially esteemed. The exact nature of a *miǎn* is unknown, as there are no surviving examples or images from the Zhōu dynasty. However, from images available from later dynasties, the *miǎn* crown that the sovereign wore probably consisted of a horizontal board above a conical cap, somewhat resembling the academic mortarboard of our own time, except that the *miǎn* board was rectangular instead of square, extending over the wearer's face, and was draped on the short ends with beaded strings of equal length, resembling a screen (see 21.7 and 29.3). The fabric is said to have been black silk, and the beads were variously colored semiprecious stones, predominantly jade. Varieties of *miǎn* may have signified distinct ranks or may have been used in distinct ritual settings. (Gao 1996; Zhou 2006; Zhao et al. 2008; Zhao and Zhang 2015) *Guān* 冠*: 10.1, Miǎn* 冕*: 4.1, 7.1, 9.11, 10.12, 21.7, 29.3, 33.3, 35.3*

Cun, Cùn 寸: See "Weights and Measures" at the beginning of the glossary.

Da Hao: See **Tai Hao.**

Dan Fu, Dǎn Fǔ 亶甫: Also known as Tài Wáng 太王. Grandfather of Zhōu King Wén. He is credited with moving the Zhōu people to the Wèi 渭 River valley and transforming them from a rustic people into a civilized state. See also **Wu (state); Zhou (dynasty).** (Loewe and Shaughnessy 1999) *4.1, 10.18*

Dance: Dance was an important part of official ceremonies and even of prognostication and archery. Unfortunately, we have few details of the exact nature of the dances, who danced them, their content, or their uses. We do know that there was a musical distinction between what we might call high and low kinds of dance, with serious dances for solemn official ceremonies being accompanied by orchestras and more lively, jovial dances being accompanied by smaller ensembles. Both kinds could have narrative elements. Confucius believed that dance, like music, could infectiously convey human emotion. See also **Music.** *19.7, 22.4, 27.1, 35.3*

Daye Marsh, Dàyě 大野: Once a vast marshland, in present-day Jùyě 巨野, Shāndōng (about 50 mi. W of Qūfù), adjacent to the famous Liáng Mountain featured in the classic novel *Outlaws of the Marsh*, or *Water Margin.* (Luo 1994; Tan 1996) *16.10*

Deputy Mao, Shàozhèng Mǎo 少正卯: Whether *shàozhèng* was a surname or a government position is uncertain. Because it appears in the historical record as a position (though only rarely) and the surname does not appear elsewhere (and Mǎo *is* a surname), we interpret it as a position and follow Knoblock (1994) in translating it as "deputy." This person is not attested elsewhere. (Kong, Sang, and Kong 1994) *2.1*

Destiny: See **Fate.**

Di (ceremony), Dì 禘: A major sacrificial ceremony to one's ancestors, performed in the ancestral temple. In the *Analects* (3.11), Confucius confesses ignorance of the exact content, though he acknowledges its power. In events recorded in CQZZ, Dì is reported as having been performed at the ancestral temple in the second, fifth, seventh, and tenth months (but not necessarily restricted to these) to ancestors of the king, including an immediately deceased ruler, and is associated with the Zhēng 烝 and Cháng 嘗 sacrifices. The focus in 27.1 and 32.12 on ancestral lines appears consistent with these passages. See also **Chang.** (Liu 1989) *27.1, 32.4, 32.12, 34.1*

Di (deity/ancestor): See **Shang Di.**

Di (people), Dí 狄(翟): A nomadic people of the northern Chinese cultural sphere during the Zhōu dynasty. They likely had a distinct language and culture but regular contact (and warfare) with their Chinese neighbors. (Qian and Dawa 1999) *10.18*

Documents: *Shū* 書, *Shū jīng* 書經, or *Shàng shū* 尚書: Early text of immense importance. It purports to record the very early history of China, and, most significantly, the military victory of the Zhōu over the Shāng and subsequent events and speeches of the Western Zhōu dynasty. It is often referred to by Confucius and is said to have been edited by him (see, e.g., 39.3). It was designated one of the Five Classics of Confucianism during the Hàn dynasty. Italicized, it refers to a single, edited collection created either by Confucius or sometime after, editions of which have been passed down to us today. When not italicized, it refers to whatever collections (e.g., the Xia shu in 18.4) of related documents existed during the time of

Confucius, prior to their arrangement into a single collection.[6] See also **Six Classics.** (Loewe 1993) *2.2, 12.1n1, 18.4, 22.5, 30.1n2, 36.2, 38.26, 39.3, 41.9, 41.16, 41.19*

Dongmen Xiangzhong, Dōngmén Xiāngzhòng 東門襄仲: Also known as Gōngzǐ Suì 公子遂. Fl. 634–601 BCE. Son of Lǔ Duke Zhuāng. Uncle of Lǔ Duke Wén. Following Duke Wén's death, Dōngmén engineered the enthronement of Duke Xuān after having two legitimate rivals murdered. (Zheng, Wu, and Yang 2000; Durrant, Li, and Schaberg 2016) *42.13*

***Dou* ritual vessel, *dòu* 豆:** A ritual vessel with a deep lid and built-in stand. They were often round, with a tall, narrow stand. During Confucius' time, they were made of bronze and were used for sacrificial ceremonies. *42.7*

Dragon, *lóng* 龍, *jiāo lóng* 蛟龍: The *lóng*, or *jiāo lóng*, is an auspicious, mythological reptile-like animal of composite characteristics, often associated with water. The *Kangxi Dictionary* provides a variety of descriptions from earlier dictionaries, which include the following: they can be hidden or out in the open; they may be small or large, and short or long; in the spring they fly into the sky, and in the fall they submerge into the depths. Some have scales, some feathers, and some horns, and some don't fly. *16.1, 16.4, 22.2, 25.4, 29.3, 32.11, 32.15*

Duanmu Ci: See **Zigong.**

Duke, *gōng* 公: Highest of the five noble titles conferred by a king. See also under **Nobility and noble titles.**

Duke of She, Shè Gōng 葉公: Shěn Zhūliáng 沈諸梁. Surname Shěn 沈, given name Zhūliáng 諸梁, *zì* Zǐgāo 子高. Fl. 505–476 BCE. The fiefdom of Shè was in northwest Chǔ south of present-day Yè 葉縣 (about 275 mi. SW of Qūfù). According to CQZZ ("Āi"), the Duke of Shè was a trusted minister of the Chǔ government and an important Chǔ general, who once saved Chǔ King Huì's life during a rebellion. The Duke of Shè appears in *Analects* 7.19, 13.16, and 13.18. (Zhang and Xia 2010) *14.1*

Duke of Zhou, Zhōu Gōng 周公: Fourth son of Zhōu King Wén. R. 1042–1036 BCE. According to the *Documents* ("Zhōu shū"), the Duke of Zhōu took control of the government after his older brother King Wǔ died prematurely and Wǔ's heir, King Chéng, was not yet of age. When civil war broke out, he successfully united the country. See also under **Cai (person).** When Chéng came of age, he handed the government over to him. He is perhaps the ruler most admired by Confucius (according to *Analects* 7.5, Confucius regularly dreamed of him). See also **Zhou (dynasty).** *2.1, 8.6, 11.1, 11.2, 13.7, 23.1, 32.2, 32.4, 33.2, 35.3, 39.1, 41.19, 41.23, 43.3, 44.3*

6. Dirk Meyer (2012) was the first that we know of to adopt this orthographic method of plain and italic font to distinguish pre-established collections from established classics. He uses it for the Documents and the Poems.

Earl, *bó* 伯: Third of the five noble titles conferred by the Zhōu king. See also under **Nobility and noble titles.**

Earl of Shao, Shào Bó (Gōng) 召(邵)伯(公): Surname Jī 姬, given name Shì 奭. One of the founding fathers of the Zhōu. Son of Zhōu King Wén. Originally enfeoffed as Earl (or Duke) at Shào 召(邵). Assisted King Wǔ in conquering Shāng. Although he was then enfeoffed as Duke of Yān in the far northeast, he gave that position to his son and remained in the capital, where he took on the role of Grand Protector of the young King Chéng. After the death of King Chéng, he stayed on to assist King Kāng, living past the age of 100. According to the *Documents* and several inscribed bronzes dating from the period, the Earl of Shào was instrumental in suppressing the Wǔ Gēng rebellion and ensuring the smooth succession of Kings Chéng and Kāng. See also 35.3n5. (Shaughnessy 1997; Zheng, Wu, and Yang 2000) *10.4n8, 34.2, 35.3*

Earl of Shēn, Shēn Bó 申伯: Zhōu King Xuān's uncle and minister. For his meritorious service, he was enfeoffed at Shēn (present-day Nányáng, Hénán). (Zheng, Wu, and Yang 2000) *36.2*

Earl of the West: See **Zhou King Wen.**

Eastern Zhou: See **Zhou King You.**

Emperor, *dì* 帝: The term *dì* 帝 refers to a paramount ruler and is applied to personages going back into the mists of prehistory. By custom, a meritorious person remains as a spiritual figure after death. By extension, *dì* also means ancestor or god. *Dì* was the preferred title for kings during the Shāng dynasty. When referring to legendary leaders prior to the Shāng, when rulers were leaders of Neolithic settlements, we translate *dì* as *chief*. For Shāng leaders, we translate it as *king;* for rulers after the Zhōu, we translate it as *emperor*. See also **Shang Di.**

Enlightened king (of the past), *míng wáng* 明王: Similar to Ancient King but also used in a prospective sense. *3.1, 3.2, 4.1, 6.1, 7.6, 8.1, 9.9, 16.10, 21.6, 24.1, 36.3, 39.3, 40.1*

***Fa xiang, Fǎ xiàng* 法象:** Normative model. This terminology is also found in the *Xì cí* 繫辭 (Commentary on the *Changes*): "易有太極, 是生兩儀, 兩儀生四象, 四象生八卦, 八卦定吉凶, 吉凶生大業。是故, 法象莫大乎天地。Changes begin in *tàijí*, which generates the two poles, from which spring the four images (*xiàng* 象), from which spring the eight trigrams, which identify the auspicious and inauspicious, from which all enterprises spring. Thus, there is no greater normative model than nature." *Image* should be understood here as a visual manifestation. The *tàijí* and the two poles (*qián* 乾 and *kūn* 坤) are forces that are too subtle to be perceived. Only when they differentiate into their four possible permutations (*qián-qián, qián-kūn, kūn-qián, kūn-kūn*), variously conceived as the four directions, four elements, four seasons, and so on, are they perceptible. Insofar as humans are to take nature as a model of behavior, these images are the normative model—*fǎ xiàng*. The term gets a decidedly Confucian elucidation in the text

Zhōng lùn 中論, written by Xú Gàn 徐幹, an older contemporary of Wáng Sù. Xú writes:

> 夫法象立，所以爲君子，法象者，莫先乎正容貌、慎威儀，是故先王之制禮也，爲冕服采章以旌之，爲珮玉鳴璜以聲之，欲.其尊也，欲其莊也，焉可懈慢也。夫容貌者，人之符表也，符表正，故情性治；情性治，故仁義存；仁義存，故盛德著；盛德著，故可以爲法象。
>
> The establishing of a normative model is what creates the *jūnzǐ*. In the normative model, nothing is prior to getting one's facial appearance and expression correct and taking care to appear serious and awe-inspiring. And so, in organizing *lǐ*, the Ancient Kings created standards through the color and presentation of apparel and headgear, and the clinking of jade belt ornaments was the aural manifestation. Wishing to project respect and dignity, how can one neglect these? Facial appearance and expression are outer expressions that tally with one's interior. When that tally is correct, it means one's inner nature and disposition are in order, which means *rén* and *yì* are present, which means an effulgence of *dé*. It is the effulgence of *dé* that can be taken as the normative model. *21.3*

Fan Chi, Fán Chí 樊遲: Fán Chí appears in six episodes in the *Analects*, prompting some of Confucius' most evocative responses. Outside of his brief biography in 38.16, he appears in two episodes of the *Dialogues*. *38.16, 41.2, 41.22*

Fan Xu: See **Fan Chi.**

Fan Xuanzi, Fàn Xuānzǐ 范宣子: Fl. 563–550 BCE. High minister of Jìn who dominated the government for a time. (Zheng, Wu, and Yang 2000) *41.15*

Fang, Fáng 防: Hill 19 mi. E of Qūfù. Burial place of Confucius' parents. *39.2, 44.3*

***Feng, fèng* 鳳, or *fènghuáng* 鳳凰:** An auspicious, mythological, composite, birdlike animal. The *Kangxi Dictionary* provides a variety of descriptions from earlier sources, which include the following: It has the shape of a crane, its markings are composed of the five colors, and its call is of the five tones; it lives in mountain caves, rests only on the firmiana tree, eats only the inner part of bamboo, drinks only fresh spring water, and appears only when the *dao* prevails in the land. It has the head of a chicken, the beak of a sparrow, the neck of a snake, the body of a goose, the tail of a fish, and wings along its spine. Sometimes *fèng* is said to be the male and *huáng* the female. *10.1, 16.4, 22.2, 25.4, 32.11, 32.15*

***Fenghuang*: See *Feng*.**

Chiefs Discussed in the *Dialogues*

Chief	Also Known As	Father	Grandfather
Yellow Chief	Xuānyuán	Shào Diǎn	
Zhuānxū	Gāo Yáng	Chāngyì	Yellow Chief
Kù	Gāo Xīn	Jiāojí	Xuánxiāo
Yáo	Táotáng	Kù	
Shùn	Yǒuyú	Gǔsǒu	Jiǎoniú
Yǔ	Xià Hòu	Gǔn	Zhuānxū

Five Chiefs, *wǔ dì* 五帝: (1) The Yellow Chief, Zhuānxū, Kù, Yáo, and Shùn. See under each entry individually, and see chapter 23 especially. *23.2, 24.1, 24.3, 24.5, 30.1* (2) A metaphor for the five elemental phases. *24.1*

Five sacrificial ceremonies, *wu si* 五祀: There are a variety of different views about the specific reference of this term. The dominant view is that the ceremonies are sacrifices to spirits associated with each of the five elemental phases, as in 24.3. According to the *Guó yǔ,* they are the ceremonies of Dì 禘, Jiāo 郊, Zōng 宗, Zǔ 祖, and Bào 報. (The difference between Zōng and Zǔ is unclear and much debated.) In another interpretation, the ceremonies are common sacrifices to spirits in and around the home, such as spirits of the doors, windows, hearth, earth, and well. (Luo 1994; Zheng, Wu, and Yang 2000) *24.3, 32.6, 32.12*

Five transformative teachings, *wǔ jiào* 五教: This locution occurs three times in the *Documents*. In the earliest mention ("Shùn diǎn"), it is associated with people at all levels who lack intimate bonds and are recalcitrant and are thus in need of instruction by the minister of education. There and elsewhere, it is associated with five ranks (*wǔ pǐn* 五品), five enduring virtues (*wǔ cháng* 五常), and five moral relationships (*wǔ lún* 五倫). The clearest explanation comes from Kǒng Yīngdá (574–648 CE), who says the five ranks are father, mother, older sibling, younger sibling, and child, and what they should be taught respectively are *yì*, compassion, friendship, reverence, and *xiào*, which, when expressed consistently over time, become the five enduring virtues. Kǒng's gloss is probably informed by passages in CQZZ and SJ, both of which make a close association between the five transformative teachings and the following roles and virtues: father's *yì*, mother's compassion, older sibling's friendship, younger sibling's reverence, and child's *xiào*. *8.1, 25.2, 30.1*

Foot: See "Weights and Measures" at the beginning of the glossary.

Fu: See **Yin Jifu.**

Fu Buqi: See **Fu Zijian.**

Fu Fuhe, Fú Fùhé 弗父何: According to the *Dialogues* and CQZZ ("Zhāo" 7), Fú Fùhé was an ancestor of Confucius and rightful heir to the Sòng throne after the death of Duke Xiāng. Older brother of Sòng Duke Lì. See also 11.1n4. *11.1, 39.1, 39.2, 39.3*

Fu Zijian, Fú Zǐjiàn 宓子賤: Surname Fú 宓, given name Bùqí 不齊, *zì* Zǐjiàn 子賤. In Fú Zǐjiàn's one brief appearance in the *Analects* (5.3), Confucius praises him. The context for that passage is provided in *Dialogues* 19.4, which ends with an encomium very similar to *Analects* 5.3. Fú receives praise from Confucius in his other appearances in the *Dialogues*, which are unusually long descriptions of his work as mayor of Shànfù. For a brief biography, see 38.15. (Luo 1994; Taiwan Academic Network 2021) *14.7, 19.4, 37.3, 38.15*

Fuzi: See **Fu Zijian.**

Gao Chai: See **Zigao.**

Gao Ting, Gāo Tíng 高庭: According to CQZZ, there was a prominent Gāo family in Qí, but a Gāo Tíng is not recorded elsewhere. *15.21*

Gao Xin, Gāo Xīn 高辛: See 23.3 for his biography. *23.3, 23.4*

Gao Yang: See **Zhuanxu.**

Gao Yao, Gāo Yáo 皋陶(繇): Trusted minister for Shùn, in charge of criminal punishment. Figures prominently in the *Documents*. *3.1, 22.8, 23.6, 30.1n2, 41.9, 41.16n47*

Gaozong, Gāozōng 高宗: Shāng dynasty king. Also known as Wǔdīng 武丁. Known for enlightened rulership. (Zheng, Wu, and Yang 2000) *38.12, 41.19*

Gengzong, Gēngzōng 庚宗: In southern present-day Sìshuǐ 泗水, Shāndōng, west of Ní Mountain (about 26 mi. WSW of Qūfù). (Zheng, Wu, and Yang 2000) *41.8*

Gong Tao: See **Nangong Jingshu.**

Gongfu Mubo, Gōngfù Mùbó 公父穆伯: Younger brother of Jì Píngzǐ. Passed away at a young age, leaving his wife, Jìngjiāng, a widow. Father of Gōngfù Wénbó. *42.18*

Gongfu Wenbo, Gōngfù Wénbó 公父文伯: Son of Gōngfú Mùbó and minister in Lǔ. *41.21, 42.18, 43.20*

Gonggong, Gònggōng 共工: Legendary prehistoric figure. Descendent of Chief Yán. Lost a battle for supremacy to Zhuānxū. (Luo 1994; Taiwan Academic Network 2021) *16.4, 24.3*

Gongliang Ru, Gōngliáng Rú 公良儒: See 38.27 for a brief biography. *22.9, 38.27*

Gongming Yi, Gōngmíng Yí 公明儀: Said to be a student of Zēngzǐ or Zǐzhāng, who apparently came to be a teacher in his own right. Quoted four times by Mencius in the *Mencius*. (Zheng, Wu, and Yang 2000) *42.20*

Gongshan Furao, Gōngshān Fúrǎo 公山弗擾: Surname Gōngshān 公山, given name Fúrǎo 弗擾 (also Bùniǔ 不狃), *zì* Zǐyì 子洩. A treacherous vassal of Jì Píngzǐ, who once attempted to assassinate him. Appears in one episode of the *Analects* (17.5). (Zhang and Xia 2010) *1.3*

Gongshu Wuren, Gōngshū Wùrén 公叔務人: Second son of Lǔ Duke Zhāo. (CQZZ "Zhāo" 29) *42.16*

Gongxi Chi, Gōngxī Chì 公西赤: Surname Gōngxī 公西, given name Chì 赤, *zì* Zǐhuá 子華. In his mini-biography (38.18) and in Zǐgòng's appraisal of him, Gōngxī Chì is praised for his skill in the protocol of entertaining guests. This is consistent with his appearance in *Analects* 5.8. In the *Dialogues*, he is also skilled in burial protocol (44.1) and is entrusted with preparing Confucius' body for burial (40.2). *12.8, 38.18, 40.2, 44.1*

Goulong, Gōulóng 勾(句)龍: Son of Gònggōng. The outline of Gōulóng's story, as related in 24.3, is all that has come down to us. Because of the great strides he made when in charge of agriculture, he was later worshipped as the god of soil (Hòu Tǔ 后土). (Zheng, Wu, and Yang 2000) *24.3, 24.5*

Grand Duke, Tài Gōng 太公: Also known as Grand Duke Wàng, Tài Gōng Wàng 太公望. Surname Lǚ 吕, given name Shàng 尚. Mentioned in BA as a general of King Wén. Mentioned in the *Poems* as general to King Wǔ in the battle to defeat the Shāng. He appears in CQZZ as the founding ruler of Qí, figuring prominently in their ritual pantheon. He is not mentioned explicitly in the *Documents*. *2.1, 35.3*

Great Inchoate, *tài yī* 太一: This term appears in a number of philosophical Warring States texts, one of which, lost and then excavated in the twentieth century, elucidates the idea. All of them describe a cosmogonic unity that is an undifferentiated mass charged with potential becoming—the "nothing" from which everything comes. The evolutionary process of differentiation depicted in *Dialogues* 32.13 tracks the process depicted in the excavated text, transitioning from the Great Inchoate to heaven and earth, *yin* and *yang*, the four seasons, and gods and spirits, except that, in the excavated text, the order is slightly different and the evolutionary steps are delineated in more detail, with the inclusion of water as the second step. Another similarity between the *Dialogues* and the excavated text is that the excavated text, which bears ideas that we often associate with Daoism, was buried among many texts traditionally associated with Confucianism. This blurring of lines between Daoism and Confucianism is also apparent in the *Dialogues*, although instead of a blurring of existing lines, the combination of ideas may instead represent an original undifferentiation. See Henricks (2000) and Meyer (2012) for translations of the excavated text. *32.13*

Guan (person), Guǎn 管: Also known as Guǎnshū 管叔. Surname Jī 姬, given name Xiān 鮮. See under **Cai (person).** *2.1, 39.1*

Guan (state), Guǎn 管: State enfeoffed by Zhōu. See under **Cai (person).** *2.1, 39.1*

Guan Longpang: Guān Lóngpáng 關龍逄(逢): According to BA, Lóngpáng was a minister of King Jié of Xià, who ultimately killed him. He is the earliest example of a loyal minister killed by a tyrannical ruler. *13.5, 20.1*

Guan Zhong, Guǎn Zhòng 管仲: Minister of Qí, 685–645 BCE. According to *Guó yǔ* and SJ, Guǎn Zhòng ascended from humble origins to be prime minister of Qí and architect of a major set of governmental reforms. These reforms had repercussions across China during his time and down through history, leading Qí to be the first superpower of the Spring and Autumn period. He was widely respected as a brilliant statesman and leader. Although neither he nor Zǐchǎn (of Zhèng) were concerned with *lǐ* and virtue in the same way that Confucius was, Confucius still specifically lauds them as outstanding officials. See also 8.9n13. (Zheng, Wu, and Yang 2000) *2.1, 8.9, 13.2, 42.7, 43.8*

***Guan*-flute, *guǎn* 管:** The word *guǎn* can refer to any simple cylindrical wind instrument, or part of a wind instrument (see 32.9, for example, where the term is used for the individual pipes of the panpipe), and as such can be regarded here as a kind of flute. A word that clearly means flute in early texts, such as the *Chǔ cí* (but not in the *Dialogues*), is *chí* 篪. Archaeologists are divided about which

Chinese word to use for flutes found in excavations from the Eastern Zhōu. (Sui County Leigudun Archaeological Team 1979; Zhang 1998; So 2000) *27.1*

Guiyin, Guīyīn 龜陰: City of Lǔ during the Spring and Autumn period. Present-day Xīntài 新泰 (55 mi. NE of Qūfù). *1.2n9*

Gun, Gǔn 鯀: According to BA, Yáo ordered Gǔn to manage the Yellow River but soon dismissed (or exiled) him, suggesting that Gǔn had bungled the job. According to separate passages in the *Documents*, Gǔn caused turmoil by damming a river and was executed by an unnamed king for it ("Hóng fàn"), and Gǔn was executed by Shùn for an unspecified reason ("Shùn diǎn"). *23.6*

Gusou, Gǔsǒu 瞽瞍: Father of Shùn. Beginning with a vague reference in the *Documents* ("Dà Yǔ mó"), the early tradition regularly praises Shùn for his heroic forbearance in the face of abusive, even murderous, treatment by his family, including his father. *15.10, 23.5*

Guzhu, Gūzhú 孤竹: A state during the Shāng dynasty. According to BA, when, in the twenty-first year of Shāng King Zhòu's reign, noble lords across the land pledged allegiance to Zhōu, Bóyí and Shūqí departed Gūzhú for Zhōu. *12.21n19*

Han River, Hàn 漢: The Hàn River flowed from the northwest corner of Chǔ in a southeast direction, emptying into the Yangtze at present-day Wǔhàn. (Tan 1996) *36.2n4, 41.16*

Han Xuanzi, Hán Xuānzǐ 韓宣子: Surname Hán 韓, given name Qǐ 起, posthumous name Xuān 宣. He entered government service in 566 BCE, and for periods of time from 542 until his death in 514 he held control of the Jìn government. In CQZZ ("Xiāng"; "Zhāo"), he is depicted as a successful general, minister, and diplomat. (Zheng, Wu, and Yang 2000) *41.9*

Heyang, Héyáng 河陽: City of Zhèng about 36 mi. NW of the Zhōu capital. Present-day Mèngzhōu 孟州. (Tan 1996) *42.1*

High ancestors: See **Shang Di.**

Hong Yao, Hóng Yāo 閎夭: According to the *Documents*, King Wén hired Tài Diān and Hóng Yāo after hearing about them. They appear across the early corpus as trusted ministers and advisers of King Wén, though details are scarce. *8.6*

Hou Ji, Hòu Jì 后稷: Hòu Jì is the purported progenitor of the Zhōu's royal Jī 姬 clan. He is said to have lived during the time of Yáo, who employed him as Minister of Agriculture; during the time of Shùn, who enfeoffed him at Tái 邰 (west of present-day Wǔgōng 武功, Shǎnxī); and during the time of Yǔ, who employed him to help with irrigation. He is traditionally credited with introducing grain agriculture into Chinese society. (Zheng, Wu, and Yang 2000) *10.18, 11.2, 29.2, 35.3*

Hua Mountain, Huá Shān 華山: Present-day Huá Mountain, in Huáyīn 華陰, Shǎnxī, about 80 mi. W of Xī'ān (Western Zhōu capital), south of the Wèi River and southwest of the main south-to-east bend of the Yellow River. (Tan 1996) *35.3*

Huan: See **Lu Duke Huan.**

Huan, Huān 歡: City on the border of Lǔ and Qí, north of the Wèn River and north of present-day Níngyáng County 寧陽縣 (about 33 mi. NNW of Qūfù). (Tan 1996) *1.2n9*

Huan Tui, Huán Tuí 桓魋: Surname Sīmǎ, given name Xiàngtuí 向魋. Because he was descended from Sòng Duke Huán, he was commonly referred to as Huán Tuí. Brother of Confucius' student Sīmǎ Lígēng 司馬黎耕. According to SJ ("Kǒngzǐ shì jiā"), Huán Tuí so disliked Confucius that he threatened to kill him with an uprooted tree. In *Analects* 7.23, Confucius says, "*Tiān* gave rise to *dé* in me. What can Huán Tuí do to me?" (Liu and Chi 2002) *38.30, 42.2*

Huangchi, Huángchí 黄池: Southwest of present-day Fēngqiū 封丘縣, Hénán, *37.2*

Hui: See **Yan Hui.**

Huo, Huò 霍: State that existed during the Shāng and was enfeoffed to a brother of King Wǔ at the beginning of the Zhōu. Present-day Huòzhōu 霍州市, Shānxī. (Zheng, Wu, and Yang 2000) *39.1*

Inch: See "Weights and Measures" at the beginning of the glossary.

Ji (place), Jì 薊: Location in the southwest corner of present-day Beijing. Became the capital of the state of Yān. *35.3*

Ji (surname): See **Jisun.**

Ji Gao: See **Zigao.**

House of Jisun in the *Dialogues*	
Jì Wǔzǐ	d. 535 BCE
Jì Píngzǐ	d. 505 BCE
Jì Huánzǐ	d. 492 BCE
Jì Kāngzǐ	d. 468 BCE

Ji Huanzi, Jì Huánzǐ 季桓子: D. 492 BCE. Surname Jì 季 (or Jìsūn 季孫), given name Sī 斯, posthumous name Huán 桓. Jì Píngzǐ's son and heir. Served under Duke Dìng. Although the duke was the sovereign head of state in Lǔ, his power had in fact been usurped by the descendants of the earlier Duke Huán (r. 711–694 BCE). They are the Jìsūn (or Jì 季), Zhòngsūn 仲孫 (or Mèngsūn 孟孫), and Shūsūn 叔孫 clans, collectively known as the Three Huáns or just the Three Families, who also had mutually antagonistic relationships. In 505 BCE, when Jì Huánzǐ was the controlling power in Lǔ, his power was effectively usurped by his household manager, Yáng Hǔ. In 498 BCE, Confucius' student Zǐlù 子路 was hired as Jì Huánzǐ's household manager. See also **Yang Hu.** (Kong, Sang, and Kong 1994; Zheng, Wu, and Yang 2000) *1.1, 16.1, 19.7, 42.14, 42.31, 43.22*

Ji Kangzi, Jì Kāngzǐ 季康子: D. 468 BCE. Surname Jì 季 (or Jìsūn 季孫), given name Féi 肥, posthumous name Kāng 康. Son and heir of Jì Huánzǐ 季桓子. In

484 BCE, Jì Kāngzǐ used a strategy from Confucius' student Rǎnyóu to defeat an invading Qí army (see 41.2). (Kong, Sang, and Kong 1994; Zheng, Wu, and Yang 2000; Durrant, Li, and Schaberg 2016) *16.8, 19.3, 24.1, 41.2, 41.17, 41.18, 41.23, 42.5, 42.14*

Ji Pingzi, Jì Píngzǐ 季平子: D. 505 BCE. Given name Yìrú 意如. Grandson of Jì Wǔzǐ. One of the most powerful men in Lǔ. Had an antagonistic relationship with Duke Zhāo. In 517 BCE, Duke Zhāo attacked Jì's city, lost the battle, fled, and died in exile in 510 BCE. Jì, in an affront to the duke, had his body buried elsewhere than the ducal cemetery. See also **Ji Wuzi.** (Kong, Sang, and Kong 1994) *41.9n31, 43.17*

Ji Wuzi, Jì Wǔzǐ 季武子: D. 535 BCE. Grandfather of Jì Píngzǐ 季平子. Controlled the government during the reigns of the Lǔ Dukes Xiāng and Zhāo. He served as ringleader when in 562 BCE, each of the Jìsūn, Shūsūn, and Mèngsūn clans established a standing army to wrest power from Duke Xiāng. In 537 BCE, he eliminated the standing army and reconstituted it into four armies, taking two of them for himself and thus effectively taking controlling power in Lǔ for generations to come. (Zheng, Wu, and Yang 2000)

Jiagu, Jiágǔ 夾谷: An area near the border between Lǔ and Qí, in the southern part of present-day Láiwú 萊蕪, Shāndōng (60 mi. NE of Qūfù). (Tan 1996; Zhang and Xia 2010) *1.2*

Jiao: See **Jiao and She.** *11.1, 19.5, 19.7, 27.1, 29.1, 29.2, 29.3, 32.4, 32.6n, 32.12, 34.1, 35.3, 41.16.*

Jiao and She, Jiāo Shè 郊社: Jiāo and Shè are topics of special concern in the *Dialogues*. Chapter 29 is devoted to Jiāo, and there is further elaboration in 32.4 and 34.1. From references in the *Dialogues*, it can be determined that the Jiāo was a major ceremony aimed at achieving a bountiful crop of grain and expressing gratitude for the people's origins. It was conducted by the ruler at the winter solstice or spring equinox on a hill on the outskirts (*jiāo*) of the city and involved *tiān*, the god Shàng Dì, the god Hòu Jì, the recently deceased, and the ancestors. The Shè ceremony, according to the *Dialogues* (27.1, 32.12), was concomitant with Jiāo and emphasized the fertility of the soil. CQZZ generally records sacrificial ceremonies only when there is something unusual about them (see "Huán" 5.5), and there are about a dozen passages regarding the Jiāo ceremony, always in the spring, summer, or fall—never in the winter, and never along with the Shè ceremony. There is little other information in either the standard textual record or archaeological record about Jiāo and Shè. Chén Mèngjiā's analysis of oracle bones, bronze inscriptions, and their relation to standard textual sources concludes that *jiāo* in Shāng times referred to a hill or the base of a hill and *shè* to a stone altar or edifice at that location used for supplication to the god Dì for rain. The god Hòu Jì, Chén says, was introduced later. See also **Sheji.** (Chen 1941) *11.1, 27.1, 32.12*

Jiaoyao, Jiāoyáo 焦僥: The Jiāoyáo are mentioned repeatedly across the early corpus as a people of particularly small stature. Locations given include the Eastern Yí region (present-day Eastern Shāndōng) and the southwest. (Zheng, Wu, and Yang 2000) *16.2*

Jiaozhi, Jiāozhǐ 交趾: A reference to southernmost China—the area south of the Nánlíng Mountains, or northern Vietnam. Alternatively, it may refer to the area near the eastern reaches of the Yangtze River. (Zheng, Wu, and Yang 2000) *23.2*

Jie, Jié 桀: Given name Guǐ 癸 or Lǚguǐ 履癸. Last king of the Xià dynasty. Defeated and deposed by Tāng, founder of the Shāng dynasty. A brief account of Jié's story appears in the *Documents* ("Tài shì zhōng"), in which he is depicted vaguely as despotic and contrary to *tiān*. The depiction of his bad behavior in BA is similarly opaque but includes a bit more detail: a number of bad events and bad omens occur during his reign, he jails a Shāng emissary and attacks Shāng after releasing him, a vassal defects to Shāng, and he executes his minister Lóngpáng. Of extant literature, the rhetorical use of Jié as a symbol of an evil tyrant begins in CQZZ, where he is alluded to repeatedly. The depictions of Jié in the *Dialogues* follow this pattern. Jié, like Zhòu (the last king of the Shāng dynasty), is a symbol of excess and cruelty. His untimely demise is a warning for rulers of the era not to do the same, at the risk of suffering the same fate, and to instead be like Yáo and Shùn or the Zhōu kings Chéng and Kāng, who were moderate, wise, and loved by the people. See also **Zhou (person).** (Zheng, Wu, and Yang 2000; Zhang and Xia 2010) *8.1, 11.2, 13.3, 13.5, 15.2, 15.8, 25.1, 31.1*

Jie Zishan, Jiè Zǐshān 介子山: More commonly known as Jiè Zǐtuī 介子推 or Jiè Zhītuī 介之推. Late seventh century BCE. He was famous for his humility and self-sacrifice, though few details have come down to us in the standard histories. According to CQZZ ("Xī" 24.1), he served under the exiled Chóngěr, future Duke Wén of Jìn, one of the Five Superpowers of the Spring and Autumn period. Chóngěr lived in hardship and exile for nineteen years before ascending the throne. Jiè Zǐshān was one of several who accompanied him during that time. After Duke Wén had ascended the throne, the duke offered rewards to all those who had stood by his side through the hardships. When asked what his reward should be, Jiè Zǐshān refused, saying that no one should take credit for the work of *tiān*. *12.21*

Jin, Jìn 晋: Vassal state of Zhōu. After conquering the state of Táng 唐, King Chéng enfeoffed his younger brother Jī Shūyú 姬叔虞 as Marquis of Táng, near present-day Yìchéng 翼城縣, Shānxī (350 mi. W of Qūfù). Shūyú's son Xiè 燮 changed the state name to Jìn. The Jìn ruler's title was elevated to duke in the year 678 BCE. Jìn gradually expanded until it encompassed most of present-day Shānxī and parts of Shǎnxī, Hénán, and Héběi, becoming one of the largest states. Under Duke Wén, it was one of the Five Superpowers of the Spring and Autumn period.

In 403 it splintered when the three leading families killed the Jìn ruler and divided Jìn into the states of Hán 韓, Wèi 魏, and Zhào 趙, all of which survived into the waning years of the Warring States period. (Zhang and Xia 2010; Zheng, Wu, and Yang 2000; Liu and Chi 2002) *12.22, 13.6, 16.7, 16.9, 20.1, 22.2, 22.9, 37.2, 38.10, 41.4, 41.5, 41.6, 41.9, 41.11, 41.14, 41.15, 42.1, 42.10*

Rulers of Jìn in the *Dialogues*	
Duke Wén	697–628 BCE
Duke Líng	r. 620–607 BCE
Duke Píng	r. 557–532 BCE

Jin Duke Ling, Jìn Líng Gōng 晉靈公: Surname Jī 姬, given name Yígāo 夷皋, posthumous name Líng 靈. Son of Duke Xiāng. R. 620–607 BCE. Infamous for his excess and cruelty, he was eventually murdered. (Huang and Zhao 1997; Zheng, Wu, and Yang 2000) *41.5*

Jin Duke Ping, Jìn Píng Gōng 晉平公: Surname Jī 姬, given name Biāo 彪, posthumous name Píng 平. Son of Duke Dào 悼. R. 557–532 BCE. Known for hiring capable and virtuous men and heeding their counsel. (Liu and Chi 2002) *12.22, 41.11*

Jin Duke Wen, Jìn Wén Gōng 晉文公: 697–628 BCE. Surname Jī 姬, given name Chóngěr 重耳, posthumous name Wén 文. Son of Duke Xiàn. R. 636–628 BCE. He fled palace intrigue and wandered among the various states for nineteen years before being escorted back to Jìn by the Qín army. As ruler of Jìn, he oversaw government, economic, labor, agricultural, and military reforms that built Jìn into a stable, prosperous, powerful state. In 635, he supressed a rebellion in Zhōu and restored the rightful king to his throne. Three years later, he fought a decisive battle with Chǔ, thereby achieving superpower status for Jìn. His success is traditionally credited to his ability to hire and heed the counsel of capable and virtuous men and his frugality in personal expenditures. See also **Jie Zishan.** (Yuan, Li, and Qi 1990; Zheng, Wu, and Yang 2000; Zhang and Xia 2010) *20.1, 41.15, 42.1*

Jingjiang, Jìngjiāng 敬姜: Wife of Gōngfù Mùbó and mother of Gōngfù Wénbó. *42.18, 43.20.*

Jisun, Jìsūn 季孫 (or Jì 季): One of the three most powerful families in Lǔ during Confucius' time. Could also refer specifically to Jì Píngzǐ 季平子, Jì Huánzǐ 季桓子, or Jì Kāngzǐ 季康子. See also **Ji Huanzi**; **Ji Kangzi**; **Ji Pingzi**; **Lu Duke Ai**; **Mengsun**; **Shusun.** *1.1, 1.3, 2.2, 5.1, 8.5, 16.7, 37.3, 38.16, 41.2, 41.9, 41.18, 41.21, 41.27, 42.5, 42.17, 42.18, 42.31, 43.7, 43.23, 44.7*

Jizi of Yanling, Yánlíng Jìzǐ 延陵季子: Given name Zhā 札. Son of King Shòumèng of Wú 吳. Jìzǐ is depicted in CQZZ ("Xiāng" 29.13) as a music aficionado and a good judge of character (the two were assumed by people of the time to be intertwined). *41.4, 42.26*

Juexiang, Juéxiàng 矍相: An area of Qūfù just west of Quèlǐ 闕里, said to be the site of an archery practice ground. (Luo 1994) *28.1*

Kang: See **Zhou King Kang.**

Kangzi: See **Ji Kangzi.**

King, *wáng* 王, *tiānzǐ* 天子, dì 帝: During the Zhōu dynasty, the term *wáng* was a title originally reserved for the Zhōu ruler, the top of the Zhōu noble hierarchy. Not long after the Zhōu moved their capital east, the ruler of Chǔ assumed the title *wáng*, and over the centuries of the Zhōu's decline, the rulers of other states followed suit. *Tiānzǐ* is another term translated here as *king*. It means child of *tiān* and refers to the cosmic legitimacy of the paramount ruler, namely, the Zhōu king. During the Shāng dynasty, the title for a king was *dì* 帝. For specific kings, see entries for their dynasty or state. See also **Emperor.**

King Cheng: See **Zhou King Cheng.**

King Dan Fu: See **Dan Fu.**

King Kang: See **Zhou King Kang.**

King Li: See **Zhou King Li.**

King Wen: See **Zhou King Wen.**

King Wu: See **Zhou King Wu.**

King Xi: See **Zhou King Xi.**

King You: See **Zhou King You.**

Kong Mie, Kǒng Miè 孔篾: Son of Confucius' older brother. *19.4, 19.10*

Kong Wenzi, Kǒng Wénzǐ 孔文子: Given name Yǔ 圉. A nobleman of Wèi 衛. Father of Kǒng Kuī 孔悝. See **Kuaikui Unrest.** (Zheng, Wu, and Yang 2000) *41.17*

Ku (Chief), Dì Kù 帝嚳: Also known as Gāo Xīn 高辛. Third of the legendary Five Chiefs. See 23.3 for his biography. *23.3, 23.4*

Kuaiji, Kuàijī 會稽: Mountain southeast of present-day Shàoxīng 紹興縣, Zhejiang Province. *16.2, 20.1, 37.2*

Kuaikui Unrest, *Kuǎikuì zhī luàn* 蒯聵之亂: In 480 BCE, the Wèi crown prince Kuǎikuì 蒯聵 (and future Duke Zhuāng 莊) returned from exile intending to claim the throne by force, but still lacked the allegiance of a key nobleman named Kǒng Kuī 孔悝 (who was also the employer of Zǐlù). Kuǎikuì's men kidnapped Kǒng Kuī, and when Zǐlù (against the advice of Zǐgāo) confronted them, he was stabbed to death. In a notable side story, one of the duke's men, in stabbing Zǐlù, severed the strap on Zǐlù's cap; before dying, Zǐlù retied the strap, saying, "A *junzi* may die but not without his cap" (CQZZ "Āi" 15.5). *43.21*

Kuang, Kuāng 匡: City southwest of present-day Chángyuán 長垣, Hénán, on the road between the capitals of Wèi 衛 and Sòng. (Luo 1994) *22.5, 22.9*

***Kui, Kuí* 夔:** (1) Mythical creature. According to the *Zhuāngzǐ*, it hops on one foot. According to the *Shān hǎi jīng*, it is strong like an ox, is bluish-green in color, has no horns, has one leg, creates storms, glows like the sun, and roars like thunder. *16.1* (2) Legendary expert in music. *23.4, 27.1*

Kun, Kūn* 坤:** The second hexagram of the *Changes*. See also ***Fa xiang; 6.2n3. *6.2, 25.4.*

Kunwu, Kūnwú 昆吾: Figure from antiquity. Kūnwú appears in BA as an enemy of the Shāng, conquered by the Shāng on their way to conquering Jié of Xià. The name Kūnwú also appears alongside the name Jié of Xià in the *Poems*. These vague references are explained in SJ, which says that Kūnwú was an abettor of Jié's tyranny. *15.8*

Lai, Lái 萊: The Lái are mentioned in the *Documents* as being a nomadic people of the north. According to CQZZ, they had their own enfeoffed state during the Spring and Autumn period in the east of Qí (near present-day Lóngkǒu 龍口, Shāndōng, about 314 mi. NE of Qūfù). CQZZ ("Xiāng" 6.7) further says that Qí Duke Líng destroyed their domain in 567 BCE, but remnants survived. A place of the same name is mentioned in CQZZ in the year 490 BCE. According to SJ ("Guǎn Yàn liè zhuàn"), Yànzǐ, the prime minister of Qí, was from Lái. See also **Yi (people).** (Chen 1987; Qian and Dawa 1999) *1.2*

Lao Dan, Lǎo Dān 老聃: Chapter 11 equates the name Lǎo Dān with Lǎozǐ. The sobriquet Lǎozǐ 老子 is commonly thought to be a nickname (meaning the elderly one or the old master). Here, Lǎo 老 functions as a surname, which is historically rare but not unknown. Alternatively, Lǎo dān could mean Old Dān, but such a familiar way of referring to a dignified figure would be unusual. Lǎozǐ is the purported author of the *Dào dé jīng*, philosophical elements of which are evident in the *Dialogues*. The name Lǎo Dān occurs in quite a number of pre-Qin texts. According to SJ, his surname was Lǐ 李, his given name was Ěr 耳, his *zì* was Dān 聃, and he acted as historian for the Zhōu royal archives. (Yuan and Du 1996) *11.1, 11.2, 12.21, 24.1, 25.3, 43.2, 43.6*

Laozi: See **Lao Dan.**

Li, Lǐ 禮 (text): When the *Dialogues* refers to the *Lǐ* as one of the classics, it is a reference to the book known today as the *Yí lǐ* 儀禮, a text that describes a variety of ceremonies for lower-level officials, ceremonies we also see in the *Dialogues*, such as the archery event and banquets. The *Dialogues* attributes its authorship or editorship to Confucius, and although the dating of the book is uncertain, it may indeed date to as early as the time of Confucius.[7] However, its contents were

7. On the point of dating, Nylan disagrees and says the *Yí lǐ* "cannot date to a time much before Han" (2001, 175).

corrupted over the centuries, and so its original contents remain mysterious. When italicized, it refers to a single, edited collection created either by Confucius or sometime after, editions of which have been passed down to us today. When not italicized, it refers to whatever collections of related documents existed during the time of Confucius, prior to their arrangement into a single collection. (Loewe 1993; Nylan 2001) *36.2, 39.3*

***Li* (measure), *Lǐ* 里:** See "Weights and Measures" at the beginning of the glossary.

Li (person): See **Zhou King Li.**

Liang Mountain, Liáng Shān 梁山: Northwest of present-day Qián 乾縣, Shǎnxī. (Tan 1996) *10.18*

Liang Zhan, Liáng Zhān 梁鱣: Liáng Zhān's *zì* was Shūyú 叔魚. Not to be confused with Yangshe Fu, whose *zi* was also Shūyú 叔魚 (see **Shuyu**). *38.32*

***Lin, Lín* 麟:** (1) Large male deer. (2) Mythical deer-like animal of composite characteristics. It was said to appear only when a sage-king presided on earth. The *Kāngxī Dictionary* provides a variety of descriptions from earlier dictionaries, which include the following: It has the body of a deer, the tail of an ox, the neck of a wolf, and the hooves of a horse. Its color is variegated, apart from its underside, which is blonde. It is a *rén* creature. It is sometimes said that the *qí* 麒 is the male of this kind of animal and the *lín* 麟 is the female. (3) The term is cognate with *lín* 麐, which is glossed in the *Ěr yǎ* as an animal having "the body of a water deer and the tail of an ox, with one horn/antler." (Luo 1994) *10.1, 16.10, 22.2, 25.4, 32.11, 32.15*

Liuxia Hui, Liǔxià Huì 柳下惠: Fl. 634 BCE. Surname Zhǎn 展, given name Huò 獲, *zì* Qín 禽 or Jì 季, posthumous name Huì 惠. Enfeoffed at Liúxià 柳下, present-day Xīntài 新泰, Shāndōng (65 mi. NE of Qūfù). Liǔxià Huì was a Lǔ aristocrat who lived two or three generations before Confucius and was widely admired as capable and virtuous. He appears in three passages of the *Analects*. (Shi, Deng, and Zhu 2005) *10.16, 12.21, 18.4*

Long, Lóng 龍: Official in charge of music for Yáo. (Yuan and Du 1996) *23.4*

Longpang: See **Guan Longpang.**

Lord Liu, Gōng Liú 公劉: Lord Liú is said to have been the great-grandson of Hòu Jì 后稷. As the Xià dynasty declined, Hòu Jì's son Bù Zhú 不窋 lost his position in the government and departed from the Xià cultural sphere. Lord Liú is credited with moving back into the Xià cultural sphere and settling the Bīn 豳 polity (west of present-day Xúnyì 旬邑, Shǎnxī), which would grow into the future Zhōu state. Lord Liú restored the prior agricultural practices and was known for being a no-nonsense hard worker. (Luo 1994; Zheng, Wu, and Yang 2000; Taiwan Academic Network 2021) *10.18*

Lu, Lǔ 魯: Vassal state of Zhōu. Zhōu King Wǔ enfeoffed his younger brother (commonly known as the Duke of Zhōu) as Duke of Lǔ. The Duke of Zhōu, remaining at the capital to complete the unfinished work of nation building, subsequently set his son up at Qūfù 曲阜 (in present-day Shāndōng) as the founding duke of the Lǔ state. Remains of the Lǔ capital at the time of Confucius have been found in present-day Qūfù 曲阜, Shāndōng. Lǔ gradually expanded to become a small- to medium-sized state, encompassing much of the western part of present-day Shāndōng Province. Known as a preserver of Zhōu culture, it was the native state of Confucius. Lǔ was absorbed by Chǔ in 255 BCE. *1.1, 1.2, 1.3, 2.1, 2.2, 5.2, 7.1, 8.2, 8.14, 8.16, 8.17, 9.4, 9.6, 10.7, 10.9, 10.16, 11.1, 12.18, 13.8, 14.6, 16.2, 16.4, 16.5, 16.6, 16.7, 16.9, 18.4, 19.3, 19.4, 19.7, 20.3, 29.2, 32.1, 32.4, 37.2, 37.3, 38.1, 38.2, 38.3, 38.5, 38.9, 38.13, 38.14, 38.15, 38.16, 38.17, 38.18, 38.19, 38.20, 38.25, 38.28, 38.29, 38.33, 38.34, 38.35, 38.40, 39.2, 39.3, 40.1, 40.2, 41.2, 41.8, 41.9, 41.18,41.25, 42.8, 42.16, 42.24, 42.31, 43.2, 43.12, 43.14, 43.18, 43.21, 43.22, 44.23* (excluding passages that merely mention Lǔ in the title of the Duke of Lǔ)

Rulers of Lǔ in the *Dialogues*	
Duke Xiào	r. 796–769 BCE
Duke Huán	r. 711–694 BCE
Duke Xī	r. 659–627 BCE
Duke Wén	r. 626–609 BCE
Duke Xuān	r. 608–591 BCE
Duke Zhāo	r. 541–510 BCE
Duke Dìng	r. 509–495 BCE
Duke Āi	r. 494–468 BCE

Lu Duke Ai, Lǔ Āi Gōng 魯哀公: Surname Jī 姬, given name Jiāng 將(蔣), posthumous name Āi 哀. R. 494–468 BCE. Son of Lǔ Duke Dìng. Duke Āi's main high ministers were first Jì Huánzǐ and then Jì Kāngzǐ, who were the real powers in control of the government and military. This mechanism can be seen in 5.1, and it is best illustrated by the fact that in 468 BCE, while the duke was planning with the help of Yuè to raise an army and assert himself against the Three Huáns, the latter made a preemptive attack, forcing the duke to flee and then deposing him. (Huang and Zhao 1997; Zheng, Wu, and Yang 2000; Zhang and Xia 2010) *4.1, 5.1, 5.2, 5.3, 5.6, 6.1, 7.1, 7.3, 7.4, 7.5, 7.6, 7.7, 10.1, 10.12, 13.1, 13.3, 13.9, 16.9, 17.1, 19.5, 26.1, 40.1, 41.17, 41.18, 41.25, 41.26*

Lu Duke Ding, Lǔ Dìng Gōng 魯定公: Son of Duke Xiāng 襄 (r. 575–542 BCE). Younger brother of Duke Zhāo. R. 509–495 BCE. Placed on the throne by the Three Huáns after Duke Zhāo was forced into exile, he employed Confucius soon afterward. (Zheng, Wu, and Yang 2000) *1.1, 1.2, 1.3, 16.5, 18.1, 29.1, 41.3, 42.3, 43.24*

Lu Duke Huan, Lǔ Huán Gōng 魯桓公: R. 711–694 BCE. Assumed the throne after assassinating his violent older brother, Duke Yǐn. Known as an effective, peace-loving ruler. Assassinated by Qí over an incestuous palace love affair (the king of Qí had an affair with Duke Huán's wife, who was also sister of the Qí duke). Ancestor of the later Three Huáns. (Zheng, Wu, and Yang 2000) *9.4, 16.6*

Lu Duke Wen, Lǔ Wén Gōng 魯文公: Son of Duke Xī. R. 626–609 BCE. It was under Duke Wen that commoners were first given control of the Lǔ government. (Zheng, Wu, and Yang 2000) *42.13n13*

Lu Duke Xi, Lǔ Xī Gōng 魯僖公: R. 659–627 BCE. (Zheng, Wu, and Yang 2000) *16.6*

Lu Duke Xiao, Lǔ Xiào Gōng 魯孝公: R. 796–769 BCE. (Zheng, Wu, and Yang 2000) *43.12*

Lu Duke Xuan, Lǔ Xuān Gōng 魯宣公: R. 608–591 BCE. Duke Xuān benefited by having two legitimate rivals for the throne murdered on his behalf. It was under Xuān that the Three Huáns gained ascendance in Lǔ. See also **Dongmen Xiangzhong; Lu Duke Ai.** (CQZZ) *42.13*

Lu Duke Zhao, Lǔ Zhāo Gōng 魯昭公: Duke Dìng's older brother and predecessor. R. 541–510 BCE. It was during the reign of Duke Zhāo that Confucius first came to prominence, but the duke's reign was marred by continuous power struggles involving the Three Huáns and especially the Jìsūn family's household manager Yáng Hǔ, who himself controlled the government for three years. In 517, Duke Zhāo raised an army to wrest control entirely from the Three Huáns, but he failed and fled into exile, dying abroad after seven years. (Zheng, Wu, and Yang 2000) *39.2, 41.3, 42.17*

Lu sovereign: Reference to the Lǔ duke. See above for specific Dukes of Lǔ. *11.1, 14.1, 19.7, 20.3, 37.3*

Marquis, *hóu* 侯: Second of the five noble titles conferred by the Zhōu king. See under **Nobility and noble titles.**

Meng Xizi, Mèng Xīzǐ 孟僖子: Surname Mèng 孟 (= Mèngsūn 孟孫 = Zhòngsūn 仲孫), given name Jué 貜, posthumous name Xī 僖. Patriarch of the Mèngsūn family, one of the Three Huáns, the main power-wielding families of Lǔ. Father of Mèng Yìzǐ 孟懿子 and Nángōng Jìngshū 南宫敬叔. *11.1, 41.3*

Meng Yizi, Mèng Yìzǐ 孟懿子: Surname Mèng 孟 (= Mèngsūn 孟孫, = Zhòngsūn 仲孫), given name Héjì 何忌, posthumous name Yì 懿. Eldest son of Mèng Xīzǐ 孟僖子 and scion of the Mèngsūn family. At his father's direction, he studied under Confucius with his younger brother Nángōng Jìngshū and went on to be a top official in Lǔ. He appears once in the *Analects*, where he is concerned with *xiào*. Although he appears in five episodes of the *Dialogues*, his topics of interest are not elaborated. In 18.6, he asks Yán Huí about *rén* and wisdom. Beyond that, we are not told much. Although in 41.3 he is unambiguously said to be a student of Confucius, he is not given his own biography in chapter 38, nor is he appraised by Zǐgòng in chapter 12. *18.6, 33.1, 33.2, 33.3, 33.4, 41.3*

Mengsun, Mèngsūn 孟孫: Surname for one of the three most powerful families in Lǔ during the time of Confucius. Interchangeable with the surname Zhòngsūn 仲孫. A shortened form of Mèngsūn is Mèng 孟. See also **Jisun**; **Lu Duke Ai**; **Shusun.** *1.3*

***Mian*:** See **Crown.**

Mieming: See **Tantai Mieming.**

Mile: See "Weights and Measures" at the beginning of the glossary.

Min Mountain, Mín Shān 岷山: In Northwest Sìchuān, on the border of present-day Sìchuān and Gānsù Provinces. (Shi, Deng, and Zhu 2005) *9.10*

Min Sun: See **Min Ziqian.**

Min Ziqian, Mǐn Zǐqiān 閔子騫: Surname Mǐn 閔, given name Sǔn 損, *zì* Zǐqiān 子騫. 536–487 BCE. Mǐn Zǐqiān appears in five passages of the *Analects*, where Confucius describes him as quiet, virtuous, *xiào,* and precise yet agreeable in his speech. His brief biography in the *Dialogues* (38.2) echoes this assessment. Interestingly, in *Analects* 6.9 he adamantly refuses to govern Jìsūn's city of Bì, and yet in *Dialogues* 25.1 he is said to be mayor of the very same Bì. In both the *Analects* and *Dialogues* (15.5), he has the honorific suffix *zǐ* appended to his surname, suggesting that he was especially respected by the community around Confucius. (Zheng, Wu, and Yang 2000) *15.5, 25.1, 38.2*

Minister of ceremony, *zōngbó* (or *zōngzhù*) 宗伯/祝: One of six cabinet-level offices of the various state governments during the Zhōu dynasty, responsible for sacrificial services and all manner of ceremonial protocol. (Zheng, Wu, and Yang 2000) *25.2, 32.5, 32.12*

Minister of education, *sītú* 司徒: One of six cabinet-level offices of the various state governments during the Zhōu dynasty, responsible for matters related to education. See also **Five transformative teachings**. *25.2.*

Minister of justice, *sīkòu* 司寇 or *dà sīkòu* 大司寇: One of six cabinet-level offices of the various state governments during the Zhōu dynasty, responsible for managing legal cases and public standards. *1.1, 2.1, 2.2, 10.7, 19.3, 25.2, 31.2, 31.3, 32.1, 38.19, 42.6*

Minister of public works, *sīkōng* 司空 (or *sīchéng* 司城): One of six cabinet-level offices of the various state governments during the Zhōu dynasty, responsible for matters pertaining to land and the construction and maintenance of roads, bridges, irrigation, and public buildings. (Luo 1994; Taiwan Academic Network 2021) *1.1, 25.2, 42.10*

Minister of security, *sīmǎ* 司馬: One of six cabinet-level offices of the various state governments during the Zhōu dynasty, responsible for military and police matters. *14.4, 25.2*

Minzi: See **Min Ziqian.**

Mourning: For Confucius, mourning is one of the most important methods of expressing sincere emotion through the forms of *lǐ*. In addition to the funeral ceremony, which is familiar to anyone today, there was also a formal period of mourning after the funeral, which, depending on one's relationship with the deceased, was longer or shorter in duration (the longest being twenty-five months—often stated as "three years") and involved such practices as fasting, taking leave from duties, and wearing simple clothing. See examples in 7.1 and 43.16 especially. In discussions of mourning in the *Dialogues*, Confucius may sometimes seem concerned with maintaining appearances—where to do it, how long to do it, what clothes to wear, and so on. But beneath the appearances, the sincere expression of emotion is always paramount. The fundamental question is about what one is moved to do, not what one should do according to some external standard. *6.2, 7.1, 8.17, 10.12, 12.15, 15.1, 15.5–6, 23.3, 24.4, 26.3–4, 27.1–3, 30.1, 32.3, 32.5, 40.2, 41.3, 42.12, 42.14–15, 42.17–30, 43.2, 43.4–6, 43.8–17, 43.20, 43.22–26, 44.1, 44.3–5*

Mourning staff, *jūzhàng* 苴杖 or *zhàng* 杖: A staff that one carries when in mourning, to bear one's weight when overcome with emotion. *10.12, 26.4, 43.14, 43.16*

Music: Music in Confucius' time can be divided into three categories. The first is orchestral music used in ceremonies. This involved enormous racks of bronze bells and chimes, along with drums, stringed instruments, and wind instruments. The second is music produced for entertainment by smaller versions of such ensembles. The third is music produced by a solitary person with a wooden string instrument, sometimes singing. We see extensive discussion of music in the *Dialogues*, which is consistent with, and expands on, Confucius' mentions in the *Analects*. For Confucius, a significant function of music is the evocation of joy and the promotion of harmony. The character for music is also the character for joy (樂), and it is often coupled with the character *lǐ* 禮. It is easy to see why *lǐ* is so closely associated with music for Confucius, because both channel human emotions (not just joy but other emotions as well) so as to harmonize relations among people. This harmony comes also in the form of movement. Orchestral music accompanied the movements of ritual (as in 35.3), small ensemble music often accompanied popular dance (as in 19.7), and a solo zither could accompany dancing (as in 22.4). Music, like emotion, is viewed as infectious and motivational. According to the *Dialogues*, Confucius played the *qín* zither and the *shēng* mouth organ (see, for example, 20.1, 44.3, 44.5). See also **Dance**; **Zither.** (Sui County Leigudun Archaeological Team 1979; So 2000) *1.2, 3.2, 5.5, 6.2, 8.1, 10.12, 11.1, 12.1, 15.5, 15.6, 15.10, 15.13, 15.19, 18.3, 19.7, 20.1, 22.2, 22.4, 22.5, 23.4, 25.3, 26.4, 27.1, 27.2, 28.1, 28.2, 31.4, 32.5, 32.9, 32.12, 32.14, 33.1, 35.1–3, 36.1–3, 37.4, 39.3, 41.4, 41.7, 41.20, 42.4, 42.23, 43.25, 44.3, 44.5, 44.6*

Music (text), *Yuè* 樂: The *Music* is listed in the *Zhuāngzǐ* (14) and *Dialogues* (39.3) as one of six texts put into order (*zhì* 治) by Confucius. The Guodian essay "Six Virtues (*Liù dé* 六德)" lists the same six texts. *Xunzi* (1; 8) has a similar grouping of five (absent the *Changes*) that appears to be a list of Confucian classics. The exact reference of "music" in these lists is unknown. Some scholars believe that a classic of music once existed as a book but is now lost, and others believe that such a reference points to the "Yuè jì" chapter of the *Lǐ jì* (or a prior version). When italicized in this translation, *Music* refers to a single, edited (now unknown) collection created either by Confucius or by someone slightly later. When not italicized, it refers to whatever collections of related documents existed during the time of Confucius, prior to their arrangement into a single collection. See also **Dance; Six Classics.** (Fang et al. 1994; Zheng, Wu, and Yang 2000; Nylan 2001) *36.2, 39.3*

Naming convention: Exact details about naming customs in Confucius' time are hard to come by, but from examples and later texts such customs can be reconstructed. What we could call a given name (*míng* 名) was provided by the father at the ancestral temple at the end of the third month after birth. When the child came of age, a *zì* 字 was adopted at the coming-of-age ceremony (see 33.1; **Capping ceremony**). Generally speaking, a person was addressed by given name only by the older generation, including one's teachers, though the given name was also used when referring to oneself (as a sign of self-deprecation). Siblings and cousins referred to each other by relationship (e.g., Older Brother) or by nickname. Taking a *zì* before going out into the world reserved a level of respect for the privileged elders, who addressed one by one's given name (hence, 33.1 says, "a boy takes on a *zì* to show due respect for his given name"), expressing a sense of familiar intimacy when used. You can see an example of this custom in reference to Confucius' son. His given name is Lǐ, which Confucius uses in the *Dialogues* to address him, but he is referred to by the narrator of the passage using his *zì*, Bóyú. When Confucius refers to himself, he uses his given name, Qiū 丘. When he addresses his students, he generally refers to them by their given name (or part of their given name), as is clear in 15.12. It was also common to give men in the upper echelons posthumous names after their death (see 42.2), by which later generations would refer to them. For example, we know the young ruler of Lǔ with whom Confucius interacted in his elder years as Duke Āi, but this appellation would have been unknown to both Confucius and the duke during their lifetimes. The attentive reader will notice that the term *zǐ* 子 occurs often in names. "Confucius" is the Latinization of Kǒng fūzǐ, which is a long form of Kǒngzǐ, the term still used today to refer to Confucius and the most common way of referring to Confucius in the *Dialogues* and *Analects* (sometimes shortened to just *zǐ*). *Zǐ* adds an aesthetic quality to an appellation and signifies respect or some level of notoriety (e.g., Nánzǐ in the *Dialogues* and Xīzǐ 西子 in the *Mencius*). In this translation, we mostly preserve the various names as they are stated in the original text, because their use preserves and demonstrates the traditional *lǐ* of naming, but occasionally we revert to a more familiar usage for clarity. (He 2012)

Nan Rongyue: See **Nangong Jingshu.**

Nangong Jingshu, Nángōng Jìngshū 南宮敬叔: Surname 南宮, given name Tāo 縚(韜) or Kuò 括(适) or Yuè 説(閱), *zì* Zǐróng 子容. The second son of Mèng Xīzǐ 孟僖子 and younger brother of Mèng Yìzǐ 孟懿子. Married Confucius' niece. In the *Analects* and the *Dialogues,* there are six names that through their similarities suggest that they belong to either one person or two people. The *Analects'* names are Nán Róng and Nángōng Kuò; the *Dialogues'* names are Nángōng Tāo, Gōng Tāo, Nángōng Jìngshū, and Nánróng Yuè. Scholars widely agree on this point. There is also little doubt among scholars that Nángōng Kuò in the *Analects* is the same person as Nán Róng, and that Gōng Tāo in the *Dialogues* is the same person as Nángōng Tāo. According to *Analects* 5.2 and 11.6, Confucius gave the daughter of his older brother in marriage to one Nán Róng. According to *Dialogues* 38.21, Confucius gave the daughter of his older brother in marriage to Nángōng Tāo. Assuming these are references to the same event, then the four names must signify the same person. How do these names fit in with the names Nán Róngyuè and Nángōng Jìngshū? There is no doubt that Nángōng Jìngshū is the younger brother of Mèng Yìzǐ (both being sons of Mèng Xīzǐ), and that they both studied with Confucius at the behest of their father. And according to *Dialogues* 41.3, Nán Róngyuè was the younger brother of Mèng Yìzǐ (both being sons of Mèng Xīzǐ) and they both studied with Confucius. Knowing that Nán Róngyuè and Nángōng Jìngshū are the same person, the similarities of those names with Nán Róng and Nángōng Tāo, respectively, are enough to tie all six names to the same person. Substantiating this conclusion, in CQZZ ("Zhāo" 7.12) Nángōng Jìngshū is identified as both the younger brother of Mèng Yìzǐ and as simply Yuè 説—the ending of Nán Róngyuè 南容説.[8] (Yang and Xu 1985; Zheng, Wu, and Yang 2000; Zhang and Xia 2010) *8.5, 11.1, 12.14, 38.21, 39.3, 41.3, 42.3, 42.19*

Nangong Tao: See **Nangong Jingshu.**

Nanwu, Nánwǔ 南武: Location uncertain, either present-day Jiāxiáng 嘉祥, Shāndōng, or Nánwǔcūn (nánwǔchéngcūn) 南武村 (南武城村) (in Píngyì 平邑县, Línyí 臨沂市), Shāndōng. See also **Wu City.** (Xu 1994; Shen 1999; Zheng, Wu, and Yang 2000; Liu and Chi 2002; Wang 2006; Zhang and Xia 2010) *38.12*

Nanzi, Nánzǐ 南子: According to the LNZ ("Nièbì") and CQZZ ("Dìng" 14.8), Nánzǐ was originally a princess of the state of Sòng, where she earned a reputation

8. We are not saying that the information in the *Dialogues* definitively settles the matter, just that the information in the *Dialogues* allows us to say, given this information, that it is safe for the purposes of this glossary to assign all these names to the same person. It is difficult to settle the matter decisively by widening the scope of the examination. Whereas the *Shi ben,* for example, supports the conclusion here, SJ raises more than one complicating factor. We believe this matter is impossible to determine definitively given the conflicting sources available. For an argument that the names represent two people, see Li Qiqian (1987).

for her beauty and her loose sexual morals. After she married Duke Líng of Wèi, the duke indulged her concupiscence. In the scene in 38.29, one must try to imagine Confucius' feelings as he follows the duke's carriage. All of the city folks would be gawking at Nánzǐ, whispering scandalous rumors, while Confucius follows behind, a mere decoration, drawn into the scandals by association and not even accorded a position of respect in the lead carriage. Nánzǐ is also mentioned in *Analects* 6:28, in which Zǐlù faults Confucius for meeting with her. See also **Qu Boyu**; **Wei Duke Ling**; **Zilu.** (Zheng, Wu, and Yang 2000) *38.29*

Ni Hill, Níqiū 尼丘: Present-day Ní Mountain 尼山, Shāndōng (15 mi. SE of Qūfù). (Tan 1996; Zheng, Wu, and Yang 2000) *39.2*

Nobility and noble titles: During the time of Confucius, China was a highly stratified society, somewhat resembling the aristocratic stratification of medieval Europe. Only a king had the authority to enfeoff someone, which, under the Zhōu, entailed autonomy over an area of land and a title. The five noble titles conferred by the Zhōu king were, in descending order of status, duke (*gōng* 公), marquis (*hóu* 侯), earl (*bó* 伯), viscount (*zǐ* 子), and baron (*nán* 男). At the beginning of the Zhōu dynasty, the title duke was not necessarily equivalent to being the head of a vassal state (e.g., the Duke of Zhōu); but by the time of Confucius, dukes enfeoffed by the Zhōu were generally the heads of state (the Duke of Shè, enfeoffed by the Chǔ king, was not a head of state). Rulers of some smaller states were of lower status (e.g., the Viscount of Tán in 16.4). The fact that three of the five noble titles were also terms for familial relationship (*gōng* 公, grandfather, or other senior or deceased male; *bó* 伯, paternal uncle, senior to one's father; and *zǐ* 子, son) speaks to how political relationships were viewed as familial relationships. See individual nobility by state, and see the introduction for further discussion.

Nong Mountain, Nóng Shān 農山: Unknown mountain. There is no Nóng Mountain today, and it is not clear from context whether the trip in 8.1 was a day trip or a longer excursion. If it was a day trip, the closest hilly areas are Jiǔxiān Mountain and Shímén Mountain, each about a four-hour walk north of Qūfù from the Sì River. Scholars' guesses include Róng 戎 Mountain, Jǐng 景 Mountain (274 mi. WSW of Qūfù in Hénán), and Náo 巙(峱) Mountain (133 mi. NE of Qūfù in Shāndōng). (Luo 1994) *8.1*

Orchid: See **Angelica and *eupatorium*.**

Panmu, Pánmù 蟠木: Thought to be islands off the east coast, perhaps present-day Japan, or simply mythical islands. (Hua 1993; Luo 1994) *23.2*

Pi, Pǐ 嚭: Surname Bó 伯, given name Pǐ 嚭, *zì* Zǐyú 子餘. Trusted (though corrupt) minister of Wú King Fūchāi. (Zheng, Wu, and Yang 2000) *16.9, 37.2*

Pingqiu, Píngqiū 平丘: Location of an important interstate summit in 529 BCE. In the eastern part of present-day Fēngqiū 封丘縣, Hénán (140 mi. WSW of Qūfù). (Tan 1996; Zheng, Wu, and Yang 2000; Liu and Chi 2002) *41.9, 41.11*

Poems: *Shī* 詩, or *Shī jīng* 詩經: Collection(s) of poems spanning from the early Zhōu to the middle of the Spring and Autumn period. They represent a diverse range of sources and geographical areas, from liturgical hymns to poems of political and leadership acumen written by the elite to folk songs about love, separation, and neglect. Many poems are quoted by Confucius as a source of instruction and moral inspiration. Confucius is credited with organizing the poems into the form of the classic we have today (39.3). This would have happened toward the end of Confucius' life, so mentions of such a collection earlier in his life may not refer to a complete compendium resembling the current *Shī jīng*. Instead, the poems probably circulated in smaller collections (such as the "Dà yǎ" mentioned in 41.3), and there may have been more poems than those in our current version of the *Poems* (the poem in 15.4, for example). For this reason, whereas many interpreters interpret references to *shī* 詩 in the *Dialogues* as references to the *Shī jīng*, we often take the term to mean classic poems more generally. The *Poems* (as a single book) was designated one of the Five Classics of Confucianism during the Hàn dynasty. Poems were viewed by Confucius to be a crucial element in a person's education, able to groom the emotions, instruct about historical facts, act as elements of effective rhetoric, provide a rich and evocative vocabulary, and offer models of exemplary behavior as well as cautions against excess. When italicized in our translation, the term refers to a single, edited collection created around the time of Confucius, editions of which have been passed down to us today. When not italicized, it refers to whatever collections (e.g., the Da ya in 41.3) of related poems existed during the time of Confucius, prior to their arrangement into a single collection. See also **Six Classics.** (Yuan and Tang 1983; Pei 1998; Loewe and Shaughnessy 1999) *2.1–2, 7.5, 8.13, 10.18, 11.2, 12.1, 12.4–6, 12.10–11, 12.14, 13.5, 13.9, 14.1, 15.4, 17.5, 19.6, 20.1, 22.1, 22.5, 27.1–2, 28.1, 29.3, 34.2, 35.2, 36.1–2, 38.10, 38.29, 38.31, 39.3, 41.3, 41.7–8, 41.11–12, 41.14, 42.10, 44.3*

Prime minister, *zhǒngzǎi* 冢宰 (or *dàzǎi* 大宰, *xiàng* 相, *lìngyǐn* 令尹, *zhèngqīng* 正卿): Said to be one of six cabinet-level offices of the various state governments during the Zhou dynasty, and the leader of all ministers and officials in the bureaucracy. (Luo 1994) *11.2, 12.4, 13.7, 14.4, 15.11, 16.9, 25.2, 33.2, 37.2, 41.5, 41.19*

Prince Bigan: See **Bigan.**

Prince Jiu: See **Qi Prince Jiu.**

Prognostication: Common in Confucius' day, prognostication took two main forms: actively seeking information about current circumstances and determining the appropriate course of action. The earliest form was called *bǔ* 卜. The sound of the word is thought to represent the popping sound of a shell or bone suddenly cracking under concentrated heat. This practice goes back thousands of years into the Neolithic age. Tens of thousands of leftover scraps of these so-called oracle bones (bovine shoulder blades and turtle plastrons) remain from the Shāng dynasty. The Chinese character *bǔ* 卜 resembles in shape the cracks on the oracle bones. The basic idea is the following: A person who wants to undertake some action in the future, such as going to war, planting a crop, or marrying a certain person, conceives a yes-or-no query. A small indentation is bored or chiseled into the bone or shell, and then the diviner heats a rod in a fire and holds it firmly in the indentation until the bone or shell cracks under the heat and pressure. The direction of the crack indicates whether the spiritual forces portend a favorable result for the intended action. An alternative term for the process was *guī* 龜, the word for turtle, which meant to prognosticate by turtle shell rather than bone. (Turtles, as we see in 25.4 and 32.11, were considered spiritually potent creatures, probably not only because of their use in divination but also because of the reputedly auspicious patterns discerned on their shells.) Turtle shells have been found in graves going back into the Neolithic age, but they were commonly used for this kind of prognostication no earlier than the Shāng dynasty. The second major kind of prognostication was by yarrow stalks, using the *Changes*. A general word for *prognosticate* is *zhān* 占 (as in 7.6). The terms *prognosticate* and *divine* are used interchangeably in this translation. See also **Changes.** (Shaughnessy 1996; K. Huang 1997; W. Zhang 2002; A. Li 2015; Ruan 2015) *7.6, 10.3, 10.8, 29.3, 31.4, 32.11, 32.12, 41.16, 42.2*

Pu, Pú 蒲: City of Wèi. Present-day Chángyuán (about 145 mi. WSW of Qūfù). *8.8, 8.18, 14.9, 22.9*

***Qi, Qì* 氣:** Like the terms *pneuma* in Greek and *prana* in Sanskrit, *qì* refers most fundamentally to the air one breathes, and the meaning was elaborated in metaphysical directions. In other early Chinese texts, *qì* can have atmospheric and cosmogonic meanings. In the *Dialogues*, we could classify *qì* as largely medical or ontic, as it refers to one's vitality, as associated with longevity and spirit. In 27.2, it is also associated, in a psychological sense, with one's aspirations. Notice how a similar crossover in Latin, *spiritus,* informs another similar crossover in English: spirit/aspiration/inspire (breathe in). *17.5, 23.1, 25.3, 27.2*

Qi (city), Qī 戚: Wèi city, just north of capital Dìqiū 帝丘, modern-day Púyáng, Hénán (125 mi. W of Qūfù). See also under **Sun Wenzi.** (Luo 1994; Tan 1996; Zheng, Wu, and Yang 2000) *41.4*

Qǐ (state), Qǐ 杞: Vassal state of the Zhōu. After conquering the Shāng, Zhōu King Wǔ sought out a direct descendant of Yǔ, founder of the Xià dynasty, and enfeoffed him as Duke of Qǐ, where the line had purportedly been moved after Xià was conquered by the Shāng. Under pressure from rivals, Qǐ moved several times until it was conquered by Chǔ in 445 BCE. During the time of Confucius, the location of Qǐ was near present-day Ānqiū 安丘, Shāndōng (168 mi. NE of Qūfù). (Tan 1996; Zheng, Wu, and Yang 2000) *6.2, 32.4, 35.3*

Qi (state), Qí 齊: Vassal state of Zhōu. Zhōu King Wǔ enfeoffed his general Jiāng Zǐyá 姜子牙 (also known as Grand Duke Wang [Tàigōng Wàng 太公望]) as

Duke of Qí at Línzī 臨淄, present-day Zībó 淄博, Shāndōng (121 mi. NNE of Qūfù). Qí gradually expanded to become a large state, encompassing much of the eastern part of present-day Shāndōng Province. Under Duke Huán, Qí was the first of the Five Superpowers of the Spring and Autumn period, initiating a prolonged period of internal political reforms across the various states. In 221 BCE, Qí became the last state to be conquered by Qín. *1.2, 8.1, 8.9, 8.10,13.2, 14.1, 14.6, 15.3, 15.4, 15.16, 16.7, 18.4, 19.7, 37.2, 37.3, 38.12, 38.32, 41.1, 41.2, 41.8, 41.13, 41.18, 41.20, 41.22, 42.4, 42.16, 42.26, 43.16* (excluding mentions that are merely identifiers of personages)

Qi (surname), Qí 祁: One of the powerful clans of Jìn during the Spring and Autumn period. *12.22, 41.14.*

Qi duke, Qí hóu 齊侯: Reference to an unspecified Qí ruler. See other entries for specific Dukes of Qí. *1.2, 14.6, 41.1, 41.11*

Qi Duke Huan, Qí Huán Gōng 齊桓公: Surname Jiāng 姜, given name Xiǎobái 小白, posthumous name Huán 桓. Younger brother of Duke Xiāng and Prince Jiū. R. 685–643 BCE. A widely admired duke of Qí, a century before Confucius. He fled to Jǔ 莒 during the chaotic reign of Duke Xiāng and returned to take the throne after Xiāng was assassinated. With the help of Guǎn Zhòng, Duke Huán built Qí into the first superpower of the Spring and Autumn period. See also **Bao Shu**; **Guan Zhong.** (Zheng, Wu, and Yang 2000) *43.8*

Rulers of Qí in the *Dialogues*	
Duke Xiāng	r. 697–686 BCE
Duke Huán	r. 685–643 BCE
Duke Líng	r. 581–554 BCE
Duke Jǐng	r. 547–490 BCE
Duke Jiǎn	r. 484–481 BCE

Qi Duke Jian, Qí Jiǎn Gōng 齊簡公: R. 484–481 BCE. Deposed and then assassinated by Chén Héng. See also **Chen Heng.** (Zheng, Wu, and Yang 2000) *41.18*

Qi Duke Jing, Qí Jǐng Gōng 齊景公: Surname Jiāng 姜, given name Chǔjiù 杵臼, posthumous name Jǐng 景. Reigned 547–490 BCE. Son of Duke Líng. Duke Jǐng was the sovereign of Qí for most of Confucius' life. According to the *Dialogues*, Confucius met with him more than once. Because Duke Jǐng employed Yàn Yīng, whom Confucius admired, the duke must have earned Confucius' esteem for at least this, though Confucius never expresses admiration for him. This is explained in *Analects* 16.12, which describes the tepid reaction of the Qí people to the duke's death. The duke had a reputation for profligate living, with little concern for the people (see *Dialogues* 14.1). In 15.3, the duke expresses admiration for Confucius. Confucius is depicted as getting the best of him in *Dialogues* 1.2. (Zheng, Wu, and Yang 2000; Zhang and Xia 2010) *1.2, 13.8, 14.1, 14.6, 15.3, 15.4, 15.16, 42.4*

Qi Duke Ling, Qí Líng Gōng 齊靈公: R. 581–554 BCE. Absorbed Lái 萊 in 567 and continued to expand eastward until Qí occupied most of the Shāndōng Peninsula. (Zheng, Wu, and Yang 2000) *41.22*

Qi Duke Xiang, Qí Xiāng Gōng 齊襄公: Surname Jiāng 姜, given name Zhūér 諸兒, posthumous name Xiāng. R. 697–686 BCE. Older brother of Prince Jiū and Duke Huán. Duke Xiāng pursued a dissolute and lavish lifestyle. This and his violent whims eventually led to an uprising and his assassination. One example of his licentious behavior (narrated in CQZZ "Zhuāng" 2) is his affair with Lǔ Duke Huán's wife, who was also Xiāng's own younger sister. (Zheng, Wu, and Yang 2000) *8.9*

Qi Mountain, Qí Shān 岐山: Northeast of present-day Qíshān 岐山縣, Shǎnxī (589 mi. WSW of Qūfù). (Luo 1994; Tan 1996) *10.18*

Qi Prince Jiu, Qí Gōngzǐ Jiū 齊公子糾: Younger brother of Qí Duke Xiāng and older brother of Duke Huán. Killed while contesting the throne. See his story under **Bao Shu.** *8.9*

Qi sovereign: Reference to an unspecified Qí ruler. See entries above for specific Dukes of Qí. *1.2, 8.10, 14.1, 41.22*

Qi Xi, Qí Xī 祁(祈)奚(傒): *Zì* Huángyáng 黄羊, enfeoffed at Qí 祁 (present-day Qí 祁縣, Shānxī). Worked as minister under Jìn dukes Lì 厲 and Dào 悼 from 573 to 570 BCE. According to CQZZ ("Xiāng" 3.4), when he was about to retire, the duke asked Qí Xī to recommend a replacement, and Qí Xī recommended an adversary (reflecting his impartiality). (Luo 1994; Zheng, Wu, and Yang 2000) *12.22*

Qian, Qián **乾:** The first hexagram of the *Changes*. See also ***Fa xiang***; 6.2n3. *6.2, 25.4*

Qianxi, Qiánxī 乾谿: Region of northern Chǔ, SE of present-day Bózhōu 亳州, Ānhuī (153 mi. SSW of Qūfù). (Tan 1996; Zheng, Wu, and Yang 2000) *41.7*

Qilin**:** See ***Lin.***

Qin Duke Mu, Qín Mù Gōng 秦穆公: R. 659–621 BCE. One of the pivotal figures in early Chinese history. Laid the groundwork for the rise of Qín in the third century BCE. Admired for his willingness to hire talented men regardless of their political or social background. (Zheng, Wu, and Yang 2000) *13.8*

Qin Lao: See **Qin Zhang.**

Qin Zhang, Qín Zhāng 琴張: See 38.33 for his biography. *38.33, 43.18*

Qu Boyu, Qú Bóyù 璩(蘧)伯玉: An older contemporary of Confucius. He was a minister of Wèi and a friend of Confucius. According to 41.17, Confucius stayed at his house while in Wèi. He was considered a capable and virtuous official and admired by Confucius. We don't know much about Qú's biography, but there is a story that fits Confucius' description of him in 12.21. According to the LNZ ("Rénzhì"), one evening when the Duke of Wèi was sitting outside on a palace terrace with his wife, they heard a horse and carriage pull up and stop outside the main gate of the palace. The wife said, "That must be Qú Bóyù." The duke asked her how she could know that, and she said that, when passing by one's lord's gate, it is proper to stop and wait in case the lord is exiting at that moment. The duke sent someone to find out, and sure enough, it was Qú. The wife's point was that Qú always did what was proper, whether or not others could see him. (Kong, Sang, and Kong 1994; Luo 1994; Liu and Chi 2002) *12.21, 22.10, 41.17, 42.12*

Queli, Quèlǐ 闕里: An area of Qūfù where Confucius is said to have taught. Many believe that the current Confucius Temple (Kǒng Miào 孔廟) was built on the site. (Zheng, Wu, and Yang 2000) *38.24*

Ran Geng, Rǎn Gēng 冉耕: Related to Rǎn Yǒu and Zhònggōng, Rǎn Gēng appears in two episodes of the *Analects* but does not appear with Confucius in the *Dialogues*. *38.3*

Ran Qiu: See **Ran You.**

Ran Yong: See **Zhonggong.**

Ran You, Rǎn Yǒu 冉有: Surname Rǎn 冉, given name Qiú 求, *zì* Zǐyǒu 子有. A relative of Zhònggōng and Rǎn Gēng, he accompanied Confucius on his travels (42.2). According to depictions in the *Dialogues*, Rǎn Yǒu was a respected and competent leader who at one time worked for Jì Kāngzǐ. It was his recommendation to Jì Kāngzǐ that prompted Confucius' return from his decade abroad (41.17). Confucius discusses the finer points of law and justice with him but faults his *lǐ*. In the *Analects* (11.17), Confucius faults him for enforcing Jì Kāngzǐ's exorbitant taxation scheme. See 12.7 for Zǐgòng's appraisal of him. In view of the honorary suffix *zi* appended to Rǎn Yǒu's name in both the *Analects* and the *Dialogues* (42.2), he must have achieved some stature in the community around Confucius. *2.2, 5.1,12.7, 30.1, 30.2, 35.2, 38.7, 41.2, 41.17, 41.23, 42.2, 42.8, 42.28*

Ranzi: See **Ran You.** (Liu and Chi 2002)

Rong (people), Róng 戎: Nomadic people of the north and northwest during the Zhōu dynasty. (Qian and Dawa 1999) *43.2n5*

Ru/Ruist, Rú 儒: Chinese word that is commonly translated into English as *Confucian*. The term appears only once in the *Analects* (6.13), where Confucius says to Zǐxià 子夏, "Be a *jūnzǐ Rú*, not a small-minded *Rú*." This passage shows us that Rú (what we would call Confucians) of Confucius' day were not necessarily admired. Though the original meaning of the term *rú* is difficult to determine from the textual record, it became attached to Confucius, and we see his clear embrace of it in chapter 5 *of Dialogues*—an eloquent and somewhat poignant discursus on the concept. (Luo 1994; Zhang and Xia 2010) *5.2, 5.3, 5.4, 5.5, 5.6*

Rui, Rui 芮: State dating from the Shāng and enfeoffed at the level of earl by the Zhōu. Absorbed by Qín in 640 BCE. Located near present-day Chāoyì 朝邑鎮, Shǎnxī (452 mi. WSW of Qūfù). (Luo 1994; Tan 1996; Zheng, Wu, and Yang 2000) *10.10*

Shanfu, Shànfù 單父: City in Lǔ during the Spring and Autumn period. Present-day Shàn 單縣, Shāndōng (83 mi. SW of Qūfù). (Luo 1994; Tan 1996; Zheng, Wu, and Yang 2000) *14.7, 37.3, 38.15*

Shang (dynasty), Shāng 商: c. 1570–1045 BCE. Second of the Three Dynasties (Xià, Shāng, and Zhōu). Said to have been founded by the virtuous Tāng 湯, it ended in iniquity under Xīn 辛, who was conquered and replaced by the Zhōu 周. In the Chinese of the *Dialogues*, the Shāng is most often referred to as Yīn 殷, an alternative name for the dynasty that was used after the Shāng moved their capital to the city of Yīn 殷, outside of present-day Ānyáng 安陽, Hénán. In the present translation, all references to Yīn are replaced with Shāng. The remains of an earlier capital have been excavated at Zhèngzhōu 鄭州, Hénán. It was during the Shāng that the Chinese writing system was established, bronze metallurgy was perfected, and ritual bronze vessels became common in sacrificial ceremonies. Although Confucius often remarks that the Zhōu culture is inherited from the Shāng, one difference was a progression of increasing humaneness in the Zhōu, as human sacrifice,[9] common during the Shāng, became increasingly rare until it entirely disappeared by the end of the Zhōu. (Loewe and Shaughnessy 1999; Wu 2006) *2.1, 6.2, 7.6, 10.18, 16.2, 16.3, 24.4, 24.5, 33.4, 34.2, 35.2, 35.3, 39.1, 39.3, 40.1, 40.2, 41.14n41, 41.25, 43.2, 43.10, 43.25, 43.26*

Shang (person): See **Zixia.**

Shang Di, Shàng Dì 上帝: May refer to high ancestors vaguely, as in 25.1; to the highest deity (transliterated as Shàng Dì); or to high chiefs, as in 24.3. This illustrates how distinctions among gods, spirits, ancient heroes, rulers, and ancestors in this period are often fluid. In 29.1, Shàng Dì appears to be synonymous with *tiān*. In 29.2, Shàng Dì is a *tiān shén* 天神, a god of *tiān*. See also **Emperor.** (Zhang, Lin, and Gao 1980; Luo 1994; Taiwan Academic Network 2021) *16.9, 24.3, 25.1, 27.2, 29.1, 29.2*

Shang King Xin: See **Zhòu (person).**

Shang King Zhòu: See **Zhòu (person).**

Shang King Yi, Dì Yǐ 帝乙: Father of Zhòu and of Wēi Viscount Qǐ. His name appears in both Shāng oracle bones and bronze inscriptions. (Zheng, Wu, and Yang 2000) *39.1*

Shang Qu, Shāng Qú 商瞿: See 38.25 for his biography. *38.25, 38.37*

9. By "human sacrifice," we mean both ceremonial sacrificial offerings and the custom of killing attendants (servants, women, soldiers, etc.) who were buried with the deceased and believed to accompany the deceased into the afterlife. By the time of Confucius, the former had largely ended, and the latter, much diminished, was in the process of being replaced by replicas of humans, made of wood, clay, or straw. See 43.25 and 44.4 for the related views of Confucius and his students. (Huang 2004; Falkenhausen 2006)

Shang Rong, Shāng Róng 商容: Said to be a capable and virtuous man of the late Shāng dynasty but not employed by the benighted last king. (Zheng, Wu, and Yang 2000) *35.3*

***Shangyang, Shāngyáng* 商羊:** This term is attested elsewhere only in the *Lùn héng*, where its dancing is also considered a sign of rain, like worms coming out of the ground. (Zhang, Lin, and Gao 1980; Luo 1994) *14.6*

Shao Dian, Shào Diǎn 少典: Father of the Yellow Chief and Chief Yán. (Luo 1994; Zheng, Wu, and Yang 2000) *23.1*

Shao Hao, Shào Hào 少(小)昊(皞/皡/皓/顥): Son of the Yellow Chief, and first ruler of the Yí people. Because he continued the work of Tài Hào (Hào the Elder), he was called Shào Hào (Hào the Younger). His capital was at Qūfù, Shāndōng. (Luo 1994; Zheng, Wu, and Yang 2000; Taiwan Academic Network 2021) *16.4, 24.1, 24.3*

She: See **Jiao and She.**

Sheji, Shèjì 社稷: *Shè* refers to the god of the soil, to the ceremonial sacrifice to the god, or to the altar used for such a ceremony. *Jì* refers to millet, grain, or the god of millet or grain. The combined form *shèjì* refers to the agrarian gods, to the ceremonial sacrifice to the agrarian gods (16.2, 32.4), or to the altar or temple for such a ceremony (42.16). Demonstrating the centrality of the ceremony to the culture of the time, *shèjì* also is a metonym for country or homeland (9.9, 32.7, 42.16). See also **Jiao and She**. (Luo 1994; Zheng, Wu, and Yang 2000; Taiwan Academic Network 2021) *4.1, 9.9, 16.2, 24.3n5, 32.4, 32.7, 42.16*

Shen: See **Zengzi.**

Shēn: See **Earl of Shēn.**

Shen Xu: See **Wu Zixu.**

***Sheng* mouth organ, *shēng* 笙:** Reed mouth organ, related to the harmonica. One of the main wind instruments in both large and small ensembles in Confucius' time. (Luo 1994; So 2000) *28.2, 44.3*

Shi: See **Zizhang.**

Shi Qiu, Shǐ Qiū 史鰌: Also known as Shǐ Yú 史魚. Redoubtable minister under Wèi Duke Líng. Associate of Qú Bóyù. Also appears in *Analects* 15.7. The similarity in name and description in accounts of Shǐ Qiū and Shǐ Yú leads scholars to commonly identify them as the same person. We follow convention here. Little is known of him outside of a few spare accounts. (Luo 1994; Zhang and Xia 2010) *13.1, 15.14, 22.10*

Shi Xiangzi, Shī Xiāngzǐ 師襄子: Little is known of Xiāngzǐ, including whether his surname was even Shī, since that is also the word for *teacher*. Some scholars say he is the same person as the chime player Xiāng in *Analects* 18.9. *35.1*

Shi Yu: See **Shi Qiu.**

Shouyang Mountain, Shǒuyáng Shān 首陽山: Mountain said to be located north of Huá Mountain 華山, south of present-day Púzhòu 蒲州, Yǒngjì 永濟縣,

Shānxī. (Luo 1994; Zheng, Wu, and Yang 2000; Taiwan Academic Network 2021) *12.21n18, 20.1*

Shu Xiang, Shū Xiàng 叔向: Surname Yángshé 羊舌, given name Xī 肸, *zì* Shūxiàng 叔向. Older brother of Shū Yú. Older contemporary of Confucius. Zhèng had Zǐchǎn, Qí had Yànzǐ, and Jìn had Shūxiàng. Although Shūxiàng, unlike Zǐchǎn and Yànzǐ, never held the reins of government, he was comparable to them in being a competent, fair-minded minister admired by Confucius. However, he appears only once in the *Dialogues* and not at all in the *Analects*. (Luo 1994; Zheng, Wu, and Yang 2000) *41.9*

Shuliang He, Shūliáng Hé 叔梁紇: Surname Kǒng 孔, given name Hé 紇, *zì* Shūliáng 叔梁. Identified in CQZZ as Hé, the man of Zōu (Zōu *rén* Hé 郰人紇; "Xiāng" 10.2) and Zōu Shūhé 郰叔紇 ("Xiāng" 17.3). Confucius' father. Official in the Lǔ city of Zōu 陬/郰/鄹. (Luo 1994; Zheng, Wu, and Yang 2000; Zhang and Xia 2010) *38.28, 39.2*

Shun, Shùn 舜: Also known as Yú 虞 and Yǒuyú 有虞 (names of his clan). Fifth of the legendary Five Chiefs. For Shùn's biography, see 23.5; for his ruling by *wú wéi*, see 3.1; for his use of capable and virtuous men, see 14.7; for his way of working with the people, see 18.1; and for his governing and his virtue, see 23.4. (Luo 1994; Zheng, Wu, and Yang 2000) *3.1, 10.1, 11.2, 12.7, 14.7, 15.10, 16.2, 18.1, 23.4, 23.5, 24.4, 24.5, 30.1n2, 30.1n5, 34.2, 35.2, 35.3, 39.3, 41.25*

Shuqi, Shūqí 叔齊: See 12.21n19 for his story. *12.21, 20.1*

Shusun, Shūsūn 叔孫: One of the three ruling families of Lǔ during Confucius' time. See also **Jisun**; **Lu Duke Ai**; **Mengsun.** *1.3, 16.10, 18.11, 41.8, 43.15*

House of Shūsūn in the *Dialogues*	
Shūsūn Mùzǐ	616–538 BCE
Shūsūn Zhāo	fl. 538–516 BCE
Shūsūn Wǔshū	fl. 502–484 BCE
Shūsūn Zhé	fl. 502–487 BCE

Shusun Muzi, Shūsūn Mùzǐ 叔孫穆子: Surname Shūsūn 叔孫, given name Bào 豹, posthumous name Mù 穆. 616–538 BCE. Father of Shūsūn Zhāo, he was murdered by his illegitimate son Niú. He was leader of the Shūsūn clan, a generation or two ahead of Confucius, and a major diplomat and general for Lǔ over a span of nearly forty years. Well-versed in ritual but a poor judge of character. (Zheng, Wu, and Yang 2000; Durrant, Li, and Schaberg 2016) *41.8*

Shusun Wushu, Shūsūn Wǔshū 叔孫武叔: Given name Zhōuchóu 州仇. Grandson of Shūsūn Zhāo. Fl. 502–484 BCE. High minister of Lǔ. He publicly doubted the abilities of Confucius. (Zhang and Xia 2010; Durrant, Li, and Schaberg 2016) *18.11, 43.15*

Shusun Zhao, Shūsūn Zhāo 叔孫昭: Son and heir of Shūsūn Mùzǐ by a concubine. Fl. 538–517 BCE. (Durrant, Li, and Schaberg 2016) *41.8*

Shusun Zhe, Shūsūn Zhé 叔孫輒: Fl. 502–487 BCE. Rebellious younger son of the Shūsūn Wǔshū during Confucius' time. It was Shūsūn Zhé's ambition to overthrow the Lǔ government, and he teamed up with Yáng Hǔ in a failed uprising. (Durrant, Li, and Schaberg 2016) *1.3*

Shuyu, Shūyú 叔魚: Surname Yángshé 羊舌, given name Fù 鮒, *zì* Shūyú 叔魚. Cf. Confucius' student Liáng Zhān Shūyú 梁鱣叔魚. (Chen and Wang 1995; Durrant, Li, and Schaberg 2016) *41.9*

Si River, Sì Shuǐ 泗水: River just outside the Lu capital. It bears the same name today and runs east to west along the north side of Qūfù, then turns southwest.

Six Classics: Books that appear as a group of five or six in Warring States texts and are designated as the Five Classics (*wǔ jīng* 五經) near the beginning of the Hàn dynasty, regarded as the most important classic representations of Confucianism: *Poems, Documents, Changes, Spring and Autumn,* and *Yí lǐ* 儀禮. Later, the *Spring and Autumn* came to include the *Zuǒ zhuàn,* and the *Yí lǐ* was replaced by the *Lǐ jì. Zhuāngzǐ* (ch. 14) and the "Six Virtues" essay of the Guodian corpus name one more, the *Music. Dialogues* 39.3 agrees with the *Zhuāngzǐ* and "Six Virtues" and attributes all the books, in one way or another, to Confucius. Michael Nylan (2001) says of such an attribution that it is "astonishing [that] no recorded tradition prior to 100 BC identifies Confucius as author, editor, or compiler of this collection" (p. 6). In fact, however, the Shanghai Museum essay "*Jūnzǐ* Performing *Lǐ*" (*Jūnzǐ wéi lǐ* 君子爲禮) (c. 350–300 BCE [Xu 2007; Hou 2018]) directly attributes the *Poems* and *Documents* to Confucius, saying that he "put them in order (*zhi* 治)" (Hou 2018, 1:254). Unfortunately, the bamboo strip is damaged directly after the word for *Documents,* so we don't know what other texts might have followed in a list. See also **Changes**; **Documents**; **Music**; **Poems.** (Luo 1994; Nylan 2001) *39.3*

Song, Sòng 宋: Zhōu vassal state. After Zhōu conquered Shāng, Zhōu King Wǔ enfeoffed the deceased Shāng King Zhòu's son Wǔgēng at a former Shāng capital in the state of Sòng, present-day Shāngqiū 商丘, Hénán (120 mi. SW of Qūfù). When King Wǔ died, Wǔgēng conspired with King Wǔ's two disaffected brothers Guǎn and Cài to mount a unified rebellion, which was suppressed by the Duke of Zhōu. After Wǔgēng was killed, Zhōu King Chéng enfeoffed the Shāng King Zhòu's older brother Wēi Viscount Qǐ as duke. See *Dialogues* 39.1 for a version of this story. Sòng grew to be a medium-sized state covering territory in present-day northeastern Hénán, and through governmental and military reforms under King Xiāng (d. 637 BCE) it became the most powerful state of its time. In 286 BCE, Sòng was conquered by a unified army of Qí, Chǔ, and Wèi. (Luo 1994; Durrant, Li, and Schaberg 2016; Taiwan Academic Network 2021) *5.2, 6.2, 11.1, 13.4, 13.11, 22.5, 22.9, 32.4, 35.3, 38.19, 38.30, 39.1, 39.2, 42.2, 42.10*

Song sovereign: Reference to an unspecified Sòng ruler. *13.11, 39.2*

***Spring and Autumn*, Chūnqiū 春秋:** Historical text chronologically cataloging key political and military events of the various states during the Spring and Autumn period. Attributed to Confucius (39.3, 42.1) and dating from about his time. The Spring and Autumn period takes its name from this book. Designated one of the Five Classics of Confucianism during the Hàn dynasty. As italicized here, it refers to a single, edited collection created either by Confucius or sometime after, editions of which have been passed down to us today. When not italicized, it refers to whatever collections of related documents existed during the time of Confucius, prior to their arrangement into a single collection. See also **Six Classics.** (Loewe 1993; Nylan 2001) *36.2, 39.3, 42.1*

Spring and Autumn period, Chūnqiū Shídài 春秋時代: The first half of the Eastern Zhōu dynasty. The Spring and Autumn period (770–481 BCE) was marked by the decline of the Zhōu throne and the rise of several major states. Although the states still deferred to the Zhōu king in principle, in fact they functioned as independent polities. It was a period of major political and social transition, as informal, aristocratic mechanisms gave way to increasing systemization and professionalization. This is also the period in which Confucius lived and was the beginning of intellectual discussions about such changes. (Loewe and Shaughnessy 1999)

Sui Wuzi, Suí Wǔzǐ 隨武子: Fl. 600 BCE. Also known as Shì Huì 士會 and Shì Jì 士季. Successively held fiefs at Suí 隨 and then Fàn 范, both of which names were attached to his as appellations, as in Suí Wǔzǐ 隨武子, Suí Huì 隨會, and Fàn Wǔzǐ 范武子. Suí Wǔzǐ was a contemporary of Zhào Wénzǐ's grandfather and worked in high levels of the government in Jìn. He was known both for his virtue and for his brilliance in military and political strategy. Earlier in his career, Suí found himself, through no fault of his own, an exile in Qín. There he served the government with honor. Later, when Jìn ventured to bring him back, he returned and served without antipathy. (Zheng, Wu, and Yang 2000; Durrant, Li, and Schaberg 2016) *12.21*

Sun Huanzi, Sūn Huánzǐ 孫桓子: Fl. 602–566 BCE. Father of Sūn Wénzǐ. Nobleman of Wèi, instrumental in creating diplomatic rapport between Wèi and Lǔ (in opposition to Qí). (Durrant, Li, and Schaberg 2016) *41.20*

Sun Wenzi, Sūn Wénzǐ 孫文子: Posthumous name Wén 文. Also known as Sūn Línfù 孫林父. Son of Sūn Huánzǐ. A couple of decades ahead of Confucius, he managed the government of Wèi off and on through the reigns of three dukes. According to CQZZ, Sūn and Wèi Duke Xiàn 獻 had a mutually antagonistic relationship. Once when the duke had sent Wén as an emissary to Lǔ, Wén unabashedly mounted the dais staircase alongside Lǔ Duke Xiāng, thereby displaying an egregious arrogance and lack of *lǐ*. This reflected poorly on Duke Xiàn (CQZZ "Xiāng" 7.7). Later, Sūn and an ally drove the duke into exile (CQZZ

"Xiāng" 14.4). After that, the son of Sūn's ally drove Sūn into the protection of Jìn and welcomed the duke back to Wèi (CQZZ "Xiāng" 26.2). (Huang and Zhao 1997; Zheng, Wu, and Yang 2000; Durrant, Li, and Schaberg 2016) *41.4*

Superpower / leader of a superpower, bà 霸 / bàwáng 霸王: The term *bà* is often translated as "overlord" or "hegemon," referring to a person or the actions of a person, but it can also refer to a state or the actions of a state (19.7, 37.2). Spring and Autumn superpowers, due to their overwhelming military might, were in the position of dictating terms of interstate peace agreements and otherwise getting their way in interstate matters. Although the superpowers were preeminent, they justified their actions in terms of maintaining the system of *lǐ* under the auspices of the Zhōu king. It is commonly said that there was a succession of five superpowers during the Spring and Autumn period, but the total number of candidates is seven, beginning with Qí (led by Guǎn Zhòng). If any states qualified as superpowers during Confucius' lifetime, they were Wǔ and Yuè, neither of which was admired by Confucius. See also 10.2n2. (Luo 1994; Durrant, Li, and Schaberg 2016) *3.1, 8.16, 13.8, 19.7, 20.1, 37.2, 37.3*

Sushen, Sùshèn 肅慎: A people once residing in present-day northeastern China in the area of the Tumen River and Paektu Mountain, ancestors of the Manchus. (Zhao 2013; Gao 2019; Guo 2019; Zhang 2019; Guo and Hu 2021) *16.3*

***Tai, Tái* 臺:** Terraces or platforms. People looking at a traditional Chinese palace (for example, in the Forbidden City) tend to focus on the building itself rather than the layers of terraces beneath it, which are actually essential to the architecture. As an architectural form, they date back to Neolithic times in China. A *tái* is set off from the surroundings, built of rammed earth, and functions as a refuge from floods and earthquakes. During the Zhōu dynasty, there was a custom among noblemen and royalty of building *tái* (sometimes outside city walls, as we see in 14.4), which had many purposes, from sites for rituals, to places for quiet contemplation, to venues for wild parties. Without a structure on top of it, a *tái* is simply a terrace, or platform. With a structure atop it, it was still often referred to in Classical Chinese as a *tái*, but in English we would focus on the structure and call it a palace, temple, observatory, tower, and the like. The archaeological record suggests that they came into fashion just before Confucius and quickly spread as status symbols. A famous example from the time of Confucius is the massive Zhānghuátái 章華臺, built by King Líng of Chǔ in 535 BCE, when Confucius was sixteen years old (see, e.g., CQZZ "Zhāo" 7.3), probably the largest and most ornate *tái* of its time. In 1.2, the term *tán* 壇, which usually means altar, is translated according to context as *terrace*. It was also common to have a *tái* inside of a building in the form of a dais, stage, or platform. Verticality within architecture indicated status. The ruler was always seated on a dais above others, and in the *Dialogues* we see repeated references to people ascending and descending staircases abutting such platforms. See also **Tower of Wuzi 武子之臺** and 5.2n2. (Bai and Wang 1995; Loewe and Shaughnessy 1999; Jingzhou Municipal Museum and Qianjiang Municipal Museum 2003; Song 2014; Wang and Chen 2019) *1.3, 14.1, 14.4*

Tai Dian, Tài Diān 太(泰/大)顛: According to the *Documents*, King Wén hired Tài Diān and Hóng Yāo after hearing about them. They appear in the early corpus as trusted ministers and advisers of King Wén, though details are scarce. *8.6*

Tai Hao, Tài (Dà) Hào 太(大)皞(昊): Mythological figure known as a great early leader. There are few details in the early literature except that his tomb is in Chén. Sometimes identified with Fú Xī 伏羲. See also **Shao Hao.** (Zheng, Wu, and Yang 2000; Zhang and Xia 2010) *16.4, 24.1, 24.2, 24.3, 24.5*

Tai Jiang, Tài Jiāng 太(大)姜: Surname Jiāng 姜. Wife of Dǎn Fǔ and grandmother of Zhōu King Wén. According to LNZ ("Mǔyí"), she was an important adviser to Dǎn Fǔ. (Zheng, Wu, and Yang 2000) *10.18, 22.1n5*

Tai Mountain, Tài Shān 泰山: Traditionally known as one of the five important mountains of China, located about fifty mi. N of Qūfù. *15.13, 39.3, 40.1, 41.13*

Tai Ren, Tài Rèn 太(大)任: Surname Rèn 任. Wife of Zhōu King Jì and mother of Zhōu King Wén. SJ ("Zhōu běn jì") describes her as a capable and virtuous woman. (Zheng, Wu, and Yang 2000) *8.6, 22.1n5*

Tai Si, Tài Sì 太姒: Surname Sì 姒. Wife of Zhōu King Wén and mother of Zhōu King Wǔ and his nine brothers. According to LNZ ("Mǔyí"), she was responsible for the excellent education of her sons until their maturity. (Zheng, Wu, and Yang 2000) *8.6, 22.1n5*

Tai Wu, Tài Wù 太(大)戊: A ruler of the Shāng reputed to have been virtuous. Little is known of him beyond the story related in 7.6, although his name does appear in the Shāng oracle bones. (Zheng, Wu, and Yang 2000) *7.6*

Tan, Tán 郯: Enfeoffed at the level of earl, Tán lay on the very eastern frontier of the Zhōu, in the territory of the Yí people. The ruling family were said to be descendants of Shào Hào, first ruler of the Yí. Tán does not appear in the historical record until the Spring and Autumn period. It was absorbed by Yuè in 414 BCE. (Zheng, Wu, and Yang 2000; Liu and Chi 2002) *8.13, 16.4*

Tang, Tāng 湯: Founding ruler of the Shāng dynasty. Also referred to as Chéng Tāng 成湯, Tāng the Accomplished, for having defeated Jié, the villainous last ruler of the Xià dynasty. He is often lauded by Confucius as one of the virtuous sage-kings of the past. If it is true that Confucius was descended from Shāng royalty, then he would also be a descendant of Tāng. See also **Jie**; **Shang (dynasty)**; **Xia (dynasty)**; and 12.15n17. (Zheng, Wu, and Yang 2000) *2.1, 11.1n2, 12.6n7, 12.15, 15.2, 23.1, 27.2, 32.2, 34.2, 39.1, 39.3, 41.19, 41.25*

Tang Shu, Táng Shū 唐叔: Surname Jī 姬, given name Yú 虞. Son of Zhōu King Wǔ and younger brother of Zhōu King Chéng. During the reign of King Chéng, the fiefdom of Táng 唐 rebelled. After being suppressed by the Duke of Zhōu, its noble line was exterminated and replaced with Jī Yú, which is why he is also known as Táng Shū. His son changed the name of the fiefdom to Jìn 晉, and so Táng Shū is also known as the progenitor of the state of Jìn. (Zheng, Wu, and Yang 2000) *41.15*

Tantai Mieming, Tántái Mièmíng 澹臺滅明: Surname Tántái 澹臺, given name Mièmíng 滅明, *zì* Zǐyǔ 子羽. Tántái Mièmíng appears only once in the *Analects* (6.14), where he is mentioned by Zǐyóu to Confucius as a particularly upright official of the Lǔ city of Wǔ 武. Perhaps he later became a student of Confucius, for in the *Dialogues* Zǐgòng identifies him as a student (12.12). There is an interesting ambiguity in 23.7, where Confucius says that Tántái cured him of judging people based on their appearance, but he does not say specifically what he means by that. The ambiguity is cleared up in 19.8, where Confucius says that Tántái has the face of a *jūnzǐ* (by which he presumably means attractive or dignified), and in the biography in 38.13 he says Tantai did not entirely live up to his potential. However, SJ ("Zhòngní dìzǐ liè zhuàn") goes in the other direction, specifically stating that Tántái was ugly but was of unimpeachable character. There may be a way to resolve this conflict. Perhaps the colorful story of Confucius being cured of his biases circulated much more broadly (or was simply more salient) than passages 19.8 and 38.13. (The biases story appears, for example, in the *Hán Fēizǐ*, the *Shuō yuàn*, and the *Lùn héng*.) And because Zǐwǒ's widely known negative behavior cured Confucius of one bias, the appearance of Tántái that cured Confucius of the other bias must also have been negative. Hence, it was widely but mistakenly believed that Tántái was ugly instead of handsome. (Zheng, Wu, and Yang 2000) *12.12, 19.8, 23.7, 38.13*

Tantai Ziyu: See **Tantai Mieming.**

Tao Forest, *Táo Lín* 桃林: East of Huá Mountain, between present-day Tóngguān 潼關 and Língbǎo 靈寶, Hénán. (Luo 1994; Tan 1996; Zheng, Wu, and Yang 2000) *35.3*

Taotang: See **Yao.**

Three Dynasties, *Sān Dài* 三代: The Xià 夏, Shāng 商, and Zhōu 周 dynasties, especially their founders. In Confucian texts, they symbolized ancient, better times. (Luo 1994; Liu and Chi 2002) *4.1, 24.4, 32.1, 36.2, 41.16*

Three Kings, Sān Wáng 三王: Founding kings of the Three Dynasties. Yǔ (of Xià), Tāng (of Shāng), and Zhōu King Wǔ (or Wén). (Luo 1994; Liu and Chi 2002) *23.2, 25.1, 33.4, 40.2*

Tian Chang: See **Chen Heng.**

Tongdi Bohua, Tóngdī Bóhuá 銅鞮伯華: Surname Yángshé 羊舌, given name Chì 赤, *zì* Bóhuá 伯華. Enfeoffed at Tóngdī 銅鞮 (south of present-day Qìn 沁縣, Shānxī). Better known as Yángshé Chì. He was a contemporary of Zhào Wénzǐ and a minister of Jìn. Only two brief episodes of his life have come down to us. According to CQZZ ("Xiāng" 3.7), he supported a proposal to punish Jìn Duke Dào's 悼 younger brother, which the duke initially opposed but then came to support. He was also falsely implicated in a plot and jailed for it (CQZZ "Xiāng" 21.5). See 12.22 and 13.7 for descriptions of Tóngdī Bóhuá not recorded in the standard histories. (Shi, Zheng, and Zhu 2005; Zhang and Xia 2010) *12.21, 13.7*

Tower of Wuzi, Wǔzǐ zhī Tái 武子之臺: A tower in the Jìsūn palace commemorating Jì Wǔzǐ 季武子. According to *Shuǐ jīng zhù*, although the tower had collapsed by the end of the Northern Wèi dynasty (386–534), the ruins still stood around twenty feet high. *1.3*

Village archery event, *xiāngshè* 鄉射: A ceremony at the local school bringing the townspeople together. It may have involved honoring recent graduates and recommending them for employment. (Zheng, Wu, and Yang 2000) *28.1, 32.3*

Viscount of Ji, Jī Zǐ 箕子: According to BA ("Dì Xīn"), the Viscount of Jī was imprisoned by the last Shāng king at the same time that the king killed Bǐgān. According to the *Documents* ("Zhōu shū"), Zhōu King Wǔ freed him after the successful conquest of Shāng. *35.3*

Viscount, *zǐ* 子: Fourth of the five noble titles conferred by the Zhōu king. See under **Nobility and noble titles.**

Viscount Qi: See **Wei Viscount Qi.**

Warring States period, Zhànguó Shídài 戰國時代: 481–221 BCE. In this period, there was an intensification of the trends of the Spring and Autumn period, with increasing sophistication of bureaucracies, professionalization, technology, intellectual speculation, and the spread of writing and education. By this time, the Zhōu throne had been entirely eclipsed, and state rulers one after another would declare themselves kings. (Loewe and Shaughnessy 1999)

Wei, Wèi 衛: A Zhōu vassal state. Zhōu King Wǔ enfeoffed his younger brother Kāngshū 康叔 at Zhāogē (present-day Qí 淇縣, Héběi). The capital started off near present-day Ānyáng 安陽 (at the former site of the Shāng capital when it was conquered), moved several times, and was at Dìqiū 帝丘, present-day Púyáng 濮陽, Hénán (about 120 mi. NW of Qūfù) during the time of Confucius. A medium-sized state covering territory in present-day southern Héběi and northern Hénán, Wèi was one of the last seven states standing toward the end of the Warring States period. It came under Qín control in 241 BCE. Of the states that Confucius visited, he spent most of his time in Wèi—approximately a decade—and thus it figures prominently in the *Dialogues*. (Zheng, Wu, and Yang 2000) *5.1, 8.4, 8.14, 12.1, 12.18, 13.1, 18.2, 20.1, 22.2, 22.9, 22.10, 34.1, 37.2, 38.6, 38.10, 38.19, 38.29, 38.33, 38.37, 41.4, 41.9, 41.17, 41.20, 42.3, 42.12, 42.21, 42.28, 42.31, 43.13, 43.18, 43.21, 44.3* (excluding mere mentions of the Duke of Wei)

Wei Duke Ling, Wèi Líng Gōng 衛 靈公: Given name Yuán 元, posthumous name Líng 靈. Son of Duke Xiāng 襄. R. 534–493 BCE. Duke Líng reigned during the decade that Confucius spent in Wèi, and although they met, the duke did not employ Confucius. See 22.9 for an account of Confucius' interaction with Duke

Líng. See also **Nanzi**; **Qu Boyu.** (Zheng, Wu, and Yang 2000) *13.1, 13.10, 22.9, 22.10, 38.29*

Wei Duke Xian, Wèi Xiàn Gōng 衛獻公: R. 576–559 and 546–544 BCE. See also under **Sun Wenzi.** (Zheng, Wu, and Yang 2000) *41.4*

Wei Marquis Wen, Wèi Wén Hóu 魏文侯: R. 445–396 BCE. Known as an enlightened ruler who employed many capable and virtuous ministers. He assumed the throne at the age of twenty and sought counsel from Zǐxià. He presided over the splintering of Jìn 晋 into Wèi 魏, Zhào 趙, and Hán 韓 in 403 BCE. (Song and Li 2000; Zheng, Wu, and Yang 2000) *38.10*

Wei Viscount Qi, Wēi Zǐ Qǐ 微子啓: Son of Shāng King Yǐ and older brother of Zhòu. According to BA ("Dì Xīn"), he fled Zhòu, and according to the *Documents* ("Zhōu shū") he was installed by Zhōu King Wǔ as founding ruler of the state of Sòng. See 39.1 for his biography. (Zheng, Wu, and Yang 2000) *39.1, 44.2*

Wei Xianzi, Wèi Xiànzǐ 魏獻子: Surname Wèi 魏, given name Shū 舒, posthumous name Xiàn 獻. D. 509 BCE. Successful general, then prime minister of Jìn. (Zheng, Wu, and Yang 2000) *41.14*

Wen: See **Zhou King Wen.**

Wen River, Wèn 汶: Known today as the Dàwèn River 大汶河, in present-day western Shāndōng Province. It ran southwest, then west, passing about 30 mi. N of the Lǔ capital. See also **Bo**; **Ying.** (Luo 1994; Tan 1996) *1.2*

Wenzi, Wénzǐ 文子: Wáng Sù identifies General Wénzǐ of Wèi 衛 as Mímóu 彌牟, a high official of Wèi. Sources differ as to his exact name and background, but there is some agreement that he was a descendant of the Wèi ruling family and an influential official in Wèi during the time of Confucius. (Zheng, Wu, and Yang 2000; Liu and Chi 2002) *12.1, 12.2, 12.3, 12.4, 12.17, 12.18, 34.1*

Wife: Ancient China was a polygynous society. Upper-class men often had more than one spouse, but only one of them could be the wife (*qī* 妻, *fēi* 妃), who was afforded a relatively high level of respect and power in the household (see 4.1). The other spouses were concubines (*qiè* 妾), meaning that they were a step below the wife in the family hierarchy, more akin to a servant than to an equal. When weddings occurred in the upper classes, it was not uncommon for extra women to be sent along as gifts. They could come from the same family (but not of the same mother) or from different families, such as nobility of other states celebrating the occasion. In both cases they were called *yìng* 媵, and in the former case the younger half-sister was called *dì* 娣. See also 15.9n10. (Wang 1997; Zheng, Wu, and Yang 2000) *qī* 妻 *1.3, 4.1, 13.3, 15.9, 22.1, 23.5, 38.12, 38.20, 38.21, 38.32, 39.2, 41.17, 41.21, 42.19, 43.4, 43.20*; *fēi* 妃 *4.1, 8.6*; *qiè* 妾 *18.4, 39.2, 43.20*; *dì* 娣 *41.17*

Wu (person): See **Zhou King Wu.**

Wu (state), Wú 吴: There are no records of Wú in the *Documents,* and it is not mentioned in BA until the reign of King Yuán of Zhōu (r. 476–469 BCE). SJ says that toward the end of the Shāng dynasty, two uncles (Tàibó 太伯 and

Zhòngyōng 仲雍) of Zhōu King Wén moved their large households to the non-Chinese southeast to indicate their wish to not contest the Zhōu throne designated for their younger brother. There they established the state of Wú 吴. After Zhōu conquered Shāng, SJ continues, Zhōu King Wǔ enfeoffed the ruler of Wú (Zhōuzhāng 周章, the great grandson of Zhòngyōng) with the noble title of viscount. CQZZ ("Mǐn" 1) alludes in the year 661 to Tàibó as if his story were common knowledge. SJ says that in 586 BCE the Wú ruler Shòumèng 壽夢 arrogated the title king for himself. Wú was a medium-sized state covering much of the territory of present-day Jiāngsū. Under King Hélǘ 闔閭 and his minister Wǔ Zǐxū (contemporaries of Confucius), Wú conquered vast areas of Chǔ, including much of present-day Ānhuī and part of Húběi. Just a few decades later (in 473 BCE), Yuè (Wú's neighbor to the south) absorbed the territory. According to the archaeological record, Wú was culturally distinct from Zhōu until 586, and the two cultures seem to have had little communication in the intervening centuries (Falkenhausen 2006). *16.2, 16.9, 37.2, 42.11, 42.26*

Wu City, Wǔ Chéng 武城: City in Lǔ, present-day Běiwǔ 北武村 (in Píngyì 平邑县, Línyí 臨沂市, Shāndōng) (49 mi. SE of Qūfù). Tāntái Mièmíng and Zǐgāo were both natives, and Zǐgāo was once mayor. Because the purported site of Wǔ City is near the border of three present-day polities, it is variously identified as being in Píngyì, Fèi 費, and Zǎozhuāng 棗莊. See also **Nanwu.** (Tan 1996; Zheng, Wu, and Yang 2000; Zhang and Xia 2010) *38.13, 38.14*

Wu King Fuchai, Wú Fūchāi Wáng: 吴王夫差: R. 495–473 BCE. During Confucius' lifetime, the real contenders for superpower status were largely in the south. Jìn and Qí were still powerful, but Chǔ, Wú, and Yuè had successfully asserted themselves as well. Accounts of actual success at achieving superpower status differ. For the latter half of Confucius' lifetime, Wú King Hélǘ was recognized, as was his son King Fūchāi, as was Yuè King Gōujiàn, who would bring about the deaths of the previous two. (Zheng, Wu, and Yang 2000) *16.9*

Wu Zixu, Wǔ Zǐxū 伍子胥: Also known as Shēn Xū 申胥. Wǔ Zǐxū came from a family of high ministers in Chǔ. When his father and elder brother were unjustly executed by Chǔ King Píng in 522 BCE, Wǔ Zǐxū vowed revenge, fled to Wú, and helped build Wú into a superpower. He achieved revenge in 506, when Wú roundly defeated Chǔ, but King Píng had already died several years earlier. In 494 BCE, Wú defeated Yuè. Wǔ Zǐxū advised King Fūchāi to destroy it and Yuè King Gōujiàn, but his advice was not heeded. In 484, when Lǔ had been attacked by Qí and Wú was contemplating teaming up with Yuè to come to Lǔ's rescue (see 37.2), Wǔ Zǐxū advised against it. Unpersuaded, the king sent Wǔ Zǐxū as emissary to Qí, at which time Wǔ Zǐxū, afraid that Wú would soon be destroyed, took along his two sons to entrust them to the Bào family of Qí. When he returned to Wú, the king had him executed. Wú was destroyed by Yuè in 473 BCE. (Zheng, Wu, and Yang 2000; Durrant, Li, and Schaberg 2016) *20.1, 37.2*

Wugeng, Wǔgēng 武庚: Son of Zhòu 紂. According to the *Documents* and BA, after the defeat of Shāng by Zhōu King Wǔ, King Wǔ enthroned Wǔgēng as the ruler of the remnants of the Shāng, and after King Wǔ died, Wǔgēng conspired with the disaffected Zhōu brothers Guǎn and Cài to rebel against Zhōu. Defeated by the Duke of Zhōu, Wǔgēng was executed. *10.18, 39.1*

Wugu: See **Baili Xi.**

Wuma Qi, Wūmǎ Qī 巫馬期: Surname Wūmǎ 巫馬, given name Shī 施, *zì* Zǐqī 子期(旗). Student of Confucius. Wūmǎ Qī appears with Confucius once in the *Analects* (7.31) and twice in the *Dialogues*. See 38.31 for his biography. (Zheng, Wu, and Yang 2000) *37.3, 38.31*

Xi: See **Lu Duke Xi.**

Xia (dynasty), Xià 夏: According to the *Documents*, the Xià was the first ruling dynasty of China—founded by the virtuous Yǔ and ended in iniquity under Jié 桀, conquered and replaced by Shāng 商. Many transmitted texts, including the *Documents* and BA, record the Xià, and although we have not found written records dating from the Xià (as we have for the Shāng), there is accumulating astronomical and archaeological evidence that (1) the Xià did indeed exist and (2) what is now known as the Érlǐtóu Neolithic culture was centered on the seat of the Xià dynasty. Customs of the Xià, vestiges of which survived into Confucius' time, were discussed by Confucius (see, e.g., 6.2, 16.8, 33.2). Chinese of Confucius' time, distinguishing themselves from other ethnicities, referred to themselves as Xià 夏 (see, e.g., 3.2). The Xià is considered the cradle of Chinese civilization, and to this day the Chinese refer to Chinese civilization as Huáxià 華夏 (splendiferous Xià). (Nivison and Pang 1990; Qian and Dawa 1999; Ji 2000; Xia-Shang-Zhou Chronology Expert Group 2000; Zheng, Wu, and Yang 2000; Li 2002; Chang and Xu 2005; Wang and Zhao 2023) *6.2, 13.3, 15.8, 15.9, 16.2, 30.1n2, 33.2, 34.2, 40.1, 40.2, 41.25, 43.25, 44.3*

Xia (people): See under **Xia (dynasty).**

***Xia* dance:** See **Dance.**

Xia Hou: See **Yǔ (person).**

Xia Ji, Xià Jī 夏姬: Daughter of Zheng Duke Mù (649–606 BCE). Married into a family of Zhèng. When her husband died, she married Xià Yùshū 夏御叔 of Chén, and she later gave birth to a son, Xià Zhēngshū 夏徵舒. After Xià Yùshū died, she was involved in affairs with Chén Duke Líng and his two ministers Kǒng Níng 孔寧 and Yí Xíngfù 儀行父, which precipitated a coup by her son. After her son was killed by the Chǔ army, she was taken to Chǔ and married. After her Chǔ husband died, she was taken to Zhèng; she later fled to Jìn. See also **Xie Ye.** (Zheng, Wu, and Yang 2000) *10.2n2*

***Xiang* archery banquets:** See ***Xiang* ceremonial banquet.** *27.1*

***Xiang* ceremonial banquet, *xiǎng* 饗 (also 鄉 or 享):** *Xiǎng* means to hold a banquet in honor of others. The basic meaning can be seen in the makeup of the character itself, which combines the character for *to eat* with the character for *village/countryside* to mean a village banquet. The original meaning, according to the earliest bronze inscriptions, was a formal ceremony to reorder the ancestral tablets in the royal ancestral temple after one king passed away and the other assumed the throne. The concomitant celebration probably included the entire clan, if not the entire populace of the capital, much like a potlatch feast of Northwest Native Americans. In the *Dialogues*, the term *xiǎng* is used in five ways: (1) as *xiǎng* (ceremonial banquet) all by itself (17.5, 30.1, 33.3, 43.23), (2) as *shíxiǎng* 食饗 (informal banquet; 27.1), (3) as *shèxiǎng* 射饗 (archery banquet; 27.1), (4) as Dà Xiǎng 大饗 (Grand Xiǎng ceremony; 27.1, 29.3), and (5) as Xiǎng in honor of the god Dì 帝 (29.3, 32.12). There does not seem to have been a hard-and-fast line between any of these uses. The essential point is that, for Confucius, a banquet is not just an occasion for eating and conviviality but an event in which the individual hierarchical position of each person in relation to each other is recognized, reverenced, and reinforced. It is an occasion to celebrate a harmonious unity of purpose across a diverse hierarchy of roles and responsibilities. Details are described in 27.1. See also 6.2, 28.2, 30.1, and 36.3 for allied ideas and depictions, and **Village archery event.** (Cooper 1982; Liu 1989) *1.2, 17.5, 27.1, 28.1, 28.2, 29.3, 30.1, 32.3, 32.12, 33.3, 43.23*

Xiang dance: See **Dance.**

Xie, Xiè 契: Legendary progenitor of the Shāng people. Surname Zǐ 子. Son of Chief Kù. Said variably to have been a minister under Yáo, Shùn, and Yǔ. Enfeoffed for meritorious deeds at Shāng. (Luo 1994; Zheng, Wu, and Yang 2000; Taiwan Academic Network 2021) *32.4, 34.2*

Xie Ye, Xiè Yě 泄冶: A minister under Chén Duke Líng. According to accounts in CQZZ ("Xuān" 9.6) and SJ ("Chén Qǐ shì jiā"), after an incident in which the king and two high officials had their way with Xià Jī 夏姬, who is represented in texts as a notorious femme fatale ("seven husbands, thrice a queen"; see under Xia Ji and 10.2n2) and played games wearing her underwear in court, Xiè Yě warned the duke that such behavior would influence the common people to also behave badly. Two of the duke's sons then killed Xiè Yě, with the duke's implicit approval. (Liu and Chi 2002) *19.6*

***Xinsi*:** See under **Calendar.**

Xinyang, Xìnyáng 信陽: City known as Yìyáng 義陽 prior to the Sòng dynasty (960–1279). South of present-day Xìnyáng, Hénán (330 mi. SW of Qūfù). (Tan 1996; Zheng, Wu, and Yang 2000) *14.8*

Xinzhu, Xīnzhù 新築: City of Wèi 衛, south of present-day Wèi 魏縣, Héběi (144 mi. NW of Qūfù). (Yang and Song 2013) *41.20*

Xu, Xú 徐/郐: A small but scrappy state of the Eastern Yí people centered in present-day Sìhóng 泗洪, Jiāngsū (183 mi. SW of Qūfù). Absorbed by Wú in 512 BCE. (Zheng, Wu, and Yang 2000) *41.7n23*

Yan (person): See **Yanzi.**

Yan (place), Yān 燕 (originally 匽 or郾): State enfeoffed by Zhōu King Wǔ to the Earl of Shào at the beginning of the Zhōu in present-day Běijīng (333 mi. N of Qūfù). The earl gave it to his son. Yān does not figure prominently in the *Dialogues* or the *Analects* but became one of the main states of the Warring States period and persisted until 222 BCE, when it was absorbed by Qín. See also **Earl of Shao.** (Zheng, Wu, and Yang 2000) *40.2*

Yan Huanzi, Yàn Huánzǐ 晏桓子: Father of Yànzǐ. D. 556 BCE. According to the CQZZ ("Xiāng" 6.7), he was the chief architect of the elimination of the Lái state in 567 BCE. See also **Yanzi.** *43.16*

Yan Hui, Yán Huí 顏回: Surname Yán 顏, given name Huí 回, *zì* Zǐyuān 子淵. 521–490/481 BCE. Yán Huí, along with Zǐgòng and Zǐlù, is one of the students most often at Confucius' side. In the *Analects*, Yán Huí is depicted as Confucius' star student—diligent, hardworking, cheerful, virtuous, and intelligent. Whereas Confucius never hesitates to criticize his other students, he rarely has a corrective word for Yán Huí (an exception seems to be in 15.12, but it is not said in Yán Huí's presence). In *Dialogues* 9.8 and 20.1, Yán Huí is pitted against Zǐlù and Zǐgòng, the latter two coming up short in Confucius' estimation and Yán Huí being right on the mark. A moving episode in *Dialogues* 20.4 demonstrates Confucius' trust in Yán Huí. Throughout the *Analects* and *Dialogues*, Confucius repeatedly praises Yán Huí, and he reportedly (*Analects* 11.9–10) feels bereft when Yán Huí passes away before reaching his potential. According to *Dialogues* 40.2, Confucius mourned Yán Huí like his own son. Yán Huí is not recorded as ever having held an official position, but he did meet with Lǔ Duke Dìng (18.1) and with the Lǔ nobleman Shūsūn Wǔshū (18.11), and the preparation for his trip to Sòng (13.4) suggests that the purpose was employment. See 12.4 for Zǐgòng's appraisal of Yán Huí, and see 38.1 for a brief biography. (Zheng, Wu, and Yang 2000; Zhang and Xia 2010) *8.1, 9.8, 12.4, 13.4, 15.12, 15.14, 18.1, 18.2, 18.3, 18.4, 18.5, 18.6, 18.7, 18.8, 18.9, 18.10, 18.11, 18.12, 20.1, 20.4, 38.1, 38.24, 40.2, 43.24, 44.5*

Yan Lu, Yán Lù 顏路: Surname Yán 顏, given name Wúyáo 無繇, *zì* Lù 路. Yán Huí's father. (Zheng, Wu, and Yang 2000) *44.5*

Yan Pingzhong: See **Yanzi.**

Yan Yan: See **Ziyou.**

Yan Ying: See **Yanzi.**

Yan You: See **Ziyou.**

Yan Yuan: See **Yan Hui.**

Yang Hu, Yáng Hǔ 陽虎 (or Yáng Huò 陽貨): Household manager of Jì Huánzǐ before Zǐlù held the position (see 1.3). In 505 BCE, he effectively usurped Jì Huánzǐ's power, but when he attempted a final coup de grace in 501, he was defeated and fled (see 16.7). Yáng Hǔ also appears in *Analects* 17.1, where, as in 43.23,

Confucius maintains his composure in a delicate interaction with him. See also **Ji Huanzi**; **Shusun Zhe.** (Kong, Sang, and Kong 1994; Zheng, Wu, and Yang 2000) *16.7, 43.23*

Yangshe, Yángshé 羊舌: One of the ruling clans of Jìn during the Spring and Autumn period. See also **Tongdi Bohua.** (Chen and Wang 1995; Durrant, Li, and Schaberg 2016) *12.21, 12.22, 41.14*

Yangtze River, Jiāng 江: The Yangtze flows roughly west to east across China and currently defines the northern border of southern China, but in the time of Confucius it was close to being the southern border of the Chinese cultural sphere. It begins in the Tibetan plateau, and after flowing through present-day Chóngqìng, Wǔhàn, and Nánjīng, it empties into the Pacific Ocean as an estuary at Shànghǎi. In the time of Confucius, it was the major waterway of the state of Chǔ, passing through its capital at Yǐng 郢 (present-day Jīngzhōu 荊州, Húběi). (Luo 1994; Tan 1996) *8.16n26, 9.10, 41.16*

Yanzi, Yànzǐ 晏子: Surname Yàn 晏, given name Yīng 嬰, *zì* Píngzhòng 平仲. D. 500 BCE. Minister of Qí who served three sovereigns for over fifty years, Yànzǐ was a somewhat older contemporary of Confucius, whom Confucius knew personally. Yànzǐ's depiction in the three stories in the *Dialogues* is consistent with his description in CQZZ. In *Dialogues* 12.21, he is depicted as independent-minded and able to preserve himself in a dangerous environment. Several stories in CQZZ portray him as unusually able to stay aloof from internal political struggles, and several depict his independence from the ruler. For example, once when he was away, the ruler of Qí had Yàn's house torn down and a much larger mansion built in its place. Upon returning home, Yàn had the mansion demolished, replacing it with the former house and the several neighboring houses that had been razed to build the mansion (CQZZ "Zhāo" 3.3). This story also demonstrates his material moderation, as depicted in *Dialogues* 42.7, and his concern for others. The story of Yàn mourning his father also appears in CQZZ ("Xiāng" 17.7). Yàn's many appearances in CQZZ show further parallels with the thinking of Confucius—namely, an emphasis on *li*, on virtue over superstition, and on harmony. One has to wonder why he doesn't appear at all in the *Analects*. In *Dialogues* 15.16, Confucius recommends that Zēngzǐ enter Qí's government under Yànzǐ. Yànzǐ is identified in SJ ("Guǎn Yàn liè zhuàn") as hailing from the Lái region. CQZZ ("Xiāng" 6.7) says that Yànzǐ's father was responsible for exterminating the Lái state. See also **Lai**; **Yan Huanzi.** (Fang et al. 1994; Zheng, Wu, and Yang 2000; Liu and Chi 2002; Zhang and Xia 2010) *12.21, 13.8, 14.5, 15.16, 37.2, 42.7, 43.11, 43.16*

Yao, Yáo 堯: Also known as Táotáng 陶唐 (the name of Yáo's clan). Son of Gāoxīn 高辛. Fourth of the legendary Five Chiefs. For his biography, see 23.4. For his ability to hire capable and virtuous men, see 14.7; for his reverence and deference in governing, see 15.8. (Zheng, Wu, and Yang 2000) *8.1, 11.2, 12.7, 14.7, 15.8, 22.8, 23.4, 23.5, 24.4, 24.5, 30.1n2, 34.2, 35.3, 39.3, 41.16*

Yellow Chief, *Huáng Dì* 黄帝: According to legend, he is the first of the Five Chiefs of prehistoric times. Son of Shào Diǎn. The appellation *Yellow* Chief comes from his association with the soil (see 24.1). The name of his state was Yǒuxióng 有熊, as was his clan. Another clan name is said to have been Xuānyuán 軒轅, the name of the hill where he lived. His original surname, Gōngsūn 公孫, was later changed to Jī 姬, which was also the surname of the Zhōu dynasty. He is said to have been the first ruler to suppress an evil regime (in the form of his half-brother, Chief Yán 炎) and bring together rival ruling houses for the benefit of society. He is also a cultural hero, credited with many innovations and inventions, such as writing, music, the calendar, palaces, boats, carriages, clothing, and the compass. Said to be the progenitor of the entire Chinese people. For his biography, see 23.1. (Luo 1994; Taiwan Academic Network 2021) *16.4, 23.1, 23.2, 24.1, 30.1n1, 35.3*

Yellow River, Hé 河: The Yellow River flows roughly east to west aross northern China, beginning in the arid west and flowing through the Ordos Desert and Loess Plateau. As it descends toward the Pacific Ocean, it deposits immense amounts of yellow loess soil. In fact, this soil created the North China Plain that it still flows trough today. The Chinese civilization arose in Neolithic settlements along the Yellow River, which is named for the color of the silt that it carries along. The river was a prominent geographical feature throughout history and also a source of disaster, because it commonly flooded and changed course. One flood occurred in the historical period concerning Confucius (in 602 BCE), but it does not figure prominently (CQZZ, in "Xuān" 10.15, records a great flood in 599 BCE, but its effects were not recorded). (Chen et al. 2012) *8.14n, 22.2, 35.3, 38.10, 41.16*

Yi (people) (or Eastern Yi), Yí 夷 (Dōng Yí 東夷): Minority people living to the east of the Central Plains, in present-day eastern Shāndōng and northern Jiāngsū. The Lái people are said to be a branch of the Yí. Shào Hào was said to be first ruler of the Eastern Yí. By the middle of the Spring and Autumn period, tombs of the Yí people had come to resemble Zhōu tombs in every way. To what extent this cultural assimilation extended to other aspects of society is difficult to know. *Yí* is translated variously according to contexts as *barbarians, non-Xia peoples, frontier people,* and so on. See also **Lai.** (Chen 1987; Qian and Dawa 1999; Falkenhausen 2006) *1.2, 3.2, 15.9, 16.3, 16.4, 37.2, 43.11*

Yi (river), Yí 沂: River south of the Lǔ capital, in present-day Shāndōng, running approximately east to west from Ní Mountain and emptying into the Sì River southwest of Qūfù. *38.23*

Yin Jifu, Yǐn Jífǔ 尹吉甫: Also, Jífǔ, or Fǔ. Not much is known about Jífǔ (it isn't even clear that Yǐn was his surname), but he seems to have been a major Western Zhōu personage during the time of King Xuān. He was famed as a successful general and as a poet, with two poems in the *Poems* attributed to him. He is very likely the successful general Jífù 吉父 whose exploits during King Xuān's reign are recorded on a bronze that still survives. (Shaughnessy 1997; Zheng, Wu, and Yang 2000) *36.2, 38.12*

Ying, Yíng 嬴: City along the Wen 汶 River northwest of present-day Láiwú (75 mi. NW of Qūfù). *42.26*

Yizi: See **Meng Yizi.**

Yongzi, Yōngzǐ 雍子: Fl. 573–528 BCE. Successful Jìn general and nobleman. Originally from Chǔ. (Zheng, Wu, and Yang 2000) *41.9*

You: See **Zhou King You.**

Yóu: See **Zilu.**

You Ruo, Yǒu Ruò 有若: Student of Confucius. Yǒu Ruò appears in only one passage in the *Dialogues* other than his mini-biography (38.17), while appearing in four passages in the *Analects*. According to SJ ("Zhòngní dìzǐ liè zhuàn"), after Confucius died, his students felt a need to fill the void left by his absence, and Yǒu Ruò was selected as his replacement because he most resembled Confucius in appearance.[10] Not surprisingly, student regret immediately set in, according to SJ. Despite the ambiguity surrounding Yǒu Ruò's role as teacher, his four brief remarks in the *Analects* stand as some of the most penetrating of the entire text. The suffix *zi* is appended to his surname in the *Analects*, indicating that he likely became a teacher or an otherwise influential figure in his own right. *38.17, 42.32*

Youling, Yōulíng 幽陵: An area spanning present-day northern Héběi and western Liáoníng. (Qian and Dawa 1999) *23.2*

Youyu, Yǒuyú 有虞: Also, Yú 虞. Name of an ancient people. Shùn was their leader, and so it is a reference either to the time of Shùn (in the sense of a dynasty) or to Shùn 舜 himself. (Zheng, Wu, and Yang 2000) *16.2, 23.5, 24.4, 24.5, 34.1, 34.2, 41.25*

Yu (person): See **Zai Wo.**

Yǔ (person), Yǔ 禹: Also known as Xià Hòu 夏后. Legendary founder of the Xià 夏 dynasty. Shùn yielded the throne to him. Viewed as a great sage-king by Confucius. During the Shāng, and again during the Zhōu, the ancestors of Yǔ were settled in the state of Qǐ 杞. See 23.6 for Yǔ's biography. *3.1, 16.2, 22.8, 23.1, 23.6, 24.5, 32.2, 32.4, 34.2, 41.16n47, 41.25*

Yú (person/period), Yú 虞: See **Youyu.**

Yu (state), Yú 虞: A state during the Shāng and Zhōu dynasties. Present-day Pínglù 平陸縣, Hénán. See also **Youyu.** (Taiwan Academic Network 2021) *10.10*

Yú Mountain, Yú Shān 嵎山: Mountain said to lie at the borders of Wú and Yuè in present-day Déqīng 德清縣, Zhèjiāng. (Luo 1994; Berman and Hays 2014) *16.2*

Yuan Si, Yuán Sī 原思: Yuán Sī appears in one episode of the *Analects* (6.5) and two of the *Dialogues*. See 38.19 for a brief biography. *38.19, 43.25*

10. D. C. Lau says, "It is not clear in what way [You Ruo] resembled Confucius" (Lau 1979, 218–19), then provides evidence from Mencius to support a claim that the resemblance was in speech.

Yuan Xian: See **Yuan Si.**

Yue, Yuè 越: The state of Yuè is mentioned in a Shāng-dynasty bronze, and in BA it appears in the early years of the Zhōu. It doesn't appear in CQZZ until 601 BCE. In 496, King Gōujiàn burst onto the scene and quickly made a name for himself, eventually conquering Wú and establishing Yuè as a superpower. At its greatest extent, its territory spanned the eastern seaboard south of Shāndōng Province all the way through present-day Guǎngzhōu 广州. Due to internal strife, Yuè gradually lost power, and by the end of the fourth century it had split in two. Its descendant states lost relevance and were absorbed by Qín in 221 BCE. (Zheng, Wu, and Yang 2000) *16.2, 20.1, 37.2*

Yue King Goujian, Yuè Gōujiàn Wáng 越王勾踐: R. 497–465 BCE. After being defeated by Wú in 494 BCE, King Gōujiàn began a self-strengthening program to turn Yuè into a major power. In 473, Gōujiàn conquered and absorbed Wú, finally achieving superpower status for Yuè. (Zheng, Wu, and Yang 2000; Durrant, Li, and Schaberg 2016) *20.1, 37.2*

Yun, Yùn 鄆: Name of two cities of Lǔ. Eastern Yùn was north of present-day Yíshuǐ 沂水縣, Shāndōng (about 105 mi. ENE of Qūfù), and western Yùn was in present-day Yùnchéng County 鄆城縣, Shāndōng (approx. 65 mi. W of Qūfù). (Luo 1994; Tan 1996; Liu and Chi 2002) *1.3n9*

Zai Wo, Zǎi Wǒ 宰我: Surname Zǎi 宰, given name Yú 予 (or Wǒ 我), *zì* Zǐwǒ 子我. 522–458 BCE. Zǎi Wǒ is a unique character among Confucius' students for being regularly criticized and never praised (except by an unnamed narrator in *Analects* 11.3). He appears in the *Analects* in five episodes, in four of which he is either corrected or criticized. Apparently, he was quite eloquent but lacked the moral qualities to match. Confucius criticizes him as not *ren* (which under one interpretation can mean downright cruel; *Analects* 17.21), and faults him for sleeping during the day (*Analects* 5.10). Confucius goes on to say that he has learned something from Zǎi Wǒ—not to trust what people say but instead to observe their behavior. The criticisms are echoed in *Dialogues* 19.8, but the *Dialogues* also shows two further facets of Zǎi Wǒ. In 19.3 he calls Confucius' own behavior into question—a rare occurrence. In several other passages (17.5 and 23.1–7), we see Zǎi Wǒ in straightforward question-and-answer sessions with Confucius like any other student, and yet at the end of chapter 23 Confucius berates Zǎi Wǒ again. One can't help but wonder if the topics of the dialogue have something to do with Confucius' dislike of Zǎi Wǒ. Confucius says repeatedly in the *Analects* that he is concerned with cultivating moral character and not concerned with metaphysical matters such as ghosts and spirits (6.22, 11.12), and yet Zǎi Wǒ asks him about exactly that topic in 17.5, and all of chapter 23 is dedicated to Zǎi Wǒ's questions about mythical figures from high antiquity. According to SJ ("Zhòngní dìzǐ liè zhuàn"), Zǎi Wǒ worked for the Qí government and was involved in Chén Huán's successful coup there. (Fang et al. 1994; Luo 1994; Zheng, Wu, and Yang 2000) *17.5, 19.3, 19.8, 23.1, 23.2, 23.3, 23.4, 23.5, 23.6, 23.7, 38.5*

Zai Yu: See **Zai Wo.**

Zang Wenzhong, Zāng Wénzhòng 臧文仲: D. 617 BCE. Also known as Zāngsūn Chén 臧孫辰. High official of Lǔ who served under four dukes (Zhuāng, Mǐn, Xī, and Wén). He was widely known for his wisdom, but, according to Confucius (18.4, 42.8) the reputation was not entirely deserved. (Fang et al. 1994) *10.8, 18.4, 42.8*

Zang Wuzhong, Zāng Wǔzhòng 臧武仲: Surname Zāngsūn 臧孫, given name Hé 紇. Grandson of Zāng Wénzhòng. A generation ahead of Confucius. A high official of Lǔ, he was widely regarded as a sage and held in high esteem by Confucius. In 569 BCE, after Zhū 邾 and Jǔ 莒 invaded Zēng 鄫, Wǔzhòng invaded Zhū in defense of Zēng but was defeated. In 556, he was trapped by Qí at Fáng and rescued by Confucius' father. In the end, animosities with the Mèngsūn and Jìsūn families prompted him to flee Lǔ. (Zheng, Wu, and Yang 2000) *10.8, 11.1, 18.4, 42.9*

Zangsun He: See **Zang Wuzhong.** (Zheng, Wu, and Yang 2000)

Zaofu, Zàofù 造父: Lived during the Western Zhōu dynasty. Famous for training horses. (Luo 1994; Zheng, Wu, and Yang 2000) *18.1*

Zeng Dian, Zēng Diǎn 曾點: Surname Zēng 曾, given name Diǎn 點, *zì* Xī 晳 (or Zǐxī 子晳). Father of Zēngzǐ. An early student of Confucius. See 38.23 for his biography. (Zheng, Wu, and Yang 2000) *38.23, 43.23*

Zeng Shen: See **Zengzi.**

Zengzi, Zēngzǐ 曾子: 505–436 BCE. Surname Zēng 曾, given name Shēn 參, *zì* Zǐyú 子輿. Zēngzǐ was one of Confucius' main students. He is mentioned in fifteen passages of the *Analects* and fourteen passages of the *Dialogues*. In the *Analects*, he is never depicted as subservient to Confucius (except perhaps in 11.13, where an unnamed person refers to him by his given name and describes him as not very bright); he never asks Confucius a question; and he often offers his own wisdom, even interpreting Confucius' words for others. He and Zǐxià are the only students in the *Analects* who are depicted with their own students. The *Dialogues* provides a more complicated picture. In 8.7, 10.11, and 20.3, Zēngzǐ offers his own wisdom, but at the end of the passages it says that Confucius heard about what Zēngzǐ said and then praised Zēngzǐ, an unusual response from Confucius with regard to hearsay regarding his students. (The only other such positive responses are in 10.8, regarding Qídiāo Píng; 41.2, regarding Rǎn Qiú; and 44.7, regarding Zǐlù.) A somewhat different description is given, however, in chapters 3 and 15, where Zēngzǐ is depicted as a typical student, deferential to Confucius and seeking wisdom. A now-lost eponymous book is attributed to Zēngzǐ. According to the *Hàn shū*, it had eighteen chapters. Ten chapters attributed to Zēngzǐ appear in the *Dà Dài lǐ jì*, in which *xiào* is a main theme, and Zēngzǐ is Confucius' interlocutor in the *Xiào jīng* (*Classic of Xiào*). Zēngzǐ is the only student of Confucius typically referred to with the honorific suffix *-zi* appended to his name in both the *Analects* and *Dialogues*, suggesting a position of authority in the community around Confucius that was second only to Confucius himself. Taking into account his youth, however (he was only twenty-six when Confucius passed away), his elevated status may have been more a function of his accomplishments after Confucius died than during Confucius' lifetime. See 38.12 for his *Dialogues* biography, and see Zǐgòng's appraisal of him in 12.9. (Gao 1991; Taiwan Academic Network 2021) *3.1, 3.2, 8.7, 10.11, 12.9, 15.10, 15.14, 15.15, 15.16, 20.3, 38.12, 38.23, 43.16, 43.25*

Zha Festival, Zhà 蜡: Little is known about this festival, but from the scant evidence available, scholars speculate that it was held after a bumper harvest and was something like a combination of Thanksgiving and pre-Lenten Carnival. It appears to have been popular in the Zhōu dynasty but waned from the Hàn onward. (Bodde 1975; Cooper 1982; Wang 2002; Li 2011; Yu 2017) *28.3, 32.1*

Zhaigong Moufu, Zhàigōng Móufù 祭公謀父: A descendant of the Duke of Zhōu. (Luo 1994) *41.7*

Zhan Qin: See **Liuxia Hui.**

Zhao: See **Shusun Zhao.**

Zhao, Zhào 趙: Zhào family. Influential aristocratic family of Jìn during Confucius' time. (Durrant, Li, and Schaberg 2016) *16.7*

Zhao Jianzi, Zhào Jiǎnzǐ 趙簡子: Surname Zhào 趙, given name Yāng 鞅. Posthumous name Jiǎn 簡. D. 475 BCE. Head of one of the leading families of Jìn. Took in Yáng Hǔ in 501 BCE after his unsuccessful uprising in Lǔ. (Zheng, Wu, and Yang 2000) *16.7, 22.2, 41.15*

Zhaoge, Zhāogē 朝歌: An alternative capital toward the end of the Shāng dynasty. First capital of Wèi. It belonged to Jìn during the Spring and Autumn period. Located in present-day Qí 淇縣, in northern Hénán (170 mi. W of Qūfù). (Tan 1996; Zheng, Wu, and Yang 2000) *39.1*

Zheng, Zhèng 鄭: Zhōu vassal state. Mentioned in the Shāng oracle bones as a contemporary fiefdom. According to BA ("You wang," "Píng wáng"),[11] Jī Duōfù 姬多父 was a prince of Zhōu. After conquering the state of Zēng 鄫 in battle in 783 BCE, he was enfeoffed by his brother Zhōu King Yōu as Duke of Zhèng, within the royal domain. Zēng got revenge by teaming up with its neighbor Shēn and the Róng people, killing King Yōu and Jī Duōfù, the new duke of Zhèng. In 770, the duke's son and heir conquered the state of Guó 虢 and moved the Zhèng capital to a nearby area between the Zhēn 溱 and Wěi 洧 rivers—that is,

11. The account in BA differs in some details from the accounts in the *Guo yu* and SJ and may be more reliable. (Shaughnessy 1997)

present-day Xīnzhèng 新鄭, Hénán (about 225 mi. SW of Qūfù). Zhèng now had room to grow, and it did so quickly to become a medium-sized state. It just as quickly fell into a persistent decline, relieved only during the decades that Zǐchǎn was influential in the government (543–522 BCE), when internal reforms and external diplomacy brought relative stability and prosperity. In 375 BCE, Zhèng was conquered by Hán. See also **Zhou King You**; **Zichan.** (Luo 1994; Tan 1996; Zheng, Wu, and Yang 2000) *8.16, 13.2, 22.8, 41.6, 41.10, 41.11, 41.12*

Zheng ceremony, Zhēng 烝: Sacrificial ceremony to the ancestors. Some sources say it was traditionally held in winter, but the earliest records in bronze inscriptions do not reflect a seasonal aspect. (Liu 1989; Xu 1991; Luo 1994; Liu and Chi 2002) *41.21*

Zhong You: See **Zilu.**

Zhongdu, Zhōngdū 中都: City of Lǔ, west of present-day Wènshàng 汶上, Shāndōng (about 35 mi. NW of Qūfù). *43.17*

Zhonggong, Zhònggōng 仲弓: Surname Rǎn 冉, given name Yōng 雍, *zì* Zhònggōng 仲弓. Born 522 BCE. A relative of Rǎn Yǒu and Rǎn Gēng. One of the main students of Confucius. According to the *Dialogues* (12.5, 38.4), Zhònggōng came from difficult circumstances but ended up quite successful. According to *Analects* 13.2, he was employed as manager of the Jìsūn household, a powerful position. Though Confucius leveled criticism at Rǎn Yǒu and Zǐlù when they worked for Jìsūn (*Analects* 16.1), he was quite complimentary toward Zhònggōng (*Analects* 5.5, 6.1, 6.6). This is consistent with Confucius' praise for him in Zǐgòng's appraisal in *Dialogues* 12.5. Apart from Zǐgòng's assessment and the *Dialogues* mini-biography (38.4), Zhònggōng appears in five passages of the *Dialogues* and in six passages of the *Analects*. In both texts, he is depicted as concerned with virtuous, level-headed governing, with a special interest in the *Dialogues* for how to handle criminal cases (31.1–31.5). (Luo 1994; Zheng, Wu, and Yang 2000) *12.5, 31.1, 31.2, 31.3, 31.4, 31.5, 38.4*

Zhonghang Wenzi, Zhōngháng Wénzǐ 中行文子: Surname Zhōngháng 中行 (or Xún 荀), given name Yín 寅, posthumous name Wén 文. A contemporary of Confucius. According to CQZZ, the Zhonghangs had a long history of service at the highest levels in Jìn. Wénzǐ was a major participant in a civil war among rival families in Jìn, which resulted in his fleeing to Qí, marking the end of the Zhōnghángs' influence in Jìn. (Zheng, Wu, and Yang 2000) *13.6, 14.3*

Zhonghangs of Jin: See **Zhonghang Wenzi.**

Zhongsun Heji: See **Meng Yizi.**

Zhou (dynasty), Zhōu 周: 1046–256 BCE. Ruling dynasty of China. Replaced the Shāng 商. Progressively weakened as a power until finally conquered by Qín 秦. Originally a vassal state of Shāng 商, Zhōu lay due west of the Shāng capital Ānyáng. According to the *Documents*, while Shāng King Xīn 辛 was busy fighting non-Chinese forces to the East and entertaining himself in the palace, the ambitious ruler of Zhōu (known to posterity as King Wén) expanded north, south, and west, conquering land and earning the fealty of a growing portion of Shāng's empire. King Wén passed away before he could finish off the Shāng, but his son (the future King Wǔ) achieved this just a few years later. Zhōu established its capital at present-day Xī'ān, Shǎnxī, and promptly enfeoffed its generals, family members, and loyal ministers in city-states across the Central Plains. These events are of paramount importance to Confucius, for in the *Documents* and the *Poems* King Wén is depicted as a ruler who gained his power through his virtue, his capability, and his care for others, deeply influencing people within his purview. Furthermore, after King Wǔ passed away prematurely, King Wǔ's brother (known to posterity as the Duke of Zhōu) controlled the government on behalf of King Wú's son King Chéng, who was still a child. The Duke of Zhōu, reportedly through virtue, capability, and care, shepherded the young empire through massive growth and a civil war, eventually bringing stability and prosperity. Another important feature attributed to the rule of King Wén and the Duke of Zhōu is their use of *lǐ*, which depended on all members of society understanding and playing their proper roles, with those lower on the hierarchy acting out of due reverence and humility while earnestly learning and cultivating virtue, and those higher in the hierarchy handling affairs virtuously and guiding others with care and concern, each generation preparing the next while revering the former. Confucius' native state of Lǔ, the rulers of which were descended from the Duke of Zhōu, is said to have best preserved the *lǐ* tradition. During Confucius' time, the Zhōu had been reduced to effectively one among several states, with its capital in what is present-day Luòyáng 洛陽. Chapter 11 of the *Dialogues* tells the story of Confucius' visit to Zhōu. See also **Bin**; **Cai (person)**; **Dan Fu**; **Duke of Zhou**; **Earl of Shao**; and the various Zhou kings. (Loewe and Shaughnessy 1999; Zheng, Wu, and Yang 2000) *3.2, 9.3, 10.18, 11.1, 11.2, 14.1, 15.4, 16.2, 24.4, 24.5, 29.2, 32.4, 33.4, 34.1, 34.2, 35.3, 36.2, 39.1, 39.3, 40.1, 40.2, 41.6, 41.11, 41.25, 42.31, 43.2, 43.10, 43.25, 43.26, 44.2*

Zhòu (person), Zhòu, 紂: The *Documents* refers to him only as Shòu 受 or King Shòu 王受. BA refers to him only as Xīn 辛 or King Xīn 帝辛. SJ introduces him as King Xīn 辛, says that everyone refers to him as Zhòu 紂 (a probable homophone of Shòu 受), and thereafter refers to him as Zhòu 紂. The tradition has preferred to call him Zhòu. Zhòu was the last ruler of the Shāng dynasty. According to his depiction in the *Documents*, he spent little time in governing because he was preoccupied with pleasures of all kinds. He is also depicted as short-tempered and vicious. He is often mentioned in the *Dialogues* along with Jié 桀, the notorious last king of the Xià dynasty, as an example of what happens when a government is allowed to go off the rails. See also **Jie**. (Luo 1994; Zheng, Wu, and Yang 2000) *11.2, 13.5, 15.2, 19.6, 25.1, 31.1, 35.2, 39.1*

Zhōu Kings in the *Dialogues*	
King Jì	dates unknown
King Wén	r. 1056–1050 BCE
King Wǔ	r. 1049–1043 BCE
King Chéng	r. 1035–1006 BCE
King Kāng	r. 1003–978 BCE
King Zhāo	r. 977–957 BCE
King Mù	r. 956–918 BCE
King Lì	r. 857–842 BCE
King Yōu	r. 781–771 BCE
King Huán	r. 719–697 BCE
King Xī	r. 681–677 BCE

Zhou King Cheng, Zhōu Chéng Wáng 周成王: Surname Jī 姬, given name Sòng 誦 (or Yōng 庸), posthumous name Chéng 成. R. 1035–1006 BCE. According to the *Documents,* King Chéng was the son and heir of Zhōu King Wǔ and assumed the throne after Wǔ's death. Since he was still a minor, the Duke of Zhōu initially acted as regent. A significant portion of the utterances in the *Documents* are attributed to King Chéng, and a number of the works in the *Poems* extol his wise leadership. On this basis, he was widely regarded as one of the great former kings, consistent with his depictions in the *Dialogues.* See also **Duke of Zhou**; **Zhou King Wu.** (Loewe and Shaughnessy 1999; Zheng, Wu, and Yang 2000) *11.2, 32.2, 33.2, 39.1, 41.19, 43.3*

Zhou King Huan, Zhōu Huán Wáng 周桓王: Surname Jī 姬, given name Lín 林, posthumous name Huán 桓. R. 719–697 BCE. Grandson of King Píng. Not much is known about King Huán except that, according to CQZZ and BA, warfare was common during his reign and he had an ongoing feud with Zhèng that ended in King Huán's defeat. (Zheng, Wu, and Yang 2000) *16.6*

Zhou King Ji, Zhōu Jì Wáng 周王季: Surname Jī 姬, given name Jìlì 季歷. Son of Dǎn Fǔ. Father of Zhōu King Wén 周文王. Leader of the Zhōu, a Shāng vassal state. Acting as general for the Shāng, he successfully battled the northern Róng tribes. He was a leader among the other Shāng states. See also **Dan Fu.** (Zheng, Wu, and Yang 2000) *8.6*

Zhou King Kang, Zhōu Kāng Wáng 周康王: Surname Jī 姬, given name Zhāo 釗, posthumous name Kāng 康. R. 1003–978 BCE. Son and heir of King Chéng. Generally regarded as a virtuous king aided by the Earl of Shào. (Loewe and Shaughnessy 1999; Zheng, Wu, and Yang 2000) *2.2n4, 31.1, 41.7n21*

Zhou King Li, Zhōu Lì Wáng 周厲王: Surname Jī 姬, given name Hú 胡 (also 𩁹), posthumous name Lì 厲. Son of King Yí 夷. R. 857–842 BCE. According to BA, in the eleventh year of King Lì's reign, the Western Róng people invaded the capital. The king lost the battle and fled to the tiny state of Zhì 彘 (northeast of present-day Huòzhōu 霍州, Shānxī). At the same time, the lower members of the royal family surrounded the palace, then captured and killed the son of Shào Duke Mù 召穆公, who was the head of the Zhōu government. The king's reign was further marred by multiple disasters. Nine heads of state died, and there were five straight years of drought. According to CQZZ ("Zhāo" 26.9), King Lì was tyrannical, and so the people rebelled and exiled him to Zhì. The nobleman who took over was presumably Shào Duke Mù, who is depicted in CQZZ ("Xī" 24.2a–b) as a virtuous leader. The *Dialogues* follows the account in CQZZ in depicting King Lì as not just having a disastrous reign but also being a disastrous person. (Loewe and Shaughnessy 1999; Zheng, Wu, and Yang 2000; Zhang and Xia 2010) *12.5n, 32.4, 41.12n36*

Zhou King Mu, Zhōu Mù Wáng 周穆王: Surname Jī 姬, given name Mǎn 满, posthumous name Mù 穆. R. 956–918 BCE. Son of King Zhāo. (Loewe and Shaughnessy 1999; Zheng, Wu, and Yang 2000) *30.1n2, 41.7*

Zhou King Wen, Zhōu Wén Wáng 周文王: Surname Jī 姬, given name Chāng 昌. Also known as *Xī Bó* 西伯, Earl of the West, a title conferred by Shāng King Zhòu. R. 1056–1050 BCE. Son of Zhōu King Jì and father of Zhōu King Wǔ. King Wén is the great hero of the *Documents*. While the Shāng dynasty was going into decline, King Wén, of the Zhōu vassal state, was quietly forming alliances and plotting its overthrow. He passed away before his final ambition could be achieved, but his sons fulfilled his wishes. King Wén is often lauded by Confucius as one of the virtuous and capable sage-kings of the past. Some specifics of his laudatory behavior are given in 17.5. See also **Zhou (dynasty)**; **Zhou King Ji.** (Loewe and Shaughnessy 1999; Zheng, Wu, and Yang 2000) *2.1, 8.6, 10.10, 15.4, 17.1, 17.5, 23.1, 28.3, 30.1, 32.2, 34.2, 35.1, 36.2, 39.3, 41.25, 44.2*

Zhou King Wu, Zhōu Wǔ Wáng 周武王: Surname Jī 姬, given name Fā 發, posthumous name Wǔ 武. R. 1045–1043 BCE. Son of Zhōu King Wén. Fulfilling his father's decades-long ambition, King Wǔ conquered the Shāng dynasty and replaced it. He is depicted in the *Documents* as a hero and virtuous ruler, and Confucius holds him up as a paragon for all subsequent rulers. See also **Zhou (dynasty).** (Loewe and Shaughnessy 1999; Zheng, Wu, and Yang 2000) *8.6, 15.2, 15.4, 16.3, 17.1, 23.1, 32.2, 33.2, 34.2, 35.3, 36.2, 39.1, 41.19, 41.25, 44.2*

Zhou King Xi, Zhōu Xī Wáng 周釐王: Surname Jī 姬, given name Húqí 胡齊, posthumous name Xī 釐 (also 僖). R. 681–677 BCE. Son of King Zhuāng. It was during his reign that the low status of the Zhōu king was cemented. In 681, Duke Huán of Qí declared superpower status in order to protect the dignity of the Zhōu throne and maintain the political status quo. King Xī appears only rarely in other texts of the period and not at all in CQZZ. In the *Dialogues*, he is portrayed as having a taste for extravagant spending. (Zheng, Wu, and Yang 2000; Durrant, Li, and Schaberg 2016) *15.4, 16.6*

Zhou King You, Zhōu Yōu Wáng 周幽王: Surname Jī 姬, given name Gōngshēng 宮湦 (or Gōngniè 宮涅), posthumous name Yōu 幽. R. 781–771 BCE. Son of King Xuān, grandson of King Lì. The Zhōu dynasty is traditionally split into two periods—the Western Zhōu and the Eastern Zhōu. The Western Zhōu begins with King Wǔ and ends with King Yōu. The essential elements of King Yōu's eleven-year reign all appear in the brief account given in BA. The state of Jìn and a Zhōu prince conquered the state of Zēng 鄫, and the prince was installed by King Yōu as duke of the new state of Zhèng 鄭. King Yōu disdained his queen and instead made a concubine named Bāo Sì 褒姒 his favorite. The crown prince Yíjiù 宜臼 fled to the state of Shēn 申 (near the conquered Zēng). King Yōu's army attacked the Róng people but was defeated. King Yōu named Bāosì's son Bófú 伯服 crown prince. Shēn formed an alliance with the Róng people and the Zēng people. The king attacked Shēn. Finally, Shēn, Zēng, and the Róng invaded the Zhōu capital, killed the king, the crown prince, and the Duke of Zhèng, kidnapped Bāosì, and installed Yíjiù as the new Zhōu king. The new king moved the capital to present-day Luòyáng, thus beginning the period known as the Eastern Zhōu. Since then, the name Yōu has been synonymous with concupiscence and disastrous leadership. See also **Zheng.** (Zheng, Wu, and Yang 2000) *12.11n, 32.4*

Zhou King Zhao, Zhōu Zhāo Wáng 周昭王: Surname Jī 姬, given name Xiá 瑕, posthumous name Zhāo 昭. R. 977–957 BCE. Son of King Kāng. (Zheng, Wu, and Yang 2000) *41.7n44*

Zhou Ren, Zhōu Rèn 周任: Unknown person. He is also quoted by Confucius in *Analects* 16.1. (Zheng, Wu, and Yang 2000; Luo 1994) *41.8, 42.10*

Zhū (state), Zhū 邾 (also Zōu 鄒): Small Zhōu vassal state about 15 mi. SE of the Lǔ capital. According to a moving story in CQZZ ("Wén" 13.3) about a ruler who put the people's needs above his own, Zhū relocated its main city to a redoubt at Yì 繹 (嶧) Mountain (about 25 mi. S of the Lǔ capital) in 614 BCE, where it managed to persist until absorbed by Chǔ late in the Warring States period. Zhū and Lǔ had a complicated relationship. Lǔ was much bigger and higher in the Zhōu hierarchy and used its military to demand fealty (and tribute) from Zhū (very much the way that Chǔ treated Lǔ). Zhū, to protect itself, often feigned friendship while forming alliances with other states for its own protection. The state of Zhū is not mentioned in the *Analects*. (Zheng, Wu, and Yang 2000; Liu, Wang, and Lu 2019) *16.5 18.4, 22.2 (as Zōu), 33.1, 33.2, 42.9, 42.15*

Zhù (state), Zhù 祝: Also called Zhùkē 祝柯 (or Zhù'ē 祝阿). Small Zhōu vassal state in the western part of present-day Jǐ'nán 濟南, Shāndōng (75 mi. N of Qūfù). According to BA ("Píng wáng"), it was absorbed by Qí toward the beginning of the Spring and Autumn period. (Tan 1996; Zheng, Wu, and Yang 2000) *35.3*

Zhū Duke Yin, Zhū Duke Yǐn 邾隱公: Duke Yǐn, a contemporary of Confucius, appears four times in CQZZ. The first appearance ("Dìng" 15.1) is an account of the episode that occurs in *Dialogues* 16.5. In 485 BCE, he fled to Lǔ and then to Qí

(CQZZ "Āi" 10.1), and twelve years later he fled from Qí to Yuè (CQZZ "Āi" 22.1). *16.5, 33.1*

Zhuansun Shi: See **Zizhang.**

Zhuanxu, Zhuānxū 顓頊: Second of the legendary Five Chiefs. Also known as Gāo Yáng 高陽. For his biography, see 23.2. (Zheng, Wu, and Yang 2000) *16.4, 23.2, 24.1, 24.3, 24.5, 34.2*

Zichan, Zǐchǎn 子產: 580–522 BCE. Surname Guó 國, given name Qiáo 僑/喬, *zì* Zǐchǎn (or Zǐměi 子美), posthumous name Chéng成. Grandson of Zhèng Duke Mù 穆. Recognized from an early age as a very capable person. Zǐchǎn was an older contemporary of Confucius and prime minister of Zhèng (from 543 BCE). Although neither he nor Guǎn Zhòng was concerned with *lǐ* and virtue in the same way that Confucius was, Confucius still specifically lauds them as model officials and as *rén* (a compliment that he uses sparingly). According to 41.12, Confucius wept when he learned of Zǐchǎn's death. See also 13.2n4 and 14.5n14. (Fang et al. 1994; Zheng, Wu, and Yang 2000) *2.1, 13.2, 14.5, 22.8, 41.6, 41.10, 41.11, 41.12, 41.24*

Zifu Bozi: See **Zifu Jingbo.**

Zifu Jingbo, Zǐfú Jǐngbó 子服景伯: Surname Zǐfú, given name Hé 何, posthumous name Jǐngbó 景伯. Zǐfú appears twice in the *Analects*, where he is depicted as an official who is protective of Confucius. (Zheng, Wu, and Yang 2000) *16.9, 44.2*

Zigao, Zǐgāo 子羔: Surname Gāo 高 (or Jì 季), given name Chái 柴, *zì* Zǐgāo子羔. Zǐgāo appears only twice in the *Analects*, once (11.18) where he is depicted as stupid, and once (11.25) where he is depicted as incapable of being the mayor of Bì. In the *Dialogues*, he is portrayed quite differently. For his mini-biography, see 38.14. For Zǐgòng's appraisal of him, see 12.15. *8.4, 12.15, 34.1, 34.2, 38.14, 43.21*

Zigong, Zǐgòng 子貢: Surname Duānmù 端木, given name Cì 賜, *zì* Zǐgòng 子貢. Native of Wèi. Born 520. Zǐgòng was one of Confucius' main students, wealthy through trade but interested in governing, and according to the *Dialogues* (14.8) he was once mayor of the Chǔ city of Xìnyáng 信陽. Though he appears in the *Analects* in thirty-eight passages, his specific intellectual interests and moral qualities remain in the background. Like Zǐlù, he is at Confucius' side through thick and thin, and the two appear to have a close relationship, and on occasion he challenges Confucius (see 2.1). He is depicted in the *Dialogues* as asking penetrating follow-up questions, and Confucius says that Zǐgòng surpasses himself in intelligence (15.12). In chapter 12 of the *Dialogues*, Zǐgòng gives his appraisal of several of Confucius' students. After Confucius passed away, Zǐgòng proposed that the students mourn Confucius as if he were their father, and he himself spent six years in mourning, twice as long as would typically be accorded a parent. (Zheng, Wu, and Yang 2000; Zhang and Xia 2010) *2.1, 8.1, 8.8, 8.17, 9.5, 9.6, 9.8, 9.9, 12.1, 12.2, 12.3, 12.4, 12.18, 12.19, 12.20, 12.22, 13.2, 14.1, 14.5, 14.8, 14.9, 15.5, 15.12, 16.5, 16.6, 16.9, 16.10, 18.12, 19.6, 20.1, 20.4, 22.1, 22.2, 22.4, 22.7, 22.8, 22.9, 23.7, 25.4, 27.1, 28.3, 36.1, 37.2, 38.6, 39.3, 40.1, 40.2, 41.6, 41.13, 42.1, 42.5, 42.6, 42.7, 42.21, 42.28, 43.9, 43.10, 43.11, 43.13, 43.14, 43.27, 44.6*

Zihan, Zǐhǎn 子罕: Surname Yuè 樂, given name Xǐ 喜. Fl. 567–544 BCE. Competent high minister of Sòng. (Fang et al. 1994; Zheng, Wu, and Yang 2000; Durrant, Li, and Schaberg 2016) *42.10, 43.26*

Zilu, Zǐlù 子路: 542–480 BCE. Surname Zhòng 仲, given name Yóu 由, *zì* Zǐlù (or Jìlù 季路). Zǐlù was a main student of Confucius, only a decade or so younger. He appears in the *Analects* in forty-one passages, where he is depicted as earnest, generous, and courageous to a fault. He accompanies Confucius on his travels, appears in settings where Confucius is most relaxed, and is at his bedside when he is ill. According to *Dialogues* 40.2, when Zǐlù passed away Confucius mourned him as if Zǐlù had been his own son. Zǐlù is said to have worked under the Wèi nobleman Kǒng Kuī 孔悝 and also as a low official in Wèi, held a major position in Chǔ, and served as the Mayor of Pú and as Jìsūn's household manager. This last post would have put him in the inner circle of power in Lǔ, since Jìsūn virtually held the puppet strings of the duke. Zǐlù was also not shy about challenging Confucius, as he did on their very first meeting (19.1) and in 2.1, 8.2, 8.8, 8.9, 8.13, 22.4, 37.4, and 42.11. (He is also the one who shows displeasure with Confucius' behavior toward Nánzǐ in *Analects* 6.28.) According to *Dialogues* 43.21, Zǐlù died protecting his employer. For a brief biography, see 38.8. For Zǐgòng's appraisal of him, see 12.6. (Kong, Sang, and Kong 1994; Zheng, Wu, and Yang 2000) *1.3, 2.1, 8.1, 8.2, 8.8, 8.9, 8.12, 8.13, 8.18, 9.4, 9.8, 9.10, 9.11, 10.5, 10.13, 10.14, 10.18, 12.6, 13.6, 13.7, 14.9, 15.9, 15.12, 16.7, 18.8, 19.1, 19.2, 19.7, 20.1, 20.2, 20.4, 22.3, 22.4, 22.5, 28.1, 35.2, 37.1, 37.2, 37.4, 38.8, 40.2, 41.20, 42.9, 42.11, 42.24, 42.25, 42.29, 43.14, 43.15, 43.21, 44.7*

Zipi, Zǐpí 子皮: Also known as Hǎnhǔ 罕虎. D. 529 BCE. Prime minister of Zhèng from 544 BCE. According to CQZZ ("Xiāng" 30.13), Zǐpí recognized the talent of Zǐchǎn and handed over the government to him. (Zheng, Wu, and Yang 2000; Zhang and Xia 2010) *13.2*

Zishi, Zǐshí 子石: Surname Gōngsūn 公孫, given name Chǒng 寵. Student of Confucius. See 38.37 for a brief biography. *37.2, 38.37*

Zither, *qín* 琴 or *sè* 瑟 (also *zhú* 筑 and *zhēng* 箏): Wooden or bamboo string instrument that is laid flat on the floor, on a table, or on one's knees when seated on the floor. It could be rectangular or trapezoidal. It could be as long as six feet or as short as two feet. It could have as many as twenty-six strings or as few as five. The strings could be plucked, strummed, or struck. In technical categorization, it is a simple chordophone. In Confucius' time, it appears in orchestras, in small ensembles, and as a personal instrument. In the *Dialogues,* we see that the *qín* is common among Confucius and his students as a vehicle for expressing personal emotion. See especially chapter 35. See also **Music.** (Sui County Leigudun Archaeological Team 1979; So 2000) *6.2, 13.1, 15.5, 15.10, 15.13, 22.5, 26.4, 35.1, 35.2, 41.4, 43.25, 44.3, 44.5*

Zixi, Zǐxī 子西: Given name Shēn 申. D. 479 BCE. Son of Chǔ King Píng. According to CQZZ ("Zhāo" 26.8), he refused the throne after the death of King Píng. From 504 BCE, he acted as prime minister of Chǔ under Kings Zhāo 昭 and Huì 惠. (Zheng, Wu, and Yang 2000) *14.4*

Zixia, Zǐxià 子夏: 507–400 BCE. Surname Bǔ 卜, given name Shāng 商, *zì* Zǐxià 子夏. One of Confucius' main students, Zǐxià is mentioned in nineteen passages of the *Analects* (where he is one of only a handful of students who is given his own independent voice in several passages) and in nineteen passages of the *Dialogues*. He and Zēngzǐ are the only students depicted in the *Analects* as having students of their own. According to the *Analects*, he was an outstanding student, a brilliant thinker, and adept at putting his learning to practical use. According to *Analects* 13.17, he held the post of mayor of the Lǔ city of Jǔfù 莒父, near present-day Jǔ 莒縣, Shāndōng (119 mi. E of Qūfù). See 12.11 for Zǐgòng's appraisal of him, and see 38.10 for a brief biography. (Tan 1996; Zheng, Wu, and Yang 2000; Zhang and Xia 2010) *8.15, 15.5, 15.8, 15.12, 25.3, 25.4, 27.2, 38.10, 40.2, 43.1, 43.2, 43.3, 43.4, 43.5, 43.6, 43.7, 43.8*

Ziyou, Zǐyóu 子游: Surname Yán 言, given name Yǎn 偃, *zì* Zǐyóu 子游, referred to in the *Dialogues* variously as Yán Yǎn 言偃, Zǐyóu子游, and Yán Yóu 言游. Zǐyóu appears eight times in the *Analects*, where he is depicted as an accomplished mayor applying Confucius' teachings, and variously concerned with *xiào*, friendship, mourning, and *rén*. In the *Dialogues*, he is depicted as singularly focused on *lǐ*. According to the *Analects* (6.14), he was once mayor of the city of Wǔ 武. SKQS adds that he accompanied Confucius to Wèi 衛. For Zǐgòng's appraisal of Zǐyóu, see 12.13. For a brief biography, see 38.9. (Zheng, Wu, and Yang 2000) *6.2, 8.16, 12.13, 27.1,32.1, 32.3, 32.4, 38.9, 40.2, 41.24, 42.3, 42.12, 42.13, 42.14, 42.17, 42.23, 42.27, 43.12, 43.19, 43.22, 43.25, 44.2, 44.4*

Ziyu: See **Tantai Mieming.**

Zizhang, Zǐzhāng 子張: Surname Zhuānsūn 顓孫, given name Shī 師, *zì* Zǐzhāng 子張. Born 503 BCE. One of Confucius' main students, who accompanied him on his travels. Zǐzhāng appears in sixteen passages of the *Analects* and is one of only a handful of students who is given his own independent voice in several passages. From the topics he mentions in the *Analects*, he had wide interests, largely practical, and focused on moral self-improvement for the purpose of earning a position of leadership in the government. The depiction of Zǐzhāng in the *Dialogues* is consistent with that in the *Analects* but provides a bit more detail. He still has wide interests that include the *Changes* and the *Documents*, but he is also focused on the practicalities of governing. In this respect, Zǐgòng says that Zǐzhāng is very accomplished and is one of a very small number of leaders whom Confucius unambiguously compliments with the term *rén* (12.10). For a brief biography, see 38.11. For Zǐgòng's appraisal of him, see 12.10. (Zheng, Wu, and Yang 2000) *10.3, 12.10, 15.12, 21.1, 21.8, 23.7, 27.1, 36.3, 37.2, 38.11, 41.19, 42.20, 42.28*

Zou, Zōu 郰/鄹/鄒: Lǔ city, 15 mi. SW of present-day Qūfù. Hometown of Confucius' father.

Zou, Zōu 鄒. See Zhū (state). (Zheng, Wu, and Yang 2000)

BIBLIOGRAPHY

Allan, Sarah. 1981. *The Heir and the Sage: Dynastic Legend in Early China*. San Francisco: Chinese Materials Center.

Allan, Sarah, 2015. *Buried Ideas: Legends of Abdication and Ideal Government in Early Chinese Bamboo-Slip Manuscripts*. Albany: State University of New York Press.

Allan, Sarah. 2016. *The Heir and the Sage: Dynastic Legend in Early China*. Revised and expanded ed. Albany: State University of New York Press.

Allred, David T. 2003. "The Circumpolar Constellations of Ancient China." M.A. thesis, Indiana University.

Ames, Roger T. 1983. *The Art of Rulership: A Study of Ancient Chinese Political Thought*. Honolulu: University of Hawaii Press.

Ames, Roger T. 2011. *Confucian Role Ethics: A Vocabulary*. Honolulu: University of Hawaiʻi Press.

Ames, Roger T. 2021. *A Conceptual Lexicon for Classical Confucian Philosophy*. Albany: State University of New York Press.

Ames, Roger T., and David L. Hall. 2001. *Focusing the Familiar: A Translation and Philosophical Interpretation of the Zhongyong*. Honolulu: University of Hawaiʻi Press.

Ames, Roger T., and Henry Rosemont Jr., trans. 1998. *The Analects of Confucius: A Philosophical Translation*. New York: Ballantine.

Anagnostopoulos, Georgios, ed. 2013. *A Companion to Aristotle*. Oxford: Wiley-Blackwell.

Appiah, Kwame Anthony. 1993. "Thick Translation." *Callaloo* 16, no. 4: 808–19. https://doi.org/10.2307/2932211.

Ariel, Yoav. 1989. *K'ung-Ts'ung-Tzu: The K'ung Family Masters' Anthology*. Princeton, NJ: Princeton University Press.

Bai, Lijuan 白丽娟, and Jingfu Wang 王景福. 1995. "浅述中国传统建筑中的'台'." 故宫博物院院刊, no. 3: 35–44.

Baxter, William H., and Laurent Sagart. 2014. *Old Chinese: A New Reconstruction*. Oxford: Oxford University Press.

Benjamin, Walter. 1997. "The Translator's Task." Translated by Steven Rendall. *TTR: Traduction, Terminologie, Rédaction* 10, no. 2: 151–65. https://doi.org/10.7202/037302ar.

Berman, Merrick Lex, and William L. Hays. 2014. "Temporal Gazetteer API." https://maps.cga.harvard.edu/tgaz/.

Bodde, Derk. 1955. "On Translating Chinese Philosophic Terms." *Far Eastern Quarterly* 14, no. 2: 231–44. https://doi.org/10.2307/2941733.

Bodde, Derk. 1975. *Festivals in Classical China*. Princeton, NJ: Princeton University Press.

Boltz, William G. 1979. "Review: Philological Footnotes to the Han New Year Rites." *Journal of the American Oriental Society* 99, no. 3: 423–39. https://doi.org/10.2307/602379.

Boltz, William G. 1997. "Manuscripts with Transmitted Counterparts." In *New Sources of Early Chinese History: An Introduction to the Reading of Inscriptions and Manuscripts*, edited by Edward L. Shaughnessy, 253–83. Berkeley: Society for the Study of Early China and Institute of East Asian Studies, University of California, Berkeley.

Brashier, K. E. 1996. "Han Thanatology and the Division of 'Souls.'" *Early China* 21: 125–58. https://doi.org/10.1017/S0362502800003424.

Brindley, Erica Fox. 2010. *Individualism in Early China: Human Agency and the Self in Thought and Politics*. Honolulu: University of Hawai'i Press.

Brooks, E. Bruce, and A. Taeko Brooks. 1998. *The Original Analects: Sayings of Confucius and His Successors; A New Translation and Commentary*. New York: Columbia University Press.

Bruya, Brian. 2001. "Qing 情 and Emotion in Early Chinese Thought." *Ming Qing Yanjiu* 2001: 151–76.

Bruya, Brian. 2010. "The Rehabilitation of Spontaneity: A New Approach in Philosophy of Action." *Philosophy East and West* 60, no. 2: 207–50.

Bruya, Brian. 2024. "Political Intimacy and Self-Governance in the *Dialogues of Confucius*: An Exploratory Study on the Philosophical Potential of the *Kongzi Jia Yu*." *Dao*, no. 23: 223–49.

Chang, Kwang-chih, and Pingfang Xu. 2005. *The Formation of Chinese Civilization: An Archaeological Perspective*. Edited and with an introduction by Sarah Allan. New Haven, CT: Yale University Press and New World Press.

Chen, Huang 陈锽. 2018. "魂舟. 魂车. 魂桥图像中的灵魂信仰探讨之三." 新美术 39, no. 9: 4–27.

Chen, Mengjia 陳夢家. 1941. "射與郊." 清華學報 13, no. 1: 115–62.

Chen, Mengjia 陳夢家. 1964. "战国度量衡略说." 考古, no. 6: 312–14.

Chen, Mingyuan 陈明远, and Minbin Jin 金岷彬. 2014. "历史考古的新观点（之二）古代弓和矢的发展历程." 社会科学论坛, no. 2: 4–23.

Chen, Mingyuan 陈明远, and Zonghu Wang 汪宗虎. 1995. 中国姓氏辞典. Beijing: 北京出版社.

Chen, Ran 陈冉, and Yang Bai 白杨. 2014. "孔安国生卒年及是否献《古文尚书》考." 赤峰学院学报(汉文哲学社会科学版) 35, no. 5: 141.

Chen, Xiao 陈筱, Hua Sun 孙华, and Ruguo Liu 刘汝国. 2020. "曲阜鲁国故城布局新探." 文物, no. 5: 48–96.

Chen, Xubo 陈绪波. 2015. "三代宫室与《仪礼》宫室结构考论." 求索, no. 8: 143–47.

Chen, Yongling 陈永龄. 1987. 民族词典. Shanghai: 上海辞书出版社.

Chen, Yunzhen, James P. M. Syvitski, Shu Gao, Irina Overeem, and Albert J. Kettner. 2012. "Socio-Economic Impacts on Flooding: A 4000-Year History of the Yellow River, China." *Ambio* 41, no. 7: 682–98. https://doi.org/10.1007/s13280-012-0290-5.

Cheng, Hao 程浩. 2013. "王肃《圣证论》体例及论说考." 古籍整理研究学刊, no. 2: 12–15.

Cheung, Martha P. Y. 2007. "On Thick Translation as a Mode of Cultural Representation." In *Across Boundaries: International Perspectives on Translation Studies*, edited by Dorothy Kenny and Kyongjoo Ryou, 22–36. Newcastle, UK: Cambridge Scholars.

Cook, Scott. 2012. *The Bamboo Texts of Guodian: A Study and Complete Translation*. 2 vols. Ithaca, NY: East Asia Program, Cornell University.

Cook, Scott 顧史考. 2021. 上博竹書孔子語錄文獻研究. Shanghai: 中西書局.

Cooper, Eugene. 1982. "The Potlatch in Ancient China: Parallels in the Sociopolitical Structure of the Ancient Chinese and the American Indians of the Northwest Coast." *History of Religions* 22, no. 2: 103–28. https://doi.org/10.1086/462915.

Corrigan, Kevin, and L. Michael Harrington. 2019. "Pseudo-Dionysius the Areopagite." In *The Stanford Encyclopedia of Philosophy*, edited by Edward N. Zalta. Winter. https://plato.stanford.edu/archives/win2019/entries/pseudo-dionysius-areopagite/.

Csikszentmihalyi, Mark. 2004. *Material Virtue: Ethics and the Body in Early China*. Leiden: Brill.

Csikszentmihalyi, Mark. 2020. "Confucius." In *The Stanford Encyclopedia of Philosophy*, edited by Edward N. Zalta. Summer. https://plato.stanford.edu/archives/sum2020/entries/confucius/.

Cua, A. S. 1969. "The Logic of Confucian Dialogues." In *Studies in Philosophy and the History of Philosophy*, vol. 4, edited by J. K. Ryan, 18–33. Washington, DC: Catholic University of America Press.

De Bary, Wm. Theodore. 1983. *The Liberal Tradition in China*. New York: Columbia University Press.

Dewey, John. 1916. *Democracy and Education: An Introduction to the Philosophy of Education*. New York: Macmillan.

Durrant, Stephen W., Wai-yee Li, and David Schaberg, trans. 2016. *Zuo tradition = Zuozhuan: Commentary on the "Spring and Autumn Annals."* Seattle: University of Washington Press.

Eifring, Halvor, ed. 2004. *Love and Emotions in Traditional Chinese Literature*. Leiden: Brill.

Eno, Robert. 2018. "The *Lunyu* as an Accretion Text." In *Confucius and the Analects Revisited: New Perspectives on Composition, Dating and Authorship*, edited by Michael Hunter and Martin Kern, 39–66. Leiden: Brill.

Falkenhausen, Lothar von. 2006. *Chinese Society in the Age of Confucius (1000–250 BC): The Archaeological Evidence*. Los Angeles: Cotsen Institute of Archaeology.

Fang, Keli 方克立, Yusan Lu 卢育三, Xichen Lü 吕希晨, and Defeng Zhou 周德丰, eds. 1994. 中国哲学大辞典. Beijing: 中国社会科学出版社.

Fong, Wen. 1980. *The Great Bronze Age of China: An Exhibition from the People's Republic of China*. New York: Metropolitan Museum of Art.

Gao, Chunming 高春明. 1996. "传统服饰形制考." 上海艺术家, no. 3: 17–35.

Gao, Song 高松. 2019. "肃慎系早期民族与其他部族往来关系探析." 黑龙江民族丛刊(民族历史与边疆学), no. 4: 37–41.

Gao, Zhuancheng 高专诚. 1991. 孔子·孔子弟子. Taiyuan, Shanxi: 山西人民出版社.

Geographical Names Board of Canada. 2012. *Principles and Procedures for Geographic Naming 2011*. Ottawa: Geographical Names Board of Canada.

Goldin, Paul R. 1999. *Rituals of the Way: The Philosophy of Xunzi*. Chicago: Open Court.

Goldin, Paul R. 2008. "When *Zhong* 忠 Does Not Mean 'Loyalty.'" *Dao* 7, no. 2: 165–74. https://doi.org/10.1007/s11712-008-9064-y.

Goldin, Paul R. 2011. *Confucianism*. Berkeley: University of California Press.

Goldin, Paul R. 2018. "Confucius and His Disciples in the *Lunyu*: The Basis for the Traditional View." In *Confucius and the Analects Revisited*, edited by Michael Hunter and Martin Kern, 92–115. Leiden: Brill.

Goldin, Paul R. 2020. *The Art of Chinese Philosophy: Eight Classical Texts and How to Read Them*. Princeton, NJ: Princeton University Press.

Goodwin, Doris Kearns. 2005. *Team of Rivals: The Political Genius of Abraham Lincoln*. New York: Simon & Schuster.

Graham, A. C. 1986. *Yin-Yang and the Nature of Correlative Thinking*. Singapore: Institute of East Asian Philosophies, National University of Singapore.

Graham, A. C. 1989. *Disputers of the Tao: Philosophical Argument in Ancient China*. La Salle, IL: Open Court.

Graham, A. C., trans. 1990a. *The Book of Lieh-Tzu: A Classic of Tao*. New York: Columbia University Press.

Graham, A. C. 1990b. *Studies in Chinese Philosophy and Philosophical Literature*. Albany: State University of New York Press.

Griffith, Samuel B., trans. 1971. *Sun Tzu: The Art of War*. New York: Oxford University Press.

Guo, Mengxiu 郭孟秀. 2019. "肃慎族系演进考." 学习与探索, no. 5: 157–66.

Guo, Mengxiu 郭孟秀, and Xiujie Hu 胡秀杰. 2021. "商周时期肃慎考古学文化考论." 中国边疆史地研究 31, no. 2: 125–35.

Guo, Qiang 郭强, and Hongxing Zhang 张洪兴. 2019. "《尸子》流变述考." 古籍整理研究学刊, no. 3: 90–93.

Hall, David L., and Roger T. Ames. 1987. *Thinking Through Confucius*. Albany: State University of New York Press.

Hao, Hong 郝虹. 2011. "《孔子家语》是否王肃伪作问题新探——从汉魏思想史角度的辨析." 孔子研究, no. 1: 89–97.

Harper, Donald. 1985. "A Chinese Demonography of the Third Century B.C." *Harvard Journal of Asiatic Studies* 45, no. 2: 459–98. https://doi.org/10.2307/2718970.

Hatzimichali, Myrto. 2016. "Andronicus of Rhodes and the Construction of the Aristotelian Corpus." In *Brill's Companion to the Reception of Aristotle in Antiquity*, edited by Andrea Falcon, 77–100. Leiden: Brill.

He, Xiaoming 何晓明. 2012. 中国姓名史. Wuhan: 武汉大学出版社.

He, Zhigang 何直刚, and Shishu Liu 刘世枢. 1981. "定县40号汉墓出土竹简简介." 文物, no. 8: 11–13.

He, Zhoude 何周德. 1996. "葫芦形器物与生育崇拜." 考古与文物, no. 3: 47–52.

Henricks, Robert G., trans. 2000. *Lao Tzu's Tao Te Ching: A Translation of the Startling New Documents Found at Guodian*. New York: Columbia University Press.

Henry, Eric, trans. 2022. *Garden of Eloquence: Shuoyuan*. Seattle: University of Washington Press.

Hermans, Theo. 2003. "Cross-Cultural Translation Studies as Thick Translation." *Bulletin of the School of Oriental and African Studies* 66, no. 3: 380–89. https://doi.org/10.1017/S0041977X03000260.

Holzman, Donald. 1956. "The Conversational Tradition in Chinese Philosophy." *Philosophy East and West* 6, no. 3: 223–30.

Hou, Naifeng 侯乃峰. 2018. 上博楚簡儒學文獻校理. Vol. 1. Shanghai: 上海古籍出版社.

Hu, Jinzhu 胡进驻. 2020. "试论周代宗庙制度及其变迁." 华夏考古, no. 1: 65–122.

Hua, Fu 华夫, ed. 1993. 中国古代名物大典. Ji'nan: 济南出版社.

Huang, H. T. 2000. *Science and Civilisation in China*. Vol. 6, *Biology and Biological Technology*, Part V: *Fermentations and Food Science*. Cambridge: Cambridge University Press.

Huang, Huaixin 黄怀信. 2009. "'五至'、'三无'说." 齐鲁学刊, no. 6: 5–10.

Huang, Huaixin 黄懷信. 2017. 漢晉孔氏家學與「僞書」公案. Taoyuan, Taiwan: 昌明文化出版社.

Huang, Huixian 黄惠贤, and Zexuan Zhao 赵泽轩, eds. 1997. 二十五史人名大辞典. Zhengzhou: 郑州古籍出版社.

Huang, Kaiguo 黄開國. 1997. "春秋時期的預占." 甘肃社会科学, no. 1: 28–32. https://doi.org/10.6309/JORP.199707_(11).0005.

Huang, Mengshan 黄梦珊. 2014. "《孔子家语》研究综述." 文教资料, no. 30: 35–38.

Huang, Xiuwen 黄秀文, ed. 1997. 中国年谱辞典. Shanghai: 百家出版社.

Huang, Zhanyue 黄展岳. 2004. 古代人牲人殉通论. Beijing: 文物出版社.

Hunter, Michael. 2012. "Sayings of Confucius, Deselected." Ph.D. diss., Princeton University. https://dataspace.princeton.edu/handle/88435/dsp01v692t624c.

Hunter, Michael. 2017. *Confucius beyond the Analects*. Leiden: Brill.

Hunter, Michael. 2018. "The *Lunyu* as a Western Han Text." In *Confucius and the Analects Revisited*, edited by Michael Hunter and Martin Kern, 67–91. Leiden: Brill.

Hunter, Michael, and Martin Kern, eds. 2018. *Confucius and the Analects Revisited: New Perspectives on Composition, Dating, and Authorship*. Leiden: Brill.

Hutchinson, A. B., trans. 1878. "The Family Sayings of Confucius, Preface." *The Chinese Recorder and Missionary Journal* 9, no. 6: 445–53.

Hutchinson, A. B., trans. 1879. "The Family Sayings of Confucius, Chs. 1–8." *The Chinese Recorder and Missionary Journal* 10, nos. 1–6: 17–23, 96–103, 175–79, 253–60, 329–37, 428–32.

Hutchinson, A. B., trans. 1880. "The Family Sayings of Confucius, Chs. 9–10." *The Chinese Recorder and Missionary Journal* 11, no. 1: 13–23.

Hutton, Eric, trans. 2014. *Xunzi 荀子: The Complete Text*. Princeton, NJ: Princeton University Press.

Ing, Michael David Kaulana. 2012. *The Dysfunction of Ritual in Early Confucianism*. New York: Oxford University Press.

James, Brenda, and William D. Rubinstein. 2007. *The Truth Will Out: Unmasking the Real Shakespeare*. New York: Harper Perennial.

Jingzhou Municipal Museum 荆州市博物馆 and Qianjiang Municipal Museum 潜江市博物馆. 2003. "湖北潜江龙湾放鹰台I号楚宫基址发掘简报." 江汉考古, no. 3: 3–15.

Jorati, Julia. 2023. "Slavery, Freedom, and Human Value in Early Modern Philosophy." In *Rethinking the Value of Humanity*, edited by Sarah Buss and Nandi Theunissen, 97–126. New York: Oxford University Press.

Judson, Lewis V. 1976. *Weights and Measures Standards of the United States: A Brief History*. NBS Special Publication 447. Washington, DC: National Bureau of Standards.

Jullien, François. 2000. *Detour and Access: Strategies of Meaning in China and Greece*. Translated by Sophie Hawkes. New York: Zone Books.

Kinney, Anne Behnke, trans. and ed. 2014. *Exemplary Women of Early China: The Lienü zhuan of Liu Xiang*. New York: Columbia University Press.

Kline, T. C., III. 2000. "Moral Agency and Motivation in the Xunzi." In *Virtue, Nature, and Moral Agency in the Xunzi*, edited by T. C. Kline III and Philip J. Ivanhoe, 155–75. Indianapolis, IN: Hackett.

Knoblock, John, trans. 1994. *Xunzi: A Translation and Study of the Complete Works*. Vol. 3, Books 17–32. Stanford, CA: Stanford University Press.

Kong, Fanjin 孔范今, Sifen Sang 桑思奋, and Xianglin Kong 孔祥林, eds. 1994. 孔子文化大典. Beijing: 中国书店.

Kong, Hua 孙华. 2020. "燕国始封地考疑." 中国典籍与文化, no. 4: 55–60.

Kong, Yingda 孔穎達, and Xuan Zheng 鄭玄, eds. 1866. 禮記正義. 武英殿十三經注疏. Guangdong: 廣東書局. https://ctext.org/library.pl?if=gb&res=77717&by_collection=8&remap=gb.

Kramers, Robert P. 1950. *K'ung Tzŭ Chia Yü: The School Sayings of Confucius*. Leiden: Brill.

Kramers, Robert P. 1991. "Review of Yoav Ariel, *K'ung Ts'ung Tzu, the K'ung Family Masters' Anthology. A Study and Translation of Chapters 1–10, 12–14*." *T'oung Pao* 77, nos. 1–3: 155–57.

Kroll, Paul W. 2015. *A Student's Dictionary of Classical and Medieval Chinese*. Boston: Brill.

Kuhn, Thomas S. 1970. *The Structure of Scientific Revolutions*. 2nd ed. Chicago: University of Chicago Press.

LaFargue, Michael. 1992. *The Tao of the Tao Te Ching: A Translation and Commentary*. Albany: State University of New York Press.

Lau, D. C., trans. 1979. *The Analects (Lun Yü)*. New York: Penguin.

Legge, James, trans. 1885. *The Lî Kî*. Parts 1 and 2. Vols. 27 and 28 of *The Sacred Books of the East*, edited by F. Max Müller. Oxford: Clarendon Press.

Legge, James, trans. (1893) 2012. *Confucian Analects, the Great Learning, and the Doctrine of the Mean*. New York: ACLS Humanities E-Book. https://www.fulcrum.org/epubs/d504rk84n?locale=en#/6/2[xhtml00000001]!/4/4/1:0.

Lewis, Mark Edward. 1999. *Writing and Authority in Early China*. Albany: State University of New York Press.

Li, Anzhu 李安竹. 2015. "论殷商龟卜之以'象'为卜." 古籍整理研究学刊, no. 6: 32–36.

Li, Feng. 2003. "'Feudalism' and Western Zhou China: A Criticism." *Harvard Journal of Asiatic Studies* 63, no. 1: 115–44. https://doi.org/10.2307/25066693.

Li, Huiling 李慧玲. 2011. "试说中国古代的狂欢节—— 蜡祭." 河南师范大学学报(哲学社会科学版) 38, no. 2: 205–8.

Li, Qiqian 李启谦. 1987. 孔门弟子研究. Ji'nan: 齐鲁书社.

Li, Rongxin. 2022. *Consultative Democracy or Consultative Authoritarianism? Understanding Chinese Consultative Politics*. Singapore: Palgrave Macmillan.

Li, Shuicheng. 2015. "Eternal Glory: The Origins of Eastern Jade Burial and Its Far-Reaching Influence." In *Death Rituals, Social Order and the Archaeology of Immortality in the Ancient World: "Death Shall Have No Dominion,"* edited by Colin Renfrew, Michael J. Boyd, and Iain Morley, 315–27. Cambridge: Cambridge University Press.

Li, Xiaocheng 李小成. 2020. "理学格局下王柏对《诗》学的反叛." 西安文理学院学报 23, no. 2: 5–10.

Li, Xueqin 李学勤. 1987. "竹简《家语》与汉魏孔氏家学." 孔子研究, no. 2: 60–64.

Li, Xueqin 李学勤. 2002. "The Xia-Shang-Zhou Chronology Project: Methodology and Results." Translated by Sarah Allan. *Journal of East Asian Archaeology* 4, no. 1: 321–33.

Littlejohn, Ronnie, and Qingjun Li. 2020. "The Concept of Dialogue in Chinese Philosophy." *Educational Philosophy and Theory* 54, no. 10: 1523–30. https://doi.org/10.1080/00131857.2020.1799945.

Liu, Jinyou 刘进有. 2019. "改革开放40年来的《孔子家语》研究综述." 济宁学院学报 40, no. 4: 7–15.

Liu, Laicheng 刘来成. 1981. "河北定县40号汉墓发掘简报." 文物, no. 8: 1–10.

Liu, Li 刘莉, Jiajing Wang 王佳静, Xingtan Chen 陈星灿, Yongqiang Li 李永强, and Wu Zhao 赵昊. 2018. "仰韶文化大房子与宴饮传统: 河南偃师灰嘴遗址F1地面和陶器残留物分析." 中原文物, no. 1: 32–43.

Liu, Li 刘莉, Jiajing Wang 王佳静, and Nan Di 邸楠. 2020. "从平底瓶到尖底瓶—— 黄河中游新石器时期酿酒器的演化和酿酒方法的传承." 中原文物, no. 3: 94–106.

Liu, Li, Jiajing Wang, Maureece J. Levin, Nasa Sinnott-Armstrong, Hao Zhao, Yanan Zhao, Jing Shao, Nan Di, and Tian'en Zhang. 2019. "The Origins of Specialized Pottery and Diverse Alcohol Fermentation Techniques in Early Neolithic China." *Proceedings of the National Academy of Sciences* 116, no. 26: 12767–74. https://doi.org/10.1073/pnas.1902668116.

Liu, Quanzhi 刘全志. 2018. "孔子之子'伯鱼出妻'说考辨." 孔学堂, no. 4: 53–59.

Liu, Wei 刘巍. 2014. 《孔子家语》公案探源. Beijing: 社会科学文献出版社.

Liu, Xuelin 刘学林, and Duo Chi 遲鐸, eds. 2002. 十三经辞典. Xi'an: 陕西人民出版社.

Liu, Yanfei 刘艳菲, Qing Wang 王青, and Guoquan Lu 路国权. 2019. "山东邹城邾国故城遗址新出陶量与量制初论." 考古, no. 2: 89–105.

Liu, Yu 劉雨. 1989. "西周金文中的祭祖礼." 考古学报, no. 4: 495–522.

Loewe, Michael. 1993. *Early Chinese Texts: A Bibliographic Guide*. Berkeley: Society for the Study of Early China and Institute of East Asian Studies, University of California, Berkeley.

Loewe, Michael, and Edward L. Shaughnessy, eds. 1999. *The Cambridge History of Ancient China: From the Origins of Civilization to 221 B.C.* Cambridge: Cambridge University Press.

Lu, Liangcheng. 2005. "The Eastern Zhou and the Growth of Regionalism." In *The Formation of Chinese Civilization: An Archaeological Perspective*, by Kwang-chih Chang and Pingfang Xu, edited by Sarah Allan, 203–47. New Haven, CT: Yale University Press and New World Press.

Luo, Zhufeng 罗竹风, ed. 1994. 汉语大词典. Shanghai: 汉语大词典出版社.

Ma, Chengyuan 马承源. 2001. 上海博物馆藏战国楚竹书. Vol. 1. Shanghai: 上海古籍出版社.

Major, John S. 1976. "A Note on the Translation of Two Technical Terms in Chinese Science: Wu-Hsing and Hsiu." *Early China* 2: 1–3. https://doi.org/10.1017/S0362502800004648.

Major, John S. 1991. "Substance, Process, Phase: Wuxing 五行 in the Huainanzi." In *Chinese Texts and Philosophical Contexts: Essays Dedicated to Angus C. Graham*, edited by Henry Rosemont Jr., 67–78. La Salle, IL: Open Court.

Makeham, John. 1996. "The Formation of *Lunyu* as a Book." *Monumenta Serica* 44, no. 1: 1–24.

Mannion, Philip D., Paul Upchurch, Xingsheng Jin, and Wenjie Zheng. 2019. "New Information on the Cretaceous Sauropod Dinosaurs of Zhejiang Province, China: Impact on Laurasian Titanosauriform Phylogeny and Biogeography." *Royal Society Open Science* 6, no. 8: 191057. https://doi.org/10.1098/rsos.191057.

Marcus Aurelius. 1983. *The Meditations*. Translated by G.M.A Grube. Indianapolis, IN: Hackett.

McGovern, Patrick E., Juzhong Zhang, Jigen Tang, et al. 2004. "Fermented Beverages of Pre- and Proto-Historic China." *Proceedings of the National Academy of Sciences* 101, no. 51: 17593–98. https://doi.org/10.1073/pnas.0407921102.

Meyer, Dirk. 2012. *Philosophy on Bamboo: Text and the Production of Meaning in Early China*. Boston: Brill.

Needham, Joseph, and Wang Ling. 1965. *Science and Civilisation in Ancient China*. Vol. 4: *Physics and Physical Technology*, Part 2: *Mechanical Engineering*. Cambridge: Cambridge University Press.

Ni, Peimin. 2016. *Confucius: The Man and the Way of Gongfu*. Lanham, MA: Rowman & Littlefield.

"Night Sky." 2022. Time and Date. https://www.timeanddate.com/astronomy/night/.

Ning, Zhenjiang 宁镇疆. 2017. 《孔子家语》新证. Shanghai: 中西書局.

Nivison, David S. 1996a. "Golden Rule Arguments in Chinese Moral Philosophy." In *The Ways of Confucianism: Investigations in Chinese Philosophy*, edited by Bryan W. Van Norden, 59–76. Chicago: Open Court.

Nivison, David S. 1996b. *The Ways of Confucianism: Investigations in Chinese Philosophy*. Edited by Bryan W. Van Norden. La Salle, IL: Open Court.

Nivison, David S., and Kevin D. Pang. 1990. "Astronomical Evidence for the Bamboo Annals' Chronicle of Early Xia." *Early China* 15: 87–95.

Nylan, Michael. 2001. *The Five "Confucian" Classics*. New Haven, CT: Yale University Press.

Ota, Yuko 太田有子. 1989. "中国古代的夫妻合葬墓." Translated by Lingyi Yang杨凌译. 华夏考古, no. 4: 103–10.

Pan, Guangdan 潘光旦. 2005. 中国民族史料汇编. Tianjin: 天津古籍出版社.

Pang, Pu 庞朴. 1963. "謹慎地对待資料辨年工作." 文史哲, no. 2: 29–30.
Pang, Pu 庞朴. 2004. "话说'至三无.'" 文史哲, no. 1: 71–76.
Pei, Puxian 裴普賢. 1998. 詩經評注讀本. 7th ed. Taipei: 三民書局.
Peng, Lin 彭林. 2019. "弓檠与弓?考辨." 考古, no. 1: 96–103.
Peng, Yushang 彭裕商. 2008. "东周青铜盆、盏、敦研究." 考古学报, no. 2: 175–94.
Pines, Yuri. 2002a. *Foundations of Confucian Thought: Intellectual Life in the Chunqiu Period (722–453 B.C.E.)*. Honolulu: University of Hawai'i Press.
Pines, Yuri. 2002b. "Lexical Changes in Zhanguo Texts." *Journal of the American Oriental Society* 122, no. 4: 691–705. https://doi.org/10.2307/3217610.
Porkert, Manfred. 1978. *The Theoretical Foundations of Chinese Medicine: Systems of Correspondence*. Cambridge, MA: MIT Press.
Pulleyblank, E. G. 1957. "The Origins and Nature of Chattel Slavery in China." *Journal of the Economic and Social History of the Orient* 1, no. 1: 185–220.
Qi, Dandan 齐丹丹. 2012. "上博简《民之父母》研究综述." 古籍整理研究学刊, no. 2: 30–35.
Qian, Muer 钱木尔, and Maiti Dawa 达瓦买提, eds. 1999. 中国少数民族文化大辞典. Beijing: 民族出版社.
Qiu, Guangming 丘光明. 1992. 中國歷代度量衡史. Beijing: 科學出版社.
Raphals, Lisa. 2016. "Sunzi versus Xunzi: Two Views of Deception and Indirection." *Early China* 39: 185–229. https://doi.org/10.1017/eac.2016.6.
Richter, Matthias L. 2013. *The Embodied Text: Establishing Textual Identity in Early Chinese Manuscripts*. Boston: Brill.
Ricket, W. Allyn. 1998. *Guanzi: Political, Economic, and Philosophical Essays from Early China*. Vol. 2. Princeton, NJ: Princeton University Press.
Rist, John M. 1982. *Human Value: A Study in Ancient Philosophical Ethics*. Leiden: Brill.
Rorem, Paul. 1993. *Pseudo-Dionysius: A Commentary on the Texts and an Introduction to Their Influence*. Oxford: Oxford University Press.
Ruan, Guoyi 阮帼仪. 2010. "《孔子家语》复音词的数量统计及语料年代分析." 西南交通大学学报（社会科学版）11, no. 1: 86–97.
Ruan, Mingyuan 陈明远. 2015. "'甲金文验古学'之三：华夏占卜和祭祀的原初史." 社会科学论坛 2015, no. 3: 17–37.
Shaughnessy, Edward L. 1991. *Sources of Western Zhou History: Inscribed Bronze Vessels*. Berkeley: University of California Press.
Shaughnessy, Edward L., trans. 1996. *I Ching: The Classic of Changes*. New York: Ballantine Books.
Shaughnessy, Edward L. 1997. *Before Confucius: Studies in the Creation of the Chinese Classics*. Albany: State University of New York Press.
Shaughnessy, Edward L. 2005. "A First Reading of the Shanghai Museum Bamboo-Strip Manuscript of the 'Zhou Yi.'" *Early China* 30: 1–24.
Shaughnessy, Edward L. 2006. *Rewriting Early Chinese Texts*. Albany: State University of New York Press.
Shaughnessy, Edward L. 2009. "Chronologies of Ancient China: A Critique of the 'Xia-Shang-Zhou Chronology Project.' In *Windows on the Chinese World. Reflections by Five Historians*, edited by Clara Wing-chung Ho, 15–28. New York: Lexington Books.
Shaughnessy, Edward L. 2015. "Unearthed Documents and the Question of the Oral versus Written Nature of the 'Classic of Poetry.'" *Harvard Journal of Asiatic Studies* 75, no. 2: 331–75.
Shaughnessy, Edward L. 2021. "A First Reading of the Anhui University Bamboo-Slip *Shi Jing*." *Bamboo and Silk* 4: 1–44.
Shen, Xiaomin 沈效敏. 1999. "曾子故里南武城考析." 济宁师专学报 20, no. 2: 76–79.
Shi, Shuaishuai 石帅帅. 2016. "毛公鼎銘文集釋." M.A. Thesis, Jilin University.
Shi, Weile 史为乐, Zixin Deng 邓自欣, and Lingling Zhu 朱玲玲, eds. 2005. 中国历史地名大辞典. Beijing: 中国社会科学出版社.
Sima, Qian 司馬遷. 1981. 史記. Taipei: 鼎文書局.

Siu, King Wai 蕭敬偉. 2004. "今本《孔子家語》成書年代新考—— 從語言及文獻角度考察." Ph.D. diss., University of Hong Kong.

Slingerland, Edward. 2018. "Review of Michael Hunter, *Confucius beyond the Analects*." *Early China* 41: 465–75.

So, Jenny F., ed. 2000. *Music in the Age of Confucius*. Washington, DC: Smithsonian Institution.

Song, Gongwen 宋公文, and Hongxing Li 红星. 2000. "魏文侯及其用人之道" 27, no. 5: 72–75.

Song, Jun 宋军. 2014. "从燕下都高台建筑看中国人的台文化." 华夏文化, no. 3: 35–37.

Song, Zhaolin 宋兆麟. 1993. "葫芦的功能与栽培技艺." 农业考古, no. 1: 138–46.

Sui County Leigudun Archaeological Team 随县擂鼓墩一号墓考古发掘队. 1979. "湖北随县曾侯乙墓发掘简报." 文物, no. 7: 1–24.

Sun, Shaohua 孙少华. 2007. "孔安国及其孔臧的生卒与学术." 中国社会科学院研究生院学报, no. 6: 89–95.

Suo, Dehao 索德浩. 2020. "中原地区封土起源再研究." 考古与文化, no. 1: 79–87.

Taiwan Academic Network. 2021. *Revised Mandarin Chinese Dictionary* 重編國語辭典修訂本. 6th ed. Taipei: Ministry of Education, R.O.C.

Tan, Qixiang 谭其骧, ed. 1996. *The Historical Atlas of China* 中國歷史地圖集. Vol. 1. Beijing: China Cartographica Publishing House 中国地图出版社.

Tang, Haipeng 汤海鹏. 2011. "《孔子家语》词汇语法现象专题研究—— 试从词汇、语法角度探讨《孔子家语》语言的时代特征." M.A. thesis, Qufu Normal University.

Tian, Xiaojuan 田小娟. 2001. "商周冠式初探." 考古与文物, no. 4: 46–54.

Van Norden, Bryan W. 2007. *Virtue Ethics and Consequentialism in Early Chinese Philosophy*. New York: Cambridge University Press.

Wang, Guowei 王国维, and Yongnian Huang 黄永年. 1997. 古本竹书纪年辑校. 今本竹书纪年疏证. Shenyang: 辽宁教育文化出版社.

Wang, Jiajing, Li Liu, Terry Ball, Linjie Yu, Yuanqing Li, and Fulai Xing. 2016. "Revealing a 5,000-Y-Old Beer Recipe in China." *Proceedings of the National Academy of Sciences* 113, no. 23: 6444–48. https://doi.org/10.1073/pnas.1601465113.

Wang, Ping 王萍. 1997. "中国古代妻妾之制述略." 三峡学刊 13, no. 4: 50–56.

Wang, Qing 王青. 2005. "礼乐文化嬗变中的鲁国祭祀." M.A. thesis, Qufu Normal University.

Wang, Tingxin 王廷信. 2002. "四时祭祖及蜡祭中的尸与扮演." 文学遗产, no. 3: 83–88, 144.

Wang, Wei 王巍, and Xiuchun Huang 黄秀纯. 1984. "1981—1983 年琉璃河西周燕国墓地发掘简报." 考古, no. 5: 405–21.

Wang, Wei 王巍, and Hui Zhao 赵辉. 2023. "'中华文明探源工程'及其主要收获." 社会科学文摘, no. 3: 5–8.

Wang, Weikun 王维坤. 2001. "隋唐墓葬出土的死者口中含币习俗溯源." 考古与文物, no. 5: 76–88.

Wang, Xiangchen 王相臣. 2006. "山东平邑县南武城故城出土铜镜." 华夏考古, no. 2: 73–77.

Wang, Xiangtian 王襄天, and Ziqiang Han 韩自强. 1978. "阜阳双古堆西汉汝阴侯墓发掘简报." 文物, no. 8: 12–33.

Wang, Xiao 王晓, and Xixi Chen 陈希茜. 2019. "基于建筑考古学的楚章华台建筑底层基本平面研究." 建筑与文化, no. 10: 155–56.

Wei, Xue 卫雪, and Yaopeng Qian 钱耀鹏. 2019. "陶尖底瓶的功能结构分析." 考古, no. 11: 76–88.

Wilkinson, Endymion. 2022. *Chinese History: A New Manual*. 6th ed. 2 vols. Cambridge, MA: Harvard University Press.

Woo, Jeong-Gil. 2019. "Revisiting the *Analects* for a Modern Reading of the Confucian Dialogical Spirit in Education." *Educational Philosophy and Theory* 51, no. 11: 1091–1105. https://doi.org/10.1080/00131857.2018.1501678.

Wu, Chengluo 吴承洛. 1984. 中国度量衡史. Shanghai: 上海书店.

Wu, Cunhao 吴存浩. 1998. "春秋战国时代墓葬习俗演变试论." 民俗研究, no. 3: 61–67.

Wu, Hong 巫鸿. 2006. "'明器'的理论和实践—— 战国时期礼仪美术中的观念化倾向." 文物, no. 6: 72–81.

Wu, Jianwei 吴建伟. 2015. "'五至'、'三无'说新释." 中国文字研究, no. 1: 93–96.
Wu, Kejing 邬可晶. 2015.《孔子家語》成書考. Shanghai: 中西書局.
Xia, Dekao 夏德靠. 2012. "先秦诸子文献的类型与文体变迁—— 以《论语》类文献为考察中心." 吉首大学学报(社会科学版) 33, no. 5: 62–70.
Xia-Shang-Zhou Chronology Project Expert Group 夏商周断代工程专家组, ed. 2000. 夏商周断代工程1996—2000 年阶段成果报告. Beijing: 世界图书出版公司.
Xu, Chuanwu 徐传武. 1994. "南武城, 今何地?" 辞书研究, no. 1: 149–52.
Xu, Jialu 许嘉璐, ed. 1991. 中国古代礼俗辞典. Beijing: 中国友谊出版公司.
Xu, Jieshun 徐杰舜, ed. 2012. 中国汉族通史. Yinchuan: 宁夏人民出版社.
Xu, Shaohua 徐少华. 2007. "论竹书《君子为礼》的思想内涵与特征." 中国哲学史, no. 2: 22–31.
Yang, Bojun 楊伯峻, ed. 2016. 春秋左传注. 4th ed. Beijing: 中华书局.
Yang, Bojun 楊伯峻, and Ti Xu 徐提. 1985. 春秋左傳詞典. Beijing: 中華書局.
Yang, Chaoming 杨朝明. 1998. "周公长于管叔考." 中国史研究, no. 3: 14–20.
Yang, Chaoming 杨朝明. 2009. "孔子'出妻'说及相关问题." 齐鲁学刊, no. 2: 10–14.
Yang, Chaoming 杨朝明. 2017. 孔子家语综合研究. Ji'nan, Shandong: 齐鲁书社.
Yang, Chaoming 杨朝明, and Lilin Song 宋立林. 2013. 孔子家语通解. Ji'nan, Shandong: 齐鲁书社.
Yang, Chunqiu 羊春秋, and Feng-wu Chou 周鳳五. 2020. 新譯孔子家語. Taipei: 三民書局.
Yang, Haizhong 杨海中. 2018. "丝绸之路与西域文明在中原的传播及影响." 地域文化研究, no. 4: 113–32, 156.
Yao, Chen 姚琛, and Zhen Wang 王阵. 2019. "葫芦形造物艺术的演化、形态及象征意义." 齐齐哈尔大学学报 (哲学社会科学版), no. 5: 161–63.
Yates, Robin. 2001. "Slavery in Early China: A Socio-Cultural Approach." *Journal of East Asian Archaeology* 3 (January): 283–331. https://doi.org/10.1163/156852301100402723.
Yee, Cordell D. K. 1994. "Reinterpreting Traditional Chinese Geographical Maps." In *The History of Cartography*. Vol. 2, Book 2, *Cartography in the Traditional East and Southeast Asian Societies*, edited by J. B. Harley and David Woodward, 35–70. Chicago: University of Chicago Press.
Yin, Qun 印群. 2001. 黄河中下游地区的东周墓葬制度. Beijing: 社会科学文献出版社.
Ylönen, Matti, and Hanna Kuusela. 2019. "Consultocracy and Its Discontents: A Critical Typology and a Call for a Research Agenda." *Governance* 32, no. 2: 241–58. https://doi.org/10.1111/gove.12369.
Yong, Xia. 2011. *The Philosophy of Civil Rights in the Context of China*. Leiden: Brill.
Yu, Lunian 俞鹿年, ed. 1992. 中国官制大辞典. Ha'erbin: 黑龙江人民出版社.
Yu, Ping 于平. 2017. "蜡祭: 从'大蜡飨农'到'岁终聚戏'." 民族艺术研究 30, no. 5: 142–48.
Yu, Yanjiao 喻燕姣, Guohui Shen 申国辉, Mingjie Li 李明洁, and Tingyan Ren 任亭燕. 2024. "马王堆汉墓出土的药物与药具." 文物天地, no. 4: 34–39.
Yu, Ying-shih 余英时. 2003. 士与中国文化. Shanghai: 上海人民出版社.
Yuan, Shiquan 袁世全, Xiusong Li 李修松, and Shuyu Qi 祁述裕, eds. 1990. 中国百科大辞典. Beijing: 华夏出版社.
Yuan, Yida 袁义达, and Ruofu Du 杜若甫. 1996. 中华姓氏大辞典. Beijing: 教育科学出版社.
Yuan, Yuying 袁愈荌, and Moyao Tang 唐莫堯. 1983. 詩經新譯注. Taipei: 木鐸出版社.
Zeng, Wuxiu 曾武秀. 1964. "中国历代尺度概述." 历史研究, no. 3: 163–82.
Zhang, Chenyang 张晨阳, and Ke Zhang 张珂, eds. 2015. 中国古代服饰辞典. Beijing: 中华书局.
Zhang, Dainian 张岱年, and Nairu Xia 夏乃儒, eds. 2010. 孔子百科辞典. Shanghai: 上海辞书出版社.
Zhang, Qiyun 張其昀, Yin Lin 林尹, and Ming Gao 高明, eds. 1980. *The Encyclopedic Dictionary of the Chinese Language* 中文大辭典. 8th ed. Taipei: Chinese Culture University Press.
Zhang, Shidong 张士东. 2019. "高句丽语与朝鲜语及后期肃慎语族关系辨析." 东疆学刊 36, no. 2: 86–90.
Zhang, Weizhong 张卫中. 2002. "春秋时期龟卜的传播功能." 浙江大学学报 (人文社会科学版) 32, no. 5: 70–76.
Zhang, Xiang 张翔. 1998. "周代乐器组合之观察." 黄钟(武汉音乐学院学报), no. 3: 48–54.

Zhang, Yanglizheng 张杨力铮, and Weihong Xu 许卫红. 2020. 陕西咸阳岩村墓地M41发掘简报. 中原文物, no. 1: 31–38.

Zhang, Yong 张勇. 2002. "明器起源及相关问题探讨." 华夏考古, no. 3: 24–30.

Zhao, Benjia 赵本加. 1993. "陶器文化与葫芦文化." 乐山师专学报 (社会科学版), no. 4: 42–44, 20.

Zhao, Congcang 赵丛苍, and Chao Zhang 张朝. 2015. "服周之冕—— 先秦时期的冕冠." 文博, no. 5: 42–46.

Zhao, Hui, Ya-Long Feng, Ming Wang, Jing-Jing Wang, Tian Liu, and Jun Yu. 1992. "The Angelica dahurica: A Review of Traditional Uses, Phytochemistry and Pharmacology." *Frontiers in Pharmacology* 13: Art. 896637. https://doi.org/10.3389/fphar.2022.896637.

Zhao, Xiaoming 赵晓明, Yun Song 宋芸, Yonggang Qiao 乔永刚, and Yongsheng Tian 田永生. 2008. "甲骨文披露薏苡酒的发明." 山西农业大学学报(社会科学版), no. 3: 232–37, 241.

Zhao, Zhan 赵展. 2013. "对肃慎及其后裔的考证."中央民族大学学报 (哲学社会科学版) 40, no. 4: 97–102.

Zheng, Tianting 郑天挺, Ze Wu 吴泽, and Zhijiu Yang 杨志玖, eds. 2000. 中国历史大辞典. Shanghai: 上海辞书出版社.

Zhou, Hong 周洪. 2006. "麻冕之升数考." 南方文物, no. 3: 142–44.

Zhou, Weirong 周卫荣, and Wei Huang 黄维. 2015. "试论青铜时代透空青铜器的工艺特色— 兼谈失蜡铸造问题."中国国家博物馆馆刊, no. 1: 147–55.

Zhou, Xiaomin 周晓敏, and Yangju Xie 谢阳举. 2021. "论春秋时期'士'含义的演变及其历史条件." 学术探索, no. 11: 89–99.

INDEX

This index provides locators for significant names and terms. For items already listed in the glossary or the introduction's philosophical lexicon (which provide locators only for the main text), locators are provided here for pages outside the main text—in the front matter, back matter, and footnotes. For items not appearing here, please go directly to the glossary. Locators in italics refer to figures.